PICTUREPEDIA

an encyclopedia on every page

PICTUREPEDIA
an encyclopedia on every page

DK LONDON

Project editor Lizzie Davey
Senior art editor Mabel Chan

Editors
Ann Baggaley, Vanessa Daubney, Sarah Macleod,
Catherine Saunders, Rona Skene, Sarah Tomley

Designers
Laura Brim, Alison Gardner, Mik Gates, Tessa Jordens,
Steve Woosnam-Savage

Managing editor Paula Regan
Managing art editor Owen Peyton Jones
Jacket design development manager Sophia MTT
Producer, pre-production Nikoleta Parasaki
Producer Mary Slater
Publisher Andrew Macintyre
Associate publishing director Liz Wheeler
Art director Karen Self
Publishing director Jonathan Metcalf

Consultants
Alexandra Black, Kim Bryan, Giles Chapman, Sheila Dickle
Robert Dinwiddie, Richard Gilbert, Sawako Irie, Philip Parker,
Penny Preston, Carole Stott, Tony Streeter, Marcus Weeks,
Philip Whiteman, Chris Woodford, John Woodward

DK DELHI

Project editor Rupa Rao
Project art editor Mahipal Singh

Editors
Deeksha Saikia, Sonam Mathur, Agnibesh Das

Art editors
Amit Varma, Vikas Chauhan, Ranjita Bhattacharji

Senior DTP designers Shanker Prasad, Harish Aggarwal
DTP designers Nityanand Kumar, Rajesh Singh Adhikari
Picture researcher Nishwan Rasool
Jacket designers Suhita Dharamjit, Dhirendra Singh
Managing jackets editor Saloni Talwar
Managing editor Kingshuk Ghoshal
Managing art editor Govind Mittal
Pre-production manager Balwant Singh
Production manager Pankaj Sharma

First published in Great Britain in 2015
by Dorling Kindersley Limited, 80 Strand, London WC2R 0RL

Copyright © 2015 Dorling Kindersley Limited, London
A Penguin Random House Company

10 9 8 7 6 5 4 3 2 1

001 – 197156 – Oct/15

A CIP catalogue record for this book is available
from the British Library.

ISBN 978-0-2411-8698-5

Printed and bound in Hong Kong

Discover more at
www.dk.com

CONTENTS

Science and technology

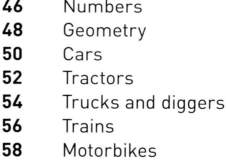

Nature

Geography

Culture

Sports and hobbies

History

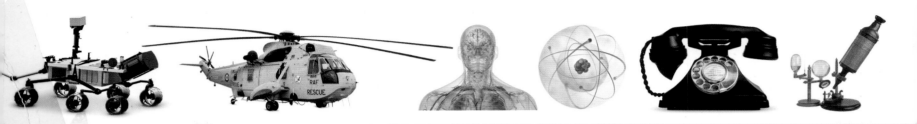

Science and technology

The Universe

The Universe is everything that exists – all of space, matter, energy, and time. It is a huge wide-open space with billions of galaxies, each containing billions of stars, and yet it is at least 99.99 per cent empty space. It has been expanding constantly since its beginning 13.8 billion years ago, when it exploded into life with the "Big Bang".

THE BIG BANG

Before the Big Bang, the entire Universe was inside a bubble that was smaller than a piece of dust. It was extremely hot and dense, and it suddenly exploded. In less than a second, the Universe became bigger than a galaxy. It carried on growing and cooling, and pure energy became matter. During the billions of years that followed, stars, planets, and galaxies formed to create the Universe as we know it.

The Universe begins, 13.8 billion years ago

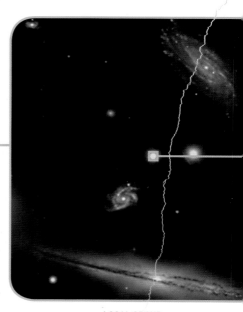

Energy turns into matter

UNIVERSE
The Universe is ever-expanding. It is full of dark energy, dark matter, and other matter such as superclusters of galaxies.

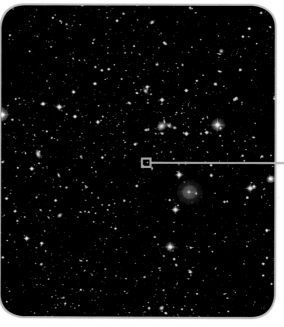

SUPERCLUSTER
Superclusters are one of the largest known structures in the Universe, made up of galaxy clusters.

LOCAL GROUP
The Local Group is a cluster of about 50 galaxies inside the Virgo Supercluster that includes the Milky Way.

GALAXIES

Galaxies are huge groups of stars, and they can be seen in the night sky using a telescope. They come in lots of different shapes, and most of them are thought to have a massive black hole at their centre.

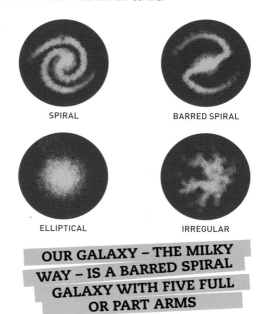

SPIRAL

BARRED SPIRAL

ELLIPTICAL

IRREGULAR

> OUR GALAXY – THE MILKY WAY – IS A BARRED SPIRAL GALAXY WITH FIVE FULL OR PART ARMS

NEBULAE

Nebulae are the "nurseries" of the Universe – they are huge clouds of gas and dust in which stars form. They may be trillions of kilometres wide and many have amazing shapes and colours.

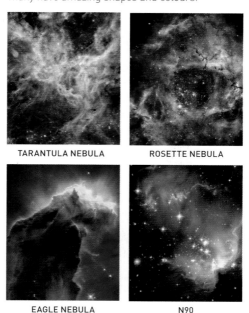

TARANTULA NEBULA

ROSETTE NEBULA

EAGLE NEBULA

N90

STARS

Stars are classified into different types depending on their temperature and brightness. Scientists use the Hertzsprung-Russell graph (shown below) to compare the size, temperature, and brightness of individual stars.

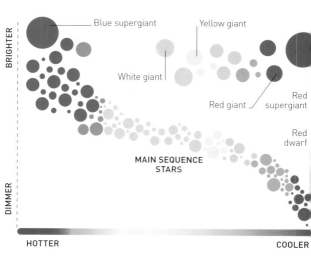

BRIGHTER

Blue supergiant

Yellow giant

White giant

Red giant

Red supergiant

Red dwarf

MAIN SEQUENCE STARS

DIMMER

HOTTER

COOLER

STAR TYPES
Most of the stars, including our Sun, are found along a part of the graph called the Main Sequence. As they age, these become giants or supergiants, and then dwarfs or supernovas.

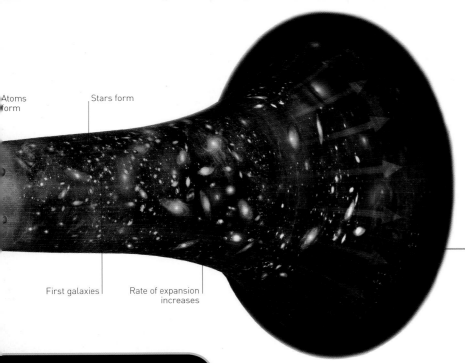

Atoms form

First galaxies

Stars form

Rate of expansion increases

WHAT MAKES UP THE UNIVERSE?

The Universe contains matter and energy. Matter is generally physical "stuff" that can be seen, like the planets, but galaxies also contain invisible matter called "dark matter". This does not give off light or heat and so can be detected only by the effects of its gravity on visible objects. Between and beyond both types of matter is "dark energy", a mysterious thing that scientists know almost nothing about.

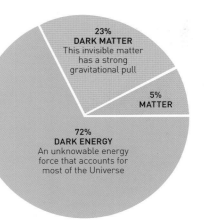

23% **DARK MATTER** This invisible matter has a strong gravitational pull

5% **MATTER**

72% **DARK ENERGY** An unknowable energy force that accounts for most of the Universe

THE SCALE OF THE UNIVERSE

The Universe is so vast that it is hard to appreciate its size. This series of pictures "zooms in" on the Universe, to show how our Solar System and planet relate to the rest of the Universe. Space is so huge that astronomers use the speed of light to measure distances. One light year is the distance light travels in a year, which is nearly 10 trillion km (6 trillion miles).

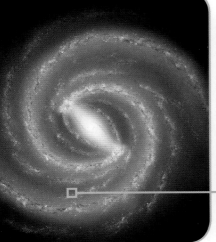

MILKY WAY GALAXY
The Milky Way has a spiral shape and holds around 200 billion stars within its gravitational pull.

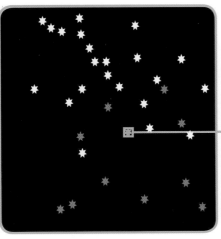

STELLAR NEIGHBOURHOOD
Our Solar System is on one of the Milky Way's spiral arms, 27,000 light years from the galaxy's centre.

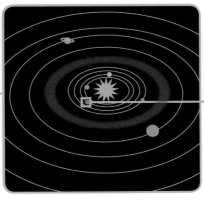

SOLAR SYSTEM
The Sun sits at the centre of our Solar System, and eight major planets orbit it.

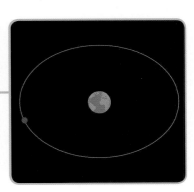

EARTH AND MOON
Earth is one of the planets orbiting the Sun, and the Moon orbits Earth.

BLACK HOLES

A black hole is a region of space where matter has collapsed in on itself. This means there is nothing to be seen, but astronomers know black holes exist because they have such a strong gravitational pull that nothing can escape them – not even light.

ARTIST'S IDEA OF A BLACK HOLE

DWARF PLANETS

Large planets have enough self-gravity to make them form into a round shape as they move through space. Smaller planets that cannot do this, but do orbit the Sun, are called "dwarf planets". Pluto is one of the largest dwarf planets in our solar system.

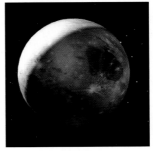

PLUTO

COMETS

Comets are small, icy worlds that orbit the Sun. They are made of frozen gases, rock, and dust. As they orbit the Sun, jets of gas and dust vaporize behind them to create long "tails" visible in space.

COMET

PLANETS

Planets are large, spherical objects that orbit a star. In our Solar System, there are eight planets: Mercury, Venus, Earth, Mars, Jupiter, Saturn, Uranus, and Neptune. Planets that occur outside our Solar System are known as exoplanets.

EARTH

MOONS

A moon is a rocky body that orbits a planet. Some planets have many moons but Earth has only one. Moons are also known as natural satellites.

EARTH'S MOON

ASTEROIDS

Asteroids are small rocky bodies that orbit the Sun. There are millions of them in space, and they are mainly made of materials that were left over from the formation of planets.

EROS, A NAMED ASTEROID

THE SUN

The Sun is the hottest and largest object in our Solar System. Its fiery surface bathes the planets around it in light, and its gravity shapes their orbits. The Sun is now about halfway through its life. In about 5 billion years it will turn into a red giant, before puffing its outer layers into space, leaving behind only a ghostly cloud called a planetary nebula.

THE SUN IS SO HUGE THAT EARTH COULD FIT INSIDE IT ONE MILLION TIMES

The planets

Around 4.6 billion years ago, a great cloud of dust and gas formed into the Sun. The parts that were not used began to form into clumps, which grew into planets orbiting the Sun. The four planets closest to the Sun formed from rock and metal. The four bigger outer planets formed from gases.

MERCURY

Mercury is the nearest planet to the Sun and the smallest in the Solar System – it is about as wide as the Atlantic Ocean. Mercury is a rocky world that has no atmosphere or water.

BRAHMS CRATER
Mercury is covered in craters made by debris crashing into its surface.

MERCURY
ROCKY PLANET

DISTANCE FROM THE SUN: 69.8 million km (43.3 million miles)

DIAMETER: 4,879 km (3,030 miles)

TIME TAKEN TO ORBIT THE SUN: 87.97 Earth days

NUMBER OF MOONS: 0

VENUS

Venus is the second planet from the Sun. It is about the same size as Earth and made from similar materials, but its atmosphere is made of carbon dioxide – the gas that we breathe out.

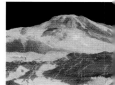
MAAT MONS
Venus has more than 1,600 volcanoes, the highest of which is Maat Mons.

VENUS
ROCKY PLANET

DISTANCE FROM THE SUN: 108.9 million km (67.6 million miles)

DIAMETER: 12,104 km (7,520 miles)

TIME TAKEN TO ORBIT THE SUN: 224.7 Earth days

NUMBER OF MOONS: 0

JUPITER

Jupiter is the largest planet in the Solar System – it could hold around 1,300 Earths. It is a giant ball of gas ringed by colourful bands of chemical gases that race around it as fierce winds.

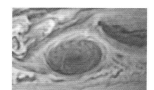
GREAT RED SPOT
This is a giant storm several times bigger than Earth, which has been raging for 300 years.

JUPITER
GAS GIANT

DISTANCE FROM THE SUN: 816 million km (507 million miles)

DIAMETER: 142,984 km (88,845 miles)

TIME TAKEN TO ORBIT THE SUN: 11.86 Earth years

NUMBER OF MOONS: 67+

SATURN

The second-largest planet in the Solar System, Saturn is not dense – it would float in a planetary-sized bathtub. It is surrounded by a system of rings that extend thousands of kilometres from the planet but are only 9 m (30 ft) thick.

RINGS OF SATURN
Saturn's rings are made up of ice crystals and rock.

SATURN
GAS GIANT

DISTANCE FROM THE SUN: 1.5 billion km (932 million miles)

DIAMETER: 120,536 km (74,900 miles)

TIME TAKEN TO ORBIT THE SUN: 29.46 Earth years

NUMBER OF MOONS: 62+

DISTANCE FROM THE SUN

The distances between the planets are huge, becoming bigger as we move out through the Solar System. If the Sun were the size of a grapefruit, Neptune would be 14.5 km (9 miles) away.

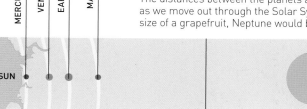
MERCURY VENUS EARTH MARS
SUN

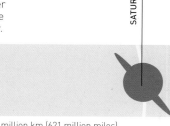
JUPITER

SATURN

500 million km (311 million miles)

1,000 million km (621 million miles)

2,000 million km (1,243 million miles)

ORBITS

All of the planets orbit the Sun anticlockwise, in an elliptical, or oval pattern. This means they are closer to the Sun at some points in their orbits than others. They are trapped by the Sun's gravity and will stay in the same plane of orbit for ever.

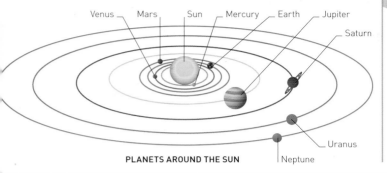

Venus Mars Sun Mercury Earth Jupiter

Saturn

Uranus

Neptune

PLANETS AROUND THE SUN

PLANET SIZES

The four rocky planets nearest to the Sun are much smaller than the gas giants. The Sun dwarfs them all, but is itself much smaller than other stars in the Universe.

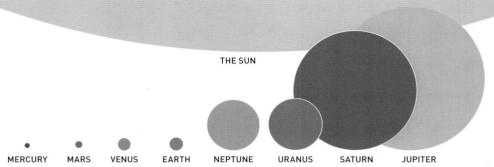

THE SUN

MERCURY   MARS   VENUS   EARTH   NEPTUNE   URANUS   SATURN   JUPITER

EARTH

Earth moves around the Sun at 30 km per second (18.6 miles per second) and takes 365 days to orbit it completely. It is the only planet known to have life on it.

HIMALAYAS
This mountain range was formed on Earth around 70 million years ago.

EARTH

ROCKY PLANET

DISTANCE FROM THE SUN: 152.6 million km (94.5 million miles)

DIAMETER: 12,756 km (7,926 miles)

TIME TAKEN TO ORBIT THE SUN: 365.26 Earth days

NUMBER OF MOONS: 1

MARS

The planet Mars is red, because its surface is covered in iron-rich dust and rock. It is about half the size of Earth and has both the highest mountain and the deepest valley of any planet in the Solar System.

OLYMPUS MONS
This mountain on Mars is about three times as tall as Earth's Mount Everest. It is also volcanic.

MARS

ROCKY PLANET

DISTANCE FROM THE SUN: 816 million km (507 million miles)

DIAMETER: 6,780 km (4,213 miles)

TIME TAKEN TO ORBIT THE SUN: 687 Earth days

NUMBER OF MOONS: 2

URANUS

Methane in Uranus's atmosphere gives it a rich blue colour. This planet is often called the "ice giant" because 80 per cent of it is made up of frozen methane, water, and ammonia.

RINGS
Uranus has very faint rings compared to the other gas giants.

URANUS

GAS GIANT

DISTANCE FROM THE SUN: 3 billion km (1.86 billion miles)

DIAMETER: 51,118 km (31,760 miles)

TIME TAKEN TO ORBIT THE SUN: 84.3 Earth years

NUMBER OF MOONS: 27

NEPTUNE

Neptune is the furthest planet from the Sun, so it gets little sunlight to warm its atmosphere. Its vivid blue colour is due to methane and an unknown compound. Neptune has the fastest winds in the Solar System.

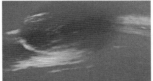

GREAT DARK SPOT
This storm, which has now dispersed, was large enough to contain Earth, and moved at 1,200 km/h (750 mph).

NEPTUNE

GAS GIANT

DISTANCE FROM THE SUN: 4.5 billion km (2.8 billion miles)

DIAMETER: 49,528 km (30,775 miles)

TIME TAKEN TO ORBIT THE SUN: 168.4 Earth years

NUMBER OF MOONS: 14

URANUS

NEPTUNE

3,000 million km (1,864 million miles)

4,500 million km (2,796 million miles)

The Moon

Always in orbit around Earth, the Moon is known as Earth's satellite. It provides Earth with light during the night, though it has no light of its own – it merely reflects the Sun's light, like a mirror. It is the closest object to Earth in space, and we can see its cratered surface even with the naked eye.

HOW THE MOON FORMED

There are many theories about how the Moon came into existence. Scientists think the most likely explanation is that something collided with Earth, sending debris into space that eventually formed the Moon.

1 IMPACT
A giant astronomical object hit the primitive molten Earth. The object was absorbed, but debris shot into space.

2 MOON FORMATION
Earth's gravity pulled the debris into orbit, and the fragments collided and clumped together, forming the Moon.

INTERNAL STRUCTURE

The Moon is made up of several layers: it has a crust, mantle, and a solid inner core surrounded by a hot and fluid outer core. There are regular "moonquakes", which last up to ten minutes.

Heat from radioactive elements has partially melted the inner mantle

Inner mantle

Outer mantle

Solid inner core

Crust

Fluid outer core

ORBITING EARTH

The Moon takes 27.3 days to orbit Earth, and the same amount of time to spin on its axis. We see some, all, or none of the Moon, depending on how much of its sunlit side faces Earth.

Moon's axis

Earth's axis

Earth's equator

Moon orbits Earth in 27.3 Earth days

CRATERS

The Moon is rocky and pockmarked with craters formed by asteroids crashing into its surface billions of years ago. The biggest craters are called "maria", or seas. They are very flat because they were filled with volcanic lava that welled up from inside the Moon and then solidified. In this Moon map, the near side is on the left and the far side is on the right.

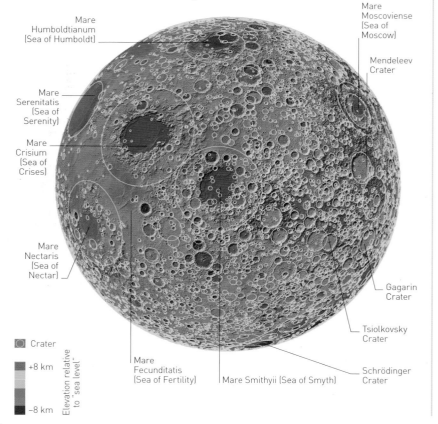

Mare Humboldtianum (Sea of Humboldt)

Mare Serenitatis (Sea of Serenity)

Mare Crisium (Sea of Crises)

Mare Nectaris (Sea of Nectar)

Mare Moscoviense (Sea of Moscow)

Mendeleev Crater

Gagarin Crater

Tsiolkovsky Crater

Schrödinger Crater

Mare Fecunditatis (Sea of Fertility)

Mare Smithyii (Sea of Smyth)

Crater

+8 km

Elevation relative to "sea level"

-8 km

FAR SIDE AND NEAR SIDE

The near side of the Moon is the side that always faces Earth, because it takes the same amount of time to rotate on its axis as it does to orbit Earth.

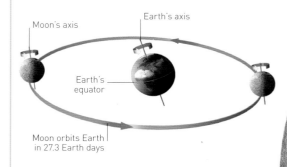

Lacus Luxuriae

Mare Moscoviense

Mare Ingenii

FAR SIDE
This side of the Moon has a thicker crust, more highlands, and fewer maria (seas).

NEAR SIDE
The near side is divided into two areas: the Lunar Highlands and maria.

HOW CRATERS FORM

When the Moon was young it was bombarded by asteroids – rocky pieces left over from the planet-making process. They blasted away the Moon's surface, forming craters, circular hollows about 10–15 times the size of the impacting asteroid.

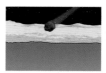

1 INCOMING SPACE ROCK
There is no atmosphere to protect the Moon from flying objects.

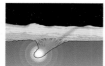

2 INITIAL IMPACT
The object strikes the ground faster than the speed of sound, breaking the crust.

3 SHOCK WAVE
On impact, the object melts and vaporizes, spewing hot rock vapour over a huge area.

4 CRATER
Some of the rock vapour (ejecta flow) settles in and around the large hole that is the crater.

PHASES OF THE MOON

The Moon seems to get larger and smaller in the sky, but this illusion is caused by the fact that we can only see the face of the Moon that faces Earth. One half of the Moon is always bathed in sunlight, but most of the time only part of the sunlit area is visible from Earth.

WAXING CRESCENT
Only a thin sliver of the sunlit part of the Moon is seen from Earth.

FIRST QUARTER
The sunlit portion increases to show half of the Moon's hemisphere lit up.

WAXING GIBBOUS
The sunlit part increases – now more than half of the Moon is visible in the sky.

FULL MOON
A full side of the Moon is now visible. This is halfway through the lunar month.

WANING GIBBOUS
Turning away from Earth again, the lit-up section of the Moon begins to decrease.

LAST QUARTER
Rising only around midnight, this half-lit Moon is brightest at dawn.

WANING CRESCENT
This marks the near completion of the Moon's orbit around Earth.

NEW MOON
The lit half of the Moon is completely hidden from Earth at this point.

Darker areas are "maria" – smooth, low-lying areas (like seas without water)

The Lunar Highlands are hilly regions with lots of craters

JOURNEY TO THE MOON

On 16 July 1969, three astronauts began a journey into space to land on the Moon. Their spacecraft was Apollo 11, which was launched into space by the three-stage Saturn V rocket. It delivered the astronauts on to the Moon in a Lunar Module.

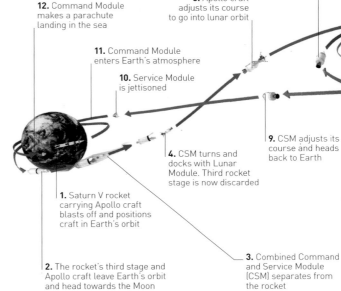

7. Third crew member continues to orbit the Moon in CSM

8. Ascent stage of Lunar Module takes astronauts back to CSM, after which it is discarded

12. Command Module makes a parachute landing in the sea

5. Apollo craft adjusts its course to go into lunar orbit

11. Command Module enters Earth's atmosphere

10. Service Module is jettisoned

4. CSM turns and docks with Lunar Module. Third rocket stage is now discarded

9. CSM adjusts its course and heads back to Earth

6. Lunar Module transports two astronauts to lunar surface

1. Saturn V rocket carrying Apollo craft blasts off and positions craft in Earth's orbit

2. The rocket's third stage and Apollo craft leave Earth's orbit and head towards the Moon

3. Combined Command and Service Module (CSM) separates from the rocket

MEN ON THE MOON

In 1972 the crew of Apollo 17 landed on the Moon and stayed there for three days. They completed three successful excursions to examine craters and the Taurus Mountains.

ASTRONAUT EUGENE CERNAN ON THE LUNAR ROVING VEHICLE, 1972

TRUE OR FALSE?

People have had theories about the Moon since they first looked up at the skies in ancient times. Modern science has helped us work out which Moon myths are true and which are false.

 FULL MOON CAUSES LUNACY
Research by scientists has proved there is no link between madness and the full moon.

 MOON AFFECTS THE OCEAN TIDES
The Moon's gravity does affect the tides of waters on Earth.

 ALIENS INHABIT THE MOON
Samples of the Moon taken by astronauts show no trace of other life, past or present.

 YOU WEIGH LESS ON THE MOON
"Weight" depends on the pull between two gravitational forces. The Moon's gravity is less than Earth's, so you would weigh less.

 THE MOON IS DRIFTING AWAY FROM EARTH
The Moon is moving away from us by 3.8 cm (1.5 in) per year.

 THE MOON HAS A DARK SIDE
The Moon spins on its axis, so every part of it is exposed to the Sun at some point during rotation.

MOON MISSIONS

In the second half of the 20th century, there was a "Space Race" between the USA and the Soviet Union (USSR) to launch crafts, satellites, and people into space. In 1959 the USSR landed a space probe on the Moon, and in 1969 the USA landed people on the Moon. Since then, other countries have sent spacecraft to find out more about the Moon.

	AGENCY	SUCCESSFUL MISSIONS
	NASA (USA)	27
	RFSA (USSR/RUSSIA)	20
	CNSA (CHINA)	3
	JAXA (JAPAN)	2
	ESA (EUROPE)	1
	ISRO (INDIA)	1

Space exploration

At the start of the 20th century, rockets were invented that were powerful enough to blast away from Earth. By the century's end, thousands of spacecraft and hundreds of people had entered space. The spacecraft of the 21st century are beginning to explore the furthest reaches of our Solar System.

APOLLO MISSION BADGES

The US space programme is run by NASA (National Aeronautics and Space Administration), and it creates a mission patch, or badge, for every space mission. The badges include elements that represent different parts of the mission: its purpose, the name of the space vehicle, and its official number.

APOLLO 1	APOLLO 7	APOLLO 8	APOLLO 9
APOLLO 10	APOLLO 11	APOLLO 12	APOLLO 13
APOLLO 14	APOLLO 15	APOLLO 16	APOLLO 17

MISSIONS TO SPACE

Space missions have landed people on the Moon and rovers on Mars. They have sampled the atmosphere of Jupiter and explored Saturn, Mercury, and even the Asteroid Belt. These missions help us understand the Solar System and our own planet.

MISSIONS TO JUPITER

NUMBER OF MISSIONS SENT: 9

KEY MISSIONS:
- **PIONEER 10:** The first craft to go through the Asteroid Belt and obtain close shots of Jupiter.
- **JUNO:** Launched on 5 August 2011, Juno is flying towards Jupiter with the aim of orbiting it for one year.

PIONEER 10   JUNO

MISSIONS TO ASTEROID BELT

NUMBER OF MISSIONS SENT: 10

KEY MISSIONS:
- **DAWN:** This spacecraft was launched in 2007 to study two bodies in the Asteroid Belt: Vesta and Ceres. It spent a year orbiting Vesta before moving on to Ceres.
- **ROSETTA:** A mission to a comet that photographed asteroids Steins and Lutetia on the way through.

ROSETTA

MISSIONS TO MERCURY

NUMBER OF MISSIONS SENT: 2

KEY MISSIONS:
- **MARINER 10:** The first craft sent to study Mercury, this was launched in 1973 and did three Mercury flybys.
- **MESSENGER:** The first craft to orbit Mercury, this was launched in 2004 and is still in operation today.

MARINER 10   MESSENGER   SOHO

MISSIONS TO THE MOON

NUMBER OF MISSIONS SENT: 100+

KEY MISSIONS:
- **APOLLO 15:** Launched in 1971, this was the first of the longer missions, where astronauts stayed for three days on the Moon.
- **LUNAR RECONNAISSANCE ORBITER:** Launched in 2009, this spacecraft is gradually mapping the entire surface of the Moon.

URANUS

THE SPACE AGE

In 1957 the Soviet Union (USSR) launched a polished aluminium ball containing a temperature control system, batteries, and radio transmitter outside Earth's atmosphere. This was the beginning of the Space Age.

1959
The USSR launches Luna 2, which crashes on the Moon, becoming the first man-made object to reach the lunar surface.

Yuri Gagarin

1961
Soviet cosmonaut Yuri Gagarin becomes the first human in space.

1965
Soviet cosmonaut Alexei Leonov becomes the first person to perform a spacewalk.

1969
The USA's Neil Armstrong and Buzz Aldrin become the first humans to walk on the Moon.

Neil Armstrong

1973
NASA's Pioneer 10 becomes the first spacecraft to travel beyond the Asteroid Belt and fly past Jupiter.

1981
NASA launches Columbia, the first "space shuttle", or reusable spacecraft.

1950

1957
The Soviet Union marks the start of the Space Age when it launches Sputnik 1, the first man-made satellite.

Sputnik 1

1958
The USA launches Explorer 1, its first satellite.

Rocket carrying Explorer 1

1965
NASA's Mariner 4 becomes the first spacecraft to fly by Mars.

Mariner 4

1971
The Soviet Union launches Salyut 1, the first space station.

Salyut series space station

1973
NASA launches its first space station, Skylab.

Skylab

1977
NASA launches Voyager 1 and 2. Over the next few years they send images and scientific data from Jupiter and Saturn.

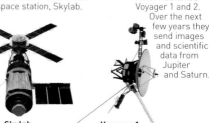

Voyager 1

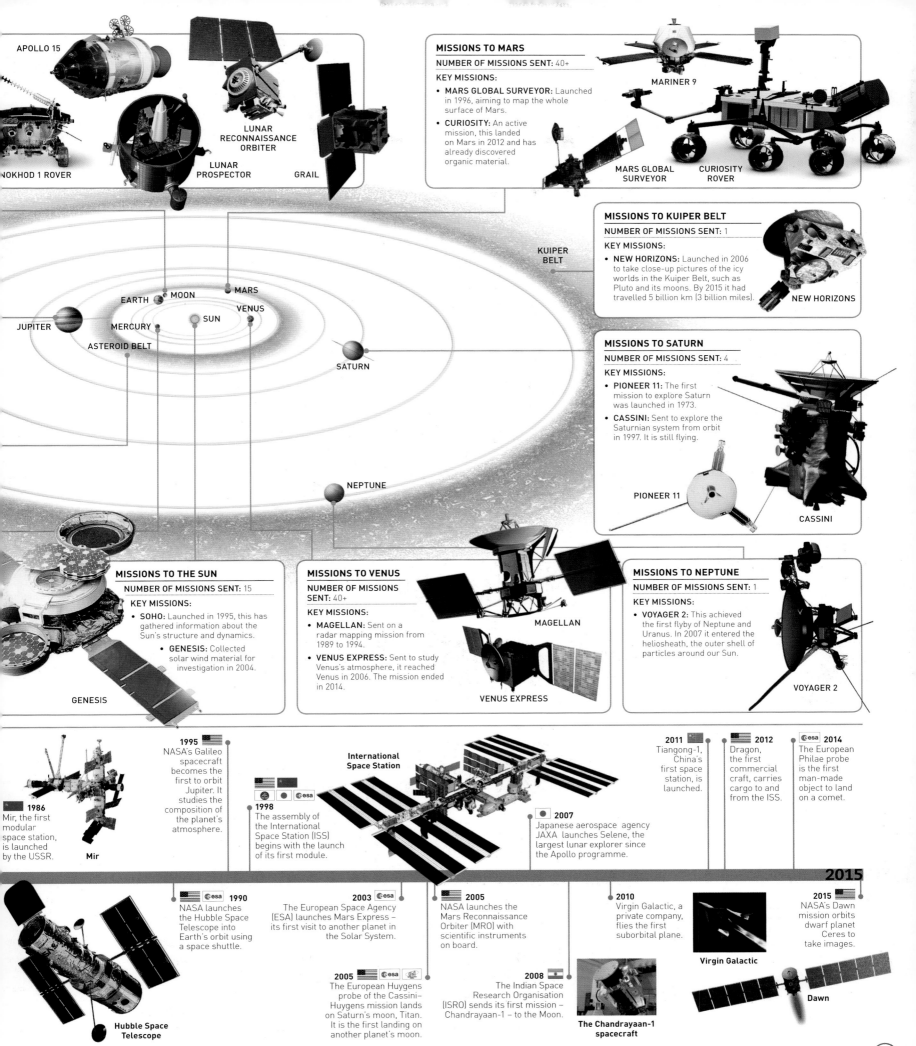

APOLLO 15

NOKHOD 1 ROVER

LUNAR RECONNAISSANCE ORBITER

LUNAR PROSPECTOR

GRAIL

MISSIONS TO MARS

NUMBER OF MISSIONS SENT: 40+

KEY MISSIONS:

- **MARS GLOBAL SURVEYOR:** Launched in 1996, aiming to map the whole surface of Mars.
- **CURIOSITY:** An active mission, this landed on Mars in 2012 and has already discovered organic material.

MARINER 9

MARS GLOBAL SURVEYOR

CURIOSITY ROVER

MISSIONS TO KUIPER BELT

NUMBER OF MISSIONS SENT: 1

KEY MISSIONS:

- **NEW HORIZONS:** Launched in 2006 to take close-up pictures of the icy worlds in the Kuiper Belt, such as Pluto and its moons. By 2015 it had travelled 5 billion km (3 billion miles).

NEW HORIZONS

KUIPER BELT

MOON   MARS

EARTH   VENUS

JUPITER   MERCURY   SUN

ASTEROID BELT

SATURN

NEPTUNE

MISSIONS TO SATURN

NUMBER OF MISSIONS SENT: 4

KEY MISSIONS:

- **PIONEER 11:** The first mission to explore Saturn was launched in 1973.
- **CASSINI:** Sent to explore the Saturnian system from orbit in 1997. It is still flying.

PIONEER 11

CASSINI

MISSIONS TO THE SUN

NUMBER OF MISSIONS SENT: 15

KEY MISSIONS:

- **SOHO:** Launched in 1995, this has gathered information about the Sun's structure and dynamics.
- **GENESIS:** Collected solar wind material for investigation in 2004.

GENESIS

MISSIONS TO VENUS

NUMBER OF MISSIONS SENT: 40+

KEY MISSIONS:

- **MAGELLAN:** Sent on a radar mapping mission from 1989 to 1994.
- **VENUS EXPRESS:** Sent to study Venus's atmosphere, it reached Venus in 2006. The mission ended in 2014.

MAGELLAN

VENUS EXPRESS

MISSIONS TO NEPTUNE

NUMBER OF MISSIONS SENT: 1

KEY MISSIONS:

- **VOYAGER 2:** This achieved the first flyby of Neptune and Uranus. In 2007 it entered the heliosheath, the outer shell of particles around our Sun.

VOYAGER 2

1986
Mir, the first modular space station, is launched by the USSR.

Mir

1995
NASA's Galileo spacecraft becomes the first to orbit Jupiter. It studies the composition of the planet's atmosphere.

International Space Station

1998
The assembly of the International Space Station (ISS) begins with the launch of its first module.

2007
Japanese aerospace agency JAXA launches Selene, the largest lunar explorer since the Apollo programme.

2011
Tiangong-1, China's first space station, is launched.

2012
Dragon, the first commercial craft, carries cargo to and from the ISS.

2014
The European Philae probe is the first man-made object to land on a comet.

2015

1990
NASA launches the Hubble Space Telescope into Earth's orbit using a space shuttle.

Hubble Space Telescope

2003
The European Space Agency (ESA) launches Mars Express – its first visit to another planet in the Solar System.

2005
The European Huygens probe of the Cassini–Huygens mission lands on Saturn's moon, Titan. It is the first landing on another planet's moon.

2005
NASA launches the Mars Reconnaissance Orbiter (MRO) with scientific instruments on board.

2008
The Indian Space Research Organisation (ISRO) sends its first mission – Chandrayaan-1 – to the Moon.

The Chandrayaan-1 spacecraft

2010
Virgin Galactic, a private company, flies the first suborbital plane.

Virgin Galactic

2015
NASA's Dawn mission orbits dwarf planet Ceres to take images.

Dawn

Stargazing

Astronomy is the branch of science that is dedicated to studying stars, planets, and all the celestial bodies that surround Earth. It seeks to explain where we came from and the beginning of the Universe itself.

PICTURING SPACE

Astronomers learn about space using telescopes. These telescopes are designed to each pick up one particular type of electromagnetic radiation from space, and use that radiation to create an image. The pictures on the right here show the Crab Nebula viewed through different types of telescopes.

INFRARED TELESCOPE
These detect heat given off by objects. They are often used in space, where they are kept cold and far from Earth (so that they do not pick up confusing heat data from objects on Earth).

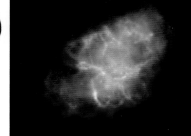

OPTICAL TELESCOPE
These use lenses and mirrors to capture light from distant objects. Reflecting and refracting telescopes are forms of optical telescopes.

ULTRAVIOLET TELESCOPE
Hot and active objects in the cosmos give off large amounts of ultraviolet energy, so they are revealed in most detail with this kind of telescope.

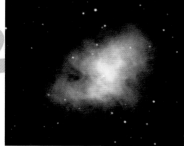

X-RAY TELESCOPE
These telescopes capture high-energy rays from extremely hot objects. X-rays from celestial objects are partly blocked by the Earth's atmosphere, so these telescopes are sent into space. They gather information from space objects as they orbit around Earth.

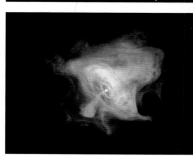

LOOKING AT THE SKY

Binoculars are a great way to start looking at the night sky, because they reveal up to ten times as much detail as the naked eye and are easy to use. Telescopes provide even greater detail.

MERCURY, VENUS, MARS, JUPITER, AND SATURN CAN BE SEEN WITH THE NAKED EYE

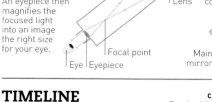

NAKED-EYE VIEW OF THE ORION NEBULA

BINOCULAR VIEW OF THE ORION NEBULA

TELESCOPE VIEW OF THE ORION NEBULA

HOW OPTICAL TELESCOPES WORK

Galileo Galilei made the first refracting telescope in 1609, and in the 1680s Isaac Newton invented the reflecting telescope, which uses mirrors to collect light and form it into an image.

REFRACTING TELESCOPE
Light enters the telescope and is focused on to the focal point by a lens. An eyepiece then magnifies the focused light into an image the right size for your eye.

Light from star enters telescope

Eye | Eyepiece

Focal point

Lens

REFLECTING TELESCOPE
In this telescope, a curved mirror captures the light and reflects it back up the tube. A small, flat mirror directs it to a focus, and the image is viewed through a magnifying eyepiece.

Eyepiece

Focal point

Light rays converge

Light from star enters telescope

Smaller mirror

Main mirror

TIMELINE

Since ancient times, people have recorded astronomical observations. As science advances, we are still trying to discover the great mysteries of the Universe.

c.330 BCE
Greek philosophers begin to believe that Earth is a sphere.

Aristotle

240 BCE
Eratosthenes, a Greek astronomer, estimates Earth's circumference with accuracy.

c.150 BCE
Claudius Ptolemy says that Earth sits at the centre of the cosmos. Belief in the Ptolemaic system continues for the next 1,400 years.

Ptolemy

1543 CE
The Polish astronomer Nicolaus Copernicus publishes his revolutionary model of the Solar System, putting the stationary Sun at the centre.

Earth

Copernicus's Solar System

1633
The Catholic Church puts Italian astronomer Galileo Galilei on trial for teaching Copernicus's heliocentric (Sun-centred) theory.

Galileo Galilei

2500 BCE

2500 BCE
Building of Stonehenge. The stones here mark the rising and setting points of the Sun at the solstices.

Stonehenge

700 BCE
Babylonians predict regular patterns of Sun and Moon eclipses.

Aristarchus's calculations

280 BCE
Ancient Greek astronomer Aristarchus calculates the size of the Sun and Moon and their distances from Earth.

240 BCE
The first certain appearance of Halley's Comet is described in the Chinese *Records of the Grand Historian*.

Halley's Comet

1054 CE
Chinese astronomers observe a supernova that is visible in the daytime. The matter blasted outwards by it remains observable as the Crab Nebula.

Elliptical orbit

1609
German mathematician Johannes Kepler calculates that the planets follow noncircular, elliptical orbits.

Isaac Newton

1687
English scientist Isaac Newton discovers that gravity keeps the Moon in orbit around Earth, and the planets in orbit around the Sun.

VIEW FROM EARTH

It is impossible to tell how large a star or planet is by looking at it from Earth, because some are huge but very far away. The Sun's diameter is 400 times that of the Moon, but it is also about 400 times further away.

SUN

MOON

MARS

POLARIS

METEOR

VENUS

SATURN

LIGHTS IN THE SKY

Sometimes we can see the interaction of light and magnetism in the skies through colourful light displays such as the northern lights.

NORTHERN LIGHTS
Also known as the aurora borealis, this light display is caused by particles from the Sun hitting Earth's magnetic field.

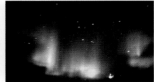
SOUTHERN LIGHTS
Also known as the aurora australis, this is similar to the northern lights but takes place above Earth's southern hemisphere.

MOONDOG
A moondog appears as a halo around the Moon. It is caused by the refraction of moonlight on ice crystals in clouds.

SUNDOG
Patches of sunlight appear at either side of the Sun. They are caused by sunlight refracting off ice crystals in clouds.

LIFE OUT THERE

The SETI (search for extraterrestrial intelligence) project was set up in 1960 to search for signs of life beyond Earth. Its powerful radio telescopes scan the skies but have not picked up an artificial (non-natural) radio signal so far.

SETI TELESCOPES

THE CELESTIAL SPHERE

The celestial sphere is an imaginary sphere around Earth. Any sky object can be mapped on to this sphere. Because Earth rotates, the celestial sphere appears to rotate. Like Earth, it has north and south poles and is divided into hemispheres by an equator.

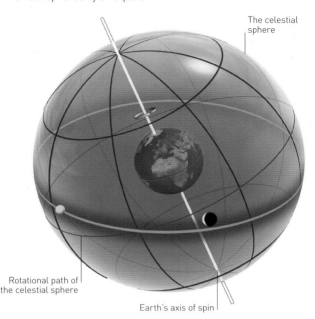

The celestial sphere

Rotational path of the celestial sphere

Earth's axis of spin

LINE OF SIGHT

Wherever you stand on Earth, you can see a portion of the celestial sphere. For example, the Plough seems to be a fixed shape, but it is actually formed by stars moving far out in space, all at different distances from the Earth.

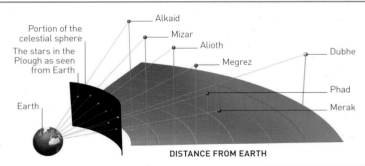

Portion of the celestial sphere

The stars in the Plough as seen from Earth

Earth

Alkaid
Mizar
Alioth
Megrez
Dubhe
Phad
Merak

DISTANCE FROM EARTH

CONSTELLATIONS

Stargazers in ancient times named groups of stars after mythical beings and animals. These star patterns are called constellations and we still use them today to find the stars. There are 88 constellations in total, and each one is only visible at certain times and from certain places.

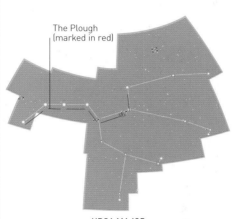

The Plough (marked in red)

URSA MAJOR
This constellation is also known as the Great Bear. It contains an asterism (smaller group of stars) known as the Plough, or the Big Dipper.

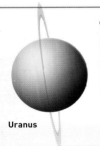
Uranus

1781
German-born astronomer, William Herschel discovers Uranus, a planet beyond Saturn, doubling the size of the known Solar System.

1933
American physicist Karl Jansky records the first radio-wave signals from space, which he concludes are from the Milky Way.

1992
Astronomers discover the first extra-solar planets (exoplanets).

Infrared Astronomical Satellite

2006
The International Astronomical Union defines the properties of a "planet" and in doing so demotes Pluto from a planet to a dwarf planet.

2018

Ceres

1801
Italian astronomer Giuseppe Piazzi comes across a rocky body orbiting between Mars and Jupiter. Named Ceres, this is the largest object in the asteroid belt, and is classified as a dwarf planet.

1843
German amateur astronomer Samuel Heinrich Schwabe observes that sunspots (areas of lower temperature) follow regular cycles.

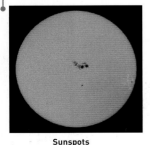
Sunspots

1922
American astronomer Edwin Hubble works out that there are more galaxies in the Universe than the Milky Way, and that they are moving apart – the Universe is expanding.

James Webb Space Telescope

2018
The James Webb Space Telescope (JWST) is a space observatory scheduled to launch in October 2018. It is a successor to the Hubble Space Telescope and will offer the clearest images ever seen of objects in space.

Northern skies

If you live north of the equator, you live in the northern hemisphere. On a dark and cloudless night, you can see a mass of glittering stars. If you know what to look for, you can pick out individual stars, constellations, and other wonders of the night sky.

KEY
This map shows stars that are visible to the naked eye. Magnitude marks how bright a star is – the lower the number, the brighter the star.

- ☆ Yellow star
- ☆ Red star
- ☆ Orange star
- ○ White star
- ○ Blue star

- ○ Magnitude brighter than 0.0
- ○ Magnitude brighter than 1.0
- ○ Magnitude brighter than 2.0
- ○ Magnitude brighter than 3.0
- ○ Magnitude brighter than 4.0
- ○ Magnitude brighter than 5.0

THINGS TO LOOK FOR

Individual stars, star clusters, and whole galaxies can be seen with binoculars or a small telescope. Here are some key sights to look out for in the northern skies.

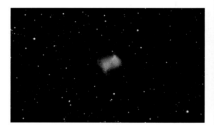

DUMBBELL NEBULA
This is a planetary nebula, which means it is made up of clouds of material shed by a star. It is in the constellation of Vulpecula.

STAR CLUSTER M13
This is the finest globular (globe-shaped) cluster in the northern skies. It lies in the Hercules constellation.

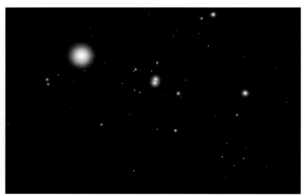

HYADES STAR CLUSTER
This star cluster makes up the face of the bull in the constellation Taurus. The brightest star here is the giant star Aldebaran, which marks the eye of Taurus.

LEO CONSTELLATION
The constellation Leo contains three spiral galaxies: M65, M66, and NGC 3628. They are known as the Leo Triplet.

PLEIADES STAR CLUSTER
This cluster in Taurus is also known as the Seven Sisters, because seven of its blue stars are visible to the naked eye.

PERSEUS CONSTELLATION
This constellation is best known for its yearly Perseid meteor shower, which takes place in mid-August. It lies just below the "W" shape of the constellation of Cassiopeia.

ORION NEBULA
This nebula marks the position of the "sword" below the "belt" of Orion in the Orion constellation.

M71 STAR CLUSTER
This loosely packed star cluster is on the edge of our galaxy. It sits in the Sagitta constellation.

REFLECTION NEBULA
This ghostly blue nebula is in the constellation of Cepheus. At its heart is a cluster of stars.

LYRA CONSTELLATION
The small constellation Lyra has one brilliant star, Vega. It is the fifth-brightest of all the stars.

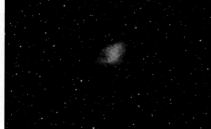

CRAB NEBULA
This is the remains of a supernova (an exploding star). It is found in Taurus, near the southerly "bull horn".

M15 STAR CLUSTER
This globular cluster is in Pegasus, northwest of Epsilon Pegasi, the constellation's brightest star.

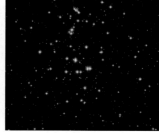

BEEHIVE CLUSTER
This swarm of stars in the constellation of Cancer is about three times the diameter of the Moon.

Altair

AQUILA

SERPENS CAUDA

OPHIUCHUS

SERPENS CAPUT

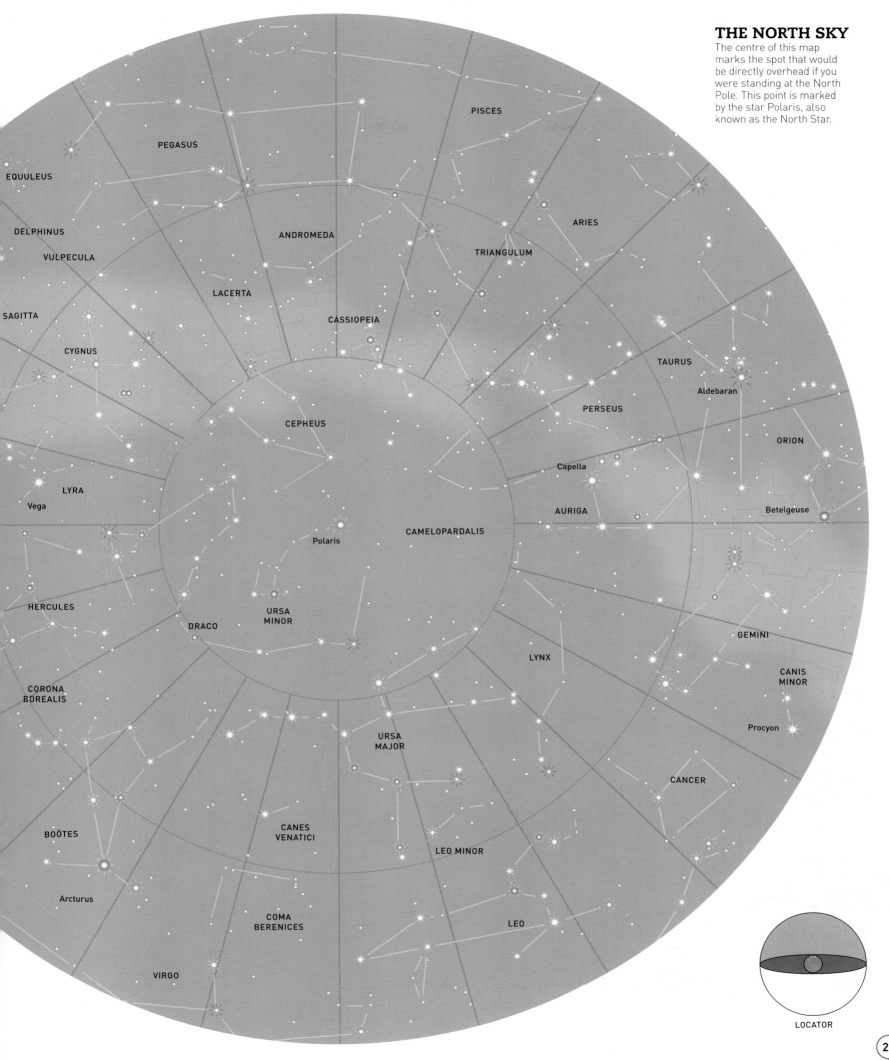

PISCES

PEGASUS

EQUULEUS

ARIES

DELPHINUS

ANDROMEDA

TRIANGULUM

VULPECULA

LACERTA

SAGITTA

CASSIOPEIA

TAURUS

CYGNUS

Aldebaran

PERSEUS

CEPHEUS

ORION

Capella

LYRA

AURIGA

Betelgeuse

Vega

CAMELOPARDALIS

Polaris

HERCULES

URSA MINOR

DRACO

GEMINI

LYNX

CORONA BOREALIS

CANIS MINOR

URSA MAJOR

Procyon

CANCER

BOÖTES

CANES VENATICI

LEO MINOR

Arcturus

COMA BERENICES

LEO

VIRGO

LOCATOR

21

Southern skies

If you live south of the equator, you live in the southern hemisphere. On a clear night, the southern skies give a fantastic view of the Milky Way, bright star clusters, constellations, colourful nebulae – and even whole galaxies.

OMEGA CENTAURI IS THE LARGEST STAR CLUSTER IN OUR GALAXY, CONTAINING AROUND TEN MILLION STARS

KEY
This map shows stars that are visible to the naked eye. Magnitude marks how bright a star is – the lower the number, the brighter the star.

- Yellow star
- Red star
- Orange star
- White star
- Blue star

- Magnitude brighter than 0.0
- Magnitude brighter than 1.0
- Magnitude brighter than 2.0
- Magnitude brighter than 3.0
- Magnitude brighter than 4.0
- Magnitude brighter than 5.0

THINGS TO LOOK FOR

The southern skies contain many night-sky objects that are not visible from the northern hemisphere, including the Magellanic clouds and the bright star cluster known as the Jewel Box.

THE JEWEL BOX CLUSTER
Shown at the bottom left here, this cluster includes a red supergiant and smaller blue stars. It is in the constellation Crux. The bright star in the upper right here is called Mimosa.

LARGE MAGELLANIC CLOUD
This small galaxy orbits our own galaxy, the Milky Way. It sits in the constellation Dorado, though part of it is in the constellation Mensa.

NGC 3603 NEBULA
This giant nebula in the constellation Carina is composed of huge glowing clouds of gas. In its centre are thousands of hot, young stars.

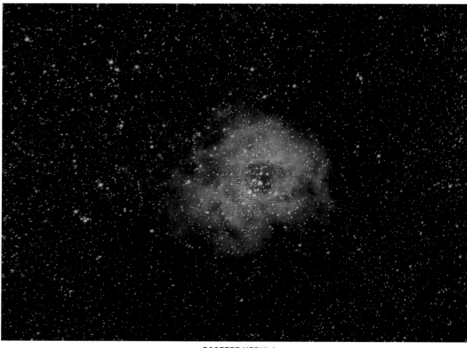

ROSETTE NEBULA
This flower-shaped nebula is a star nursery – stars are being created within it – and there is a cluster of new stars at its centre. It can be seen with a small telescope in the constellation Monoceros.

OMEGA CENTAURI CLUSTER
This is the largest and brightest globular cluster visible from Earth – it appears as a fuzzy star to the naked eye. It is in the centre of the Centaurus constellation.

ERIDANUS

Rigel

LEPUS

CANIS MAJOR

Sirius

MONOCEROS

M4 GLOBULAR CLUSTER
This cluster is around 12.2 billion years old. It is found near the bright star Antares, in the constellation Scorpius.

47 TUCANAE GLOBULAR CLUSTER
This huge star cluster is around 16,700 light years from Earth, in the constellation of Tucana. It contains several million stars but looks like a single hazy star to the naked eye.

CORVUS CONSTELLATION
Corvus, the crow, is made up of four bright stars, shown in the lower-right half of this image. It sits close to the very bright double star known as Spica (top left).

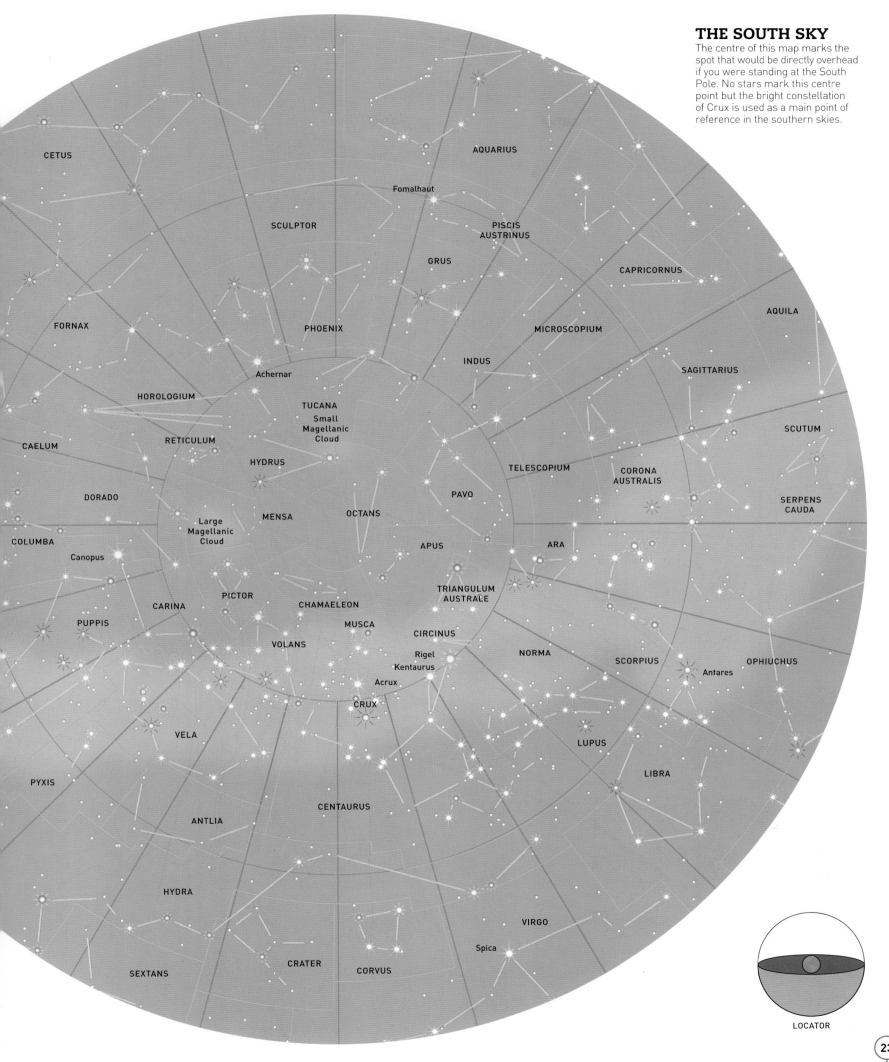

CETUS

AQUARIUS

Fomalhaut

SCULPTOR

PISCIS AUSTRINUS

GRUS

CAPRICORNUS

PHOENIX

MICROSCOPIUM

AQUILA

FORNAX

INDUS

Achernar

SAGITTARIUS

HOROLOGIUM

SCUTUM

TUCANA

Small Magellanic Cloud

CAELUM

RETICULUM

HYDRUS

TELESCOPIUM

CORONA AUSTRALIS

SERPENS CAUDA

DORADO

PAVO

OCTANS

Large Magellanic Cloud

MENSA

APUS

ARA

COLUMBA

Canopus

PICTOR

TRIANGULUM AUSTRALE

CARINA

CHAMAELEON

PUPPIS

MUSCA

CIRCINUS

VOLANS

NORMA

SCORPIUS

OPHIUCHUS

Rigel Kentaurus

Antares

Acrux

CRUX

LUPUS

VELA

LIBRA

PYXIS

CENTAURUS

ANTLIA

HYDRA

VIRGO

Spica

SEXTANS

CRATER

CORVUS

LOCATOR

23

Physics

How do forces, such as gravity and magnetism, affect matter – the stuff all around us? And how does energy make that possible? The answers to these questions are found in physics. Physicists try to unravel the rules of the Universe to explain why the world works as it does.

GRAVITY

Gravity is the force that keeps us held fast on the planet, even while Earth spins at up to 1,670 km/h (1,037 mph). Gravity pulls together all matter, but larger things with more mass have more gravitational force.

Earth pulls apple down

Force of gravity makes apple fall

Apple pulls Earth up a tiny amount

Earth and apple pull together

FALLING APPLE

GRAVITY KEEPS EARTH AND THE OTHER PLANETS IN THE SOLAR SYSTEM ORBITING AROUND THE SUN

MASS AND WEIGHT

The mass of something is the amount of matter it contains, and mass always stays the same, wherever the object is. But weight changes depending on where an object is, because weight is determined by gravity.

Man of 75 kg (165 lb) mass, weighs 12.5 kg (27.5 lb) on the Moon

MOON

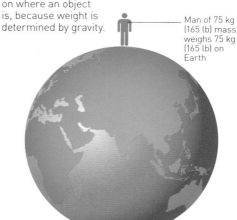

Man of 75 kg (165 lb) mass, weighs 75 kg (165 lb) on Earth

EARTH

FORCE

A force is something that pushes or pulls objects – whenever something moves, it has been moved by a force. Forces can change the speed of an object, alter its direction, or change its shape.

CHANGING SPEED

The force of the golf club hitting the ball makes the ball move. The ball gains energy and takes off down the golf course.

The harder the ball is hit, the more force is used, and the further it travels

CHANGING DIRECTION

When a force is applied to a moving object like a tennis ball, it can move it in a different direction.

Ball moves in one direction towards the racket

Hitting the ball with the racket applies force, changing the ball's direction

CHANGING SHAPE

A force may cause something to change shape if the force is strong enough and the atoms inside the object cannot resist it.

Bending a bar rearranges the atoms inside it, altering its shape

MAGNETISM

Magnetism is a powerful invisible force that is created by electric currents. Magnetic objects have the power to attract other magnetic objects or push them away, depending on how their ends (poles) are lined up.

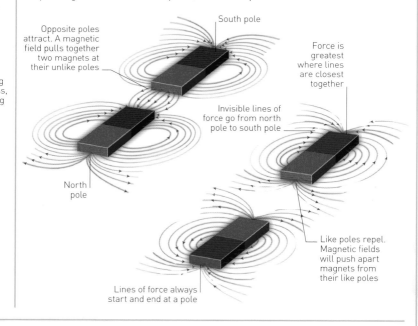

Opposite poles attract. A magnetic field pulls together two magnets at their unlike poles

South pole

Force is greatest where lines are closest together

Invisible lines of force go from north pole to south pole

North pole

Like poles repel. Magnetic fields will push apart magnets from their like poles

Lines of force always start and end at a pole

LAWS OF MOTION

All motion is caused by forces pushing and pulling. The scientist Isaac Newton described three laws of motion. The first says that all things will stay still or move at a steady speed unless a force acts on them. The second says that when a force acts on something it makes it accelerate. The third says that when a force operates on something (action), there is always an opposing and equal force (reaction).

FIRST LAW
Before take-off, the only force acting on a rocket is gravity.

SECOND LAW
The main engines and booster rockets create a huge downward force that accelerates the rocket upwards.

THIRD LAW
The exhaust gas firing down (the action) makes the rocket shoot up (the reaction). The rocket does not push against the air; it moves up because of the force of the exhaust blasting down.

FRICTION

This force occurs when one object is dragged over the surface of another object. The rougher a surface is, the more friction it produces. Even smooth surfaces have tiny bumps that will produce some friction.

Surface A
Surface B

FRICTION
As two rough objects slide over one another, their surfaces catch, slowing the sliding down.

Surface A
Surface B

LUBRICATION
Putting a slippery material such as oil between two surfaces lets them move past one another more easily.

TYPES OF ENERGY

There are many different kinds of energy, and most of them can be converted into other forms. For example, when you burn coal it changes the chemical energy stored in the coal into heat energy.

SOUND ENERGY
Energy we can hear, made when things vibrate.

KINETIC ENERGY
The energy objects have because they are moving.

ELECTRICAL ENERGY
The energy carried by electricity as it flows down a wire.

LIGHT ENERGY
Energy carried in electromagnetic waves.

CHEMICAL ENERGY
Released by a reaction between different chemicals.

NUCLEAR ENERGY
Generated by atoms splitting apart or joining together.

POTENTIAL ENERGY
Energy that is stored and yet to be released.

HEAT ENERGY
Energy stored or moved by molecules jiggling around.

HEAT

Heat is a form of energy, so when you heat something, you are increasing its stored energy. Objects store heat by jostling molecules or atoms inside them. Even large, cold objects can have heat energy.

HEAT IS USUALLY ON THE MOVE – IT TRAVELS ABOUT, SO COLD THINGS GET HOT AND HOT THINGS GET COLD

ICEBERGS
Icebergs are freezing cold but they still have some heat energy.

ELECTROMAGNETIC SPECTRUM

The Sun's heat and light is carried to Earth by electromagnetic waves. These are just part of a spectrum that includes radio waves, microwaves, and X-rays. All waves travel at the speed of light but they vary in wavelength, frequency, and energy.

MICROWAVES
Microwaves can be used to cook food.

INFRARED RAYS
Infrared radiation is a kind of "hot light". It shows up on thermal (heat-sensitive) cameras.

GAMMA RAYS
These are made when atoms split apart in nuclear explosions.

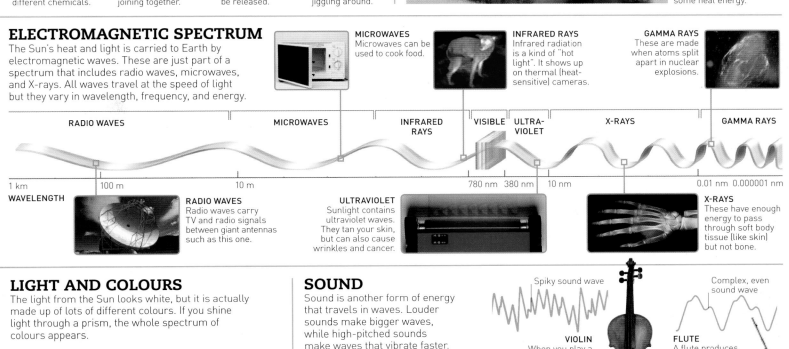

RADIO WAVES | MICROWAVES | INFRARED RAYS | VISIBLE | ULTRA-VIOLET | X-RAYS | GAMMA RAYS

1 km   100 m   10 m   780 nm   380 nm   10 nm   0.01 nm   0.000001 nm
WAVELENGTH

RADIO WAVES
Radio waves carry TV and radio signals between giant antennas such as this one.

ULTRAVIOLET
Sunlight contains ultraviolet waves. They tan your skin, but can also cause wrinkles and cancer.

X-RAYS
These have enough energy to pass through soft body tissue (like skin) but not bone.

LIGHT AND COLOURS

The light from the Sun looks white, but it is actually made up of lots of different colours. If you shine light through a prism, the whole spectrum of colours appears.

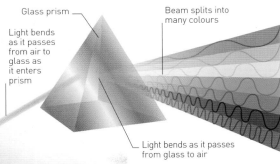

Glass prism

Light bends as it passes from air to glass as it enters prism

Beam splits into many colours

Light bends as it passes from glass to air

SOUND

Sound is another form of energy that travels in waves. Louder sounds make bigger waves, while high-pitched sounds make waves that vibrate faster. The various noises we hear are produced by sound waves of different shapes and sizes.

Spiky sound wave

Complex, even sound wave

VIOLIN
When you play a violin, the strings vibrate, setting the air moving inside the hollow wooden case. A violin's sound wave is a sharp and spiky wave.

FLUTE
A flute produces sound when you blow into it, making waves inside the pipe. The sound waves are similar to a sine wave.

Smooth, even sound wave

TUNING FORK
A tuning fork makes one simple, regular, up-and-down sound wave pattern called a "sine" wave. Each fork produces only one note.

CYMBAL
Percussion instruments make sounds when you hit them. Their sound waves are more like a short burst of random noise (white noise) than a precise wave.

A bigger cymbal vibrates a greater volume of air so it sounds louder

TINY SCIENCE

Our whole planet and all its people are made of atoms. The nucleus of an atom consists of protons and neutrons, and these are made of even smaller things called quarks. It is unclear what those are made of, but some scientists think that they may be vibrations of matter or energy, which scientists refer to as "strings". This science is known as quantum physics.

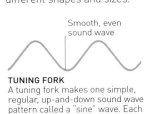

Quark

Proton

ATOM

GREAT PHYSICISTS

People have tried to explain our world and the Universe since ancient times. In the last 400 years, physicists have invented theories that underpin much of what we know.

○ **ISAAC NEWTON (1643–1727)**
Newton discovered that sunlight contains all the colours of the rainbow. He also devised the laws of gravity and motion.

○ **ERNEST RUTHERFORD (1871–1937)**
Rutherford proved that the atom was not solid but contained electrically charged electrons orbiting a nucleus.

○ **ALBERT EINSTEIN (1879–1955)**
Einstein discovered many things, but he is most famous for his theory of relativity.

○ **RICHARD FEYNMAN (1918–88)**
Feynman is best known for introducing the world to quantum physics.

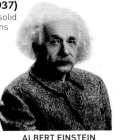
ALBERT EINSTEIN

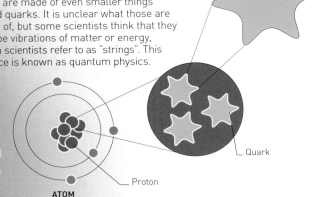

Electricity

We use electricity to power all sorts of things, from factories and trains to the many small appliances in our homes. The energy it contains comes from charged electrons that whizz around inside every atom.

ELECTRICITY IN NATURE

Electricity is not only generated in power stations – it is also found in nature, from high-energy lightning strikes to inside our own bodies. Our brains use electric signals to tell our muscles to move.

LIGHTNING
A bolt releases as much energy as a power station makes in one second.

AURORA
These lights in the sky are streams of electrically charged particles.

NERVOUS SYSTEMS
Human nerves communicate by electric signals.

ELECTRIC EEL
This eel discharges electricity in water to kill fish for food

ELECTRIC CURRENT

When electrons flow down wires, they carry energy from place to place. So in a torch, electrons march around the wire from the battery to the lamp, where their power lights up the bulb.

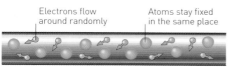
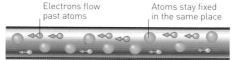

Electrons flow past atoms — Atoms stay fixed in the same place

CURRENT FLOWING
When the power is switched on, the electrons move along in a line, forming an electric current.

Electrons flow around randomly — Atoms stay fixed in the same place

NO CURRENT FLOWING
When the power is switched off, there's nothing to move the electrons in a line, so they just jig about randomly.

CIRCUITS

The path that electrons travel along is called a "circuit". A circuit carries power from a power source (such as a wall socket) to something that needs electricity to run (such as a lamp). There are two types of circuit.

SERIES CONNECTION
All the power moves through each part of the circuit, in a line.

PARALLEL CONNECTION
The power splits into two as it reaches two lamps wired like this.

SWITCHES

If you attach a wire to both ends of a battery, and connect a lightbulb to the wire at some point, the electricity would continually flow and always light the bulb. A switch is used to break the circuit, so the bulb can be switched on and off.

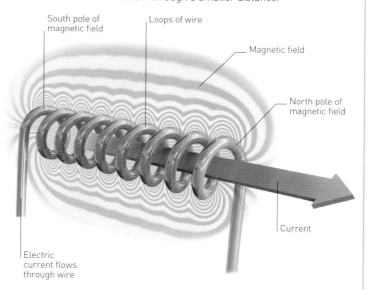

If the circuit is not broken, the electricity flows back into the battery

A switch can be used to make a break in the circuit

Electrons flow from the negative end of the battery

The lightbulb forms part of the circuit

BATTERIES

Batteries make their own electricity by using chemicals. When you connect a battery, chemical reactions take place that generate electrons.

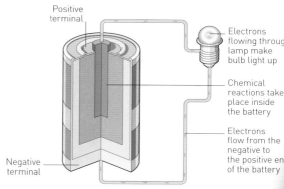

Positive terminal

Electrons flowing through lamp make bulb light up

Chemical reactions take place inside the battery

Electrons flow from the negative to the positive end of the battery

Negative terminal

LIGHTNING BOLTS ARE LARGE-SCALE STATIC SHOCKS

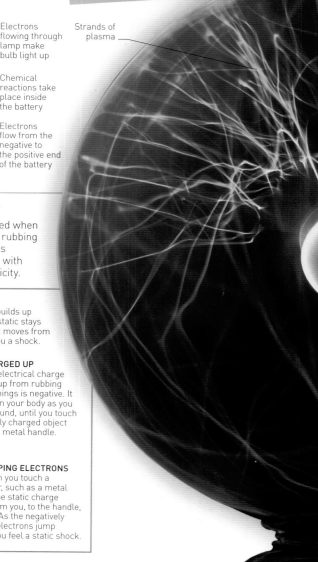

Strands of plasma

ELECTROMAGNETISM

When an electric current flows through a wire, it creates a magnetic field around it. The strength of the magnetic field can be increased by coiling the wire in loops, because that allows more current to flow through a smaller distance.

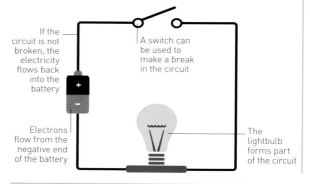

South pole of magnetic field

Loops of wire

Magnetic field

North pole of magnetic field

Current

Electric current flows through wire

STATIC ELECTRICITY

Static electricity is sometimes created when two things are rubbed together. The rubbing creates an electrical charge, which is released when it comes into contact with something else that conducts electricity.

GETTING A SHOCK

Static shocks occur because your body builds up static when you rub against things. The static stays until you touch something metal, when it moves from you through the metal to Earth, giving you a shock.

1 CHARGED UP
The electrical charge you pick up from rubbing against things is negative. It will stay in your body as you move around, until you touch a positively charged object such as a metal handle.

2 JUMPING ELECTRONS
When you touch a conductor, such as a metal handle, the static charge jumps from you, to the handle, to Earth. As the negatively charged electrons jump across, you feel a static shock.

CONDUCTORS AND INSULATORS

Electricity is a flow of electrons, so materials that do not allow the flow cannot pass along electricity. These are called "insulators". Materials that do allow the flow of electricity are called "conductors".

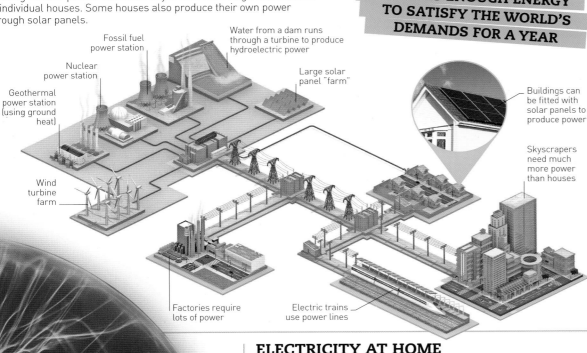

INSULATORS — **SEMICONDUCTORS** — **CONDUCTORS**

RUBBER   WOOD   SILICON   WATER   COPPER

POWER TO THE HOME

Electricity is produced for homes in several ways, such as burning coal or using nuclear power. The electricity is then fed though sub-stations to individual houses. Some houses also produce their own power through solar panels.

Fossil fuel power station

Nuclear power station

Geothermal power station (using ground heat)

Wind turbine farm

Water from a dam runs through a turbine to produce hydroelectric power

Large solar panel "farm"

Buildings can be fitted with solar panels to produce power

Skyscrapers need much more power than houses

Factories require lots of power

Electric trains use power lines

ONE MINUTE OF SUNLIGHT PROVIDES ENOUGH ENERGY TO SATISFY THE WORLD'S DEMANDS FOR A YEAR

ELECTRICITY AT HOME

We use electricity at home from the moment we get up (perhaps switching on a light or using an electric toothbrush), to when we go to bed. Homes need energy for heat, light, cooking, and washing machines, as well as lots of personal items, such as hairdryers and mobile phones.

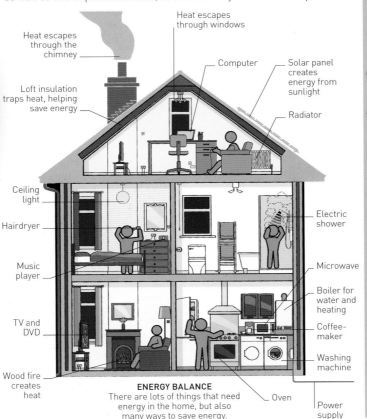

Heat escapes through windows

Heat escapes through the chimney

Loft insulation traps heat, helping save energy

Computer

Solar panel creates energy from sunlight

Radiator

Ceiling light

Hairdryer

Music player

TV and DVD

Wood fire creates heat

Electric shower

Microwave

Boiler for water and heating

Coffee-maker

Washing machine

Oven

Power supply

ENERGY BALANCE
There are lots of things that need energy in the home, but also many ways to save energy.

PLASMA SPHERE
The streams of plasma here are created by the release of static electricity, which flows as a current from the centre to the edge of the glass sphere.

VOLTAGE

Voltage is a kind of force that makes electricity move through a wire. The bigger the voltage, the more current will shoot through the wire. Bigger voltages and currents deliver more electrical power, but they are also more dangerous.

PYLONS
These hold up overhead lines that carry electricity across long distances. The largest ones use 400,000-volt cables. Cables on wooden poles use 400–11,000 volts.

ELECTRIC TRAIN CABLES
Trains take power from cables above them. One train needs less than 1,000 volts, but the cables are about 25,000 volts. This means many trains can use the line at once.

ELECTRICITY AT HOME
Voltage in the home differs from country to country, but generally lies at 110–250 volts. Factories need higher voltages because they have bigger machines.

BATTERY CHARGERS
A laptop or phone charger needs 10–20 volts to charge its battery. Laptops need higher voltages than phones because they have bigger screens and circuits that use more energy.

TORCH BULBS
Bulbs for torches and lamps are rated by the voltage and current needed to operate them. The standard AA, C, and D batteries all deliver 1.5 volts each.

PIONEERS

Electricity has been around forever, because it exists naturally in the world. However, some people were important in finding out how to harness its power.

○ **BENJAMIN FRANKLIN (1706–90)**
Franklin discovered that lightning is electricity, and that there are positive and negative charges.

○ **ALESSANDRO VOLTA (1745–1827)**
A professor of experimental physics, Volta invented the first battery, called the Voltaic Pile.

○ **GEORG SIMON OHM (1789–1854)**
Ohm discovered electrical resistance. The unit of resistance – ohm – is named after him.

○ **MICHAEL FARADAY (1791–1867)**
Faraday discovered that if you move a magnet near wire, the wire becomes electrified. This is known as electromagnetic induction.

○ **THOMAS ALVA EDISON (1847–1931)**
Edison built the first electric power stations and invented the lightbulb, sound recorder (phonograph), and movie camera.

○ **NIKOLA TESLA (1856–1943)**
Tesla discovered alternating currents, hydroelectric power, radio waves, and radar. He invented transformers, a long-distance power system, electric motors, and X-ray machines.

NIKOLA TESLA

Chemistry

Chemists dig deep. They begin with the elements that make up all matter, and break them down into tiny atoms. They analyse what the atoms are, how they change state, and how they react when they mix.

CHEMISTRY IN ACTION

In ancient times, people used the natural materials around them, such as wood and stone, to make objects. Since then, scientists have discovered thousands of chemicals, some of which can be used to make new materials.

HOUSEHOLD CHEMICALS
We use lots of chemicals in our homes, from the paint on our walls to the shampoo for our hair.

BIOCHEMISTRY
This looks at chemical processes inside living things or affecting them.

ORGANIC CHEMISTRY
This branch of chemistry focuses on carbon-based compounds and their uses.

MATERIALS SCIENCE
This science uses physics and chemistry to create new materials.

ENGINEERING
Engineers use their knowledge of material. to design things.

INSIDE AN ATOM

Even though an atom is tiny, it has even smaller things inside it – protons, neutrons, and electrons. Protons and neutrons combine to form the atom's nucleus. Electrons fill the space around the nucleus.

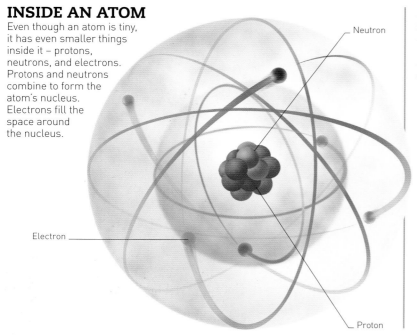

Neutron

Electron

Proton

STRUCTURE OF AN ATOM

Some particles in the atom are electrically charged. The protons in the nucleus are positively charged and the orbiting electrons are negatively charged. There are always equal numbers of protons and electrons.

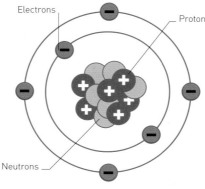

Electrons

Protons

Neutrons

CARBON ATOM
The number of protons inside an atom determines what kind of atom it is. For example, a carbon atom has six electrons and six protons.

MOLECULES

Atoms of the same sort or different atoms can clump together to make molecules. A molecule can be as simple as just two atoms, as in hydrogen, or lines of thousands of atoms, as in some plastics.

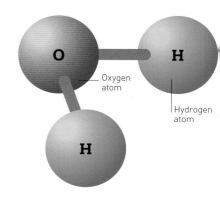

O

H

Oxygen atom

Hydrogen atom

H

WATER MOLECULE
A molecule of water is made up of two different kinds of atoms: two hydrogen (H) atoms and one oxygen (O) atom.

STATES OF MATTER

All matter can change state. Water, for instance, can be a liquid, gas (steam), or solid (ice). Its state depends upon the way its atoms move around. As a solid, its atoms lock tightly together. As a liquid, they move further apart, and as a gas they move freely and independently.

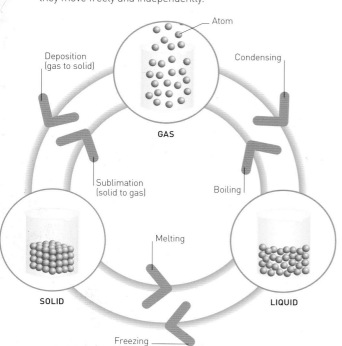

Atom

Deposition (gas to solid)

Condensing

GAS

Sublimation (solid to gas)

Boiling

Melting

SOLID

LIQUID

Freezing

MIXTURES

A mixture is made when two substances are combined, but no chemical reaction takes place. The ingredients are said to combine, rather than to bond.

SOLUTION
Fruit concentrate (solute) dissolves in water (the solvent) to make a drink.

SUSPENSION
A mixture between a liquid and particles of a solid, such as water and soil.

COARSE MIXTURE
An unevenly distributed mixture of different types of larger particles.

ALLOY
A mixture of a metal with other elements that create a stronger material.

SEPARATING MIXTURES

The substances in a mixture are not bonded together, so they can be separated. However, the more similar the properties of each substance are to one another, the harder it is to separate them.

FLOATING
Shaken together these substances mix. Left for a time, they separate back out.

MAGNETIZING
Magnetic substances will be drawn to stick to the magnet.

CHROMATOGRAPHY
Using a substance that attracts some particles more than others separates the two.

FILTERING
Solid particles will collect on the filter during the filtration process.

ACIDS AND BASES

All liquids and solutions fall somewhere on the acids and bases scale, which is measured as a pH level. Those at each end of the scale are very reactive and dangerous.

| 0 | 1 | 2 | 3 | 4 | 5 | 6 | 7 | 8 | 9 | 10 | 11 | 12 | 13 | 14 |

STRONG ACID
e.g. gastric acid

WEAK ACID
e.g. tomato juice

NEUTRAL
e.g. water

WEAK BASE
e.g. baking soda

STRONG BASE
e.g. bleach

THE pH SCALE

WHAT IS A CHEMICAL REACTION?

In the natural world, atoms and molecules are constantly joining together or breaking down to form new things. This can also be done in a laboratory. When scientists add one ingredient (called a reactant) to another, they create a chemical reaction. The molecules of the reactants split apart, rearrange themselves, and then form a new bond – the product of the reaction.

REACTANT 1   REACTANT 2   REACTION   PRODUCT

SWIRLS AND FUMES
The product of a chemical reaction can be very different from the original reactants. This mix reacts quickly, swirling and giving off fumes.

TYPES OF CHEMICAL REACTION

Although the product of a chemical reaction is very different from the reactants, none of the atoms are destroyed – there are the same number before as after the reaction. There are three types of chemical reaction.

SYNTHESIS REACTION
Two or more reactants join together to make a new compound.

DECOMPOSITION REACTION
One reactant breaks apart into two products to make two compounds.

> **GRAPHITE CAN BE CHANGED INTO DIAMOND THROUGH HEAT AND PRESSURE**

REPLACEMENT REACTION
Atoms of one type swap places with those of another to make a new compound.

COMBUSTION

Car engines and power stations are powered by a chemical reaction called combustion (burning). The reactants are fuel, such as petrol or coal, and oxygen from the air. Adding heat (setting fire to the fuel) starts the reaction.

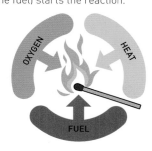

OXYGEN   HEAT   FUEL

MATERIALS

The materials we use for making everyday objects need to have the right properties for the object's function. For example, wood is robust and good for building a chair but would be a poor choice for a frying pan, because it would catch fire.

WOOD
Hard, strong, and rigid, burns readily, and is a good insulator.

METAL
Good conductor of heat and electricity. It is strong and inflexible.

PLASTIC
Strong, waterproof, and can be made into any shape. Good insulator.

CERAMIC
Fragile if knocked but can withstand high temperatures.

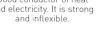

GLASS
Transparent and can be made into any shape. Breaks easily if thin.

SYNTHETIC FIBRE
Plastic-based fibres are strong and waterproof.

KEVLAR®
High-strength material that withstands high impact and extremes of temperatures.

GREAT CHEMISTS

The discoveries of great chemists have contributed to human progress in everything from medicine to space travel.

ROBERT BOYLE (1627–91)
The author of *The Sceptical Chymist* was the first to develop rigorous scientific techniques for his experiments in the field of chemistry.

ANTOINE LAVOISIER (1743–94)
The first chemist to demonstrate that water is made of oxygen and hydrogen, and to show that oxygen is needed for combustion.

MARIE CURIE (1867–1934)
Twice winner of the Nobel prize, Curie discovered radium.

LINUS PAULING (1901–94)
American scientist who worked out how molecules bond together.

LINUS PAULING

DOROTHY HODGKIN (1910–94)
A pioneer in X-ray techniques who discovered the atomic structure of penicillin.

29

The elements

The building blocks of every single thing on Earth are pure chemical substances called elements. Put a few elements together by joining their atoms and you can get anything from a flea to a space rocket. Carbon-based elements are found in all living things, while water has just two elements – hydrogen and oxygen.

THE PERIODIC TABLE

Elements with a similar atomic structure sit together in the grid, which predicts how they will behave. Most of the 118 elements occur in rocks or in the atmosphere, but scientists have also built new ones by smashing smaller atoms together.

WHAT IS THE PERIODIC TABLE?

Elements are listed in a chart called the periodic table. Each entry shows the element's name, short chemical symbol, atomic number, and atomic mass.

ATOMIC NUMBER
An element's atomic number refers to the number of protons in the nucleus of an atom of the element. Titanium has 22.

22	47.867
Ti	
TITANIUM	

ATOMIC MASS
This is the number of protons and neutrons inside an atom.

CHEMICAL SYMBOL
This scientific symbol is a short version of the element's name.

NAME
This is the element's name. Titanium is a strong, light metal that is found in abundance in Earth's crust.

MAN-MADE ELEMENTS
Elements with a higher number than uranium (92) do not occur naturally. These transuranic elements have to be created in particle accelerators or nuclear reactors. They include plutonium, which was used to make the atomic bomb.

96 PER CENT OF THE HUMAN BODY IS MADE UP OF JUST FOUR ELEMENTS: OXYGEN, CARBON, HYDROGEN, AND NITROGEN

Periodic table

Group 1

1	1.0079
H	
Jupiter	
HYDROGEN	

Group 2

3	6.941		4	9.0122
Li			**Be**	
Watermelon tourmaline			Aquamarine	
LITHIUM			BERYLLIUM	

11	22.990		12	24.305
Na			**Mg**	
Salt			Peridot	
SODIUM			MAGNESIUM	

Groups 3–9

3	4	5	6	7	8	9

19	39.098	20	40.078	21	44.956	22	47.867	23	50.942	24	51.996	25	54.938	26	55.845	27	58.93
K		**Ca**		**Sc**		**Ti**		**V**		**Cr**		**Mn**		**Fe**		**Co**	
Banana		Cheese				Benitoite gemstone		Vanadinite		Chrome tap		Spessartine		Iron horseshoe		Blue glass	
POTASSIUM		CALCIUM		SCANDIUM		TITANIUM		VANADIUM		CHROMIUM		MANGANESE		IRON		COBALT	

37	85.468	38	87.62	39	88.906	40	91.224	41	92.906	42	95.94	43	(96)	44	101.07	45	102.9
Rb		**Sr**		**Y**		**Zr**		**Nb**		**Mo**		**Tc**		**Ru**		**Rh**	
Fireworks		Strontium				Zircon stone		Rocket engine		Steel girder						Rhodium-plated buckle	
RUBIDIUM		STRONTIUM		YTTRIUM		ZIRCONIUM		NIOBIUM		MOLYBDENUM		TECHNETIUM		RUTHENIUM		RHODIUM	

55	132.91	56	137.33	57-71		72	178.49	73	180.95	74	183.84	75	186.21	76	190.23	77	192.2
Cs		**Ba**		**La-Lu**		**Hf**		**Ta**		**W**		**Re**				**Ir**	
Caesium atomic clock		Crystals				Nuclear reactor control rod		Capacitor		Filament in light bulb		Jet turbine blades		Tip of fountain pen / **Os**		Surgical needle	
CAESIUM		BARIUM		LANTHANIDE		HAFNIUM		TANTALUM		TUNGSTEN		RHENIUM		OSMIUM		IRIDIUM	

87	(223)	88	(226)	89-103		104	(261)	105	(262)	106	(266)	107	(264)	108	(277)	109	(26#)
Fr		**Ra**		**Ac-Lr**		**Rf**		**Db**		**Sg**		**Bh**		**Hs**		**Mt**	
FRANCIUM		RADIUM		ACTINIDE		RUTHERFORDIUM		DUBNIUM		SEABORGIUM		BOHRIUM		HASSIUM		MEITNERIUM	

57	138.91	58	140.12	59	140.91	60	144.24	61	(145)	62	150.3
La		**Ce**		**Pr**		**Nd**		**Pm**		**Sm**	
Monazite		Cerium oxide		Permanent magnet		Earphones				Samarskite	
LANTHANUM		CERIUM		PRASEODYMIUM		NEODYMIUM		PROMETHIUM		SAMARIUM	

89	(227)	90	232.04	91	231.04	92	238.03	93	(237)	94	(244)
Ac		**Th**		**Pa**		**U**		**Np**		**Pu**	
						Nuclear power plant				Atomic bomb	
ACTINIUM		THORIUM		PROTACTINIUM		URANIUM		NEPTUNIUM		PLUTONIUM	

e table has horizontal rows called periods and vertical
lumns called groups. Atoms get bigger and heavier
wards the bottom of each group because they have more
rotons and more electrons in the shells (rings) around
em. As you move along the rows from left to right, atoms
in protons and electrons, and become more tightly packed.

PERIODIC TABLE KEY

- **Alkali metals** Soft reactive metals, usually in compounds.
- **Alkaline earth metals** Very reactive metals not found as pure elements.
- **Transition metals** Malleable, ductile metals that are good conductors.
- **Rare earth metals** Toxic, radioactive metals often man-made.
- **Noble gases** Stable gases that do not react naturally.
- **Other metals** Malleable, ductile, solid, dense metals.
- **Metalloids** Share properties with metals and non-metals.
- **Non-metals** Poor solid conductors, brittle, with no metallic lustre, and gases.
- **Halogens** These exist in solid, liquid, and gas forms.
- **Unknown** Newly discovered synthetic element.

GROUP In the vertical groups, a shell is added with each step down. The elements are similar because they all have the same number of electrons in their outer shell.

RIOD e elements in a period ve different chemical d physical properties t all have the same mber of shells.

THE RUSSIAN SCIENTIST DMITRI MENDELEEV INVENTED THE PERIODIC TABLE IN 1869

Group	13	14	15	16	17	18
						2 · 4.0026 · **He** · Helium balloon · HELIUM
	5 · 10.811 · **B** · Soap · BORON	6 · 12.011 · **C** · Diamond · CARBON	7 · 14.007 · **N** · Coffee beans · NITROGEN	8 · 15.999 · **O** · Oxygen cylinder · OXYGEN	9 · 18.998 · **F** · Fluorite · FLUORINE	10 · 20.180 · **Ne** · Helium-neon laser · NEON
	13 · 26.982 · **Al** · Foil · ALUMINIUM	14 · 28.086 · **Si** · Silicon chip · SILICON	15 · 30.974 · **P** · Matchbox · PHOSPHORUS	16 · 32.065 · **S** · Sulphur · SULPHUR	17 · 35.453 · **Cl** · Carnallite · CHLORINE	18 · 39.948 · **Ar** · Light bulb · ARGON

10	11	12	13	14	15	16	17	18
8 · 58.693 · **Ni** · Spoon · NICKEL	29 · 63.546 · **Cu** · Wire · COPPER	30 · 65.39 · **Zn** · Sphalerite · ZINC	31 · 69.723 · **Ga** · Solar thermal panel · GALLIUM	32 · 72.64 · **Ge** · Camera lens · GERMANIUM	33 · 74.922 · **As** · Arsenic · ARSENIC	34 · 78.96 · **Se** · SELENIUM	35 · 79.904 · **Br** · Bromine · BROMINE	36 · 83.80 · **Kr** · Fluorescent lamp · KRYPTON
5 · 106.42 · **Pd** · Catalytic converter · ALLADIUM	47 · 107.87 · **Ag** · Silver pendant · SILVER	48 · 113 · **Cd** · Yellow paint · CADMIUM	49 · 114.82 · **In** · Light emitting diode (LED) · INDIUM	50 · 118.71 · **Sn** · Tin-plated can · TIN	51 · 121.76 · **Sb** · Bullet · ANTIMONY	52 · 127.60 · **Te** · Compact disc (CD) · TELLURIUM	53 · 126.90 · **I** · Liquid iodine · IODINE	54 · 131.29 · **Xe** · Arc lamp · XENON
8 · 195.08 · **Pt** · Ring · PLATINUM	79 · 196.97 · **Au** · Necklace · GOLD	80 · 201 · **Hg** · Thermometer · MERCURY	81 · 204.38 · **Tl** · Rat poison · THALLIUM	82 · 207.2 · **Pb** · Lead battery · LEAD	83 · 208.96 · **Bi** · Crystal · BISMUTH	84 · (209) · **Po** · POLONIUM	85 · (210) · **At** · ASTATINE	86 · (222) · **Rn** · RADON
0 · (281) · **Ds** · ARMSTADTIUM	111 · (272) · **Rg** · ROENTGENIUM	112 · 285 · **Cn** · COPERNICUM	113 · 284 · **Uut** · UNUNTRIUM	114 · 289 · **Uuq** · UNUNQUADIUM	115 · 288 · **Uup** · UNUNPENTIUM	116 · 293 · **Uuh** · UNUNHEXIUM	117 · 294 · **Uus** · UNUNSEPTIUM	118 · 294 · **Uuo** · UNUNOCTIUM

3 · 151.96 · **Eu** · Xenotime · EUROPIUM	64 · 157.25 · **Gd** · GADOLINIUM	65 · 158.93 · **Tb** · Green fluorescent lamp · TERBIUM	66 · 162.50 · **Dy** · Fergusonite crystals · DYSPROSIUM	67 · 164.93 · **Ho** · Gadolinite · HOLMIUM	68 · 167.26 · **Er** · Fibre optic cable · ERBIUM	69 · 168.93 · **Tm** · THULIUM	70 · 173.04 · **Yb** · Atomic clock · YTTERBIUM	71 · 174.97 · **Lu** · LUTETIUM
5 · (243) · **Am** · Smoke detector · AMERICIUM	96 · (247) · **Cm** · CURIUM	97 · 231.04 · **Bk** · BERKELIUM	98 · (251) · **Cf** · CALIFORNIUM	99 · (252) · **Es** · EINSTEINIUM	100 · (257) · **Fm** · FERMIUM	101 · (258) · **Md** · MENDELEVIUM	102 · (259) · **No** · NOBELIUM	103 · (262) · **Lr** · LAWRENCIUM

Biology

Biology is the science of all life, from microscopic bacteria that cannot be seen with the naked eye to enormous animals such as elephants and whales. It includes their form and function, origin and growth, and evolution and distribution.

NEEDED FOR LIFE

All life forms need the same essentials to survive. Few forms of life can exist without most of these basic necessities.

WATER
All living things are made of cells, which need water to exist – most life forms are mainly made up of water.

ENERGY SOURCE
Life forms need energy to grow and move around. Plants use sunlight to make energy. Animals get energy by eating plants or each other.

OXYGEN
Oxygen in air or water is necessary for all life.

ESSENTIAL CHEMICALS
The chemicals hydrogen, nitrogen, and carbon are essential for life. Plants get them from soil, while animals absorb them from food.

THE RIGHT TEMPERATURE
Few living things can exist in extremely hot or cold temperatures.

WHAT IS A CELL?

Cells are the building blocks of life. The cells of all living things except archaea and bacteria contain a nucleus, mitochondria, and other organelles. Cells can be specialized to perform different functions – for example, we have nerve, muscle, and bone cells. The human body has around 75 trillion cells, whereas less complex organisms may have only one.

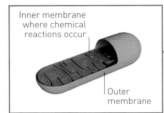

Inner membrane where chemical reactions occur

Outer membrane

MITOCHONDRION
This is the part of the cell that releases energy from food molecules within the body.

ANIMAL CELL
An animal cell contains lots of "machines" called organelles that perform special jobs (such as the mitochondrion).

Vacuoles store nutrients or waste

Ribosomes are the protein builders of the cell

A jelly-like fluid called cytoplasm fills the space between the organelles

The nucleus is the cell's control centre. It sends chemical instructions to other parts of the cell

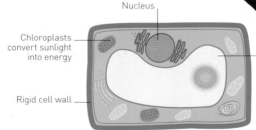

Nucleus

Chloroplasts convert sunlight into energy

Rigid cell wall

Large vacuole filled with cell sap

PLANT CELL
These have much in common with animal cells, but they also have rigid cell walls and chloroplasts.

CHROMOSOMES

Within the nucleus of each cell there are chromosomes that carry DNA. DNA contains genes that determine how an organism looks and functions. Humans have 46 chromosomes (23 pairs).

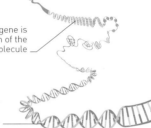

Each chromosome is made up of tightly coiled DNA

Each gene is a section of the DNA molecule

DNA is a long molecule arranged in a double-helix shape

GENES

Our genes are inherited from our parents – half from mum and half from dad – and they dictate things like eye colour. Each person has two versions of each gene, called alleles, which together make up their genotype. One allele is often dominant over another, which means that that feature is the one seen in the person.

KEY

■ **b** The recessive allele. A child must have two b alleles to have blue eyes.

■ **B** The dominant allele – a child with one or two B alleles will have brown eyes.

BLUE-EYED FATHER

BROWN-EYED MOTHER

Each parent carries a different combination of genes for eye colour

Parents' genes

Possible genetic combinations of children

Children's possible eye colours

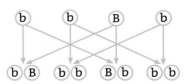

GENETICS IN ACTION
The mother here has one recessive and one dominant allele. The father has two recessive alleles. This means it is equally likely that they have a brown- or blue-eyed child.

CELL DIVISION

Organisms develop from a single cell, which divides again and again. Over the organism's lifetime, its cells are continually replaced in a process called mitosis.

Cell splits into two daughter cells, each with a full set of chromosomes

Doubled chromosomes are pulled apart

Chromosomes

Chromosomes duplicate

    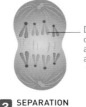

1 FIRST STAGE
The cell contains chromosomes that can be copied to make new identical chromosomes.

2 CHROMOSOMES ALIGN AND COPY
The wall of the nucleus breaks down and chromosomes line up in the middle of the cell.

3 SEPARATION
The doubled chromosome is pulled in half, so one chromosome moves to each end of the cell.

4 "DAUGHTER" CELLS FORM
Cell splits into two identical cells and the nuclear wall reforms.

CLASSIFICATION OF LIFE

All living things shared a common ancestor in the distant past. Over time, many organisms have evolved and become extinct. Today, there are six kingdoms of life – bacteria, archaea, and four eukaryotic groups – animals, fungi, protists, and plants.

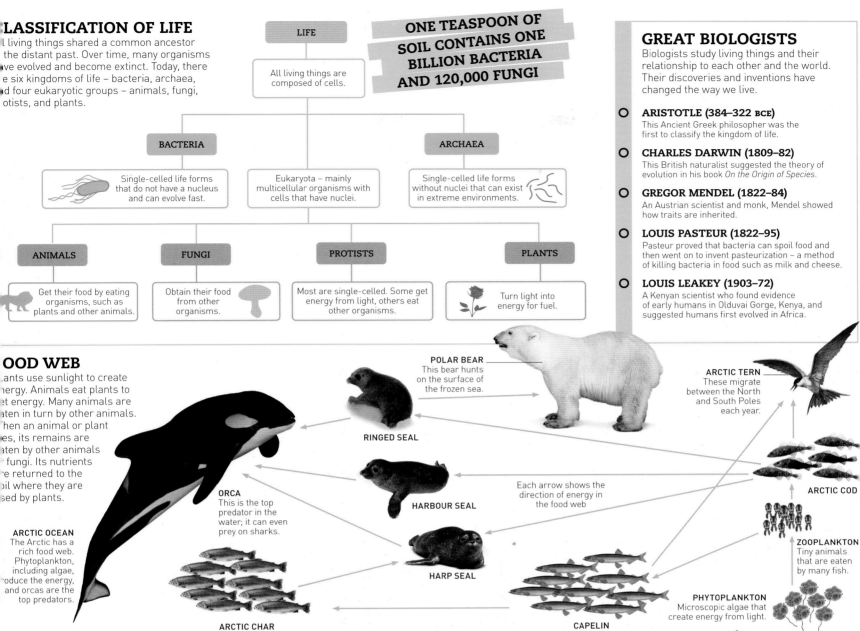

LIFE
All living things are composed of cells.

BACTERIA
Single-celled life forms that do not have a nucleus and can evolve fast.

Eukaryota – mainly multicellular organisms with cells that have nuclei.

ARCHAEA
Single-celled life forms without nuclei that can exist in extreme environments.

ANIMALS
Get their food by eating organisms, such as plants and other animals.

FUNGI
Obtain their food from other organisms.

PROTISTS
Most are single-celled. Some get energy from light, others eat other organisms.

PLANTS
Turn light into energy for fuel.

ONE TEASPOON OF SOIL CONTAINS ONE BILLION BACTERIA AND 120,000 FUNGI

GREAT BIOLOGISTS

Biologists study living things and their relationship to each other and the world. Their discoveries and inventions have changed the way we live.

- **ARISTOTLE (384–322 BCE)**
  This Ancient Greek philosopher was the first to classify the kingdom of life.
- **CHARLES DARWIN (1809–82)**
  This British naturalist suggested the theory of evolution in his book *On the Origin of Species*.
- **GREGOR MENDEL (1822–84)**
  An Austrian scientist and monk, Mendel showed how traits are inherited.
- **LOUIS PASTEUR (1822–95)**
  Pasteur proved that bacteria can spoil food and then went on to invent pasteurization – a method of killing bacteria in food such as milk and cheese.
- **LOUIS LEAKEY (1903–72)**
  A Kenyan scientist who found evidence of early humans in Olduvai Gorge, Kenya, and suggested humans first evolved in Africa.

FOOD WEB

Plants use sunlight to create energy. Animals eat plants to get energy. Many animals are eaten in turn by other animals. When an animal or plant dies, its remains are eaten by other animals or fungi. Its nutrients are returned to the soil where they are used by plants.

ARCTIC OCEAN
The Arctic has a rich food web. Phytoplankton, including algae, produce the energy, and orcas are the top predators.

POLAR BEAR
This bear hunts on the surface of the frozen sea.

RINGED SEAL

ORCA
This is the top predator in the water; it can even prey on sharks.

HARBOUR SEAL

Each arrow shows the direction of energy in the food web

HARP SEAL

ARCTIC CHAR

CAPELIN

ARCTIC TERN
These migrate between the North and South Poles each year.

ARCTIC COD

ZOOPLANKTON
Tiny animals that are eaten by many fish.

PHYTOPLANKTON
Microscopic algae that create energy from light.

EVOLUTION

Individuals that are best suited to the environment in which they live are the ones most likely to survive and reproduce. They then pass on the genes that favour their existence to their offspring. Over time, this leads to change. This process is known as evolution by natural selection.

FISH ON LAND
Over time, lobe-finned fish evolved in a way that allowed them to move out of the water and live on the land.

WATER — **LOBE FIN**

ONTO LAND — **LEG-LIKE FIN**

LAND — **FORELIMB WITH HAND**

ADAPTATION

Animals adapt to suit their environment, and birds' beaks, or bills, are a perfect example of this. The birds pictured here have all evolved from the same ancestor, but their bills have become perfectly adapted to help them catch and eat food in different habitats.

Probing bill for eating leaves

Pointed bill is used to peck insects from leaves

Grasping bill lets bird use stick to dig prey out from under bark

Ancestor cracked seeds with thick bill

Hooked bill slices into soft fruits and buds

Overbite is useful for digging up grubs

EXTINCTION

The dying out of a species is known as "extinction". Scientists believe that we are now undergoing the biggest wave of extinctions since the dinosaurs disappeared.

CLIMATE CHANGE
Only animals that suit their environments survive. Smilodon became extinct when the climate changed 11,000 years ago.

GEOLOGICAL EVENTS
Meteor strikes and volcanic eruptions can cause extinctions. Dinosaurs are thought to have been wiped out by a meteor or volcanic activity.

HUNTED TO DEATH
Overhunting by humans can cause animals to become extinct. This happened to the easily caught and very tasty dodo of Mauritius.

HABITAT DESTRUCTION
Habitat destruction and fragmentation has led to species such as the panda being in danger of extinction.

POACHING
The tiger is threatened due to use of its body parts in traditional Chinese medicine.

The human body

The human body is a complex machine, made up of tissues and organs. These work together through joined-up systems that communicate with each other through electrical messages, which travel to and from the brain.

BUILDING A BODY

Microscopes show that everything in the human body is made up of tiny cells, which are different depending on where they are and what they do. They grow in the right way for their tasks because they all contain DNA, which is like an internal instruction manual.

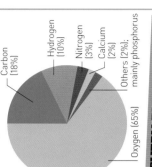

CELL
There are more than 37 trillion cells in a human body.

DNA
Cells contain spirals of DNA, which tell them how to grow.

ORGANS
Tissue forms into organs, such as the heart (shown here).

TISSUE
Cells form into tissue, such as muscle tissue.

WHAT IS THE BODY MADE OF?

More than half of the body's weight is water. The rest is made up of different kinds of tissue, from the soft tissue that lines our intestines to the hard tissue that forms our bones. Water and tissues themselves are made up of around six elements, as shown in the diagram below.

Carbon (18%)
Hydrogen (10%)
Nitrogen (3%)
Calcium (2%)
Others (2%): mainly phosphorus
Oxygen (65%)

EVERY ELEMENT IN THE BODY COMES FROM STARDUST

THE SKIN

The skin is a protective layer that goes all around the body. It is tough but flexible and it is very sensitive, sending messages back to the brain. It also helps the body stay at a constant temperature.

Skin hairs rise to keep the body warm

The outer layer, the epidermis, is tough and protective

The dermis has touch sensors

The third layer of skin is made up of fat

Blood vessels widen to help

HUMAN ANATOMY

The "anatomy" of something shows its structure, so a diagram of human anatomy shows the internal structure of a person. This diagram shows how the different systems in the body fit together.

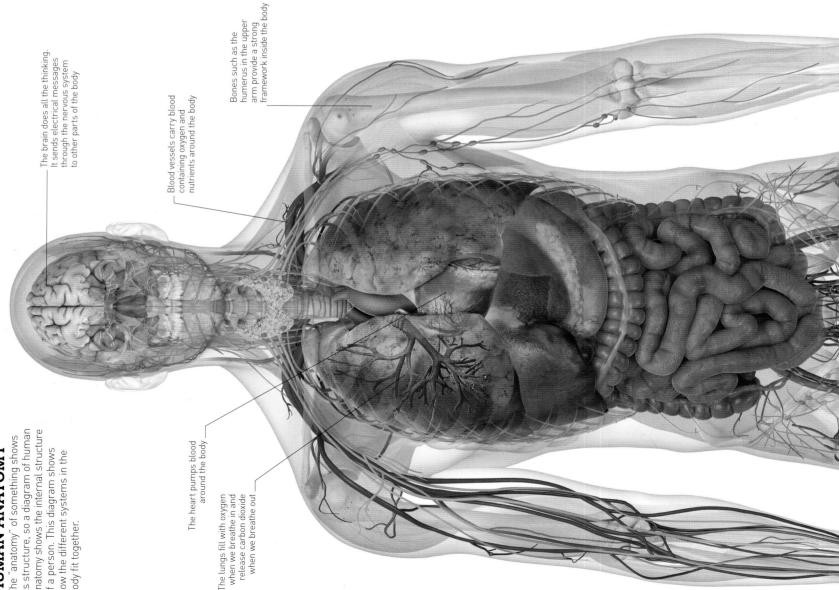

The brain does all the thinking. It sends electrical messages through the nervous system to other parts of the body

Blood vessels carry blood containing oxygen and nutrients around the body

Bones such as the humerus in the upper arm provide a strong framework inside the body

The heart pumps blood around the body

The lungs fill with oxygen when we breathe in and release carbon dioxide when we breathe out

BODY SYSTEMS

Inside the body, complex systems of tissues and organs work together to help the body perform. Each system has a particular task, such as digesting food or fighting off disease. There are 11 different systems in the body.

NERVOUS
This is a messaging system between the brain and other parts of the body.

MUSCULAR
The muscles allow the bones and organs of the body to move.

SKELETAL
The bones and joints give the body its basic framework.

RESPIRATORY
This is the system that allows us to breathe in and out.

DIGESTIVE
Food is broken down into vital nutrients by this system.

LYMPHATIC AND IMMUNE
This helps us fight off disease and infection.

CARDIOVASCULAR
Blood runs through this system, all around the body.

ENDOCRINE
This produces chemicals called hormones, which can affect other systems.

MALE
FEMALE
REPRODUCTIVE
This is the system that allows people to produce children together. It is different in men and women.

URINARY
This system allows the body to filter out the waste and water it doesn't need.

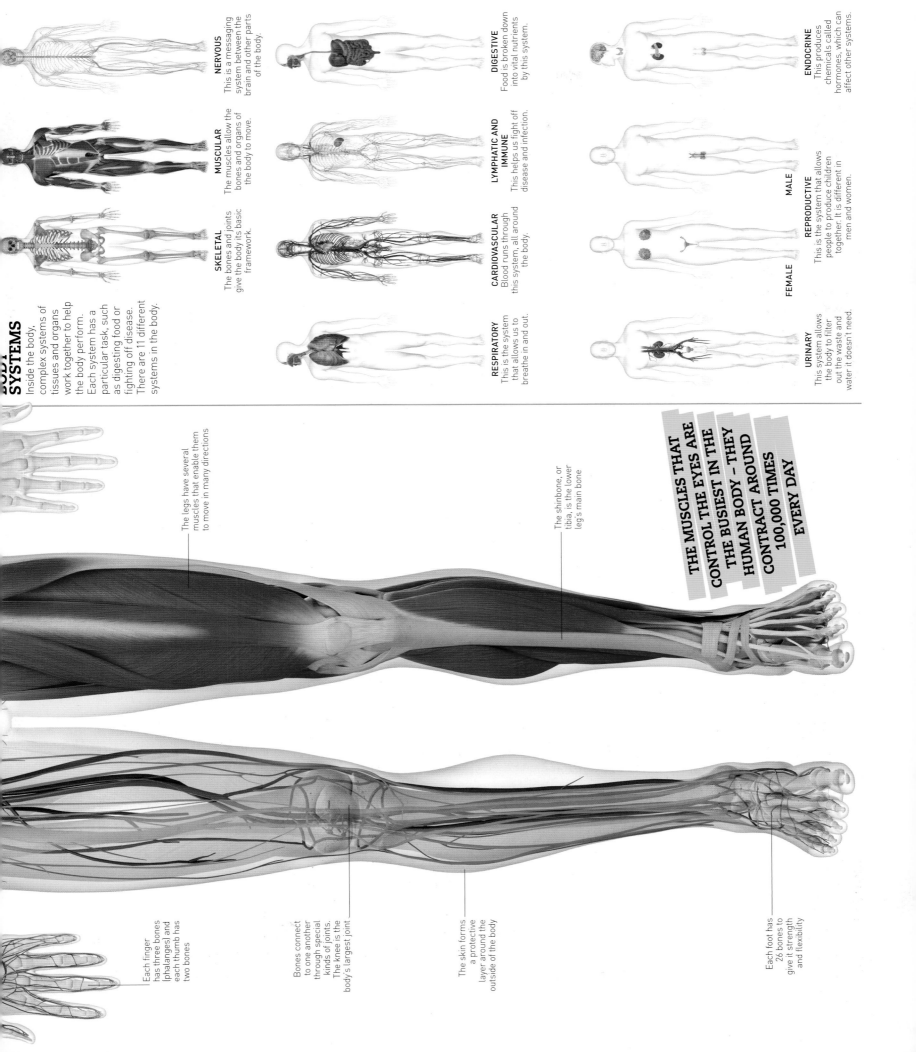

Each finger has three bones (phalanges) and each thumb has two bones

The legs have several muscles that enable them to move in many directions

Bones connect to one another through special kinds of joints. The knee is the body's largest joint

The skin forms a protective layer around the outside of the body

The shinbone, or tibia, is the lower leg's main bone

Each foot has 26 bones to give it strength and flexibility

THE MUSCLES THAT CONTROL THE EYES ARE THE BUSIEST IN THE HUMAN BODY – THEY CONTRACT AROUND 100,000 TIMES EVERY DAY

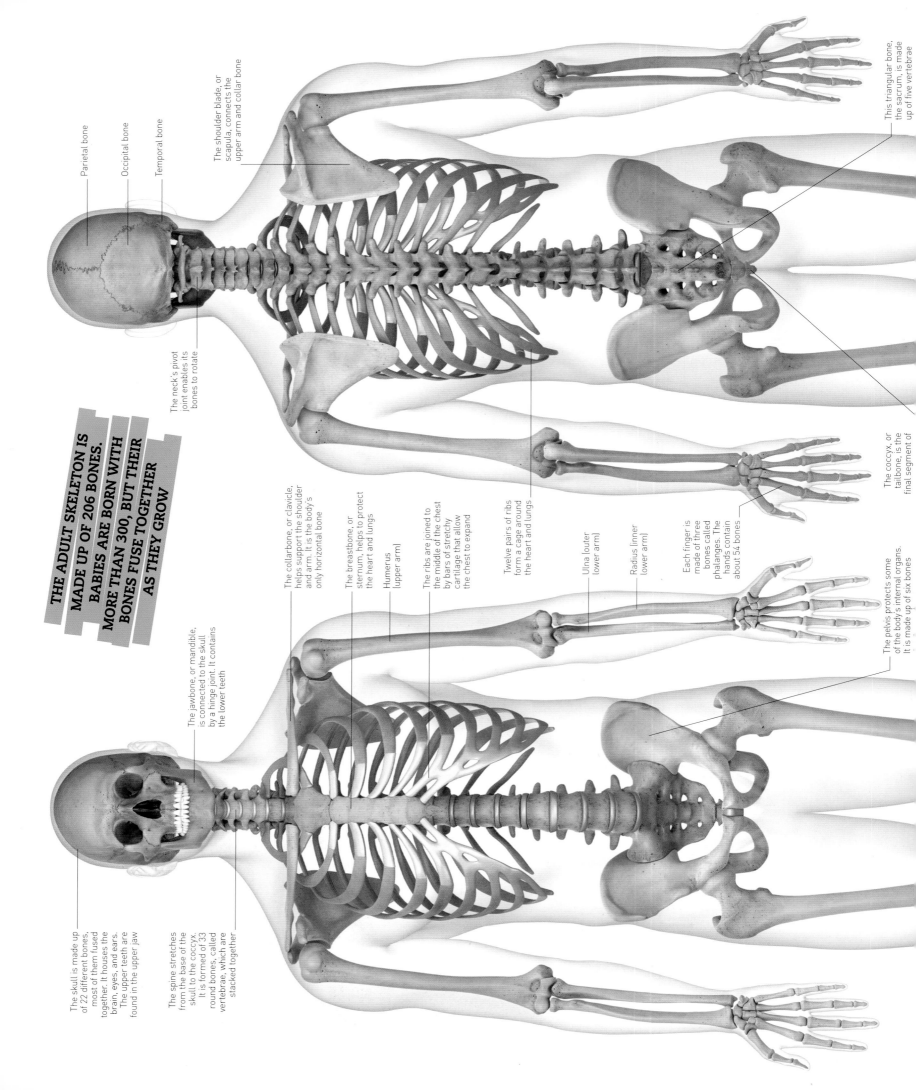

THE ADULT SKELETON IS MADE UP OF 206 BONES. BABIES ARE BORN WITH MORE THAN 300, BUT THEIR BONES FUSE TOGETHER AS THEY GROW

Parietal bone

Occipital bone

Temporal bone

The shoulder blade, or scapula, connects the upper arm and collar bone

This triangular bone, the sacrum, is made up of five vertebrae

The neck's pivot joint enables its bones to rotate

The coccyx, or tailbone, is the final segment of

The collarbone, or clavicle, helps support the shoulder and arm. It is the body's only horizontal bone

The breastbone, or sternum, helps to protect the heart and lungs

Humerus (upper arm)

The ribs are joined to the middle of the chest by bars of stretchy cartilage that allow the chest to expand

Twelve pairs of ribs form a cage around the heart and lungs

Ulna (outer lower arm)

Radius (inner lower arm)

Each finger is made of three bones called phalanges. The hands contain about 54 bones

The jawbone, or mandible, is connected to the skull by a hinge joint. It contains the lower teeth

The pelvis protects some of the body's internal organs. It is made up of six bones

The skull is made up of 22 different bones, most of them fused together. It houses the brain, eyes, and ears. The upper teeth are found in the upper jaw

The spine stretches from the base of the skull to the coccyx. It is formed of 33 round bones, called vertebrae, which are stacked together

Skeleton

The skeleton is the body's scaffolding – it gives us shape and support. It has other important functions, too. Along with muscles, it enables us to move around. It also protects our inner organs and produces red blood cells.

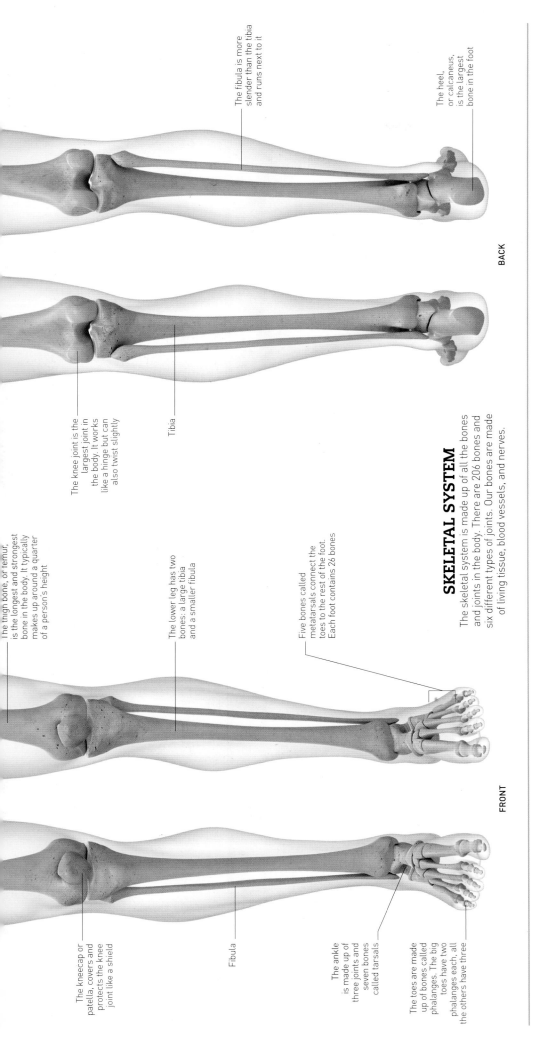

FRONT

The thigh bone, or femur, is the longest and strongest bone in the body. It typically makes up around a quarter of a person's height

The kneecap or patella, covers and protects the knee joint like a shield

The lower leg has two bones: a large tibia and a smaller fibula

Fibula

Five bones called metatarsals connect the toes to the rest of the foot. Each foot contains 26 bones

The ankle is made up of three joints and seven bones called tarsals

The toes are made up of bones called phalanges. The big toes have two phalanges each, all the others have three

The knee joint is the largest joint in the body. It works like a hinge but can also twist slightly

Tibia

The fibula is more slender than the tibia and runs next to it

The heel, or calcaneus, is the largest bone in the foot

BACK

SKELETAL SYSTEM

The skeletal system is made up of all the bones and joints in the body. There are 206 bones and six different types of joints. Our bones are made of living tissue, blood vessels, and nerves.

INSIDE A BONE

Inside the solid outer bone is lighter, honeycomb-like spongy bone. In big bones the centre is filled with jelly-like marrow, which makes red blood cells.

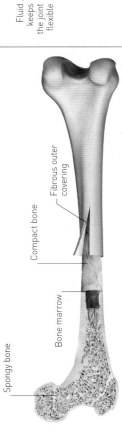

Spongy bone

Compact bone

Fibrous outer covering

Bone marrow

WHAT IS A JOINT?

Where bones meet, they are held together by joints, tissues that allow them to move. Without joints we wouldn't be able to move our bodies. The movement a joint allows depends on the shape of the bones.

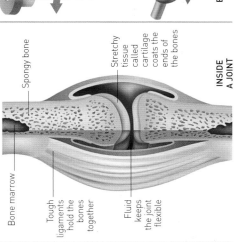

Bone marrow

Spongy bone

Tough ligaments hold the bones together

Stretchy tissue called cartilage coats the ends of the bones

Fluid keeps the joint flexible

INSIDE A JOINT

SYNOVIAL JOINTS

Synovial joints are the most common type of joints. There are six types of synovial joints, each allowing a different range of movement, depending on how the bones fit together.

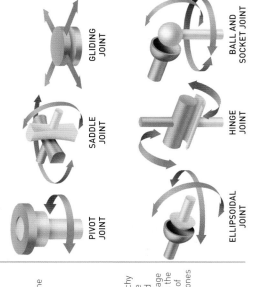

GLIDING JOINT

BALL AND SOCKET JOINT

SADDLE JOINT

HINGE JOINT

PIVOT JOINT

ELLIPSOIDAL JOINT

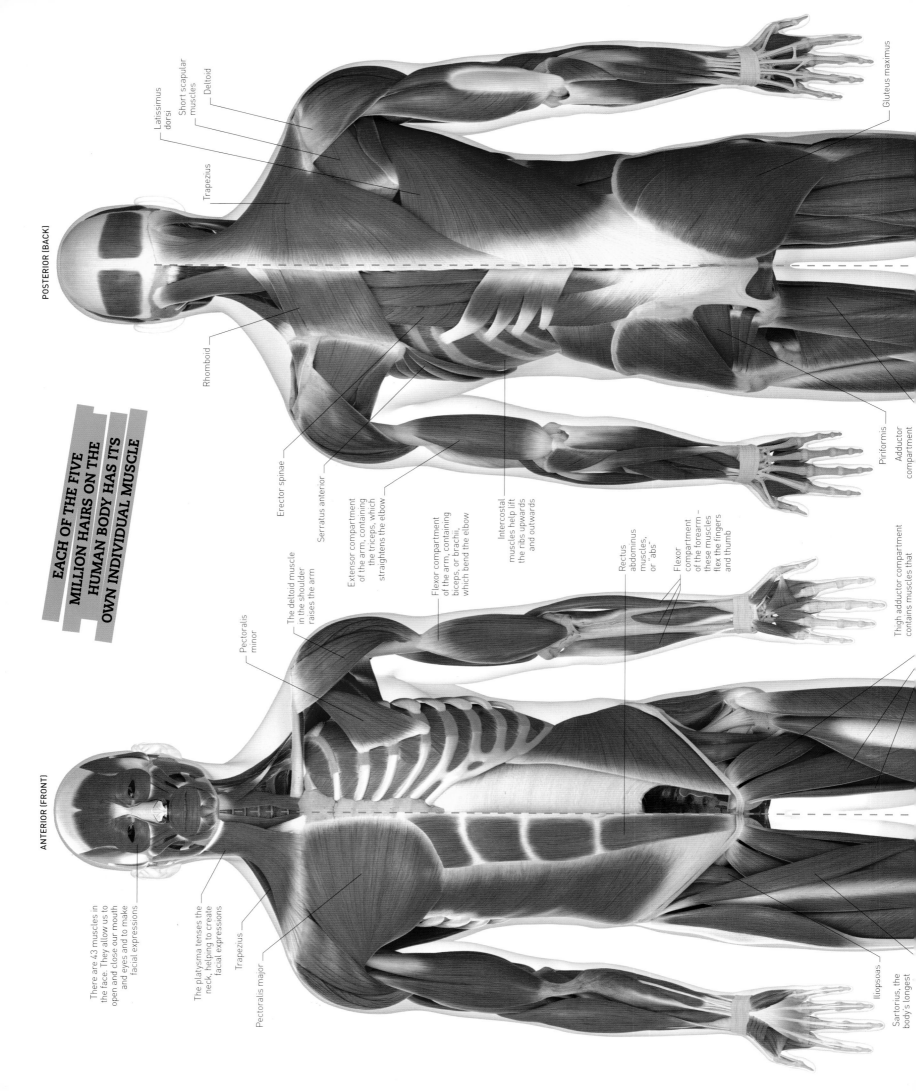

POSTERIOR (BACK)

ANTERIOR (FRONT)

EACH OF THE FIVE MILLION HAIRS ON THE HUMAN BODY HAS ITS OWN INDIVIDUAL MUSCLE

Latissimus dorsi

Short scapular muscles

Deltoid

Trapezius

Gluteus maximus

Rhomboid

Erector spinae

Serratus anterior

Piriformis

Adductor compartment

Pectoralis minor

The deltoid muscle in the shoulder raises the arm

Extensor compartment of the arm, containing the triceps, which straightens the elbow

Flexor compartment of the arm, containing biceps, or brachii, which bend the elbow

Intercostal muscles help lift the ribs upwards and outwards

Rectus abdominus muscles, or "abs"

Flexor compartment of the forearm – these muscles flex the fingers and thumb

Thigh adductor compartment contains muscles that

There are 43 muscles in the face. They allow us to open and close our mouth and eyes and to make facial expressions

The platysma tenses the neck, helping to create facial expressions

Trapezius

Pectoralis major

Iliopsoas

Sartorius, the body's longest

Muscles

Every movement we make, from blinking an eye to running a race, is powered by muscles. Even the movements we are not aware of, such as the beating of our heart or the digestion of food, are actually controlled by muscles.

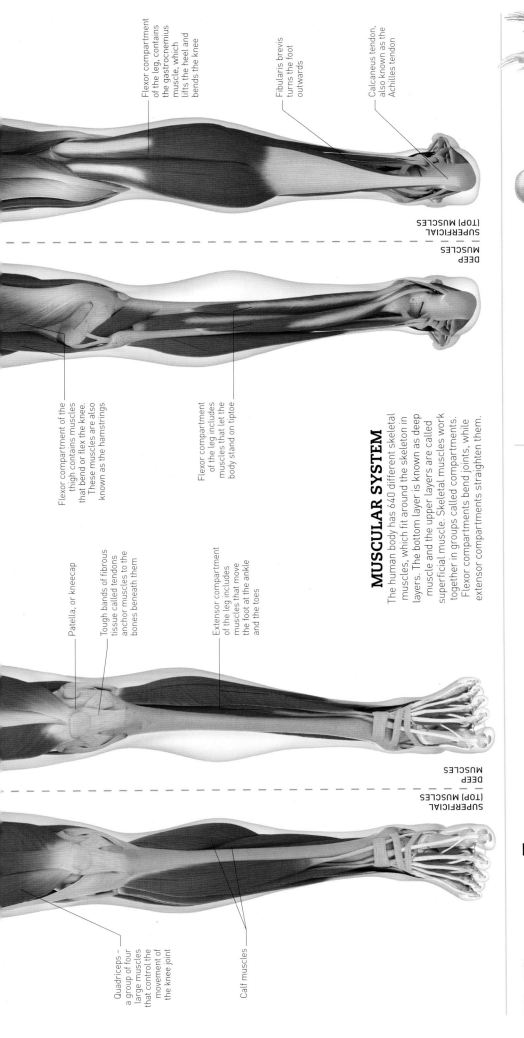

Flexor compartment of the leg, contains the gastrocnemius muscle, which lifts the heel and bends the knee

Fibularis brevis turns the foot outwards

Calcaneus tendon, also known as the Achilles tendon

SUPERFICIAL (TOP) MUSCLES

DEEP MUSCLES

Flexor compartment of the thigh contains muscles that bend or flex the knee. These muscles are also known as the hamstrings

Flexor compartment of the leg includes muscles that let the body stand on tiptoe

Patella, or kneecap

Tough bands of fibrous tissue called tendons anchor muscles to the bones beneath them

Extensor compartment of the leg includes muscles that move the foot at the ankle and the toes

Quadriceps – a group of four large muscles that control the movement of the knee joint

Calf muscles

SUPERFICIAL (TOP) MUSCLES

DEEP MUSCLES

MUSCULAR SYSTEM

The human body has 640 different skeletal muscles, which fit around the skeleton in layers. The bottom layer is known as deep muscle and the upper layers are called superficial muscle. Skeletal muscles work together in groups called compartments. Flexor compartments bend joints, while extensor compartments straighten them.

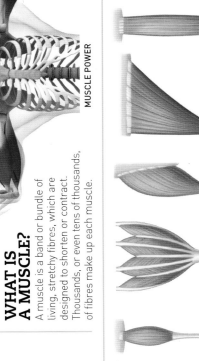

Triceps contracts to straighten the arm

Biceps contracts to bend the arm

MUSCLE POWER

WHAT IS A MUSCLE?

A muscle is a band or bundle of living, stretchy fibres, which are designed to shorten or contract. Thousands, or even tens of thousands, of fibres make up each muscle.

MUSCLE SHAPES

There are many different shapes of skeletal muscle in our bodies. They vary in size and structure depending on their specific function.

CIRCULAR (MOUTH)

STRAP (INNER THIGH)

TRIANGULAR (CHEST)

UNIPENNATE (FINGER)

MULTIPENNATE (SHOULDER)

FUSIFORM (BICEPS)

MUSCLE TYPES

Skeletal muscles move the body's bones in response to conscious messages from the brain. Cardiac and smooth muscles work without conscious thought.

SKELETAL MUSCLE
Also called striped or striated muscle, this is connected to the bones.

SMOOTH MUSCLE
This muscle is found in the intestines and other organs.

CARDIAC MUSCLE
Makes the heart beat by contracting rhythmically.

The brain

The brain is the most complex organ in the body. Safely encased inside the skull, it controls our actions and all the body functions that keep us alive. It also monitors the world around us, stores our memories, and enables us to plan for the future.

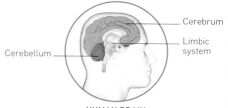

PLANNING
THINKING
JUDGING
SPEECH
FEELING
TASTE
SMELL

NERVOUS SYSTEM

The brain is linked to the rest of the body through a network of nerves, known as the nervous system. This network acts as a kind of information highway, carrying messages between the brain and the body. Part of the system, known as the autonomic nervous system (ANS), makes sure all our "automatic" body actions, such as breathing, keep functioning correctly.

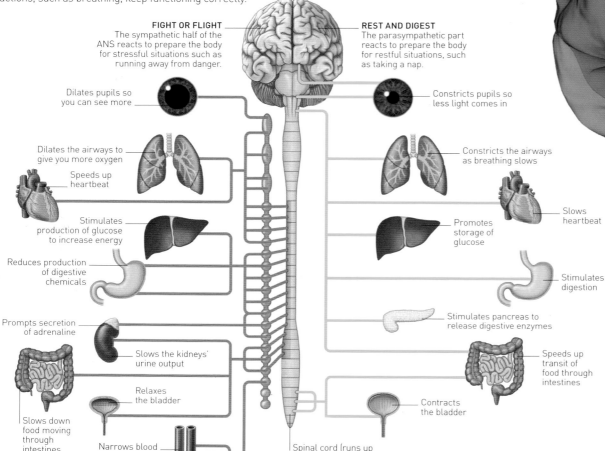

FIGHT OR FLIGHT
The sympathetic half of the ANS reacts to prepare the body for stressful situations such as running away from danger.

REST AND DIGEST
The parasympathetic part reacts to prepare the body for restful situations, such as taking a nap.

Dilates pupils so you can see more

Constricts pupils so less light comes in

Dilates the airways to give you more oxygen

Constricts the airways as breathing slows

Speeds up heartbeat

Slows heartbeat

Stimulates production of glucose to increase energy

Promotes storage of glucose

Reduces production of digestive chemicals

Stimulates digestion

Prompts secretion of adrenaline

Stimulates pancreas to release digestive enzymes

Slows the kidneys' urine output

Speeds up transit of food through intestines

Relaxes the bladder

Contracts the bladder

Slows down food moving through intestines

Narrows blood vessels to move blood faster around the system

Spinal cord (runs up the inside of the spine)

BRAIN JOBS

The brain allows you to sense, think, learn, remember, and much more. Different areas of the brain have different jobs.

■ **SENSES**
There are five main sense areas in the brain. They process the signals from the sense organs – eyes, ears, skin, tongue, and nose.

■ **LANGUAGE**
One part of the brain known as Broca's area controls your speech. Two other parts, known as Geschwind's territory and Wernicke's area, help you to learn and understand language.

■ **MEMORIES**
The hippocampus is where your brain makes and stores memories.

■ **MOVEMENT**
This part of the brain is called the motor cortex and it sends signals to your muscles to tell them to move your body.

■ **THOUGHTS**
The large area known as the prefrontal cortex processes your thoughts. It turns them into plans, judgements, and ideas, and also helps you to understand other people's feelings.

HOW NERVES SEND MESSAGES

The nervous system is made up of billions of cells called neurons. These odd-looking cells have branches called axons that carry electric messages, or impulses, down to lots of smaller branches. These pass the message on to another neuron.

Signal travels onwards towards another neuron

Axon

NEURON

Dendrites

Signal passes from one neuron to another

Axon of neuron sending signal

Electrical impulse (the message)

The message takes chemical form

Chemicals move across to the other neuron

Receiving neuron

TRANSMITTING MESSAGES
There is a gap between neurons called the synapse. The electrical impulses convert to a chemical form to travel across the gap.

BRAIN AREAS

The human brain has many different parts, but it can be divided into three main areas. The large cerebrum deals with thoughts, language, and behaviour. The limbic system processes emotions, and the cerebellum coordinates movement.

Cerebrum

Limbic system

Cerebellum

HUMAN BRAIN
The human brain has lots of wrinkles, which hold all its information. If the surface of your brain was unfolded, it would be more than twice as big.

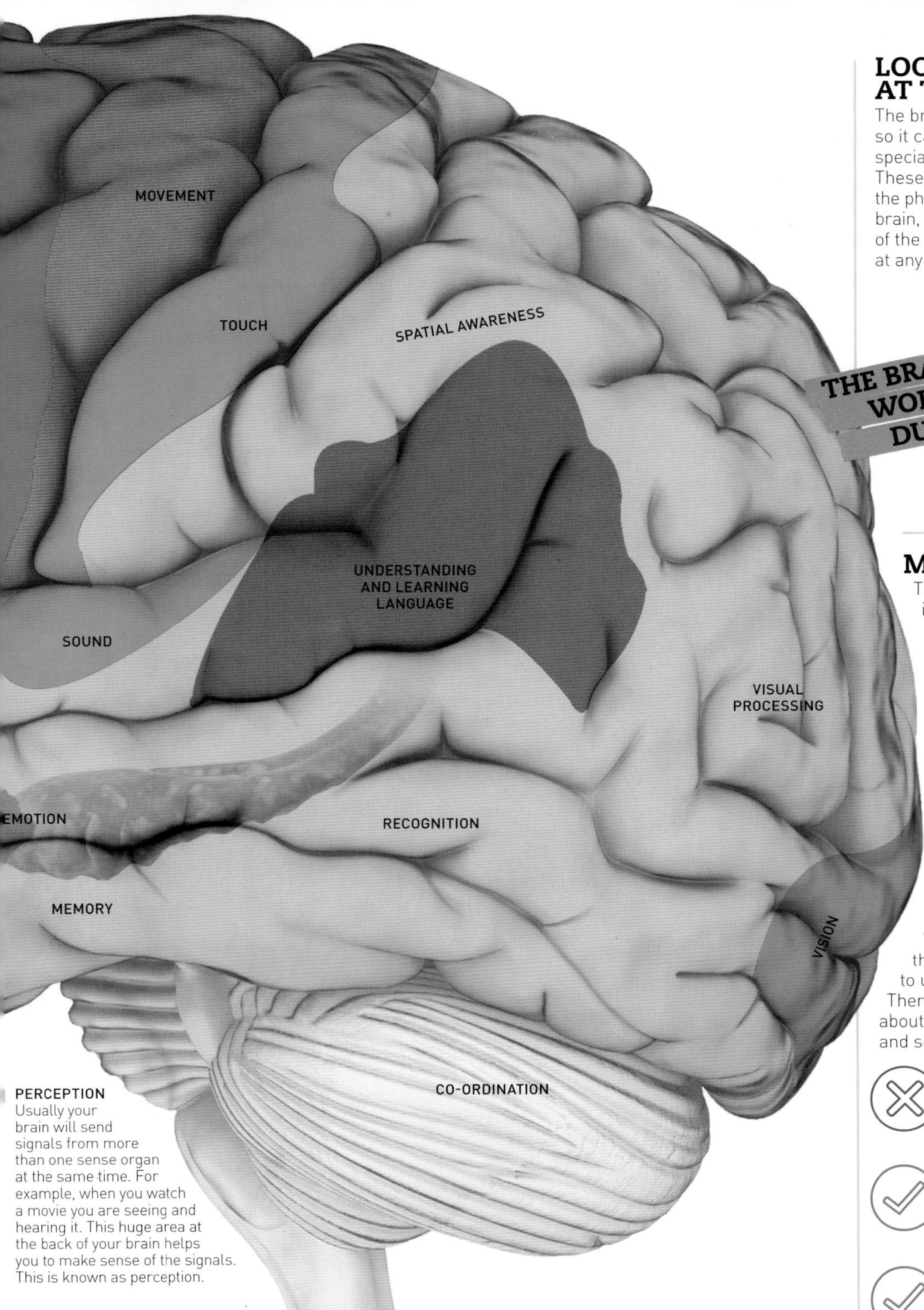

Labels on brain diagram:

MOVEMENT

TOUCH

SPATIAL AWARENESS

UNDERSTANDING AND LEARNING LANGUAGE

SOUND

VISUAL PROCESSING

EMOTION

RECOGNITION

MEMORY

VISION

CO-ORDINATION

LOOKING AT THE BRAIN

The brain is inside the skull, so it can only be seen using special scanning machines. These can be used to show the physical make-up of the brain, or to highlight the parts of the brain that are working at any moment.

THE BRAIN IS ALWAYS WORKING, EVEN DURING SLEEP

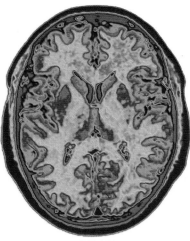

MRI SCAN
An MRI scan uses magnetism to produce images of different sections of the brain.

MAKING MEMORIES

The brain absorbs information from the senses, processes all of it into an image or thought, and then stores that image or thought as a memory. Memories can be short-term, such as a phone number you use once, which is held for just as long as you need it, or long-term, such as your first day at school, which you may remember for many years.

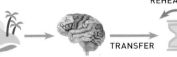

SENSORY INPUT → SENSORY MEMORY → TRANSFER → SHORT-TERM MEMORY ⇄ RETRIEVAL / REHEARSAL → LONG-TERM MEMORY

PERCEPTION
Usually your brain will send signals from more than one sense organ at the same time. For example, when you watch a movie you are seeing and hearing it. This huge area at the back of your brain helps you to make sense of the signals. This is known as perception.

EMOTIONS
The amygdala is where the brain turns the information it receives into emotions.

CO-ORDINATION
The cerebellum at the base of your brain helps to coordinate your muscles, so that they work together.

TRUE OR FALSE?

The brain is so complex that we are only beginning to understand how it works. There are many popular beliefs about the brain – some are true and some are false.

WE ONLY USE 10 PER CENT OF OUR BRAINS
The truth is that we use all of our brains to complete normal daily tasks.

30,000 NEURONS WOULD FIT ON THE HEAD OF A PIN
This is true, and the brain contains around 100 billion neurons in total.

THE BRAIN DOES NOT FEEL PAIN
The brain does not have pain receptors, so it cannot feel pain.

EINSTEIN'S BRAIN WAS BIGGER THAN AVERAGE
Einstein's brain was a bit smaller than average. Size does not affect intelligence.

SOME UNUSUAL BRAINS

When parts of the brain do not function or function differently, it can affect the way that individuals make sense of the world.

○ **AMNESIA**
This is a loss of memory due to a physical or emotional trauma.

○ **SYNAESTHESIA**
People with this disorder experience mixed-up senses. For example, some people see colours when they read or hear numbers.

○ **DEMENTIA**
This is a set of problems, including difficulties with thinking, memory, problem-solving, and language. It usually affects older adults.

○ **OBSESSIVE–COMPULSIVE DISORDER (OCD)**
This is a disorder where people worry about things all the time and repeat actions over and over again.

EMOTIONS

The brain processes our feelings. As it does so, signals move through the body so that those feelings become visible to other people. There are six primary emotions, and they all show on the face in a particular way. These facial expressions are the same in everyone – a smile means the same thing whether you live in the Sahara desert or New York City.

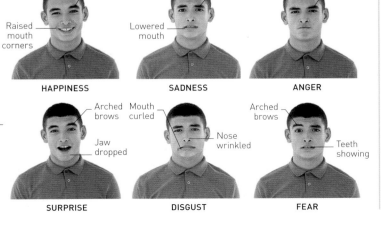

HAPPINESS — Smooth brow, Raised mouth corners

SADNESS — Raised inner brows, Lowered mouth

ANGER — Brows lowered

SURPRISE — Arched brows, Jaw dropped

DISGUST — Mouth curled, Nose wrinkled

FEAR — Arched brows, Teeth showing

TRICKS OF THE MIND

Sometimes you cannot believe your eyes – or more accurately, you cannot believe what your brain thinks it is seeing. The brain can be fooled.

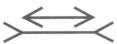

WHICH LINE IS LONGER?
Do you see one of these lines as longer? This is a visual illusion – the lines are both the same length.

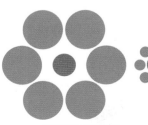

WHICH IS BIGGER?
The red dot on the right looks bigger, but it is not. Your brain judges it in relation to the blue dots around it.

Computers

Computers are electronic machines that we can use to do many different things, just by changing the programs they are running. Today, computers have become indispensable because they are used to run our world – from global air traffic control to personal mobile phones.

2000 BCE

c.2000 BCE
The Chinese invent the abacus, the world's first counting machine.

Abacus

166●
Samuel Morland invents a machine that can add and subtract

Morland's calculating machine

COMPUTER HISTORY

The first calculating machines were invented to add numbers, which was important for buying and selling goods. They were continually improved, until we arrived at the modern computer.

1642
Blaise Pascal invents the Pascaline, a mechanical and automatic calculator.

Pascaline

HOW COMPUTERS WORK

Computers work by processing information: they take in information (data), store it (memory), process it in whichever way they have been programmed to do, then display the result (output).

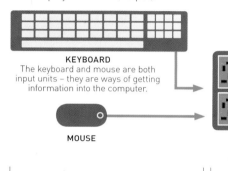

KEYBOARD
The keyboard and mouse are both input units – they are ways of getting information into the computer.

MOUSE

INPUT

PROCESSOR CHIP
A computer's processor is like the brain of the computer. It uses a chip – a piece of silicon that can hold billions of components – to perform its computing tasks.

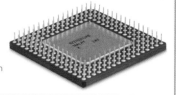

MEMORY
Computers use two different kinds of memory: ROM (read-only memory), and RAM (memory you can change).

STORAGE AND PROCESSING

SCREEN
Computers have LCD screens to display the result of the processing that has taken place.

OUTPUT

SOFTWARE

Software is the name for ready-made programs we use to make one computer do many things. Software allows us to write, edit photos, use the internet, and so on, without having to program a computer ourselves.

```
0010 0011 1000 1100
1000 0110 0100 1001
0100 1001 0001 0101
```

1 BINARY CODE
Computers only understand binary code, which is made up of 0s and 1●

```
IDLE  File  Edit  Shell  Debug  Window  Help

# Ghost Game
from random import randint
print ( 'Ghost Game' )
feeling_brave=True
Score=0
While feeling_brave:
    ghost_door=randint( 1,3 )
    print('Three doors ahead...')
```

2 PROGRAMMING LANGUAGE
Programming languages are used to lay out sets of instructions for computers to follow.

3 SOFTWARE
Programming languages are used to write computer programs (software)

SHRINKING SIZES

The 1949 EDSAC computer took up a whole room and was arranged over 12 racks. Today's personal computers (PCs) perform calculations millions of times faster, but they can sit easily on someone's desk or lap.

EARLY COMPUTER
1949

THE WORLD'S SMALLEST COMPUTER IS JUST ONE MILLIMETRE CUBED

DESKTOP COMPUTER
1980

LAPTOP COMPUTER
1983

TABLET
1993

NETWORKS

A network is a number of things connected in some way. There are three main forms of computer networks, which can connect computers and peripherals, such as printers.

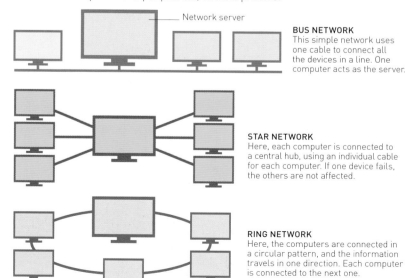

Network server

BUS NETWORK
This simple network uses one cable to connect all the devices in a line. One computer acts as the server.

STAR NETWORK
Here, each computer is connected to a central hub, using an individual cable for each computer. If one device fails, the others are not affected.

RING NETWORK
Here, the computers are connected in a circular pattern, and the information travels in one direction. Each computer is connected to the next one.

SUPERCOMPUTERS

Some scientific problems are so vast that they need huge amounts of processing power, delivered by "supercomputers". Some of these have tens of thousands of processors all working on one thing at the same time.

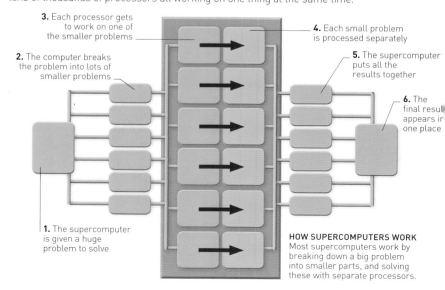

3. Each processor gets to work on one of the smaller problems

2. The computer breaks the problem into lots of smaller problems

4. Each small problem is processed separately

5. The supercomputer puts all the results together

6. The final resul● appears in one place

1. The supercomputer is given a huge problem to solve

HOW SUPERCOMPUTERS WORK
Most supercomputers work by breaking down a big problem into smaller parts, and solving these with separate processors.

1801
Joseph Jacquard's loom uses a program (run by punched cards) to weave fabric.

1906
The vacuum tube, an essential part of modern computers, is invented.

Vacuum tube

1943
British engineer Thomas Flowers builds Colossus: the first electronic, digital computer.

1946
ENIAC is created – the world's first general-purpose electronic computer. It weighs 100 tonnes and contains 18,000 electronic switches.

1962
Computer company IBM sets up SABRE, a system that connects up 1,500 computer terminals.

1971
Intel 404, the first single-chip microprocessor, is invented.

Microchip

1995
A USB is used for the first time to connect other devices to a computer.

USB

2015

1822
Charles Babbage's engine has an input, a memory, and a number-cruncher (processor).

Babbage Engine

1886
Herman Hollerith builds the first punched-card tabulating and sorting machine.

Herman Hollerith

1941
German Konrad Zuse designs the Z3, the world's first working, programmable, fully automatic digital computer.

1947
The transistor is invented. It would allow electronic devices to become much smaller.

Transistor

1976
The world's first supercomputer, CRAY–1, is built.

1981
IBM launches a PC that uses MS-DOS as an operating system.

1991
The World Wide Web is made publicly available.

2014
The first 8-terabyte hard drive is released.

THE INTERNET

The Internet is a computer network that stretches round the world, linking most computers on the planet. Every computer has its own Internet or IP address, so that digital things (such as email) can be sent to or from it.

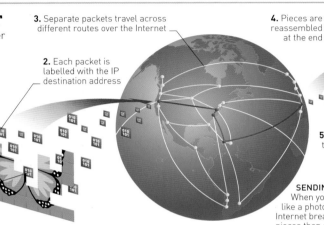

3. Separate packets travel across different routes over the Internet

2. Each packet is labelled with the IP destination address

4. Pieces are reassembled at the end

5. Receiver sees the final picture exactly as sent

1. Sender's computer breaks photo into many tiny digital pieces, or "packets"

SENDING A PHOTO
When you send something like a photo by email, the Internet breaks it into small pieces then reassembles it.

WHAT WE DO ONLINE?

We now use the Internet for all sorts of activities where we want to connect with someone else – either for fun or for business.

EMAIL
Emails are an instant way to send a digital letter.

GAMES
We can play games with distant friends via the Internet.

SHOPPING
We can buy things online from anywhere in the world.

SOCIAL NETWORKING
Groups of people can communicate easily online.

COMPUTERS EVERYWHERE

Computers are used in all sorts of devices, from personal music players and phones to microwave ovens and surveillance cameras.

PORTABLE GPS

PORTABLE MEDIA PLAYER

SMARTPHONE

DIGITAL TELESCOPE

DIGITAL RADIO

SURVEILLANCE CAMERA

MICROWAVE OVEN

CYCLE COMPUTER

DIGITAL CLOCK

NAO ROBOT

Inventions

The work of inventors is all around you. Not just your phone and games console – the chair you are sitting on, the car outside, even the light bulb above your head was invented by somebody. Some early inventions, like the wheel, will be used for ever. Others, such as the spear, have been replaced by newer, more effective models.

FLINT HAND AXE

HAND AXE

Flint is a special kind of rock because it breaks into sharp pieces. Stone-Age people discovered that its hard, sharp edges made it very useful as a tool. Shaped into an axe, it could be used for cutting meat, scraping skins (to make clothes), chopping wood, and as a weapon.

SPEAR

The problem with hand-held weapons was that hunters had to stand very close to their prey, which was dangerous. The invention of the spear solved this problem. The hunter could stand back some distance, take aim, and throw the weapon. Early spears had flint heads. Later ones used metal heads, shaped into long, thin blades.

SHORT SPEARS

ANCIENT EGYPTIAN JAR

POTTERY

Chinese inventors realized they could dig clay from the ground, shape it into pots, and harden them in hot ashes. The pots were watertight so they could be used to carry or heat up water and food.

◀ 1876 ◀   1862   ◀ 1834   ◀ 1759   ◀ 1712

ROTARY PHONE

TELEPHONE

Early in the 19th century people found they could send signals through wires, but it was not until the invention of the telephone by Alexander Graham Bell in 1876 that voices could be sent along wires at long distance. This invention revolutionized the ways in which we communicate.

PLASTIC

British inventor Alexander Parkes was trying to create a synthetic material that could be easily shaped when hot, but would be hard when cold. In 1862 he exhibited Parkesine, the world's first type of plastic.

MODERN PLASTIC BOTTLES

REFRIGERATOR

Until 1834 people kept food cool in insulated boxes filled with ice, which was delivered to their door. Then Jacob Perkins of Philadelphia, USA, invented a water-freezing machine that led to the first domestic fridge.

1950s REFRIGERATOR

OPTICAL SEXTANT

SEXTANT

As explorers continued their long journeys across oceans, there was a need for accurate instruments for navigation. In 1759 British instrument maker John Bird perfected the sextant, which is still kept on ships today as a back-up device in case GPS (satnav) navigation fails.

▶ 1878 ▶   1886   ▶ 1895   ▶ 1903   ▶ 1923

LIGHT BULB

Scientists across the world experimented with lamps and light in the 19th century, but it was Thomas Edison in the USA, who created a light bulb that could last for more than 1,200 hours. Light bulbs have since been redesigned to use less energy.

EDISON'S LAMP

CAR

Karl Benz of Germany built the first stationary petrol engine in 1879, and decided to work out how to use this in a "horseless carriage". By 1885 he had invented a two-seater vehicle with a compact, single-cylinder engine. The patent for this car, filed in 1886, is seen as the "birth certificate" of the motor car.

1900 BENZ IDEAL

CABINET WIRELESS RADIO, 1932

RADIO COMMUNICATION

In 1895 Italian inventor Guglielmo Marconi managed to send Morse code signals using radio waves instead of wires. The instrument he used became known as the radio.

AEROPLANE

Orville Wright from the USA first took to the skies with an aeroplane powered by a small petrol engine in North Carolina in 1903. He flew for 12 seconds over a distance of 37 m (120 ft). He and his brother Wilbur had spent five years in their workshop in Ohio designing machines that were strong, light, and had enough balance and control to fly.

MODEL OF THE WRIGHTS' 1903 FLYER

TV SET FROM THE 1950s

TELEVISION

John Logie Baird, from Scotland, was the first person to transmit a TV picture in 1923. In 1927 American Philip Farnsworth created the first form of electronic television.

8000 BCE

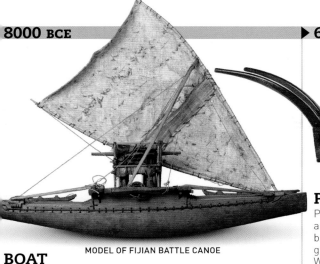

MODEL OF FIJIAN BATTLE CANOE

BOAT
Early people needed some form of floating raft to take them fishing and from one island to another. The earliest boats were wooden logs or bamboo trunks tied together, but by around 3000 BCE, people had developed metal tools to cut tree trunks into wooden planks to build the first ships.

▶ 6000 BCE

WOODEN PLOUGH

PLOUGH
People hunted for food until around 8500 BCE when they began to farm the land to grow grains, such as wheat. Wooden ploughs were invented to make use of animal power. Ploughs could be joined to oxen and used to dig up much bigger areas of land.

▶ 3500 BCE

WHEEL
The first wheels were solid wooden discs with a hole through the centre. People needed sharp metal tools to chisel the round shape, which explains why this major invention took a while to arrive. The wheels were connected by a rod called an axle.

WOODEN WHEEL

▶ 900 CE

GUNPOWDER BURNING

GUNPOWDER
Chinese alchemists (early chemists) had been experimenting with chemicals for centuries when a group discovered that a mix of saltpetre, sulphur, and charcoal exploded into flame. The mix was used in fireworks to scare away evil spirits and later in weapons. The recipe was kept from the rest of the world until the 13th century.

◀ 1590

STEAM ENGINE
The first steam machine was designed by Spanish inventor Jerónimo de Ayanz in 1606 to push water out of mines. Other machines followed, but it was not until Scotsman James Watt added a condenser (for cooling the steam back to water) and gears (for making the engine faster) that the steam engine became a useful form of power for factories, mines, farming, and transport.

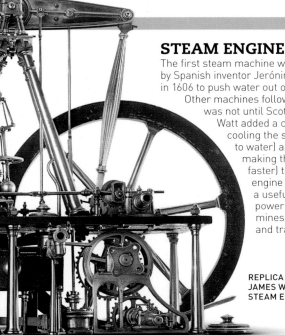

REPLICA OF JAMES WATT'S STEAM ENGINE

COMPOUND MICROSCOPE
Zacharias Janssen, the son of a spectacles maker in Holland, invented the microscope using a long tube and a mix of curved lenses. In 1665 the Englishman Robert Hooke improved the design and added an oil lamp to light up the specimens. Microscopes have been used by scientists ever since.

REPLICA OF ROBERT HOOKE'S MICROSCOPE

◀ 1300

EYE GLASSES

EYE GLASSES
Early peoples such as the Vikings used rock crystals to act as lenses and increase their viewing power. Wearable lenses in the form of eye glasses were invented in the 14th century – probably in Italy, where glassblowing techniques were advanced. These early spectacles were made of two magnifying lenses set into bone, metal, or leather mountings, and were balanced on the nose.

1928

ANTIBIOTIC PILLS

ANTIBIOTIC
Alexander Fleming's discovery that a mould juice (now known as penicillin) could kill a wide range of bacteria changed the course of modern medicine. Today, there are many types of antibiotics, targeting bacteria, fungi, and parasites.

▶ 1946

COMPUTER
Developed for the US government, the world's first electronic general-purpose computer was called ENIAC: Electronic Numerical Integrator and Computer. This huge computer led the way for smaller and more powerful computers in the decades to come.

COMMODORE (PERSONAL) COMPUTER FROM 1977

▶ 1957

SPACE SATELLITE
The Soviet Union put the first satellite into space on 4 October 1957. Called Sputnik 1, it was the size of a beach ball, and took 98 minutes to orbit Earth. This marked the beginning of the Space Age.

SPUTNIK 1

▶ 1973

1990s MOBILE PHONE

MOBILE PHONE
Martin Cooper, working at Motorola in the USA, developed and demonstrated the first mobile phone. It was the size of a brick and would not be sold to the general public for another ten years, but it marked the start of mobile personal communication systems.

▶ 1989

WORLD WIDE WEB
In the 1970s Vinton Cerf developed a system that allowed mini-networks of computers all over the world to send files to each other. Then in 1991 Tim Berners-Lee introduced a World Wide Web of information that anyone with an online computer could access, and helped to create the Internet we know and use today.

▶ 2010

3-D BODY PARTS
Invented in the USA, 3-D printing has been used since the 1980s to build up three-dimensional objects in layers from digital information. More recently, scientists have been developing 3-D printers to make human organs and body tissue.

2.4 BILLION OF THE 7 BILLION PEOPLE ON EARTH USE THE INTERNET

Numbers

Numbers are symbols that are used to represent a quantity of something. They have been used for thousands of years to answer the question "how many?". At first people only used whole numbers (integers), but then came the idea of fractions and negative numbers.

NUMBER SYMBOLS

Many ancient civilizations used some form of number system. The modern Hindu-Arabic system is the simplest and most useful for mathematical calculations.

Modern Hindu-Arabic	1	2	3	4	5	6	7	8	9	10
Mayan	•	••	•••	••••	—	•̲	••̲	•••̲	••••̲	☰
Ancient Chinese	一	二	三	四	五	六	七	八	九	十
Ancient Rome	I	II	III	IV	V	VI	VII	VIII	IX	X
Ancient Egypt	Ɩ	ƖƖ	ƖƖƖ	ƖƖ̸	ƖƖ̸	ƖƖƖ̸	ƖƖƖƖ	ƖƖƖ̸	ƖƖƖƖ̸	∩
Babylonian	𒁹	𒈫	𒐲	𒑄	𒑋	𒑌	𒑏	𒑐	𒑑	<

ADDITION

Numbers can be added together to find the total of two or more quantities. Additions are written as equations by placing "+" between the numbers being added.

Sign for addition

Equals sign leads to answer

$$1 + 3 = 4$$

FIRST NUMBER — NUMBER TO ADD — TOTAL, RESULT, OR SUM

SUBTRACTION

Subtraction is a mathematical way of working out how many are left if you take some of an original quantity away. It uses the "−" sign.

Sign for subtraction

Equals sign leads to answer

$$4 - 3 = 1$$

FIRST NUMBER — NUMBER TO SUBTRACT — TOTAL, RESULT, OR SUM

MULTIPLICATION

Multiplication is useful for repeated addition. To find the total people in 9 rows, for instance, where each row has 13 people, you could add 9 to itself 13 times, or calculate 9 x 13.

$$9 \times 13$$

Sign for multiplication

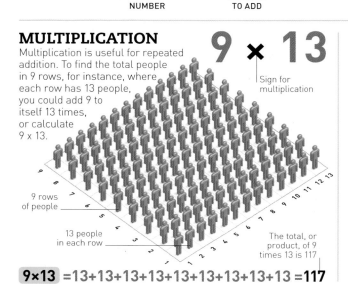

9 rows of people

13 people in each row

The total, or product, of 9 times 13 is 117

$9 \times 13 = 13+13+13+13+13+13+13+13+13 = 117$

DIVISION

Division is used to divide up a total number of things into several equal bundles, or amounts. This example shows how to divide ten sweets among three people. It is not possible to do this evenly, so after giving the three people three sweets each, there is still one left over (known as the "remainder").

$$10 \div 3$$

Division sign

DIVIDEND
This is the number that is being divided by (or shared out among) another number.

Sign for division

DIVISOR
The number that is used to divide the first number (the dividend).

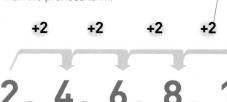

$10 \div 3 = 3$ remainder 1

QUOTIENT
The result of the division.

POWERS

A "power" is the number of times a number is multiplied by itself. So "5 x 5 x 5 x 5" is said to be "five to the power of four" which is written mathematically as 5^4.

5^3

This is the power, which shows how many times to multiply the number (5^3 means $5 \times 5 \times 5$)

This is the number that the power relates to

One example of 5^2 would be 5 rows with 5 units in each row

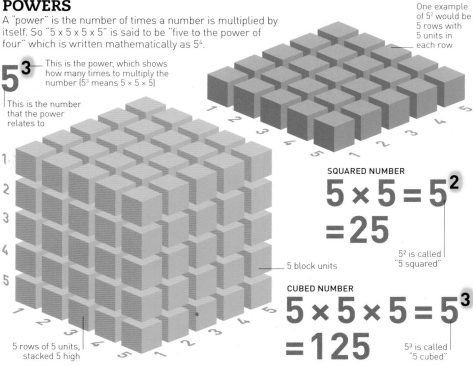

5 block units

SQUARED NUMBER
$$5 \times 5 = 5^2 = 25$$
5^2 is called "5 squared"

CUBED NUMBER
$$5 \times 5 \times 5 = 5^3 = 125$$
5^3 is called "5 cubed"

5 rows of 5 units, stacked 5 high

NUMBER SEQUENCES

A sequence of numbers is a series of numbers that follow one another according to a pattern, such as each number being two higher than the previous term.

Each number in this sequence is 2 higher than the number before

A BASIC SEQUENCE
The rule for this sequence is that each number equals the previous number plus 2.

+2 +2 +2 +2

Fifth number is 10

$$2, 4, 6, 8, 10 ...$$

First number is 2, so the next will be 2+2

Dots show sequence continues

FIBONACCI SEQUENCE
This is a very famous number sequence that appears in lots of natural formations such as flower petals and spiral galaxies.

Each number in this sequence is the sum of the two numbers before it

1+1 1+2 2+3 3+5 5+...

$$1, 1, 2, 3, 5, 8, ...$$

Sequence starts with 1

Sequence continues in same way indefinitely

POSITIVE AND NEGATIVE NUMBERS

Positive numbers count up from zero; negative numbers count down from zero. This means they are less than zero. If you had £5 in your bank account and withdrew £10 from a cash machine, your bank balance would show as –£5.

| –5 | –4 | –3 | –2 | –1 | 0 | 1 | 2 | 3 | 4 | 5 |

NEGATIVE NUMBERS · POSITIVE NUMBERS

DECIMALS

Decimals are a way of expressing parts of things or numbers as tenths or hundredths of a whole number.

The number to the left of the decimal point is a whole number (here it is 1,234)

The decimal point

The numbers to the right of the decimal point are parts of a number; here 5 tenths and 6 hundredths

1,234.56

FRACTIONS

Fractions are a way of expressing parts of an object or number. If you cut a cake, for instance, into 2 equal parts, each piece is now 1 of 2 parts; this is written as 1 over 2, like this: "½".

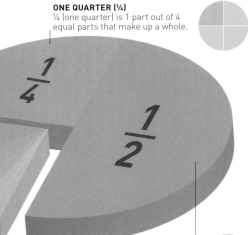

ONE QUARTER (¼)
¼ (one quarter) is 1 part out of 4 equal parts that make up a whole.

EIGHTH (⅛)
⅛ (one eighth) is 1 part out of 8 equal parts that make up a whole.

SIXTEENTH (¹⁄₁₆)
¹⁄₁₆ (one sixteenth) is 1 part out of 16 equal parts that make up a whole.

ONE THIRTY-SECOND (¹⁄₃₂)
¹⁄₃₂ (one thirty-second) is 1 part out of 32 equal parts that make up a whole.

ONE SIXTY-FOURTH (¹⁄₆₄)
¹⁄₆₄ (one sixty-fourth) is 1 part out of 64 equal parts that make up a whole.

ONE HALF (½)
If you divide a cake into 2 equal parts, each piece is 1 of 2 parts. This is written mathematically as ½.

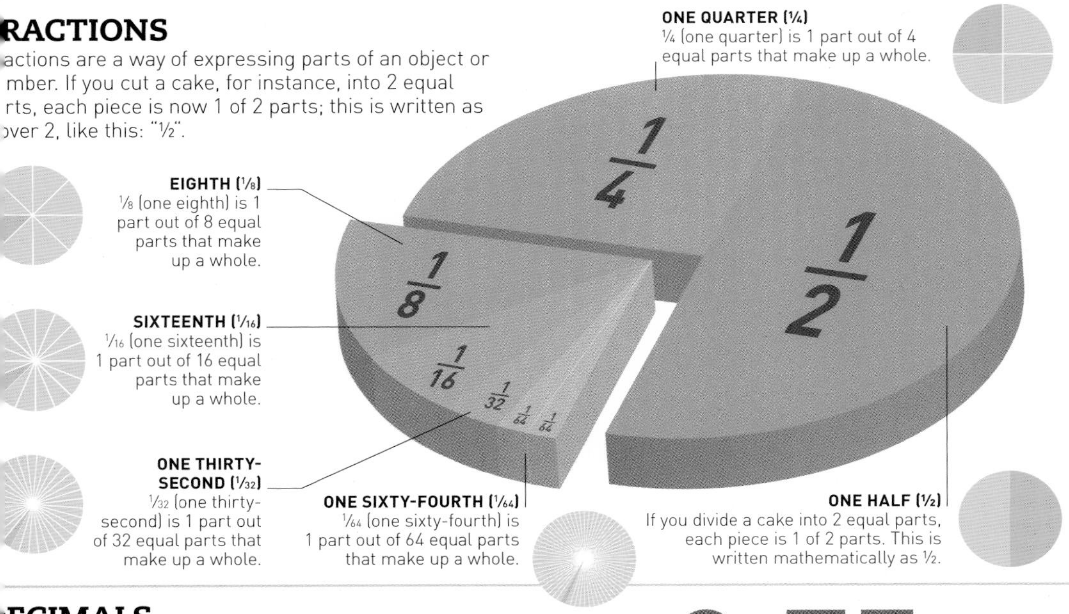

PERCENTAGES

Percentages are another way of talking about parts of an object or number. Here, the whole (such as the whole of a school class) is said to be 100 per cent, or 100%. Half the class is therefore half that: 50%. The whole can be broken into very fine parts up to 100%.

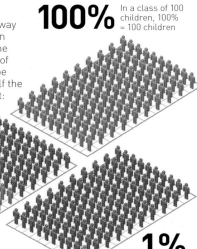

100%
In a class of 100 children, 100% = 100 children

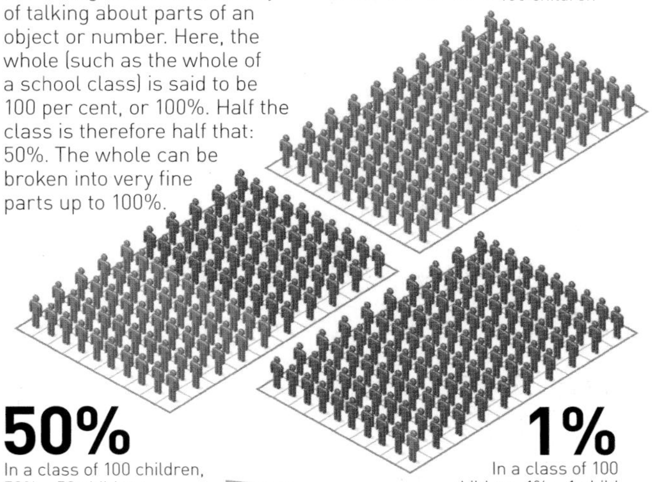

50%
In a class of 100 children, 50% = 50 children

1%
In a class of 100 children, 1% = 1 child

DECIMALS, FRACTIONS, AND PERCENTAGES

These are all ways of talking about parts of a number, or something that is less than a whole (such as half a cake, 5% of a class, or 0.5 of a metre). We can "translate" fractions, decimals, or percentages into each other. For instance, ¾ is the same as 75% or 0.75.

0.75

DECIMAL
A decimal shows a number as tenths and hundredths of a whole.

75%

PERCENTAGE
A percentage shows a number as a proportion of 100.

FRACTION
A fraction shows a number as part of an equally divided whole.

¾

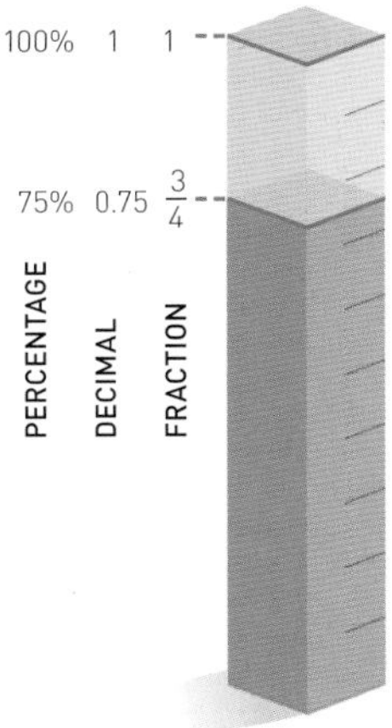

100% 1 1
75% 0.75 ¾

PERCENTAGE · DECIMAL · FRACTION

DECIMALS, FRACTIONS, AND PERCENTAGES ARE DIFFERENT WAYS OF SAYING THE SAME THING

COMMON NUMBERS
The table below shows some commonly used fractions, decimals, and percentages.

Decimal	Fraction	%	Decimal	Fraction	%
0.1	¹⁄₁₀	10%	0.625	⁵⁄₈	62.5%
0.125	⅛	12.5%	0.666	⅔	66.7%
0.25	¼	25%	0.7	⁷⁄₁₀	70%
0.333	⅓	33.3%	0.75	¾	75%
0.4	²⁄₅	40%	0.8	⁴⁄₅	80%
0.5	½	50%	1	1	100%

PRIME NUMBERS

These are special numbers that cannot be divided by any other number except themselves and 1. For example, 13 cannot be divided by any number other than 13 or 1. Numbers that can be divided by others are known as "composite numbers".

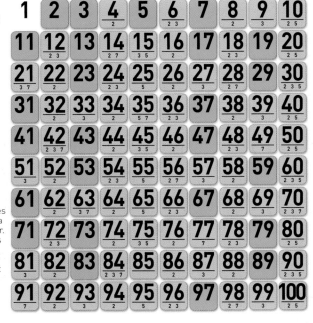

KEY TO TABLE

17

PRIME NUMBER
A green box on the table indicates that the number is a prime number.

42
2 3 7

COMPOSITE NUMBER
A blue box indicates that a number is a composite number. The numbers it is divisible by are given as smaller numbers below it (2, 3, 7 in the example above).

ALGEBRA

When mathematicians are trying to work out a missing number in an equation, they use a symbol to represent the missing number. In this example, we know that 2 plus something (here called "b") equals 8.

VARIABLE
An unknown number or quantity represented by a letter is known as the "variable".

2 + ?b = 8

EXPRESSION
An expression is a statement written in algebraic form, such as 2 + b = 8.

The answer is:
b = 6

AVERAGES

An average is the middle value of a set of data. The most common type of average is the mean, which is found by adding up a set of numbers then dividing the total by the amount of numbers in the set.

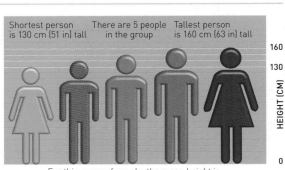

Shortest person is 130 cm (51 in) tall

There are 5 people in the group

Tallest person is 160 cm (63 in) tall

160
130

HEIGHT (CM)

0

For this group of people, the mean height is:
(130 + 140 + 150 + 160 + 160) ÷ 5 = 148 cm

Geometry

Geometry is the part of maths that looks at lines, angles, shapes, and space. It is used to work out distances, areas, and volumes in a wide range of tasks from building houses to astronomy.

COMMON ANGLES

If you draw a line out from a centre point and move it around 360°, it will return to the starting point. So the angles surrounding a point make up a whole turn, and they add up to 360°. The angles on a straight line make up a half turn and add up to 180°.

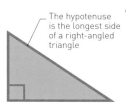

0/360°
45°
90°
270°
180°
WHOLE TURN

Angle less than 90°
ACUTE ANGLE

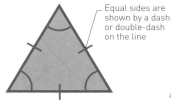
90°
RIGHT ANGLE

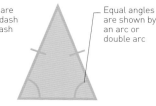
Angle greater than 90° but less than 180°
OBTUSE ANGLE

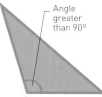
Angle greater than 180° less than 360°
REFLEX ANGLE

TRIANGLES

Shapes made of straight lines are called polygons. Triangles are the simplest polygons, because they are made from three straight lines joined at three corners. All three angles inside a triangle always add up to 180°. There are several different types of triangles.

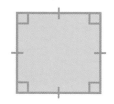
Equal sides are shown by a dash or double-dash on the line

EQUILATERAL TRIANGLE
This triangle has three equal sides and three equal angles (each 60°).

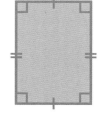
Equal angles are shown by an arc or double arc

ISOSCELES TRIANGLE
This triangle has two equal sides. The angles opposite these sides are equal.

The hypotenuse is the longest side of a right-angled triangle

RIGHT-ANGLED TRIANGLE
This triangle has one angle that is 90° (a right angle). It also has a hypotenuse.

Angle greater than 90°

OBTUSE TRIANGLE
This triangle has one angle that is greater than 90° (more than a right angle).

SCALENE TRIANGLE
This triangle has sides different lengths and three different-sized angles

QUADRILATERALS

Shapes that are made from four straight lines are called quadrilaterals. They have four vertices (points where the sides meet) – each of these is called a vertex. The interior angles of a quadrilateral always add up to a total of 360°. There are several different types of quadrilaterals.

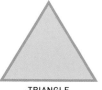
SQUARE
This quadrilateral has four equal sides and four equal angles (right angles). The opposite sides of a square are parallel.

RECTANGLE
This is like a long version of the square: it has four right angles and two pairs of sides, but one pair is longer than the other. Opposite sides are parallel.

RHOMBUS
This quadrilateral has four sides of equal length, and two pairs of opposite angles that are also equal.

PARALLELOGRAM
This has two pairs of equal-length sides and two pairs of equal angles. The opposite sides are parallel.

Parallel sides

TRAPEZIUM
A trapezium (or trapezoid) has one pair of opposite sides that are parallel but not equal in length.

KITE
A kite has two pairs adjacent sides (sides that are next to each other) are equal in length, and pair of equal angles

POLYGONS

A polygon is a closed two-dimensional shape that has three or more sides. It is usually named according to how many sides it has. For example, *hexa* is Greek for "six", so a hexagon is a polygon with six sides. Every type of polygon has the same number of sides as it has angles. The shapes may be regular – with equal length sides and angles – or irregular, with unequal sides and angles.

TRIANGLE
3 sides and angles

SQUARE
4 sides and angles

PENTAGON
5 sides and angles

HEXAGON
6 sides and angles

HEPTAGON
7 sides and angles

OCTAGON
8 sides and angles

NONAGON
9 sides and angles

DECAGON
10 sides and angles

HENDECAGON
11 sides and angles

DODECAGON
12 sides and angles

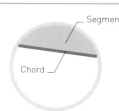
PENTADECAGON
15 sides and angles

ICOSAGON
20 sides and angles

CIRCLES

A circle is a closed curved line surrounding a central point, where every point along the curved line is the same distance from the centre point. In maths, the parts of a circle all have their own names.

RADIUS
A straight line that runs from the centre point of a circle to any point on its edge.

DIAMETER
A straight line that runs from one side of a circle to the other, through the centre point.

CIRCUMFERENCE
The circumference is the total length of the outside edge of a circle.

Arc
Sector
ARC AND SECTOR
A sector is a space enclosed by two radii (the plural of radius). An arc is a section of the circumference.

Segment
Chord
CHORD AND SEGMENT
A chord is a straight line linking two points on a circle's circumference. A segment is the area between a chord and the arc of the circle.

AREA
The total amount of space inside a circle's circumference.

PI

If you divide the circumference of a circle by its diameter, the answer is always 3 and a bit, or pi (π). It is impossible to write pi precisely, because the numbers after the decimal point continue forever.

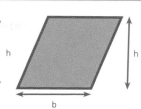

π = 3.141592653

PI SYMBOL

FINDING AREA

The area of a two-dimensional shape is the amount of space inside it. There are formulae that can be used to work out how much space there is inside any polygon.

 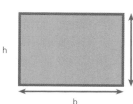 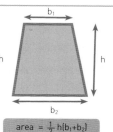 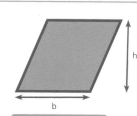

area = πr^2	area = $\frac{1}{2}$bh	area = bh	area = bh	area = $\frac{1}{2}$h(b$_1$+b$_2$)	area = bh
CIRCLE	**TRIANGLE**	**RECTANGLE**	**PARALLELOGRAM**	**TRAPEZIUM**	**RHOMBUS**

CIRCLE
The area of a circle is pi (3.14) multiplied by the square of the circle's radius.

TRIANGLE
To find the area of a triangle, multiply the base by the height, then halve your answer.

RECTANGLE
The area of a rectangle can be found by multiplying its base by its height.

PARALLELOGRAM
Find the area of a parallelogram by multiplying its base by its vertical height.

TRAPEZIUM
Find the area by adding the two parallel sides, multiplying the total by the height, then dividing by 2.

RHOMBUS
The area of a rhombus can be found by multiplying its base by its vertical height.

PYTHAGORAS'S THEOREM

This theory is named after an Ancient Greek mathematician called Pythagoras. He observed that if you draw squares from each side of a right-angled triangle, the area of the two smaller squares added together is equal to the area of the largest square.

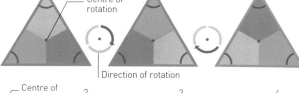

"GEOMETRY" COMES FROM GREEK: "GEO" MEANING EARTH AND "METRIA" MEANING MEASURE

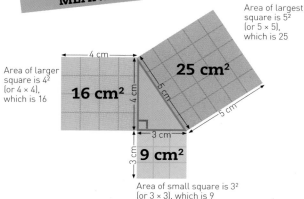

Area of larger square is 4² (or 4 × 4), which is 16

16 cm²

Area of largest square is 5² (or 5 × 5), which is 25

25 cm²

Area of small square is 3² (or 3 × 3), which is 9

9 cm²

USING THE THEOREM
Pythagoras's theorem can be used to find the length of the longest side of a right-angled triangle (c), if you know the length of the two shorter sides (a and b).

$a^2 + b^2 = c^2$

FINDING VOLUME AND SURFACE AREA

Volume is the amount of space enclosed within a three-dimensional (3-D) object. Surface area is the total area around the outside of a 3-D object.

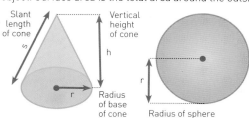

Slant length of cone — s
Vertical height of cone — h
Radius of base of cone — r
Radius of sphere — r
Radius of cylinder — r
h, height (or length) of cylinder

surface area = $\pi rs + \pi r^2$	surface area = $4\pi r^2$	surface area = $2\pi r$ (h+r)
volume = $\frac{1}{3}\pi r^2 h$	volume = $\frac{4}{3}\pi r^2$	volume = $\pi r^2 h$
CONE	**SPHERE**	**CYLINDER**

CONE
Find the surface area of a cone using the radius of its base, its height, and its slant length. Find the volume using the height and radius.

SPHERE
You can find the surface area and volume of a sphere using only its radius, because the other part of the equation, pi, is a constant number (3.14).

CYLINDER
The surface area and volume of a cylinder can be found from its radius and height (or length).

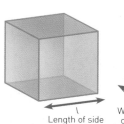 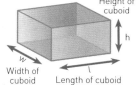 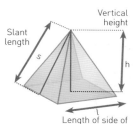

Length of side
Height of cuboid
Width of cuboid
Length of cuboid
Vertical height
Slant length — s
Length of side of base of pyramid

surface area = $6l^2$	surface area = 2(lh+lw+hw)	surface area = $2ls+l^2$
volume = l^3	volume = lwh	volume = $\frac{1}{3}l^2 h$
CUBE	**CUBOID**	**SQUARE PYRAMID**

CUBE
The surface area and volume of a cube can be found by using only the length of its sides. No other information is needed.

CUBOID
The surface area or volume of a cuboid can be found if you know its length, width, and height.

SQUARE PYRAMID
Find the surface area of a square pyramid by using the lengths of its slant and the side of its base. Its volume can be found from its height and the side of its base.

ROTATIONAL SYMMETRY

If a shape can be moved around a centre point and still fit its original outline exactly, it is said to have rotational symmetry. The order of rotational symmetry is the number of ways a shape can fit into its original outline when rotated.

EQUILATERAL TRIANGLE
An equilateral triangle has rotational symmetry of order 3 – when rotated, it fits its original outline in three different ways.

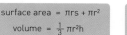

Centre of rotation

Direction of rotation

SQUARE
When rotated around its centre, a square fits its original outline in four different ways – its rotational symmetry is order 4.

Centre of rotation

REFLECTIVE SYMMETRY

A reflection shows a shape in its mirror image, like a mountain reflection in a lake. When a flat shape can be divided in half so that each half is the exact mirror image of the other, it is said to have reflective symmetry. The line that divides the shape to perform the reflection is called a line of symmetry.

ISOSCELES TRIANGLE
This is symmetrical across a central line: the sides and angles on either side of the line are equal, and the line cuts the base in half at right angles.

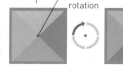

Line of symmetry

EQUILATERAL TRIANGLE
An equilateral triangle has a line of symmetry through the middle of each side – not just the base.

TANGRAMS

Any shape that is made of straight sides can be split into triangles. If you were to cut up a piece of paper into triangles, for instance, you could reassemble the pieces in different ways to create new shapes. The game of Tangrams is a puzzle that uses a square shape split into seven polygons, most of which are triangles.

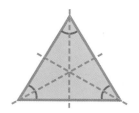 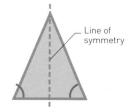   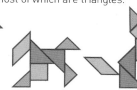

TANGRAM   **POSSIBLE SHAPES USING TANGRAM PIECES**

Cars

The first cars were invented more than 130 years ago. Originally known as "horseless carriages", these early models were slow, open-topped vehicles, but today's cars are fast, stylish, and can be powered by petrol, diesel, or electricity.

HOW A CAR WORKS

The power that turns a car's wheels comes from the car's internal combustion engine. Combustion is a kind of burning that takes place inside the engine when air is mixed with petrol or diesel, compressed, and ignited with a spark.

1. INSIDE THE ENGINE
Air and petrol (or diesel) are sucked into cylinders inside the engine by pistons, which then compress the mixture. A spark plug ignites it, providing energy.

2. IN GEAR
The pistons move very fast, but a car needs more force and less speed to start moving. Gears control the force and speed the car receives.

3. TURNING WHEELS
The gears turn rods called axles. Wheels are attached to these axles, so they turn too.

4. MOVING FORWARD
The wheels are much bigger than the axles, so as they turn they cover a lot of ground quickly, moving the car forward

BESTSELLING CARS

In 1901 only 600 cars were sold around the world. By 2014 yearly car sales had reached 71 million. Some models have sold in huge numbers, as shown below.

1 TOYOTA COROLLA
The world's bestselling car, over 40 million of this Japanese model have been sold since 1966.

2 FORD F-SERIES
Ford have sold more than 35 million of these chunky pick-up trucks since they were introduced in 1948.

FORD F-SERIES 1948

3 VOLKSWAGEN GOLF
Introduced in 1974, the Golf has been consistently popular – 27.5 million have been sold.

4 VOLKSWAGEN BEETLE
First produced in 1933, 23.5 million Beetles have been sold worldwide.

VOLKSWAGEN BEETLE 1948

5 FORD ESCORT
These family cars were produced from 1968. Sales eventually topped 20 million.

6 HONDA CIVIC
Honda was about to stop making cars before creating the Civic in 1972. 18.5 million have sold.

7 HONDA ACCORD
The first Japanese car produced in the USA, Honda has sold 17.5 million Accords since 1976.

8 FORD MODEL T
The original affordable car, Ford sold 16.5 million of these between 1908 and 1927.

9 VOLKSWAGEN PASSAT
Seven generations of Passat have seen total sales of above 15.5 million since 1973.

10 CHEVROLET IMPALA
Chevrolet have sold 14 million of these since the car was introduced in 1958.

CHEVROLET IMPALA 1960

THE FERRARI LAFERRARI CAN REACH 100 KM/H (62 MPH) IN UNDER THREE SECONDS

MASERATI GRANTURISMO MC STRADALE 2011

FERRARI LAFERRARI 2013

SUPERCARS

Cars that are designed to be faster, sleeker, and more powerful than normal cars are called supercars. They use cutting-edge materials and technology, and are very expensive. They are the cars that make onlookers say "Wow!".

CARS THROUGH TIME

The first petrol-fuelled cars reached a top speed of 19 km/h (12 mph). Since then, technology has given us affordable, faster, and safer cars with speeds of up to 435 km/h (270 mph).

1886

Benz Motorwagen

1886
Benz Motorwagen is the first petrol-fuelled automobile.

1901
Lohner-Porsche produces the first hybrid cars, which can run on an electric battery and petrol.

1908
The Ford Model T is the first affordable car.

1913
Ford operates first moving car assembly line.

1928
Bentley wins Le Mans race.

Bentley 4½ Litre

1954
Mercedes-Benz 300 SL "Gull Wing" is first production car to exceed 241 km/h (150 mp)

1893
Duryea Motor Wagon is the first successful car powered by petrol.

1903
Mercedes Simplex 60HP can reach 120 km/h (75 mph).

Mercedes Simplex 60HP

1910
First four-wheel brake system is patented by Argyll Motors, Scotland.

Argyll Landaulette

1934
Citroën Traction Avant is first successful front-wheel-drive made for the mass-market.

Citroën Traction Avant

1948
Jaguar XK120 reaches 200 km/h (124.6 mph).

OFF-ROAD ADVENTURERS

These cars are specially built to travel along difficult terrain, such as muddy or very uneven roads. They are also known as "four-by-fours" because all four wheels are powered by the engine. This gives each wheel the ability to pull the vehicle out of a sticky position.

WILLYS MB JEEP
1941

LAND ROVER SERIES 1
1949

MERCEDES-BENZ G300D
1993

RANGE ROVER
2002

HUMMER H3
2008

THE FUTURE IS GREEN

Hybrid cars have two kinds of energy sources: a petrol or diesel engine and an electric motor. When the car is using the petrol or diesel engine, it also charges up the electric motor, which can then be used to drive. These cars use less energy and cause less pollution than other cars.

FORD ESCAPE HYBRID
2009
New York City, USA, is now using more and more hybrid taxicabs.

TESLA ROADSTER
2007
This car is purely electric.

BMW I8
2014
This hybrid sports car can reach speeds of up to 250 km/h (155 mph).

RACING DEMONS

Racing cars come in several shapes and sizes. Each one is built to suit a particular kind of race, such as Formula 1, rallying, endurance, or stock car racing.

MCLAREN F1 GT
1997

BUGATTI VEYRON
2005

KOENIGSEGG AGERA RS
2015

LAMBORGHINI HURACÁN
2014

PORSCHE 918 SPYDER
2015

FORMULA 1 RACING: 2008 MCLAREN-MERCEDES
Driven by 2008 World Champion Lewis Hamilton.

TOURING CAR RACING: 2003 MERCEDES BENZ
This won nine of the ten races in Germany's Touring Car Masters (DTM).

ENDURANCE RACING: 2009 PEUGEOT
Winner of Le Mans 24-hour race; driven by a team of three.

STOCK CAR RACING: 2009 TOYOTA CAMRY
Brian Vickers won the Carfax 400 in this hybrid car.

RALLYING: 2000 SUBARU IMPREZA
Winner of the Safari Rally; driven by Richard Burns.

RECORD BREAKERS

Over the years, manufacturers have tried to outdo each other with new refinements. Here are some remarkable record-breaking cars.

FIRST AFFORDABLE CAR
In the early years of motoring, cars were driven only by wealthy people. Henry Ford changed this in 1908, when he produced the affordable Model T.

FORD MODEL T

LAND SPEED RECORD
Thrust SSC (SuperSonic Car) used two turbojets to drive faster than sound in 1997 in the Nevada Desert, USA, reaching 1,228 km/h (763 mph).

THRUST SSC

SMALLEST ROADWORTHY CAR
Built by Austin Colson in the USA in 2012, this car measures just 63.5 cm (25 in) high x 65.41 cm (25.8 in) wide x 126.47 cm (50 in) long. It is just big enough to be allowed on roads.

MOST EXPENSIVE CAR
In 2013 Lamborghini unveiled the world's most expensive car: the Veneno Roadster. It costs £3.3 million (US$4.95 million) and has a top speed of 356 km/h (221 mph). Lamborghini said that only nine cars would ever be produced.

FASTEST PRODUCTION CAR
The fastest series production car is the Hennessey Venom GT. It reached a speed of 435.31 km/h (270.49 mph) in 2014, and is powered by a 7.0-litre, twin-turbo V8 engine.

...rcedes-Benz ...0 SL "Gull Wing"

1959
The space-saving, compact Mini changes thinking about economy cars.

Mini

1971
Chrysler Imperial introduces a reliable electronic four-wheel anti-lock braking system, called Sure-Brake.

1982
Bosch produces the first fully digital electronic fuel injection system.

Fuel injection system

2014
Hennessey Venom does 435 km/h (270.49 mph).

2015

1958
Aston Martin DB4 achieves 227 km/h (141 mph).

Aston Martin DB4

1966
Lamborghini Miura reaches 275 km/h (171 mph).

Lamborghini Miura

1973
Catalytic converter invented.

Catalytic converter

1997
Toyota Prius is the first mass-produced hybrid car.

Toyota Prius

2010
Bugatti Veyron 16.4 Super Sport does 434 km/h (269.86 mph).

Tractors

A tractor is a vehicle designed to pull things – especially large farm machinery. Tractors have engines with a special gearbox that allows them to use all the engine's power for strength, not speed. Once fuelled by coal, they now run on diesel.

MODERN MACHINE ANATOMY

Modern tractors are very large and powerful. They have four huge wheels with grooved tyres that allow them to travel over wet, muddy ground, and reinforced cabs to keep the driver safe even if the tractor tips over. Other farm machinery can be attached using linkage and pick-up hitches, and powered via the tractor's PTO (power take off) shaft.

SOCKETS
These can be used to power things like brake lights on machinery.

HYDRAULICS
These allow the tractor to raise and lower heavy items.

THREE-POINT LINKAGE
Other machinery can be attached to the tractor here.

PICK-UP HITCH
The driver can use this to hook up equipment.

PTO SHAFT
This takes power from the tractor to any farm machinery attached.

A YEAR ON THE FARM

Farmers work with the seasons, as seeds and crops will grow only when conditions are right. Tractors are useful at every stage of the process, from preparing the land to harvesting the crops.

1 PLOUGHING AND CULTIVATING
After the harvest, tractors are used to pull ploughs, preparing the soil for seeding.

2 PLANTING SEEDS
Seeds are sown on to the fields using a tractor seeder. Modern machines make sure that lines of seeds don't overlap.

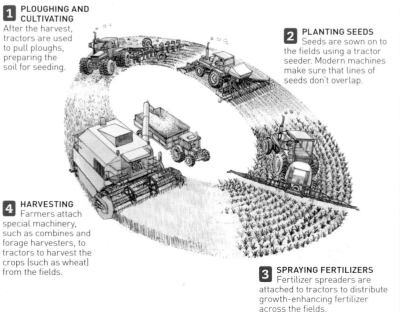

4 HARVESTING
Farmers attach special machinery, such as combines and forage harvesters, to tractors to harvest the crops (such as wheat) from the fields.

3 SPRAYING FERTILIZERS
Fertilizer spreaders are attached to tractors to distribute growth-enhancing fertilizer across the fields.

FIRST TRACTORS

Tractors were invented in the 1860s to do the job of horses around the farm. They had steam engines, large metal wheels, and a seat at the back.

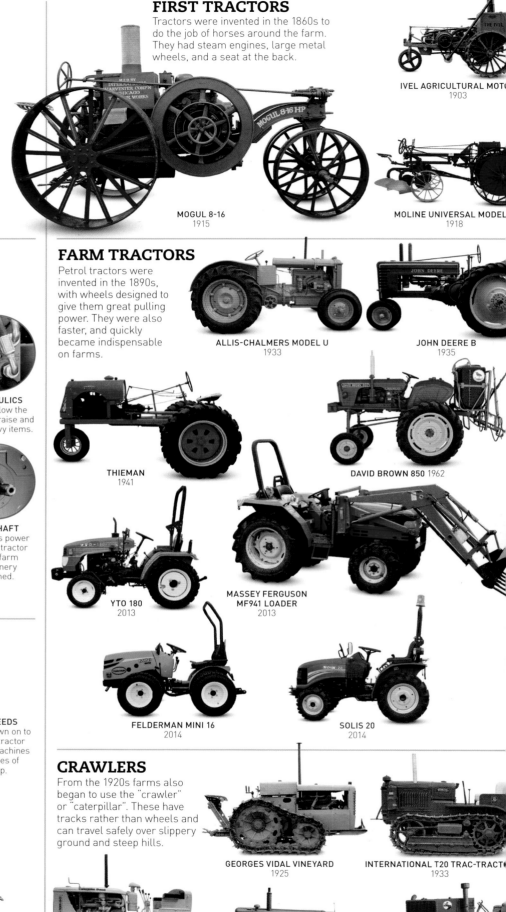

IVEL AGRICULTURAL MOTO
1903

MOGUL 8-16
1915

MOLINE UNIVERSAL MODEL
1918

FARM TRACTORS

Petrol tractors were invented in the 1890s, with wheels designed to give them great pulling power. They were also faster, and quickly became indispensable on farms.

ALLIS-CHALMERS MODEL U
1933

JOHN DEERE B
1935

THIEMAN
1941

DAVID BROWN 850 1962

YTO 180
2013

MASSEY FERGUSON MF941 LOADER
2013

FELDERMAN MINI 16
2014

SOLIS 20
2014

CRAWLERS

From the 1920s farms also began to use the "crawler" or "caterpillar". These have tracks rather than wheels and can travel safely over slippery ground and steep hills.

GEORGES VIDAL VINEYARD
1925

INTERNATIONAL T20 TRAC-TRACT
1933

CATERPILLAR D7
1948

JOHN DEERE MC
1950

BREDA 50TCR
1952

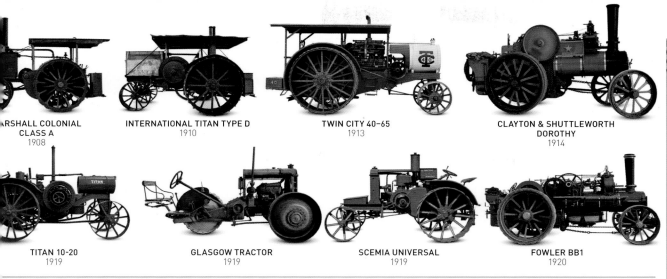

MARSHALL COLONIAL
CLASS A
1908

INTERNATIONAL TITAN TYPE D
1910

TWIN CITY 40–65
1913

CLAYTON & SHUTTLEWORTH
DOROTHY
1914

TITAN 10-20
1919

GLASGOW TRACTOR
1919

SCEMIA UNIVERSAL
1919

FOWLER BB1
1920

MASSEY-HARRIS
101 JUNIOR
1939

Roll-bars over
the cab area
protect the
driver should the
tractor tip over

Thick treads,
or grooves,
provide grip
on muddy
ground

The engine
is hidden under
the bonnet

MASSEY FERGUSON 7619
2013

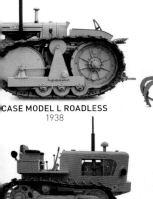

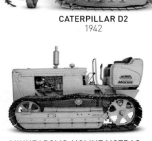

CASE MODEL L ROADLESS
1938

CATERPILLAR D2
1942

TRACK-MARSHALL
1958

MINNEAPOLIS-MOLINE MOTRAC
1960

INTERNATIONAL TD14
1944

TRACTOR HISTORY

Today's powerful tractors are the
result of the gradual development
of the tractor since its invention in
the late 19th century.

1892
John Froelich builds first petrol
engine that can move forwards
and backwards.

1896
A Hornsby-Akroyd
engine is used to
power the first
petrol tractor.

**Hornsby-
Akroyd Tractor**

1908
Australia's
tractor industry
begins with the
building of the
first McDonald
Imperial.

McDonald Imperial

Pavesi America

1913–17
As Europe prepares for WWI,
the Pavesi company realizes the
demand for military tractors to
replace horses for pulling heavy
loads. The result is the US model
known as Pavesi America.

1918
The Fordson Model F
becomes the first
mass-produced and
affordable tractor.

Fordson Model F

1924
International Harvester launches the
Farmall model, introducing the idea of
a general-purpose row-crop tractor.

1931
The Caterpillar 60 Atlas
is the first diesel tractor by the
Caterpillar Tractor Company.

Caterpillar 60

1940
Tractors capable of towing aircraft
are supplied to the RAF in the UK
during WWII.

1958
Sir Edmund Hillary arrives at
the South Pole on a tractor.

Doe Triple-D

1964
Doe Triple-D is the first double
tractor; built by British farmer
George Pryor.

1990
JCB launches the
Fastrac, which has
a top speed of
64 km/h (40 mph).

JCB Fastrac

2013
India becomes the world's
largest tractor producer.

1880

2015

53

Trucks and diggers

People are often fascinated by the vehicles they see on our roads and hard at work on construction sites. These machines come in all shapes and sizes, and do very different jobs.

WHAT ARE THEY FOR?

Trucks carry every kind of load. Oil and other liquids are transported in tankers, while huge transporters carry other vehicles. Some trucks, such as road gritters, refuse trucks, and ambulances, provide vital services.

CONSTRUCTION
Cement mixers, diggers, and bulldozers are vital for building work.

EMERGENCY VEHICLES
Specialized trucks, such as fire engines and police vans, respond to emergencies.

HAULAGE
Large trucks and tankers haul their heavy loads over long distances.

SPECIALIST
Highly specialized machines, such as tracked diggers, do specific jobs.

LIGHT TRUCKS

While some light trucks may only be car-sized, they are hardwearing, practical vehicles. These trucks are useful for carrying small loads and operating in small spaces.

FORKLIFT

THREE-WHEELER

SMALL FLATBED

PICK-UP TRUCK

MINI DUMPER

MEDIUM TRUCKS

Local delivery vehicles and trucks providing public services, such as rubbish collection or breakdown recovery, are usually medium-sized.

STREET-SWEEPER VEHICLE

PICK-UP TRUCK WITH SMALL CRANE

DELIVERY TRUCK

REFUSE TRUCK

HEAVY TRUCKS

These huge vehicles have very powerful engines and strong structures to support their heavy cargoes. They are often "articulated", meaning a tractor unit pulls a trailer. The largest trucks are mining dump trucks, used to shift huge loads of earth and rocks.

MONSTER TRUCK

HAULAGE TRUCK

TIMBER TRUCK

CEMENT MIXER

Cars are loaded on to the transporter's decks

TRANSPORTER

TANKER

BIG RIG

DUMP TRUCK

HYDRAULICS

Hydraulics means powering a machine using liquid-filled pipes. Liquids cannot be squeezed into a smaller space, so a pipe filled with oil can be used to exert force. If the pipe is wider at one end than the other, the force is increased.

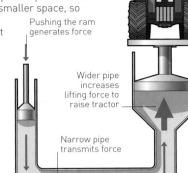

Pushing the ram generates force

Wider pipe increases lifting force to raise tractor

Narrow pipe transmits force

HOW A HYDRAULIC RAM WORKS

Since the lift pipe is wider than the ram pipe, the lifting force is multiplied.

CRANES

Truck-mounted cranes move very heavy items around building sites. The engine of this crane powers a hydraulic pump that lifts the main crane boom up and down.

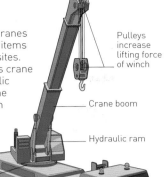

Pulleys increase lifting force of winch

Crane boom

Hydraulic ram

Turntable swings the boom over a large area

Hydraulic stabilizers stop the crane from tipping over

MIGHTY MACHINES

The world's biggest dump trucks – or ultra class haulers – stand at around 8 m (26 ft) high. These mechanical monsters are used in mines and can carry a staggering 500 tonnes of debris – the weight of 38 elephants. At 10 m (33 ft) high, the largest hydraulic diggers weigh around 980 tonnes. They can shovel nearly 1,000 tonnes of material an hour.

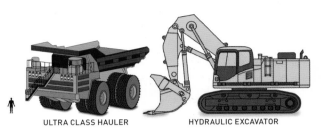

ULTRA CLASS HAULER

HYDRAULIC EXCAVATOR

EMERGENCY VEHICLES

The most important trucks are those that save lives. Fire engines are equipped with ladders, water tanks, and other tools. Armoured SWAT trucks are used by the military and police, while ambulances ferry the sick and injured to hospital.

MOTOR HOME

AIRCRAFT TOW TRUCK

AMBULANCE

POLICE VAN

SWAT TRUCK

FIRE CHIEF'S CAR

BOMB DISPOSAL TRUCK

LADDER 17

FIRE ENGINE

DIGGERS

Also known as excavators, these machines use a bucket on the end of a hinged arm (boom) to dig into the ground. Wheeled diggers are suitable for moving across hard surfaces, while tracked wheels are best for mud. Loaders are used to scoop up loose material, such as gravel, from the ground.

Cab where the driver sits

BACKHOE LOADER

FRONT LOADER

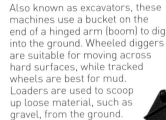

TRACKED LOADER

MINI DIGGER

WHEELED EXCAVATOR

DEERE

160D LC

TRACKED DIGGER

SKILLED OPERATORS USE BACKHOE LOADERS TO PERFORM STUNTS CALLED "DIGGER DANCING"

Trains

In 1804 British engineer Richard Trevithick tried attaching a steam engine to a wagon, a job that before then had been done by horses. It easily pulled enormous weights, and the steam railway was born. Today's trains use diesel, electricity, or magnetic levitation to run fast and cleanly.

DIESEL TRAINS

Steam engines polluted the air and were inefficient, so people began to look for better ways of powering trains. In 1892 the German engineer Rudolf Diesel invented the diesel engine that ran on a liquid type of fuel.

BOXLEY WHITCOMB 30-DM-31
1941

ENGLISH ELECTRIC DELTIC
1955

> **ONE EARLY DIESEL PASSENGER TRAIN WAS CALLED THE FLYING HAMBURGER**

STEAM POWER

A steam engine runs on the heat energy that is produced by burning coal or other fuel. Inside the steam engine there is a fire that heats a boiler filled with water. The steam that is produced goes into cylinders and pushes pistons backwards and forwards. The pistons are connected to the driving wheels, and push and pull them round.

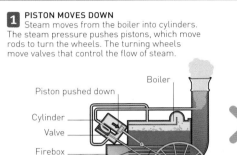

1 PISTON MOVES DOWN
Steam moves from the boiler into cylinders. The steam pressure pushes pistons, which move rods to turn the wheels. The turning wheels move valves that control the flow of steam.

Boiler
Piston pushed down
Cylinder
Valve
Firebox
Valve control rod
Connecting rod
Wheel

2 PISTON MOVES UP
When the piston nears the bottom of the cylinder, the valve swaps the steam flow from the top to the bottom. The steam pushes the piston up, pulling the connecting rod to turn the wheel back to where it started.

Piston pushed up
Wheel rotates

STEAM ENGINES

Steam engines were the first form of locomotives. They were used in the UK from the early 1800s, spreading quickly to the rest of the world. The early trains were quite slow, but in 1934 a steam engine called *Flying Scotsman* reached 160 km/h (100 mph) on a test run between Leeds and London.

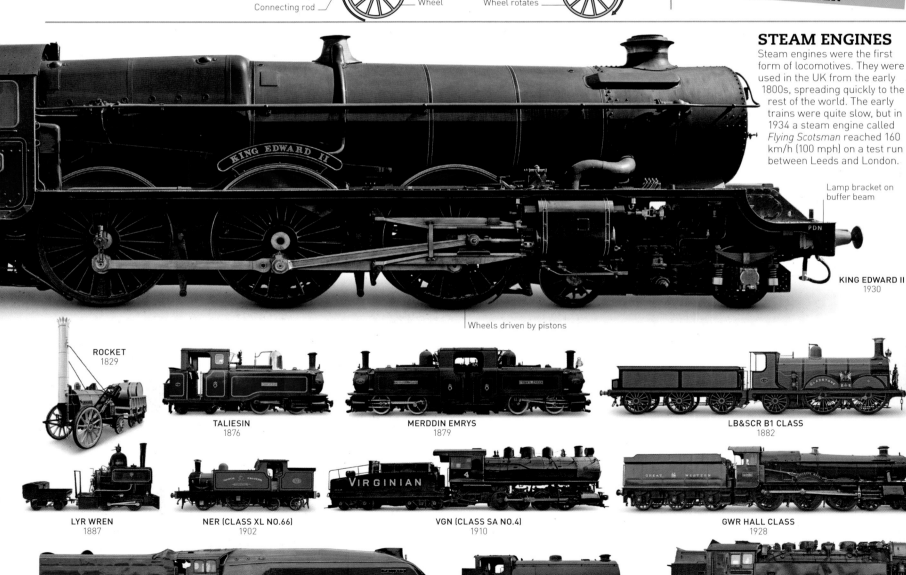

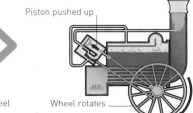

Lamp bracket on buffer beam

KING EDWARD II
1930

Wheels driven by pistons

ROCKET
1829

TALIESIN
1876

MERDDIN EMRYS
1879

LB&SCR B1 CLASS
1882

LYR WREN
1887

NER (CLASS XL NO.66)
1902

VGN (CLASS SA NO.4)
1910

GWR HALL CLASS
1928

MALLARD
1938

HUNSLET AUSTERITY
1944

DR (CLASS 99.73-76)
1954

UGATTI RAILCAR
1932/33

DR (CLASS Kö)
1934

GHE T1
1934

MA&PA GM EMD TYPE NWZ
1946

ALDWIN S12 SWITCHER
1950

BR CLASS 08
1953

BR (CLASS 05)
1954

NORFOLK AND WESTERN 41
1958

N&W EMD GP9 CLASS
1955

DR V15 (CLASS 101)
1959

DR V60 (CLASS 105)
1961

CONRAIL NO.2233
1963

BR D9500 (CLASS 14)
1964

PRESTON DOCKS SENTINEL
1968

ELECTRIC TRAINS

Electric trains run on electricity that is provided by an overhead line or an electrified rail. They do not give off smoke and can travel very fast.

ENGLISH ELECTRIC, 0-4-0
1930

READING MULTIPLE UNIT N0.800
1931

DR EO4
1933

PRR (CLASS GG1)
1934

DR (CLASS 243)
1982

BR (CLASS 92)
1993

GATWICK ADTRANZ C-100
1987

EUROTUNNEL LE SHUTTLE
1994

JAVELIN NO.395 017
2009

FASTEST TRAINS

An early record-setting train was *Stephenson's Rocket*, at 46 km/h (29 mph). In the 1960s, Japan opened the world's first high-speed rail line, capable of carrying "bullet trains" that travelled at around 210 km/h (130 mph). Some trains today can travel even faster.

MAGLEV: SHANGHAI METRO, CHINA
UP TO 430 KM/H (267 MPH)

HARMONY CRH 380A: BEIJING TO SHANGHAI, CHINA
UP TO 380 KM/H (236 MPH)

AGV ITALO: NAPLES TO MILAN, ITALY
360 KM/H (224 MPH)

AVE S 103: BARCELONA TO MADRID, SPAIN
350 KM/H (217 MPH)

TALGO 350: MADRID TO LLEIDA, SPAIN
350 KM/H (217 MPH)

MAGNETIC TRAINS

Maglev trains use magnetic levitation to move trains along without having to touch the ground or any form of rail. Magnets allow them to rise and then travel extremely fast above special rails.

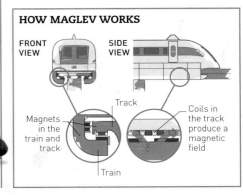

MAGLEV TRAIN

HOW MAGLEV WORKS

FRONT VIEW

SIDE VIEW

Track

Magnets in the train and track

Coils in the track produce a magnetic field

Train

1808
Trevithick runs a steam engine in Bloomsbury, London.

Trevithick's "Puffing Billy"

1829
Stephenson's Rocket becomes the fastest train when it reaches 46 km/h (29 mph).

1869
The transcontinental railway opens, making the USA a dominant economic power. Railways create big business in America, driving the Industrial Revolution.

1914–18
Large armies are moved by train during World War I.

1964
Japan introduces a super-fast "bullet" train.

Japanese bullet train

1800

2000s

1804
Trevithick's Penydarren locomotive is tried in South Wales.

1812
First successful commercial use of steam, in Yorkshire, England.

1863
Underground railway opens in London, UK.

1913
Sweden uses the first diesel-powered main line trains.

1960s
USA phases out steam engines.

2014
Japan's Maglev trains run faster than 480 km/h (300 mph).

1890
First use of electric locomotives on London's underground.

London Underground map

East German Battery shunter
1966

TRAIN HISTORY

Trains have changed significantly over their 200-year history. The first trains were steady and steam-powered. Modern trains are usually electric and can reach very high speeds.

Motorbikes

A popular means of transport for nearly 100 years, motorbikes can move faster than any other road vehicles. There are specialized bikes for almost every purpose, from town riding to fun sports and racing.

FASTEST BIKES

Some specially built motorcycles can travel at more than 560 km/h (350 mph). Such high speeds are not allowed on public roads.

TOP 1 ACK ATTACK – 605.697 KM/H (376.363 MPH)

SUZUKI HAYABUSA – 399 KM/H (248 MPH)

MTT TURBINE SUPERBIKE Y2K – 365.3 KM/H (227 MPH)

SPORT BIKES

These bikes are designed for thrills. They have fast acceleration, powerful brakes, and can take corners at high speed. Some models are used for road riding as well as racing.

HONDA VFR700F
INTERCEPTOR 1987

YAMAHA YZF600R
THUNDERCAT 1998

STUNTS

Motorcycle stunt riding is a sport in which riders perform daring tricks, often making their bikes leave the ground. Lightweight sports bikes are most commonly used.

STOPPIE

ONE-HAND
STOPPIE

STAND-UP
WHEELIE

CLOTHING

Riders need protective clothes that will help save them from injury if they fall off their bikes. The most vital piece of equipment is the helmet.

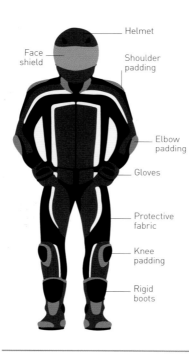

- Helmet
- Face shield
- Shoulder padding
- Elbow padding
- Gloves
- Protective fabric
- Knee padding
- Rigid boots

STANDARD BIKES

These bikes have little or no extra bodywork. They let riders sit upright, allowing them to see well ahead. This improves safety, especially in busy towns. Standard bikes are often the first choice for new riders.

BMW R32 1923

COVENTRY EAGLE
FLYING 8 1925

NORTON INTERNATIONAL 1948

TRIUMPH TROPHY
TR6 1958

ROYAL ENFIELD
INTERCEPTOR 1965

HONDA CB250 K4 1972

DUCATI M900
MONSTER 1994

CRUISERS

Modern cruisers are powerful luxury bikes, at their best on open roads. They are built to look stylish, but many riders find them less comfortable than touring bikes.

Low, wide seat

TOURERS

Comfortable rather than ultra-fast, touring bikes provide an easy ride over long distances. They are also popular for everyday travel.

ROYAL ENFIELD CONSTELLATION
AIRFLOW 1959

IVY THREE 1924

SUNBEAM S7
DE LUXE 1949

HARLEY-DAVIDSON
FLH DUO-GLIDE 1960

SUZUKI T500 1975

SIDECARS

A sidecar is a small, one-wheeled vehicle that attaches to the side of a bike. It usually provides a passenger seat and some luggage space.

ZUNDAPP KS750
WEHRMACHT
SIDECAR 1940

NSU 18PS SPORT 1924

EXCELSIOR JAP SPEEDWAY 1949

WESLAKE HOBBIT DRAGSTER 1978

HONDA RC30
1988

HONDA CBR900RR
FIREBLADE 1992

SUZUKI
GSX-R1100 1994

KAWASAKI ZX7R
1995

KAWASAKI NINJA ZX-12R
2000

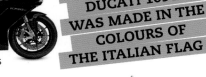

TRIUMPH DAYTONA 675
2006

DUCATI 1098S
2007

A SPECIAL EDITION OF THE DUCATI 1098S WAS MADE IN THE COLOURS OF THE ITALIAN FLAG

HISTORY OF MOTORBIKES

The motorbike had its beginnings in the late 19th century, when inventors discovered how to power bicycles with fuel-driven engines.

Daimler Reitwagen

- **1885** A gas-powered wooden bike is designed and built by German inventors Gottlieb Daimler and Wilhelm Maybach.

- **1894** The Hildebrand & Wolfmüller Motorrad is the first real motorcycle to come off a production line.

Hildebrand & Wolfmüller Motorrad

- **1908** The first-ever motorcycle race is held at Brooklands, Surrey, in England, and won by a 944cc NLG Peugeot bike.

NLG Peugeot

- **1936** The first scooters are made in the USA. The Cushman Auto-Glide is produced in 1938 and later adapted for wartime use.

Auto-Glide Model 1

- **1969** Honda launches the first superbike – the Honda CB750. It is the first standard bike to offer features such as an overhead-camshaft four-cylinder engine and front disc brake.

Honda CB750

- **1977** Raced by builder Brian Chapman, "Mighty Mouse" is the first dragster to cover 400 m (1,312 ft) in less than nine seconds.

Mighty Mouse

RANCIS-BARNETT
CRUISER 1933

HONDA VF500C
MAGNA 1983

HARLEY-DAVIDSON
XLH883 SPORTSTER 1987

Brake disc

HONDA VT 750C2
SHADOW 1998

SUZUKI M1800R
INTRUDER 2007

MOTO GUZZI CALIFORNIA EV 2001

TRIUMPH AMERICA 2012

Triumph Thunderbird 1600

- **2010** The world's biggest parallel-twin engine appears when the Triumph Thunderbird 1600 comes off the production line.

- **2011** The Triumph Rocket III Roadster features the biggest production motorcycle engine ever built.

KIRBY BSA RACING
SIDECAR 1968

WARTIME SPACE SAVER

During World War II, the British Army used a lightweight bike that could be dropped by parachute. Named the Welbike, it weighed just 34 kg (75 lb) and fitted into a small canister.

SCOOTER FOLDED INTO CANISTER

BMW R50
COMBO 1957

WELBIKE SCOOTER 1942

FIGHTER PLANES

Small, fast, and agile, fighter planes are designed for attacking other aircraft. The first fighters appeared during World War I. Today's planes have highly sophisticated tracking and weapons systems.

FOKKER DVII

FOCKE-WULF FW190

MESSERSCHMITT ME262

SOPWITH PUP

SOPWITH F.1 CAMEL

BRISTOL BULLDOG

P-38 LIGHTNING

F-86 SABRE

NIEUPORT 17

FOKKER DR.1

SUPERMARINE SPITFIRE

P-51 MUSTANG

F-4 PHANTOM II

ROYAL AIRCRAFT FACTORY S.E.5A

SOPWITH DOLPHIN

A6M ZERO

YAKOVLEV YAK-9

HAWKER HUNTER

BOMBERS AND STRIKE AIRCRAFT

The role of these aircraft is to strike ground and sea targets. Heavy bombers carry out long-range strategic missions. Low-flying strike aircraft can attack battlefield targets, such as tanks and troops, with great precision.

DE HAVILLAND MOSQUITO

B-52 STRATOFORTRESS

ROYAL AIRCRAFT FACTORY B.E.2C

B-25 MITCHELL

A-4 SKYHAWK

VICKERS VIMY

AVRO LANCASTER

JUNKERS JU 87B

AVRO 698 VULCAN

B-17 FLYING FORTRESS

F-117A NIGHTHAWK

VICKERS WELLINGTON X

B-58A HUSTLER

Aircraft

Aviation has come a long way since the first powered aircraft flight took place in 1903. Today, huge planes can carry hundreds of passengers halfway around the world, while supersonic fighter jets can fly faster than the speed of sound.

HOW PLANES FLY

All aeroplanes have wings and an engine. In order to fly, a plane must engage in a "tug-of-war" between the forces of lift versus weight, and thrust versus drag.

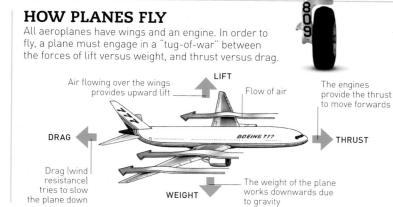

Air flowing over the wings provides upward lift

LIFT

Flow of air

The engines provide the thrust to move forwards

DRAG

THRUST

Drag (wind resistance) tries to slow the plane down

WEIGHT

The weight of the plane works downwards due to gravity

PASSENGER PLANES

The first commercial flight took place in 1914, with just one paying passenger. Today's largest airliner, the Airbus A380, can carry up to 853 passengers.

F-14 TOMCAT

AV-8B HARRIER II

F-35 LIGHTNING II

FOKKER F27 FRIENDSHIP

BOEING 737-800

DOUGLAS DC3

CONCORDE

LOCKHEED L-1049 G SUPER CONSTELLATION

DE HAVILLAND DH106 COMET 4C

AIRBUS A380

PRIVATE AIRCRAFT

A range of light, propeller-driven aircraft are privately flown for both pleasure and transport. Some business travellers use private, often luxurious jets as air taxis.

BOEING STEARMAN MODEL 75

AUSTER J/1 AUTOCRAT

CESSNA F177RG CARDINAL

B-2 SPIRIT

GIPSY MOTH

PITTS S1-S

BOMBARDIER LEARJET 45

A-10 THUNDERBOLT II

HELICOPTERS

The rotating blades of helicopters allow them to take off and land vertically, hover, and fly in all directions. These agile aircraft can land in small spaces and reach isolated locations.

BELL JETRANGER

WESTLAND WS-61 SEA KING

BELL UH-1D IROQUOIS

SIKORSKY UH-60 BLACK HAWK

WESTLAND WESSEX

WESTLAND LYNX

DESIGNED TO BE INVISIBLE TO RADAR, THE NIGHTHAWK WAS THE WORLD'S FIRST "STEALTH" AIRCRAFT

BREAKING THE SOUND BARRIER

Supersonic jets flying faster than the speed of sound create a shock wave called a "sonic boom". To slice through the air at such incredible speed, these planes need a slim body, thin wings, and a sharp nose.

1 SLOWER THAN SOUND Ordinary planes trail behind their own sounds so you can hear them coming.

2 AT THE SPEED OF SOUND As a supersonic plane nears the speed of sound, sound waves bunch together to form a shock wave.

3 FASTER THAN SOUND Shock waves trail behind the plane, creating a loud sonic boom.

HOW HELICOPTERS FLY

The rotor blades on a helicopter are like spinning plane wings. As each blade rotates, air is forced over its curved surface and pushed down. This produces the upward force called "lift".

Tilted blade produces more lift for takeoff

Flatter blade produces less lift while landing

Tilted blade in rear produces more lift

Flatter blade in front produces less lift

TAKEOFF When the lift produced by the tilted blades is greater than the aircraft's weight, the helicopter rises.

LANDING The helicopter descends when the lift produced by the flattened blades is less than the aircraft's weight.

STRAIGHT AHEAD When the rotor is tilted forwards, the resulting thrust propels the helicopter forwards.

The story of flight

From the first balloon and glider flights to the launch of a solar-powered aircraft, people have always been fascinated by the idea of flying. The invention of aircraft that can carry people was one of the 20th century's great triumphs, and helped to shape the modern world.

▶ C.200 BCE

The wings are moved by the pilot's legs and arms

ORNITHOPTER

KONGMING LANTERN
The Chinese-invented sky lantern (a hot-air balloon made from paper) is named the Kongming lantern. It is used for signalling between military troops.

▶ C.1488 CE

LEONARDO DA VINCI
An ornithopter – a wing-flapping aircraft – is designed by Leonardo da Vinci. He also sketches flying machines such as helicopters and parachutes (although he does not build them), and studies airflows and streamlined shapes.

▶ 1783

FIRST MANNED FLIGHT
The first recorded manned flight – lasting about 25 minutes – takes place in a hot-air balloon built by the Montgolfier brothers. The balloon is made of linen lined with paper.

MONTGOLFIER BROTHERS' HOT-AIR BALLOON

◀ 1947

FIRST SUPERSONIC FLIGHT
US Air Force captain Charles "Chuck" Yeager becomes the first pilot to travel faster than the speed of sound in the Bell X-1. This rocket-powered aircraft does not take off from the ground but is launched from the belly of a Boeing B-29 at an altitude of 7000 m (23,000 ft).

◀ 1944

FIRST COMBAT JET
In July the British Gloster Meteor Mk1 becomes the world's first operational jet fighter. It is followed closely by Nazi Germany's Messerschmitt Me262s, which begin attacking American bombers in October the same year.

GLOSTER METEOR F MK8

◀ 1939

FIRST HELICOPTER FLIGHT
Russian-born Igor Sikorsky makes the first flight in his VS-300 helicopter, establishing the single main rotor and smaller tail rotor layout that is now so familiar.

SIKORSKY'S LATER R-4 HELICOPTERS WERE USED IN WORLD WAR II

◀ 1932

AMELIA EARHART
The first woman to fly solo across the Atlantic, Amelia Earhart faces strong winds and mechanical problems on her 15-hour journey from Newfoundland to Ireland. The flight is made in a bright red Lockheed Vega 5B.

AMELIA EARHART

▶ 1952

DE HAVILLAND DH106 COMET 4C

FIRST JETLINER
The de Havilland Comet 1, the world's first ever jetliner, enters service. There are 36 passengers on the maiden flight between London and Johannesburg, South Africa. The journey, including stops, takes 23 hours, 38 minutes, and the return fare costs £315.

▶ 1967

X-15

FASTEST MANNED AIRCRAFT
An experimental rocket-powered aircraft, the X-15, achieves 7273 km/h (4520 mph) – nearly seven times the speed of sound. This remains the record for a manned aircraft.

▶ 1969

FIRST SUPERSONIC AIRLINER
Concorde, the world's first supersonic airliner, makes its maiden flight. The jet will enter service in 1976, with a typical London-to-New-York journey taking just under three and a half hours. However, Concorde's huge operating costs will make the price of tickets very expensive.

CONCORDE

▶ 1976

FASTEST JET AIRCRAFT
The Lockheed SR-71 Blackbird sets the official air speed record for a manned jet aircraft with a speed of 3530 km/h (2193 mph).

SR-71 BLACKBIRD

British airways

1853
FIRST MANNED GLIDER
English engineer Sir George Cayley is the first person to understand the forces acting upon an aircraft wing. In 1853 he transports his coachman across a small valley in what he calls a "governable parachute" – the first man-carrying glider.

AS A RESULT OF HIS RESEARCH, GEORGE CAYLEY IS OFTEN CALLED THE "FATHER OF FLIGHT"

▶ 1896
OTTO LILIENTHAL
After making over 2,000 glides in weight-shift controlled gliders, German pioneer Otto Lilienthal dies in hospital after his glider stalls and he crashes from a height of 15 m (50 ft). His scientific data on flight would inspire many others.

OTTO LILIENTHAL'S HANG-GLIDER

▶ 1900

1928 ZEPPELIN

FIRST AIRSHIP
LZ1, the first rigid airship (designed by Ferdinand, Graf von Zeppelin), makes its initial flight from a floating hangar on Lake Constance near Friedrichshafen, Germany. Carrying five people, it stays airborne for 17 minutes.

▶ 1903
FIRST POWERED FLIGHT
The first controlled, powered aeroplane flight is achieved by American inventors the Wright brothers. It lasts just 12 seconds and covers 36.5 m (120 ft).

WRIGHT FLYER

▶ 1909
FIRST CHANNEL CROSSING
Flying his Type XI monoplane, Frenchman Louis Blériot crosses the English Channel for the first time in a heavier-than-air aircraft. He crash-lands in a field above the cliffs of Dover on the English coast.

1930
AMY JOHNSON
The first woman to fly solo from England to Australia makes the journey in a Gipsy Moth named "Jason". With only experience of flying from London to Hull in England, Amy Johnson makes her epic 18,000 km (11,000 miles) trip in a small, low-powered biplane more suited to club flying.

GIPSY MOTH

◀ 1927
FIRST TRANSATLANTIC SOLO FLIGHT
American pilot Charles Lindbergh takes 33.5 hours to complete the first solo, nonstop, transatlantic flight, travelling from New York to Paris. Flying in a single-engine aircraft, he encounters fog and icy conditions, though his biggest challenge is staying awake for the entire journey.

◀ 1919
FIRST TRANSATLANTIC FLIGHTS
In May an NC-4 commanded by Albert C Read crosses the Atlantic in several stages from Long Island, USA, to Portugal. In June John Alcock and Arthur Brown fly nonstop from Newfoundland to Ireland.

CURTISS NC-4

◀ 1917

EUGENE JACQUES BULLARD

FIRST BLACK COMBAT PILOT
Georgia-born Eugene Jacques Bullard – who was denied entry into the US Army Air Corps because of his race – serves throughout World War I in the French Flying Corps. He is awarded the Legion of Honour.

◀ 1910
FIRST TAKEOFF FROM A SHIP
In November American flight pioneer Eugene Burton Ely successfully takes off from the deck of a ship. Two months later, he makes the first successful landing aboard a ship.

FOR PROTECTION, ELY WORE A PADDED AMERICAN FOOTBALL HELMET AND A LIFE JACKET MADE FROM PARTS OF BICYCLE TYRES

▶ 1988

HEAVIEST AIRCRAFT
Designed to transport the Soviet Union's 250-tonne Buran space shuttle, the six-engined Antonov An-225 takes the record for the world's biggest and heaviest aircraft. It also has the largest wingspan of any aircraft in operational service.

THE AN-225 HOLDS THE RECORD FOR AIRLIFTING THE HEAVIEST CARGO

ANTONOV AN-225

▶ 1991

F-117 NIGHTHAWK

FIRST STEALTH FIGHTER
The American Lockheed F-117 Nighthawk sees its first active service during Operation Just Cause in Panama.

▶ 2005

AIRBUS A380

LARGEST MASS-PRODUCED AIRCRAFT
The double-deck, four-engine Airbus A380 is launched. This airliner can transport 853 passengers and can carry enough fuel to fly nonstop from Sydney, Australia, to Dallas, USA, – a distance of 13,804 km (8,577 miles).

▶ 2015
SOLAR IMPULSE 2 SETS OFF
Using only energy from the Sun, Solar Impulse 2 leaves on an epic round-the-world flight. Its wingspan is larger than a Boeing 747's, though the aircraft weighs no more than a small van.

Bicycles

Millions of people around the world use bicycles as an efficient means of transport. Cheap to buy, they are easy to run and produce no pollution. Cyclists can select special types of bikes for different terrains or tracks.

HOW A BIKE WORKS

A bike converts 90 per cent of energy from pedalling into forward motion. Changing gear – moving the chain from one cog to the other – makes pedalling more energy-efficient.

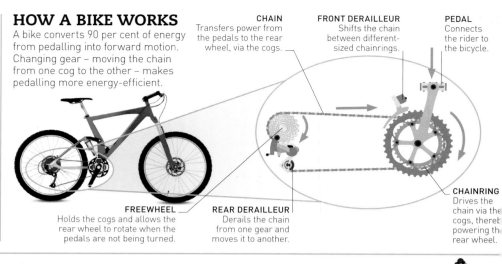

CHAIN Transfers power from the pedals to the rear wheel, via the cogs.

FRONT DERAILLEUR Shifts the chain between different-sized chainrings.

PEDAL Connects the rider to the bicycle.

FREEWHEEL Holds the cogs and allows the rear wheel to rotate when the pedals are not being turned.

REAR DERAILLEUR Derails the chain from one gear and moves it to another.

CHAINRING Drives the chain via the cogs, thereby powering the rear wheel.

OFF-ROADERS

These hardy bikes are built to withstand tough, off-road conditions. They have a strong frame, knobbly tyres for extra grip on rough ground, and are usually equipped with a good range of gears.

FAT CHANCE

TREK 6000

TREK 8900 PRO

DMR TRAILSTAR

MARIN PALISADES TRAIL

STUMPJUMPER FSR PRO

ROCKY MOUNTAIN VERTEX TEAM

KONA STAB PRIMO

Saddle

Stem

Handlebars

Seat post

Top tube

Gear cable

Suspension fork

Seat post quick release

Cassette

Down tube

Pedal

Chainring

Rear derailleur

MARIN MOUNT VISION

SPECIALIST BIKES

Like any great invention, the bicycle has been adapted over the years. Recumbent bikes enable the cyclist to lean back in a more efficient and comfortable riding position. Tandem cycling is a good way for people of different abilities to ride together.

Pedals assisted by an electric motor

SINCLAIR C5

WINDCHEETAH SL MARK VI

VELOCA

KINGCYCLE BEAN

KINGCYCLE

DAWES GALAXY TWIN

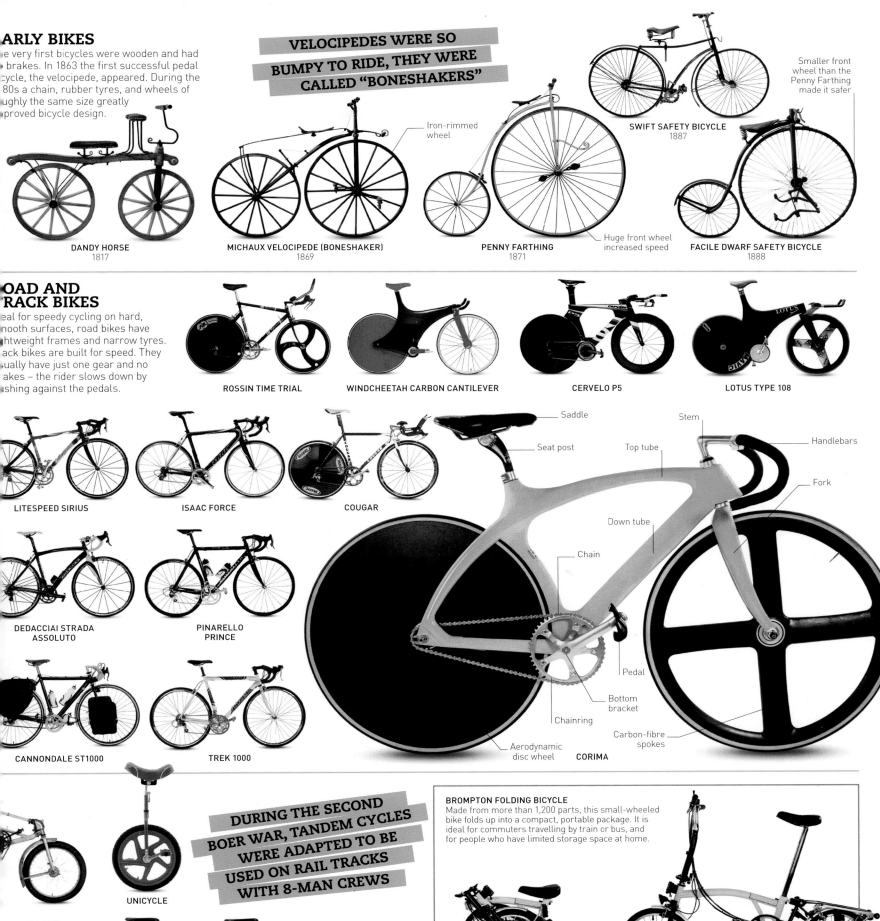

~ARLY BIKES

~e very first bicycles were wooden and had ~ brakes. In 1863 the first successful pedal ~cycle, the velocipede, appeared. During the ~80s a chain, rubber tyres, and wheels of ~ughly the same size greatly ~proved bicycle design.

VELOCIPEDES WERE SO BUMPY TO RIDE, THEY WERE CALLED "BONESHAKERS"

Smaller front wheel than the Penny Farthing made it safer

Iron-rimmed wheel

SWIFT SAFETY BICYCLE
1887

DANDY HORSE
1817

MICHAUX VELOCIPEDE (BONESHAKER)
1869

PENNY FARTHING
1871

Huge front wheel increased speed

FACILE DWARF SAFETY BICYCLE
1888

~OAD AND ~RACK BIKES

~eal for speedy cycling on hard, ~nooth surfaces, road bikes have ~htweight frames and narrow tyres. ~ack bikes are built for speed. They ~ually have just one gear and no ~akes – the rider slows down by ~shing against the pedals.

ROSSIN TIME TRIAL

WINDCHEETAH CARBON CANTILEVER

CERVELO P5

LOTUS TYPE 108

LITESPEED SIRIUS

ISAAC FORCE

COUGAR

Saddle

Seat post

Top tube

Stem

Handlebars

Fork

Down tube

Chain

DEDACCIAI STRADA ASSOLUTO

PINARELLO PRINCE

Pedal

Bottom bracket

Chainring

Carbon-fibre spokes

Aerodynamic disc wheel

CORIMA

CANNONDALE ST1000

TREK 1000

UNICYCLE

DURING THE SECOND BOER WAR, TANDEM CYCLES WERE ADAPTED TO BE USED ON RAIL TRACKS WITH 8-MAN CREWS

Drop handlebars

SANTANA TRIPLET

BROMPTON FOLDING BICYCLE
Made from more than 1,200 parts, this small-wheeled bike folds up into a compact, portable package. It is ideal for commuters travelling by train or bus, and for people who have limited storage space at home.

1 FOLDED
The bike can be folded in less than 20 seconds, and is carried by grasping the saddle or frame.

2 UNFOLDED
All models have a full-sized frame, made mainly from steel. The Brompton provides an upright riding position, and is designed to be light, agile, and speedy.

Nature

Rhinos and tapirs

Even-toed hoofed animals

Carnivores
(Meat-eaters)

Clams and oysters

SEA SPONGES ARE THE SIMPLEST ANIMALS, WITH NO BRAIN, NO DIGESTIVE ORGANS, AND NO NERVOUS SYSTEM

Centipedes

Crustaceans
(Crabs and lobsters)

Mushrooms

Whales

Squid and octopus

MOLLUSCS
(Animals with a soft unsegmented body and sometimes a shell)

Snails

ARTHROPODS
(Animals with an outer skeleton)

Spiders and scorpions

Insects

Lichens
(Organisms composed of a fungus and...)

Bats

Earthworms

Rodents

Rabbits and relatives

SPONGES

Hedgehogs

Dugongs and manatees

Echinoderms
(For example starfish and sea urchins)

Primates
(Apes – including humans – monkeys, and others)

INVERTEBRATES
(Animals without a backbone)

ANIMALS

Elephants

Sharks and rays

FISH

VERTEBRATES
(Animals with a backbone)

Frogs and toads

Armadillos and anteaters

Ray-finned fish
(For example perch)

AMPHIBIANS

Newts and salamanders

Marsupials
(Includes mammals with pouches)

REPTILES

Crocodiles

Egg-laying mammals

MAMMALS

Turtles

Lizards

Snakes

Tree of life

The first living things that appeared on Earth, billions of years ago, were tiny organisms made of just one cell. This "tree" shows how such simple beginnings led to the development of the wonderful variety of life we know today.

BRANCHING OUT

For well over two centuries, scientists have been using diagrams similar to this one to explain how life evolved. By following the "branches", we can trace the relationships of the main groups of animals, plants, and fungi to the earliest types of life. Only living species are shown here. Extinct animals, such as dinosaurs, are not included.

HOW MANY SPECIES

There are far more species of animals than there are of plants, fungi, and protists added together. No one could possibly count up all the bacteria and archaea because there are simply too many millions of them.

ESTIMATED NUMBER OF SPECIES

- PLANTS 300,000
- PROTISTS 64,000
- FUNGI 611,000
- ANIMALS 7,770,000

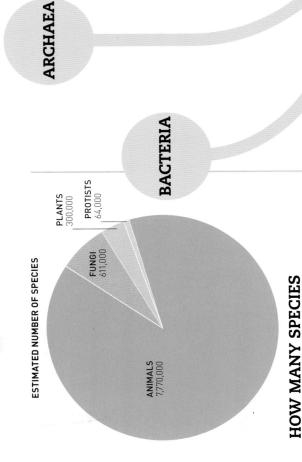

FLOWERING PLANTS

Gingko trees

Conifers

Ferns

Yeasts

Mosses

Birds

FUNGI

PLANTS

PROTISTS (Single-celled organisms and algae)

ARCHAEA

BACTERIA

BEGINNING OF LIFE: SINGLE-CELLED ORGANISMS

THE SIX KINGDOMS

The tree of life is divided into six main branches, which scientists call kingdoms. Three kingdoms are mainly made up of tiny single-celled organisms. The others are fungi, plants, and animals.

ARCHAEA
Early life, made of one cell. Can live in extreme habitats, such as those that are very hot or salty.

PROTISTS
Single cells with a nucleus. Some make their own food, others must feed on other organisms.

BACTERIA
Cells similar to archaea but not suited to their extreme habitats. Many are vital to life, others cause diseases.

FUNGI
Some are single-celled, but the best known are mushrooms. They break down organic matter.

PLANTS
From tiny mosses to big trees, all plants use sunlight to make food and release oxygen into the air.

ANIMALS
These eat other organisms. Most use their senses for finding food. Some have backbones.

CLASSIFICATION OF LIFE

Starting with the kingdoms, all living things are arranged, or classified, into further groups according to how they are related. This works in stages: the group called a phylum is divided into classes, classes are split into orders, and so on. Shown below is how a tiger (scientific name *Panthera tigris*) is classified.

KINGDOM	PHYLUM	CLASS	ORDER	FAMILY	GENUS	SPECIES

1 ANIMALS
Multi-celled living things that feed on other organisms. Most are able to move around.

2 CHORDATES
Animals with a rod-like structure in their bodies. Includes vertebrates, which have a backbone.

3 MAMMALS
Warm-blooded vertebrates with hair whose females feed their young on milk.

4 CARNIVORES
Mostly mammals that hunt other animals for food and have special teeth for cutting through meat.

5 CATS
Agile, specialized hunters. Many have sheathed toes into which their claws can disappear.

6 BIG CATS (PANTHERA)
The largest and most powerful members of the cat family, including lions, tigers, and leopards.

7 TIGER (TIGRIS)
The largest and heaviest of the forest-dwelling big cats, with distinctively striped fur.

How life began

The very first life forms appeared on Earth around 3.5 billion years ago. Fossils preserved in rock help us chart the story of life from the first single-celled bacteria to the modern humans who roam Earth today.

DIVISION OF TIME

Earth's geological history can be divided into blocks of time. An era represents several hundred million years and is split into smaller periods. Earth is currently in the Quaternary Period of the Cenozoic Era.

	PRE-CAMBRIAN 4.6 BYA–541 MYA
	PALAEOZOIC ERA 541–252 MYA
	MESOZOIC ERA 252–65 MYA
	CENOZOIC ERA 65 MYA–PRESENT DAY

BYA = Billion years ago
MYA = Million years ago

▶ 4.6 BYA–541 MYA

PRE-CAMBRIAN

This represents 80 per cent of total geological time. Volcanic activity on the new Earth produced water. Simple lifeforms appeared, and some produced oxygen.

VOLCANIC EARTH

541–485 MYA

CAMBRIAN

Many types of marine life evolved in the so-called "Cambrian explosion". They included molluscs, sponges, and animals with jointed legs (arthropods).

TRILOBIT

ECHMATOCRINUS

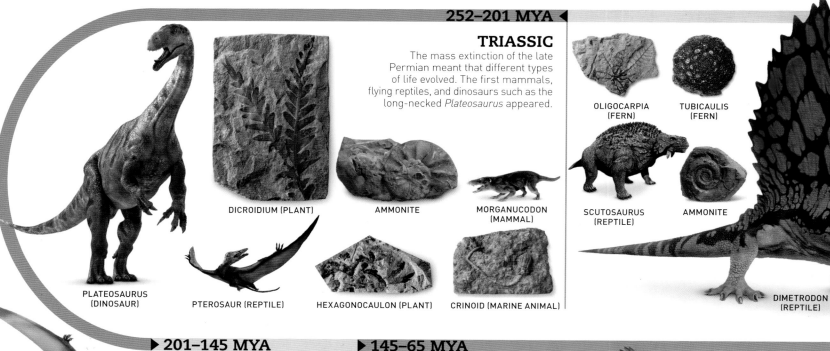

252–201 MYA ◀

TRIASSIC

The mass extinction of the late Permian meant that different types of life evolved. The first mammals, flying reptiles, and dinosaurs such as the long-necked *Plateosaurus* appeared.

PLATEOSAURUS (DINOSAUR)

DICROIDIUM (PLANT)

AMMONITE

MORGANUCODON (MAMMAL)

PTEROSAUR (REPTILE)

HEXAGONOCAULON (PLANT)

CRINOID (MARINE ANIMAL)

OLIGOCARPIA (FERN)

TUBICAULIS (FERN)

SCUTOSAURUS (REPTILE)

AMMONITE

DIMETRODON (REPTILE)

▶ 201–145 MYA

JURASSIC

Reptiles began to dominate the land and sea, and some took to the air. Many different dinosaurs roamed Earth, from giant plant-eaters to fierce predators.

PTERODACTYL (REPTILE)

EOCAECILIA (AMPHIBIAN)

DAKOSAURUS (REPTILE)

WILLIAMSONIA (PLANT)

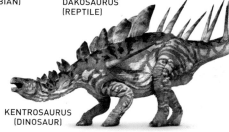

KENTROSAURUS (DINOSAUR)

▶ 145–65 MYA

CRETACEOUS

The climate was mostly warm, but cooled towards the end of the period. Flowering plants spread. The period ended with the mass extinction of the big dinosaurs.

EOMAIA (MAMMAL)

VEGAVIS (BIRD)

CONFUCIUSORNIS (BIRD)

ARCHAEANTHUS (PLANT)

ARCHELON (TURTLE)

HOPLOPTERYX (FISH)

PROTOSTEGA (TURTLE)

SCAPHITES (AMMONITE)

CARCHARODONTOSAURUS (DINOSAUR)

485–443 MYA
ORDOVICIAN
The first fish appeared, such as the scaly, jawless *Astraspis*. Molluscs and corals dominated the oceans. The period ended with mass extinctions.

SPONGE

MARRELLA

HALLUCIGENIA

TRILOBITE

BRACHIOPOD (SHELL)

FALSE MUSSEL

SEA MAT

ASTRASPIS (FISH)

443–419 MYA
SILURIAN
Plants, such as the leafless *Cooksonia*, grew on land. In the seas, there were more fish, and spiny animals called echinoderms thrived. Early scorpions may have left the oceans for land.

COOKSONIA (PLANT)

ECHINODERM

CORAL

LOGANELLIA (FISH)

419–358 MYA
DEVONIAN
Many new types of fish evolved, such as the *Tiktaalik*. This was a lobe-finned fish belonging to the group from which the amphibians eventually evolved.

TIKTAALIK (FISH)

SOLICLYMENIA (AMMONITE)

DISCALIS (PLANT)

STENACANTHUS (SHARK)

298–252 MYA ◄
PERMIAN
The hot, dry conditions of this period favoured reptiles, such as *Dimetrodon*. At the end of this period a catastrophic mass extinction wiped out 70 per cent of land species and 90 per cent of marine life.

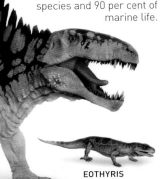

ECHINODERM

CORAL

EOTHYRIS (REPTILE)

358–298 MYA ◄
CARBONIFEROUS
As lush swamp forests grew, life on Earth flourished. Reptiles such as *Spinoaequalis* and *Ophiacodon* evolved.

SPINOAEQUALIS (REPTILE)

ODONTOPTERIS (FERN)

OPHIACODON (REPTILE)

CLUB MOSS

AMPHIBAMUS (AMPHIBIAN)

COCKROACH

► 65–23 MYA
PALEOGENE
With the dinosaurs extinct, mammals and birds evolved rapidly. Most of the main groups of mammals had their beginnings in this period.

AMMONITE

CHAMA AND XENOPHORA (MOLLUSCS)

OSMUNDA (FERN)

ROTULARIA (WORMS)

ICARONYCTERIS (BAT)

UINTATHERIUM (MAMMAL)

► 23–2 MYA
NEOGENE
The first humans, or hominins, evolved in this era. More modern types of mammals, such as kangaroos and giraffes, appeared.

THYLACOSMILUS (MAMMAL)

CARCHARODON (SHARK)

► 2 MYA–PRESENT DAY
QUATERNARY
Ice ages with warmer phases in between have dominated the last two million years. Modern humans (*Homo sapiens*) arose in eastern Africa and spread across the world.

NEPTUNEA (SEA SNAIL)

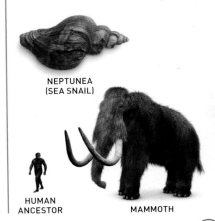
HUMAN ANCESTOR

MAMMOTH

Fossils

Fossils are clues preserved in rocks, amber (tree resin), tar, or ice. They show us what plants and animals looked like thousands or millions of years ago and can sometimes tell us where and how they lived.

HOW FOSSILS FORM

Fossils form when a plant or animal is buried quickly and deeply after it dies. The sediment that surrounds the animal gradually turns its body into rock over thousands of years. This is called fossilization.

1 AFTER DEATH
The body of an ancient land animal falls into a lake or is buried by soil and begins to decompose.

2 BARE BONES
The bones and other hard parts of the body become covered by sediment, such as mud or sand.

3 BONE TO MINERAL
Minerals from the sediment replace the minerals in the animal's bones.

4 TIME PASSES
The minerals crystallize and the sediment around them solidifies into rock, forming foss

PLANTS

Fossil plants are usually fossils of parts of the plant, rather than the whole thing. They include leaves, flowers, cones, bark, and wood.

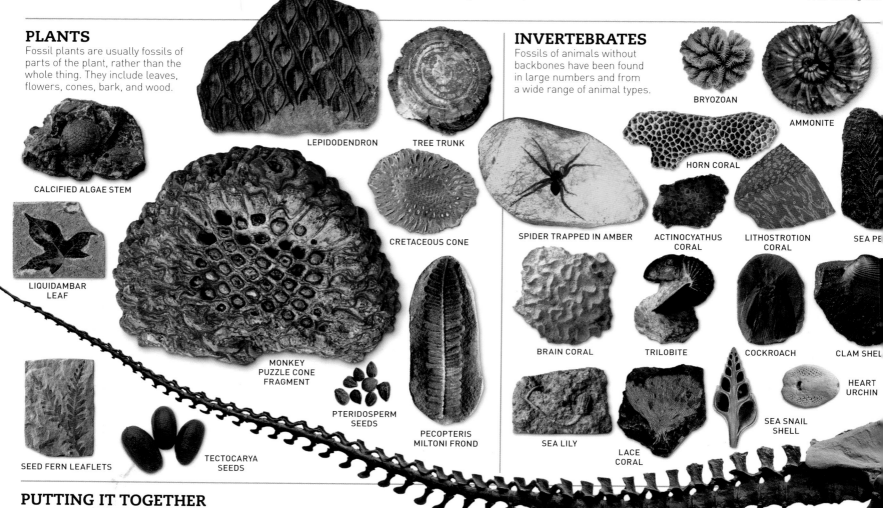

LEPIDODENDRON

TREE TRUNK

CALCIFIED ALGAE STEM

CRETACEOUS CONE

LIQUIDAMBAR LEAF

MONKEY PUZZLE CONE FRAGMENT

PTERIDOSPERM SEEDS

PECOPTERIS MILTONI FROND

SEED FERN LEAFLETS

TECTOCARYA SEEDS

INVERTEBRATES

Fossils of animals without backbones have been found in large numbers and from a wide range of animal types.

BRYOZOAN

AMMONITE

HORN CORAL

SPIDER TRAPPED IN AMBER

ACTINOCYATHUS CORAL

LITHOSTROTION CORAL

SEA PE

BRAIN CORAL

TRILOBITE

COCKROACH

CLAM SHEL

SEA LILY

LACE CORAL

SEA SNAIL SHELL

HEART URCHIN

PUTTING IT TOGETHER

Dinosaur bones can be found scattered over a large area and scientists then work out how they are pieced together. Dinosaur skeletons are very like bird and reptile skeletons, which helps to work out which bone goes where.

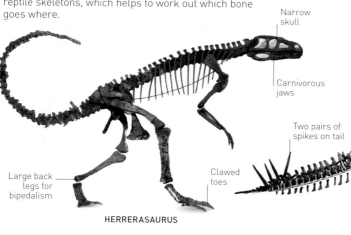

Narrow skull

Carnivorous jaws

Triangular back plates

Ischium (part of the pelvis)

Neck plates with rounded tops

Tibia

Two pairs of spikes on tail

Horny beak

Ribcage

Large back legs for bipedalism

Clawed toes

Pedal phalanges (toe bones)

HERRERASAURUS

TUOJIANGOSAURUS

5 SURFACE EROSION Fossilized remains of creatures begin to be revealed as the land is eroded slowly over thousands of years.

6 EXCAVATION Fossils are excavated by being carefully freed from the rock that has long surrounded them.

FOSSIL SITES
Some parts of the world are especially rich in fossils. This map shows some areas where lots of fossils have been discovered.

KEY
- Green river, USA
- Joggins, Canada
- Santana, Brazil
- Jurassic coast, UK
- Karoo, South Africa
- Gobi desert, Mongolia
- Gogo formation, Australia
- Kolyma river, Russia

FOSSIL TYPES
Fossils may be formed from the remains of plants or animals, or from traces of their activities during life.

○ TRACE FOSSIL
These are fossils showing animal activity, such as footprints, burrows, or nests.

○ IMPRESSIONS
These are fossils where the animal or plant body has decayed completely but left an impression in the sediment.

○ PETRIFICATION
This type of fossil is formed when minerals crystallize inside the body cells, preserving them in stone.

○ NATURAL CAST
In cast fossils, sediment hardens in natural gaps inside an animal, such as the inside of a shell.

VERTEBRATES
Fossils of vertebrate animals are some of the most exciting fossils ever found. They reveal species – such as dinosaurs and flying reptiles – that existed millions of years ago.

PARADOXIDES

CONSTELLARIA

AMMONITE

REMAINS OF HOMOEOSAURAS

BONY RAY-FINNED FISH

DINOSAUR VERTEBRA

DINOSAUR VERTEBRA

PLIOSAUR SKULL

MAMMAL-LIKE REPTILE SKULL

SHARK TOOTH

JAW OF THECODONTOSAURUS

FOOT SKELETON OF PLATEOSAURUS

UPPER CHEEK TOOTH OF A MAMMOTH

GALLIMIMUS SKULL

PRIMITIVE FROG

PANTHERA LOWER JAW

OVIRAPTOR PHILOCERATOPS EGG

THUMB CLAW OF BARYONYX THEROPOD

Cervical vertebrae

Manual phalanges (finger bones)

Mandible (jaw bone)

Ribcage

TYRANNOSAURUS REX

Very long tail

Long, powerful legs

Long, thin hand claws

STRUTHIOMIMUS

DINOSAUR FOSSILS HAVE BEEN DISCOVERED ON EVERY CONTINENT, INCLUDING ANTARCTICA

Ilium

Femur

Scapula

Large, bony frill

Tail vertebrae

Ribcage

Ulna, radius

TRICERATOPS

Plant-eating dinosaurs

Plant-eating dinosaurs roamed Earth for more than 140 million years. There were many different kinds, and they included some of the largest land creatures the world has ever seen.

HERBIVORE ANATOMY

Many herbivorous (plant-eating) dinosaurs were quadrupeds – they walked on all fours. The largest herbivores had powerful muscles and strong bones to support their weight. Their digestive systems were adapted for eating plants, which are more difficult to digest than meat.

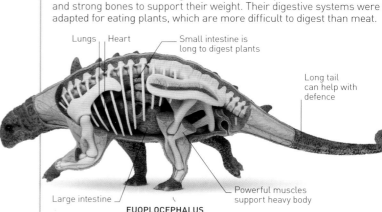

Lungs Heart — Small intestine is long to digest plants

Long tail can help with defence

Large intestine

Powerful muscles support heavy body

EUOPLOCEPHALUS

SAUROPODS AND PROSAUROPODS

Palaeontologists – people who study fossils – divide dinosaurs into various types. Sauropods, such as *Diplodocus*, had long necks and tails and tiny heads, with small brains. Their ancestors, prosauropods, were often able to walk on two legs and included *Plateosaurus*.

ANCHISAURUS

VULCANODON

LUFENGOSAURUS

GIRAFFATITAN

About 15 elongated vertebrae support the long neck

EFRAASIA

CAMARASAURUS

APATOSAURUS

MAMENCHISAURUS

ISANOSAURUS

SALTASAURUS

ARGENTINOSAURUS

DIPLODOCUS

SHUNOSAURUS

STEGOSAURS

Large and slow-moving, stegosaurs had spiky tails and strange bony plates running along their backs. These were embedded into the dinosaur's skin, not the bone. Stegosaurs appeared during the Jurassic period (201–145 million years ago).

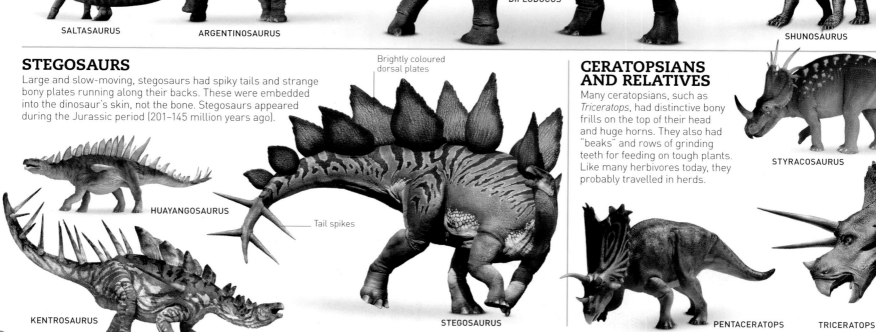

Brightly coloured dorsal plates

HUAYANGOSAURUS

Tail spikes

KENTROSAURUS

STEGOSAURUS

CERATOPSIANS AND RELATIVES

Many ceratopsians, such as *Triceratops*, had distinctive bony frills on the top of their head and huge horns. They also had "beaks" and rows of grinding teeth for feeding on tough plants. Like many herbivores today, they probably travelled in herds.

STYRACOSAURUS

PENTACERATOPS

TRICERATOPS

ELF-DEFENCE

en the largest plant-eating dinosaurs risked being hunted and
led by meat-eating dinosaurs. Over time herbivores developed
ecialized body defences for survival. These included horns, spikes,
ines, and heavy tails that could inflict terrible injuries.

BONY PLATES
Covering the head of *Euplocephalus*, these bony plates provided protection against the jaws and teeth of meat-eating dinosaurs.

SPINY SKULL
A thick skull topped with spines protected a *Sauropelta's* vulnerable brain.

SHARP HORNS
Huge plant-eater *Triceratops* had extremely long, sharp horns, which it used to fight off predators, such as the giant meat-eating *Tyrannosaurus*.

TAIL CLUB
Some plant-eaters, particularly ankylosaurs, had heavy, club-like tails made of fused bone that could break a predator's leg.

SPIKY TAIL
The *Stegosaurus* had very sharp spikes on the end of its tail that could inflict terrible injuries on an opponent.

WHIP-LIKE TAIL
It is suggested that the mighty *Diplodocus* used its long tail like a whip to defend itself against attackers.

THE HORNS OF TRICERATOPS WERE AN AMAZING 1 M (3 FT) IN LENGTH

HEAVYWEIGHTS

Like humans, elephants, and other animals, dinosaurs were vertebrates: they had an internal skeleton with a backbone to support their bodies. Many, though, were much heavier. At 70 tonnes, *Argentinosaurus* was 15 times heavier than an elephant.

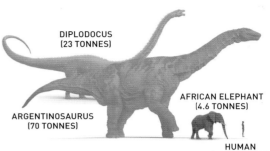

DIPLODOCUS (23 TONNES)

ARGENTINOSAURUS (70 TONNES)

AFRICAN ELEPHANT (4.6 TONNES)

HUMAN (80 KG/176 LB)

ORNITHOPODS

Ornithopods, including *Iguanodon*, lived 145–66 million years ago. They could stand on two legs to reach into trees and could chew plants very efficiently. *Corythosaurus*, for instance, had hundreds of teeth for grinding plants.

TITANOSAURUS

BARAPASAURUS

PLATEOSAURUS

DICRAEOSAURUS

LESOTHOSAURUS

LEAELLYNASAURA

HETERODONTOSAURUS

DRYOSAURUS

HYPSILOPHODON   MUTTABURRASAURUS

CORYTHOSAURUS

PARASAUROLOPHUS

IGUANODON

EDMONTOSAURUS

TENONTOSAURUS

MAIASAURA

ANKYLOSAURS AND RELATIVES

Looking rather like prehistoric armoured tanks or armadillos, ankylosaurs had bony plates over their head and shoulders to protect them from predators. They had short, thick legs to support their heavy bodies.

PSITTACOSAURUS

PROTOCERATOPS

GARGOYLEOSAURUS

GASTONIA

MINMI

EUOPLOCEPHALUS

SAUROPELTA

ANKYLOSAURUS

EDMONTONIA

Meat-eating dinosaurs

Dinosaurs appeared on Earth about 245 million years ago. They spread to every continent and dominated Earth for millions of years before dying out. Many were powerful meat-eating predators, with bodies built for attack.

CARNIVORE ANATOMY

Meat-eaters evolved into highly efficient predators, able to hunt and digest their prey. Large dinosaurs could tackle large herbivorous dinosaurs, such as *Triceratops*. Smaller dinosaurs hunted smaller prey, or hunted together in groups.

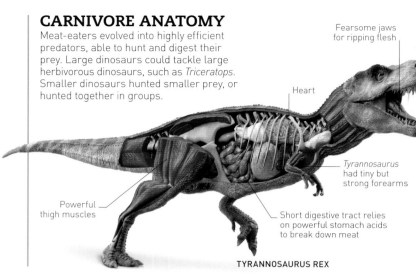

Fearsome jaws for ripping flesh

Heart

Tyrannosaurus had tiny but strong forearms

Powerful thigh muscles

Short digestive tract relies on powerful stomach acids to break down meat

TYRANNOSAURUS REX

THEROPODS

Carnivorous (meat-eating) dinosaurs belong to a group known as theropods. Meaning "beast-footed", theropods stood on their hind legs. They ranged from huge carnivores such as *Allosaurus* to the smaller feathery *Citipati* and *Alxasaurus*.

EORAPTOR

CERATOSAURUS

BARYONYX

SINOSAUROPTERYX

THERIZONOSAURUS

GALLIMIMUS

VELOCIRAPTOR

CAUDIPTERYX

COELOPHYSIS

ALXASAURUS

DEINONYCHUS

SPINOSAURUS

SUCHOMIMUS

CITIPATI

STRUTHIOMIMUS

MONOLOPHOSAURUS

GASOSAURUS

AUCASAURUS

LILIENSTERNUS

CRYOLOPHOSAURUS

IRRITATOR

DIET

[Th]eropods were [th]e most powerful [p]redators on land. [Th]ey fed on insects, [fi]sh, other dinosaurs, [s]mall mammals, and [bi]rd-like creatures.

INSECTS
Insects evolved more than 350 million years ago.

FISH
Oceans and rivers teemed with fish.

DINOSAURS
Plant-eating dinosaurs provided food.

EARLY MAMMALS
Rodent-like mammals existed with dinosaurs.

EARLY BIRDS
Birds evolved from earlier theropod dinosaurs.

TEETH

Scientists can learn about dinosaurs from their fossilized skulls and teeth, which are often the only remaining parts. Carnivorous dinosaurs had lethal claws and sharp teeth.

SHARP POINTS
Baryonyx and other fish-eating theropods had pointed needle-like teeth that pierced fish skin.

KNIFE-LIKE
Theropods such as *Allosaurus* had sharp teeth that they used to slice meat from the bone.

CRUSHING BONES
The large teeth of *Tyrannosaurus rex* crushed straight through bone.

PACK HUNTING

A pack of *Deinonychus* attacks a large plant-eating *Tenontosaurus*. Evidence from fossilized dinosaur footprints suggests that some dinosaurs hunted in packs. Probably they did not herd prey but worked together to bring down larger dinosaurs.

DUBREUILLOSAURUS

CARCHARODONTOSAURUS

ALBERTOSAURUS

Stiff, pointed tail counterbalances huge head and allows dinosaur to turn quickly

ALLOSAURUS

Powerful legs with four clawed toes, only three of which are weight-bearing

TYRANNOSAURUS REX

DEEP BITES FROM TYRANNOSAURUS HAVE BEEN FOUND IN FOSSILIZED TRICERATOPS BONES

Prehistoric animals

The first signs of life appeared more than 3.5 billion years ago when tiny single-celled organisms evolved in the oceans. Over millions of years, other organisms evolved, moved on to land, and even took to the air.

TYPES OF PREHISTORIC ANIMALS

We use the term "prehistoric" for creatures that existed before recorded history. They were very diverse. The dinosaurs are probably the best known and most familiar, but there were also fish, invertebrates (animals without backbones), reptiles, amphibians, and mammals.

INVERTEBRATES
This squid-like belemnite lived in the prehistoric oceans some 200 million years ago.

SCIENTISTS THINK THAT EITHER AN ASTEROID STRIKE OR ERUPTING VOLCANOES CAUSED A MASS EXTINCTION OF PREHISTORIC ANIMALS

IN THE AIR

Many prehistoric creatures took to the air. They included pterosaurs, such as *Dimorphodon* and *Eudimorphodon*, which were flying reptiles. As time passed, birds and flying mammals also appeared.

ANUROGNATHUS

RHAMPHORYNCHUS

PETEINOSAURUS

DIMORPHODON

EUDIMORPHODON

PTERODAUSTRO

ORNITHOCHEIRUS

IBEROMESORNIS

ICARONYCTERIS

ARGENTAVIS

TERATORNIS

ON LAND

Plant life developed on land about 472 million years ago. Creatures crawled out of the seas to become amphibians, reptiles, and dinosaurs.

OPHIACODON

ROBERTIA

DIMETRODON

LYSTROSAURUS

EUPARKERIA

DINOSAUR (HERRERASAURUS)

SIMOSUCHUS

STAGONOLEPIS

ORNITHOSUCHUS

PLACERIA

IN THE WATER

Prehistoric seas were full of life. Early organisms such as *Wiwaxia*, *Opabinia*, and *Anomalocaris* seem very strange to us. However, later fossil fish such as *Megalodon* and *Hybodus* look a lot like the fish and sharks around today.

SHONISAURUS

LIOPLEURODON

ICHTHYOSAURU

WIWAXIA

OPABINIAI

ANOMALOCARIS

GONIATITES

ENCRINUS

TEMNODONTOSAURUS

DITOMOPYGE

HAIKOUICHTHYS

ASTRASPIS

PLACODUS

MIXOSAURUS

LARIOSAURUS

NOTHOSAURUS

GEOSAURUS

FISH
The very first vertebrates (animals with backbones) to evolve were fish.

AMPHIBIANS
Like frogs today, prehistoric amphibians could breathe air but bred in fresh water.

REPTILES
The earliest reptiles evolved from amphibians about 315 million years ago. They had scaly skin.

MAMMALS
The first mammals appeared on Earth about 220 million years ago.

TRANSITION TO MODERN ANIMALS
About 65 million years ago a huge catastrophe wiped out many prehistoric creatures. Birds and some animals survived. Later, new animals emerged, including the ancestors of the mammals we know today.

MOERITHERIUM
This pig-sized relative of the elephant family lived in African swamps and woodlands more than 35 million years ago.

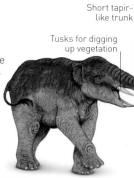

Tusks for digging up vegetation
Short tapir-like trunk

PHIOMIA
Appeared around 35 million years ago. Like modern elephants, it had air-filled spaces in its skull to reduce its weight.

DEINOTHERIUM
Standing 4.5 m (14.8 ft) high, *Deinotherium* roamed Africa, Asia, and Europe around 24 million years ago.

Unlike modern elephants, curved tusks point downwards

ELEPHANT
The modern elephant, the largest living land animal, has features in common with its prehistoric ancestors, including its trunk.

PROTOSUCHUS

PHENOSUCHUS

PLIOHIPPUS

NEMEGTBAATAR

UINTATHERIUM

DIRE WOLF

SMILODON

WOOLLY MAMMOTH

GLYPTODON

WOOLLY RHINOCEROS

PLIOPLATECARPUS

HYBODUS

LEEDSICHTHYS

ISCHYODUS

MOSASAURUS

KRONOSAURUS

ELASMOSAURUS

MEGALODON

Plants

There are around 400,000 species of plants on Earth. Plants make their food using sunlight, water, and carbon dioxide, and they are an important food source for all land animals. They also produce oxygen, which is vital to all life.

HOW PLANTS GROW

In spring, seeds get warm, absorb water, and start to sprout (germinate). Roots begin to grow downwards to get water and nutrients from the soil, while shoots grow upwards, towards the light.

Outer coat

1 GERMINATION
A small pore (the micropyle) in the seed coat takes in water and the seed swells.

Seed sprouts

2 NEW PLANT
The plant starts to grow beneath the ground, shooting in two directions.

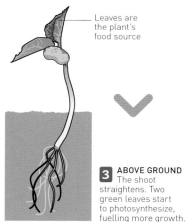
Leaves are the plant's food source

3 ABOVE GROUND
The shoot straightens. Two green leaves start to photosynthesize, fuelling more growth.

PHOTOSYNTHESIS

Plants make their own food (glucose) through a process called photosynthesis. They soak up water from the soil and take in carbon dioxide from the air. They then use the Sun's energy to produce glucose.

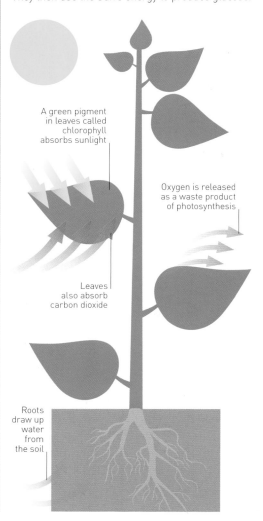

A green pigment in leaves called chlorophyll absorbs sunlight

Oxygen is released as a waste product of photosynthesis

Leaves also absorb carbon dioxide

Roots draw up water from the soil

SEED DISPERSAL

Plants need to spread their seeds as far away from themselves as possible, so they do not end up overcrowded. There are different ways that seeds can be dispersed.

BY BURSTING
When the seeds are ripe, they burst out, away from the parent plant.

BY WIND
Some seeds have shapes that make them fly easily in the wind.

BY WATER
Some fruits (seeds) are waterproof and can float, such as the coconut.

BY ANIMALS
Seeds can be eaten and excreted, or carried on animal coats.

BY HUMANS
Humans discard seeds after eating fruit or carry them on their clothes.

NON-FLOWERING PLANTS

These evergreen plants tend to like damp, shady places. They reproduce by releasing spores. Spores from coniferous plants are carried by the wind to special cones, where seeds develop.

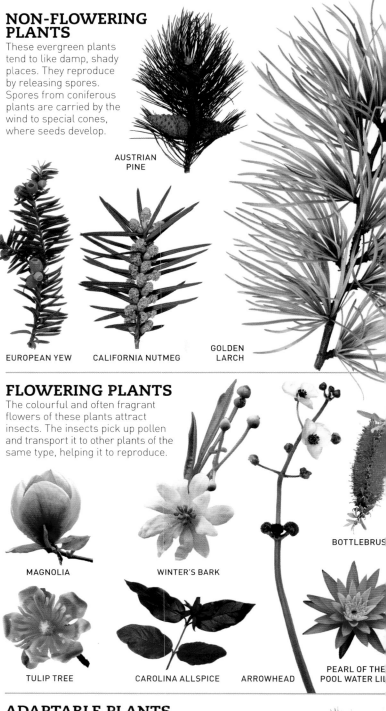

AUSTRIAN PINE

EUROPEAN YEW   CALIFORNIA NUTMEG   GOLDEN LARCH

FLOWERING PLANTS

The colourful and often fragrant flowers of these plants attract insects. The insects pick up pollen and transport it to other plants of the same type, helping it to reproduce.

MAGNOLIA   WINTER'S BARK   BOTTLEBRUS[H]

TULIP TREE   CAROLINA ALLSPICE   ARROWHEAD   PEARL OF THE POOL WATER LIL[Y]

ADAPTABLE PLANTS

Plants cannot protect themselves from animals or harsh weather conditions by moving, so they have other adaptations that help them survive. Plants in hot deserts can live with very little water, for instance, while those near the sea are very salt-tolerant.

CACTI
Cacti live in very hot places, so they have small spines instead of leaves, which do not allow so much water to evaporate. Their stems also store water.

CONIFERS
Coniferous plants stay green all year round. They have long, thin needles that need less water and can withstand freezing weather.

MANGROVES
These grow near the sea, but their leaves are able to get rid of (secrete) excess salt. If the salt levels become too high, the leaves just fall off.

TONGALAND CYCAD

ALPINE
WOODFERN

EASTERN CAPE
BLUE CYCAD

SILVER LIP
FERN

SPHAGNUM

MEXICAN
HORNCONE

MOORE'S MACROZAMIA CYCAD

FLOATING FERN

HORSETAIL

ADDER'S
TONGUE FERN

GINKGO

COMMON
LIVERWORT

HORNWORT

HIBISCUS

DAHLIA

PANSY

DAFFODIL

AMARYLLIS

POPPY

AFRICAN
LILY

ROUND-
HEADED
LEEK

HOLLYHOCK

GLADIOLUS

TULIP

ENGLISH
BLUEBELL

BIRD-OF-PARADISE

DYER'S
TILLANDSIA

CARNIVOROUS PLANTS

Some plants grow in soil that does not have many nutrients, so they get additional nutrients from animal prey, such as insects. Many attract their prey using colour and smell and then trap it. The plant's digestive juices break down the prey so it can be absorbed.

BUTTERWORT
This plant's leaves are covered with an insect-trapping sap. Small insects, such as gnats, get stuck, and their struggle releases the plant's digestive juices.

COBRA LILY
The traps on this plant look like snake heads. It contains cells that give off light and attractive smells to tempt hungry insects.

PITCHER PLANT
This tropical plant has cups (pitchers) that hang from trees and contain water to attract prey. Thirsty insects fall in – and become plant food.

☠ POISONOUS PLANTS

Some plants use poison as a protective device, so that people and animals do not eat them. These plants are among the deadliest to humans.

○ **OLEANDER**
The whole oleander plant is poisonous. Even smoke from burning oleander is highly toxic.

○ **WATER HEMLOCK**
The most deadly plant in North America, a tiny dose of this plant can be lethal if eaten. One species also occurs in Europe.

○ **ROSARY PEA**
These bright red seeds contain the most deadly plant poison known to humankind.

○ **DEADLY NIGHTSHADE**
All parts of this plant contain deadly toxins. The roots are the most dangerous part.

○ **CASTOR BEAN**
These contain ricin, one of the deadliest plant toxins. It is more toxic when inhaled than eaten.

CATCHING PREY

The Venus flytrap catches its insect prey very fast – it snaps shut in a tenth of a second. If an insect lands on the plant and touches sensory hairs, the plant snaps into action.

1 PRIMED
The plant has sensory hairs on the inside ready for its prey.

2 TRIGGERED
A landing insect touches the hairs and sends electrical signals to the plant cells.

3 SHUT
The plant lobes snap together, trapping the insect. Digestive juices are released.

Flowers

Flowers, often colourful and scented, play a vital role in a plant's life cycle. They contain organs that produce pollen and seeds. Pollen is taken from one flower to another in various ways. The flower receiving the pollen is fertilized (pollinated) and then forms seeds to make new plants.

STRUCTURE OF A FLOWER

The parts of a flower are centred around the task of reproduction. Flower petals surround an ovary that produces eggs, and a stigma that is ready to accept pollen. When eggs and pollen meet, they create seeds.

Petal

Stigma

Anther filled with pollen grains

Pollinating insect

Style (links stigma to ovary)

Filament

Ovary

Sepals

Stem

MONOCOTS

This group of flowers has several features in common: their petals are always in multiples of three; they have one main stem, which has very few leaves; and their stems contain veins that run in parallel lines.

LILY

TORCH LILY

IRIS

HYACINTH

HUME'S ROSCOEA

CHINESE YELLOW BANANA

LIPPEROSE MOTH ORCHID

DARK-RED HELLEBORINE

QUEEN'S SPIDERWORT

BOG ASPHODE

CLUSTER FLOWERS

Some plants have a cluster of flowers on each stem called an inflorescence. Such clusters are found in both monocots and eudicots. The flowers may branch out at intervals from the main stem or group together on the tip.

BARBADOS PRIDE

BRITISH BLUEBELL

GREEN FLOWERS

Plants with green flowers use wind pollination, as they are less attractive to insects. The flowers also tend to be small and not always easy to see. Their pollen-containing parts are positioned to catch the breeze.

COMMON HOGWEED

GLADIOLUS

RED CLOVER

WILD DAISY

WHITE WILLOW

STINKING HELLEBORE

FAT HEN

POLLINATION

Flowers reproduce by pollination – pollen being taken from one flower to another. Some plants self-pollinate, but animals, wind, and water often play a part.

ANIMAL
Many flowers contain nectar that attracts animals such as bees. While drinking the nectar the animal gets coated with pollen, which it carries to other flowers.

WIND
Some plants, such as grasses, rely on wind for pollination. They produce lots of pollen to increase the chances of it landing in the right places.

WATER
A small number of aquatic plants are pollinated by water. Pollen is released into the water and carried to other plants by water currents.

SELF
Some plants self-pollinate by either transferring pollen from the anther to the stigma of the same flower, or to another flower on the same plant.

FRUITS

Fruits are the parts of a plant that contain seeds. Some fruits change colour and become juicy when ripe, which makes them attractive to animals. If a fruit is eaten, its seeds pass through the animal's digestive tract and are dispersed in its droppings. Some types of fruit have wings or hooks and are carried on the wind or stuck in an animal's fur.

1 SEEDS AT BASE After pollination, seeds form in this melon flower's ovary.

2 OVARY SWELLS The flower petals fall away and the ovary begins to swell.

3 SMALL FRUIT The skin hardens; the ovary is now a small fruit.

4 RIPENING Over the growing season, the fruit gets bigger and ripens.

5 MATURE FRUIT The melon is ripe. If an animal eats it the seeds will be dispersed.

EUDICOTS

These complex flowers have flower petals in multiples of four or five. They also have lots of branches coming off the main stem, and their leaves have branching veins.

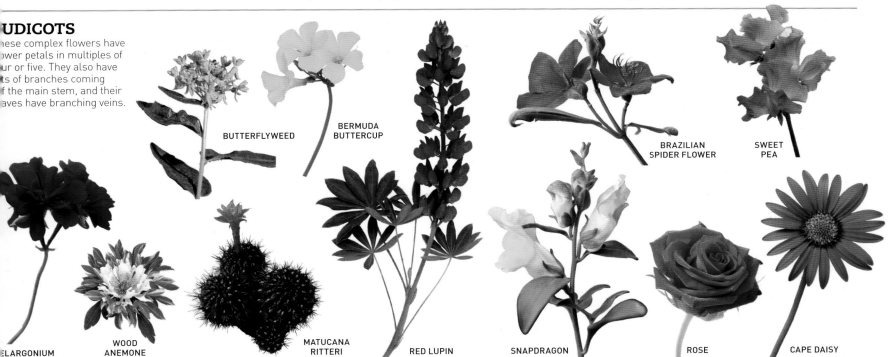

PELARGONIUM | WOOD ANEMONE | BUTTERFLYWEED | BERMUDA BUTTERCUP | MATUCANA RITTERI | RED LUPIN | BRAZILIAN SPIDER FLOWER | SWEET PEA | SNAPDRAGON | ROSE | CAPE DAISY

PLANTS WITH GREEN FLOWERS ARE A MAJOR CAUSE OF HAY FEVER BECAUSE THEY PRODUCE LOTS OF POLLEN AT CERTAIN TIMES OF THE YEAR

GREEN BRISTLEGRASS | GRASS FLOWERS | SEA BEET | NAVELWORT

THE GREAT PRETENDERS

Some flowers have evolved in ways that would make them at home in fairy tales. Among them are flowers that look like insects. Others smell of bad meat or the foul scent sprayed by skunks. Such strange adaptations have a good reason – they are tricks to attract pollinators.

RAFFLESIA
This is also known as the "corpse flower" because it smells like a rotten carcass. It has no roots or leaves, and lives off other plants, taking their nutrients and water.

BEE ORCHID
This flower has petals that look like a bee. Real bees are fooled into trying to mate with it, so they pick up and disperse the pollen.

WESTERN SKUNK CABBAGE
The tiny flowers are surrounded by a vivid yellow structure called a "spathe". Some insects love the skunky smell of this plant.

STINK LILY
The long black spike (spadix) on this plant stinks of rotten meat – which attracts flies hoping for a meal.

Trees

The largest plants on Earth, trees have been here for millions of years. They are vital to the planet's survival. Their leaves absorb harmful substances from the atmosphere and produce oxygen. Trees keep the air moist, which helps to create rainfall, and provide homes and food for wildlife.

TREE SHAPES
The shape of a tree is called its habit. Typical habits include widely spreading branches, narrow columns, and neat cones. Tree species can often be recognized by their habit, even if leafless in winter.

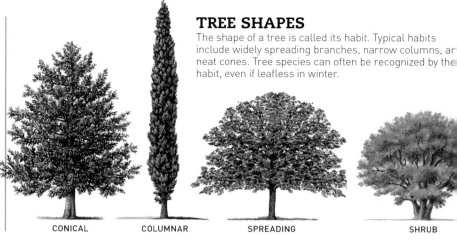

CONICAL   COLUMNAR   SPREADING   SHRUB

WHAT IS A TREE?
A tree is a tall plant with, usually, a woody stem called a trunk that divides into ever-smaller, leaf-bearing branches. A network of roots anchors the tree to the ground and draws up water and nutrients from the soil.

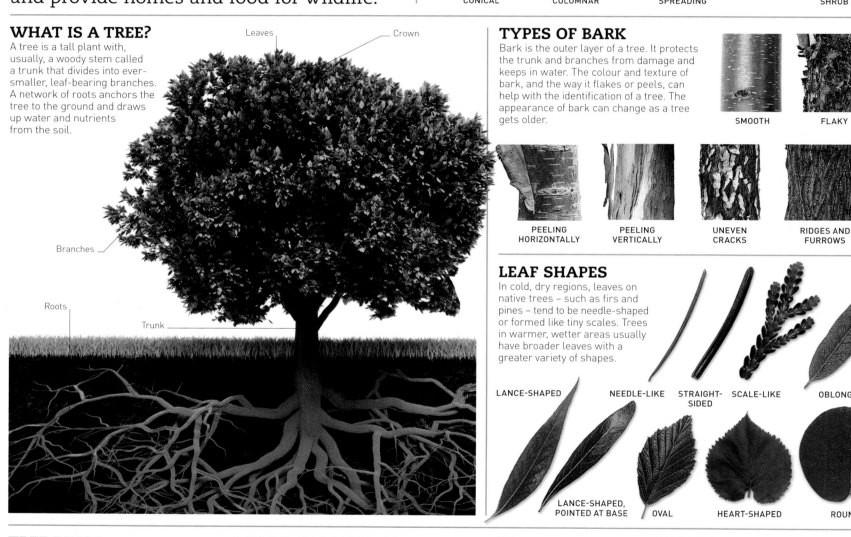

Leaves — Crown

Branches

Roots

Trunk

TYPES OF BARK
Bark is the outer layer of a tree. It protects the trunk and branches from damage and keeps in water. The colour and texture of bark, and the way it flakes or peels, can help with the identification of a tree. The appearance of bark can change as a tree gets older.

SMOOTH   FLAKY

PEELING HORIZONTALLY   PEELING VERTICALLY   UNEVEN CRACKS   RIDGES AND FURROWS

LEAF SHAPES
In cold, dry regions, leaves on native trees – such as firs and pines – tend to be needle-shaped or formed like tiny scales. Trees in warmer, wetter areas usually have broader leaves with a greater variety of shapes.

LANCE-SHAPED   NEEDLE-LIKE   STRAIGHT-SIDED   SCALE-LIKE   OBLONG

LANCE-SHAPED, POINTED AT BASE   OVAL   HEART-SHAPED   ROUNDE

TREE RINGS
Every year that a tree grows it adds a new layer of wood beneath its bark. If the tree is cut down, these layers can be seen as dark and light rings. By counting the dark rings, it is possible to work out the age of the tree.

Bark   Rings in cut trunk

FOUR SEASONS
Many types of trees have a cycle of growth that follows seasonal weather changes. They produce leaves and flowers in spring, then seeds through the summer. As the hours of daylight shorten in autumn, the trees stop growing and drop their leaves. In winter, the trees have a period of rest.

Leafless branches

LEAF CHANGE
In autumn, leaves change appearance. The green vanishes, and reds, yellows, and browns make woodlands glow with colour.

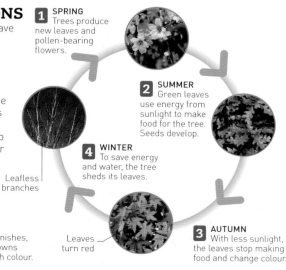

1 SPRING
Trees produce new leaves and pollen-bearing flowers.

2 SUMMER
Green leaves use energy from sunlight to make food for the tree. Seeds develop.

4 WINTER
To save energy and water, the tree sheds its leaves.

Leaves turn red

3 AUTUMN
With less sunlight, the leaves stop making food and change colour.

TALLEST TREES
The evergreen trees known as Coastal Redwoods grow taller than any other species of tree. They grow naturally only along the Pacific coast of northern California, USA. The very tallest redwood is an amazing 116 m (380 ft) high. Named Hyperion, its exact location is secret.

STATUE OF LIBERTY 93 m (305 f

HYPERION REDWOOD 116 m (380 ft)

DECIDUOUS TREES

Trees that lose all their leaves for part of the year – for example, oaks and beeches – are called deciduous. They have flat leaves of many shapes that are usually shed in cold or dry seasons. The tree remains bare until warmer weather returns, when new leaves grow. Deciduous trees are found in many regions of the world.

COMMON ALDER   SILVER BIRCH   COMMON HORNBEAM   SWEET CHESTNUT   COMMON BEECH

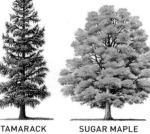

MANNA ASH   TAMARACK   SUGAR MAPLE   QUAKING ASPEN   CHERRY   WHITE WILLOW   ROWAN   ENGLISH ELM

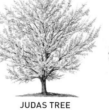

WHITE MULBERRY   ENGLISH OAK   QUINCE   JUDAS TREE   COMMON FIG   TURPENTINE TREE

EVERGREEN TREES

These trees have leaves all year round. Although old leaves fall off, they are constantly replaced by new ones. Evergreens include firs, pines, cedars, and spruces. Many grow in northern regions, where they thrive in harsh, cold climates.

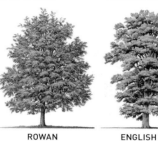

THE WORLD'S MOST ANCIENT TREE IS A BRISTLECONE PINE IN CALIFORNIA, DATED AT 4,789 YEARS OLD

SILVER FIR   GIANT FIR   MONKEY PUZZLE   YLANG YLANG   ITALIAN CYPRESS

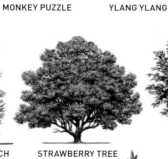

NORWAY SPRUCE   BLUE SPRUCE   BLUE GUM   MAGELLAN'S BEECH   STRAWBERRY TREE   LEMON TREE   CEDAR OF LEBANON   WELLINGTONIA

COCOA TREE   CHINESE EVERGREEN MAGNOLIA   COMMON MANGO   COMMON JUNIPER   SCOTS PINE   COMMON YEW   EASTERN HEMLOCK

ANCIENT TREES

The first tree-like plants that grew on Earth, about 380 million years ago, were spore trees. These reproduced not from seeds but from cells called spores on the underside of their leaves. The only spore trees living today are the tree ferns. Another ancient tree is the Ginkgo, a survivor from before the age of dinosaurs.

TREE FERNS   GINKGO

BONSAI

The ancient oriental art of bonsai creates tiny replicas of large trees. Techniques such as wiring roots and branches stop the tree from reaching its full growth. Bonsai can be used on any type of tree to produce a miniature version small enough to keep in a pot.

JAPANESE MAPLE   DWARF CRAB APPLE

Wart

BAY CUP

LEMON DISCO

GREEN ELFCUP

YELLOWING CUP

Cap

LEMON PEEL FUNG

FRUITING BODY

Gills (spore-carrying tissues)

CAP-AND-STEM MUSHROOM

Stem or "stipe"

Base

Root-like threads

The mushroom seen growing in grass or woodland is called a "fruiting body". Another part of the fungus is hidden underground. The best-known mushrooms have a rounded cap with a central stem. Under the cap are thin, flat tissues known as gills, where spores – tiny reproductive cells – are produced.

Cup carries spores

Deeply cup-shaped fruiting body

COMMON EARTH-CUP

TOOTHED CUP

ORANGE PEEL FUNGUS

ANEMONE CUP

JELLY EA

Ring (remains of tissue that covered baby mushroom)

BLISTERED CUP

Spore-producing tissue

CUP-LIKE

There are many varieties of mushrooms shaped like cups or discs. The inner surface of the cup carries the spores. These fungi grow from the ground or on damp wood.

LARGE PURPLE DROP

SCARLET ELFCUP

BEECH JELLYDISC

BALL-SHAPED

Some fungi are round like balls. They range in size from tiny ones clustering on stems to giants as large as a football. The type called puffballs split open to release the spores stored inside.

Spores sit on the inner surface

GREY PUFFBALL

PESTLE-SHAPED PUFFBALL

CRAMP BALLS

COMMON EARTHBALL

STUMP PUFFBALL

SPINY PUFFBALL

MEADOW PUFFBALL

SUMMER TRUFFLE

GIANT PUFFBALL

RE CAG

CAP-AND-STEM

The most easily recognized fungi are the "umbrella" or cap-and-stem type. They come in all shapes and sizes. Some are small and spindly, others have fat stems and thick, fleshy caps.

MEADOW WAXCAP

AMETHYST DECEIVER

Bun-shaped cap

FALSE MOREL

SPLENDID WEBCAP

SCARLET WAXCAP

VIOLET WEBCAP

SICKENER

CONIFER TUFT

FLY AGARIC

PANTHERCAP

FIELD BLEWIT

LILAC BONNET

Mushrooms

Although they look like plants, mushrooms are quite different and belong to a separate scientific group – the fungi. They come in many shapes and colours, and all of them feed on organic matter. Some mushrooms are edible but others are deadly poisonous.

LIFECYCLE OF A MUSHROOM

The real growth of a fungus takes place out of sight. Beneath the ground, a web of fine threads develops from the mushroom's spores (reproductive cells) and spreads to produce more mushrooms.

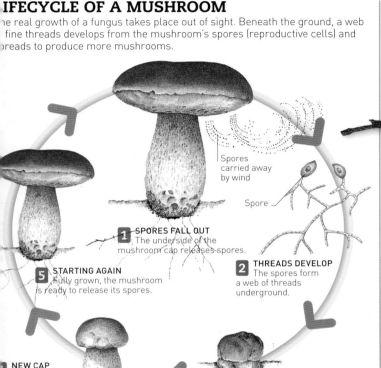

Spores carried away by wind

Spore

1 SPORES FALL OUT
The underside of the mushroom cap releases spores.

5 STARTING AGAIN
Fully grown, the mushroom is ready to release its spores.

2 THREADS DEVELOP
The spores form a web of threads underground.

4 NEW CAP EMERGES
The young mushroom appears above the ground.

3 MUSHROOM SPROUTS
The threads stick together, forming a small knot – a new mushroom.

WHERE FUNGI GROW

Finding and identifying fungi means knowing the right places to look. For example, some fungi grow by certain trees.

FALLEN BRANCHES
The common brown cup mushroom grows on oak bark.

FIR CONES
The earpick fungus grows directly out of decaying fir cones.

LEAVES
Redleg club fungi appear on the ribs and stalks of ash, maple, or alder leaves.

UNDER TREES
The hazel bolete mushroom grows in leaf beds under hazel and hornbeam trees.

ON OTHER MUSHROOMS
Silky piggyback mushrooms grow on the rotting bodies of other fungi.

☠ DANGEROUS MUSHROOMS

Some poisonous mushrooms look very like the ones used in cooking. No one should pick a mushroom without being quite sure what type it is.

- **DEATHCAP**
  One of the deadliest fungi in the world, the deathcap can be fatal if eaten.

- **BROWN ROLLRIM**
  The poison in the rollrim can damage red blood cells and lead to kidney and liver failure.

  Short stem

  Cap rolls inwards

- **JEWELLED AMANITA**
  This cream-coloured or yellow mushroom can cause sickness and stomach pains less than an hour after being eaten.

- **FUNERAL BELL**
  Found on rotting wood, the yellowish-brown funeral bell contains a poison that causes liver damage and, without fast treatment, death.

- **DEADLY WEBCAP**
  This is very dangerous because it looks like the edible chanterelle mushroom. If eaten, the webcap damages the liver and kidneys.

BRACKET-LIKE

These types of fungi are found on trees or dead wood. They grow like shelves, sometimes forming row on top of row. Bracket fungi can eventually kill living trees by attacking their tissues.

BEESWAX BRACKET

CHICKEN OF THE WOODS

OYSTER MUSHROOM

OAK MAZEGILL

TOOTHED JELLY

JELLY ROT

STAR-SHAPED

In these fungi, the spores are held in a round case. To release the spores, the outer layer of the case splits open like a many-pointed star.

DWARF EARTHSTAR

DEVIL'S FINGERS

COLLARED EARTHSTAR

CORAL-LIKE

Often brightly coloured, the clustered, branching stalks of coral fungi look very similar to the corals found in tropical seas.

CLUB-SHAPED

With their upright shapes and no noticeable cap, club fungi can be hard to recognize as mushrooms. Some types grow in clumps.

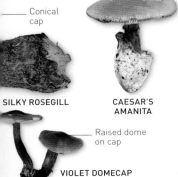

Conical cap

Raised dome on cap

SILKY ROSEGILL

CAESAR'S AMANITA

VIOLET DOMECAP

SCARLET CATERPILLAR CLUB

BOG BEACON

SCALY EARTHTONGUE

DEAD MAN'S FINGERS

YELLOW CLUB

PIPE CLUB

CANDLESNUFF FUNGUS

UPRIGHT CORAL

ROSSO CORAL

YELLOW STAGSHORN

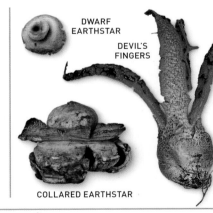

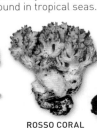

SPIDERS

There are about 4,200 species of spiders. They have eight legs, and six or eight eyes. Most spiders can live for up to one year, if they avoid disease and predators. Some big spiders, such as the tarantula, can live for up to 20 years.

NURSERY WEB SPIDER

DADDY LONG-LEGS SPIDER

NORTH AMERICAN TRAPDOOR SPIDER

GIANT HOUSE SPIDER

WATER SPIDER

CAVE SPIDER

NORTHERN SPITTING SPIDER

AMERICAN GOLDEN SILK ORB-WEAVER

CHACO TARANTULA

BROWN JUMPING SPIDER

NORTHERN BLACK WIDOW SPIDER

FUNNEL-WEB SPIDER

EUROPEAN WOLF SPIDER

Spiders and scorpions

Spiders and scorpions are part of the arachnid family – invertebrate animals with eight legs. They are alike in many ways, but a scorpion has a venomous stinger in its tail, while spiders have venomous fangs.

ANATOMY OF A SPIDER

A spider's body is divided into two parts. The first part includes the eyes, fangs, stomach, and legs, while the second part contains the silk glands, known as spinnerets. Spiders have four pairs of legs, and use the hairs on these to pick up smells, sounds, and vibrations.

Digestive glands

Heart

Intestine

Eye

Ovary

Silk gland, or spinneret, for making webs

Book lung

Fang with venom canal

SCORPLINGS

Young scorpions develop inside their mother's body. After birth, they climb on to her back until their external skeleton moults for the first time.

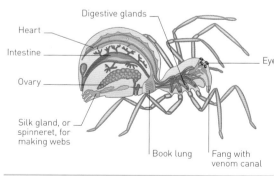

Scorplings

External skeleton will be shed five to seven times before adulthood

SCORPIONS

A scorpion's body is encased in a tough shell-like covering. Claws near the head are used to seize prey and fight predators, while its tail ends in a venomous stinger.

YELLOW THICK-TAIL SCORPION

IMPERIAL SCORPION

CHILEAN BURROWING SCORPION

OTHER ARACHNIDS

The arachnid family includes other animals such as mites, ticks, and harvestmen. They are often mistaken for insects, but they are not, mainly because they all have eight legs, not six, and two body segments, instead of three.

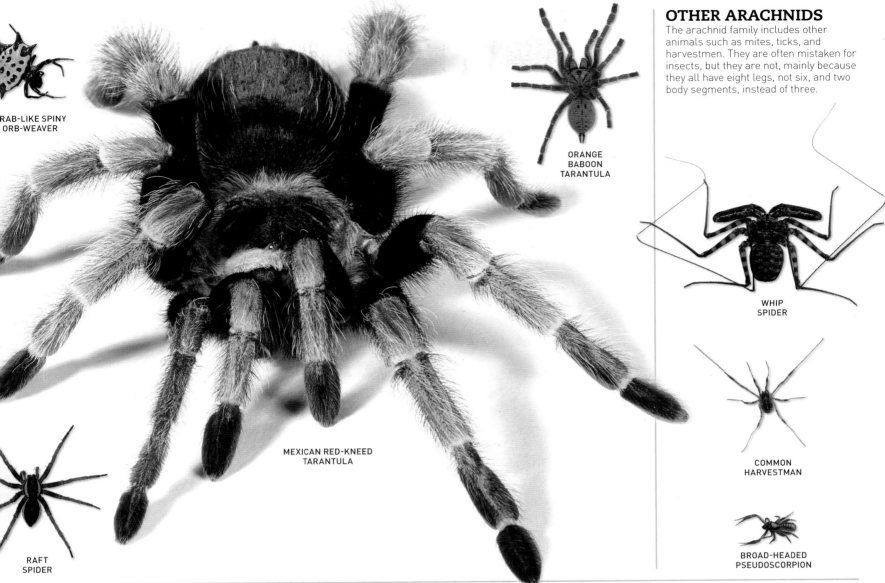

RAB-LIKE SPINY
ORB-WEAVER

MEXICAN RED-KNEED
TARANTULA

RAFT
SPIDER

ORANGE
BABOON
TARANTULA

WHIP
SPIDER

COMMON
HARVESTMAN

BROAD-HEADED
PSEUDOSCORPION

WEB TYPES

Different species of spider produce different types of webs. Orb spiders produce the most widely recognized web.

ORB WEB
Spun by orb web spiders, this type of web needs repairing every day.

TRIANGULAR WEB
This type is spun by non-venomous cribellate orb weaver spiders.

COBWEB
Also known as a "tangled web", this type is made by house spiders.

FUNNEL-WEB
This tubular style is built by funnel-web spiders.

THE OLDEST WEB
IS A 110-MILLION-
YEAR-OLD FOSSIL

BUILDING A WEB

Orb spiders produce a strong silk "thread" from their abdomen, which they use for spinning webs. The finished web is sticky, so that it can trap insects that pass by for the spider to eat.

1 FRAMEWORK
The spider lets out a thread, which catches on a twig. It then attaches the other end to another twig. Next, it attaches a looser thread to the same spot and then suspends itself from a third thread in the middle.

2 SPIRAL THREADS
Once the third thread is attached, the spider spins spiral threads to complete the web. These threads are not sticky.

3 STICKY THREADS
Finally, the spider replaces the spiral threads with sticky threads, ready to catch its prey. It then eats the non-sticky threads.

SPIDER SIZES

The world's smallest spider, the Patu Digua, has a body about the size of a pin head. The largest spider, the Goliath Birdeater Tarantula, has a leg span of 28 cm (11 in).

PATU DIGUA
SPIDER

GOLIATH BIRDEATER
TARANTULA

FEEDING

Spiders use fangs to kill their prey. Many also "spit" digestive fluids over the prey, to turn it to liquid, and then suck it up. All spiders eat insects, but some big spiders also eat lizards, frogs, and even fish.

☠ DANGEROUS SPIDERS

Only a small number of spiders are a danger to humans.

○ **BRAZILIAN WANDERING SPIDER**
The world's most poisonous spider wanders across jungle floors at night in search of food.

○ **SYDNEY FUNNEL-WEB**
When prey comes into contact with its web, this spider rushes out and delivers lots of bites, very quickly.

○ **BROWN RECLUSE**
Also known as "violin spiders", these bite with flesh-eating venom for which there is no cure.

○ **BLACK WIDOW SPIDER**
This spider's venom is very poisonous, but its bite is small.

Crustaceans

The animals called crustaceans are a varied group that includes crabs, lobsters, prawns, and shrimps. Most of them live in water. Among the few found on land are tiny woodlice. Crustaceans have an outer skeleton that does not grow when their bodies do, so they shed it regularly to allow a new, larger one to develop.

THE BODY OF A CRUSTACEAN

Lobsters and crabs have three body regions: the head, the thorax or mid-section, and the abdomen. They have five pairs of legs, which in some species form pincers.

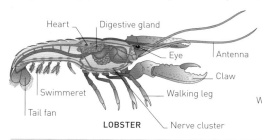

Heart — Digestive gland — Eye — Antenna — Claw — Walking leg — Swimmeret — Tail fan — Nerve cluster

LOBSTER

Eye — Antenna — Nerve cord — Claw — Stomach — Gills — Walking leg — Heart — Swimming leg

CRAB

LIFECYCLE OF A CRAB

Like most crustaceans, newly hatched crabs look very different from their parents. They develop into adults through several stages. A female crab lays millions of eggs, of which only a handful survive.

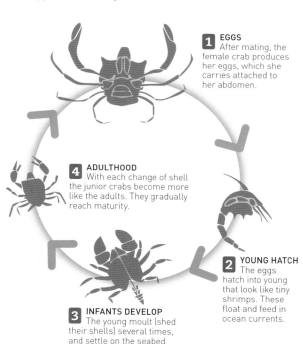

1 EGGS
After mating, the female crab produces her eggs, which she carries attached to her abdomen.

4 ADULTHOOD
With each change of shell the junior crabs become more like the adults. They gradually reach maturity.

2 YOUNG HATCH
The eggs hatch into young that look like tiny shrimps. These float and feed in ocean currents.

3 INFANTS DEVELOP
The young moult (shed their shells) several times, and settle on the seabed.

SURVIVAL TACTICS

Crabs are a tasty meal for many other sea creatures. They often dodge predators by hiding under rocks or in a tangle of seaweed. If cornered a long way from shelter, a crab uses different tactics to get out of trouble.

MOCK ATTACK
The crab rears up and waves its pincers, trying to make itself look as large as possible.

CROUCH
Another trick the crab may try is to crouch down low, so that it is seen less easily by the waiting predator.

ESCAPE
With luck, the crab confuses the attacker and has time to scuttle off to safety.

DEADLY BUBBLE

The 5 cm (2 in) long pistol shrimp makes a big noise for its size. Meeting prey, the shrimp opens the larger of its claws and snaps it shut at lightning speed. The snap creates an air bubble, which bursts with a bang loud enough to stun the victim.

1 CLAW OPENS
The shrimp opens its hinged claw wide.

2 CLAW SHUTS
The claw snaps shut, creating a bubble.

3 PREY STUNNED
The sound of the bubble bursting stuns the prey.

CRABS

All but a few crabs live in the sea. Most of them have flat bodies and a wide shell. The soft-bellied hermit crabs protect themselves by living in the empty shells of other marine animals. Crabs move by walking sideways.

WARTY BOX CRAB

EDIBLE CRAB

SPLENDID ROUND CRAB

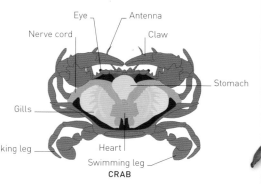

SPINY SPIDER CRAB

MASKED CRAB

GHOST CRAB

LOBSTERS AND OTHER FAMILIES

Like most crabs, lobsters live in the sea. These large animals have a hard upper shell and powerful tails. Smaller crustaceans include numerous shrimps, both marine and freshwater. Sea slaters and woodlice belong to a large family whose members are found on land as well as in water.

BROAD LOBSTER

VERNAL POOL TADPOLE SHRIMP

AESOP SHRIMP

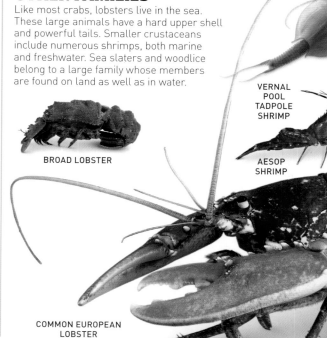

COMMON EUROPEAN LOBSTER

RED LAND CRAB

Eyestalk

FURROWED CRAB

ANEMONE HERMIT CRAB

COMMON HERMIT CRAB

Tiny hairs act as sensors

DUNGENESS CRAB

VELVET SWIMMING CRAB

PANAMIC ARROW CRAB

Empty shell used as a portable home

WHITE-SPOTTED HERMIT CRAB

PORCELAIN ANEMONE CRAB

RED REEF HERMIT CRAB

ORANGE FIDDLER CRAB

COMMON EUROPEAN CRAB

ATLANTIC BLUE CRAB

SCULPTURED SLIPPER LOBSTER

PEACOCK MANTIS SHRIMP

COMMON MARBLE SHRIMP

COMMON SHRIMP

NORWAY LOBSTER

MORETON BAY BUG LOBSTER

HAIRY SQUAT LOBSTER

SEA SLATER

ANTARCTIC KRILL

WHITE-CLAWED CRAYFISH

STRIPED-LEG SPINY LOBSTER

PILL WOODLOUSE

SPINY SQUAT LOBSTER

TIGER PRAWN

91

RECOGNIZING AN INSECT

Insects come in many forms. Most have wings, and there are other features that make them easier to recognize, too.

THREE BODY SEGMENTS

OFTEN HAVE WINGS

OUTER SKELETON

COMPOUND EYES

FEELERS

SIX JOINTED LEGS

INSECTS WERE THE FIRST ANIMALS TO FLY, 400 MILLION YEARS AGO

Insects

Out of all the animals on Earth, insects are the biggest success story. There are greater numbers, living in more places, than any other type of creature. More than a million insect species have been identified – and there may be millions still to discover.

THE BODY OF AN INSECT

Insects have three main body segments: the head; the thorax, or midsection, to which the legs, and maybe wings, are attached; and the abdomen or belly. All these parts are protected by a hard outer skeleton.

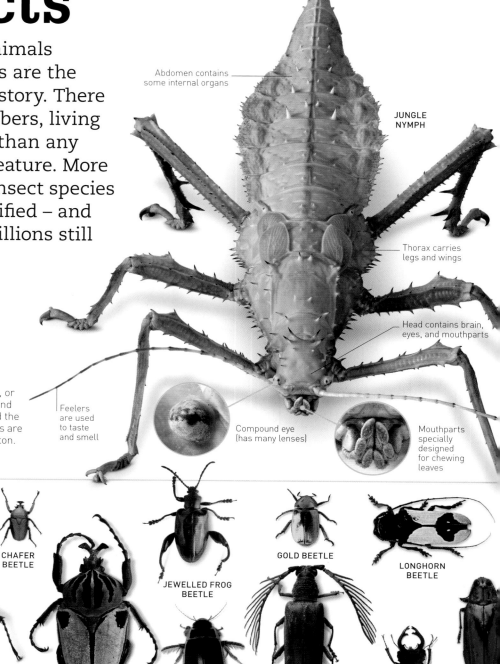

Abdomen contains some internal organs

JUNGLE NYMPH

Thorax carries legs and wings

Head contains brain, eyes, and mouthparts

Feelers are used to taste and smell

Compound eye (has many lenses)

Mouthparts specially designed for chewing leaves

BEETLES

About one in every three insects is a beetle. At least 370,000 species are known. They all have hard front wings that fold shut to form a protective case.

RED GIRAFFE WEEVIL

GREEN JUNE BEETLE

CHAFER BEETLE

JEWELLED FROG BEETLE

GOLD BEETLE

LONGHORN BEETLE

SCARLET LILY BEETLE

CLICK BEETLE

TWENTY-TWO SPOT LADYBIRD

WEEVIL

HERCULES BEETLE

GOLIATH BEETLE

GREAT DIVING BEETLE

WALLACE'S LONGHORN BEETLE

STAG BEETLE

JEWEL BEETLE

TRUE BUGS

Not all so-called bugs are true bugs. These are a group of insects with long beak-like mouthparts made for piercing and sucking juices from plants and animals.

Large head shaped like a peanut shell

PEANUT-HEADED BUG

BED BUG

FIREBUG

THORN BUG

HAWTHORN SHIELD BUG

WATER SCORPION

GIANT WATER BUG

WART-HEADED BUG

WHITE SPOTTED ASSASSIN BUG

GRASSHOPPERS AND CRICKETS

A grasshopper makes its loud chirp by rubbing its hindlegs against its wings. Crickets "sing" by rubbing their wings together. Both types of insect fly and jump.

OAK BUSH CRICKET

SPECKLED BUSH CRICKET

COMMON BLACK CRICKET

DESERT LOCUST

STRIPE-WINGED GRASSHOPPER

COMMON FIELD GRASSHOPPER

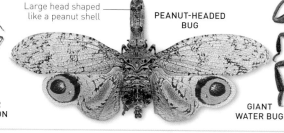
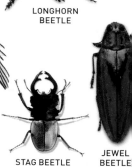

ANTS, BEES, AND WASPS

These groups of insects include many that sting. Ants and nearly all types of bees and wasps live in organized colonies.

WOOD ANT

ARMY ANT

COMMON WASP

ASIAN CARPENTER BEE

TAWNY MINING BEE

FLIES

There are thousands of species of flies around the world. Although some types are disease-carrying pests, many are useful as pollinators of plants.

BLUEBOTTLE   TIMBER FLY   HOUSE FLY

GIANT BLUE ROBBER FLY

DRAGONFLIES AND DAMSELFLIES

Slender bodies and large wings make these the flying aces of the insect world. They are skilful predators, darting through the air to catch other insects.

PLAINS CLUBTAIL

COMET DARNER

MEDITERRANEAN DAMSELFLY

FLAME SKIMMER

TWIN-SPOTTED SPIKETAIL

Transparent wings

AZURE DAMSELFLY

GRAY PETALTAIL

Compound eyes

Appendages at end of abdomen

PRINCE BASKETTAIL

BROAD-BODIED CHASER

EMPEROR DRAGONFLY

SOUTHERN HAWKER DRAGONFLY

ILLINOIS RIVER CRUISER

BANDED DEMOISELLE

GIANT HAWKER

WHITE-LEGGED DAMSELFLY

BUTTERFLIES AND MOTHS

Often colourful, butterflies are daytime flyers. Moths are usually duller and most fly at night. Both have tiny scales on their wings.

ORANGE OAKLEAF BUTTERFLY

MONARCH BUTTERFLY

GARDEN TIGER MOTH

MADAGASCAN SUNSET MOTH

LIFECYCLE

All insects start life as an egg. Once they hatch out, their bodies go through changes as they grow into adults. The lifecycle of the ladybird, shown here, is how many beetles develop.

1 EGGS The female may lay hundreds of eggs over the spring and early summer.

2 LARVA Each egg hatches into a larva (young, undeveloped insect).

3 SKIN CHANGES The larva eats and grows, shedding its skin multiple times over several weeks.

4 PUPA When the larva is full size, its skin splits to reveal the pupa (non-feeding stage).

5 ADULT Inside a tight wrapping, the pupa changes, and an adult ladybird emerges.

TITAN LONGHORN BEETLE 16.7 CM (6.5 IN)

FAIRYFLY 0.139 MM (0.005 IN)

BIGGEST AND SMALLEST

One of the largest insects in the world is the South American Titan Longhorn Beetle, which can fill the palm of a hand. The tiniest insects are fairyflies, barely visible without a magnifying glass.

ALL-ROUND VISION

Insects have compound eyes. While a human eye has one lens, a compound eye has hundreds or thousands of lenses. This allows insects to look in many directions at once.

Large compound eyes are very sensitive to movement

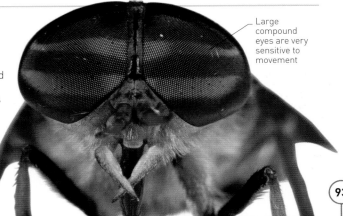
HORSEFLY

Butterflies and moths

With their delicate shape and often stunning colours, butterflies and moths are beautiful insects. All have four wings covered in tiny scales that create a mosaic of exquisite patterns. Most butterflies and moths feed on nectar from flowers and are important for pollinating plants.

WHAT'S THE DIFFERENCE?

Most butterflies fly by day and are brightly coloured. At rest, they usually fold their wings upright. Moths fly largely at night and most have duller colouring. They have furry bodies and feathery antennae. When resting, moths either hold their wings apart or fold them close to the body.

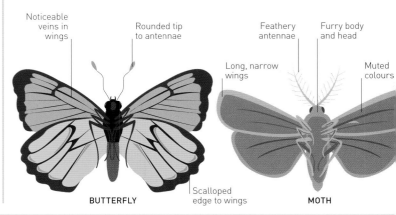

Noticeable veins in wings

Rounded tip to antennae

Feathery antennae

Furry body and head

Long, narrow wings

Muted colours

BUTTERFLY

Scalloped edge to wings

MOTH

BUTTERFLIES

There are butterflies nearly everywhere in the world. The biggest wings and boldest patterns are seen mostly in species from tropical regions. A butterfly's colours not only attract mates but also provide protection. To a predator, bright wings are a warning that the prey could be poisonous to eat.

MOTHS

There are many more moths than butterflies. Most are less eye-catching, but spectacular species do occur. The gigantic moon moths can have wingspans of up to 30 cm (12 in).

LARGE COPPER

BROWN-VEINED WHITE

WESTERN PYGMY BLUE

ADONIS BLUE

ORANGE-BARRED GIANT SULPHUR

IMPERIAL WHITE

LEAFWING

BLUE NIGHT BUTTERFLY

REGENT SKIPPER

MOORLAND CLOUDED YELLOW

MECHANITIS MIMIC

QUEEN ALEXANDRA'S BIRDWING

BRAZILIAN DYNASTOR

TIGER SWALLOWTAIL

BLUE TRIANGLE

PEACOCK BUTTERFLY

APOLL

PROVENCE BURNET

MADAGASCAN SUNSET MOTH

INFANT MOTH

ORNATE MOTH

GOLDEN EMPEROR

SMOOTH EMERALD

ORIZABA SILKMOTH

LIFECYCLE OF A BUTTERFLY

Butterflies and moths change from caterpillars to adults in a process called metamorphosis. Their life stages vary according to species. Some caterpillars change inside a silk cocoon rather than the hard case shown here.

1 EGG
A butterfly begins life as an egg the size of a pin head. Butterfly eggs may be laid singly or in clusters.

2 CATERPILLAR
A caterpillar hatches from the egg. It eats and eats and sheds its skin (moults) several times as its body gets bigger.

3 CHRYSALIS
The final moult reveals a hard case, or chrysalis, inside which the caterpillar stays as its body changes.

4 ADULT BUTTERFLY
A colourful butterfly emerges out of the chrysalis. In turn, it will lay its own eggs.

LARGEST AND SMALLEST

The female Queen Alexandra's Birdwing is the world's biggest butterfly with a wingspan of up to 28 cm (11 in). The Western Pygmy Blue has a wingspan of less than 2 cm (0.5 in), making it one of the world's smallest.

WESTERN PYGMY BLUE

QUEEN ALEXANDRA'S BIRDWING

CATERPILLAR MOVEMENT

Caterpillars have three pairs of legs at the front and between two and five pairs of false legs, which provide grip, at the hind end. They move with a wave-like motion.

Two pairs of false legs

Three pairs of walking legs

1 FRONT MOVES
The caterpillar moves its front part forwards, leaving the rear anchored.

2 REAR CATCHES UP
It draws its hind end forwards while holding on with the front legs.

3 FRONT MOVES AGAIN
It then moves its front again, gripping with the false legs at the back.

CATERPILLARS

Different species of caterpillars vary greatly in appearance, but all are big eaters. Most feed on plants, often of one type only. Less usual foods include wool and the horns of dead cattle.

DEATH'S HEAD HAWK-MOTH

OAK LEAFROLLER

PUSS MOTH

POSTMAN BUTTERFLY

SWALLOWTAIL

TIGER MOTH

CHINESE OAK SILK MOTH

COMMON CLUBTAIL

HEWITSON'S BLUE HAIRSTREAK

LARGE BLUE

PURPLE HAIRSTREAK

GUAVA SKIPPER

BHUTAN GLORY

MARBLED WHITE

PIRATE BUTTERFLY

JULIA

EUROPEAN MAP BUTTERFLY

PAINTED LADY

GRIZZLED SKIPPER

EIGHTY-EIGHT BUTTERFLY

MONARCH

CATTLE HEART SWALLOWTAIL

MALACHITE

AFRICAN MOON MOTH

GREEN SILVER-LINES MOTH

COMMON EPICOMA MOTH

LIME HAWK-MOTH

GIANT LEOPARD MOTH

ELEPHANT HAWK-MOTH

LARGE MAPLE SPANWORM MOTH

HARTIG'S BRAHMAEA

BASKER

LAND SLUGS

With no shell to retreat into, slugs have to hide, emerging at night to feed. Some live underground. Although seen as pests for devouring garden plants and farm crops, slugs play a useful part in breaking down rotting vegetation.

COMMON GARDEN SLUG

KERRY SPOTTED SLUG

BLACK SLUG

SEA SLUGS

As wobbly as jelly and often as brightly coloured, sea slugs creep over seabeds and corals. Some can swim in a clumsy fashion. They carry gills, or breathing organs, such as feathers or spikes on their backs.

ELEGANT SEA SLUG

Gills

VARICOSE SEA SLUG

SPANISH DANCER

Smell or taste orga

ANNA'S SEA SLUG

HEADSHIELD SLUG

OPALESCENT SEA SLUG

LAND SNAILS

Among the best-known animals on Earth, land snails range from species no bigger than a pinhead to the giant African land snail, which can reach 30 cm (15.5 in) long and weigh up to 900 g (2 lb). Their shells are more than portable homes. The colours and patterns provide camouflage by blending into the snail's habitat.

SOME TYPES OF SNAILS ARE HUNTERS THAT PREY ON WORMS, SLUGS, AND EVEN OTHER SNAILS

BROWN-LIPPED SNAIL

ROMAN SNA

Eye at the end of the tentacle

Sensory tentacles

HAIRY SNA

MANUS ISLAND SNAIL

WHITE-LIPPE SNAIL

COMMON GARDEN SNAIL

ROSY WOLFSNAIL

GIANT AFRICAN LAND SNA

Slugs and snails

Leaving pathways of shining slime made by their own bodies, land slugs and snails are familiar in damp places almost all over the world. Less often seen, except sometimes as aquarium pets, are slugs and snails that live in water. Many of these, especially species from warm oceans, are vividly coloured or have fantastically shaped shells.

WHAT'S THE DIFFERENCE?

The bodies of slugs and snails look very alike, but a telltale feature lies beneath a snail's shell. This is a small hump containing most of the snail's internal organs. Some slugs have a tiny internal shell that serves as a calcium store.

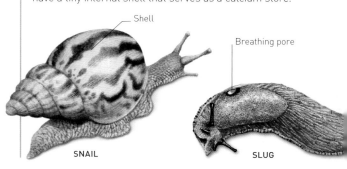

Shell

Breathing pore

SNAIL

SLUG

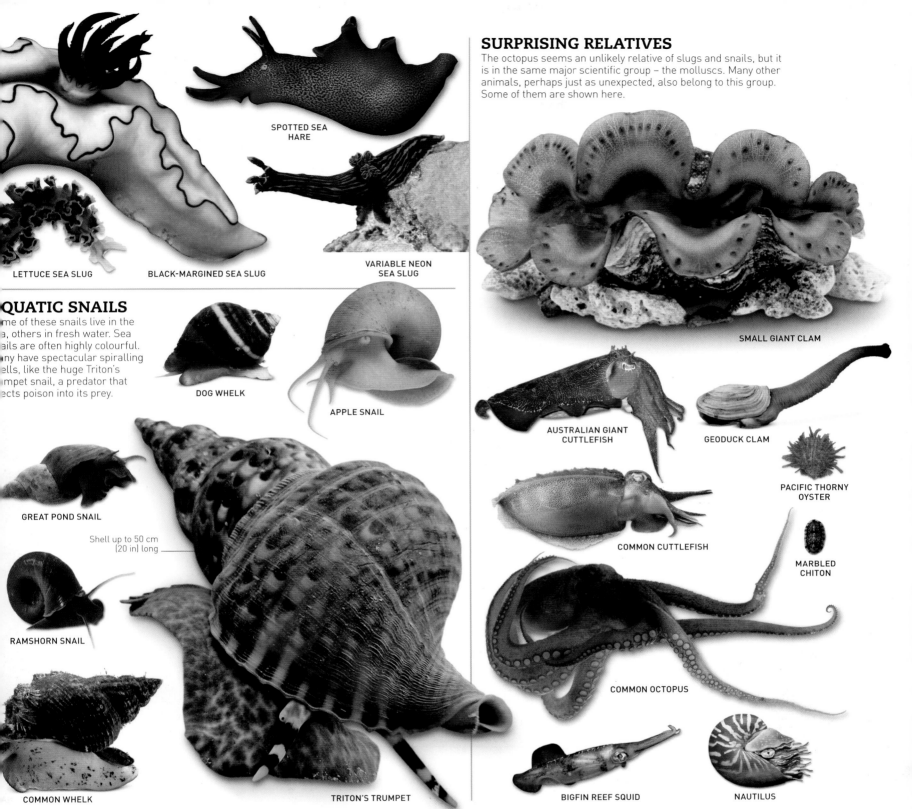

LETTUCE SEA SLUG

SPOTTED SEA HARE

BLACK-MARGINED SEA SLUG

VARIABLE NEON SEA SLUG

SURPRISING RELATIVES

The octopus seems an unlikely relative of slugs and snails, but it is in the same major scientific group – the molluscs. Many other animals, perhaps just as unexpected, also belong to this group. Some of them are shown here.

SMALL GIANT CLAM

QUATIC SNAILS

me of these snails live in the
a, others in fresh water. Sea
ails are often highly colourful.
ny have spectacular spiralling
ells, like the huge Triton's
mpet snail, a predator that
ects poison into its prey.

DOG WHELK

APPLE SNAIL

AUSTRALIAN GIANT CUTTLEFISH

GEODUCK CLAM

PACIFIC THORNY OYSTER

GREAT POND SNAIL

Shell up to 50 cm
(20 in) long

COMMON CUTTLEFISH

MARBLED CHITON

RAMSHORN SNAIL

COMMON OCTOPUS

COMMON WHELK

TRITON'S TRUMPET

BIGFIN REEF SQUID

NAUTILUS

ONELESS BODIES

ugs and snails have no bones. Their soft bodies consist
a head, a central part containing the organs, and an
derside, or "foot", that they use for moving. The head
rries one or two pairs of tentacles that contain eyes and
her sense organs.

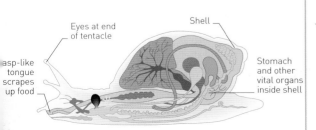

Eyes at end
of tentacle

Shell

asp-like
tongue
scrapes
up food

Stomach
and other
vital organs
inside shell

SHELL SHAPES

Most snails have spiral shells, which come in many shapes and sizes. More unusual types of shells usually belong to sea snails. Among the variations are elegantly twisted cones, irregular shapes bristling with spikes, and flat shells like caps.

SPINDLE SHAPE   IRREGULAR   SPIRAL SHAPE

CLUB SHAPE   PEAR SHAPE   CAP SHAPE   EGG SHAPE

HABITATS

There are tens of thousands of different slugs and snails living in a wide variety of habitats. They are found on mountains and seabeds, and in rivers, forests, and gardens.

SEA
Many slugs and snails live on coral reefs and in warm seas. A few occur at great depths.

FRESH WATER
Ponds, lakes, streams, and rivers are all common habitats for freshwater snails.

LAND
Few snails can survive in a dry habitat. Most, like slugs, thrive only in damp places.

SALTWATER FISH

Fish that live in the sea are known as saltwater, or marine, fish. There are around 16,000 marine species.

HARLEQUIN TUSKFISH

CROWNED SQUIRRELFISH

BUTTERFLY BLENNY

FOXFACE

TURBOT

BANDED ARCHER FISH

COMMON BLUESTRIPE SNAPPER

CLOWN TRIGGERFISH

SEAHORSE

EUROPEAN PLAICE

BLUEFISH

ATLANTIC MACKEREL

RED MULLET

ROCKLING

JOHN DORY

SPOTTED BOXFISH

VARIEGATED LIZARDFISH

LONG-SPINED SEA SCORPION

MEDITERRANEAN PARROTFISH

WEEDY SEADRAGON

LONG-SPINE PUFFERFISH

BLUE-SPOTTED SEA BREAM

BROWN MEAGRE

EMPEROR ANGELFISH

ROYAL GRAMMA

HARLEQUIN SWEETLIPS

COMMON SOLE

RED BANDFISH

FLYING GURNARD

STONEFISH

TASSELLED SCORPIONFISH

CLOWN ANEMONEFISH

TIGER SHARK

Fish

Fish can be found in nearly every type of watery environment, from mountain streams to the deepest oceans. They range from 12 mm (0.5 in) to 16 m (53 ft) in length, and there are more than 30,000 species.

ANATOMY

Most fish have streamlined bodies, so they can move easily through the water. They are covered in scales and breathe through gills – organs on each side of the head that collect oxygen from water.

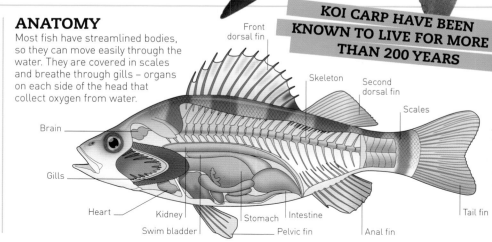

KOI CARP HAVE BEEN KNOWN TO LIVE FOR MORE THAN 200 YEARS

Front dorsal fin

Skeleton

Second dorsal fin

Scales

Brain

Gills

Heart

Kidney

Stomach

Intestine

Swim bladder

Pelvic fin

Anal fin

Tail fin

FRESHWATER FISH

Around 14,000 fish species live in fresh (non-salty) water in lakes, streams, rivers, and ponds. Some fish, known as euryhaline fish, can adapt to live in salty or fresh water.

ZEBRA MORAY

SARGASSUM FISH

GLASS CATFISH

RIVER HATCHETFISH

CHIPOKAE

GOLDFISH

SIAMESE FIGHTING FISH

UMPETFISH

POWDER BLUE SURGEON FISH

ELEPHANT NOSE FISH

SPOTTED CLIMBING PERCH

MEXICAN TETRA

SPOTTED GARDEN EEL

KOI CARP

LONGSNOUT DISTICHODUS

GREEN SUNFISH

GARFISH

TIGER SHOVELNOSE CATFISH

STRIPED ANOSTOMUS

WHITE SPOTTED PUFFER

CLOWN KNIFEFISH

RED PIRANHA

EUROPEAN EEL

CLOWN LOACH

ARCTIC CHAR

EUROPEAN PERCH

ATLANTIC COD

PADDLEFISH

NILE TILAPIA FISH

RED LIONFISH

RAINBOW TROUT

BURBOT

TYPES OF FISH

here are three main types fish: jawless, bony, and rtilaginous. Bony species ake up the highest number 7,000), then cartilaginous (970), d finally the jawless species (100).

JAWLESS FISH
This is the oldest type of fish. They have no jaws or scales.

BONY FISH
These are the only fish with a skeleton made of bone.

CARTILAGINOUS FISH
These are similar to bony fish, but have a skeleton made of cartilage.

CARING FATHERS

Fish don't usually take care of their young. However, for a few species, including the seahorse, the male carries the fertilized eggs in a pouch until they hatch.

Eggs kept safely in pouch

MALE SEAHORSE

DEFENCE

ost fish do not have eapons (such as spines) n their bodies to defend emselves, so they do ever things to make emselves look bigger disappear from view.

SWIMMING IN GROUPS
A group of fish swimming in a school looks to a predator like one big fish.

BURIED IN SAND
Flat fish can alter the colour and pattern of their skin so they can hide by lying flat in the sand.

HIDING IN ANEMONE
Clownfish hide in the stinging tentacles of sea anemones to avoid predators.

BALLOONING UP
When threatened porcupinefish inflate their bodies to make sharp spines stand up.

Sharks

Sharks have prowled the oceans for 400 million years, which means they existed before the dinosaurs. In all that time they have hardly changed at all, perhaps because they are so perfectly suited to their environment. There are around 500 different species of sharks.

ANATOMY

Sharks have a skeleton made of cartilage, not bone. Most species have eight fins, and many rows of teeth. A strong tail provides them with movement and direction.

First dorsal fin

Skin made up of rough, tooth-like scales

Eyes adapted to see in dark water

Skeleton made of cartilage

Second dorsal fin

Upper lobe of tail

Lower lobe of tail

Pelvic fin

5–7 gill slits

SHARP TEETH

TYPES OF SHARKS

Sharks vary in size enormously. The slow-moving whale shark is about 8 m (26 ft) long, while the dwarf lanternshark is smaller than a human hand. Some eat large animals, such as seals, while others feed on tiny plankton.

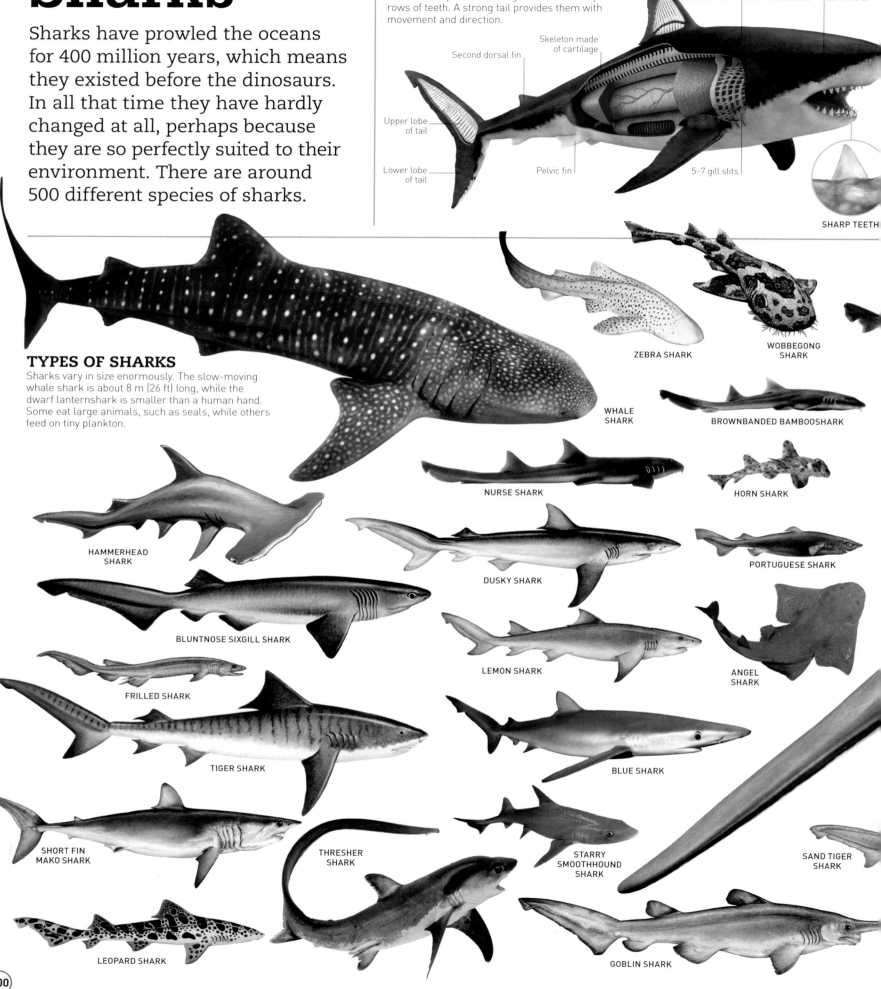

ZEBRA SHARK

WOBBEGONG SHARK

WHALE SHARK

BROWNBANDED BAMBOOSHARK

NURSE SHARK

HORN SHARK

HAMMERHEAD SHARK

DUSKY SHARK

PORTUGUESE SHARK

BLUNTNOSE SIXGILL SHARK

LEMON SHARK

ANGEL SHARK

FRILLED SHARK

TIGER SHARK

BLUE SHARK

SHORT FIN MAKO SHARK

THRESHER SHARK

STARRY SMOOTHHOUND SHARK

SAND TIGER SHARK

LEOPARD SHARK

GOBLIN SHARK

ENSES

As well as having excellent eyesight, hearing, and sense of smell, sharks have an extra sense that humans do not have: electrical sensing. Special pores in their skin pick up electrical fields generated by other animals.

SNOUT
Two nasal cavities give the shark an acute sense of smell.

Nasal cavities

EYES
A shark's eyes are about 10 times more sensitive to light than human eyes.

Highly sensitive eyesight

Ampullae of Lorenzini (electroreceptors)

ELECTRICAL SENSORS
The snout contains cells that sharks use to "receive" electric signals from nearby creatures.

LETHAL JAWS

To catch its prey, a great white shark lifts its snout, drops its upper jaw, sticks out its lower jaw, and takes a large bite. Sharks' teeth are sharp, often serrated, so they can rip through flesh easily.

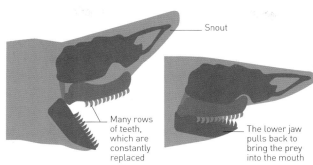

Snout

Many rows of teeth, which are constantly replaced

The lower jaw pulls back to bring the prey into the mouth

MISTAKEN IDENTITY

Although there are around 500 shark species, only 25 have been known to attack humans. This may be because they mistake people for fish, seals, sea lions, or turtles.

SEA TURTLE

SEA LION

HUMAN SURFER

SHARKS USUALLY LET GO AFTER EACH BITE THEY TAKE OUT OF THEIR PREY

RELATIVES

Rays, skates, and sawfish are flattened fish that are related to sharks. They too have a skeleton made of cartilage. These fish have existed on Earth for at least 150 million years.

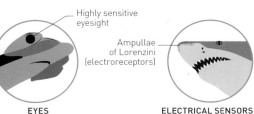

PORT JACKSON SHARK

MEGAMOUTH SHARK

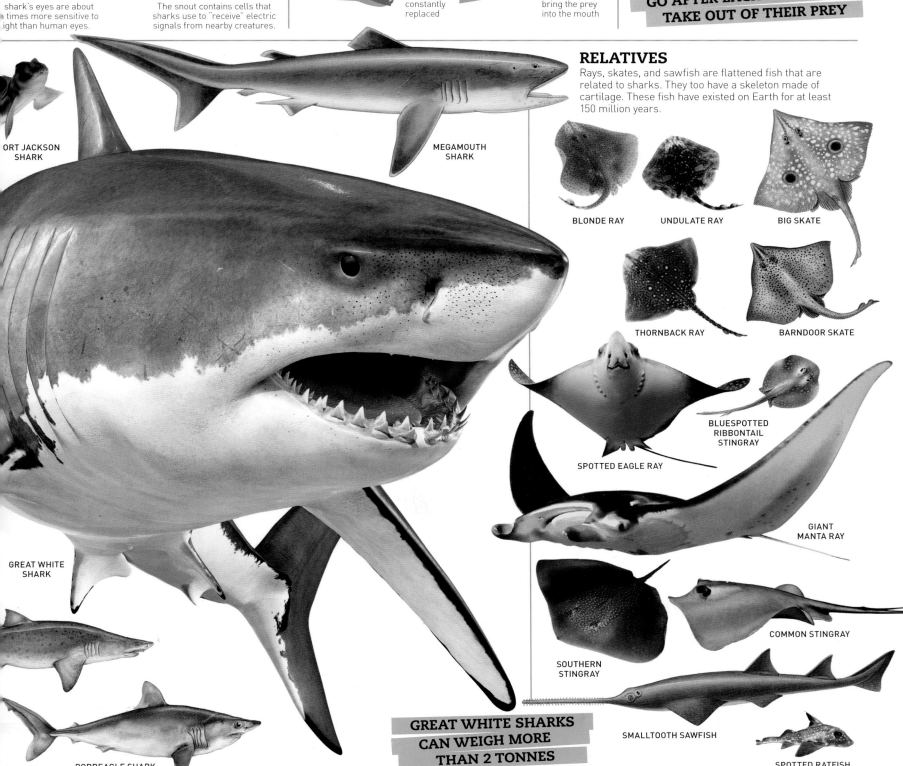

GREAT WHITE SHARK

GREAT WHITE SHARK

PORBEAGLE SHARK

GREAT WHITE SHARKS CAN WEIGH MORE THAN 2 TONNES

BLONDE RAY

UNDULATE RAY

BIG SKATE

THORNBACK RAY

BARNDOOR SKATE

BLUESPOTTED RIBBONTAIL STINGRAY

SPOTTED EAGLE RAY

GIANT MANTA RAY

SOUTHERN STINGRAY

COMMON STINGRAY

SMALLTOOTH SAWFISH

SPOTTED RATFISH

Seashells

The shells that wash up on beaches are the empty homes of soft-bodied sea animals called molluscs. Shells come in amazing shapes and colours. Some have two joined halves, others are in one piece, often a coil or a spiral. No two, even of the same type, are ever identical.

WHO NEEDS A SHELL?

Molluscs have easily damaged bodies and are too slow moving to hurry away from danger. A rigid shell provides a safe place to retreat into or close up tightly when predators are around. Empty shells make useful shelters for other animals.

THERE ARE MORE THAN 50,000 KNOWN SPECIES OF MOLLUSCS

LIMPET
Tucked beneath its shell, a limpet clinging tightly to a rock is very difficult to dislodge.

Two parts open on a hinge

FLAME SCALLOP
It is hard for a predator to open a scallop shell once the hinged halves are firmly shut.

Snail's large foot emerges

COMMON WHELK
Like its land-based cousins, this sea snail pulls itself into its shell to escape danger.

HERMIT CRAB
This soft-bellied crab makes its home in discarded sea snail shells.

SHORE CRAB
Crabs regularly shed their own shells. Until a new one hardens, a "borrowed" scallop shell can provide protection.

INSIDE A SHELL

The whorls or coils of a spiral seashell form around a central inner pole, or pillar. As the animal inside grows bigger, further whorls are added. The smallest and oldest whorls are at the top of the shell.

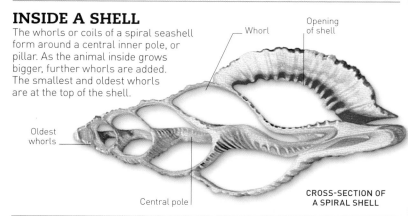

Whorl

Opening of shell

Oldest whorls

Central pole

CROSS-SECTION OF A SPIRAL SHELL

SIZE COMPARISON

The biggest molluscs on Earth are the giant clams, which can weigh as much as 227 kg (500 lb). The smallest shells belong to some minute sea snails, several of which would fit on a thumbnail.

LARGEST SHELL: GIANT CLAM
1.2 m (4 ft)

SMALLEST SHELL: SEA SNAIL
1 mm (0.04 in)

HINGED SHELLS

Many sea animals – such as clams, scallops, and oysters – are bivalves. Their shells are divided into two parts called valves that are joined by a hinge. The animal opens the shell to feed and closes it to take refuge.

CHICKEN VENUS

AUSTRALIAN BROOCH CLAM

GIANT RAZOR SHELL

PACIFIC THORNY OYSTER

PEARL OYSTER

SNAIL SHELLS

The largest group of seashells are those of the sea snails. These are endlessly varied in size, shape, and pattern. There are species that twist like corkscrews, while others coil or look like caps or shiny eggs. The animals that live in these shells creep slowly about on a large fleshy foot.

COMMON EGG COWRIE

HUMPBACK COWRIE

EYED COWRIE

HONEY COWRIE

TROSCHEL'S MUREX

SCARLET CONE

TEXTILE CONE

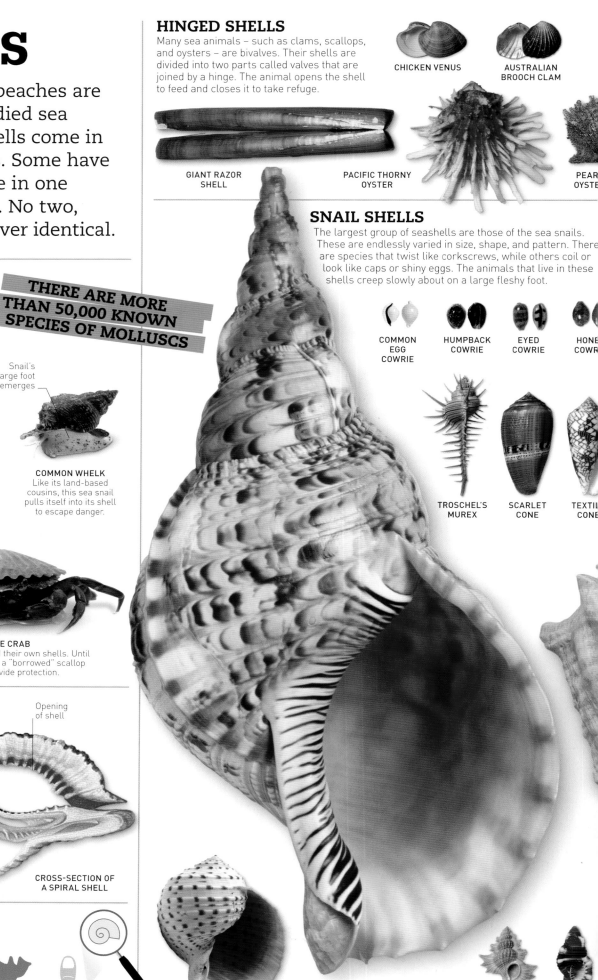

TRITON'S TRUMPET

SPOTTED TUN

MAPLE LEAF TRITON

ROBIN REDBREAST TRITON

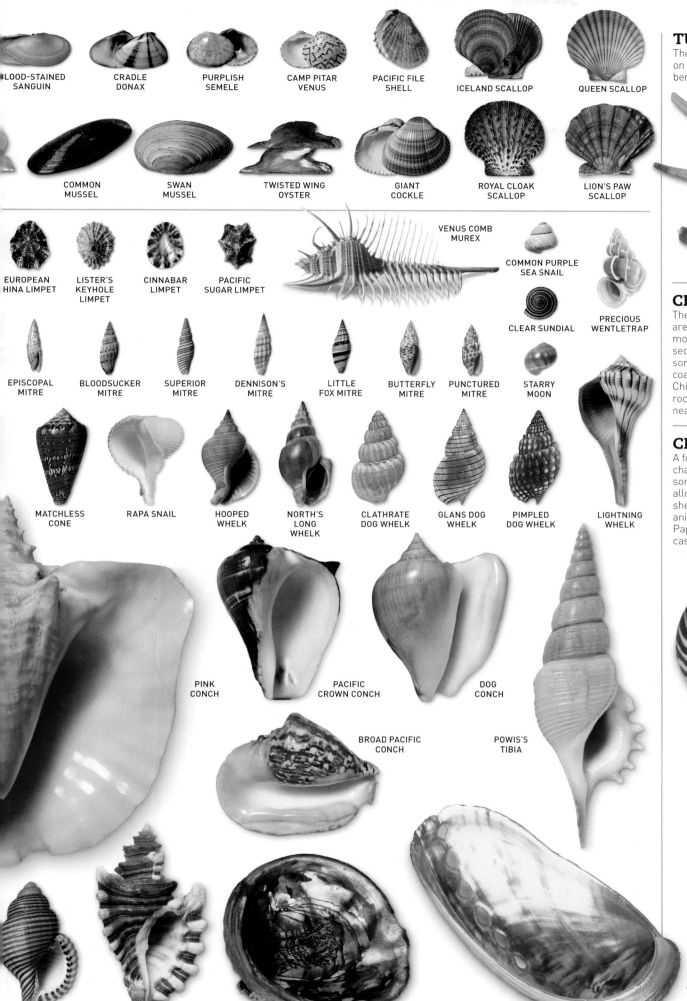

BLOOD-STAINED SANGUIN

CRADLE DONAX

PURPLISH SEMELE

CAMP PITAR VENUS

PACIFIC FILE SHELL

ICELAND SCALLOP

QUEEN SCALLOP

COMMON MUSSEL

SWAN MUSSEL

TWISTED WING OYSTER

GIANT COCKLE

ROYAL CLOAK SCALLOP

LION'S PAW SCALLOP

EUROPEAN HINA LIMPET

LISTER'S KEYHOLE LIMPET

CINNABAR LIMPET

PACIFIC SUGAR LIMPET

VENUS COMB MUREX

COMMON PURPLE SEA SNAIL

CLEAR SUNDIAL

PRECIOUS WENTLETRAP

EPISCOPAL MITRE

BLOODSUCKER MITRE

SUPERIOR MITRE

DENNISON'S MITRE

LITTLE FOX MITRE

BUTTERFLY MITRE

PUNCTURED MITRE

STARRY MOON

MATCHLESS CONE

RAPA SNAIL

HOOPED WHELK

NORTH'S LONG WHELK

CLATHRATE DOG WHELK

GLANS DOG WHELK

PIMPLED DOG WHELK

LIGHTNING WHELK

PINK CONCH

PACIFIC CROWN CONCH

DOG CONCH

BROAD PACIFIC CONCH

POWIS'S TIBIA

LESSER GIRDLED TRITON

ANGULAR TRITON

RED ABALONE

DONKEY'S EAR ABALONE

TUSK SHELLS

These seashells are not often found on the beach. Most of them live buried beneath the sand in deep water.

ELEPHANT TUSK

EUROPEAN TUSK SHELL

BEAUTIFUL TUSK

CHITONS

The shells of chitons are made of eight movable, overlapping sections. They are sometimes called coat-of-mail shells. Chitons live under rocks and stones near the shore.

WEST INDIAN CHITON

MARBLED CHITON

CHAMBERED SHELLS

A few shells are divided inside into chambers. In the squid-like Nautilus, some chambers are gas-filled, which allows the shell to float. The chambered shell of the Spirula squid is inside the animal, not outside. The similar-looking Paper-nautilus "shell" is the empty egg case of an animal called an argonaut.

NAUTILUS

COMMON SPIRULA

PAPER-NAUTILUS

FROGS AND TOADS
There are around 5,860 species of frogs and toads in total. They live on every continent except Antarctica.

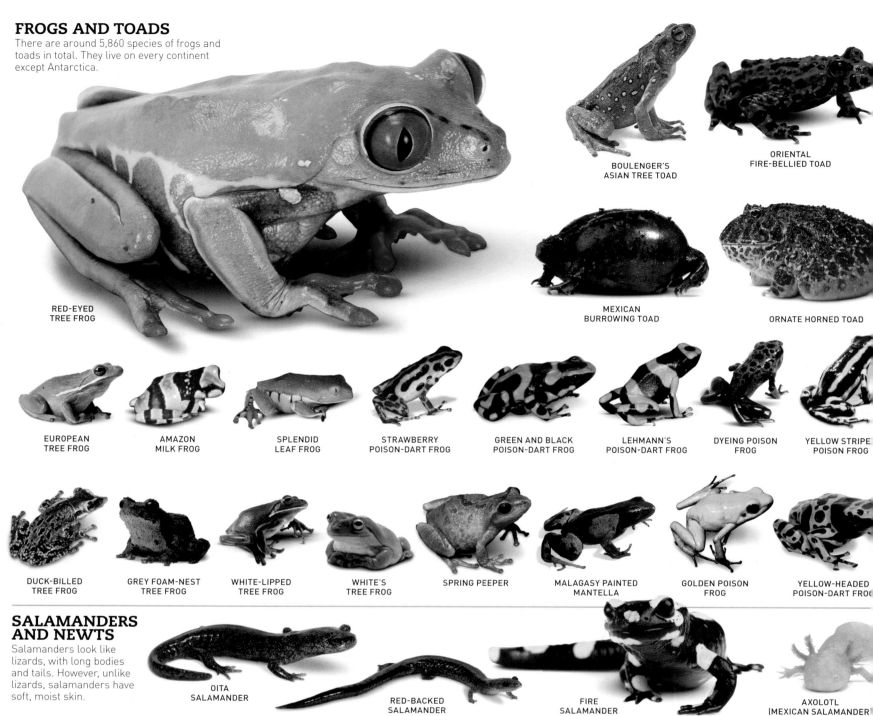

RED-EYED
TREE FROG

BOULENGER'S
ASIAN TREE TOAD

ORIENTAL
FIRE-BELLIED TOAD

MEXICAN
BURROWING TOAD

ORNATE HORNED TOAD

EUROPEAN
TREE FROG

AMAZON
MILK FROG

SPLENDID
LEAF FROG

STRAWBERRY
POISON-DART FROG

GREEN AND BLACK
POISON-DART FROG

LEHMANN'S
POISON-DART FROG

DYEING POISON
FROG

YELLOW STRIPE
POISON FROG

DUCK-BILLED
TREE FROG

GREY FOAM-NEST
TREE FROG

WHITE-LIPPED
TREE FROG

WHITE'S
TREE FROG

SPRING PEEPER

MALAGASY PAINTED
MANTELLA

GOLDEN POISON
FROG

YELLOW-HEADED
POISON-DART FROG

SALAMANDERS AND NEWTS
Salamanders look like lizards, with long bodies and tails. However, unlike lizards, salamanders have soft, moist skin.

OITA
SALAMANDER

RED-BACKED
SALAMANDER

FIRE
SALAMANDER

AXOLOTL
(MEXICAN SALAMANDER)

Amphibians

Amphibians are cold-blooded vertebrates that start life in the water, where they breathe using gills. As adults they develop lungs, which allow them to live on the land too. Frogs, toads, newts, and salamanders are all amphibians.

FEATURES
Most amphibians share some key features. They start life as eggs and then aquatic larvae, and need to live close to water as adults.

COLD-BLOODED

HAVE MOIST SKIN

MANY HATCH
AS TADPOLES

LAY EGGS TO
REPRODUCE

LIFECYCLE OF A FROG
Frogs lay hundreds of eggs because many of them get eaten by predators. Those that survive undertake remarkable changes, becoming tadpoles then frogs in a cycle that lasts 11 weeks.

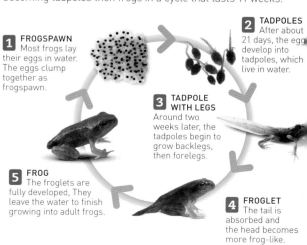

1 FROGSPAWN
Most frogs lay their eggs in water. The eggs clump together as frogspawn.

2 TADPOLES
After about 21 days, the eggs develop into tadpoles, which live in water.

3 TADPOLE WITH LEGS
Around two weeks later, the tadpoles begin to grow backlegs, then forelegs.

4 FROGLET
The tail is absorbed and the head becomes more frog-like.

5 FROG
The froglets are fully developed, They leave the water to finish growing into adult frogs.

EUROPEAN GREEN TOAD

RAUCOUS TOAD

NATTERJACK TOAD

GREEN CLIMBING TOAD

AFRICAN SQUARE-MARKED TOAD

MAJORCAN MIDWIFE TOAD

EUROPEAN COMMON TOAD

CHILEAN RED-SPOTTED TOAD

AMERICAN TOAD

MARSH FROG

BANDED BULLFROG

WOOD FROG

TUNGARA FROG

EDIBLE FROG

GOLIATH FROG

PARADOXICAL FROG

PICKEREL FROG

CANE TOAD

CROCODILE NEWT

SMOOTH NEWT

MARBLE NEWT

CAECILIANS

These limbless, worm-like amphibians are rarely seen. They live in soil, burrows, sor underwater and use their sharp, curved teeth to catch worms.

ASIAN CAECILIAN

HUNTING

A hunting frog usually [si]ts still until it sees [a] bug or worm [w]ithin range. Then [it] jumps or leans [fo]rward, catching [it]s prey on its long, [s]ticky tongue.

Tongue used to catch prey and deliver it to the frog's mouth

Large webbed feet provide power

PARENTAL CARE

Female midwife toads lay strings of eggs and pass them to the male during mating. The male carries the eggs on his back until they are ready to hatch.

Eggs

MOST TOXIC

The world's most poisonous frogs live in foliage and on the ground, in the hot, damp forests of Central and South America.

1 GOLDEN POISON-DART FROG
One of the most toxic animals on Earth, this frog only carries about 1 mg of poison, but that is enough to kill 10 humans. It lives in Colombia and stores poison in its skin.

2 BLACK-LEGGED DART FROG
A cousin of the golden poison-dart frog, this frog is also found in Colombia. Its poison is used on the tips of hunting darts.

3 PHANTASMAL POISON FROG
This bright red and white frog lives in Equador. It is tiny – only 1–4 cm (0.4–1.6 in) – but deadly. Despite its size, it carries enough toxin to kill a human.

HOW FROGS SWIM

[M]ost frogs propel [th]emselves through water [b]y pushing back against it [w]ith their webbed back feet. [T]he smaller forelimbs help [to] change direction.

1 PULL
The frog pulls its back legs towards its body by contracting its thigh muscles.

2 KICK
It pushes its forelimbs down to its sides as it begins to kick backwards.

3 STEER
As the legs finish the kick, the forelimbs reach forwards to steer through the water.

TURTLES

Most turtles spend nearly all their lives in water. For a few species, this is the sea, but there are also freshwater turtles, some of which are called terrapins. With streamlined shells and webbed feet or flippers, turtles are well made for swimming and diving.

Webbed feet with long toenails

LOGGERHEAD
SEA TURTLE

BLANDING TURTL

Wing-like
flippers

BIG-HEADED TURTLE

COMMON
SNAPPING TURTLE

SPOTTED
TURTLE

MISSISSIPPI
MAP TURTLE

NORTHERN
RED-BELLIED TURTLE

EUROPEA
POND TURTL

TORTOISES

These slow-moving land-dwellers have strong shells, often with a high dome that is difficult for predators to bite. They have short, bent legs and strong, stumpy feet.

RED-FOOTED
TORTOISE

SPUR-THIGHED
TORTOISE

HORSEFIELD
TORTOISE

GALAPAGOS TORTOISES, THE LARGEST IN THE WORLD, CAN GROW UP TO 1.2 M (4 FT) LONG AND WEIGH UP TO 270 KG (595 LB)

DESERT TORTOISE

ELONGATED
TORTOISE

SERRATED HINGE-
BACK TORTOISE

PANCAKE
TORTOISE

GALAPAGOS TORTOISE

LEOPARD TORTOISE

Turtles and tortoises

There were turtles and tortoises on Earth even before the dinosaurs. They all belong to the same scientific group. The main difference between them is that turtles live in water and tortoises on land. All have shells and lay eggs.

INSIDE THE SHELL

Turtles and tortoises have an unusual skeleton. Their ribs, spine, and some other bones form part of the shell. In nearly all species, the shell has a bony inner layer covered by thin plates of keratin, the same material as human fingernails.

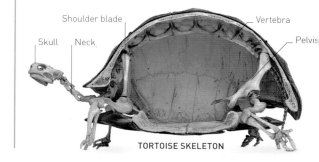

Shoulder blade

Vertebra

Skull

Neck

Pelvis

TORTOISE SKELETON

COMMON SNAKE
NECKED TURTLE

YELLOW SLIDER

WEST AFRICAN
BLACK TURTLE

RED-EARED
SLIDER

POND TERRAPIN

CHINESE SOFT-SHELLED TURTLE

COMMON MUSK TURTLE

LITTLE PAINTED TURTLE

WOOD TURTLE

The shell can grow
up to 122 cm (48 in)
in length

DIAMONDBACK
TERRAPIN

GOLDEN COIN
TURTLE

ALDABRA GIANT
TORTOISE

RADIATED TORTOISE

INDIAN STARRED
TORTOISE

HERMANN'S TORTOISE

LIFECYCLE OF A TURTLE

All sea turtles come ashore to lay their eggs. They visit the same nesting beaches year after year. Depending on the species, the female may lay 50–200 eggs.

1 LAYING EGGS
The female lays her soft-shelled eggs in a scraped-out nesting chamber.

2 HATCHLINGS HEAD OUT
The newly hatched babies dig their way out of the nest and crawl to the sea.

4 RETURN JOURNEY
Between 25 and 50 years of age, the adults make their first egg-laying trip back to the beach where they hatched.

3 OCEAN LIFE
The young turtles spend many years entirely at sea, eating and growing.

HIDING FROM DANGER

Tortoises move too slowly to run away from their natural predators, which include ravens, foxes, and dogs. Fortunately, they carry their own hiding place, which often keeps them safe until the danger has passed.

1 DETECTS A THREAT
A tortoise has a keen sense of smell that tells it when a likely predator is lurking nearby.

2 RETREATS INTO SHELL
Pulling in its legs and long, flexible neck, the tortoise disappears right into its shell. It is safe from the predator.

Lizards

With more than 5,500 species, lizards are the largest group of reptiles on Earth. They are cold-blooded animals that live in every continent except Antarctica. Lizards are useful predators of insect pests.

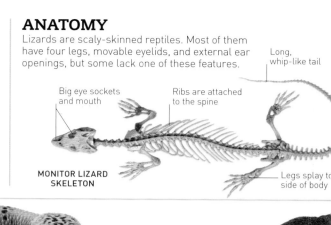

GECKOS

These small lizards have about 500,000 hairs on each foot that provide them with good adhesion for climbing smooth surfaces. They eat spiders and mosquitoes. Some make a clicking noise that sounds like "gecko".

TURQUOISE DWARF GECKO

LEOPARD GECKO

RING-TAILED GECKO

KUHL'S FLYING GECKO

TOKAY

MARBLED GECKO

WONDER GECKO

PALM GECKO

CRESTED GECKO

MEDITERRANEAN GECKO

MADAGASCAR DAY GECKO

AFRICAN FAT-TAILED GECKO

COMMON HOUSE GECKO

WESTERN BANDED GECKO

MONITOR LIZARDS

These large lizards are strong, powerful, and fast swimmers. They have a forked tongue that can detect scent in the air and water. The largest lizard on Earth, the Komodo dragon, is a monitor lizard.

DUMERIL'S MONITOR LIZARD

ASIAN WATER MONITOR

SPINY-TAILED MONITOR LIZARD

SAVANNA MONITOR LIZARD

GREEN TREE MONITOR LIZARD

KOMODO DRAGON

IGUANAS

Iguanas live in the tropical rainforests and deserts of the Americas, Fiji, and Madagascar. They can use their long tails like a whip for defence. The Marine Iguana is the only lizard that finds food in the sea, where it eats seaweed.

GREEN SPINY IGUANA

MARINE IGUANA

MADAGASCAN COLLARED IGUANA

BLACK IGUANA

GREEN IGUANA

NEW TAIL

[So]me lizards can detach their tails [to] escape from or deter a predator. [Af]ter the tail has fallen off, the area [he]als like a wound. After about ten [da]ys a new tail begins to grow.

> A LIZARD'S DETACHED TAIL GOES ON MOVING FOR A WHILE TO DISTRACT THE PREDATOR

1 TAIL FALLS OFF
The lizard detaches the end of its tail when attacked or threatened. The point of breakage begins to heal.

2 GROWING BACK
Within 10 days or so, a new tail starts growing. By about day 25, the new tail is strong enough for the lizard to flick it.

3 NEW FOR OLD
After about 60 days, the new tail is complete. It is not exactly the same as the original tail, as it uses cartilage instead of bone.

SIZE COMPARISON

The world's smallest lizard fits on a fingernail. The biggest weighs about 70 kg (154 lb) and can hunt down large animals.

BRITISH VIRGIN ISLAND DWARF GECKO
18 mm (0.75 in) long

KOMODO DRAGON
3.1 m (10 ft) long

CHAMELEONS

[C]hameleons mainly live in trees. [Th]ey have long tongues for catching [in]sects and protruding eyes that [m]ove independently of one another. [Th]e chameleon can swivel each [ey]e around to look at two different [thi]ngs at once.

JACKSON'S CHAMELEON

MEDITERRANEAN CHAMELEON

COLOUR CHANGE
Chameleons have special skin cells containing tiny sacs of different coloured pigments. The lizard's moods – such as anger and fear – cause changes in its body that trigger the release of colour from the sacs.

PANTHER CHAMELEON
A calm chameleon is usually a pale green colour. When it wants to show off to a possible mate, the chameleon may display all sorts of colours at once.

Protruding eyes that move in different directions

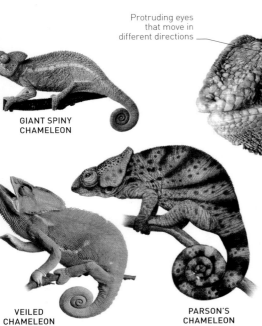

GIANT SPINY CHAMELEON

VEILED CHAMELEON

PARSON'S CHAMELEON

Two groups of toes on each foot help the chameleon hang on to the branch

PANTHER CHAMELEON

LEGLESS LIZARDS

These lizards look like snakes, but can be distinguished from them by several features. Unlike snakes, they have eyelids, external ear openings, and a tail that can break off if the lizard is attacked by a predator.

SLOW WORM

SLENDER GLASS LIZARD

EUROPEAN GLASS LIZARD

SKINKS

Skinks have very long, rounded bodies and pointed heads. Their legs are short, or even absent, and they like to burrow into soft, sandy ground. They eat snails, slugs, and insects.

FIVE-LINED SKINK

SANDFISH SKINK

PERCIVAL'S LANCE SKINK

FIRE SKINK

OTHER LIZARDS

There are many types of lizards. Some are small families, such as the seven tegu species, while others are large, such as the 391 species of anole lizards.

KNIGHT ANOLE

GREEN ANOLE

THAI WATER DRAGON

FRILLED LIZARD

RED TEGU

Snakes

There are several thousand different types of snakes. Most of them are not venomous or dangerous to people, and many are beautiful, with bright colours and patterns. All snakes swallow their prey whole.

INSIDE A SNAKE

A snake's inner organs are designed to fit in a long, narrow space. These organs are very stretchy, allowing prey to be swallowed whole.

A SNAKE'S HEART CAN SHIFT AROUND TO AVOID INJURY FROM SWALLOWED PREY

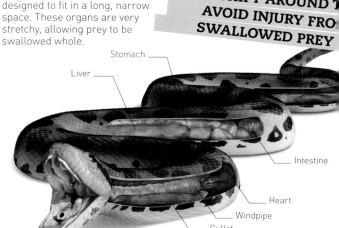

Stomach
Liver
Intestine
Heart
Windpipe
Gullet

WHAT MAKES A SNAKE?

Snakes are cold-blooded and need outside heat, like the Sun, to keep warm. A snake smells with its tongue and "hears" by picking up vibrations.

LIDLESS EYES   COLD-BLOODED   NO EARS   FORKED TONGUE

COLUBRIDS

With their diverse colours and sizes, the colubrids make up a very large group. Few of them are venomous. Some kill by constriction.

EASTERN PINE SNAKE

DIADEM SNAKE

CALIFORNIA KINGSNAKE

LAVENDER STRIPED KINGSNAKE

RED CORNSNAKE

VIPERS

Found in nearly all countries, vipers are venomous. They have squat bodies and broad heads. Some have infrared sensors under their eyes that help them hunt in the dark.

 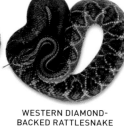   

MALAYAN PIT VIPER   GABOON VIPER

WESTERN DIAMOND-BACKED RATTLESNAKE

TAYLOR'S CANTIL VIPER

FER-DE-LANCE

BOAS

These include the biggest snakes in the world. Most boas live in the Americas or Africa. They kill prey by squeezing (constricting) it.

ROSY BOA

COOK'S TREE BOA

RUBBER BOA

RAINBOW BOA

EAST AFRICAN SAND BOA

COBRAS AND RELATIVES

All cobras are venomous. Some have very fast-acting poisons strong enough to kill large animals, or a human.

ALBINO MONOCLED COBRA

EGYPTIAN COBRA

CENTRAL AMERICAN CORAL SNAKE

RED SPITTING COBRA

KING COBRA

PYTHONS

These often very big constricting snakes come from Asia and Africa. Some types are popular as pets.

BURMESE PYTHON

ALBINO BURMESE PYTHON

SPOTTED PYTHON

MOST DEADLY

Many people die from snake bites. These five snakes are among the most venomous.

FER-DE-LANCE
The most feared snake in South America, it tends to live dangerously close to humans.

PUFF ADDER
Thick-bodied and slow, this African viper blows up its body and hisses if it feels threatened.

AUSTRALIAN TAIPAN
Anyone bitten by this taipan needs immediate medical treatment.

KING COBRA
This long snake is found in India and Southeast Asia. Just one of its bites could kill an elephant.

BLACK MAMBA
The fast-moving mamba is responsible for many human deaths in its native Africa.

THE BIG SQUEEZE
A constrictor, like a python or boa, catches its prey by striking fast and seizing the animal with its sharp teeth. Then the snake wraps its body around the victim and suffocates it by gradually tightening its coils.

1 GETTING A GRIP
The snake squeezes its victim to death.

2 HEAD FIRST
Its prey held head first, the snake is ready to eat.

3 SWALLOWING DOWN
Mouth open wide, the snake gulps down its meal.

A POISONOUS BITE
Venomous snakes have hollow fangs through which poison is squirted from glands in their mouth. In some species, the fangs move forwards on a hinge when the snake bites its victim.

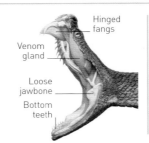

Hinged fangs
Venom gland
Loose jawbone
Bottom teeth

COLOSSAL CONSTRICTOR
A 60-million-year-old fossil of a monster snake was found in Colombia. Named Titanoboa, it was 15 m (50 ft) long and weighed 1,130 kg (2,500 lb).

Titanoboa:
Length 15 m (50 ft)

Average human:
Height 1.8 m (6 ft)

YELLOW RATSNAKE

RUTHVEN'S KINGSNAKE

CALIFORNIA MOUNTAIN KINGSNAKE

BROWN TREESNAKE

ROUGH GREEN SNAKE

BANDED FLYING SNAKE

COMMON GARTER SNAKE

HORNED DESERT VIPER

ORSINI'S VIPER

PRAIRIE RATTLESNAKE

COPPERHEAD

PUFF ADDER

COMMON ADDER

ASP VIPER

PARAGUAYAN ANACONDA

GREEN ANACONDA

DUMERIL'S BOA

CALABAR GROUND BOA

COMMON BOA

AFTER A LARGE MEAL A BOA MAY NOT EAT AGAIN FOR WEEKS OR EVEN MONTHS

WHAT'S THE DIFFERENCE?

The crocodile's snout is more pointed than the alligator's and the fourth tooth on the crocodile's lower jaw sticks out when the mouth is closed. Gharials have narrow, greatly elongated jaws.

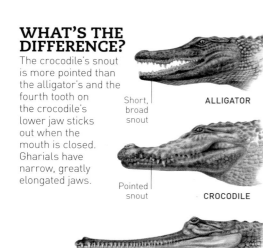

Short, broad snout

ALLIGATOR

Pointed snout

CROCODILE

Long, narrow snout

GHARIAL

ARMOURED BODY

A crocodilian's long body and tail are covered in tough scales. The short legs allow limited movement on land. With eyes, ears, and nostrils on top of its head, a crocodilian can hunt while almost fully under water. The lungs hold enough oxygen for a 15-minute dive.

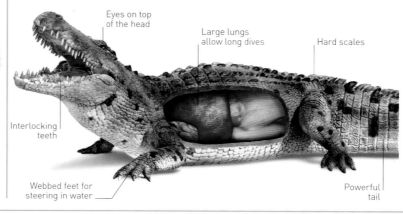

Eyes on top of the head

Large lungs allow long dives

Hard scales

Interlocking teeth

Webbed feet for steering in water

Powerful tail

PARENTING

Eggs are laid in a nest built and fiercely guarded by the female. After the eggs have hatched, the mother usually remains with her young for a time to protect them.

JUST HATCHED
The mother carries her newly hatched young in her mouth to take them to the water.

Crocodiles and alligators

Crocodilians – crocodiles, alligators, and gharials – have been around since the time of the dinosaurs. They use stealth to ambush prey and their ferocious jaws to kill. These reptiles live partly in water and partly on land.

SURPRISE AMBUSH

Feeding on fish, birds, reptiles, and mammals, crocodilians are masters of the surprise attack. Small prey is swallowed whole, but larger animals must first be drowned before they can be eaten.

1 WAITS
With just eyes, ears, and tip of snout above the water, a crocodile waits almost motionless for unsuspecting prey to come near.

2 LUNGES
Without warning, the crocodile launches itself from the water and seizes its victim with powerful jaws that snap shut around the animal.

3 KILLS
With a strong grip on its prey, the crocodile dives down beneath the water and waits for the animal to drown.

CROCODILES

Found in tropical regions, these reptiles occupy both freshwater and saltwater habitats. The two largest and most dangerous species are the saltwater crocodile and the Nile crocodile.

SALTWATER CROCODILE

WITH THE STRONGEST BITE OF ANY LIVING CREATURE, A MALE SALTWATER CROCODILE CAN CRUSH A BUFFALO'S SKULL

Sharp teeth to tear prey

HARIALS

[Th]e endangered gharial occurs only in the rivers of India. Its long
[ja]ws are ideal for catching fish. Unlike other crocodilians, the female
[do]es not carry her young but she does give them some care.

LLIGATORS

[Ap]art from the rare Chinese alligator, alligators are found only
[in t]he USA. Their close relatives, the caimans, live in Central and
[So]uth America. All these creatures live in freshwater swamps
[an]d rivers, and feed on fish, birds, and mammals.

GHARIAL

AMERICAN ALLIGATOR

CUVIER'S DWARF CAIMAN

CHINESE ALLIGATOR

YACARE CAIMAN

BROAD-SNOUTED CAIMAN

SPECTACLED CAIMAN

CUBAN CROCODILE

DWARF CROCODILE

Large scales
armoured with
bony deposits

SIAMESE CROCODILE

FRESHWATER CROCODILE

Powerful tail propels
crocodile through water

NILE CROCODILE

Eggs

The young of many animals develop inside eggs, which provide protection and food. All birds and most fish and insects are egg-layers. Others include reptiles, frogs and toads, slugs and snails, and even a few mammals.

EGG SHAPES

Most commonly, bird eggs are oval-shaped. Seabirds nesting on cliffs lay pear-shaped eggs, which roll in a circle but not off an edge. A few birds, including some owls, lay round eggs.

OVAL
Typical shape for most birds' eggs.

PEAR-SHAPED
Unlikely to roll right off a bare ledge.

SPHERICAL
Usually laid by birds that build deep nests.

CONICAL
These eggs pack closely in the nest for equal warmth.

INSIDE AN EGG

The developing bird, which is known as the "embryo", is cushioned inside a sac or bag full of fluid. The yellow yolk provides the embryo with most of its food, but the albumen, or "white", also gives it protein and water.

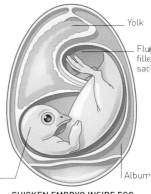

Yolk

Flu fille sac

Embryo (developing bird)

Album

CHICKEN EMBRYO INSIDE EGG

BIRD EGGS

Eggs come in lots of different colours and patterns, which may help to camouflage them from predators. The colours partly depend on the diet of the bird. If it eats plenty of calcium – which it might get from foods such as insects – it produces a lighter, whiter egg.

RUBY-THROATED HUMMINGBIRD

RUFOUS HUMMINGBIRD

PLAIN PRINIA

WOOD WARBLER

GREAT TIT

CETTI'S WARBLER

MARSH WARBLER

ROCK WREN

BLUE SHORTWING

BLACK BULBUL

MANILA NIGHTJAR

LESSER NIGHTHAWK

GREEN BROADBILL

AMERICAN ROBIN

QUAIL

COMMON STARLING

MAGNIFICENT RIFLEBIRD

GREY BUTCHERBIRD

KENTIS PLOVE

GREATER GOLDEN PLOVER

MASKED FINFOOT

CHICKEN

PEREGRINE FALCON

OSPREY

COMMON OYSTERCATCHER

EGYPTIAN VULTURE

COMMON GUILLEMOT

MUTE SWAN

BROWN KIWI

AUSTRALIAN EMU

INCUBATING AN EGG

The embryo inside an egg cannot develop without warmth. Parent birds provide this by sitting on their eggs until the chicks hatch out. The process is called incubation. A mother hen such as this one will sit for 21 days.

HEN INCUBATING HER EGGS

HATCHING OUT

The pictures below show a Japanese quail hatching out of its egg. First, the emerging chick starts chipping away at the shell with its beak. Eventually, the shell cracks apart and the chick kicks itself free of the egg.

1 STARTING TO HATCH The young chick starts chipping through the shell.

2 CRACKING OPEN The shell cracks open and falls into two parts.

3 KICKING FREE Using its legs and body, the chick struggles out.

4 HATCHED The exhausted chick rests for a while after hatching.

DUNNOCK

ANDEAN SPARROW

COMMON KINGFISHER

RICHARD'S PIPIT

CUCKOO SHRIKE

COMMON CUCKOO

GREEN WOOD-HOOPOE

HAWFINCH

JUNGLE CROW

RINGED PLOVER

JACKDAW

GUIRA CUCKOO

BARN OWL

CHIMANGO

NORTHERN LAPWING

GREY TINAMOU

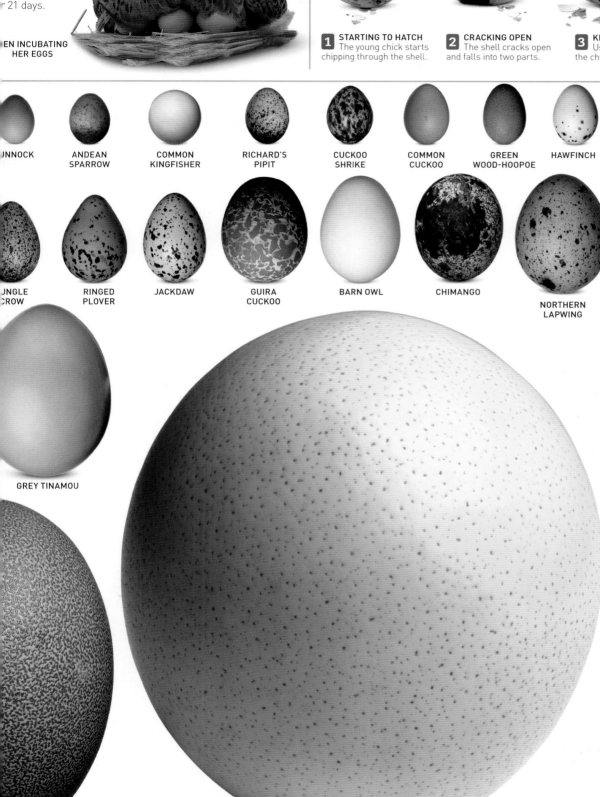

SOUTHERN CASSOWARY

OSTRICH

REPTILE EGGS

Most reptiles lay eggs. Crocodiles and tortoises have hard-shelled eggs – like birds' eggs – while the eggs of turtles, snakes, and lizards are soft and leathery.

AFRICAN DWARF CROCODILE

SPUR-THIGHED TORTOISE

GALAPAGOS GIANT TORTOISE

NILE MONITOR LIZARD

GRASS SNAKE

RAT SNAKE

AFRICAN HOUSE SNAKE

OTHER EGGS

Fish, insects, and slugs are among other egg-layers. Most produce very tiny eggs in large numbers. In some species, such as the dogfish, the eggs are held in a protective case.

GOLDFISH

RAINBOW TROUT

CHINESE OAK SILK MOTH CATERPILLAR

OWL BUTTERFLY CATERPILLAR

SLUG

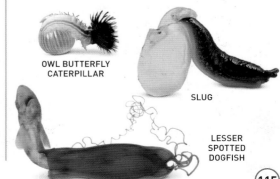

LESSER SPOTTED DOGFISH

Birds

Birds occupy almost every kind of habitat around the world – from hot deserts to the icy polar regions. Of the 10,200 species, some are larger than people while others are barely bigger than bees. All birds have feathers and most of them can fly.

WHAT IS A BIRD?

Any animal that has feathers is a bird. All birds have wings, even those species that cannot fly. Most birds also have very good eyesight and hearing.

EGGS
Birds reproduce by laying eggs and many build nests.

FEATHERS
These enable flight and also provide warmth.

FLIGHT
While most birds can fly, some only walk.

WARM-BLOODED
Like mammals, birds create their own body heat.

TOOTHLESS BEAK
Having no teeth, birds grind their food in a "gizzard".

CLAWED FEET
Feet and claws come in many different shapes.

INSIDE A BIRD

Birds have strong yet lightweight skeletons, and large chest muscles to power their wings. Flying burns energy and needs a lot of oxygen. Birds have a series of air sacs in their body to keep up the flow of oxygen through their lungs.

Birds have excellent eyesight

Crop, where food is stored

Lightweight bones enable flight

Lungs

Special air sacs pump air through the lungs

Gizzard

Clawed feet

FLIGHTLESS BIRDS

The largest of all birds, ostriches are too heavy to fly. They escape predators by running on strong legs. The smallest flightless birds are the chicken-sized kiwis. Their tiny wings are invisible beneath their thick plumage.

Long, powerful legs

KIWI

OSTRICH

OSTRICHES CAN SPRINT FASTER THAN MOST HORSES CAN GALLOP, REACHING SPEEDS OF UP TO 70 KM/H (43 MPH)

GAME BIRDS

These birds are hunted for food or sport. Most are ground-dwellers, taking flight only to escape from danger. They have strong feet and toes for scraping the ground to find food, and they can run fast.

INDIAN PEACOCK

SPRUCE GROUSE

GREY PARTRIDGE

COMMON PHEASANT

CALIFORNIAN QUAIL

TURKEY

CUCKOOS AND TURACOS

Turacos live only in Africa, whereas cuckoos are more widespread. Some cuckoo species trick other birds into raising their chicks by laying eggs in their nests.

GREAT SPOTTED CUCKOO

GREATER ROADRUNNER

RED-CRESTED TURACO

OWLS

These night hunters have forward-facing eyes and see well in poor light. Fringed feathers allow owls to fly without making a sound.

EURASIAN EAGLE OWL

LITTLE OWL

TOUCANS AND WOODPECKERS

These tree-living birds have strong gripping feet, with two toes pointing backwards and two forwards.

PILEATED WOODPECKER

GREAT SPOTTED WOODPECKER

RED-HEADED BARBET

TOCO TOUCAN

BIRDS OF PREY

Eagles, hawks, and falcons are all birds of prey. These swift predators have three things in common: hooked beaks, long talons, and superb eyesight.

RED KITE

BALD EAGLE

PENGUINS

Expert swimmers, penguins have wings that have evolved into flippers. Many species live in the icy waters around Antarctica. A few penguins live in warmer waters further north.

EMPEROR PENGUIN ANO CHICK

STORKS, IBISES, AND HERONS

These wading birds stalk prey in shallow waters. Storks and herons make lightning strikes for fish and insects, while ibises probe in mud and under plants.

GREEN HERON

SCARLET IBIS

GREY HERON

EUROPEAN WHITE STORK

PELICANS

The long-beaked pelicans, and their relatives the gannets, are fisheaters. Pelicans scoop up their catch in a large throat pouch.

BROWN PELICAN

NORTHERN GANNET

EAK VARIETY

bird's beak reflects its
et. For example, the
oonbill sweeps its beak
rough water like a shovel
 locate food. The sharp
eak of a woodpecker is
erfect for chiselling off
ee bark to reach insects.

SWEEPING IN WATER

CATCHING FLYING INSECTS

PICKING UP SURFACE PREY

TEARING MEAT

CUTTING FRUIT

CHISELLING WOOD

STABBING AND SPEARING PREY

PROBING MUD AND SAND

MULTI-PURPOSE

ABY BIRDS

mily life is usually
rief but very busy
riod. Most birds lay
eir eggs in a nest.
atchlings need
nstant feeding and
ow very quickly.
ce baby birds have
astered flying, they
ave the nest for good.

1 EGGS
Most birds sit on their eggs to keep them at the right temperature.

> **2 HATCHLINGS**
Blind and naked, the hatchlings rely on their parents for care and food.

> **3 FIVE-DAY-OLD CHICKS**
Now called "nestlings", the chicks' eyes open and small "pin" feathers develop.

> **4 NINE-DAY-OLD CHICKS**
The nestlings are now nearly feathered and their eyes are wide open.

> **5 READY TO FLEDGE**
At two weeks, the fledglings are ready to leave the nest and learn to fly.

IGEONS AND DOVES

th their round bodies, small bobbing
eads, and short beaks, pigeons
d doves are easily
cognized.

MOURNING DOVE

SPECKLED PIGEON

SOUTHERN CROWNED PIGEON

PARROTS AND COCKATOOS

These vibrantly coloured
tropical birds are well
known for their intelligence.

BLUE-CROWNED HANGING PARROTS

OLIVE-HEADED LORIKEET

RED-FAN PARROT

HUMMINGBIRDS AND SWIFTS

he tiny, acrobatic hummingbirds are
mong the smallest of all bird species.
vifts, known for their speed, can be
recognized by their very short
legs and small feet.

RAZILIAN RUBY

LUCIFER HUMMINGBIRD

WHITE-THROATED SWIFT

KINGFISHERS

Brightly coloured kingfishers
and their relatives are mostly
"sit-and-wait" predators, swooping
down from perches to snatch prey.

PIED KINGFISHER

LAUGHING KOOKABURRA

JAMAICAN TODY

WHITE-THROATED BEE-EATER

DUCKS, GEESE, AND SWANS

Found across the world, these water
birds have webbed feet and flattened
beaks. Nearly all species nest on or
beside the water.

PLUMED WHISTLING DUCK

BAIKAL TEAL

KING EIDER DUCK

BLACK SWAN

BAR-HEADED GOOSE

LONG-TAILED DUCK

PARROTS CAN COPY MANY SOUNDS, INCLUDING HUMAN WORDS AND LAUGHTER

CRANES

raceful cranes and their many relatives
e in both dry and wet habitats.
anes perform impressive
ourtship displays.

PURPLE GALLINULE

ORNCRAKE

AMERICAN COOT

LITTLE BUSTARD

GREY-CROWNED CRANE

WADERS, GULLS, AND AUKS

Auks, such as puffins, are
sea swimmers, while gulls
hunt on the wing. Waders
feed along muddy shores.

ATLANTIC PUFFIN

COMMON REDSHANK

HEERMAN'S GULL

EURASIAN OYSTERCATCHER

PIED AVOCET

PERCHING BIRDS

Most birds are perching birds – their
unique feet can grip even very slender
branches. Many species are songbirds.

BARN SWALLOW

EASTERN YELLOW ROBIN

LESSER BIRD OF PARADISE

EURASIAN SKYLARK

YELLOW WARBLER

DUNNOCK

WRENTIT

Birds of prey

Also known as "raptors", birds of prey have exceptional vision, grasping talons, and a sharp, hooked beak. Found on every continent apart from Antarctica, these spectacular hunters are divided into day-flying raptors and night-flying raptors, or owls.

WHAT MAKES A BIRD A RAPTOR?

Day-flying raptors in particular have excellent eyesight that allows them to spot prey from a distance and to calculate exactly when to strike. Many owls rely more on their keen hearing. Strong feet and talons are a raptor's main tools of attack, while the hooked beak is used for tearing meat.

CURVED BEAK
Powerful beaks can pierce prey, rip off skin, and tear flesh into chunks.

KEEN EYESIGHT
Large, forward-facing eyes enable raptors to detect and capture their prey.

KILLING FEET
Long, curved talons are designed to grasp prey such as rabbits.

AN EAGLE'S VISION IS AT LEAST FOUR TIMES MORE POWERFUL THAN THAT OF A HUMAN

SOARING HIGH

The large wings of some hawks and eagles allow them to soar high in the sky by riding warm air currents called thermals. Using little energy, they can glide for long periods while searching for prey.

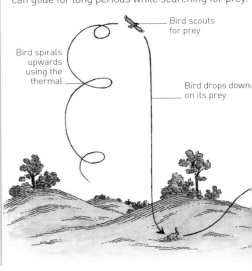

Bird scouts for prey

Bird spirals upwards using the thermal

Bird drops down on its prey

DAY-FLYING RAPTORS

As well as airborne hunters like hawks, eagles, and falcons, this group also includes the largely ground-dwelling secretary birds. Vultures, such as the Andean Condor, rarely kill prey and instead feed on dead animals.

GOLDEN EAGLE

WHITE-BELLIED SEA EAGLE

BALD EAGLE

BATELEUR

LIZARD BUZZARD

LONG-LEGGED BUZZARD

EURASIAN BUZZARD

AFRICAN HAWK EAGLE

NORTHERN HARRIER

HARRIS'S HAWK

NORTHERN GOSHAWK

OSPREY

RUPPELL'S VULTURE

TURKEY VULTURE

Uses a stone to break an egg

EGYPTIAN VULTURE

RED-TAILED HAWK

Large wingspan makes this the largest bird of prey

ANDEAN CONDOR

PALM NUT VULTURE

OWL PELLETS

Owls usually swallow their prey whole. They are unable to digest fur and bones, so they bring up pellets containing these undigested remains. The tawny owl pellet below reveals that the owl had dined on voles.

INSIDE A PELLET
All the bones shown here came from inside a single owl pellet.

WHOLE PELLET

VOLE SKULLS

LOWER JAWBONES

CURVED RIBS

VERTEBRAE

LEG BONES

HIP BONES

FRONT-LIMB BONES

SHOULDER BLADES

SNAIL KITE

MISSISSIPPI KITE

WHITE-TAILED KITE

AMERICAN KESTREL

LANNER FALCON

AFRICAN PYGMY FALCON

COMMON KESTREL

CRESTED CARACARA

STRIATED CARACARA

Diet includes snakes

Powerful legs are used to stamp on prey

SECRETARY BIRD

OWLS

Most owls are nocturnal, although some hunt at dawn and dusk. Only a very few are active in the daytime. Owls have superb hearing and they can see well in the dark. Flying silently on softly feathered wings, owls use stealth rather than speed to hunt their prey.

GREAT GREY OWL

URAL OWL

BENGAL EAGLE OWL

GREAT HORNED OWL

BARN OWL

BUFFY FISH OWL

SNOWY OWL

BURROWING OWLS

SPECTACLED OWL

NORTHERN HAWK OWL

SHORT-EARED OWL

LONG-EARED OWL

BLACK-AND-WHITE OWL

FERRUGINOUS PYGMY OWL

EASTERN SCREECH OWL

SOUTHERN WHITE-FACED OWL

BOOBOOK OWL

COLLARED SCOPS OWL

TAWNY OWL

EURASIAN SCOPS OWL

CUBAN PYGMY OWL

NORTHERN SAW-WHET OWL

ELF OWL

TROPICAL SCREECH OWL

Feathers

Birds have spread to every continent on Earth, partly because of their ability to fly. Feathers play a vital role in their flight, and help birds to stay warm, attract mates, and be camouflaged. Feathers come in many shapes and sizes, and have different functions.

WHAT ARE FEATHERS FOR?

Feathers allow flight, keep birds warm, provide camouflage, and help attract a mate. In many nesting birds, an area of feathers moults to allow more heat to pass from the mother bird to the eggs.

FLIGHT
Stiff wing and tail feathers aid flight.

TEMPERATURE CONTROL
Downy base of feather traps air for warmth.

ATTRACTION
Bright colours can help attract a mate.

CAMOUFLAGE
Patterns help bird blend into background.

TYPES OF FEATHERS

Birds have two main types of feathers: down feathers for warmth, and contour feathers for flight. The feathers grow in areas called tracts, with bare skin in between. The bare areas are hidden by the feathers.

PRIMARIES
These are flight feathers, attached to the front section of the wing.

TAIL FEATHERS
For balance, braking, and elevating in flight.

GAME BIRDS

Game birds spend most of their time on the ground, preferring to walk rather than fly. Their flight feathers have a very pronounced curve, or camber, to provide explosive lift and quick bursts of flight.

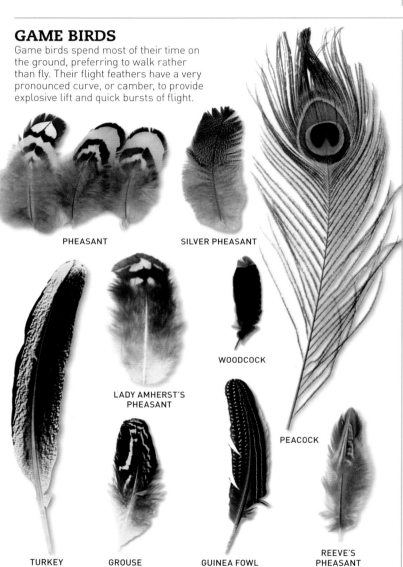

PHEASANT

SILVER PHEASANT

WOODCOCK

LADY AMHERST'S PHEASANT

PEACOCK

TURKEY

GROUSE

GUINEA FOWL

REEVE'S PHEASANT

COLOURFUL DISPLAY

Male peacocks have amazingly colourful tail feathers that spread up and around into a fan shape behind them when they want to attract a mate. The females choose a mate depending on how many eye spots are on his tail – the more the better.

TAIL FEATHERS DOWN

TAIL FEATHERS ON DISPLAY

PARROTS AND COCKATOOS

Parrots use their brightly coloured feathers to attract the opposite sex. The vivid colours may also help disguise these birds against the vibrant green of the forests where they live.

REGENT PARROT

COCKATIEL

AFRICAN GREY PARROT

BUDGERIGAR

MACAW

BIRDS OF PREY

There are two families of birds of prey: falcon-like birds that are awake in the daytime, and owls that are awake at night. Some can soar for hours to look for food, others achieve great speed when they dive down to catch their prey.

BARN OWL

MERLIN

KESTREL

BUZZARD

HAWK

EAGLE OWL

GOLDEN EAGLE

TOUCANS AND WOODPECKERS

Woodpeckers and toucans do not have any soft down feathers, even when they are chicks.

GREEN WOODPECKER

ARACARI

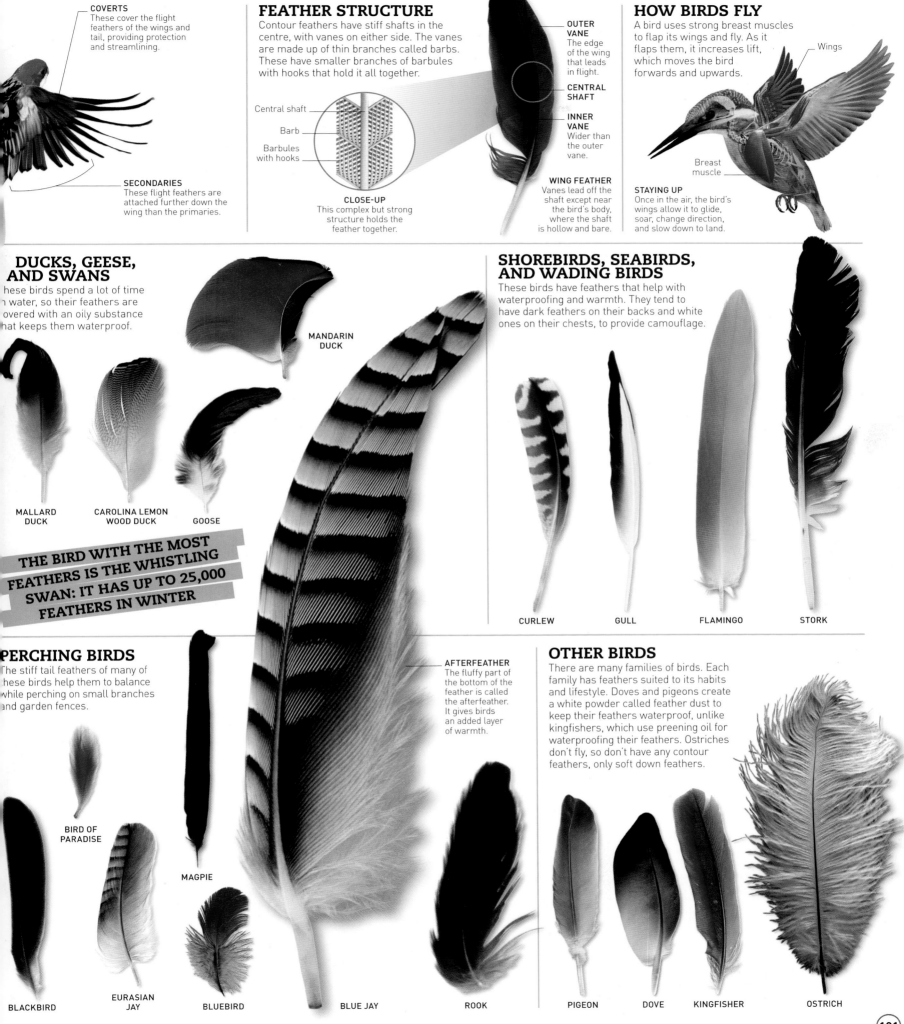

COVERTS
These cover the flight feathers of the wings and tail, providing protection and streamlining.

SECONDARIES
These flight feathers are attached further down the wing than the primaries.

FEATHER STRUCTURE
Contour feathers have stiff shafts in the centre, with vanes on either side. The vanes are made up of thin branches called barbs. These have smaller branches of barbules with hooks that hold it all together.

Central shaft
Barb
Barbules with hooks

CLOSE-UP
This complex but strong structure holds the feather together.

OUTER VANE
The edge of the wing that leads in flight.

CENTRAL SHAFT

INNER VANE
Wider than the outer vane.

WING FEATHER
Vanes lead off the shaft except near the bird's body, where the shaft is hollow and bare.

HOW BIRDS FLY
A bird uses strong breast muscles to flap its wings and fly. As it flaps them, it increases lift, which moves the bird forwards and upwards.

Wings

Breast muscle

STAYING UP
Once in the air, the bird's wings allow it to glide, soar, change direction, and slow down to land.

DUCKS, GEESE, AND SWANS
These birds spend a lot of time in water, so their feathers are covered with an oily substance that keeps them waterproof.

MANDARIN DUCK

MALLARD DUCK

CAROLINA LEMON WOOD DUCK

GOOSE

THE BIRD WITH THE MOST FEATHERS IS THE WHISTLING SWAN: IT HAS UP TO 25,000 FEATHERS IN WINTER

SHOREBIRDS, SEABIRDS, AND WADING BIRDS
These birds have feathers that help with waterproofing and warmth. They tend to have dark feathers on their backs and white ones on their chests, to provide camouflage.

CURLEW

GULL

FLAMINGO

STORK

PERCHING BIRDS
The stiff tail feathers of many of these birds help them to balance while perching on small branches and garden fences.

BIRD OF PARADISE

MAGPIE

AFTERFEATHER
The fluffy part of the bottom of the feather is called the afterfeather. It gives birds an added layer of warmth.

OTHER BIRDS
There are many families of birds. Each family has feathers suited to its habits and lifestyle. Doves and pigeons create a white powder called feather dust to keep their feathers waterproof, unlike kingfishers, which use preening oil for waterproofing their feathers. Ostriches don't fly, so don't have any contour feathers, only soft down feathers.

BLACKBIRD

EURASIAN JAY

BLUEBIRD

BLUE JAY

ROOK

PIGEON

DOVE

KINGFISHER

OSTRICH

Animal journeys

Every year, some animals move huge distances from one area to another. This is known as "migration" and may involve groups numbering millions. Such journeys are undertaken to ensure a species' survival.

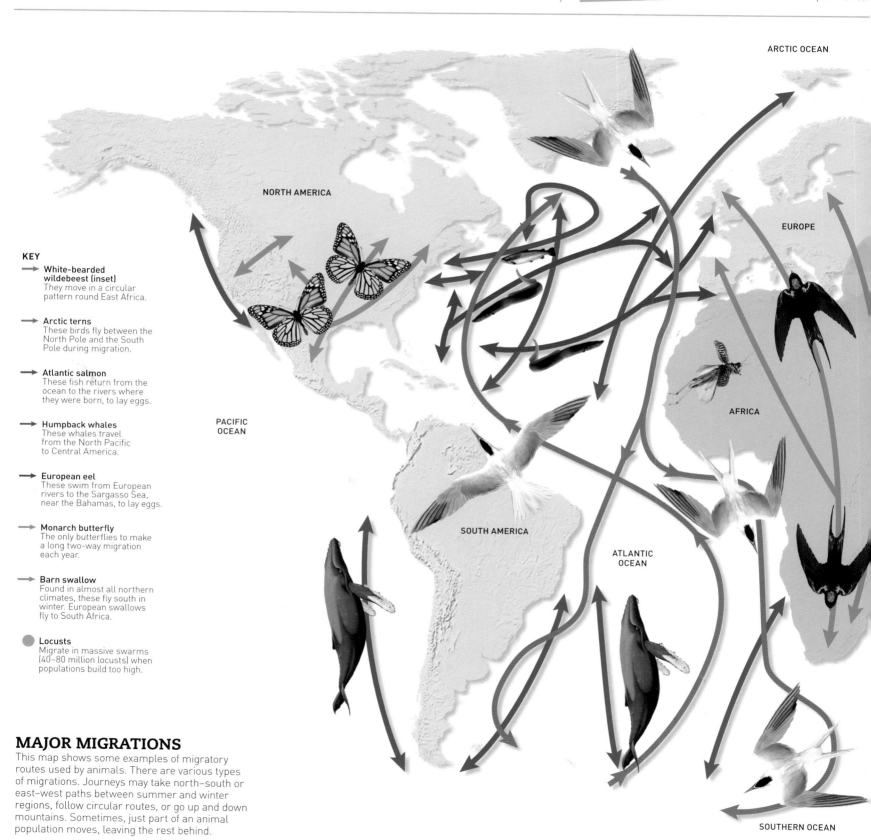

ARCTIC OCEAN

NORTH AMERICA

EUROPE

PACIFIC OCEAN

AFRICA

SOUTH AMERICA

ATLANTIC OCEAN

SOUTHERN OCEAN

KEY

White-bearded wildebeest (inset)
They move in a circular pattern round East Africa.

Arctic terns
These birds fly between the North Pole and the South Pole during migration.

Atlantic salmon
These fish return from the ocean to the rivers where they were born, to lay eggs.

Humpback whales
These whales travel from the North Pacific to Central America.

European eel
These swim from European rivers to the Sargasso Sea, near the Bahamas, to lay eggs.

Monarch butterfly
The only butterflies to make a long two-way migration each year.

Barn swallow
Found in almost all northern climates, these fly south in winter. European swallows fly to South Africa.

Locusts
Migrate in massive swarms (40–80 million locusts) when populations build too high.

MAJOR MIGRATIONS

This map shows some examples of migratory routes used by animals. There are various types of migrations. Journeys may take north–south or east–west paths between summer and winter regions, follow circular routes, or go up and down mountains. Sometimes, just part of an animal population moves, leaving the rest behind.

FOR PRODUCTION
animals may migrate to find a mate, lay eggs, give birth, and raise their young.

TO AVOID EXTREME WEATHER
In harsh wintry conditions, animals may move to areas where there is more food and warmer weather.

TO AVOID OVERCROWDING
When a population gets too big, animals may make a mass move. Locusts are one example.

BIRD MIGRATION

Bird migration takes place in spring and late autumn. The movement is triggered by changes in hours of daylight and temperature. Many migrating birds fly in V-shaped formations. The journey can last weeks or even months.

GETTING READY
Birds release a hormone to help them store fat in the weeks before they migrate.

NORMAL BODY FAT

READY TO MIGRATE

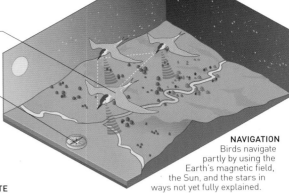

Height depends on wind patterns and landforms

The Sun and stars help to set the course

NAVIGATION
Birds navigate partly by using the Earth's magnetic field, the Sun, and the stars in ways not yet fully explained.

TRACKING MIGRATION

Scientists can track migrating animals by attaching ultra-light radio transmitters to them in various ways, such as on their legs. The little radios send signals to satellites in space, building up maps of the animals' movements. Birds are also given leg rings with unique numbers that are used to track movement.

INCA TERN

Migration ring

RECORD MIGRATIONS

When animals migrate, they can travel astonishing distances, often without stopping for food or drink. Here are some world-record holders.

○ **ARCTIC TERN**
Longest round trip: 71,000 km (44,000 miles) This tiny bird migrates further than any other animal in the world, zigzagging between Greenland and Antarctica.

○ **BAR-TAILED GODWIT**
Longest nonstop flight: 11,500 km (7,145 miles) One of these shorebirds covered this distance in eight days without a break for food.

○ **LEATHERBACK TURTLE**
Longest recorded aquatic journey: 20,558 km (12,774 miles) These travel across the Pacific Ocean to the beach where they were born.

○ **WHITE-BEARDED WILDEBEEST**
Largest land migration: 1.3 million wildebeest Vast herds can travel 1,610 km (1,000 miles) in a year.

○ **BAR-HEADED GOOSE**
Highest journey: 7,290 m (23,9170 ft) Flying at extreme altitude, these birds fly with only ten per cent of the oxygen found at sea level. They have been tracked flying for 17 hours without stopping.

○ **DESERT LOCUST**
Largest air migration: 69 billion locusts in one swarm In 2004, the swarm crossed Morocco and devastated crops in parts of northwest Africa.

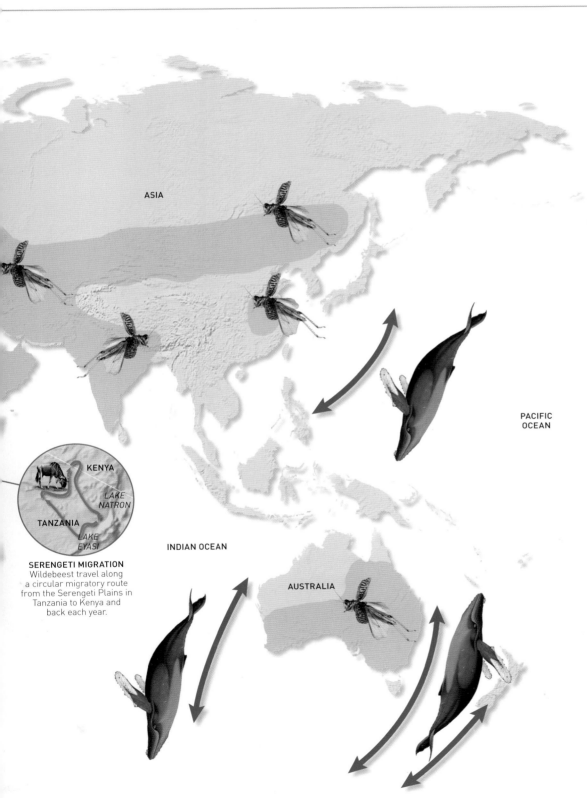

ASIA

PACIFIC OCEAN

INDIAN OCEAN

AUSTRALIA

KENYA

LAKE NATRON

TANZANIA

LAKE EYASI

SERENGETI MIGRATION
Wildebeest travel along a circular migratory route from the Serengeti Plains in Tanzania to Kenya and back each year.

Rodents

There are few places in the world where rodents cannot live. Mostly small, these animals fit themselves into many different habitats, and often flourish in huge numbers. Rodents are gnawing animals that must constantly wear down their ever-growing front teeth.

WHAT MAKES A RODENT?

A compact body, long whiskers, and a long tail are common rodent features, although there are many variations in this big group. Rodents' teeth make them different from other animals. They have four sharp front teeth, or incisors, and just a few molars at the back of the mouth.

Spine

Ribcage

Long tail aids balance

Sharp incisors continue to grow throughout life

Long, narrow hindfeet have five toes

Forefeet have four toes and a small thumb

SQUIRREL SKELETON

SUITABLE BODIES

Many rodents have special body adaptions to suit their various lifestyles. These include extra-flexible joints in the feet for climbing trees, protruding teeth for digging and tunnelling, and webbed toes for swimming.

CLIMBERS
Swivelling joints in their ankles make squirrels one of the few mammals that can climb head first down a tree.

BURROWERS
Mole-rats dig with their sticking-out front teeth, and push the soil behind them with their wide, flat hindfeet.

SWIMMERS
Beavers have webbed feet and a flat tail that is used as a rudder. Thick underfur keeps them warm in water.

HOW SQUIRRELS "FLY"

The rodent group includes the flying squirrels. As they move between trees, these animals travel through the air in what appears to be real flight. In fact, they are gliders. A flying squirrel has thin, loose skin between its legs that spreads out like a parachute to keep it aloft. To steer in midair, the squirrel moves its front legs. When preparing to land, it raises its fluffy tail as a brake.

Parachute-like skin

Front legs used for steering

Tail acts as brake

A FLYING SQUIRREL CAN GLIDE FOR UP TO 50 M (165 FT)

MOUSE-LIKE RODENTS

Mice and rats, gerbils, hamsters, lemmings, and voles are among the most numerous animals in the world. Various species of these rodents are found in nearly every country. Some make popular pets, but others are serious pests in homes and agricultural areas.

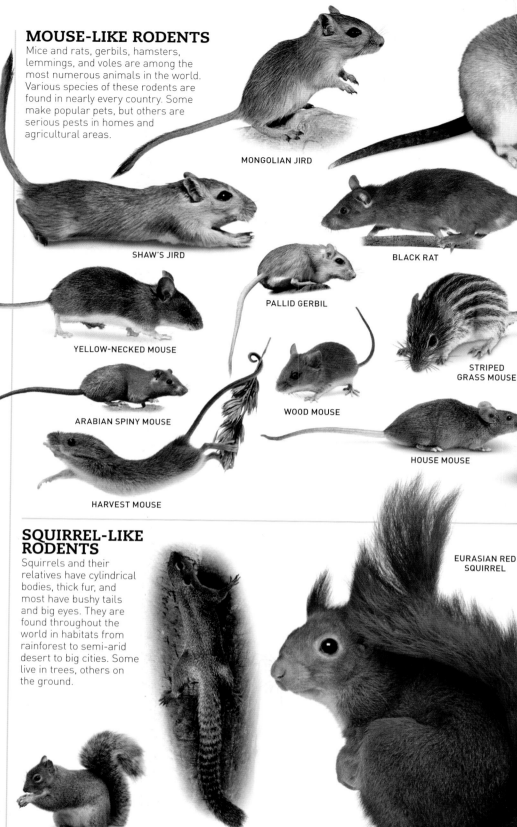

MONGOLIAN JIRD

SHAW'S JIRD

BLACK RAT

PALLID GERBIL

YELLOW-NECKED MOUSE

STRIPED GRASS MOUSE

ARABIAN SPINY MOUSE

WOOD MOUSE

HOUSE MOUSE

HARVEST MOUSE

SQUIRREL-LIKE RODENTS

Squirrels and their relatives have cylindrical bodies, thick fur, and most have bushy tails and big eyes. They are found throughout the world in habitats from rainforest to semi-arid desert to big cities. Some live in trees, others on the ground.

EURASIAN RED SQUIRREL

GREY SQUIRREL

GAMBIAN SUN SQUIRREL

CAVY-LIKE RODENTS

The best known of these rodents is the guinea pig, or cavy. It has a big head, sturdy body, short tail, and slender legs, which are common features among this varied group. Cavy relatives include porcupines, the capybara – the biggest rodent in the world – and the almost hairless, nearly blind mole-rat, which lives underground.

DOMESTIC GUINEA PIG

LONG-HAIRED GUINEA PIG

AGOUTI

BROWN AGOUTI GUINEA PIGS

STRIPED DWARF
HAMSTER

COMMON HAMSTERS

ALAGASY
ANT RAT

ROBOROVSKY'S
DESERT HAMSTER

GOLDEN HAMSTER

SYRIAN HAMSTER

ORKNEY VOLE

NORWEGIAN
LEMMING

MUSKRAT

BANK VOLE

FOREST
DORMOUSE

BROWN RAT

AFRICAN
DORMOUSE

HAZEL
DORMOUSE

COMMON VOLE

SOUTH AFRICAN
GROUND SQUIRREL

HARRIS'S ANTELOPE
SQUIRREL

HOPI
CHIPMUNK

NORTHERN
FLYING SQUIRREL

EASTERN
CHIPMUNKS

RED BUSH
SQUIRREL

YELLOW-BELLIED
MARMOT

BLACK-TAILED PRAIRIE DOG

BEAVERS

There are two species of beavers: North American
and Eurasian. Both are river-dwellers. They create
waterways for their own
purposes by building
dams out of
branches, mud,
and stones.

MOLE-RAT

CHINCHILLA

MARA

CRESTED
PORCUPINE

CAPYBARA

EURASIAN BEAVER

Monkeys and apes

Like humans, monkeys and apes are primates. They use their hands as we do, placing their thumbs against their fingers to grasp things. Monkeys and apes have good vision and large brains for their size. A tail helps to identify which animals are which: most monkeys have tails, apes do not.

MOVING AROUND

Some apes, such as gorillas, spend a lot of time on the ground, while others are skilled climbers and leapers. Monkeys scamper and run on all fours, using their tails for balance or as a fifth limb.

ON TWO FEET
Apes are able to walk on their hindlimbs for short periods of time.

ON FOUR FEET
Monkeys move on all fours, and their limbs are of roughly equal length.

KNUCKLE-WALK
Gorillas and chimpanzees put their weight on the knuckles of their forelimbs.

SWINGING
Some apes use their long arms to swing from branch to branch.

TOOL USE

Apes are intelligent and can make and use tools. Chimpanzees have been observed using rocks to crack nuts, and making "sponges" from leaves and moss to collect water. They also push sticks into termite mounds and trees to "fish" for insects.

GROUP BEHAVIOUR

Most apes and monkeys live in groups, which helps keep them safe from predators. They communicate with each other by using body language and sounds. Chimpanzees even work together to hunt and then share the food among the group.

CARE OF YOUNG
Monkeys and apes have one to two infants at a time, and may devote years to rearing their offspring.

SOCIAL LIFE
Grooming is important not only for cleaning fur, but also for bonding between group members.

MONKEYS

New World monkeys live in South and Central American rainforests. They have fairly broad noses with nostrils that open sideways. Many have gripping tails. Old World monkeys live in Asia and Africa. They have narrower noses than New World monkeys and downward-pointing nostrils. Most are tree-dwellers, although baboons live mainly on the ground.

WEEPER CAPUCHIN

NORTHERN NIGHT MONKEY

COMMON SQUIRREL MONKEY

GOLDEN LION TAMARIN

COTTON-TOP TAMARIN

PYGMY MARMOSET

COMMON MARMOSET

RED HOWLER MONKEY

GREY WOOLLY MONKEY

PIG-TAILED MACAQUE

BARBARY MACAQUE

APES

Found in Africa and Southeast Asia, apes have a more upright body posture than monkeys and do not have a tail. Gorillas, chimpanzees, orangutans, and humans are all "great apes", while gibbons are "lesser apes".

BORNEAN ORANGUTAN

RVET MONKEY

MONA MONKEY

GUEREZA

OTHER PRIMATES
Many other species belong to the order of primates. Lemurs are found only on the island of Madagascar in Africa. Other relatives of apes and monkeys include galagos, bandros, and bushbabies, which are all nocturnal.

BROWN GREATER GALAGO

SENEGAL BUSHBABY

AMADRYAS BABOON

GUINEA BABOON

BANDRO

VERREAUX'S SIFAKA

B-EATING MACAQUE

RHESUS MACAQUE

TOQUE MACAQUE

MANDRILL

BLACK LEMUR

GREATER BAMBOO LEMUR

LAR GIBBON

PILEATED GIBBON

WHITE-CHEEKED CRESTED GIBBON

SIAMANG

RING-TAILED LEMUR

MONGOOSE LEMUR

BONOBO

COMMON CHIMPANZEE

RED-BELLIED LEMUR

WESTERN GORILLA

BLACK AND WHITE RUFFED LEMUR

RED-COLLARED LEMUR

Wild cats

Sleek, stealthy, patient, and intelligent, wild cats are natural killers. Most of them hunt on their own, using their claws and teeth to catch, stab, and cut up their prey. They are athletic, with supple, muscular bodies that are well adapted to running, climbing, leaping, and even swimming. They live in various habitats across Africa, Asia, Europe, and the Americas.

CONSERVATION

The threats to wild cats vary according to where they live, but the main ones are poaching and the loss of their habitat. Most of the big cats are now vulnerable or endangered.

KEY

- ■ Critically endangered
- ■ Endangered
- ■ Vulnerable
- ■ Near threatened
- ■ Least concern

- AMUR LEOPARD
- SNOW LEOPARD
- ASIATIC LION
- BENGAL TIGER
- AMUR TIGER
- AFRICAN LION
- INDOCHINESE CLOUDED LEOPARD
- DIARD'S CLOUDED LEOPARD
- JAGUAR

SMALL WILD CATS

More than three-quarters of the world's wild cats are classified as "small". The 30 different species have adapted to their environments – their colours help them blend in. Domestic cats were derived from the North African wildcat.

SERVAL

GEOFFROY'S CAT

IBERIAN LYNX

EUROPEAN WILDCAT

EURASIAN LYNX

COLOCOLO

CARACAL

FISHING CAT

BIG CATS

Lions, tigers, jaguars, and leopards are classed as cats. They all live alone, except for lions, which live in a big group known as a pride. The largest cats in the world are the Bengal and Amur tigers, which can weigh the same as 100 domestic cats.

LIONESS

CLOUDED LEOPARD

LION

UILT FOR SPEED

e cheetah is the fastest land mammal on Earth –
an run at 113 km/h (70 mph). Strong muscles, large
gs, and a large heart mean it can take in lots of
ygen very fast and so accelerate very quickly.
has to rest after about 20–60 seconds.

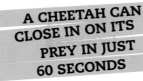

STARTING LEAP
A cheetah can run fast over
ort distances only. It stalks its
y until it is very close, then
ddenly rushes out of cover.

2 STRAIGHTENING OUT
The cheetah's unusually
long and flexible spine
means it can cover 7–8 m
(23–26 ft) in one single stride.

3 FLEXED TO LAND
The powerful back legs propel
the cheetah forward so well that the
back feet overtake the forefeet,
ready to spring again.

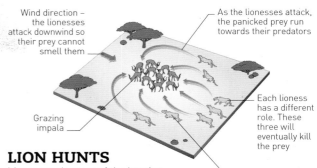

Wind direction –
the lionesses
attack downwind so
their prey cannot
smell them

Grazing
impala

As the lionesses attack,
the panicked prey run
towards their predators

Each lioness
has a different
role. These
three will
eventually kill
the prey

The lionesses fan
out to surround
their prey

LION HUNTS
Lionesses do most of the hunting.
Once killed the prey is feasted upon by
all that can get near enough. Youngsters
usually give way to older members and
all are subordinate to the males.

LEOPARD CAT

JUNGLE CAT

BOB CAT

MARGAY

SAND CAT

PUMA

OCELOT

INDIAN DESERT CAT

CHEETAH

CANADIAN LYNX

A tiger's stripes are
unique – no two tigers will
ever have the same pattern

BENGAL TIGER

AMUR TIGER

SNOW LEOPARD

AMUR LEOPARD

BLACK LEOPARD

JAGUAR

Whales and dolphins

Although they live in water, whales, dolphins, and porpoises are all mammals. At intervals, they rise to the surface to breathe in fresh air and exhale stale air through blowholes, similar to nostrils, on the top of their head.

TEETH AND FILTERS

Some whales have teeth for catching prey such as fish or squid. Filter-feeding whales have comb-like plates called baleen hanging from their upper jaw. As they swim, baleen whales gulp water and the plates trap tiny prey.

Single blowhole

Pair of blowholes

Baleen plates instead of tee

TOOTHED WHALE

Row of conical teeth

BALEEN WHALE

WHALES

There are several distinct groups of whales. Some are baleen whales, or filter feeders. These include the blue whale, the biggest mammal in the world. Others have teeth and sometimes beaks as well. Depending on type, whales can be found from coastal waters to the deep ocean.

HUMPBACK WHALE

SPERM WHALE

SEI WHALE

BRYDE'S WHALE

MINKE WHALE

Small, stubby dorsal fin

PYGMY RIGHT WHALE

GRAY WHALE

FIN WHALE

DOLPHINS

Apart from a few river species, dolphins are ocean-dwellers. They come in many patterns. Common dolphin features include a beak and a bulging forehead.

HECTOR'S DOLPHIN

HOURGLASS DOLPHIN

WHITE-BEAKED DOLPHIN

TUCUXI

STRIPED DOLPHIN

MELON-HEADED WHALE

RISSO'S DOLPHIN

KILLER WHALE

ATLANTIC WHITE-SIDED DOLPHIN

BOTTLENOSE DOLPHIN

PYGMY KILLER WHALE

FALSE KILLER WHALE

ROM LAND TO SEA

y million years ago (MYA) the ancestors of whales were not
mming in seas but living on land and walking on four legs.
se animals gradually started spending more time feeding
ater. Slowly, their bodies changed and whales eventually
dry land forever.

Whale-like ear bones

Flippers replace legs

PAKICETUS (50 MYA)
About the size of a large dog,
animal sometimes swam
fish. Its fossilized ear bones
ch those of modern whales.

2 DORUDON (38 MYA)
Able to swim well, this early whale
had front flippers, tiny hindlimbs, and
a flexible tail. The nostrils had shifted
to the top of the head as blowholes.

3 MODERN WHALE
Perfectly adapted for ocean life, the
whale has a streamlined body, powerful
flippers, and a flat tail to aid propulsion.
The hindlegs have vanished.

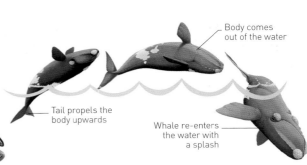

Body comes
out of the water

Tail propels the
body upwards

Whale re-enters
the water with
a splash

THE BLUE WHALE CAN MEASURE UP TO 30.5 M (100 FT) LONG

BREACHING

Whales often leap high out of the water
and plunge back with a large splash. This
is called breaching, and scientists are not
sure why whales do it. Possibly it is a form
of signalling or helps to dislodge parasites.

BAIRD'S BEAKED WHALE

CUVIER'S BEAKED WHALE

GERVAIS' BEAKED WHALE

PYGMY SPERM WHALE

NORTHERN
BOTTLENOSED WHALE

BLAINVILLE'S BEAKED WHALE

SHEPHERD'S BEAKED WHALE

GRAY'S BEAKED WHALE

BLUE WHALE

HUBBS' BEAKED WHALE

STRAP-TOOTHED WHALE

GINKGO-TOOTHED BEAKED WHALE

NARWHAL

SOUTHERN
RIGHT WHALE

Outgrowths of hard skin
develop on head

BELUGA

BOWHEAD WHALE

SOUTHERN RIGHT WHALE DOLPHIN

ROUGH-TOOTHED DOLPHIN

INDUS RIVER DOLPHIN

PORPOISES

Most of this group are smaller and rounder-
bodied than their rwelatives. Porpoises are
usually found in shallow seas near the coast.

LONG-FINNED PILOT
WHALE

ATLANTIC SPOTTED
DOLPHIN

FRANCISCANA

DALL'S PORPOISE

SPECTACLED PORPOISE

PEALE'S DOLPHIN

COMMON DOLPHIN

AMAZON RIVER
DOLPHIN

HARBOUR PORPOISE

VAQUITA

arge, broad
flippers

COMMERSON'S DOLPHIN

FRASER'S DOLPHIN

DUSKY DOLPHIN

FINLESS PORPOISE

BURMEISTER'S PORPOISE

Animal skeletons

Without a skeleton, most animals would be a shapeless blob. Vertebrates, such as mammals and birds, have a strong internal skeleton. Many invertebrates, such as insects, have a protective external skeleton, called an exoskeleton.

WHAT DOES THE SKELETON DO?

A skeleton provides an animal's body with strength, shape, and protection. Muscles are attached to the bones, and joints between bones enable movement. Bones also store vital minerals and produce red blood cells.

SUPPORT
The skeletal framework gives shape and strength to an animal's body.

PROTECTION
Bones such as the ribcage and skull protect vital organs from injury.

MOVEMENT
Bones act as levers and are points of attachment for the muscles.

INNER SKELETONS

All vertebrates have an inner skeleton that supports the body and protects the organs. The skeleton is usually made of bone, although some animals – such as sharks – have a skeleton made of flexible cartilage.

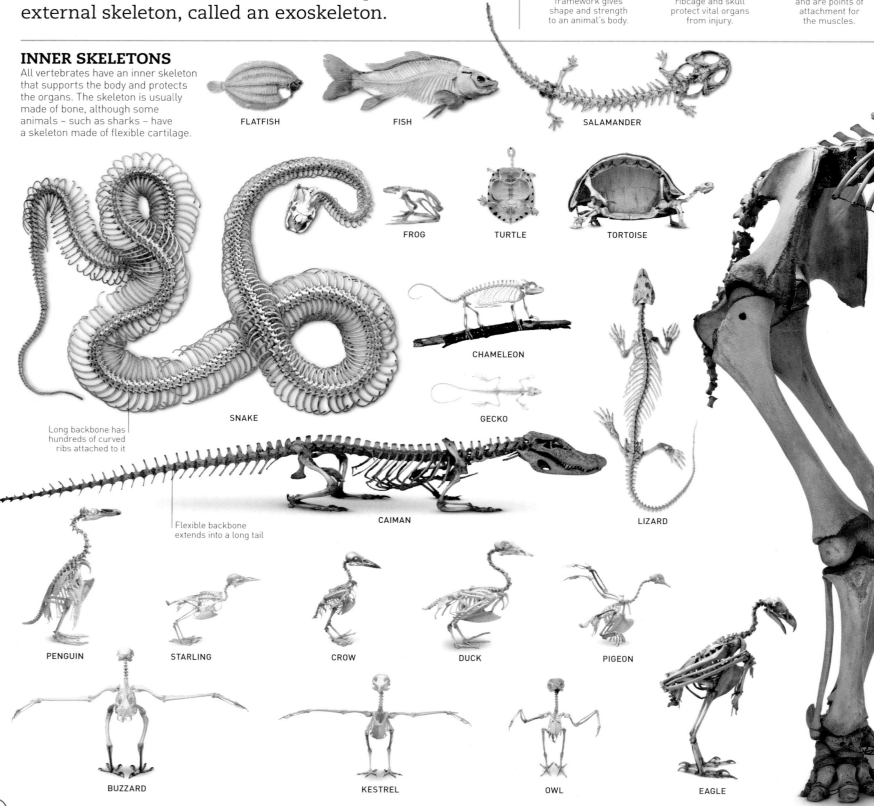

FLATFISH

FISH

SALAMANDER

FROG

TURTLE

TORTOISE

Long backbone has hundreds of curved ribs attached to it

SNAKE

CHAMELEON

GECKO

LIZARD

Flexible backbone extends into a long tail

CAIMAN

PENGUIN

STARLING

CROW

DUCK

PIGEON

BUZZARD

KESTREL

OWL

EAGLE

UTER KELETONS

veral groups of ertebrates have an mour-like external eleton. The rigid casing otects inner organs from mage and possibly m predators. When sects or creatures such crabs grow, they shed eir exoskeleton and make new one.

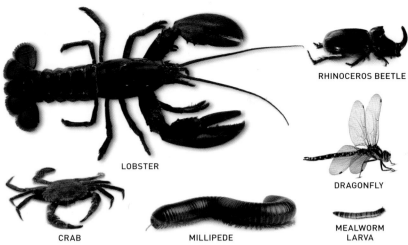
LOBSTER

RHINOCEROS BEETLE

ARANTULA

CRAB

MILLIPEDE

DRAGONFLY

MEALWORM LARVA

ECHINODERM SKELETON

Echinoderms include marine invertebrates like sea urchins and starfish. They have an exoskeleton made of plates, covered by a thin layer of skin. When these animals grow, their skeleton grows with them.

SEA URCHIN

HYDROSTATIC SKELETON

The shape of many soft-bodied invertebrates is supported by a water-based "skeleton" consisting of a fluid-filled cavity surrounded by a muscular wall.

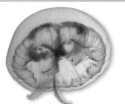
JELLYFISH

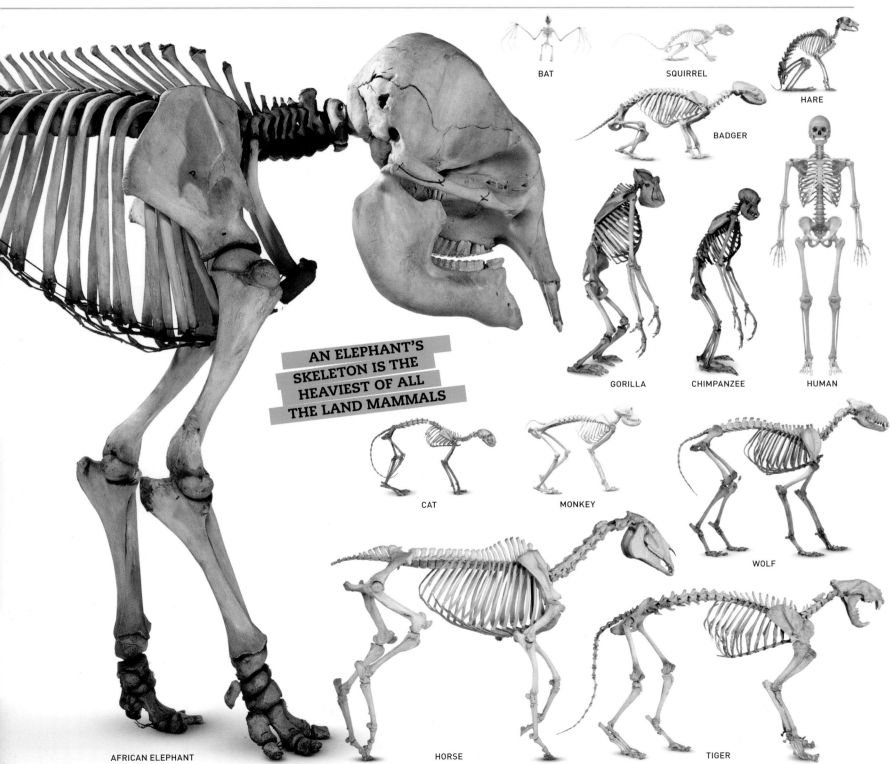

BAT

SQUIRREL

HARE

BADGER

GORILLA

CHIMPANZEE

HUMAN

AN ELEPHANT'S SKELETON IS THE HEAVIEST OF ALL THE LAND MAMMALS

CAT

MONKEY

WOLF

AFRICAN ELEPHANT

HORSE

TIGER

Dogs

People and dogs have been together for at least 12,000 years. All dogs are descendants of grey wolves that left the wild for the camps of prehistoric hunters. Since those distant times, hundreds of different dog breeds have been created in all sizes and types.

BODY DESIGN
Dogs can be big or small, tall or short, shaggy or hairless. The variations are many, but the basic body design of a dog is the same for all.

Shoulder

Breastbone

Upper thigh

Belly

Foreleg

Hock

Wrist

Toes

EVOLUTION
There are around 500 million dogs worldwide. All of them a related to each other throug their ancestor, the grey wolf.

WOLVES
Tribespeople all over the ancient world began to tame wolves as useful hunting companions.

DOGS
People began to breed dogs for specific purposes and in doing so changed and standardized their form.

CLOSE TO WOLVES
After centuries of change, most dogs are no longer at all like their wolf ancestors. Just a few are still close to the original wolf form. Some are popular pets and others are semi-wild.

IBIZAN HOUND

PHARAOH HOUND

PORTUGUESE PODENGO

MEXICAN HAIRLESS

CANAAN

PERUVIAN INCA ORCHID

NEW GUINEA SINGING DOG

CAROLINA

BASENJI

PERUVIAN HAIRLESS

SPITZ DOGS
The most famous spitz dogs are breeds such as the husky, which was once used for sled-pulling on polar expeditions. Spitz dogs have immensely thick, double coats and furry feet.

SIBERIAN HUSKY

GREENLAND DOG

SAMOYED

CHOW CHOW

LAIKA

TERRIERS
Bold and lively, terriers come in many different sizes and types. They are strong-willed and must be trained properly to prevent bad habits, such as chasing other pets. The favourite game of many terriers is digging holes.

SCOTTISH TERRIER

WEST HIGHLAND WHITE TERRIER

FOX TERRIER

JACK RUSSELL TERRIER

YORKSHIRE TERRIER

CAIRN TERRIER

NORFOLK TERRIER

BOSTON TERRIER

MANCHESTER TERRIER

WHEATEN TERRIER

BEDLINGTON TERRIER

BULL TERRIER

RUSSIAN BLACK TERRIER

GUNDOGS
These dogs were developed to work with hunters. Some are used for locating prey. Other gundogs drive game birds out of cover and pick up those that are shot.

SPANISH WATER DOG

LAGOTTO ROMAGNOLO

BRITTANY

COCKER SPANIEL

HUNGARIAN VIZSLA

GOLDEN RETRIEVER

IRISH SETTER

CHESAPEAKE BAY RETRIEVER

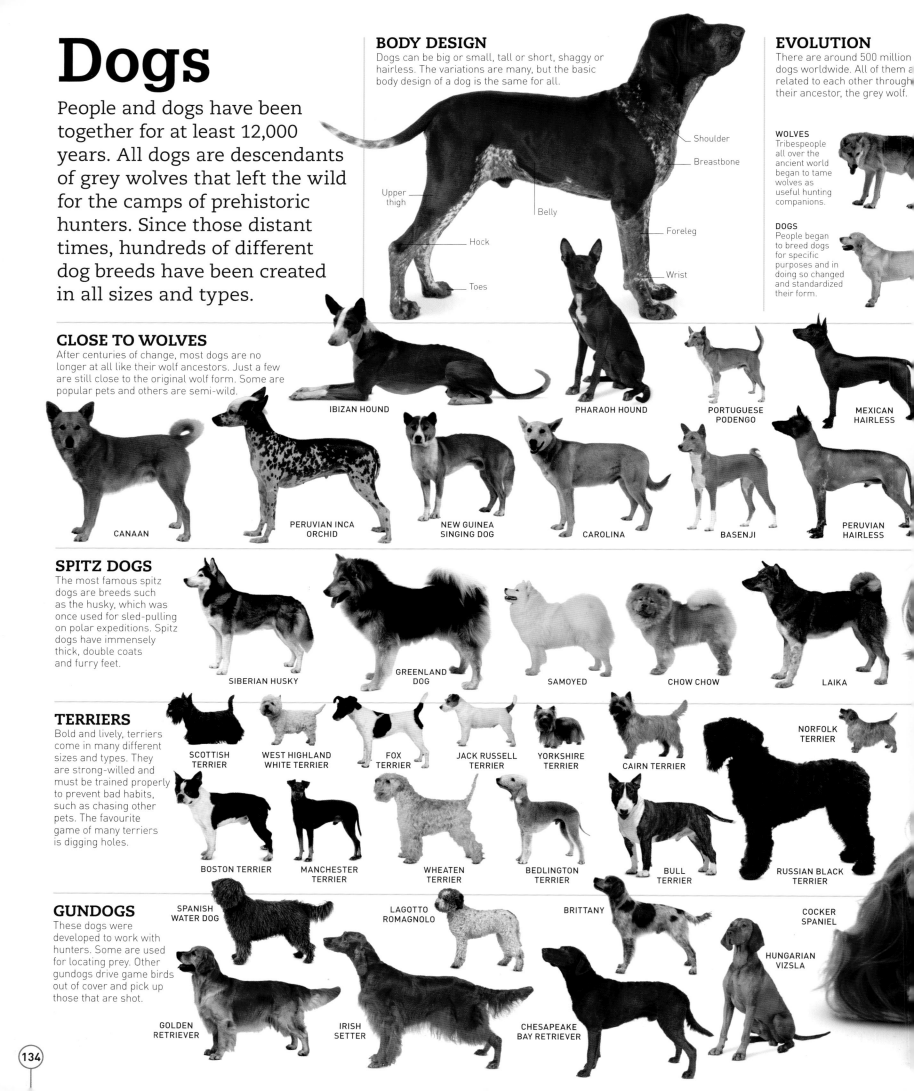

KEEN NOSES

The nose of a dog is packed with hundreds of millions of smell sensors. These pick up detailed messages about the world.

	SMELL SENSORS (IN MILLIONS)
HUMAN	5
CAT	200
DOG	300

0   100   200   300   400
SMELL SENSORS (IN MILLIONS)

EARS

There are a large variety of dog ear shapes. Most dogs have good hearing, and pointy-eared dogs hear better than droopy-eared breeds.

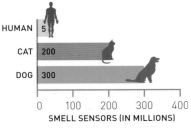

ERECT   CANDLE FLAME   ROSE

BUTTON   DROP   PENDANT

A DOG'S-EYE VIEW

Dogs have a wider field of vision than humans, so can see more without moving their heads. They see detail clearly, have good 3-D vision, and can see movement at long range.

Range seen by left eye   Range seen by right eye

Range seen by both eyes

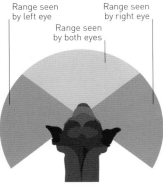

RANGE OF VISION

BEHAVIOUR

When pet dogs do things such as stopping to mark a tree, they are behaving as a wolf would in the wild. Dogs and wolves also use the same body language.

HOWLING
Dogs don't howl often. They howl if they are shut in alone, possibly because they want company.

MARKING TERRITORY
Dogs leave scent markings to communicate with other dogs.

NOSE LICKING
A lick of the nose is usually a sign that a dog is calming itself down.

YAWNING
Yawning is a calming signal. Dogs yawn to deflect threats and avoid conflict.

DIGGING
Dogs dig to bury things and to reach animals that live underground.

WORKING DOGS

Herding sheep and cattle, guarding property, and rescuing lost people are some of the jobs done by working dogs. Many of these breeds make very good pets.

MASTIFF   PEMBROKE WELSH CORGI   HUNGARIAN PULI   ROUGH COLLIE   ST BERNARD

SCENT HOUNDS

With the best noses of all dog breeds, scent hounds have been used for centuries to track prey. They have strong hunting instincts and some work well in a pack.

BASSET HOUND

DACHSHUND   BEAGLE   RHODESIAN RIDGEBACK   BILLY   DOBERMANN

SIGHT HOUNDS

Slender and long-legged, these hounds are swift hunters that follow prey by sight. They are mainly kept today for racing and as pets.

IRISH WOLFHOUND   SALUKI   GREYHOUND   AFGHAN HOUND

COMPANION DOGS

Many breeds, most of them small, have been specially produced to make good companions. They are designed to have appealing looks and affectionate natures.

RUSSIAN TOY   CHIHUAHUA   FRENCH BULLDOG   DALMATIAN   BICHON FRISE

LHASA APSO   THAI RIDGEBACK   KING CHARLES SPANIEL   PUG   POODLE   HIMALAYAN SHEEPDOG

CROSSBREEDS

Some dogs are the result of a planned cross between two recognized breeds. Dogs with unknown parentage are called mixed breeds.

GOLDENDOODLE   LABRADOODLE   BULL BOXER   LUCAS TERRIER   COCKERPOO   LURCHER   BICHON YORKIE

135

Cats

Tens of millions of pet cats are kept worldwide. Some of these are pedigrees – breeds "designed" with a special look, such as a striking coat pattern or long hair. Most people love cats just for their appealing personalities and independent ways.

The first cats to be kept as pets, probably about 4,000 years ago, were short-haired. This type is the favourite with cat owners today. Colours and markings show up clearly on short hair and the coat is easy to groom.

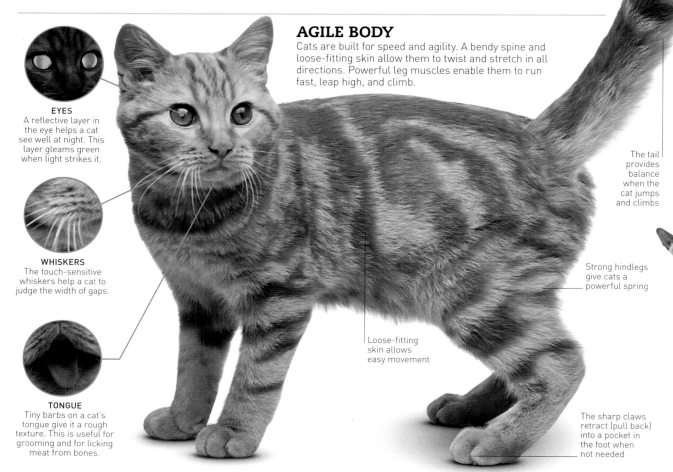

AGILE BODY
Cats are built for speed and agility. A bendy spine and loose-fitting skin allow them to twist and stretch in all directions. Powerful leg muscles enable them to run fast, leap high, and climb.

EYES
A reflective layer in the eye helps a cat see well at night. This layer gleams green when light strikes it.

WHISKERS
The touch-sensitive whiskers help a cat to judge the width of gaps.

TONGUE
Tiny barbs on a cat's tongue give it a rough texture. This is useful for grooming and for licking meat from bones.

The tail provides balance when the cat jumps and climbs

Strong hindlegs give cats a powerful spring

Loose-fitting skin allows easy movement

The sharp claws retract (pull back) into a pocket in the foot when not needed

CHARTREUX   KHAO MANI

MUNCHKIN

SIAMESE

LONG-HAIRED CATS
These cats are shaggy, silky, or fluffy, depending on type. Some longhairs, such as the Persian, have an immensely thick underlayer to their coat that needs daily brushing and combing.

TURKISH VAN

TAIL LANGUAGE
A cat uses its tail to give out messages about its feelings. Learning to read this "language" helps us to understand cats.

A MOTHER CAT HOLDS HER TAIL UPRIGHT AS A SIGN TO HER KITTENS TO FOLLOW HER

PLEASED/EXCITED
Pointing straight up and quivering.

WATCHFUL
Twitching slightly from side to side.

READY TO ATTACK
Held bristling over the back.

ANXIOUS
Upright and fluffed out.

TRUE OR FALSE?
Cats are mysterious animals. It is not surprising that people wonder what to believe about them. These are some popular sayings.

(X) **CATS HAVE NINE LIVES**
False. Cats are good at landing on their feet after a fall or getting out of trouble but they have only one life.

(✓) **CATS SPEND MOST OF THEIR TIME SLEEPING**
True. Even an active cat sleeps on average for about two-thirds of its day.

(X) **BLACK CATS BRING BAD LUCK**
False. This is folklore that is repeated in many regions. Some people say black cats are lucky.

(✓) **CATS CAN BE RIGHT-PAWED OR LEFT-PAWED**
True. Female cats are more likely to use the right paw, while male cats tend to use the left.

(X) **CATS USE THEIR WHISKERS FOR BALANCE**
False. Cats' whiskers are "feelers" for finding the way, not for balancing.

SIBERIAN

KITTENS
Born blind and helpless, kittens turn into cats in a very short time. At about 10 weeks old they no longer rely on their mother. They can wash themselves, climb, jump, and hunt pretend prey.

1 FOUR DAYS
Although its eyes are glued shut, the kitten can sense its surroundings.

2 TWO WEEKS
The eyes have opened, but the kitten cannot see very well.

3 FOUR WEEKS
Already toddling about, the kitten uses its tail for balance.

4 EIGHT WEEKS
Very active, the kitten is learning how to be a grown-up cat.

5 TEN WEEKS
The kitten is nearly independent and ready to leave its mother.

NORWEGIAN FOREST CAT

BOMBAY

EXOTIC SHORTHAIR

TONKINESE

ABYSSINIAN

EGYPTIAN MAU

BURMESE

OCICAT

SAVANNAH

DEVON REX

SNOWSHOE

BRITISH SHORTHAIR

MANX

RUSSIAN BLUE

SCOTTISH FOLD

AUSTRALIAN MIST

ORIENTAL

JAPANESE BOBTAIL

HAIRLESS CATS

A few breeds of cats are almost completely hairless. One of the best known is the Sphynx, which has just a fine fuzz covering its body.

SPHYNX

ENGAL

KORAT

ASIAN

SINGAPURA

SELKIRK REX

KINKALOW

KURILIAN BOBTAIL

PIXIEBOB LONGHAIR

BIRMAN

SOMALI

AMERICAN CURL

PERSIAN

TURKISH ANGORA

LAPERM LONGHAIR

SCOTTISH FOLD LONGHAIR

CYMRIC

MUNCHKIN LONGHAIR

RAGDOLL

CHANTILLY TIFFANY

TIFFANIE

MAINE COON

BALINESE-JAVANESE

137

Horses

People are thought to have first tamed wild horses for riding and pulling loads around 6,000 years ago. Until modern times, the horse was the fastest form of transport available and an essential part of farming life. Today, horses are mostly used for leisure riding and other sports. There are hundreds of different breeds of all sizes.

NAMING PARTS

The various parts of a horse's body have special names, which riders and other people who work with horses always use. These parts are often referred to as the "points" of a horse.

Forelock

Crest (topline of neck)

EVOLUTION OF THE HORSE

Forerunners of the horse first appeared 55 million years ago (MYA). These animals, about the size of a small dog, looked very different from modern horses. The pictures here show some of the stages of the horse's evolution.

MODERN HORSES EVOLVED DURING THE LAST ICE AGE

1 HYRACOTHERIUM (55–45 MYA)
This little forest-dwelling animal had padded toes instead of hoofs.

2 MIOHIPPUS (32–25 MYA)
Some prehistoric horses were growing taller by this period.

3 MERYCHIPPUS (17–11 MYA)
The size of a pony, *Merychippus* lived on grassy plains.

4 PLIOHIPPUS (12–6 MYA)
Pliohippus looked more like the horses we know today.

5 EQUUS (5 MYA–PRESENT)
Modern horses appeared first in North America and then spread widely.

Withers (highest point of shoulders)

HEAVY HORSES

Also called draught or working horses, these large, strongly built animals are bred for hauling heavy loads. They were once widely used for farm work but most of them are now kept for showing and other competitions.

Flank

SHIRE   CLYDESDALE   POITEVIN   ARDENNAIS

PERCHERON   NORMAN COB   SUFFOLK PUNCH   JUTLAND

LIGHT HORSES

These horses are smaller and less powerful than draught horses. They are widely used for leisure riding and in sports such as racing, showjumping, and carriage driving.

THOROUGHBRED   ANDALUCIAN   ARABIAN

DANISH WARMBLOOD   KNABSTRUP   KARABAKH   APPALOOSA

Hock (joint similar to human ankle)

Fetlock joint

Hoof

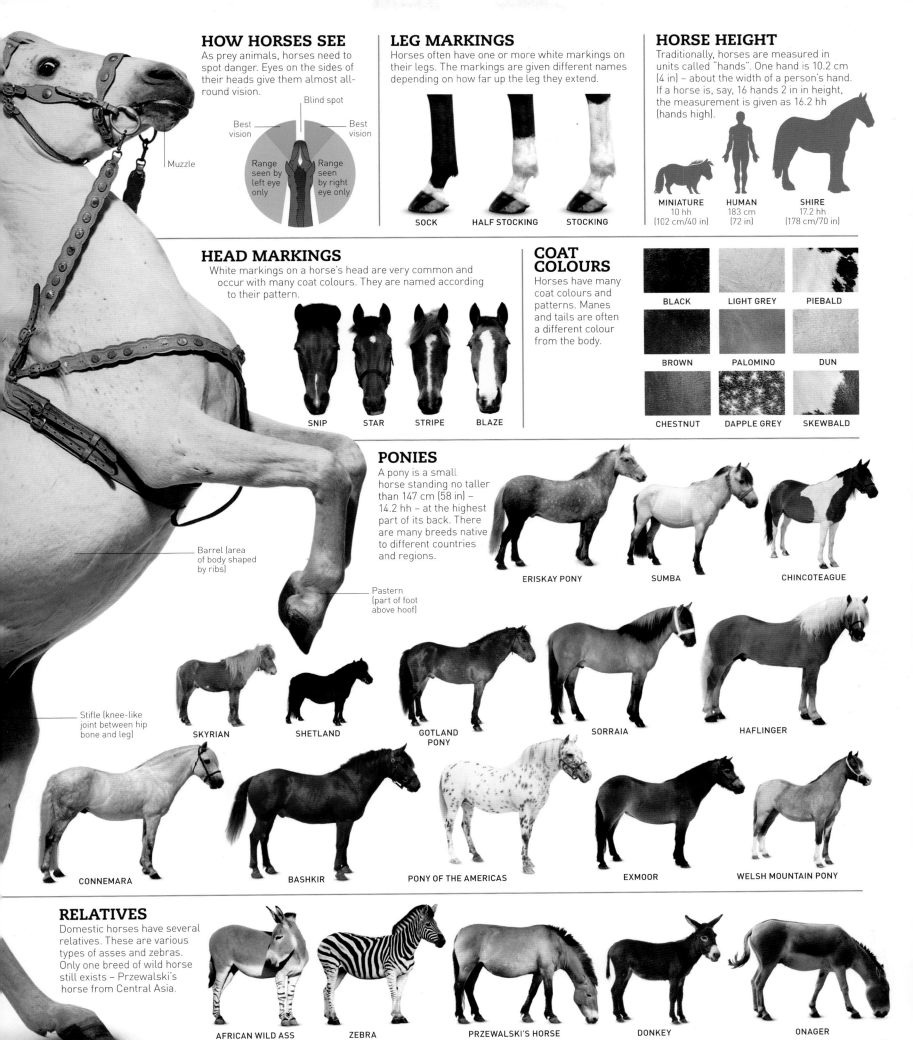

HOW HORSES SEE

As prey animals, horses need to spot danger. Eyes on the sides of their heads give them almost all-round vision.

Muzzle

Blind spot

Best vision

Best vision

Range seen by left eye only

Range seen by right eye only

LEG MARKINGS

Horses often have one or more white markings on their legs. The markings are given different names depending on how far up the leg they extend.

SOCK

HALF STOCKING

STOCKING

HORSE HEIGHT

Traditionally, horses are measured in units called "hands". One hand is 10.2 cm (4 in) – about the width of a person's hand. If a horse is, say, 16 hands 2 in in height, the measurement is given as 16.2 hh (hands high).

MINIATURE
10 hh
(102 cm/40 in)

HUMAN
183 cm
(72 in)

SHIRE
17.2 hh
(178 cm/70 in)

HEAD MARKINGS

White markings on a horse's head are very common and occur with many coat colours. They are named according to their pattern.

SNIP

STAR

STRIPE

BLAZE

COAT COLOURS

Horses have many coat colours and patterns. Manes and tails are often a different colour from the body.

BLACK

LIGHT GREY

PIEBALD

BROWN

PALOMINO

DUN

CHESTNUT

DAPPLE GREY

SKEWBALD

PONIES

A pony is a small horse standing no taller than 147 cm (58 in) – 14.2 hh – at the highest part of its back. There are many breeds native to different countries and regions.

Barrel (area of body shaped by ribs)

Pastern (part of foot above hoof)

Stifle (knee-like joint between hip bone and leg)

ERISKAY PONY

SUMBA

CHINCOTEAGUE

SKYRIAN

SHETLAND

GOTLAND PONY

SORRAIA

HAFLINGER

CONNEMARA

BASHKIR

PONY OF THE AMERICAS

EXMOOR

WELSH MOUNTAIN PONY

RELATIVES

Domestic horses have several relatives. These are various types of asses and zebras. Only one breed of wild horse still exists – Przewalski's horse from Central Asia.

AFRICAN WILD ASS

ZEBRA

PRZEWALSKI'S HORSE

DONKEY

ONAGER

DUCKS AND GEESE

These birds are kept for meat and eggs, and sometimes their soft downy feathers are used for quilted bedding and clothing. Large and noisy, geese are wary of anything suspicious and make very good "watchdogs".

KHAKI CAMPBELL DUCK

MUSCOVY DUCK

WHITE PEKIN DUCK

INDIAN RUNNER DUCK

EMBDEN GOOSE

TOULOUSE GOOSE

CHICKENS

Farmers around the world raise about 50 billion chickens a year. Some birds are reared for their meat and others as egg-layers.

BRAHMA

PEKIN BANTAM

BUFF ORPINGTON

CUCKOO MARANS

LIGHT SUSSEX

GOLDEN-LACE WYANDOTTE

Farm animals

Many animals that were once wild are now reared on farms to provide us with food or materials. Some farms specialize in one type of animal – for example, cows, pigs, or chickens – while others rear a variety of livestock.

CATTLE

There are many types of cattle, some kept for milking, others for providing beef. After thousands of years of careful breeding, domestic cattle look very little like their wild ancestors.

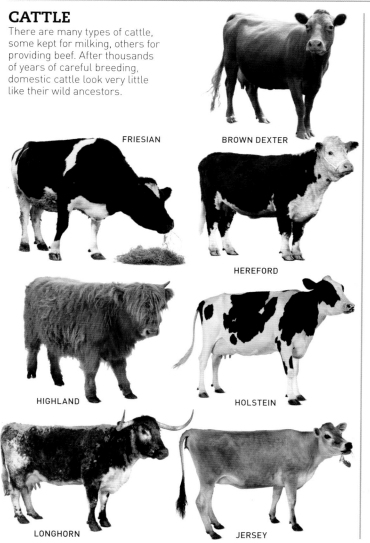

FRIESIAN

BROWN DEXTER

HEREFORD

HIGHLAND

HOLSTEIN

LONGHORN

JERSEY

GREYFACE DARTMOOR

SHEEP

Usually given more freedom to roam than most farm animals, sheep are kept, sometimes in huge numbers, for meat and wool. Some breeds are shorn of their thick coats, known as fleeces, every year.

COTSWOLD

LINCOLN LONGWOOL

WENSLEYDALE

TEXEL CROSS

HEBRIDEAN

JACOB

THE FIRST FARM ANIMALS

Farming developed over thousands of years, as people gradually learned which animals could be useful to them. They also found out how to handle the larger, more dangerous ones such as horses and camels. The dates when most animals were first farmed are not known exactly.

8500 BCE Goats and sheep – Asia

8000 BCE Cattle – Asia, North Africa

4500 BCE Llama – South America

3000 BCE Camels – Asia

400 BCE Rabbits – France

8500 BCE

400 CE

8000 BCE Chickens – South and Southeast Asia

7000 BCE Pigs – Middle East

5000 BCE Alpaca and guinea pigs – South America

4000 BCE Donkey – North Africa Horse – Europe and Asia

HERDWICK

MANX LOAGHTAN

GOATS

Worldwide, goats are popular for their milk, meat, and hair. Easier to keep and feed than cattle, they are particularly important to many small farmers in Asia and Africa.

GOLDEN GUERNSEY

BAGOT

ANGORA

BRITISH ALPINE

PYGMY

PIGS

Most domestic pigs are used for producing pork, ham, and bacon, while a few are kept for showing. The largest numbers of pigs are farmed in China.

BRITISH SADDLEBACK

GLOUCESTER OLD SPOT

LARGE BLACK

PIETRAIN

LARGE WHITE

OTHER FARM ANIMALS

Donkeys or camels are often the main milk providers in countries where there are few cattle. Instead of rearing large animals for meat, some farms breed small ones such as guinea pigs and rabbits. Turkey is a popular alternative to chicken meat, and quails are raised for meat and eggs. Alpacas and llamas are bred for their fine wool.

DONKEY

QUAIL

GUINEA PIG

RABBIT

TURKEY

CAMEL

ALPACA

LLAMA

A HONEYBEE MAY VISIT 100 FLOWERS IN ONE TRIP TO COLLECT POLLEN OR NECTAR

BEEKEEPING

Many people keep bees for fun, but beekeeping is also run as a farming business. Some beekeepers look after hundreds of hives and sell their honey and beeswax to big customers such as supermarkets.

Forest

About 30 per cent of the world's land area is forest. These large areas of trees form dense canopies, which restrict the amount of light that reaches the ground. The types of trees in the forest vary with the climate, but all are home to a range of plants and animals.

WHERE ON EARTH?

Forests grow wherever the climate is warm and rainy enough to support large numbers of trees. This allows forest of different types to grow on every continent, except Antarctica – from the hot, tropical rainforests near the equator to the cooler, snowy forests in the Arctic region.

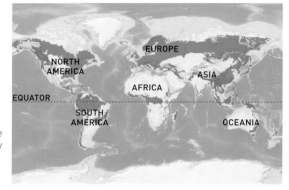

BIODIVERSITY

Every natural forest has a variety of trees and other plants, and provides homes for many animals. In regions with cold winters and warm summers, many trees lose their leaves in winter. Animals survive by lying low or moving somewhere warmer, but the new spring growth feeds masses of insects that support birds and other animals.

Red kite

Oak tree

Silver birch tree

Chaffinch

Red deer and fawn

Sapling (young tree)

Badger sett with badger cubs

European badger

Foxgloves

Roosting tawny owl

Wood anemones

Den with fox cubs

Fly agaric fungus

Red fox

Nettles

Blackbird

Mistlethrush

Leaf litter

Rabbits

Campion

Dogwood

Greater spotted woodpecker

Grey squirrel

TYPES OF FORESTS

Some forests contain many different species of trees, while others contain large groups of the same type. In some parts of the world, trees need special adaptations to survive cold, hot, dry, or wet seasons.

TEMPERATE DRY
These forests have hot, dry summers and mild, wet winters. Trees can be evergreen or deciduous.

TEMPERATE DECIDUOUS
A deciduous tree has large, thin leaves that make food in summer. In winter, when the weather is cold and there is little sun, deciduous trees shed their leaves.

BOREAL EVERGREEN
In cold regions, the summer is too short for deciduous trees to grow well. Here, most of the trees are conifers, with tough, needle-shaped leaves that are resistant to the cold.

MAMMALS

Many forest mammals feed on leaves, fruit, nuts, and seeds. Others, including many bats, prey on insects. Small mammals are targeted by bigger hunters such as foxes, and some forests support packs of wolves.

POLECAT

AMERICAN MIN[K]

OTTER

EURASIAN BADGER

BEECH MARTEN

HEDGEHOG

RACCOON

STRIPED SKUN[K]

BIRDS

In forests with cold winters, many of the birds are summer visitors from warmer regions. They nest, raise their young, then leave. Other birds stay in the forest all year round.

COAL TIT

BARN OWL

ROBIN

PLANT LIFE

Many different types of trees grow in forests. They shelter a variety of smaller plants that can grow in shady conditions. In deciduous forests, some small plants flower in spring before they are shaded by the new leaves growing on the trees.

MOSS

ENGLISH OAK

MONTPELLIER MAPLE

DORMOUSE

BANK VOLE

NOCTULE BAT

EURASIAN WILD BOAR

SIKA DEER

KOALA

ROE DEER

EURASIAN LYNX

RED FOX

RED PANDA

COYOTE

GREY WOLF

BROWN BEAR

MAGPIE

MANDARIN DUCK

BLACKBIRD

COMMON
CROSSBILL

GREEN
WOODPECKER

EURASIAN
BULLFINCH

KINGFISHER

NORTHERN
GOSHAWK

MALLARD

EURASIAN
SPARROWHAWK

WOOD DUCK

INVERTEBRATES

Most forest animals are
insects, spiders, snails,
worms, and other invertebrates.
They flourish in summer, but
most of them hide away or
die off in winter.

TIGER SWALLOWTAIL
BUTTERFLY

LADYBIRD

WOOD ANT

HORNET

STAG BEETLE

COMMON
WASP

DANDELION

STINGING
NETTLE

HART'S
TONGUE FERN

LADY
FERN

WAKE ROBIN

WOOD
ANEMONE

BRITISH
BLUEBELL

WOOD SORREL

FUNGI AND
LICHENS

Dead leaves and
other plant remains
are recycled by
mushrooms and other
fungi. They break down
the tough plant tissue
and turn it into food for
other plants. Lichens are
relatives of fungi that can
make their own food.

LICHEN

BEECH

EUCALYPTUS

COMMON ASPEN

BEACH PINE

SCOTCH PINE

CEDAR

MUSHROOMS

ORANGE LICHEN

EMERGENT LAYER

The forest has many layers, which give animals different places to live. Soaring above the rest of the forest, a few extra-tall trees form the highest layer. These giants make good perches for birds.

SUNLIGHT

HARPY EAGLE
Mexico to South America

BLUE MORPHO BUTTERFLY
Central and South America

SCARLET MACAW
Mexico to South America

HANGING PARROT
Southeast Asia

DENDROBIUM ORCHID
Southeast Asia

CANOPY

Most of the forest trees have broad crowns that form a continuous layer of branches called the canopy. This is where many of the animals live and feed, high above the forest floor.

SUNLIGHT

SHINING-GREEN HUMMINGBIRD
South America

WHITE-THROATED TOUCAN
South America

AFRICAN GREY PARROT
West and Central Africa

BLUE POISON-DART FROG
South America

RED-EYED TREE FROG
Central America

GREEN TREE PYTHON
New Guinea; Australia

MISTLETOE CACTUS
Central America

UNDERSTOREY

Beneath the canopy is a layer of smaller trees and shrubs that can grow in the shade of the tall trees. It is alive with insects, lizards, and tree-living snakes.

SUNLIGHT

FRANQUET'S FRUIT BAT
West and Central Africa

KUHL'S FLYING GECKO
Southeast Asia

PARSON'S CHAMELEON
Madagascar

MAGNIFICENT BIRD OF PARADISE
Papua New Guinea

EMERALD TREE BOA
South America

CHIMPANZEE
West to Central Africa

FOREST FLOOR

The dim light at ground level means that few plants can grow, except in clearings. Fallen fruit and seeds provide food for small animals, which are hunted by predators such as jaguars.

SUNLIGHT

TIGER CENTIPEDE
Southeast Asia

GOLDEN SCARAB
South America

WESTERN GORILLA
Central Africa

EMPEROR SCORPION
Africa

RAFFLESIA
Southeast Asia

KING COBRA
South and Southeast Asia

MANDRILL
Central Africa

RIVER

Thick vegetation grows along the sunlit banks of rivers. In the rainy season, some rivers swell so high that they overflow and flood vast areas of the surrounding forest.

SUNLIGHT

MATAMATA TURTLE
South America

PIRANHA
South America

CAPYBARA
South America

NILE CROCODILE
Africa

MADAGASCAN TOMATO FROGS
Madagascar

EMERGENT LAYER

CANOPY

UNDERSTOREY

FOREST FLOOR

RIVER

VAMPIRE BAT
Mexico to South America

KAPOK TREE
Mexico; Central and South America; West Africa

BRAZIL NUT TREE
South America

BLACK SPIDER MONKEY
South America

MALAYAN FLYING FOX
Southeast Asia

KINKAJOU
Mexico to South America

MALACHITE
North to South America

TAWNY RAJAH
South Asia

GUEREZA
West and central Africa

PILEATED GIBBON
Southeast Asia

ANT PLANT
Southeast Asia; Australia

PITCHER PLANT
Southeast Asia; Australia

POSTMAN BUTTERFLY
Central and South America

JUNGLE NYMPH
Southeast Asia

BROMELIAD PLANT
Mexico to South America

COCOA TREE
Central and South America

SOUTH AMERICAN COATI
South America

GIANT ANTEATER
Central and South America

JAGUAR
Central and South America

SCARLET IBIS
South America; Caribbean

ANACONDA
South America and Trinidad

Rainforest

Tropical rainforests grow in regions that are always warm and wet, so trees and other plants can grow, flower, and produce seeds and fruit all year round. The trees provide homes and food for an amazing variety of animals, with more different species than anywhere else on Earth.

WHERE IN THE WORLD?

Tropical rainforests grow near the equator. The climate here is hot and wet all year round, and has no cold winters or dry summers. The biggest areas of rainforest are in Central and South America, Central Africa, Southeast Asia, and New Guinea. There are smaller patches in Madagascar, India, and northern Australia.

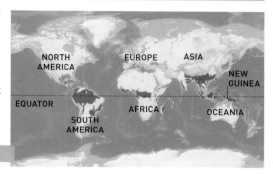

NORTH AMERICA · EUROPE · ASIA · NEW GUINEA · EQUATOR · AFRICA · OCEANIA · SOUTH AMERICA

THE AMAZON TROPICAL RAINFOREST IS THE LARGEST IN THE WORLD

☠ DEADLY LIFE IN THE RAINFOREST

The forests provide homes for many dangerous animals and plants. This list includes some of the most deadly.

STRAWBERRY POISON-DART FROG

○ **POISON-DART FROG**
These tiny, but vividly coloured frogs from tropical America release toxins through their skin.

○ **GABOON VIPER**
This heavy-bodied venomous snake lurks in ambush on the African forest floor.

○ **CURARE**
Extracted from various South American plants, curare was used to poison the tips of blow darts for hunting.

GABOON VIPER

○ **BRAZILIAN WANDERING SPIDER**
This big, long-legged hunter is the world's most deadly spider.

○ **BULLET ANT**
Native to Central and South America, this giant ant has such a painful sting that people say it feels like being hit by a bullet from a gun.

TYPES OF RAINFORESTS

The nature of rainforests depends on where they grow. The tallest trees grow in the warm lowlands, while smaller trees and different types of plants grow higher up in the mountains where the climate is cooler.

LOWLAND RAINFOREST
The warm, wet lowland rainforest has the most plant and animal life, and the richest variety of species.

CLOUD FOREST
Mountain forests are often hidden in the clouds. The trees are always wet and covered with mosses.

FLOODED RAINFOREST
Every year, forests near rivers become flooded. The trees are surrounded by water inhabited by fish and turtles.

LOSING THE RAINFORESTS

At least half the world's rainforests have been cut down for timber or to make way for farms. An area the size of a football pitch is cut down every second. If people carry on doing this, the forests will disappear.

AGRICULTURE
Trees are felled so crops can be grown on the land. Some crops are used to make fuel for our cars.

CATTLE RANCHES
Meat for burgers is produced on ranches – fields of grass created on land that was once rainforest.

LOGGING
Many rainforest trees are cut down for valuable timber called hardwood, which is sold worldwide.

MINING
Minerals such as copper are mined from huge pits dug in the forest. These can cause river pollution.

Savanna

Tropical regions of the world that are too dry for dense rainforest support open grasslands with scattered trees are known as savannas. In the tropical wet season, they are lush and green, but for half the year they are hot, dry, and scorched by wildfires.

WHERE IN THE WORLD?

Tropical grasslands form in warm regions near the equator that have long dry seasons. They include the African savannas, and similar grasslands in South America, India, and northern Australia.

AROUND THE WORLD

Many tropical grasslands are dry with just a few trees. Others are more thickly wooded, or become flooded by seasonal rains. Some have plants adapted for life on high mountains.

SHORTGRASS SAVANNA
The Serengeti in east Africa is a sea of grass dotted with trees.

WOODED SAVANNA
This savanna in Australia is more like open woodland.

FLOODED SAVANNA
Much of the Llanos in South America floods in the rainy season.

MONTANE SAVANNA
Above the tree line it is cooler than in shortgrass savanna.

UNDER THREAT

The wild animals and plants of the savanna are threatened by poaching, habitat loss and fragmentation, farming, and climate change.

○ **HUNTING**
Illegal hunting of savanna animals such as elephants, rhinos, and gazelles is endangering some species. These animals will become extinct if it continues.

○ **OVERGRAZING**
Many farmers keep goats and cattle on the savanna. If there are too many animals, they eat all the wild plants, and the grassland will turn into a barren desert.

○ **FARMING**
More of the savanna is being turned into farmland. Almost half of the wild tropical grassland in South America is now planted with crops such as maize.

○ **WATER LOSS**
Farm crops need regular watering to survive the tropical dry season. The water is taken from natural sources, so there is not enough left for wild animals and plants.

○ **CLIMATE CHANGE**
Global climate change may result in more grasslands turning to desert. But it may also cause some rainforest regions to dry out and become savanna grasslands.

BROWSERS AND GRAZERS

The plant life of the savannas provides food for a wide variety of animals. Some are browsers, which gather the leaves of trees and bushes. Others are grazers, which mainly eat grass and often live in big herds.

GRANT'S GAZELLE

IMPA

EMU

HIPPOPOTAMUS

HUNTERS AND SCAVENGERS

Powerful hunters such as lions prey on the big plant-eating animals. Others, including the giant anteater, hunt insects. Scavengers eat the remains of dead animals.

BLAC
VULTU

SERVAL

LION

REPTILES, AMPHIBIANS, AND INSECTS

The savanna grasslands swarm with insects such as flies, beetles, and termites. There are also many species of frogs, lizards, and snakes.

AFRICAN ROCK PYTHON

NILE MONITOR

LIFE IN THE SAVANNA

The plants and animals of typical savannas are adapted to survive months without rain. Many of the plants are able to avoid losing too much moisture, and the animals learn where to find supplies of vital drinking water.

IN THE DRY SEASON, THE AFRICAN SAVANNA ONLY RECEIVES AROUND 10 CM (4 IN) OF RAIN

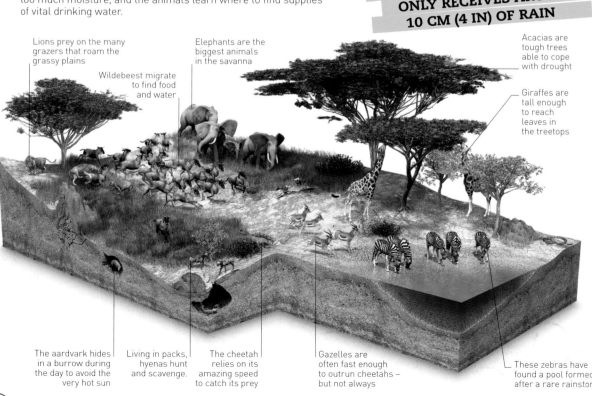

Lions prey on the many grazers that roam the grassy plains

Wildebeest migrate to find food and water

Elephants are the biggest animals in the savanna

Acacias are tough trees able to cope with drought

Giraffes are tall enough to reach leaves in the treetops

The aardvark hides in a burrow during the day to avoid the very hot sun

Living in packs, hyenas hunt and scavenge.

The cheetah relies on its amazing speed to catch its prey

Gazelles are often fast enough to outrun cheetahs – but not always

These zebras have found a pool formed after a rare rainstorm

MARSH DEER

GNU

EASTERN GREY
KANGAROO

AFRICAN SAVANNA
ELEPHANT

FRICAN
FFALO

WHITE RHINOCEROS

GIRAFFE

CAPYBARA

PLANTS

Grasses and other small plants survive the dry season by allowing the parts above ground to die back. When rain comes, they sprout from roots or seeds. Acacia trees are tough enough to avoid drying up, while baobab trees store water in their trunks.

FRICAN WHITE-
ACKED VULTURE

GIANT
ANTEATER

MANED WOLF

AFRICAN
WILD DOG

ACACIA

JAGUAR

SPOTTED
HYENA

SPOTTED HYENAS LIVE IN LARGE GROUPS CALLED CLANS, WHICH ARE LED BY FEMALES

TERMITE

TSETSE FLY

DUNG
BEETLE

AFRICAN
BULLFROG

CANE TOAD

TASMANIAN BLUE GUM

SAVANNA
MONITOR

COMMON EGG-
EATING SNAKE

LEOPARD TORTOISE

AGAMA LIZARD

BAOBAB

Deserts

Deserts are the driest habitats on Earth, with less than 25 cm (10 in) of rainfall a year. They may be hot, cold, or coastal, depending on their geographic position, but all are dry. Desert animals and plants must be able to survive with little or no water and endure significant daily ranges in temperature.

WHERE IN THE WORLD?

The biggest deserts are in the hot, dry parts of north Africa, Arabia, and Australia. Other deserts have formed in Asia and the Americas, in places that are far from oceans, or cut off by mountain ranges.

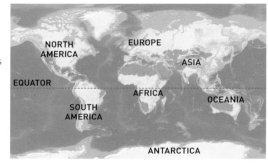

NORTH AMERICA · EUROPE · ASIA · EQUATOR · AFRICA · OCEANIA · SOUTH AMERICA · ANTARCTICA

TYPES OF DESERTS

All deserts share one feature – they are very dry. But they form in many ways, and each desert is different. Many are sandy, others are rocky, and a few are snowy. Some are not as dry as others, and have a lot of plant life.

HOT DESERT
In deserts such as the Sahara, heat makes any moisture dry up. These deserts are hot by day and cold by night. They can be sandy or stony.

COLD DESERT
Cold deserts are far from oceans. They are much cooler than hot deserts, with short summers and heavy snowfall in the winter.

COASTAL DESERT
Where deserts occur by the sea they may be covered in fog but still go for years without rainfall, remaining very dry.

SAND DUNES

The desert wind can blow dry sand into heaps called dunes. When the wind loses strength, it drops the sand suspended in it. The shape the resulting dunes form depends on wind direction and sand texture.

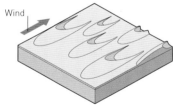

Wind

CRESCENT DUNES
These dunes have less sand at their edges, meaning those parts of the dune move faster, giving a distinctive crescent shape.

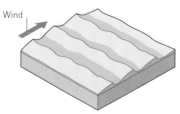

Wind

TRANSVERSE DUNES
Constant winds form long ridges of sand that look like waves on the sea. The crests lie across the direction of the wind.

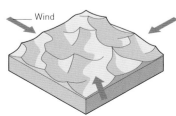

Wind

STAR DUNES
Where the wind blows from different directions, it heaps up sand in irregular shapes. These dunes can grow very big.

MAMMALS

Most desert mammals are small animals that hide in burrows during the day to avoid the heat. Larger mammals such as camels are adapted to withstand the heat and retain water.

MEERKAT · CARACAL · CHINESE HAMSTER · ARABIAN SPINY MOUSE · AFRICAN WILD ASS · FENNEC FOX · BACTRIAN CAMEL · SHORT-BEAKED ECHIDNA · RED KANGAROO

REPTILES

The scaly, waterproof bodies of lizards and other reptiles stop them drying out under the desert sun. Many snakes have a venomous bite, so that they can kill prey quickly without using too much energy.

GREY-BANDED KINGSNAKE · SIDEWINDER · DESERT TORTOISE · DABB LIZARD

SINALOAN MILK SNAKE · RED SPITTING COBRA · DIADEM SNAKE · GILA MONSTER · FRINGE-TOED LIZARD · THORNY DEVIL

PLANTS

Most desert plants have very deep or wide-spreading roots to gather water – some have both. Cactus plants, euphorbias, and others have spongy stems that store water. Other plants survive as seeds, which sprout after rare rainfall.

MESCAL CACTUS · PRICKLY PEAR · DESERT ROSE · HEDGEHOG CACTUS · EUPHORBIA · CARDON CACTUS

IRDS

rds are well-equipped
life in deserts,
cause most can fly
find water, prey, or
ants that have seeded
ter local rainstorms.
e ostrich cannot
, but is able to walk
ng distances.

ROADRUNNER

GALAH

GILA
WOODPECKER

LANNER FALCON

OSTRICH

BURROWING
OWL

TURKEY
VULTURE

NVERTEBRATES

sects, spiders, and scorpions have
rd-shelled bodies that do not dry
t easily. Many can go for days without
ting at all, which helps them survive
here food is scarce.

HARVESTER ANT

JEWEL WASP

DESERT
LOCUST

DESERT
CRICKET

DARKLING
BEETLE

DOMINO
BEETLE

MEXICAN
RED-KNEED
TARANTULA

CRAB
SPIDER

FALSE WHIP
SCORPION

SCORPION

LIFE IN THE DESERT

Only a few types of plants and animals can survive in deserts with
extremely dry climates. In some deserts a little rain falls each year –
these deserts provide a habitat for a wide variety of plants and animals,
from tiny insects to big hunters like the coyote. In parts of other deserts
rain has never been recorded.

AFTER IT RAINS, THE
DESERT SPRINGS TO LIFE,
WITH MANY PLANTS
FLOWERING AT ONCE

The fierce great
horned owl preys on
small mammals, and
may nest in a cactus

The coyote eats
fruit and insects as
well as larger prey

The giant saguaro
cactus has a pleated
stem that expands
to store water

Brittlebush has
hairy leaves that
reduce water loss

Venomous
rattlesnakes catch
small mammals,
sometimes in their
own burrows

The kangaroo rat
can use its long back
legs to roam widely
in search of food

Globemallow has flat
orange flowers that
attract butterflies and
bees in the summer

Polar habitats

In winter, there is little sunlight near the cold North and South poles. In summer, the seas teem with life, which supports large numbers of fish and other animals. Many land animals live in the Arctic, but only a few tiny invertebrates live in Antarctica.

WHERE ON EARTH?

The polar regions consist of the Arctic Ocean and nearby land, and the continent of Antarctica and the surrounding ocean. Large areas of the seas in these regions are frozen in winter.

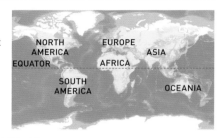

NORTH AMERICA
EUROPE
ASIA
EQUATOR
AFRICA
SOUTH AMERICA
OCEANIA

POLAR REGIONS

There are two different polar regions on Earth. The Arctic is at Earth's North Pole, and Antarctica at the South Pole.

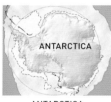

THE ARCTIC
The Arctic is an icy ocean with land all around it, where animals can live.

ASIA
EUROPE
ARCTIC OCEAN

ANTARCTICA
Antarctica is an icy continent, and most of its animals live in the ocean.

ANTARCTICA

POLAR SEASONS

As Earth spins, most places experience day and night. But because of the tilt of Earth's axis, the polar regions are always dark in midwinter, and stay light in midsummer. This is one reason why polar winters are so bitterly cold.

NORTHERN WINTER
In December, the Arctic is in almost constant darkness.

FOOD WEB

In the Antarctic, all the animals get their food from the sea. Tiny drifting algae (phytoplankton) feed swarms of krill, which are in turn eaten by baleen whales, seals, penguins, and birds. Fish are eaten by seals and birds, while orcas eat anything they can catch.

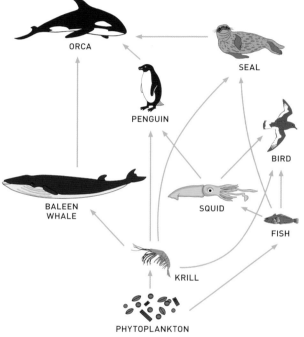
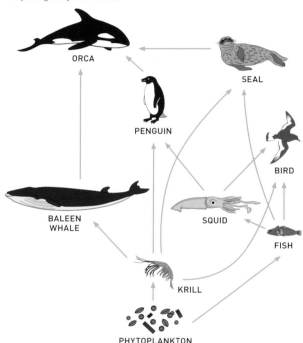

ORCA
SEAL
PENGUIN
BIRD
BALEEN WHALE
SQUID
FISH
KRILL
PHYTOPLANKTON

LAND MAMMALS

The Arctic is the only polar region with land mammals. Some are summer visitors, but others such as the musk ox live in the Arctic all year round. Polar bears live mainly on the sea ice.

ARCTIC HARE

COLLARED PIKA
SNOWSHOE HARE

ERMINE
ARCTIC LEMMING

MARINE LIFE

Giant whales cruise the polar oceans, eating vast numbers of krill and fish. Smaller whales and seals hunt fish, squid, and shellfish.

BOWHEAD WHALE

LIFE IN THE ARCTIC

The Arctic has a greater diversity of life than the Antarctic, because it has many different types of land animals. Arctic seas are also rich in food and marine life.

Arctic foxes have thick fur coats to keep out the cold

Ptarmigan

Musk oxen dig through the snow to find food

Snowy owls seize lemmings from their runs under the snow

Ermine

Arctic hare

In winter and spring, polar bears prowl the sea ice in search of seals

Lemmings live and feed under the snow

The walrus hunts shellfish on the seabed

Polar bear cubs

The male narwhal has a long spiral tusk. Narwhals eat squid and large fish such as cod

Ringed seal

Orcas hunt seals and big fish in the open sea

BIRDS

Many land birds range over the Arctic, but all Antarctic birds, such as penguins, find their food in the ocean.

ALBATROS

SNOWY OWL

PEREGRINE FALCON

WOLVERINE

ARCTIC FOX

ARCTIC WOLF

REINDEER

MUSK OX

POLAR BEAR

BEARDED SEAL

LEOPARD SEAL

WALRUS

HARP SEAL

BELUGA

ORCA

NARWHAL

GREENLAND SHARK

PLANTS

Only the toughest plants can survive the extreme cold of a polar winter. Most are low-growing, so they are sheltered from the wind, and there are no tall trees. In the Arctic, all the plants flower at once when spring arrives to make the most of the short summer.

ARCTIC TERN

ARCTIC SKUA

SOUTH POLAR SKUA

AMERICAN GOLDEN PLOVER

LITTLE AUK

PUFFIN

ROCK PTARMIGAN

SNOW BUNTING

COTTONGRASS

ARCTIC WILLOW

BALD EAGLE

CANADA GOOSE

KING PENGUIN

ARCTIC POPPY

PASQUE FLOWER

SUNLIT ZONE

TWILIGHT ZONE

DARK ZONE

ABYSSAL ZONE

HADAL ZONE

SUNLIT ZONE

Near the ocean surface, sunlight provides vital energy that fuels the growth of tiny organisms drifting in the water. The algae feed swarms of small animals that are eaten by fish and other marine life.

CANDY STRIPE FLATWORM

BOTTLENOSE DOLPHIN

KILLER WHALE

LONGNOSED HAWKFISH

HERMIT CRAB

FLAMBOYANT CUTTLEFISH

SPOTTED SEAHORSE

FLYING GURNARD

SEA LION

GARFISH

SUNLIGHT

DUGONG

CLOWN TRIGGERFIS

TWILIGHT ZONE

Below 200 m (660 ft) there is only faint blue light. Algae that need light cannot survive, so there is not much food for small animals. Bigger animals hunt each other.

OCTOPUS

RED LIONFISH

SUNLIGHT

SEAL

LIZARDFISH

DARK ZONE

Deeper than 1,000 m (3,300 ft), the water is dark apart from the eerie glow produced by luminous animals. Life is scarce, but some deep divers visit from the surface.

SPERM WHALE

SUNLIGHT

PELICAN EEL

FRILLED SHARK

ABYSSAL ZONE

This is the deepest part of the dark zone, and includes the ocean floor. Most of the animals here feed on dead algae and scraps that drift down from above.

THE ABYSSAL ZONE IS COLD, DARK, AND THE PRESSURE IS SO INTENSE THAT IT WOULD CRUSH A HUMAN

STOPLIGHT LOOSEJAW

SUNLIGHT

PACIFIC GRENADIER

NURSE SHARK

SEAMOTH

WHITETIP REEF SHARK

TIGER SHARK

ROYAL ANGELFISH

STONEFISH

SPOTTED BOXFISH

HUMPBACK GROUPER

BLUE CHROMIS

BLUE-SPOTTED RIBBONTAIL RAY

WARTY FROGFISH

TIGER PRAWN

SPOTTED CLEANER SHRIMP

PRICKLY PACIFIC DRUPE

PANAMIC ARROW CRAB

SEA STRAWBERRY SOFT CORAL

FLUTED GIANT CLAM

BROWN TUBE SPONGE

ANTARCTIC KRILL

ATLANTIC HORSESHOE CRAB

BRITTLE STAR

GIANT SQUID

ORANGE ROUGHY

LONGNOSE LANCETFISH

VIPERFISH

COMMON FANGTOOTH

CUSK EEL

ANGLERFISH

SNAILFISH

SUNLIGHT

HADAL ZONE

In some places, deep ocean trenches plunge deeper than the ocean floor. Some animals live in this zone, but very little is known about them.

Ocean

The oceans form the biggest environment for wildlife on the planet. Most organisms live near the sunlit surface, especially in shallow water near land, where the water is rich in food. But some animals are able to live in the ocean depths, where there is no light and very little to eat.

WHERE ON EARTH?

The five interconnected oceans cover more than two-thirds of the planet. The biggest ocean is the Pacific, while the smallest is the Arctic Ocean at the North Pole. The Atlantic extends all the way from the Arctic to the Southern Ocean around Antarctica. All the oceans, whether cold or warm, are teeming with life.

ARCTIC OCEAN

ATLANTIC OCEAN

EQUATOR

PACIFIC OCEAN

PACIFIC OCEAN

INDIAN OCEAN

SOUTHERN OCEAN

ANIMAL RELATIONSHIPS

The oceans are full of dangers, so some animals join forces to improve their chances of survival. Others tag along with larger animals to feast on scraps of food that their big partners ignore.

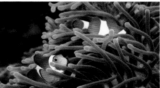

CLOWNFISH AND ANEMONE
The stinging tentacles of a big sea anemone do not affect the clownfish, but they protect it from predators.

MANTA RAY AND REMORA FISH
A sucker on its head allows the remora to cling to big fish, like this manta ray, as they cruise the oceans.

BOXER CRAB AND ANEMONES
This tiny tropical crab holds a stinging sea anemone in each claw. It uses them for defence, and to stun prey.

GROUPS OF FISH

Many open-water fish travel in big groups called shoals or schools. Some contain thousands of fish. Living together like this makes it difficult for big hunters such as sharks to pick out individual fish.

BLACK SMOKERS

In some of the deepest parts of the ocean, water seeps into the ocean floor and is heated by hot volcanic rock. The hot water forms a spring on the ocean floor, which erupts. As the hot water hits the cold sea, the minerals turn into solid particles that build up to form smoking "chimneys" up to 55 m (180 ft) high. Amazingly, there are unique animals, including some tubeworms, that can survive this extreme heat.

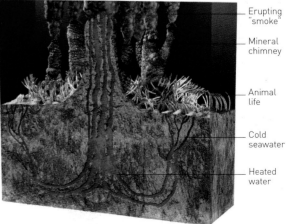

Erupting "smoke"

Mineral chimney

Animal life

Cold seawater

Heated water

Coral reef

Tropical coral reefs are the most complex of all underwater habitats. They are created by simple animals called corals that live in big colonies and have hard, stony skeletons. The coral colonies shelter an amazing variety of marine life, including many kinds of fish and invertebrates.

WHERE IN THE WORLD?

Coral reefs grow in clear, shallow, warm water near tropical shores. Most of them lie in the western Pacific and Indian oceans.

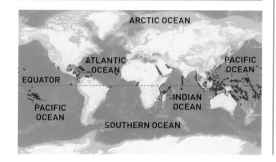

ARCTIC OCEAN
ATLANTIC OCEAN
PACIFIC OCEAN
EQUATOR
PACIFIC OCEAN
INDIAN OCEAN
SOUTHERN OCEAN

TYPES OF REEFS

Many reefs grow around islands, forming fringes of coral in the shallow water. If an island is an extinct volcano, it gradually sinks, while the reef keeps growing upwards. This creates a barrier reef. Eventually, the island sinks from sight, leaving a coral atoll.

FRINGING REEF
This tropical volcanic island is surrounded by a fringing reef. The extinct volcano slowly starts to sink.

The island sinks, but the coral keeps growing

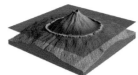

BARRIER REEF
As the island continues to sink, the reef grows upwards, forming a barrier reef around a ring-shaped lagoon.

Reef encloses a shallow central lagoon

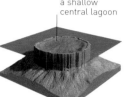

ATOLL
The original island sinks below the waves, leaving behind a ring of coral – an atoll.

BIG VISITORS

The animals living on the reefs attract big hunters such as giant groupers, sharks, and dolphins. These usually hunt in the deeper channels between the corals. Sea turtles may visit to lay their eggs in the coral sand of the lagoon beaches.

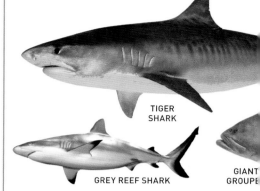

TIGER SHARK

GREY REEF SHARK

GIANT GROUPE

REEF FISH

The water around the coral is alive with small fish that may swim in shoals. Some live in crevices in the reefs, and slip out to feed when it is safe. Most of them feed on small animals, but some nibble seaweed.

PORCUPINE FISH

SURGEON FISH

FIREFISH

MANTA RAY

LIFE IN A CORAL REEF

Reef corals have stinging cells that capture food. They also have tiny algae living in their tissues – the coral uses some of the sugar the algae produce, and in return provides the algae with a safe environment to live in. Corals also provide food for many other types of animals – reefs swarm with colourful fish, starfish, shrimps, crabs, and even sea snakes.

Banded sea krait (a sea snake)

Sea grass growing in coral sand

Golf ball sponge

Royal angelfish

Table coral – one of the biggest types of reef coral

Cloth of gold cone shell – a venomous hunter

Finger coral

Tube sponge filters water for food

Giant grouper

Sea slug grazing on coral

REEF INVERTEBRATES

As well as corals, many other invertebrates live on the reefs. Sponges, sea squirts, and clams filter the water for food, while sea slugs, shrimps, and crabs search for scraps and living prey.

SCARLET CLEANER SHRIMP

GIANT CLAM

CORALS

Every coral reef is made up of many different types of coral. They include brain corals, staghorn corals, and sea fans. Each one is a colony of animals sharing a hard, stony skeleton.

MUSHROOM CORAL

BRAIN CORAL

BLACKTIP REEF
SHARK

HAWKSBILL TURTLE

WHALE SHARK

BOTTLENOSE
DOLPHIN

HAMMERHEAD
SHARK

ORCA

PARROTFISH

GREAT BARRACUDA

MANDARIN
FISH

**THE DWARF SEAHORSE IS
THE SLOWEST FISH IN THE
WORLD, WITH A TOP SPEED
OF 1.5 M (5.25 FT) PER HOUR**

BLUE-SPOTTED
RIBBONTAIL RAY

CLOWN TRIGGER FISH

QUEEN ANGELFISH

YELLOW
SHRIMP GOBY

DAMSELFISH

ELECTRIC
RAY

CORAL TROUT

THREADFIN
BUTTERFLY FISH

YELLOW TANG

SEAHORSE

JEWELFISH

LION FISH

CLOWN FISH

LONGNOSED
HAWKFISH

RED HERMIT
CRAB

SEA
SQUIRT

SEA SLUG

SEA SPONGE

SOFT CORAL

STAGHORN CORAL

SEA FAN

CORAL REEF
Live coral grows on top of
the stony remains of dead
coral to build the reef.

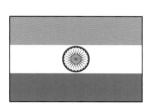

Geography

Earth

Formed more than 4.5 billion years ago, Earth is the only place in the Universe known to support life. Its breathable atmosphere, liquid-water oceans, and large areas of dry land support a rich diversity of living things.

MAGNETIC FIELD

With its iron core, Earth acts like an enormous bar magnet with north and south poles. As Earth spins, swirling currents occur in the molten metal within its outer core. This movement generates a powerful magnetic shield.

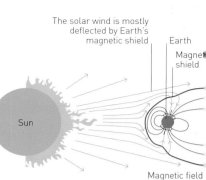

The solar wind is mostly deflected by Earth's magnetic shield

Sun

Earth

Magnetic shield

Magnetic field

EARTH'S STRUCTURE

Earth is made up of many different layers. At its centre is a hot, metallic core surrounded by a thick layer of solid but slowly moving rock, called the mantle. Earth's thin crust sits on top.

INNER CORE
This solid iron-nickel alloy core is boiling hot but stays solid due to the extreme pressure at Earth's centre.

OUTER CORE
A layer of liquid iron and nickel surrounds the inner core. It is in constant motion.

MANTLE
The mantle is solid but slowly moves around.

CRUST
The solid outer layer of Earth is the only part we can see.

OCEAN
Saltwater oceans cover almost three-quarters of Earth's surface.

ATMOSPHERE
Earth is surrounded by a layer of gases known as the atmosphere, which gradually merge into space.

Over a quarter of Earth's surface is land made up of continental crust. This is thicker than the oceanic crust that occurs under the oceans

HABITATS

Plants and animals live in natural environments on Earth, called habitats. These habitats vary, depending on rainfall, temperature, and location.

OCEAN
The largest habitat on Earth, the ocean is home to as many as a million types of plants and animals.

CORAL REEF
Formed in clear, warm, shallow waters, coral reefs are like beautiful underwater gardens, teeming with marine life.

POLAR REGIONS
With freezing temperatures, the Arctic and Antarctic are the most inhospitable places on Earth.

GRASSLAND
Found on every continent except Antarctica, grassland covers about one-third of Earth's land surface.

INSIDE EARTH'S CRUST

The rocky crust layer that makes up Earth's continents and ocean floors contains many different chemical elements. Most of the crust is formed of silicon dioxide, which consists of joined-together silicon and oxygen atoms.

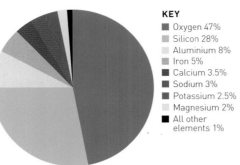

KEY
- Oxygen 47%
- Silicon 28%
- Aluminium 8%
- Iron 5%
- Calcium 3.5%
- Sodium 3%
- Potassium 2.5%
- Magnesium 2%
- All other elements 1%

ELEMENTS IN EARTH'S CRUST

ATMOSPHERE

Earth is surrounded by a thick blanket of gases that make up its atmosphere. Without it, life on Earth would not exist. Around 20 per cent of the atmosphere consists of oxygen, the rest is mostly nitrogen, with just small amounts of other gases, such as carbon dioxide.

EXOSPHERE
This is the outer zone. Gas molecules can escape into space from here.

THERMOSPHERE
In this zone, temperature increases with height.

MESOSPHERE
A zone where temperature decreases with height.

STRATOSPHERE
Absorption of ultraviolet sunlight adds energy to the stratosphere, so temperature increases with height here.

Weather balloon

TROPOSPHERE
All weather occurs in this layer.

Clouds

- 500 km (310 miles)
- Aurora
- 80 km (50 miles)
- Meteors
- 50 km (30 miles)
- 16 km (10 miles)
- Aeroplane

LAYERS OF ATMOSPHERE

TECTONIC PLATES

Earth's crust is broken into pieces, or tectonic plates, that fit together like a jigsaw puzzle. These plates float on the mantle – solid but slowly moving rock with pockets of liquid magma. When the mantle moves, so do the plates.

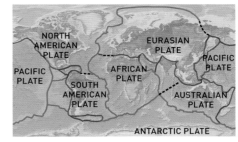

NORTH AMERICAN PLATE
PACIFIC PLATE
SOUTH AMERICAN PLATE
EURASIAN PLATE
AFRICAN PLATE
PACIFIC PLATE
AUSTRALIAN PLATE
ANTARCTIC PLATE

KEY
- Convergent
- Divergent
- Uncertain
- Transform

ON THE MOVE
Earth's plates are constantly moving towards, away from, or alongside one another.

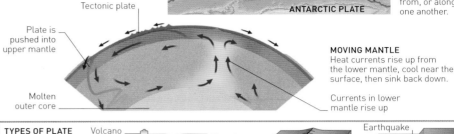

Tectonic plate

Plate is pushed into upper mantle

Molten outer core

MOVING MANTLE
Heat currents rise up from the lower mantle, cool near the surface, then sink back down.

Currents in lower mantle rise up

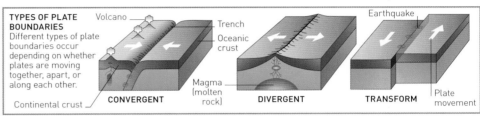

TYPES OF PLATE BOUNDARIES
Different types of plate boundaries occur depending on whether plates are moving together, apart, or along each other.

Volcano
Trench
Oceanic crust
Earthquake
Magma (molten rock)
Continental crust
Plate movement

CONVERGENT   **DIVERGENT**   **TRANSFORM**

MOUNTAIN BUILDING

Most mountains are "fold mountains" that have been created over millions of years by the movement of tectonic plates across Earth's surface. Many mountain ranges, such as the Himalayas, are still being pushed upwards.

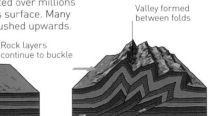

Rock layers are pushed horizontally
Thrust fault
Rock layers continue to buckle
Valley formed between folds

1 FAULT FORMS
As two plates meet, the rock of Earth's crust lifts up, forming a thrust fault.

2 SECOND FAULT FORMS
The plates continue to converge, leading to further faulting and folding upwards.

3 THIRD FAULT FORMS
Over time, a complex of fractured and buckled rock layers form a mountain range.

HIGHEST AND DEEPEST

At 8,848 m (29,029 ft), the top of Mount Everest, part of the Himalaya mountain range in Asia, is Earth's highest point. By contrast, the Mariana Trench, in the Pacific Ocean, is the deepest, reaching 10,920 m (35,829 ft) below sea level.

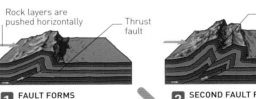

9,000 M — MT EVEREST — K2
6,000 M
3,000 M
0 M
3,000 M
6,000 M
9,000 M — TONGA TRENCH
12,000 M — MARIANA TRENCH

LIFE ON EARTH

More than 3.5 billion years ago, life on Earth began. Over time, it has evolved and diversified to suit its natural environment.

ARCHAEA
A very early form of life, consisting of single cells.

BACTERIA
Microscopic bacteria live in most habitats. Some cause diseases.

PROTISTS
Made of single cells with nuclei, some protists can make their own food.

FUNGI
Fungi get their nutrients from dead organic matter.

PLANTS
Plants use sunlight to make food, and release oxygen into the air.

ANIMALS
Animals get their food from eating other organisms.

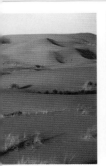

DESERT
With sparse rain and extreme temperatures, little life survives here.

RIVER AND WETLAND
Despite covering less than one per cent of Earth's surface, freshwater rivers and wetland support a lot of plants and animals.

MOUNTAIN
Wildlife is plentiful on warm, lower mountain slopes, but at higher altitudes, temperatures drop, and little can survive.

FOREST
Forests are made up of the biggest plants on Earth – trees. They provide shelter and food to a vast array of life.

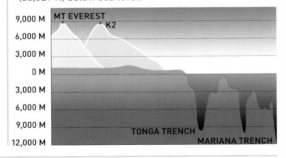

Volcanoes

Deep inside Earth are pockets of hot, molten rock. Now and then, this fluid surges up to the surface and pours out in a volcanic eruption. Some volcanoes stay active over millions of years, whereas others erupt only for a few years.

WHAT IS A VOLCANO?

A volcano is an opening in Earth's surface through which a mixture of gases and molten rock, or magma, escapes from an underground chamber. The outflow cools and sets, shaping the volcano.

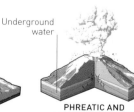

Ash cloud

Main opening through whi magma escapes

Magma is called lava when it flow on the surfa

Bedrock

HOW A VOLCANO GROWS

A volcano builds itself up out of its own erupted materials, such as lava and ash. Red-hot when it flows out, this matter cools to form solid rock.

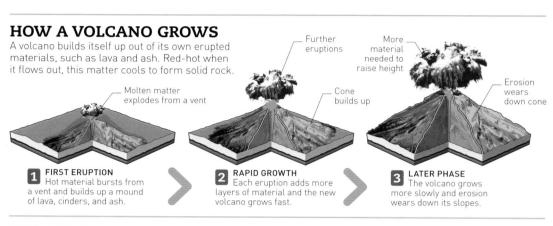

Molten matter explodes from a vent

Further eruptions

More material needed to raise height

Cone builds up

Erosion wears down cone

1 FIRST ERUPTION
Hot material bursts from a vent and builds up a mound of lava, cinders, and ash.

2 RAPID GROWTH
Each eruption adds more layers of material and the new volcano grows fast.

3 LATER PHASE
The volcano grows more slowly and erosion wears down its slopes.

VOLCANO TYPES

Not all volcanoes have a steep "smoking mountain" shape. Other forms include shield volcanoes – which look like huge, upturned dinner plates – and small cindery cones. Calderas are craters that appear when a volcano collapses.

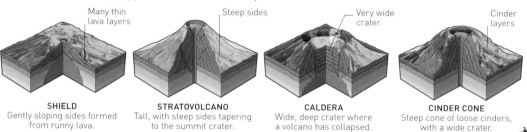

Many thin lava layers

Steep sides

Very wide crater

Cinder layers

SHIELD
Gently sloping sides formed from runny lava.

STRATOVOLCANO
Tall, with steep sides tapering to the summit crater.

CALDERA
Wide, deep crater where a volcano has collapsed.

CINDER CONE
Steep cone of loose cinders, with a wide crater.

LARGEST ACTIVE SHIELD VOLCANOES

LOCATION	SHAPE	SUMMIT HEIGHT	MAXIMUM WIDTH OF BASE
Mauna Loa, Hawaii		4,169 m (13,677 ft)	95 km (59 miles)
Erta Ale, Ethiopia		613 m (2,011 ft)	80 km (50 miles)
Sierra Negra, Galápagos		1,500 m (4,921 ft)	50 km (31 miles)
Nyamuragira, Democratic Republic of Congo		3,058 m (10,033 ft)	45 km (28 miles)
Kilauea, Hawaii		1,247 m (4,091 ft)	50 km (31 miles)

ERUPTIONS

Volcanoes have many different eruption styles. They may produce lava in short bursts, start erupting with a terrific bang, or pump out mushroom clouds of ash.

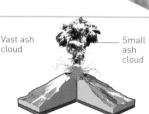

Vast ash cloud

Small ash cloud

Lava flows from crack

PLINIAN
Steady, powerful blast.

STROMBOLIAN
Short lava showers.

FISSURE OR ICELANDIC
Erupts from crack in ground

Red-hot volcanic "bombs"

Ash explodes out of sea

Flow or surge of material

Underground water

VULCANIAN
Starts with a bang.

SURTSEYAN
Erupts below the sea surface.

PELEAN
Flows and surges of gas and ash.

PHREATIC AND PHREATOMAGMATIC
Molten rock meets water.

VOLCANIC FALLOUT

An eruption blasts a lot of dangerous material into the air. Molten lava "bombs", hot cinders, rocks, and ash fly upwards then fall to the ground. Poisonous, suffocating gases are also given off.

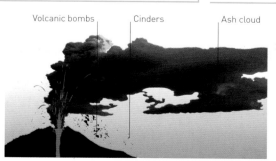

Volcanic bombs

Cinders

Ash cloud

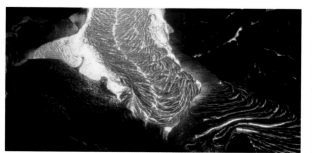

LAVA

The red-hot flow that pours from a volcano is lava – the name given to molten rock, or magma, once it reaches the surface. The hottest lavas are thin and runny, and flow a long way before cooling and solidifying. Others are thick and sticky, and creep just a short way before coming to a stop.

CALDERAS

A caldera is a vast bowl in the ground. Calderas form when a volcano comes apart during an eruption, and the surface collapses into the emptying magma chamber.

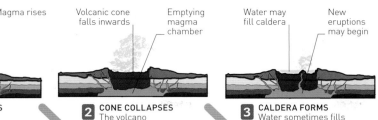

1 VOLCANO ERUPTS
Magma explodes upwards, emptying the inner chamber.

2 CONE COLLAPSES
The volcano collapses into the emptying chamber.

3 CALDERA FORMS
Water sometimes fills a caldera to form a lake. A new volcano may arise.

Magma rises · *Volcanic cone falls inwards* · *Emptying magma chamber* · *Water may fill caldera* · *New eruptions may begin*

LIVING NEAR A VOLCANO

Many people spend their lives next door to a volcano. They are prepared to put up with the risk of danger because there are a few advantages, too.

POSITIVES

TOURISM
Sightseers bring in money.

AGRICULTURE
Volcanic soil is good for growing crops.

ENERGY
Hot underground water is used by industry.

NEGATIVES

DEATH
Eruptions can kill people and ruin land.

MUDFLOWS
Violent floods wash down volcanic debris.

REFUGEES
People lose their homes and livelihoods.

A THICK LAVA FLOW CAN TAKE YEARS TO COOL DOWN COMPLETELY

Magma erupts from surface crack

1,200°C (2,190°F) The temperature at Earth's surface of the hottest lavas.

600°C (1,112°F) The flame temperature of a lighted match.

100°C (212°F) The boiling point of water at sea level.

chamber full of molten rock, or magma

RED-HOT

Scientists are exploring ways of tapping into the huge energy produced by hot magma. One day, this could provide the world with a big new source of power.

FLOWS AND SURGES

Pyroclastic flows are lethal currents of hot gas, ash, and rocks. These currents race down a volcano, destroying everything in their path. Just as deadly are billowing, choking clouds called pyroclastic surges. They contain more gas than pyroclastic flows and can move faster.

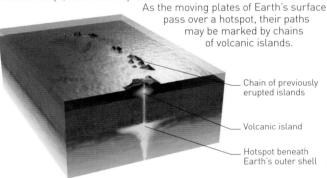

FLOW Dense currents of rock, ash, and gas

SURGE Faster and more turbulent than a flow

VOLCANIC ISLAND CHAINS

Beneath some ocean floors are volcanic areas, or "hotspots". If these erupt, lava builds up until it rises out of the sea as an island. As the moving plates of Earth's surface pass over a hotspot, their paths may be marked by chains of volcanic islands.

- Chain of previously erupted islands
- Volcanic island
- Hotspot beneath Earth's outer shell

MOST DEADLY

These are 10 of the biggest volcanic disasters. The worst, Tambora, killed more than 70,000 people. The most famous is Vesuvius's eruption in 79 CE.

1 MOUNT TAMBORA, 1815
Sumbawa island, Indonesia. Ejected ash blocked the sun and lowered global temperatures.

2 KRAKATOA, 1883
Krakatoa island, Indonesia. Made the loudest bang ever recorded and blew up most of the island.

3 MT PELEE, 1902
Martinique, Caribbean Islands. Ash and gas flowed at speeds of more than 600 kph (370 mph).

4 NEVADO DEL RUIZ, 1985
Colombia. Gigantic mudflows overwhelmed an entire town.

5 MOUNT UNZEN, 1792
Japan. Created a landslide and a tsunami.

6 LAKI, 1783
Iceland. Poisonous gas killed half of Iceland's farm livestock.

7 KELUT, 1919
Java, Indonesia. Mudslides destroyed more than 100 villages.

8 SANTA MARIA, 1902
Guatemala. Ash detected 4,000 km (2,500 miles) away.

9 GALUNGGUNG, 1882
Java, Indonesia. Destroyed 114 villages.

10 VESUVIUS, 79 CE
Italy. The cities of Herculaneum and Pompeii were wiped out. An eruption in 1631 caused further deaths.

CAST OF A POMPEII DISASTER VICTIM

SUPERVOLCANOES

These are the monsters, capable of eruptions thousands of times larger than those of any other kind of volcano. Luckily, there aren't many of them. Here are some of the most important.

YELLOWSTONE This map shows the vast area of North America affected in one of Yellowstone's ancient eruptions.

Yellowstone caldera

YELLOWSTONE CALDERA
Wyoming, USA. Makes up much of Yellowstone Park.

LONG VALLEY CALDERA
California, USA. Recent uplifting of ground observed.

VALLES CALDERA
New Mexico. Hot springs are a sign of volcanic activity.

LAKE TOBA
Sumatra, Indonesia. World's largest volcanic lake.

LAKE TAUPO
New Zealand. Has erupted 28 times.

AIRA CALDERA
Japan. Contains a currently active volcanic cone.

WHERE IN THE WORLD?

Volcanoes emerge in clusters in just a few places around the world. There are large numbers in the area called the "Ring of Fire" that circles the Pacific Ocean. Iceland, East Africa, and the Caribbean are big volcanic regions, too.

IN SPACE

Earth is not the only body in the Solar System to have volcanoes. Some of our neighbours in space have many volcanic regions.

OLYMPUS MONS / MT EVEREST

SLEEPING GIANT
Olympus Mons, a vast volcano on Mars, is three times as high as Mount Everest. It is not active at the moment.

TRITON
Volcanic eruptions on Neptune's biggest moon can last a whole year.

IO
This moon of Jupiter has many active volcanoes.

VENUS
The planet's surface is made almost entirely of volcanoes.

NEPTUNE · URANUS · SATURN · JUPITER · MARS · EARTH · VENUS · MERCURY

Earthquakes

Earth's surface is broken up into different sections, called tectonic plates. These are always on the move, and sometimes shift in ways that cause violent vibrations. Such vibrations are called earthquakes.

EARTHQUAKE-PRONE ZONES

Some countries are more affected by earthquakes than others because they lie on the boundaries of tectonic plates. The ten countries shown here have the highest death rates in the world due to violent earthquakes.

WHAT CAUSES EARTHQUAKES?

The plates on Earth's surface move in ways that makes one plate push over or slide past another. If the rocky surface is not strong enough to bear the stress, it breaks. This sends out vibrations called "seismic waves" that travel outwards from the breaking point (the focus).

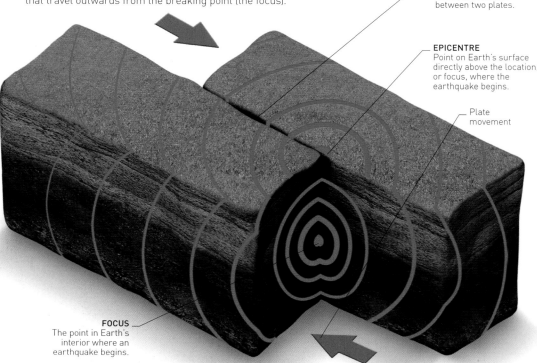

FAULT LINE
Line of movement on Earth's surface between two plates.

EPICENTRE
Point on Earth's surface directly above the location, or focus, where the earthquake begins.

Plate movement

FOCUS
The point in Earth's interior where an earthquake begins.

FAULT TYPES

Faults are the boundaries between two moving tectonic plates. They are often the sites of earthquakes. The blocks of rock on either side of a fault can shift and slide past each other in various ways.

NORMAL FAULT
Rock on one side of the fault moves down, so it is lower than the rock on the other side of the fault.

REVERSE FAULT
One block is pushed up relative to the other, so it ends up at a higher level.

STRIKE-SLIP FAULT
The rocks on either side of the fault move in different directions, scraping side by side.

OBLIQUE-SLIP FAULT
The rocks on either side of the fault move sideways and up or down relative to each other.

SEISMIC WAVES

Two types of seismic waves created by an earthquake can travel right through Earth's interior. P-waves pass through both solid and liquid layers. S-waves, slower but more dangerous waves, move only through solid rock.

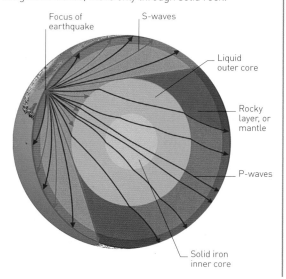

Focus of earthquake

S-waves

Liquid outer core

Rocky layer, or mantle

P-waves

Solid iron inner core

HOW SEVERE?

The Mercalli scale, below, is one way of measuring the intensity of an earthquake. For more precise estimates, scientists use the "moment magnitude" scale, which measures the amount of energy released during a quake.

I–II
Hardly felt by people, but can be measured by instruments.

III–IV
Felt indoors as a quick vibration that makes hanging objects shake.

V–VI
Rocking motion felt by people; also makes buildings tremble.

VII–VIII
Buildings shake badly, and tree branches break and fall.

IX–XI
Buildings crack and some fall; underground pipes torn apart.

XII
Most buildings are destroyed; rivers are forced to change course.

MAJOR EARTHQUAKES

Earthquakes can cause terrible devastation. The following have some of the highest-ever measurements on the moment magnitude scale.

1 CHILE, 22 MAY 1960
Registering at magnitude 9.5, this is the largest recorded earthquake. It occurred in the Pacific Ocean and caused a series of tsunamis that left two million people homeless.

2 PRINCE WILLIAM SOUND, ALASKA, 28 MARCH 1964
This huge earthquake (magnitude 9.2) caused a tsunami that rose to 67 m (220 ft) and hit Hawaii, Canada, and the USA. In the first day there were 11 aftershocks with magnitudes greater than 6.0.

3 NORTHERN SUMATRA, 26 DECEMBER 2004
This ruptured the longest fault of any recorded quake, spanning 1,500 km (900 miles) in ten minutes. More than 227,000 people were killed by the resulting tsunami.

4 HONSHU, JAPAN, 11 MARCH 2011
This 9.0-magnitude earthquake occurred off the coast of Japan and reached depths of 24.4 km (15 miles). The resulting tsunami caused more than 15,800 deaths.

5 KAMCHATKA, RUSSIA, 4 NOVEMBER 1952
Registering a magnitude of 8.2, this earthquake set off a Pacific-wide tsunami that hit Peru, Chile, New Zealand, many Pacific islands, and California, USA.

MEASURING EARTHQUAKES

Scientists measure earthquake vibrations with an instrument called a seismometer. In various forms, the seismometer has been in use for thousands of years.

1855
Italian physicist Luigi Palmieri designs a seismometer that can record the direction, intensity, and duration of earthquakes too small for humans to notice.

Palmieri's seismometer

1902
Italian scientist Giuseppe Mercalli invents a scale for measuring earthquakes based on observation of effects.

1925
Americans Harry Wood and James Anderson's seismometer is precise enough to be used ten years later for the Richter scale.

Seismograph, recorded 1920s

AROUND 500,000 EARTHQUAKES ARE RECORDED BY INSTRUMENTS EVERY YEAR

1700   2015

1703
French inventor Jean de Hautefeuille builds a basic seismometer by filling a bowl with mercury and noting the amount and direction of spill during an earthquake.

1751
Italian teacher Andrea Bina uses a pendulum with a pointer to trace movement in the sand below during an earthquake.

Bina's pendulum

1880
While working in Japan, British geologist John Milne develops the first accurate seismometer.

1907
German physicist Emil Wiechert builds a machine that records an earthquake using an oscillating pendulum.

Wiechert's pendulum

1934
American seismologist Charles Richter develops a widely used scale that measures the energy released by an earthquake.

1979–PRESENT
The moment magnitude scale is introduced as a more accurate version of the Richter scale.

EARLY WARNING SYSTEMS

Early warning systems act to protect people, animals, and property by alerting people of incoming seismic waves from an earthquake. This gives people time to take cover, businesses and power stations time to make equipment safe, and emergency services time to prepare for action.

1 MOVEMENT DETECTED
Early warning systems quickly detect the first signs of an earthquake, estimate the location and magnitude, and calculate areas under threat.

2 ALERT DISPATCHED
The time between the first alert and the arrival of strong tremors is short. Warnings are transmitted to as many broadcasting stations as possible.

EARTHQUAKE DRILL

One simple emergency drill has been proven to reduce injuries from earthquakes: Drop, Cover, Hold On. This is because most injuries come from falling objects such as lamps and glass, rather than from building collapse.

1 DROP
Drop to the ground immediately to protect yourself as much as possible where you are.

2 COVER
Take cover under a sturdy desk or table if possible; if not, move to the corner of the room.

3 HOLD ON
Hold on to the desk or table while covering your head and neck with your arms.

RESISTING EARTHQUAKES

While no structure can be guaranteed completely safe from earthquake damage, the buildings listed here have proven to be very resistant to massive ground shakes.

CHECHEN ITZA, MEXICO
The Mayan pyramid of El Castillo at Chechen Itza is very strong as it has a base much broader than its summit.

TOMB OF CYRUS, IRAN
Built in 400 BCE, this uses "base-isolation" to survive shakes: its base moves independently of its foundations.

YOKOHAMA LANDMARK TOWER, JAPAN
This skyscraper has a mass damper system, sits on rollers, and is made from flexible materials.

TRANSAMERICA PYRAMID, USA
Rising to 260 m (853 ft), this skyscraper in San Francisco has foundations that reach 16 m (52 ft) into the ground.

TAIPEI 101, TAIWAN
Stretching twice as high as the Transamerica Pyramid, this relies on a huge mass damper to resist movement.

TAIPEI 101

MASS DAMPER

One way to help skyscrapers cope with an extreme ground shake is to install a mass damper – a huge steel sphere – at the centre, suspended by cables. It moves back and forth to counter any motion by the building itself.

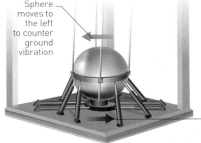

Sphere moves to the right to counter ground vibration

Hydraulic rams to move sphere

Ground shakes to the left

MOVEMENT OF BUILDING
During an earthquake, the entire building moves with the horizontal vibrations from the ground.

Sphere moves to the left to counter ground vibration

Ground shakes to the right

COUNTER MOVEMENT OF DAMPER
The huge sphere moves in the opposite direction to the shake to keep the building secure.

TSUNAMIS

When an earthquake occurs in the seafloor, it can cause a part of the seabed to rise upwards, triggering a tsunami wave on the surface of the sea.

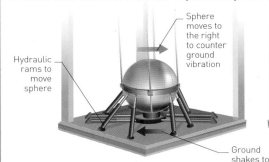

A block of seafloor shoots up

In the open ocean, each wave is not very high and may pass unnoticed

The top of a large tsunami wave usually forms as it approaches the shore

Sometimes water is drawn away from the shore a few minutes before a tsunami wave arrives

Powerful vibrations spread out from the epicentre in all directions

Epicentre (the spot on the seafloor above the point in Earth's interior where the rupture started)

Tsunami waves are evenly spaced at distances of up to 200 km (120 miles)

As each wave passes, there is a circular movement of seawater under it

As the seabed rises, the wave slows down and gains in height

MAJOR TSUNAMIS

Tsunamis are assessed according to the size of their waves, how many occur in one event, how far they come on shore, and how much damage they cause.

1 SUMATRA, INDONESIA, 26 DECEMBER 2004
This tsunami's waves reached 50 m (164 ft) and killed more than 227,000 people, affecting 14 countries.

2 NORTH PACIFIC COAST, JAPAN, 11 MARCH 2011
Travelling at 800 km/h (497 mph), the 10 m (33 ft) high waves of this tsunami forced 450,000 people from their homes.

3 PORTUGAL, 1 NOVEMBER 1755
Set off by an 8.5-magnitude earthquake, this tsunami hit Portugal, Morocco, and Spain with waves 30 m (98 ft) high.

4 KRAKATOA, INDONESIA, 27 AUGUST 1883
Caused by the eruption of the Krakatoa Caldera volcano, this tsunami created multiple waves reaching 37 m (121 ft) high.

5 ENSHUNADA SEA, JAPAN, 20 SEPTEMBER 1498
Waves from this tsunami were powerful enough to cross a section of land separating Lake Hamana from the sea.

Shaping the land

Earth's surface changes constantly but so gradually we can hardly see it. Wind, waves, moving ice, and other forces wear away rocks and mountains and create valleys. At the same time, Earth's plates move, forming mountains and continents.

EROSION

Water, wind, and ice wear down rocks and soil. They also move the resulting materials to new places, and in doing so change the shape of the land. The process is called erosion. Natural forces cause most erosion but human activity, such as deforestation, also contributes.

GLACIER
Huge ice masses called glaciers scrape away rocks and earth as they move down mountain valleys.

WATER
Moving water erodes coasts, cliffs, and riverbanks, picking up and transporting rocks, pebbles, and soil.

WIND
A powerful erosive force, wind blows away the top surface of soil and wears away rock.

EROSION AND DEPOSITION

Rivers and streams mould the landscape. From glacier beginnings, a river travels fast, picking up rocky debris and carving deep into valleys. The river slows but continues to erode the landscape and also deposits some material along the way. When it reaches the sea, it drops silt to form deltas and beaches.

U-SHAPED VALLEY
Moving glacier ice erodes rock to form U-shaped valley.

GORGE
Fast-moving river or waterfall deepens valley or gorge.

RIVERS DUMP ABOUT 20 BILLION TONNES OF SEDIMENT INTO THE SEA EVERY YEAR

FLOODPLAIN
Sediment deposited by river creates flat floodplain.

KETTLE LAKE
Melting ice from retreating glacier forms shallow lake.

MEANDER
River bend caused by erosion on one side and silt deposits on the other.

TERMINAL MORAINE
Ridge of rock, gravel, and soil at final point of glacier's advance.

POOL
Cascading water forms pool at base of waterfall.

ARCH
Pounding waves form arch in headland.

GLACIERS

Icy glaciers flow through mountain valleys, reshaping them. They move slowly, usually less than 1 m (3.3 ft) a day, but are so large they carve out vast depressions in the rock and U-shaped valleys.

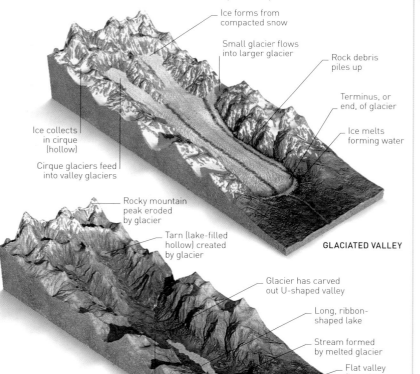

Ice forms from compacted snow

Small glacier flows into larger glacier

Rock debris piles up

Terminus, or end, of glacier

Ice collects in cirque (hollow)

Cirque glaciers feed into valley glaciers

Ice melts forming water

Rocky mountain peak eroded by glacier

Tarn (lake-filled hollow) created by glacier

GLACIATED VALLEY

Glacier has carved out U-shaped valley

Long, ribbon-shaped lake

Stream formed by melted glacier

Flat valley floor that floods periodically

Flat-bottomed valley eroded by glacier

AFTER THE GLACIER

DELTA
A delta forms where a slow-moving river deposits sediment where it meets the sea.

BEACH
Beaches are created from eroded material carried by the sea.

SAND SPIT
On the coast, sandy deposits settle and project out into the sea.

WATERFALL FORMATION

A waterfall forms when a river pours over a rocky edge. The water flow erodes the rock, creating a pool and undermining the ledge. Soft rock erodes more quickly than hard rock so the amount of erosion varies, as does the height and flow of the water.

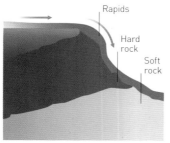

Rapids

Hard rock

Soft rock

RAPIDS
Rapids occur when the flow of a shallow river is broken up by hard rock projecting out of the water.

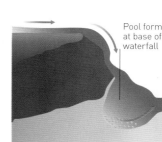

Pool forms at base of waterfall

WATERFALL
When a river erodes soft rock, beyond the rapids, it carves out a pool into which the water cascades.

WATER EROSION

Helped by strong winds, ocean waves batter against coastal landforms. Dislodged rocks and pebbles are ground down and rub abrasively against headlands, cliffs, and standing rocks.

ERODED ROCK, LOCH ARD GORGE, AUSTRALIA

ARCHES AND STACKS

As waves approach a headland, they curve around, attacking the sides. In a process called corrosion, stones flung up by the waves erode the sides, causing cracks. Compressed air brought in by waves expands, enlarging cracks and forming arches and stacks.

ARCHES AND STACKS ARE CREATED BY A MIXTURE OF WIND AND WATER EROSION

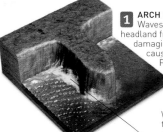

1 ARCH FORMATION
Waves batter the headland from both sides, damaging rock and causing cracks. Pressure of water enters cracks to form an arch.

Water penetrates through headland creating an arch

2 STACK FORMATION
A sea stack is formed when waves continue to erode the headland and a pillar of rock (the stack) becomes separated.

Water pressure collapses arch leaving sea stack

LIMESTONE LANDSCAPES

Deep below Earth's surface are large cave systems. Rainwater, which is slightly acidic, gradually dissolves the limestone, creating cracks. Flowing water widens the cracks, forms channels, and eventually creates cave systems.

1 LIMESTONE WEAKENS
Only rainwater can dissolve limestone. Over centuries, the slow drip of rainwater weakens limestone, forming cracks.

2 CAVE SYSTEM
As water continues to erode the limestone, cracks widen to become large cavities or caves. Rock falls help the process.

3 GORGE
Eventually, the roof collapses, creating sinkholes. These merge to form large sunken regions called gorges.

INSIDE A CAVE

Limestone caves are wondrous places. Over centuries, erosion has created huge chambers, often containing many incredibly shaped pillars, and river-filled tunnels. Caves vary in size. Some are shallow but the deepest, in France, lies nearly 1.5 km (1 mile) below ground.

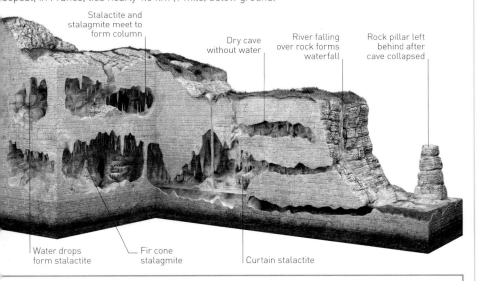

Stalactite and stalagmite meet to form column

Dry cave without water

River falling over rock forms waterfall

Rock pillar left behind after cave collapsed

Water drops form stalactite

Fir cone stalagmite

Curtain stalactite

STALACTITES AND STALAGMITES

Slim, beautifully shaped stalactites hang down from the roof of a cave. Stalagmites rise up from the floor of the cave. Both form from a mineral in the rocks called calcite that dissolves in drops of water seeping through the roof. Over time, they form fantastic shapes.

1 WATER SEEPS IN
Mineral-saturated water drips through the cave roof. The water dries, leaving a mineral residue.

2 STALACTITE FORMS
Water continues seeping. The residue builds up and a stalactite forms, hanging down from the roof.

3 STALAGMITE FORMS
Some water lands on the floor. It dries and leaves deposits that gradually form a stalagmite.

4 PILLAR FORMS
Over time, the stalactite and stalagmite continue forming until they join to create a pillar.

OXBOW LAKES

On low-lying land, snake-like meanders may form when the course of a river bends and may eventually become oxbow lakes. Meanders have two sets of curves: one side is formed by erosion as the river erodes the land, the other side forms from deposits of silt and sediment.

Steady bend in river

River wears away land

River straightens out

Old loop of river gets cut off

1 RIVER MEANDERS
A river curves slightly. Water erodes the far bank and deposits sediment on the inner bank.

2 BEND TIGHTENS
As the erosion and deposits of sediment increase, the meander, or curve, tightens into a C-shaped loop.

3 BEND IS CUT OFF
River flows through neck of meander cutting it off. Sediment deposits close ends and an oxbow lake is formed.

WIND EROSION

Wind is a powerful erosive agent. It blows away soil, sand, and other light substances, depositing them at different locations, often sculpting new landforms. Wind erosion can be destructive, particularly for farmers. Trees and terraces help protect land.

CONICAL FORMATIONS, TURKEY
In some parts of the world the impact of wind has changed landscapes, eroding rocks into new forms.

SANDSTONE SWIRLS, USA
Wind, and the sand particles it carries, erode sedimentary rocks such as sandstone, creating fantastic swirls.

MUSHROOM-SHAPED ROCKS, EGYPT
Desert winds fling sand about, which causes erosion. The sand blasts against rocks, producing strange shapes.

Rocks and minerals

The outer layers of Earth are mostly solid rock. This is easy to see where there are mountains or canyons, but much more rock is hidden under the soil and the sea. Rocks are made of minerals. They can be changed or destroyed by weather or water at the surface, or by heat and pressure inside Earth.

WHAT'S THE DIFFERENCE?

Minerals are natural chemical substances that usually form as solid crystals. Each type can be recognized by its hardness, colour, and atomic structure. Rocks are a mixture of minerals locked together. For example, granite is made of the minerals quartz, feldspar, and mica.

MINERAL: QUARTZ

IGNEOUS ROCKS

Formed from volcanic material as it cools down, igneous rocks are of two types. Some, such as pegmatites, form deep underground. Others, such as andesite, form when volcanic lavas cool at Earth's surface.

PUMICE

ANDESITE

OBSIDIAN

PINK GRANODIORITE

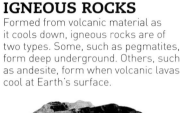
TOURMALINE PEGMATITE

RHYOLITE

PORPHYRY

SEDIMENTARY ROCKS

These rocks form mostly at the bottom of seas and lakes. They are made from grains of sand and clay worn away from older rocks by wind and water. Over a very long period of time, the grains settle into layers of mud, or sediment. These layers are buried and eventually harden into new rock.

GREYWACKE

LIMESTONE WITH FOSSILS

FLINT

OIL SHALE

SHALE

PUDDINGSTONE

MINERALS

There are thousands of different minerals, though only about 30 make up most rocks. They usually form from water solutions and molten rock, sometimes deep inside Earth. Some, such as diamonds, are cut and polished to make gemstones.

ENARGITE

TENNANTITE

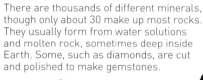
CHRYSOPRASE

MAGNETITE

COCKSCOMB BARITE

ARSENOPYRITE

HORNBLENDE

BROOKITE

CHALCOCITE

HALITE

CHALCOPYRITE

NAILHEAD CALCITE

GALENA

CORUNDUM

SULPHUR

GOLD

MEASURING MINERALS

A test called the "Mohs scale" was invented more than 200 years ago to measure a mineral's hardness. The scale is based on how scratch-resistant one mineral is compared to others.

HARD

SOFT

ABSOLUTE HARDNESS SCALE

DIAMOND

CORUNDUM

TOPAZ
QUARTZ
ORTHOCLASE
APATITE
FLUORITE
CALCITE
GYPSUM
TALC

MOHS HARDNESS SCALE

ROCK: PINK GRANITE

ROCK CYCLE

Rocks are made and remade in an endless cycle. Molten rock rises from inside Earth to the surface. Weathering breaks down surface rock into grains. The grains build new rocks, which are buried and then melted by heat.

Glaciers carry away cool volcanic rock

Rain and snow fill streams

Volcano

Streams and winds carry away rock grains

Molten rock forced up to surface

Rock grains reach the coast as sediment

Rock becomes molten

Sedimentary rock changes under heat and pressure

Sediment sinks

Pressure turns sediment into rock

METAMORPHIC ROCKS

Intense heat or pressure deep inside Earth can change the minerals in rocks from one type to another or may rearrange the mineral grains. This process produces what are called metamorphic rocks.

LIMESTONE BRECCIA

DOLOMITE

CLAYSTONE

SKARN

RED MARL

CHALK

LOESS

MYLONITE

ECLOGITE

MIGMATITE

IRONSTONE

SANDSTONE

GREEN MARBLE

SERPENTINITE

SLATE

GNEISS

DIAMOND

PURPLE FLUORITE

REALGAR

ROSE QUARTZ

SPHALERITE

AZURITE

HEMATITE

NICKELINE

PROUSTITE

STIBNITE

BOTRYOIDAL ARSENIC

COVELLITE

ORPIMENT

CHRYSOBERYL

RUTILE

BERYL

RHODOCHROSITE

SMOKY QUARTZ

BLUE SAPPHIRE

HEMIMORPHIITE

MALACHITE

BORNITE

Gems

A gemstone, or gem, is a mineral that has been polished and shaped by a skilled craftsperson in order to enhance its beauty. The most highly prized gems are hard-wearing and rare. There are more than 5,000 known minerals on Earth, but fewer than 100 are used as gemstones.

GEM SHAPES

Gemstones can be shaped in many ways. Some shapes, or "cuts", are very popular for rings, especially diamond rings. More than three-quarters of all diamonds today are cut into the "round brilliant" shape.

ROUND BRILLIANT · CUSHION · SQUARE

SCISSORS · PEAR · STEP

EMERALD · HEART · OVAL BRILLIANT

BIRTHSTONES

Some gemstones are traditionally associated with certain months of the year. It is believed to be lucky to wear the gem for your birth month.

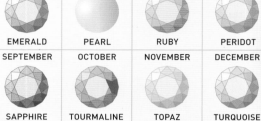

JANUARY	FEBRUARY	MARCH	APRIL
GARNET	AMETHYST	AQUAMARINE	DIAMOND
MAY	JUNE	JULY	AUGUST
EMERALD	PEARL	RUBY	PERIDOT
SEPTEMBER	OCTOBER	NOVEMBER	DECEMBER
SAPPHIRE	TOURMALINE	TOPAZ	TURQUOISE

PRECIOUS STONES

Traditionally, gems such as opal, emerald, sapphire, ruby, and diamond were named "precious" stones. This was because their rarity made them the most valuable. Today, gems are valued in several different ways. The term "precious" is outdated, although jewellers still find it useful.

FIRE OPAL · MILKY OPAL · BLACK OPAL · MULTICOLOURED OPAL · PINK AND TURQUOISE OPAL · WHITE OPAL · HELIODORE · GREEN EMERALD · MORGANITE · YELLOW SAPPHIRE · GREEN SAPPHIRE

SEMI-PRECIOUS STONES

Gems found in large quantities were once said to be "semi-precious" and had a lower value than rare stones. However, a gem's beauty and popularity are now also considered part of its value. Some "semi-precious" stones sell for more money than "precious" ones.

CLEAR FLUORITE · GREEN FLUORITE · YELLOW FLUORITE · PINK TOURMALINE

AMBLYGONITE · BLUE APATITE · YELLOW APATITE · DANBURITE · GREEN TOURMALINE

PINK-VIOLET KUNZITE · LABRADORITE · PREHNITE · RHODONITE · SCAPOLITE · BLUE TOURMALINE · GREEN-YELLOW TOURMALINE

QUARTZ GEMS

Quartz is one of the most common and varied minerals on Earth. It comes in an amazing number of colours and intricate patterns.

TIGER'S EYE QUARTZ · PALE YELLOW CITRINE · DENDRITIC AGATE · RUTILE QUARTZ · HAWK'S EYE QUARTZ · SARDONYX · PHANTOM QUARTZ · ONYX · AVENTURINE QUARTZ · HONEY-COLOURED CITRINE

ACETING A DIAMOND

hen mined, gemstones often ok dull; they must be cut and lished to shine. The best way maximize the beauty of a ansparent gem is to cut the rface into a series of flat, flective faces called facets.

1 SELECTION
A gem-quality piece of rough diamond – an octahedral crystal – is selected for cutting.

2 ROUNDED
The stone is rounded on a lathe using another diamond and the top facet, called the table, is cut.

Table facet

3 "MAIN" CUTS
The 16 "main" facets or planes are then cut above and below the mid-point, or girdle.

Girdle

Crown

4 INCREASING SHINE
Thirty two facets are cut into the crown (top) and pavilion (bottom) to increase brilliance and shine.

Pavilion

5 FINISHED BRILLIANT CUT
The final "brilliant cut" emphasizes the brightness of the gem.

MINING

emstones are und in different eas across e world. They e sometimes ought to the arth's surface volcanic uptions.

KEY
- Diamond
- Emerald
- Sapphire
- Ruby
- Aquamarine
- Topaz
- Opal

BIGGEST GEMS

Gemstones can be huge. The Olympic Australis opal weighs 3.45 kg (7.5 lb); the American Golden topaz is 4.57 kg (10 lb); and the largest colourless diamond, the Cullinan, is 10 cm (4 in) long.

CULLINAN DIAMOND

AMERICAN GOLDEN TOPAZ

OLYMPIC AUSTRALIS OPAL

LUE SAPPHIRE

PADPARADSCHA SAPPHIRE

LIGHT BLUE TOPAZ

WHITE SAPPHIRE

PINK TOPAZ

SHERRY TOPAZ

AQUAMARINE

DIAMOND

RUBY

JASPER

AZURITE

GREEN PERIDOT

MOONSTONE

DRAVITE

CUPRITE

HOWLITE

HEMATITE

RED GARNET

TURQUOISE

BLUE ZIRCON

BLUE TANZANITE

SPHENE

SUNSTONE

KYANITE

ALEXANDRITE

MALACHITE

MAUVE SPINEL

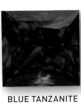
RED SPINEL

PINK SPINEL

VESUVIANITE

SUGILITE

ORGANIC GEMSTONES

Organic gemstones are made from animal or plant materials. For instance, coral is formed from sea creatures, pearls develop in certain shellfish such as oysters, and amber is made of fossilized tree resin.

DUMORTIERITE IN QUARTZ

AMETHYST

VIOLET CORAL

BLACK PEARL NEXT TO PEARL OYSTER

WHITE PEARL

AMBER

MILKY QUARTZ

ROSE QUARTZ

SMOKY QUARTZ

YELLOW-GREY CAT'S EYE QUARTZ

Water on Earth

ABOUT 97 PER CENT OF THE WORLD'S WATER LIES IN THE OCEANS

Water is the most common substance on Earth's surface – it fills the colossal oceans, swirls in clouds as water vapour, and falls as rain on land. It is vital to all life and is why our planet is unique: water vapour and ice may exist on other planets but only Earth has oceans of liquid water.

WATER TEMPERATURE

Deep-ocean water is permanently cold, but the temperature of surface water varies. It is warmest around the equator, where the Sun's heat is more intense. But in the polar region the Sun is less powerful, resulting in permanently cold water

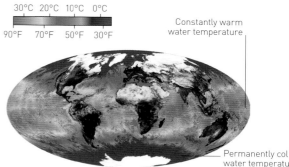

30°C 20°C 10°C 0°C
90°F 70°F 50°F 30°F

Constantly warm water temperature

Permanently col water temperatu

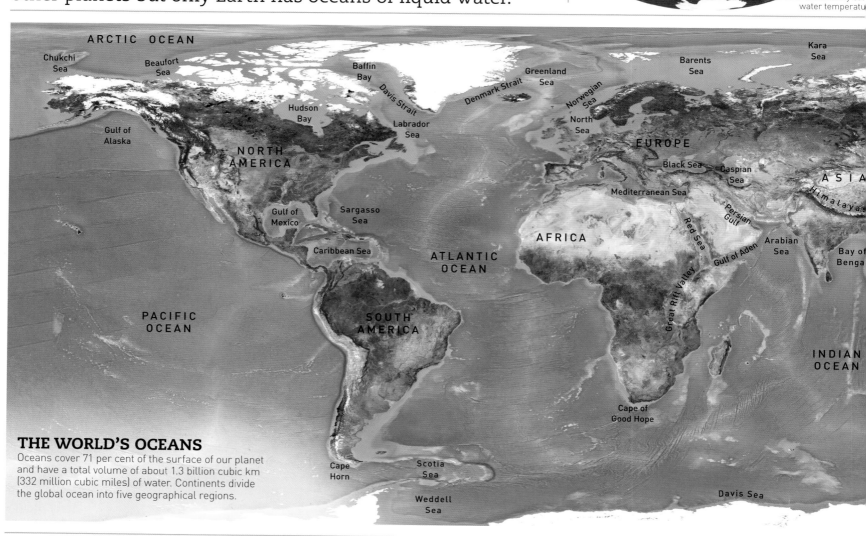

THE WORLD'S OCEANS

Oceans cover 71 per cent of the surface of our planet and have a total volume of about 1.3 billion cubic km (332 million cubic miles) of water. Continents divide the global ocean into five geographical regions.

OCEAN FLOOR

The ocean floor is not just a featureless plain filled with water. Underwater volcanoes, towering mountains, vast plains, and the deepest trenches on Earth lie hidden beneath the waves.

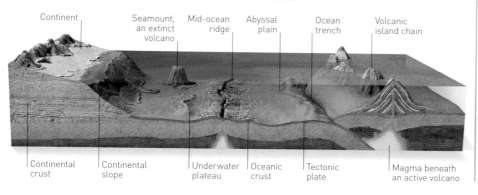

Continent

Seamount, an extinct volcano

Mid-ocean ridge

Abyssal plain

Ocean trench

Volcanic island chain

Continental crust

Continental slope

Underwater plateau

Oceanic crust

Tectonic plate

Magma beneath an active volcano

SALT WATER

Most of Earth's water is salty. Over millions of years, rain pouring down on the land weathered the rocks and carried dissolved minerals on its journey to the seas. The minerals included sodium chloride (common salt). This process is still happening today.

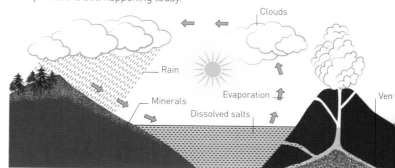

Clouds

Rain

Minerals

Evaporation

Dissolved salts

Ven

WATER CYCLE

Powered by the Sun's heat, the water cycle circulates between sea, air, and land. The Sun-warmed surface water is constantly evaporating (turning into water vapour). The rising vapour cools and condenses, forming clouds that may be carried over land. Here, it falls back as rain or snow, and flows over the land before the water finds its way back to the sea.

Water returns to land in the form of rain or snow

Clouds blow over land

Rising water vapour cools and forms clouds made of tiny droplets of water

Plants release moisture into the air

Sun draws moisture from the ground into the air

Some of the water evaporates and rises into the air as water vapour

Rain and melting ice feed rivers and lakes

Some of the water seeps into the ground

Rivers carry water back to the sea

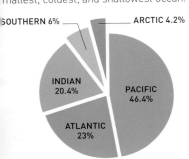

ARCTIC OCEAN
Laptev Sea
East Siberian Sea
Sea of Okhotsk
Sea of Japan (East Sea)
East China Sea
Philippine Sea
PACIFIC OCEAN
Arafura Sea
Coral Sea
AUSTRALIA
Tasman Sea
SOUTHERN OCEAN
ANTARCTICA

LARGEST LAKES

Some lakes are just shallow pools that eventually dry out, while others are so vast that they are like inland seas.

1 CASPIAN SEA
Area: 371,000 sq km (143,000 sq miles) This lake was once part of the Mediterranean Sea; it was cut off when sea levels fell during the last ice age.

2 SUPERIOR
Area: 82,414 sq km (31,820 sq miles) One of the five Great Lakes of North America, and the largest freshwater lake in the world.

3 VICTORIA
Area: 69,485 sq km (26,828 sq miles) The waters of Lake Victoria in Africa fill a shallow basin in the centre of a plateau.

4 HURON
Area: 59,600 sq km (23,000 sq miles) This is the second largest of the North American Great Lakes.

5 MICHIGAN
Area: 58,000 (22,000 sq miles) Also one of the five Great Lakes but located entirely within the USA.

LAKE TYPES

Lakes form in various ways, depending on how the hollow on Earth's surface was created, and most contain fresh water. They are found in a number of environments, including mountains, deserts, and plains. Some lakes are millions of years old but most are much younger.

 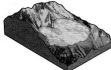 

FAULT LAKE
Tectonic movement of Earth's crust creates long hollows, which fill with water. These are among the oldest and deepest lakes on Earth.

KETTLE LAKE
Depressions left behind when an underground block of ice melts creating a steep-sided circular lake.

CALDERA LAKE
This type of lake forms when rain fills the huge crater left after an eruption has blown away the top of a volcano.

MAN-MADE LAKE
Some lakes are man-made to provide a reservoir of clean water for homes and industry, or to create hydroelectricity.

RIVERS

Most rivers begin life as small, fast-flowing streams that join up to form bigger, slower ones. They start life in higher ground, where rainwater or melting snow collects and trickles downhill. Some rivers also form when lakes overflow or from springs.

Fast-moving water is cooler and clearer near the source

Mid-speed flow of water

Slow-flowing murkier water

MOUTH

SOURCE

Meander

UPPER COURSE
The water at the source of a river is fast-flowing, and full of gravel and pebbles. This in turn erodes and deepens the stream channel.

MIDDLE COURSE
On flatter ground, the river slows down. Winding curves called meanders form, and as the flow cuts away the outside of the curve, the meanders become more extreme.

LOWER COURSE
As a river reaches lower ground, it widens and slows, then flows into a lake or a sea. The sediment carried by the water is left behind at the mouth of the river.

LONGEST RIVERS

Earth has some incredibly long rivers that snake across its surface. These are the five longest rivers of the world.

1 NILE
Length: 6,670 km (4,145 miles) Africa's River Nile has two major tributaries (branches): the Blue Nile and the White Nile.

2 AMAZON
Length: 6,450 km (4,005 miles) More water flows through South America's mighty Amazon than any other river.

3 YANGTZE
Length: 6,378 km (3,964 miles) China's Yangtze River is the world's deepest river as well as the third-longest river.

4 MISSISSIPPI-MISSOURI
Length: 5,970 km (3,710 miles) The Mississippi and Missouri rivers combine to form North America's longest river system.

5 YENISEI
Length: 5,539 sq km (3,445 sq miles) The Yenisei River starts in Mongolia and flows through Russia.

OCEAN SIZES

This chart shows the total area covered by each ocean. The Pacific is the deepest and by far the largest ocean, covering almost half the Earth. The Arctic is the smallest, coldest, and shallowest ocean.

SOUTHERN 6%
ARCTIC 4.2%
INDIAN 20.4%
PACIFIC 46.4%
ATLANTIC 23%

WATER POWER

Earth's essential resource can move with considerable force, and modern techniques have been developed to harness this incredible power into energy.

HYDROELECTRIC
Hydroelectric dams are built to convert a river's kinetic energy (energy of movement) into electrical power.

TIDAL SURGE
Tidal barrages work in a similar way to hydroelectric dams, generating power from rising and falling tides.

HYDROELECTRIC ENERGY
Hydroelectric power stations use the force of moving water to produce electrical energy. The amount of energy created is determined by the flow of water.

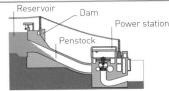

Reservoir
Dam
Power station
Penstock

1 WATER IS RELEASED
Water is stored in a reservoir and released into giant tubes (penstocks) inside the dam.

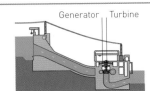

Generator
Turbine

2 WATER PRESSURE
The force of the water spins the blades of the turbines, which are connected to electricity generators.

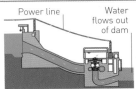

Power line
Water flows out of dam

3 ELECTRICITY IS PRODUCED
Power lines carry away electricity, while the water flows off downstream, away from the dam.

Climate and weather

Sunshine, air, and water interact to create the constantly changing conditions we call weather. Weather can change fast within a day and slowly from season to season. The average weather pattern in one place is what makes up its climate.

WORLD'S CLIMATE

The world is divided into climate zones, each one with a pattern of temperature and rainfall, and distinct vegetation. They range from a hot and wet climate near the equator to a cold and dry one at the poles.

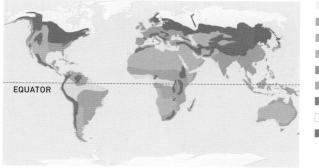

EQUATOR

- Hot, with rain all year
- Hot, with a dry and a wet season
- Hot, with one rainy season
- Hot desert
- Cool coastal climate
- Warm, with winter rain
- Cold, with warm summers
- Very cold and dry
- Mountain climate

SEASONS

Seasons differ in the northern and southern hemispheres due to a tilt in Earth's spin axis. In summer, the hemisphere tilted towards the Sun has longer, warmer days.

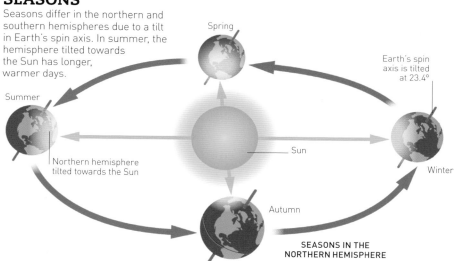

Spring

Summer

Northern hemisphere tilted towards the Sun

Earth's spin axis is tilted at 23.4°

Sun

Winter

Autumn

SEASONS IN THE NORTHERN HEMISPHERE

CLIMATE CHANGE

Climate is made up of interactions between the land, ocean, and atmosphere. Human activity can also alter these interactions and cause climate change.

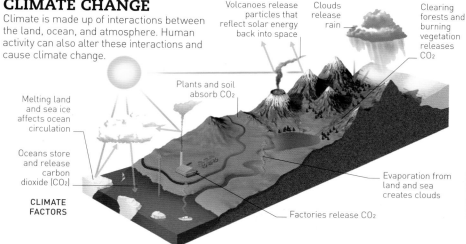

Volcanoes release particles that reflect solar energy back into space

Clouds release rain

Clearing forests and burning vegetation releases CO_2

Plants and soil absorb CO_2

Melting land and sea ice affects ocean circulation

Oceans store and release carbon dioxide (CO_2)

Evaporation from land and sea creates clouds

CLIMATE FACTORS

Factories release CO_2

WHAT IS CLIMATE?

A climate is the average weather pattern in an area, influenced by factors such as the region's distance from the equator.

TEMPERATURE
Places tend to be colder the further they are from the equator.

PRECIPITATION
There are zones of high and low rainfall around the Earth.

WEATHER SYSTEM

Local air masses have their own temperature, moisture content, density, and pressure. A weather front occurs when one air mass meets another.

WARM FRONT
Cold air is replaced by warm air, which slowly rises to form clouds and then rain as the air cools.

COLD FRONT
Cold air pushes i warm air, forcing upwards to creat storm clouds and heavy rain.

ATMOSPHERIC CIRCULATION

Air is always on the move, and this creates the circulation of the atmosphere around the globe. Hot air close to the equator is carried to high latitudes, and cool air is returned to the tropics. In each hemisphere, three "cells" with separate circulations create winds that blow from specific directions. These in turn produce surface currents in the oceans.

Polar easterli blow away fro the North Po

Polar-front jet stream moves in different seasons

Subtropical jet stream flows at about 30°N all year round

Direction of Earth's rotation

THE ROARING FORTIES, FURIOUS FIFTIES, AND SHRIEKING SIXTIES ARE FIERCE SOUTH WINDS

Cool air subsides at the South Pole

ATIONARY FRONT
...occurs where
...masses push
...ainst one another
...hout moving. Can
...use heavy rain.

CLUDED FRONT
...st-moving cold air
...rtakes a warm
...nt, and lifts the
...rm air mass. It
...rain for days.

Lines called isobars join points with the same pressure

An area with low pressure is called a depression

A WEATHER MAP

POLAR CELL
Cold air at the pole flows south then returns.

Winds produced by Ferrel Cells flow from the west

Northeasterly trade winds

HADLEY CELL
Moist air rises at the equator and subsides at the subtropics.

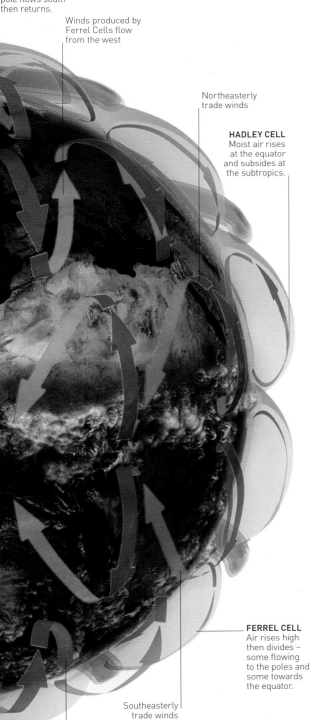

FERREL CELL
Air rises high then divides – some flowing to the poles and some towards the equator.

Southeasterly trade winds

Roaring forties wind

PRECIPITATION
All precipitation is simply falling moisture. Whether water falls from a cloud as rain, hail, or snow depends on how cold the air is.

RAIN
Droplets in clouds fall when they are too heavy to float.

SLEET
Sleet is a mix of snow and rain in air above freezing.

HAIL
Ice pellets form from crystals in storm clouds.

SNOW
Snowflakes are clusters of frozen water droplets.

FOG
Fog forms when warm, moist air hits cold ground.

WIND
Air moving between high and low pressure areas is called wind. Wind speed – from still air to a hurricane – is measured on the Beaufort scale.

CALM	LIGHT AIR	LIGHT BREEZE	GENTLE BREEZE	MODERATE BREEZE	FRESH BREEZE	STRONG BREEZE	NEAR GALE	GALE	STRONG GALE	STORM	VIOLENT STORM	HURRICANE
0	1	2	3	4	5	6	7	8	9	10	11	12

BEAUFORT SCALE

RECORD-BREAKING WEATHER
Some places have extreme climates, or weather events that are talked about for years.

○ **WINDIEST**
The fastest wind speed in a tornado was 450 km/h (280 mph), recorded at Wichita Falls, USA, in 1958.

○ **HOTTEST**
The hottest land-surface temperature ever recorded (by satellite measurement) was 70.7°C (159.3°F) in the Lut Desert, Iran, in 2005.

○ **COLDEST**
The coldest recorded temperature was −93°C (−136°F), measured in Antarctica's eastern highlands in 2010.

○ **WETTEST**
The highest rainfall recorded in one day was 18.25 cm (71.9 in) in Foc-Foc, Reunion Island, in the Indian Ocean in 1966, during a tropical cyclone.

○ **DRIEST**
Arica, Chile is the populated area with the lowest average annual rainfall in the world at 0.76 mm (0.03 in).

ARICA, CHILE

CLOUDS
All clouds fall into three main groups, although each type has many different shapes. Cumulus form pillowy heaps; stratus have flat layers; and cirrus are wispy streaks.

CLOUD NAMES
Clouds are named according to their size, shape, and height.

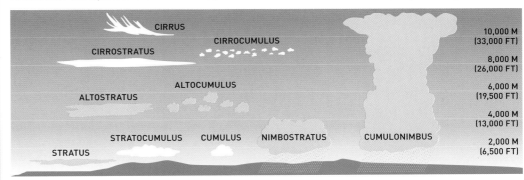

CIRRUS
CIRROCUMULUS
CIRROSTRATUS
ALTOCUMULUS
ALTOSTRATUS
STRATOCUMULUS   CUMULUS   NIMBOSTRATUS   CUMULONIMBUS
STRATUS

10,000 M (33,000 FT)
8,000 M (26,000 FT)
6,000 M (19,500 FT)
4,000 M (13,000 FT)
2,000 M (6,500 FT)

HOW CLOUDS FORM

1 MOISTURE
When the Sun shines, moisture in the ground and sea rises into the air as water vapour.

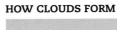

2 VAPOUR CONDENSES
As the vapour rises and cools, it condenses and forms clouds made of tiny water droplets.

3 CLOUDS RISE
During cloud formation, heat is released into the surrounding air and lifts the cloud higher.

WATCHING THE WEATHER
Weather stations are at work all over the world, gathering information about local and global weather patterns. They use a range of instruments from simple thermometers and rain gauges to weather balloons and satellites, which use sensors to monitor Earth's atmosphere.

DOPPLER RADAR
This type of radar uses microwaves to track moving bands of rain.

WEATHER BALLOON
Helium-filled balloons carry sensors high into the atmosphere.

SATELLITE
Satellites orbit from pole to pole or sit above one region.

Extreme weather

Tornadoes, hurricanes, and flash floods destroy homes and countryside. Long dry spells cause water shortages and parched crops. There have always been episodes of extreme weather, but now it seems likely that the increase in freak events all around the world is due to climate change.

CAUSES OF EXTREME WEATHER

The Sun's heat is a key factor, creating excessively high and low atmospheric pressure that can lead to extreme weather conditions. Dust from volcanoes can cause major disturbance, and global warming may play a part.

GLOBAL WARMI
Since 1970 glob
temperatures ha
risen by 0.5°C
(0.9°F), adding h
that may alter
weather patterr

WHAT IS EXTREME WEATHER?

Many parts of the world experience wide variations in their weather, so when does it become extreme? In India torrential monsoons are normal, as is a big freeze in the far North. Put simply, extreme weather is weather that is windier, hotter, colder, wetter, or more destructive than usual.

THE USA HAS THE MOST TORNADOES IN THE WORLD – ABOUT 1,000 EVERY YEAR

THUNDERSTORM
Thunderclouds form in hot, humid weather and bring heavy rain, hail, lightning, and thunder.

MONSOON
These torrential rains that last for weeks are just seasonal weather in subtropical regions.

FLOOD
Too much rain in a short time may cause flash floods in valleys and near rivers and the sea.

TORNADO
These twisting columns of wind can flatten houses and pick up vehicles.

HURRICANE
The Earth's most powerful weather systems bring huge winds and rain.

DUST STORM
In very dry places, sand and soil is picked up in the wind that grows into a suffocating dust storm.

HEATWAVE
During a heatwave, temperatures soar, reservoirs dry up, and water is in short supply.

DROUGHT
If there is high pressure for long periods, no clouds form and there is no rain. Vital crops fail.

SEVERE FOG
The thickest fogs occur in polluted areas. Tiny droplets of water settle on particles in the air.

HAILSTORM
Showers of large hailstones can break glass and leave drifts of ice.

SNOWSTORM
A snowstorm is a rapid fall of snow, 15 cm (6 in) deep or more, that disrupts daily life.

COLD WAVE
This dramatic dip in temperature to well below freezing can threaten lives.

MONSOON

Massive monsoon winds bring torrential rain to subtropical regions in summer. This rain is essential for crops to grow. The winds change direction in winter to bring dry, cooler weather.

SUMMER
The South Asian monsoon blows from the Indian Ocean, bringing rain across India.

WINTER
Fine, dry weather spreads across India when the South Asian monsoon reverses.

THUNDERSTORMS

In hot, humid weather, an enormous cloud called a cumulonimbus, can rapidly build up. This towering cloud brings gusty winds, torrential rain, hail, and lightning. Flashes of lightning happen after droplets, ice crystals, and hail in the cloud become electrically charged. The flashes superheat the air, creating claps of thunder.

Huge cumulonimbus cloud has an anvil-shaped top

Warm, humid air rises from the ground

1 CLOUDS BUILD
Humid air is heated on the surface and causes thermal currents. As these cool down they produce a towering cloud.

Up- and downdraughts create a violent storm

2 MATURE STAGE
An updraught pulls more warm air upwards. High in the sky the drops become rain, hail, or snow and fall in a downdraught.

Thermals begin to die down

Downdraughts block warm air The rain stops

3 ON THE WANE
The strong downdraught takes over. Cool air spills over the surface of the cloud and it begins to disappear.

LIGHTNING STROKES

It takes a huge voltage of electricity to overcome the resistance of the air, but once the process starts, strokes of lightning zig-zag towards the ground. When a leader stroke makes contact with a high point like a tree, it lights up with a brighter stroke called the return stroke.

CLOUD-TO-CLOUD LIGHTNING
This most common type of lightning flashes from cloud to cloud then disappears in the air.

CLOUD TO GROUND
Electricity in the lightning joins currents rising from the ground.

RIBBON LIGHTNING
Return strokes flowing back up the first stroke create a ribbon effect.

SHEET LIGHTNING
Lightning flashing inside a cloud looks like a sheet of light.

SOLAR HEAT
The intensity of the sun fluctuates day-to-day and its heat causes changes in atmospheric pressure.

AIR PRESSURE
Low atmospheric pressure causes storms and strong winds. Prolonged high pressure can cause drought.

EXCITING WEATHER PHENOMENA
Weather can produce some amazing phenomena and rare sights.

○ **SPRITES, ELVES, AND JETS**
Sprites and elves are dancing red lightning flashes in the sky. Jets are cones of blue light on thunderclouds.

○ **BALL LIGHTNING**
This glowing orb lasts for only seconds. It may be caused when elements in the soil vaporize and react with oxygen in the air.

○ **KATABATIC WINDS**
These winds occur at night on mountain slopes. Dense, cold air is pushed down the slope by gravity.

○ **NONAQUEOUS RAIN**
Spiders, frogs, and even jellyfish can be whipped up in strong winds and then fall as rain.

○ **ST ELMO'S FIRE**
This electric spark is like the glow in a plasma ball but it occurs naturally on things like masts and lampposts during thunderstorms.

GIANT HAILSTONE
This whopper fell in Vivian, South Dakota, USA, during a July storm in 2010. Hailstones can gather ice layers as winds in storm clouds whip them upwards again and again.

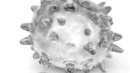

RECORD HAILSTONE
This hailstone weighed 1 kg (2.2 lb) and was 20 cm (8 in) across – three times the size of a tennis ball.

HURRICANES
Hurricanes are violent tropical storms that develop over a warm ocean. Up to 4,000 km (2,500 miles) across, with winds of more than 300 km/h (185 mph), they can leave a trail of destruction across islands and coastal regions.

AIRFLOWS
Warm air on the top spirals out from the eye, then cools and descends.

> **HURRICANES USUALLY HAVE GIRLS' OR BOYS' NAMES BUT SOME ARE NAMED AFTER ANIMALS, OR EVEN FOODS**

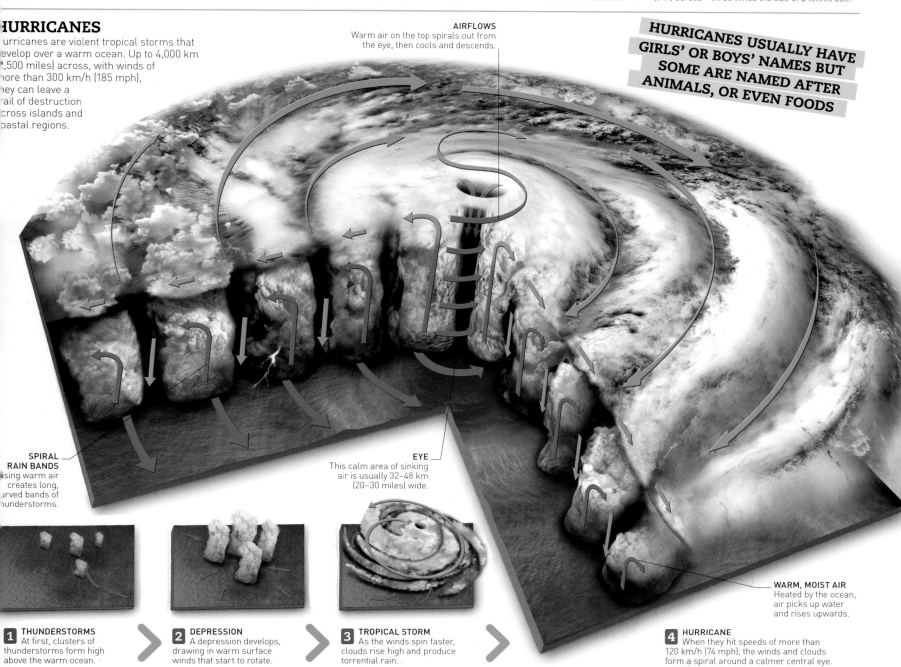

SPIRAL RAIN BANDS
Rising warm air creates long, curved bands of thunderstorms.

EYE
This calm area of sinking air is usually 32–48 km (20–30 miles) wide.

WARM, MOIST AIR
Heated by the ocean, air picks up water and rises upwards.

1 THUNDERSTORMS
At first, clusters of thunderstorms form high above the warm ocean.

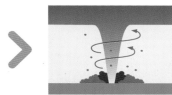

2 DEPRESSION
A depression develops, drawing in warm surface winds that start to rotate.

3 TROPICAL STORM
As the winds spin faster, clouds rise high and produce torrential rain.

4 HURRICANE
When they hit speeds of more than 120 km/h (74 mph), the winds and clouds form a spiral around a calmer central eye.

TORNADOES
These spinning columns of air reach from the clouds down to the ground. They are shaped like a funnel with a core of air that can spin at anything up to 480 km/h (300 mph). Nicknamed "twisters" in the USA, they form during summer storms and can destroy crops and buildings.

1 STEADY SPIN
As warm air rises from the ground it starts to spin. The base of a cloud forms a funnel.

2 FUNNEL GROWS
When the funnel reaches the ground it draws in more hot air and begins to spin faster.

3 PEAK PROGRESS
At its peak, the column can be several kilometres wide and destroy everything in its path.

4 COLUMN DIES
After a while the column spins more slowly. It narrows and is drawn up into the cloud.

Environment in danger

Pollution, deforestation, and the burning of fossil fuels are all changing the environment and making it difficult for many species of plants and animals to survive. However, there are plenty of ways to slow down these harmful effects on the environment, from thinking carefully about what can be recycled to finding new, greener sources of energy.

GREENHOUSE EFFECT

Some gases, such as carbon dioxide, make the atmosphere behave like the glass of a greenhouse, trapping solar heat. This process, which keeps Earth at a comfortable temperature, is called the "greenhouse effect".

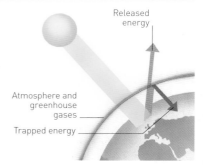

Released energy

Atmosphere and greenhouse gases

Trapped energy

GLOBAL WARMING
Burning fossil fuels like coal and oil releases more greenhouse gases into the atmosphere, warming the planet.

GLOBAL WARMING

The warming up of the Earth may sound like a good thing at first, but it actually has severe consequences. Even a tiny shift of one or two degrees in temperature can change the balance of the planet and eventually lead to the loss of wildlife habitats, farmland, and even human lives.

SEA-LEVEL RISES
As the ice in polar regions melts and sea levels rise, coastal land and homes will be lost.

OCEAN BECOMES MORE ACIDIC
Sea creatures, including coral reefs, are dying as their environment changes.

EXTREME WEATHER
Global warming leads to destructive storms, floods, and droughts.

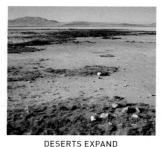

DESERTS EXPAND
An increase in global temperature will lead to more desert areas, destroying habitats and farmland.

POLLUTION

Human activities cause extensive pollution around the world every day. The environment may be affected on a small scale, or pollution may contribute to wider problems, like the greenhouse effect. Pollution affects all forms of life on the planet, from animals on the land to plant life in the sea.

MOUNTAINS
The air and streams are much cleaner in the mountains.

ACID RAIN
Some pollutant gases acidify water in the atmosphere. Rain formed from this water can destroy trees.

PESTICIDES
Chemicals used by farmers on their crops can wash off fields and into nearby water sources.

RUBBISH
Most rubbish is buried in the ground in landfill sites. It can release dangerous chemicals and gases.

CLEANING CHEMICALS
Chemicals are released into water from household cleaning products.

FUEL
Cars powered by fossil fuels release greenhouse gases from their exhausts.

SOOT
Soot, caused by burning coal or oil, pollutes the air.

GAS EMISSIONS
As well as non-polluting steam, many power stations produce invisible gases that contribute to the greenhouse effect and global warming.

CHEMICALS
Chemicals from industrial processes can make their way into rivers and the sea.

SEWAGE
Some waste from sewage plants is dumped in the sea, harming marine life.

MARINE LIFE
If plants on the seabed are killed by pollution, there is little for other marine life to eat.

HAZARDOUS WASTE
Waste dumped in the sea or buried can leak harmful pollutants.

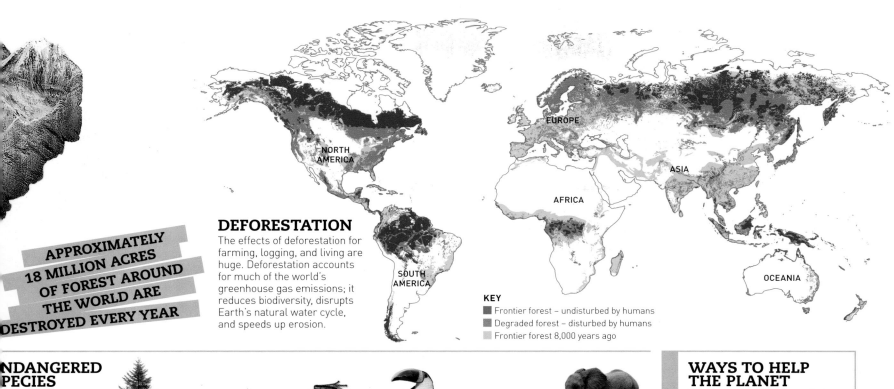

DEFORESTATION

The effects of deforestation for farming, logging, and living are huge. Deforestation accounts for much of the world's greenhouse gas emissions; it reduces biodiversity, disrupts Earth's natural water cycle, and speeds up erosion.

KEY
- Frontier forest – undisturbed by humans
- Degraded forest – disturbed by humans
- Frontier forest 8,000 years ago

APPROXIMATELY 18 MILLION ACRES OF FOREST AROUND THE WORLD ARE DESTROYED EVERY YEAR

ENDANGERED SPECIES

Habitat loss, disease, and hunting cause hundreds, or potentially thousands, of species to become extinct every year.

PLANTS
There are more than 10,000 endangered plant species.

REPTILES
About half of all turtle species are endangered.

AMPHIBIANS
Around 43 per cent of amphibians are threatened.

BIRDS
About 13 per cent of bird species are vulnerable.

FISH
Millions of sharks are killed for their fins each year.

MAMMALS
Around 26 per cent of mammal species are threatened.

EVERYDAY CONSUMERS

There are many things people use every day that can have a big impact on the environment. Using one plastic bag in a shop might seem small, but if other people around the world do this also, the effects on the planet can be huge.

OIL
Spills from tankers and oil rigs are life-threatening to sea creatures.

COTTON
Cotton is treated with pesticides and harmful chemicals.

BATTERIES
Batteries can release dangerous chemicals if they are not disposed of safely.

PLASTIC BAGS
Millions of marine animals die each year from swallowing plastic bags.

GADGETS
Fifty million tonnes of electrical waste is thrown out every year.

THE INTERNET
The internet produces about 300 million tonnes of carbon dioxide each year.

MEAT
Around 18 per cent of all greenhouse gas emissions comes from producing meat.

CHOCOLATE
About 25,000 litres of water is needed to make just 1 kg (2.2 lb) of chocolate.

WATER BOTTLES
Around 50 billion plastic water bottles are used each year in the USA.

RECYCLING

Materials like plastic and glass can take hundreds or thousands of years to break down in a landfill site. Recycling these items can save resources and energy, while also being healthier for the environment.

PLASTIC
Plastic can be recycled into park benches, drain pipes, or even fleece jackets.

GLASS
Recycling 1 tonne of glass releases 315 kg (695 lb) less carbon dioxide than the production of new glass.

PAPER
Recycling paper uses 70 per cent less energy than producing it from raw materials.

ALUMINIUM
Recycling aluminium uses just 5 per cent of the energy needed to make new aluminium.

WAYS TO HELP THE PLANET

There are things we can all do to help reduce our impact on the planet. If everyone takes a few small steps, it can have a greatly positive effect overall.

○ **SWITCH OFF**
Save electricity by turning off lights and computers when they are not in use.

○ **TRAVEL SMART**
Try to walk, cycle, or use public transport, instead of cars.

○ **SAVE WATER**
Ban baths, take shorter showers, and turn off the tap when brushing teeth.

○ **AVOID WASTE**
Buy products with less packaging, so it is not wasted.

○ **RECYCLE**
Many things can be recycled, including paper, glass, and plastic.

○ **REUSE WASTE**
Create compost from food waste.

○ **DON'T LITTER**
Littering harms animals, and litter can end up in the sea, where it stays for a very long time.

○ **PLANT A TREE**
Trees and plants absorb carbon dioxide, a greenhouse gas.

○ **WATCH WHAT YOU EAT**
Buy local and seasonal food. Eat less meat.

○ **SPREAD THE WORD**
Encourage your friends and family to help the environment.

RENEWABLE ENERGY

Fossil fuels provide most of the world's energy, but this has serious environmental impacts and these fuels will become more scarce. There are other sources of cleaner, renewable energy that can be used instead.

WIND
Wind can power turbines that convert the wind energy into electricity.

SOLAR
Energy from the Sun is caught by solar panels and turned into electricity.

TIDAL
As tides rise and fall, they move turbines that convert the movement into energy.

HYDROELECTRIC
When water is channelled through a dam, turbines are turned, which creates energy.

GEOTHERMAL
Cool water is pumped underground through pipes, to absorb the Earth's heat.

BIOFUELS
Fuel can be produced from organic matter, like plants, which are burned to provide energy.

WOOD
Specially grown wood can be burned for heat and light. Trees must be replanted.

SHIPWRECK
Objects like sunken ships on the seabed can release harmful material from their cargo.

Our physical world

Most of Earth's surface is covered in water. The rest is occupied by seven vast landmasses, called continents: Europe, Africa, North America, South America, Asia, Australasia/Oceania, and Antarctica. The tilt of Earth's axis and its orbit of the Sun means that some places are much hotter and drier than others.

SURFACE AREA

The entire surface of the Earth is 510,066,000 sq km (196,937,000 sq miles). Water makes up more than 70% of the surface area, most of which is salt water in the oceans.

29.2% LAND

70.8% WATER

> THE CIRCUMFERENCE OF THE EARTH AROUND THE EQUATOR IS 40,075 KM (24,901 MILES)

CONTINENT SIZES

Tens of millions of years ago, all land on Earth was joined together in one huge continent called Pangea. Over time, this broke apart and the continents we know today gradually moved to their present locations.

Oceania
8,525,989 sq km
(3,291,903 sq miles)

Europe
10,498,000 sq km
(4,053,309 sq miles)

Antarctica
14,000,000 sq km
(5,405,430 sq miles)

South America
17,819,000 sq km
(6,879,000 sq miles)

Asia
43,608,000 sq km
(16,838,365 sq miles)

North America
24,247,000 sq km
(9,361,791 sq miles)

Africa
30,335,000 sq km
(11,712,434 sq miles)

LATITUDE AND LONGITUDE

The equator is an imaginary line that divides the Earth into northern and southern hemispheres. Latitude shows how far north or south a location is in relation to the equator. Longitude gives the east/west position from the prime meridian, which runs between the North and South Poles through London, England.

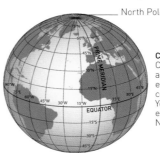

North Pole

COORDINATES
Combining latitude and longitude gives every location a coordinate. New York City, for example, is 40.7° N, 74°W.

KEY
ELEVATION

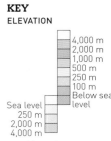

4,000 m
2,000 m
1,000 m
500 m
250 m
100 m
Below sea level

Sea level
250 m
2,000 m
4,000 m

▲ Mountain
▼ Lowest point

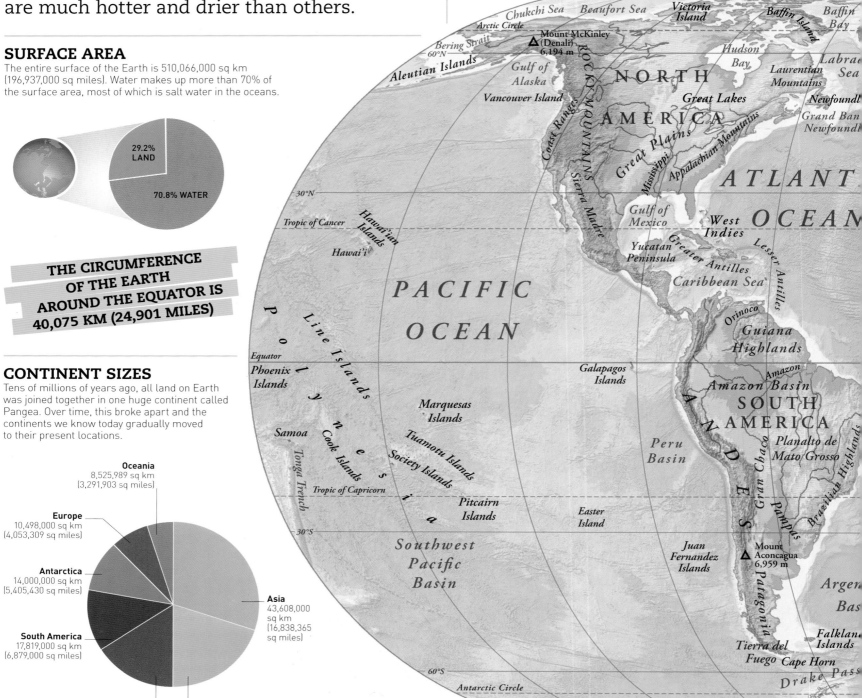

EXTREME PLACES

The place with the hottest average temperature on Earth is Dallol in Ethiopia, at 24.4°C (93.9°F). The place with the coldest average temperature, measuring −58.3°C (−72.9°F), is the highest point on the East Antarctic Ice Sheet, called Dome A. Mawsynram in India is the wettest place in the world, with an average annual rainfall of 1,187 cm (467 in). The driest place is the Dry Valleys in Antarctica, which receive no rain, snow, or hail.

DRIEST PLACE: DRY VALLEYS, ANTARCTICA

WETTEST PLACE: MAWSYNRAM, INDIA

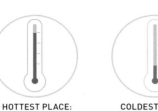

HOTTEST PLACE: DALLOL, ETHIOPIA

COLDEST PLACE: DOME A, ANTARCTICA

TALLEST MOUNTAINS

Slow, but gigantic, movements in Earth's crust form mountains. The tallest mountain range is the Himalayas in Asia, which contains the ten highest mountains in the world. The longest mountain range is the Andes in South America, stretching for 7,200 km (4,500 miles).

MT EVEREST	K2	KANGCHENJUNGA	LHOTSE 1	MAKALU 1
8,848 m (29,029 ft)	8,611 m (28,251 ft)	8,586 m (28,169 ft)	8,485 m (27,838 ft)	8462 m (27,766 ft)

TOP FIVE TALLEST MOUNTAINS

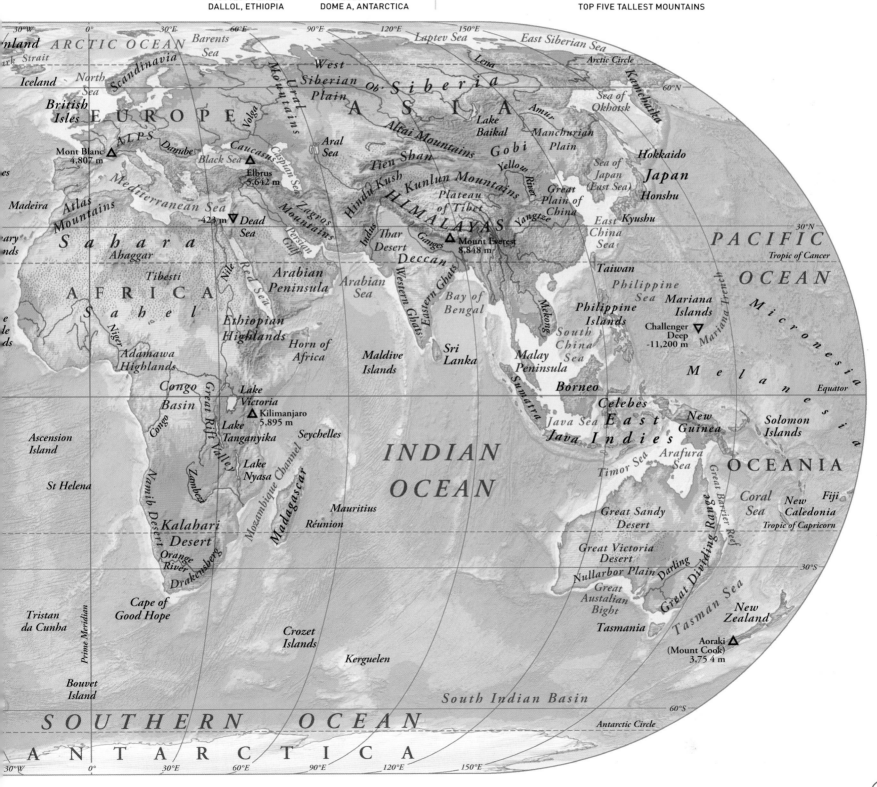

Our political world

There are 196 independent countries in the world today, all differing from each other in size, shape, population, language, government, and culture. The size of a country, its boundaries, and natural resources, such as oil and gas, are just some elements that affect both its internal organization and its relationship with other countries.

POPULATION

There are more than 7 billion people in the world today. United Nations' estimates of what the population will be in 2040 range from about 8 to 9.7 billion. Some areas of the world are more populated than others because of their climate, terrain, and natural and economic resources. Over half the world's population live in cities, most in Asia, as a result of mass migration from rural areas in search of jobs.

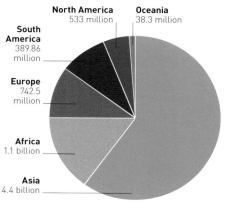

North America 533 million
Oceania 38.3 million
South America 389.86 million
Europe 742.5 million
Africa 1.1 billion
Asia 4.4 billion

POPULATION CHART

TIME ZONES

The world is divided into more than 24 time zones. From the prime meridian (0° longitude), which runs through Greenwich, London, for every 15° you move west or east, you generally lose or gain an hour. At the equator a day is about 12 hours year round. Moving away from the equator, the day can increase to 24 hours or decrease to zero, depending on the time of year. Countries on similar latitudes have the same day lengths.

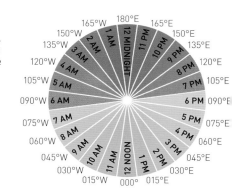

COUNTING TIME
The time zone change is counted at 15° intervals, because Earth rotates 15° each hour.

MEGACITIES

A megacity is an urban area with more than 10 million inhabitants. The top five megacities by population are in Asia.

1 TOKYO
Japan: 37,843,000

2 JAKARTA
Indonesia: 30,539,000

3 NEW DELHI
India: 24,998,000

4 MANILA
Philippines: 24,123,000

5 SEOUL
South Korea: 23,480,000

EUROPE

BIGGEST AND SMALLEST COUNTRIES

Covering a vast expanse of land, the Russian Federation is the world's largest country. It has 11 time zones and shares land borders with 14 other countries. Vatican City, the centre of the Catholic Church, is located within the Italian city of Rome and is the world's smallest country.

BIGGEST COUNTRIES	SMALLEST COUNTRIES
1 RUSSIAN FEDERATION 17,098,242 sq km (6,601,668 sq miles)	**1 VATICAN CITY** 0.44 sq km (0.17 sq miles)
2 CANADA 9,984,670 sq km (3,855,103 sq miles)	**2 MONACO** 2 sq km (0.7 sq miles)
3 UNITED STATES 9,629,091 sq km (3,717,813 sq miles)	**3 NAURU** 21 sq km (8 sq miles)
4 CHINA 9,598,094 sq km (3,705,845 sq miles)	**4 TUVALU** 26 sq km (10 sq miles)
5 BRAZIL 8,514,877 sq km (3,287,612 sq miles)	**5 SAN MARINO** 61 sq km (24 sq miles)

Asia

The largest of Earth's seven continents, Asia occupies one-third of the world's total landmass. It claims both the lowest and the highest points on the planet's surface. More than 4 billion people live here and it is home to the world's two most populous countries, China and India.

PETRA, JORDAN

Once a thriving trading centre, this unique city was carved into the pink sandstone rock face more than 2,000 years ago. Rediscovered in 1812, the entrance today is through the Siq, a long, narrow gorge flanked by high cliffs.

IMMENSE CARVING
The Monastery at Petra is beautifully carved and so huge that even the doorway is several stories high.

ANGKOR WAT, CAMBODIA

The temple of Angkor Wat is covered with exquisite carvings. Part of a vast complex of sacred monuments spread over 400 sq km (155 sq miles), it was constructed between the 9th and 14th centuries. Parts of the complex are now grown over by trees.

HINDU COSMOS
The temple is an earthly representation of the Hindu cosmos. Its five towers, shaped like lotus buds, form a pyramidal structure symbolizing the mythical Mount Meru, home of the Hindu gods.

RIVER GANGES, INDIA

Starting in the Himalayas and finishing at the Bay of Bengal, the River Ganges is worshipped by Hindus as the goddess Ganga. The river is a lifeline for the people who live alongside it, but it has become heavily polluted by human and industrial waste.

HOLY BATHING
Pilgrims gather to bathe in the River Ganges at Haridwar, the "Gateway to God". It is one of the seven holiest places for Hindus.

KEY
ELEVATION

	4,000 m
	2,000 m
	1,000 m
	500 m
	250 m
	100 m
	Below sea level
Sea level	
250 m	
2,000 m	
4,000 m	

△ Mountain
▽ Lowest point

POPULATION
■ Capital city
⦿ Over 1 million
◉ 500,000 to 1 million
◎ 100,000 to 500,000
○ below 100,000

TAJ MAHAL

The Taj Mahal was commissioned by Mughal emperor Shah Jahan in 1632 to house the tomb of his beloved wife Mumtaz Mahal.

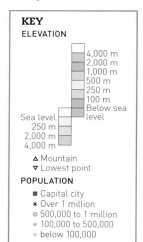

MARBLE MONUMENT
Made of white marble, the colour of the building appears to change depending on the time of day.

IT TOOK 22 YEARS AND MORE THAN 20,000 CRAFTSMEN AND ARTISANS TO BUILD THE TAJ MAHAL

CHERRY BLOSSOM, JAPAN

Spring is celebrated in Japan with the arrival of the cherry blossom, a symbol of hope and renewal. Japanese people get together to marvel at these brilliant, fragrant displays of colour. It is thought that the blossoms help us to remember that lives should be lived to the full.

BLOSSOMING SOUTH TO NORTH
The cherry blossom season begins in Okinawa in January and moves northwards to Kyoto and Tokyo at the end of March.

THE GREAT WALL OF CHINA

Built to protect against raids from the north, the Great Wall of China is made up of different sections, built by various Chinese dynasties. The longest structure ever built, much of the wall was constructed in the 14th century during the Ming Dynasty.

BIG BUILD
The outside of the wall was built with stones and fired bricks and the inside filled with stones and mud. Sections were up to 7.5 m (25 ft) wide and stretched for thousands of kilometres.

MOUNT EVEREST, NEPAL

At 8,848 m (29,029 ft) high, this is the highest mountain in the world. In 1953 climbers Edmund Hillary from New Zealand and Nepalese Sherpa Tenzing Norgay became the first people to reach the summit of Everest.

TOUGH CLIMB
To date, more than 4,000 people have climbed Mount Everest. Climbers have to face avalanches, freezing temperatures, storms, altitude sickness, and a lack of oxygen.

NEW HEIGHTS
With the movement of tectonic plates, Everest continues to increase in height by approximately 4 mm (0.16 in) every year.

ORANGUTANS, BORNEO

Borneo is one of only two remaining natural habitats for orangutans. An endangered species, they live in the tropical canopy, eating fruit and sleeping in nests made of branches.

SWING TIME
Orangutans have long arms and a strong grip.

FAST FACTS

More than half the world's population lives in Asia. The biggest cities are also found here.

○ **AREA:**
43,608,000 sq km (16,838,365 sq miles)

○ **POPULATION:**
4,426,683,000

○ **NUMBER OF COUNTRIES:**
49

○ **LARGEST COUNTRY BY AREA:**
Russian Federation 17,075,400 sq km (6,592,846 sq miles)

○ **LARGEST COUNTRY BY POPULATION:**
China 1,340,000,000

○ **LARGEST CITY BY POPULATION:**
Tokyo, Japan 38,000,000

○ **HIGHEST POINT:**
Mount Everest 8,848 m (29,029 ft)

○ **LOWEST POINT:**
Dead Sea, Israel –413 m (–1,378 ft)

○ **LONGEST RIVER:**
Yangtze, China 6,299 km (3,915 miles)

North America

North America is the third largest of the continents. It is a hugely diverse land with mountains, plains, deserts, and ice. To the north is Greenland, the world's largest island. To the southeast are the tropical islands of the Caribbean and central American rainforests.

DENALI NATIONAL PARK

This national park in Alaska is 19,187 sq km (7,408 sq miles) of tranquil wilderness with taiga forest, alpine tundra, and snowy mountains. Grizzly and black bears roam, and more than 100 bird species call the park home for the summer.

GRIZZLY BEAR

MOUNT MCKINLEY

Situated near the Pacific Ocean and the Arctic Circle, Mount McKinley, known locally as Denali, has some of the harshest weather conditions in the world.

NIAGARA FALLS

Three waterfalls on the border of the United States and Canada are known as the Niagara Falls. They are renowned for their majestic beauty, and millions of people visit them every year. The combined force of their power is also a valuable source of hydroelectricity.

FANTASTIC FALLS

Around 567,811 litres (150,000 US gallons) of water flow over Niagara Falls every second.

KEY

ELEVATION

4,000 m
2,000 m
1,000 m
500 m
250 m
100 m
Below sea level

Sea level
250 m
2,000 m
4,000 m

▲ Mountain
▼ Lowest point

POPULATION

■ Capital city
◉ Over 1 million
◎ 500,000 to 1 million
○ 100,000 to 500,000
○ below 100,000

St.John's

Newfoundland

St Pierre & Miquelon (to France)

Lawrence

Greenland (to Denmark)

Labrador Sea

NUUK

Labrador

Laurentian Mountains

Baffin Bay

Iqaluit (Frobisher Bay)

Hudson Strait

C A N A D A

Ellesmere Island

Baffin Island

Foxe Basin

Hudson Bay

O C E A N

A R C T I C

Victoria Island

Great Bear Lake

Yellowknife

Great Slave Lake

Lake Athabasca

Reindeer Lake

Lake Winnipeg

Saskatoon

Beaufort Sea

Mackenzie

Mackenzie Mountains

R o c k y

Edmonton

Brooks Range

Whitehorse

ASIA

Bering Strait

UNITED STATES OF AMERICA (Alaska)

Mount McKinley (Denali) 6,194 m

Anchorage

Juneau

Bering Sea

Aleutian Islands

Gulf of Alaska

Queen Charlotte Islands

PACIFIC

YELLOWSTONE

This national park is best known for its collection of thermal features, more than 500 of which are geysers, and the active super-volcano the Yellowstone Caldera. It is also home to grizzly bears, bison, and elk.

LIKE CLOCKWORK
Old Faithful ejects hot water and steam every 35 to 120 minutes for 1.5 to 5 minutes at a time. It is the park's biggest regular geyser.

GOLDEN GATE

One of the top construction achievements of the 20th century, the Golden Gate Bridge opened in San Francisco in 1937. It is 2.7 km (1.7 miles) long and took four years to build.

SUPER SUSPENSION
The Golden Gate Bridge is a suspension bridge with cables between towers to carry its weight.

GRAND CANYON

Carved by the Colorado River, the immense and dramatic Grand Canyon is 446 km (277 miles) long, up to 29 km (18 miles) wide, and 1.6 km (1 mile) deep.

NATURAL WONDER
Erosion has exposed many colourful rock layers, creating an inspirational landscape.

CHICHEN ITZA

The native American Maya people built temples and monumental cities, such as Chichen Itza, in the jungles of the Yucatán Peninsula in Mexico from c.200 ce.

EL CASTILLO
This pyramid temple stands in the centre of Chichen Itza.

THE MAYA'S ASTRONOMICAL SKILLS WERE SO ADVANCED THEY COULD EVEN PREDICT SOLAR ECLIPSES

FLORIDA EVERGLADES

The Everglades are a vast area of semi-tropical wetland, home to mangrove, mahogany, bay, and eucalyptus trees. The swampy conditions are perfect for alligators and crocodiles.

WILDLIFE WATCHING
Alligators, turtles, and egrets are just some of the wildlife that can be seen.

IN THE PINK
Flamingos turn pink from the colour pigments in the algae and shrimp they eat.

AMERICAN CROCODILE

COSTA RICA RAINFOREST

In the Costa Rica rainforest in central America, tall trees covered with orchids, vines, ferns and moss rise into the sky. The rainforest teems with life and is home to many exotic animal and plant species.

TREE FROG
The red-eyed tree frog is one of 133 species of frogs and toads that are found in Costa Rica.

BUTTERFLIES
The country has an assortment of butterflies including this beautifully coloured Metalmark butterfly.

ORCHIDS
The Costa Rica rainforest supports a huge collection of orchids. There are more species here than anywhere else on Earth.

Map labels

ATLANTIC OCEAN

UNITED STATES OF AMERICA

MEXICO

Gulf of Mexico

Caribbean Sea

Gulf of California

CUBA
THE BAHAMAS
JAMAICA
HAITI
DOMINICAN REPUBLIC
Puerto Rico (to US)
Turks & Caicos Islands (to UK)
Virgin Islands (to US)
British Virgin Islands (to UK)
Anguilla (to UK)
ANTIGUA & BARBUDA
Guadeloupe (to France)
DOMINICA
Martinique (to France)
ST LUCIA
ST VINCENT & THE GRENADINES
BARBADOS
GRENADA
TRINIDAD & TOBAGO
ST KITTS & NEVIS
Montserrat (to UK)
Aruba (to Neth.)
Curaçao (to Neth.)
Bonaire (to Neth.)
Cayman Islands (to UK)

West Indies
Greater Antilles
Lesser Antilles

SOUTH AMERICA

GUATEMALA
BELIZE
HONDURAS
EL SALVADOR
NICARAGUA
COSTA RICA
PANAMA

Appalachian Mountains
Great Plains
Sierra Madre Oriental
Sierra Madre Occidental
Coast Ranges
Rocky Mountains

Lake Superior
Lake Michigan
Lake Huron
Lake Erie
Lake Ontario
Great Salt Lake
Salt Lake City

Yucatán Peninsula

Mississippi Delta
Mississippi
Missouri
Arkansas
Ohio
Colorado
Columbia
Rio Grande
Lake Nicaragua

California
Lower California

Death Valley -86 m ▽
Volcán Pico de Orizaba 5,700 m ▲

Cities:
Boston, Hartford, Albany, New York, Philadelphia, Baltimore, WASHINGTON DC, Richmond, Raleigh, Columbia, Jacksonville, Tampa, Miami, Atlanta, Montgomery, Nashville, Columbus, Cleveland, Detroit, Toronto, Chicago, Indianapolis, Memphis, Jackson, New Orleans, Baton Rouge, Houston, San Antonio, Austin, Dallas, Little Rock, Oklahoma City, Kansas City, Saint Louis, Des Moines, Lincoln, Saint Paul, Denver, Albuquerque, El Paso, Phoenix, Las Vegas, Reno, Sacramento, San Jose, San Francisco, Oakland, Los Angeles, San Diego, Boise, Tijuana, Mexicali, Hermosillo, Chihuahua, Ciudad Juárez, Monterrey, León, Guadalajara, Querétaro, MEXICO CITY, Puebla, Acapulco, Mérida

NASSAU, HAVANA, PORT-AU-PRINCE, SANTO DOMINGO, SAN JUAN, KINGSTON, Guantánamo Bay, BELMOPAN, GUATEMALA CITY, SAN SALVADOR, TEGUCIGALPA, MANAGUA, SAN JOSÉ, PANAMA CITY, PORT-OF-SPAIN

South America

Most of the continent of South America lies south of the equator. Its different climates and habitats mean it is home to many unique animal species.

ANGEL FALLS

Angel Falls is the world's highest uninterrupted waterfall at 979 m (3,212 ft). The falls lie on the Gauja River, in the Canaima National Park in Venezuela. The indigenous name for the falls is *Kerepakupai Vená*, which means "waterfalls of the deepest place".

BEAUTY SPOT
Angel Falls is one of Venezuela's top tourist attractions.

GALAPAGOS ISLANDS

The 19 islands of the Galápagos were formed by volcanoes on the ocean floor. They are now strictly controlled to protect the many animal and bird species that live on them.

FRIGATEBIRD
Male frigatebirds have impressive red throat pouches, which they inflate to attract females.

GIANT TORTOISE
These huge reptiles can weigh as much as 300 kg (660 lbl) and grow up to 1.2 m (4 ft) in length.

LAND IGUANA
The Galápagos land iguana may look ferocious, but it is actually a herbivore.

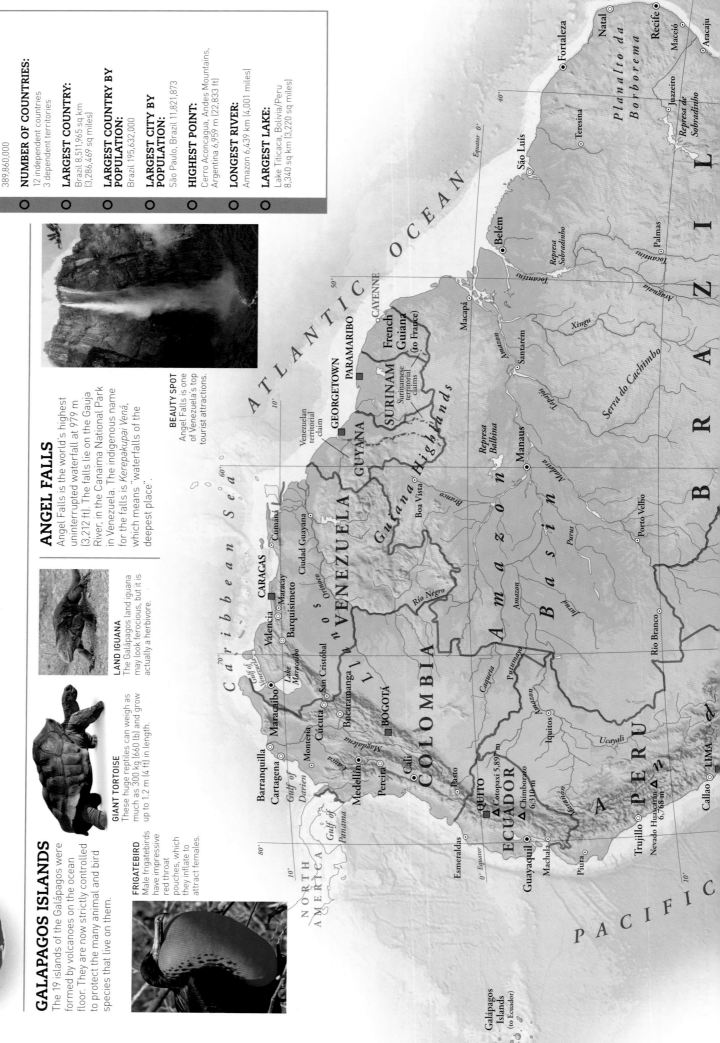

KEY

ELEVATION

4,000 m
2,000 m
1,000 m
500 m
250 m
100 m
Below sea level

Sea level
250 m
2,000 m
4,000 m

▲ Mountain
▼ Lowest point

POPULATION

■ Capital city
◉ Over 1 million
◎ 500,000 to 1 million
⊙ 100,000 to 500,000
○ below 100,000

AMAZON RAINFOREST

More than 55 million years old, the Amazon rainforest accounts for approximately 50 per cent of the world's total rainforest. It contains one in ten of every known plant and animal species in the world.

LONGEST RIVER
The Amazon River carries more water than any other river and can be seen from space.

TOP PREDATOR
Jaguars are some of the most fearsome predators in the Amazon. Their spots help to camouflage them against the jungle around them.

ENORMOUS SNAKE
Anacondas keep growing their whole lives. They can reach lengths of up to 6.5 m (21 ft).

ARGENTINE BEEF

Rearing cattle for beef production is a major industry in Argentina. The country has the second-highest consumption of beef, and is the third-largest exporter of beef in the world.

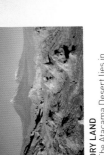

PRIZE WINNERS
Producing the best cattle is a competitive business in Argentina.

GAUCHOS
In Argentina, cattle herders, or gauchos, live on the Pampas grasslands and look after the herds of cattle.

THE FIRST EVIDENCE OF HUMANS EXISTING IN SOUTH AMERICA DATES BACK TO APPROXIMATELY 9000 BCE

LAKE TITICACA

Situated between Peru and Bolivia, Lake Titicaca is the world's highest navigable lake, lying at a height of 3,812 m (12,507 ft) above sea level.

FLOATING HOMES
The Uros people live on the lake on floating islands made out of reeds.

SALT PLAINS

The Salar de Uyuni is the world's largest salt pan, an area of ground that is crusty and covered in salt and minerals. It is located in the Altiplano plateau in Bolivia.

BATTERY POWER
As well as providing salt, the Salar de Uyuni is also the source of more than 50 per cent of the world's lithium, which is used to power batteries and other devices.

THE ANDES MOUNTAINS

Running through seven countries in South America for 7,250 km (4,505 miles), the Andes form the longest continental mountain range in the world. They contain the world's highest volcanoes.

WOOLLY WONDERS
There are many herds of alpacas in the Andes. They are bred for their wool, which is made into blankets, sweaters, and other clothes.

DRY LAND
The Atacama Desert lies in a plateau west of the Andes and is the driest non-polar desert in the world.

Map labels

Vitória
Belo Horizonte
Brazilian Highlands
Goiânia
Nova Iguaçu
Rio de Janeiro
São Paulo
Santos
Osasco
Campinas
Ribeirão Preto
Londrina
Campo Grande
Curitiba
Florianópolis
Porto Alegre
Serra do Mar
Santa Maria
Tacuarembó
MONTEVIDEO
URUGUAY
Río de la Plata
Mar del Plata
La Plata
Uruguay
Mesopotamia
PARAGUAY
ASUNCIÓN
Ciudad del Este
Posadas
Paraguay
Resistencia
Paraná
Gran Chaco
Pilcomayo
BUENOS AIRES
Rosario
Paraná
Córdoba
Salta
Cerro Ojos del Salado 6,880 m
La Rioja
SUCRE
Santa Cruz
Cochabamba
Lago Poopó
Altiplano
Atacama Desert
Iquique
Arica
Antofagasta
Coquimbo
Mendoza
Salado
Cerro Aconcagua 6,959 m
SANTIAGO
Concepción
Valdivia
Puerto Montt
CHILE
ARGENTINA
Pampas
Colorado
Bahía Blanca
Río Negro
Rawson
Lago Colhué Huapí
Gulf of San Jorge
Deseado
Patagonia
Laguna del Carbón -105 m
Bahía Grande
Río Gallegos
Punta Arenas
Ushuaia
Magellan
Beagle Channel
Cape Horn
Golfo de Penas
Chubut
STANLEY
Falkland Islands (to UK)
Tropic of Capricorn
ATLANTIC OCEAN
PACIFIC OCEAN

Europe

The continent of Europe is rich in cultural diversity, with a history of wealth, industry, and empire building. There are 23 official languages spoken across the 47 European countries.

FAST FACTS

Europe is the second smallest continent. It contains the world's smallest country, Vatican City, with a population of only 800.

- **AREA:**
  10,498,000 sq km
  (4,053,309 sq miles)

- **POPULATION:**
  742,452,000

- **NUMBER OF COUNTRIES:**
  47

- **LARGEST COUNTRY BY AREA:**
  Russian Federation 3,960,000 sq km (1,528,560 sq miles)

- **LARGEST COUNTRY BY POPULATION:**
  Russian Federation 110,000,000

- **LARGEST CITY BY POPULATION:**
  Istanbul, Turkey (14,377,000)

- **HIGHEST POINT:**
  Mount El'brus, Russian Federation 5,642 m (18,510 ft)

- **LONGEST RIVER:**
  Volga, Russian Federation 3,690 km (2,293 miles)

- **LARGEST LAKE:**
  Lake Ladoga, Russian Federation 18,390 sq km (7,100 sq miles)

KEY
ELEVATION

4,000 m
2,000 m
1,000 m
500 m
250 m
100 m
Sea level   Below sea level
250 m
2,000 m
4,000 m

△ Mountain
▽ Lowest point

POPULATION
- ■ Capital city
- ● Over 1 million
- ◉ 500,000 to 1 million
- ◎ 100,000 to 500,000
- ○ below 100,000

NORWAY'S FJORDS

Norway's fjords (steep-sided waterways) were created by the movement of ice and rock during successive ice ages. When the glaciers retreated, seawater flooded these U-shaped valleys. Norway has the highest concentration of fjords in the world.

DRAMATIC VIEW
Norway's fjords offer views of snow-capped mountains, ancient glaciers, and remote fishing villages.

THE ALPS

The highest mountain range entirely within Europe is 1,200 km (750 miles) long. The Alps formed millions of years ago when two tectonic plates collided. Mont Blanc, on the French–Italian border, is the Alps' highest mountain at 4,810 m (15,781 ft).

ALPINE FUN
The Alps are a popular winter destination for skiing, with lots of ski slopes and resorts.

RIVER DANUBE

The River Danube is the second longest river in Europe. It starts in the Black Forest mountains of Germany and flows 2,850 km (1,770 miles) to the Black Sea, passing through ten countries on the way.

RIVERSIDE CITIES
The Danube flows through four capital cities: Vienna, Bratislava, Budapest (shown here), and Belgrade.

GREAT WHITE PELICAN
More than 50 per cent of Eurasian great white pelicans live in the Danube delta.

EIFFEL TOWER, FRANCE

The Eiffel Tower was built as part of the 1889 World Fair, to celebrate 100 years since the French Revolution. An engineering achievement, it has become a cultural icon of Paris and France. It is 324 m (1,063 ft) high.

RECORD-HOLDER
The tower was the world's tallest man-made structure for 41 years until the Chrysler Building in New York City was built in 1930.

ROME, ITALY

Once the centre of the vast Roman Empire, Rome is one of Europe's most historical cities. With classical ruins, Renaissance buildings, and Baroque sculptures, the city is a showcase for many amazing engineering and artistic achievements.

DRAMATIC SETTING
The Colosseum was built as an arena for all kinds of Roman entertainment: combats between gladiators, re-enactments of battles, and even executions.

THE ACROPOLIS, GREECE

The ancient ruins of the Acropolis sit above the city of Athens and are visited by millions of people each year. The Acropolis is said to symbolize the greatest achievements of the Ancient Greeks.

TEMPLE TO ATHENA
The Parthenon – one of the Acropolis's most famous buildings – was a temple built to honour Athena, the goddess of wisdom and knowledge. It once contained a huge statue of her.

THE MEDITERRANEAN

This sea separates Europe from Africa. It has been a focal point for empires and civilizations, which is reflected in the diverse cultures of the people living in this coastal region.

BEACH LIFE
With hot, dry summers and calm, blue sparkling sea, the Mediterranean region is a hugely popular tourist destination.

EUROPE WAS NAMED AFTER THE BEAUTIFUL PRINCESS EUROPA IN GREEK MYTHOLOGY

Novaya Zemlya
Kara Sea
Vorkuta
Arctic Circle
Ural Mountains
USSIAN
ERATION
Perm'
Kirov
Vologda
Ufa
Yaroslavl'
Kazan'
Nizhniy Novgorod
Ul'yanovsk
Tol'yatti
Orenburg
MOSCOW
Samara
Central Russian Upland
Tula
Saratov
oronezh
Kharkiv
Volgograd
Volga
NE
Dnipropetrovs'k
Astrakhan'
50°
Donets'k
Rostov-na-Donu
-28 m
Caspian Sea
Sea of Azov
Stavropol'
Novorossiysk
Grozny
Caucasus
ol'
(annexed by Russia, 2014)
El'brus 5,642 m
ck Sea
60°
70°
60°
40°

Africa

The world's second largest continent, Africa is rich in history, language, culture, and geographic diversity. With a stunning collection of animals, reptiles, birds, and insects, it is also where human beings first appeared on Earth.

FAST FACTS

Africa makes up around 20 per cent of Earth's land mass. It contains the world's longest river – the Nile.

○ **AREA:**
30,335,000 sq km (11,712,434 sq miles)

○ **POPULATION:**
1,136,239,000

○ **NUMBER OF COUNTRIES:**
54

○ **LARGEST COUNTRY:**
Algeria 2,381,741 sq km (919,595 sq miles)

○ **LARGEST COUNTRY BY POPULATION:**
Nigeria 177,155,754

○ **LARGEST CITY BY POPULATION:**
Lagos, Nigeria 21,000,000

○ **HIGHEST POINT:**
Mount Kilimanjaro, Tanzania 5,895 m (19,336 ft)

○ **LONGEST RIVER:**
Nile River 6,695 km (4,160 miles)

○ **LARGEST LAKE:**
Lake Victoria, Uganda, Kenya, Tanzania 68,880 sq km (26,560 sq miles)

PYRAMIDS AT GIZA

During the 4th Dynasty (2613–2494 BCE), Giza became a royal burial ground for the Ancient Egyptians. Three pyramid complexes serve as tombs for their dead kings. The Sphinx was added to guard the pyramids, and each king's royal family and courts were buried nearby.

BUILDING BLOCKS
The construction methods of the Pyramids are unknown. More than 2 million blocks of stone were used just to make the largest, the Great Pyramid.

THE SPHINX
The Sphinx is modelled on a mythical animal with the head of a human and the body of a lion.

SAHARA DESERT

The Sahara covers much of North Africa and is the world's largest hot desert. Constantly shaped by the wind, around 25 per cent of the desert is sand dunes. The rest is made up of a barren, rocky landscape with very little water. The highest peak is Emi Koussi (3,145 m/ 11,294 ft) in the Tibesti Mountains.

SAHARA TRANSPORT
Camels' feet allow them to move quickly and easily through sand. Camels can last up to 17 days without food or water.

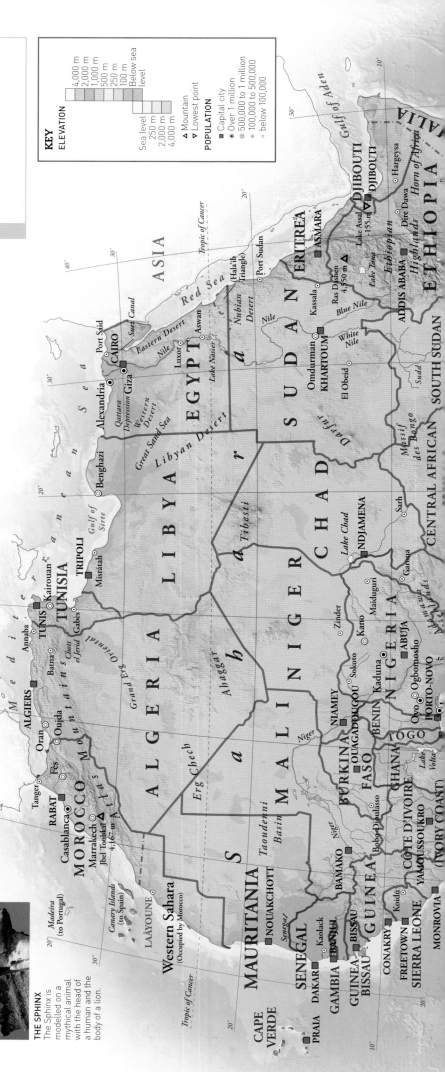

KEY

ELEVATION

4,000 m
2,000 m
1,000 m
500 m
250 m
100 m
Below sea level

Sea level
250 m
2,000 m
4,000 m

▲ Mountain
▼ Lowest point

POPULATION

■ Capital city
◉ Over 1 million
◎ 500,000 to 1 million
◉ 100,000 to 500,000
○ below 100,000

Gulf of Aden

ASIA

EUROPE

Mediterranean Sea

Red Sea

Gulf of Sirte

Tropic of Cancer

Tropic of Cancer

Equator

ATLANTIC OCEAN

Places on map

MOROCCO — RABAT, Casablanca, Marrakech, Tanger, Fes, Oujda, Oran, Ibel Toubkal 4,167 m ▲

Atlas Mountains

ALGERIA — ALGIERS, Annaba, Batna

TUNISIA — TUNIS, Kairouan, Gabes

LIBYA — TRIPOLI, Misratah, Benghazi

EGYPT — CAIRO, Alexandria, Port Said, Suez Canal, Giza, Luxor, Aswan

Qattara Depression, Western Desert, Eastern Desert, Libyan Desert, Great Sand Sea

Nubian Desert, Lake Nasser

SUDAN — KHARTOUM, Omdurman, El Obeid, Kassala, Port Sudan, Darfur

Sahara

Grand Erg Occidental, Grand Erg Oriental, Erg Chech, Chott el Jerid, Taoudenni Basin

MAURITANIA — NOUAKCHOTT

WESTERN SAHARA (Occupied by Morocco) — LAÂYOUNE

CAPE VERDE — PRAIA

SENEGAL — DAKAR, Kaolack

GAMBIA — BANJUL

GUINEA-BISSAU — BISSAU

GUINEA — CONAKRY, Koidu

SIERRA LEONE — FREETOWN

MONROVIA

CÔTE D'IVOIRE (IVORY COAST) — YAMOUSSOUKRO, Bobo-Dioulasso

MALI — BAMAKO, Niger

BURKINA FASO — OUAGADOUGOU

GHANA — Volta

TOGO

BENIN — PORTO-NOVO

NIGER — NIAMEY, Zinder

NIGERIA — ABUJA, Sokoto, Kaduna, Kano, Maiduguri, Oyo, Ogbomosho, Lagos

CHAD — NDJAMENA, Lake Chad, Sarh, Tibesti

Mandara Mts, Garoua

CENTRAL AFRICAN

CAMEROON — Massif des Bongo

SOUTH SUDAN, Sudd, White Nile, Blue Nile

ERITREA — ASMARA

ETHIOPIA — ADDIS ABABA, Dire Dawa, Ethiopian Highlands, Lake Tana, Ras Dashen 4,550 m ▲

DJIBOUTI — DJIBOUTI, Hargeysa

Horn of Africa

Lake Assal 155 m ▼

(Halaib Triangle)

Canary Islands (to Spain), Madeira (to Portugal), Senegal, Niger, Nigr

Madrid

MAASAI MARA

Between July and October, wildebeest migrate to the Maasai Mara nature reserve in Kenya from Tanzania's Serengeti. They are hunted by lions, cheetahs, leopards, and hyenas. The plains are also full of zebras, impalas, giraffes, hippos, and gazelles. Many tourists visit to view the wildlife.

ZEBRA
No two zebras have the same pattern of stripes.

WILDEBEEST
A type of antelope, wildebeest keep together in huge herds. They eat constantly.

HIPPOPOTAMUS
Hippos spend most of the day in the water, so they don't get too hot in the Sun.

OKAVANGO DELTA

Starting in the mountains of Angola, the Okavango River flows into the Kalahari desert, forming a great inland wetland that is home to a variety of wildlife. Seasonal flooding swells the size of the delta, attracting animals from far away to this oasis. It is a perfect wildlife-viewing destination: herds of antelopes, zebras, buffaloes, elephants, crocodiles, hippopotamuses, lions, and cheetahs all thrive here.

LIFE SUPPORT
Situated in region of Botswana that is dry for much of the year, this large inland delta attracts lots of wildlife.

CAPE TOWN

One of the most popular African cities for tourists to visit, Cape Town is famous for its huge harbour. The big, flat-topped Table Mountain overlooks the city.

ACTIVE HARBOUR
Cape Town harbour is one of the busiest ports in South Africa.

CATTLE HERDERS

Living in Kenya, the Samburu people are traditionally cattle herders, and may also keep sheep, goats, and camels. Cattle are highly prized, and ownership determines status and wealth.

NOMADIC HERDERS
The Samburu often graze their herds far from settlements in order to find water and vegetation.

MOUNT KILIMANJARO

The highest peak in Africa, and the tallest free-standing mountain in the world, Mount Kilimanjaro rises to 5,895 m (19,336 ft). It is a dormant volcano with three volcanic cones. Around 25,000 visitors trek up its slopes each year.

AFRICA'S PEAK
The snow-capped summit of Mount Kilimanjaro is surrounded by dry, flat scrubland.

VICTORIA FALLS

Forming the border between Zambia and Zimbabwe, the Zambezi River is transformed into a ferocious torrent as it thunders over a wide, basalt cliff, forming Victoria Falls. Columns of spray can be seen from miles away as the river plummets over the edge into a gorge over 108 m (360 ft) below.

GIANT FALLS
The combination of its great height and enormous width make Victoria Falls the world's largest sheet of falling water.

MINERAL RICH, ABOUT 65% OF THE WORLD'S DIAMONDS COME FROM AFRICA

SEYCHELLES
VICTORIA

MAURITIUS
PORT LOUIS
Réunion (to France)

MADAGASCAR
ANTANANARIVO
Fianarantsoa
Toamasina
Mahajanga
Antsiranana

COMOROS
MORONI
Mayotte (to France)

INDIAN OCEAN

Mozambique Channel

Tropic of Capricorn

MOZAMBIQUE
MAPUTO
Beira
Nacala

SWAZILAND
MBABANE
MANZINI

Kismaayo
Mombasa
NAIROBI
Kirinyaga 5,200 m
Kilimanjaro 5,895 m
Zanzibar
Dar es Salaam
DODOMA

TANZANIA
Lake Victoria
KIGALI
RWANDA
BUJUMBURA
BURUNDI
Bukavu
Lake Tanganyika
Kalemie
Lake Nyasa

MALAWI
LILONGWE
Blantyre
Zambezi

DEM. REP. CONGO
Mbandaka Basin
KINSHASA
Ilebo
Mbuji-Mayi
Lualaba
Lubumbashi

ZAMBIA
LUSAKA
Kitwe
Zambezi

ZIMBABWE
HARARE
Bulawayo
Limpopo

BOTSWANA
GABORONE
Kalahari Desert
Okavango Delta

NAMIBIA
WINDHOEK
Namib Desert
Walvis Bay
Lüderitz

ANGOLA
LUANDA
Bié Plateau
Lubango
Namibe
ANGOLA (Cabinda)

GABON
BRAZZAVILLE
Port-Gentil
SÃO TOMÉ

Equator

ATLANTIC OCEAN

Tropic of Capricorn

Orange River

SOUTH AFRICA
PRETORIA
Johannesburg
Kimberley
Welkom
BLOEMFONTEIN
Pietermaritzburg
MASERU
LESOTHO
Mahalapye
Mbombela
East London
Port Elizabeth
CAPE TOWN
Cape of Good Hope

Great Rift Valley

Oceania

Oceania is the collective name for Australia, New Zealand, and the island groups in the Pacific Ocean, including Melanesia, Micronesia, and Polynesia. Australia dominates the region in size, population, and economic strength.

PACIFIC ISLANDS

There are more than 20,000 islands in the Pacific Ocean. These palm-covered paradises are either volcanic or part of natural reefs. While they may look similar, they are quite diverse in human culture.

ISLAND PARADISE
The Fijian archipelago (group of islands) is made up of more than 330 beautiful islands.

ABORIGINAL CULTURE

Aboriginal people have been living in Australia for more than 50,000 years. They have a tribal culture of storytelling and art, and a strong spiritual belief tying them to the land. Many still live in the Australian outback, where rocks feature their paintings.

ROCK ART
Some of the oldest Aboriginal paintings are more than 20,000 years old.

ULURU
Particularly sacred to the Anangu Aboriginal people, this massive red monolith dominates the surrounding landscape.

SYDNEY OPERA HOUSE

The Sydney Opera House is a performing arts centre designed by Danish architect Jorn Utzon in 1957. It opened in 1973, and today is visited by more than seven million people every year.

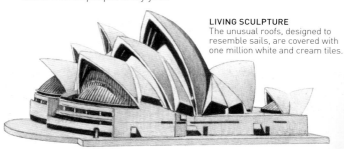

LIVING SCULPTURE
The unusual roofs, designed to resemble sails, are covered with one million white and cream tiles.

SURFING

Australia is a first-class surfing destination, famous for both the quality and the variety of its waves. The coastline has plenty of beach, reef, and point breaks to challenge the experienced surfer, and easy rolling swells for beginners.

SURF CULTURE
With its world-renowned beaches, surfing and beach culture is a popular part of Australian life.

WILDLIFE

The islands of Oceania are a long way from other landmasses, so they contain a diverse range of animals and birds, many of which are not found anywhere else in the world. Some birds, like the emu and kiwi, evolved into flightless specivvves due to the lack of predators.

TASMANIAN DEVIL
Australia

KOALA
Australia

EMU
Australia

PLATYPUS
Australia

KIWI
New Zealand

KANGAROO
Australia

A JOEY (BABY KANGAROO) STAYS IN ITS MOTHER'S POUCH FOR UP TO TEN MONTHS

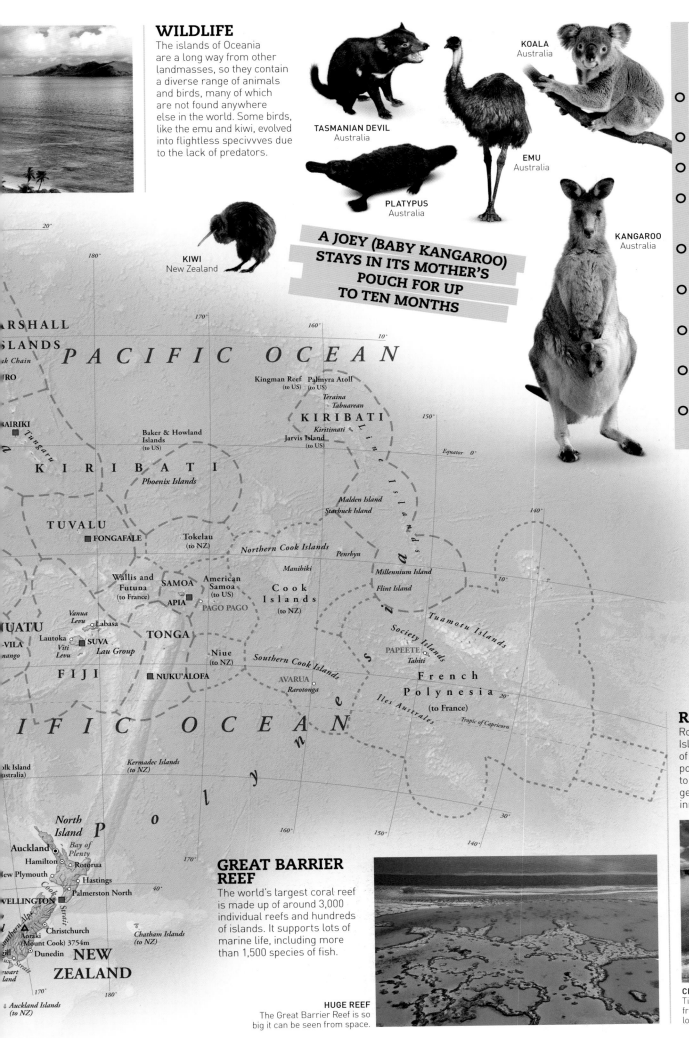

PACIFIC OCEAN

MARSHALL ISLANDS
ak Chain
RO

KIRIBATI

Kingman Reef (to US) Palmyra Atoll (to US)
Teraina
Tabuarean

KIRIBATI
Kiritimati
Jarvis Island (to US)

Baker & Howland Islands (to US)

Equator 0°

AIRIKI
Tungaru

K I R I B A T I
Phoenix Islands

Malden Island
Starbuck Island

TUVALU
FONGAFALE

Tokelau (to NZ)

Northern Cook Islands
Penrhyn

Manihiki

Millennium Island

Flint Island

Line Islands

Wallis and Futuna (to France)
SAMOA
APIA
American Samoa (to US)
PAGO PAGO

Cook Islands (to NZ)

Tuamotu Islands

Society Islands
PAPEETE
Tahiti

Vanua Levu Labasa

UATU
-VILA
nango

Lautoka SUVA
Viti Lau Group
Levu

TONGA

Niue (to NZ)

Southern Cook Islands

French Polynesia (to France)

FIJI
NUKU'ALOFA
AVARUA
Rarotonga

Iles Australes

Tropic of Capricorn

IFIC OCEAN

olk Island ustralia)

Kermadec Islands (to NZ)

North Island
Auckland Bay of Plenty
Hamilton Rotorua
New Plymouth Hastings
Palmerston North
WELLINGTON
Southern Alps
Aoraki (Mount Cook) 3754m
Christchurch
Chatham Islands (to NZ)
Dunedin
wart land
NEW ZEALAND

Auckland Islands (to NZ)

KEY
ELEVATION

4,000 m
2,000 m
1,000 m
500 m
250 m
100 m
Below sea level

Sea level
250 m
2,000 m
4,000 m

△ Mountain
▽ Lowest point

POPULATION

■ Capital city
◉ Over 1 million
◎ 500,000 to 1 million
◦ 100,000 to 500,000
○ below 100,000

ROTORUA

Rotorua on New Zealand's North Island is a natural theme park full of steam clouds, bubbling mud pools, and soothing hot springs to bathe in. It is an area of great geothermal activity, where Earth's inner heat rises to the surface.

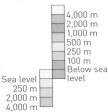

GREAT BARRIER REEF

The world's largest coral reef is made up of around 3,000 individual reefs and hundreds of islands. It supports lots of marine life, including more than 1,500 species of fish.

HUGE REEF
The Great Barrier Reef is so big it can be seen from space.

CHAMPAGNE POOL
Tiny bubbles of carbon dioxide rising from the Earth make this hot spring look like a warm glass of champagne.

193

Antarctica

The continent of Antarctica sits under huge masses of ice called ice sheets. This ice holds 90 per cent of Earth's fresh water. Beneath it lies a continent of valleys, mountains, and lakes but only about 2 per cent is visible above the ice. The only people in Antarctica are scientists and staff working in research stations, and tourists.

EARLY EXPEDITIONS

By the late 19th century, Antarctica remained the last unexplored continent, and the race was on to reach the most remote spot on Earth – the South Pole. In 1909 Ernest Shackleton got within 180 km (111 miles) of the Pole before having to turn back. It was finally reached by explorers Roald Amundsen and Robert Scott in 1911 and 1912.

SHACKLETON'S HOOD

KEY
— Amundsen's route
— Scott's route
☐ Ice shelves

RACE TO THE POLE
The Norwegian Roald Amundsen beat the Englishman Robert Falcon Scott by 33 days, to reach the South Pole on 15 December 1911.

COMPASS, SCOTT'S EXPEDITION

BANJO, SHACKLETON'S EXPEDITION

ICY FEATURES

Antarctica is covered in ice. It has huge masses of glacial ice that are known as ice sheets. Where the ice sheets meet the ocean floating areas of ice form, which are called ice shelves. The edges of these shelves can break away, forming smaller lumps of floating ice called icebergs.

KEY
ELEVATION

4,000 m
2,000 m
1,000 m
500 m
250 m
100 m
Below sea level

Sea level
250 m
2,000 m
4,000 m

△ Mountain
▽ Lowest point
● Research station

COLLAPSE
Impressive crevasses from the glacier of the melting Larsen B ice shelf, which collapsed in 2002.

ICEBERGS
Immense flat-topped icebergs are formed when blocks of ice break away from the main ice shelf.

GETTING AROUND

Working and living in Antarctica is a tough experience, as it is one of the most extreme environments on the planet. Most residents stay on Antarctica for the summer only, from November to March or April.

DRIVING CONDITIONS
Vehicles built to withstand extreme temperatures over long distances are used in Antarctica.

WILDLIFE

The Antarctic continent is quite inhospitable to life. The sea, rather than the land, supports the most wildlife. The Antarctic is the true home for the Emperor and Adélie penguins, and three other types breed on the northern tip of the Antarctic Peninsula.

EMPEROR
PENGUIN

ADELIE
PENGUIN

GENTOO
PENGUIN

FUR SEAL

ORCA

FAST FACTS

No one country owns Antarctica. The international Antarctic Treaty provides agreement for the care and use of the continent.

○ **AREA:**
14,000,000 sq km (5,405,430 sq miles)

○ **POPULATION:**
No permanent residents

○ **HIGHEST POINT:**
Vinson Massif, 4,897 m (16,066 ft)

○ **LONGEST RIVER:**
Onyx 40 km (25 miles)

○ **LARGEST KNOWN LAKE:**
Lake Vostok, 15,690 sq km (6,100 sq miles)

Flags

Every country in the world has a unique flag. Each nation picks its own patterns and colours, which are usually of historical or political significance. A flag is a powerful symbol. It fosters pride in a country or cause and unites people in times of war and peace.

ANCIENT SYMBOLS

Flags have been displayed since ancient times as symbols of loyalty to a country or person. In battle, a flag rallied the troops. Early flags were made of wood or metal. Cloth was first used by the Romans.

Decorative shape for carrying legion's badge

Symbol of legion

Silver ornaments

ROMAN FLAG
This is a modern copy of a flag once carried by a Roman legion.

TYPES OF FLAGS

Variations on common flag patterns such as stripes and crosses turn up again and again all over the world. Often, the only difference between one flag and another is its colour. These are some of the common patterns.

SALTIRE

QUARTERED

SCANDINAVIAN CROSS

CANTON

CROSS

TRICOLOUR

TRIANGLE

TRIBAR

BICOLOUR

BORDERED

NORTH AMERICA

 CANADA

UNITED STATES OF AMERICA

MEXICO

BELIZE

COSTA RICA

EL SALVADOR

GUATEMALA

HONDURAS

NICARAGUA

PANAMA

ANTIGUA AND BARBUDA

BAHAMAS

BARBADOS

CUBA

DOMINICA

DOMINICAN REPUBLIC

GRENADA

HAITI

JAMAICA

ST KITTS & NEVIS

SAINT LUCIA

ST VINCENT & THE GRENADINES

TRINIDAD & TOBAGO

THE STUDY OF FLAGS IS CALLED VEXILLOLOGY

SOUTH AMERICA

COLOMBIA

GUYANA

SURINAME

VENEZUELA

BOLIVIA

ECUADOR

PERU

BRAZIL

ARGENTINA

URUGUAY

CHILE

PARAGUAY

AFRICA

ALGERIA

LIBYA

MOROCCO

TUNISIA

BURUNDI

DJIBOUTI

EGYPT

ERITREA

ETHIOPIA

KENYA

RWANDA

SOMALIA

SOUTH SUDAN

SUDAN

TANZANIA

UGANDA

BENIN

BURKINA FASO

CAPE VERDE

IVORY COAST

GAMBIA

GHANA

GUINEA

GUINEA-BISSAU

LIBERIA

MALI

MAURITANIA

NIGER

NIGERIA

SENEGAL

SIERRA LEONE

TOGO

CAMEROON

CENTRAL AFRICAN REPUBLIC

CHAD

CONGO

DEMOCRATIC REPUBLIC OF CONGO

EQUATORIAL GUINEA

GABON

SAO TOME & PRINCIPE

ANGOLA

BOTSWANA

COMOROS

LESOTHO

MADAGASCAR

MALAWI

MAURITIUS

MOZAMBIQUE

NAMIBIA

SEYCHELLES

SOUTH AFRICA

SWAZILAND

ZAMBIA

ZIMBABWE

THE JOLLY ROGER

The pirate flag known as the "Jolly Roger" was used widely in the 18th century. With its ghoulish designs, it was meant to terrorize a victim into handing over his ship without a fight. The flags belonging to four famous pirates are shown here.

 HENRY EVERY

 "BLACK SAM" BELLAMY

 "CALICO JACK" RACKHAM

 BLACKBEARD

FLAG SIGNALS

Before modern technology, ships at sea "talked" to one another by signalling with flags. They used semaphore, a code in which flags are held in different patterns to represent letters and numbers.

SIGNAL "H" SIGNAL "E" SIGNAL "L" SIGNAL "P"

ANSWERING SIGN SIGNAL   ERROR SIGNAL   END OF WORD SIGNAL   NUMBERS FOLLOW SIGNAL

THERE ARE SIX AMERICAN FLAGS ON THE MOON

PLANTING FLAGS

For centuries, flags have been used by explorers to claim ownership of new land. The national flags planted at such places as the South Pole, the summit of Mount Everest, and even on the Moon all proclaimed "We were here first".

THE MOON
In 1969 the first men on the Moon, astronauts Neil Armstrong and Buzz Aldrin, planted the US flag at their landing site.

SOUTH POLE
Norwegian explorer Roald Amundsen led the first expedition to reach the South Pole in 1911. He left his country's flag on the top of a tent.

MOUNT EVEREST
In 1953 Edmund Hillary and Tenzing Norgay, the first men to stand on top of Mt Everest, planted the flags of the United Kingdom, United Nations, Nepal, and India.

ASIA

AUSTRALIA AND OCEANIA

EUROPE

ICELAND · DENMARK · FINLAND · NORWAY · SWEDEN · BELGIUM · LUXEMBOURG · NETHERLANDS · IRELAND

UNITED KINGDOM · FRANCE · MONACO · ANDORRA · PORTUGAL · SPAIN · AUSTRIA · GERMANY · LIECHTENSTEIN

SLOVENIA · SWITZERLAND · ITALY · MALTA · SAN MARINO · VATICAN CITY · CZECH REPUBLIC · HUNGARY · POLAND

SLOVAKIA · ALBANIA · BOSNIA & HERZEGOVINA · CROATIA · KOSOVO · MACEDONIA · MONTENEGRO · SERBIA · CYPRUS

BULGARIA · GREECE · BELARUS · ESTONIA · LATVIA · LITHUANIA · MOLDOVA · ROMANIA · UKRAINE · RUSSIAN FEDERATION

AUSTRALIA AND OCEANIA

FIJI · KIRIBATI · MARSHALL ISLANDS

MICRONESIA · NAURU · PALAU

PAPUA NEW GUINEA · SAMOA · SOLOMON ISLANDS

TONGA · TUVALU · VANUATU

AUSTRALIA · NEW ZEALAND

ASIA

KAZAKHSTAN · ARMENIA · AZERBAIJAN · GEORGIA · TURKEY · ISRAEL · JORDAN · LEBANON

SYRIA · BAHRAIN · IRAN · IRAQ · KUWAIT · OMAN · QATAR · SAUDI ARABIA

UNITED ARAB EMIRATES · YEMEN · AFGHANISTAN · KYRGYZSTAN · TAJIKISTAN · TURKMENISTAN · UZBEKISTAN · CHINA

MONGOLIA · NORTH KOREA · SOUTH KOREA · TAIWAN · JAPAN · INDIA · SRI LANKA · MALDIVES

PAKISTAN · BANGLADESH · BHUTAN · NEPAL · CAMBODIA · LAOS · MYANMAR · THAILAND

VIETNAM · BRUNEI · EAST TIMOR · INDONESIA · MALAYSIA · PHILIPPINES · SINGAPORE

Where food comes from

Long ago, people only ate what could be grown locally. Today, with modern transportation, people in richer countries can find food from all around the world – such as coffee from Brazil, rice from India, and olives from Italy – in supermarkets. Tropical places export crops such as mangoes and bananas, while countries with huge farmlands supply the world with cereals.

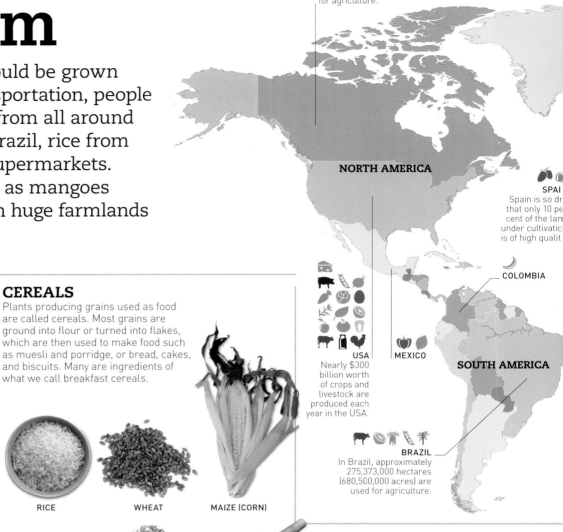

CANADA
Although Canada is the second largest country in the world by area, only 6.8 per cent is used for agriculture.

NORTH AMERICA

SPAIN
Spain is so dry that only 10 per cent of the land under cultivation is of high quality.

COLOMBIA

USA
Nearly $300 billion worth of crops and livestock are produced each year in the USA.

MEXICO

SOUTH AMERICA

BRAZIL
In Brazil, approximately 275,373,000 hectares (680,500,000 acres) are used for agriculture.

BASIC FOOD CROPS

Crops like rapeseed and sugar cane are grown in vast amounts because they can be used in many different ways, not just as foods, but also for products such as fuel. After they are harvested they are usually processed and sent to manufacturers to make other foods or goods.

SUGAR CANE
After sugar cane is harvested, it is processed to extract sucrose (ordinary sugar). It can be eaten as it is but more often is used to sweeten other foods.

SUGAR BEET
The sugar syrup extracted from sugar beet is used in many products, including drinks, feed for animals, and even fuels known as biofuels.

SOYA BEANS
A great source of protein and vitamins, soya beans can be used to make milk, textured vegetable protein, tofu, and flavourings such as soy sauce.

RAPESEED
Fields of yellow rape produce rapeseed, which is usually turned into oil for cooking or used in food products. It is also used in animal feed and biofuels.

PALM OIL
Palm oil is semi-solid at room temperature. It is used in everything from ice-cream to pizza dough, as well as in products like soap and cosmetics.

SUNFLOWER SEEDS
We can snack on raw sunflower seeds but most of the crop is processed to produce oil for cooking or to be turned into spreads like margarine.

CEREALS

Plants producing grains used as food are called cereals. Most grains are ground into flour or turned into flakes, which are then used to make food such as muesli and porridge, or bread, cakes, and biscuits. Many are ingredients of what we call breakfast cereals.

RICE   WHEAT   MAIZE (CORN)

MILLET   OATS   TRITICALE

SORGHUM   BARLEY   RYE

DAIRY

The most popular milk produced around the world is cow's milk. It is used in drinks and in cooking and also to produce cheese, butter, ghee, and yogurt. Water buffalo milk, used in Italy to make mozzarella cheese, is the second most popular milk globally.

COW'S MILK   MOZZARELLA (FROM WATER BUFFALO MILK)

CHEESE

VEGETABLES

Although many people like to grow vegetables in their garden, most of us buy them in greengrocer shops and supermarkets. Potatoes are popular in many parts of the world because they can be used in many ways. Vegetables like cassava and yams are part of a traditional diet in Africa but are now exported to countries with multicultural populations.

POTATOES   CASSAVA   SWEET POTATOES   CABBAGES AND OTHER BRASSICA

PEAS   LETTUCE   BEANS   SPINACH   GARLIC

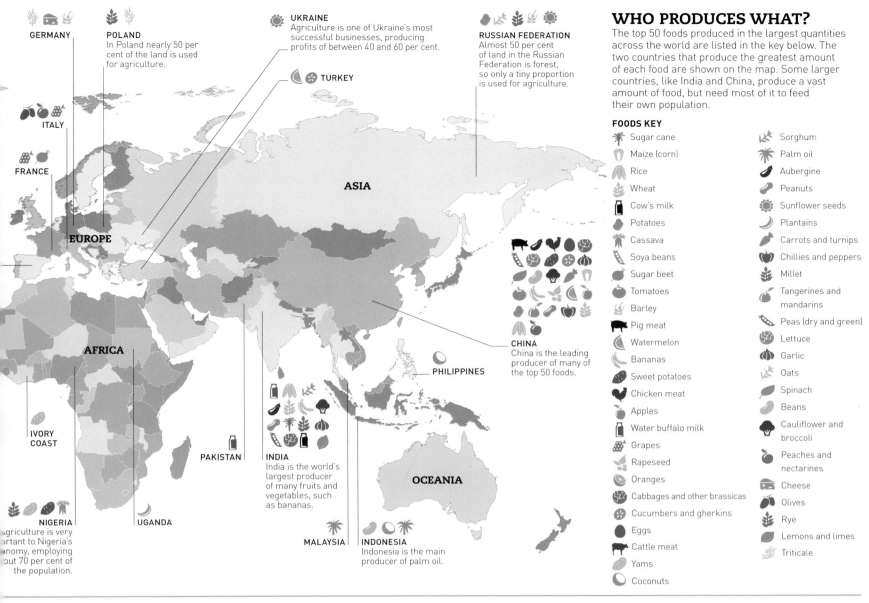

GERMANY

POLAND
In Poland nearly 50 per cent of the land is used for agriculture.

UKRAINE
Agriculture is one of Ukraine's most successful businesses, producing profits of between 40 and 60 per cent.

TURKEY

RUSSIAN FEDERATION
Almost 50 per cent of land in the Russian Federation is forest, so only a tiny proportion is used for agriculture.

ITALY

FRANCE

EUROPE

ASIA

AFRICA

CHINA
China is the leading producer of many of the top 50 foods.

PHILIPPINES

IVORY COAST

PAKISTAN

INDIA
India is the world's largest producer of many fruits and vegetables, such as bananas.

OCEANIA

NIGERIA
Agriculture is very important to Nigeria's economy, employing about 70 per cent of the population.

UGANDA

MALAYSIA

INDONESIA
Indonesia is the main producer of palm oil.

WHO PRODUCES WHAT?
The top 50 foods produced in the largest quantities across the world are listed in the key below. The two countries that produce the greatest amount of each food are shown on the map. Some larger countries, like India and China, produce a vast amount of food, but need most of it to feed their own population.

FOODS KEY

- Sugar cane
- Maize (corn)
- Rice
- Wheat
- Cow's milk
- Potatoes
- Cassava
- Soya beans
- Sugar beet
- Tomatoes
- Barley
- Pig meat
- Watermelon
- Bananas
- Sweet potatoes
- Chicken meat
- Apples
- Water buffalo milk
- Grapes
- Rapeseed
- Oranges
- Cabbages and other brassicas
- Cucumbers and gherkins
- Eggs
- Cattle meat
- Yams
- Coconuts

- Sorghum
- Palm oil
- Aubergine
- Peanuts
- Sunflower seeds
- Plantains
- Carrots and turnips
- Chillies and peppers
- Millet
- Tangerines and mandarins
- Peas (dry and green)
- Lettuce
- Garlic
- Oats
- Spinach
- Beans
- Cauliflower and broccoli
- Peaches and nectarines
- Cheese
- Olives
- Rye
- Lemons and limes
- Triticale

MEAT
For thousands of years, animals have been reared to provide meat. Most large farms specialize in just one type of animal, raising cattle (cows and bulls) for beef, pigs for pork, sheep for lamb and mutton, and deer for venison. Pigs are the most popular because their meat can be used in many ways.

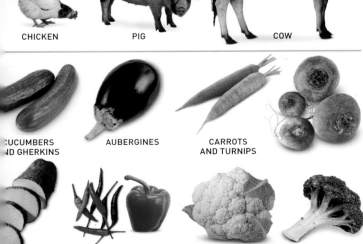

CHICKEN

PIG

COW

CUCUMBERS AND GHERKINS

AUBERGINES

CARROTS AND TURNIPS

YAMS

CHILLIES AND PEPPERS

CAULIFLOWER AND BROCCOLI

FRUIT, NUTS, AND SEEDS
Tropical fruit like bananas and coconuts, and Mediterranean fruit like oranges, lemons, and limes need sunshine and warmth to grow. These major crops in warm countries are exported (sent abroad) to colder places that do not have the right climate to grow them. Fruit can be picked and eaten straight away, used to make juices, or added to recipes. Grapes are also harvested to make wine, and olives to make oil for salads and cooking.

BANANAS

PLANTAINS

PEACHES AND NECTARINES

OLIVES

GRAPES

TOMATOES

PEANUTS

TANGERINES AND MANDARINS

APPLES

ORANGES

LEMONS AND LIMES

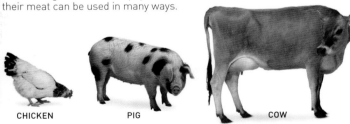

THE FIRST RECORD OF A WATERMELON HARVEST DATES FROM NEARLY 5,000 YEARS AGO IN EGYPT

WATERMELONS

COCONUTS

Culture

World religions

A religion is a collection of beliefs that attempts to explain the meaning of life. Most religions recognize a supreme power, usually a god or gods. There are many different faiths worldwide, most with their own laws and history set down in sacred books. The followers of a faith unite through prayer, rituals, and beliefs.

WHICH FAITH?

Christianity is the largest of the world religions. The number of followers of any religion changes all the time, as people decide to join or leave a faith, or to convert from one to another.

RELIGION CAN BE TRACED BACK TO THE STONE AGE, THROUGH SUCH EVIDENCE AS BURIAL SITES, TOTEMS, AND MONUMENTS

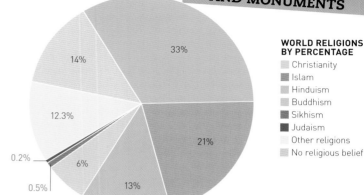

33%
14%
12.3%
0.2%
0.5%
6%
13%
21%

WORLD RELIGIONS BY PERCENTAGE
- Christianity
- Islam
- Hinduism
- Buddhism
- Sikhism
- Judaism
- Other religions
- No religious belief

CHRISTIANITY

SYMBOL
Cross

Christians believe in one God and in his son, Jesus Christ. Their holy text, the Bible, tells how Jesus was born on Earth to be the saviour of humankind. His teachings gave rise to Christianity, of which there are various branches. These include the Protestant, Roman Catholic, and Orthodox churches. Each has a different form of worship, but they all pray to the same God.

ICONS
The Orthodox Christian church uses icons – often paintings such as this one of the infant Christ with his mother Mary – as a focus for prayers.

ST PETER'S SQUARE
The square lies at the heart of the Vatican City, in Rome, where the Pope, head of the Catholic Church, lives.

CANTERBURY CATHEDRAL
This English cathedral is one of the oldest and most important Christian buildings in the world.

HINDUISM

SYMBOL
Letter for the sacred sound "OM"

There are hundreds of millions of Hindus worldwide. Their religion includes many gods and goddesses, the greatest being Brahma. Hindus believe in reincarnation: the cycle of life, death, and rebirth that continues until the soul is set free. Most of them worship by saying individual prayers, and do not attend communal services, although they join together at festivals.

GANESH
Elephant-headed Ganesh is the Hindu god of learning and new ventures.

NADI TEMPLE
Hindu temples are built in many styles. This one is the Nadi temple in Fiji.

KRISHNA
Usually shown with blue skin, Krishna is one of the best-loved Hindu gods.

ISLAM

SYMBOL
Crescent and star

The people who belong to this religion are called Muslims. They live according to the Five Pillars of Islam: faith, prayer, fasting, alms-giving, and pilgrimage. Their holy book is the Qur'an, which contains the word of the one Muslim God, Allah, as told to the Prophet Muhammad. Muslims pray at five set times every day. On Fridays, Muslims gather for prayers at a mosque.

FACING MECCA
At prayer, Muslims kneel facing the direction of the holy city of Mecca, to which all aim to make a pilgrimage.

JUMEIRAH MOSQUE
The mosque is the centre of a Muslim community – a place for people to pray, meditate, and learn.

QUR'AN
In this copy of the Qur'an the text is surrounded by ornate borders.

BUDDHISM

SYMBOL
Wheel of law

Buddhists do not worship a single, creator god. They follow a way of thinking based on the teachings of Siddhartha Gautama, born a prince in 5th-century India, who became known as the Buddha. Through recurring lifecycles, Buddhists hope to reach a state called Nirvana – freedom from all suffering.

BUDDHIST NOVICE
Boys as young as seven years may enter Buddhist monasteries as trainees, or novices.

STUPA
Dome-shaped mounds called stupas were built all over Asia to house Buddhist relics. This one is in Sri Lanka.

GIANT BUDDHA
This giant-sized statue of the Buddha in Uva Province, Sri Lanka, is carved from solid rock.

PRAYER FLAGS
Buddhist flags, fluttering in the mountains of Nepal, carry prayers into the wind.

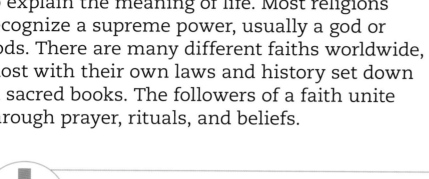

JAINISM

SYMBOL
Hand and wheel

JAIN LAL MANDIR TEMPLE
Built in 1658, this is one of the oldest temples in New Delhi, India. Within the ornate buildings there is also a hospital for birds.

Followers of this faith, who are called Jains, mostly live in India. They believe, in common with members of many other religions, that we die and are reborn in a repeating cycle. If a person can become truly spiritual, the soul becomes free. Jains respect all life, including plants and insects, and reject violence.

BAHA'I

SYMBOL
Nine-pointed star

LOTUS TEMPLE
Built in the shape of a lotus flower, the Baha'i Temple in New Delhi, India, is open to people of all faiths.

One of the world's newest religions, Baha'i began in Persia (now Iran) in the mid-19th century. The aim of the faith is to achieve world peace and to strive for justice and equality among people of all religions.

SHINTO

SYMBOL
Sacred gate

Arising out of Japanese folklore, Shinto developed as a religion more than 2,000 years ago. Followers believe in the existence of divine spirits, or *kami*. At Shinto places of worship, called shrines, people pay respect to the *kami*, and honour them with many rites and festivals.

GATEWAY
The gateway, known as a *torii*, to the Shinto shrine on Miyajima Island in Japan stands in the sea.

TAOISM

SYMBOL
Yin and Yang
(two opposites)

Tao means "the way" – the natural force or power that controls the Universe. According to Taoism, people must accept this power, while trying to lead peaceful and unselfish lives. Believers hope they will eventually be able to free their spirits and become immortal.

TAO FESTIVAL
People gather outside a colourful Chinese Taoist temple in Thailand to celebrate the Vegetarian Festival.

SIKHISM

SYMBOL
Circle and swords

The faith was founded in northern India, where many Sikhs today live or have family links. In Sikhism, there is one God, who makes his will known through gurus (teachers). Believers worship regularly in temples known as *gurdwaras*. At a Sikh service there are prayers, a sermon, and hymns from the sacred Sikh book called the Guru Granth Sahib. Meditation is an important part of the religion.

DRESS RULES
Male Sikhs always have a beard. Their long hair, which is never cut, is fastened in a bun and covered with a turban.

GOLDEN TEMPLE
Built in the state of Punjab, northern India, at the beginning of the 17th century, this famous Sikh temple is sited in the middle of a lake.

THE GURU GRANTH SAHIB
The Sikh holy text contains hymns written or collected by gurus.

ZOROASTRIANISM

SYMBOL
Guardian angel

ZOROASTER
The prophet believed that his God, Ahura Mazda, had appeared to him in visions.

Founded by Zoroaster, a prophet who lived in ancient Persia (now Iran), Zoroastrianism is more than 2,500 years old. Followers believe in Ahura Mazda, the Supreme Creator of the world, and the eternal struggle between good and evil. Their holy book is called the Avesta. Zoroastrians worship in temples, where they hold many ceremonies.

CONFUCIANISM

SYMBOL
The Chinese character for water (a life source) is sometimes used.

This religious philosophy comes from the teachings of Confucius, a 5th-century Chinese thinker and reformer. Kindness, honourable behaviour, and respect for family are key beliefs.

GREAT THINKER
A statue of Confucius stands at the entrance to the Confucian Temple in Shanghai, China.

JUDAISM

SYMBOL
Star of David

This is the religion of the Jewish people, who can trace their roots back to the Hebrews who lived in the Middle East almost 4,000 years ago. Judaism has one God. Followers worship in buildings known as synagogues under the guidance of spiritual leaders called rabbis. Teachings on Judaism are found in the Torah, or Hebrew Bible, and the Talmud, which is the Jewish code of law.

THE WESTERN WALL
Also known as the Wailing Wall, this stone wall in the city of Jerusalem is considered a holy site by Jewish people.

TORAH SCROLL
The scroll, which contains the Torah handwritten in Hebrew, is read in the synagogue.

MENORAH
The menorah, or seven-branched candlestick, is an important Jewish symbol.

CAO DAI

SYMBOL
Divine Eye

Originating in Vietnam, Cao Dai was founded in 1926. The faith takes some of its practices from other religions, including Roman Catholicism and Buddhism. Followers of Cao Dai would like to see all people living at peace with each other. They worship a Supreme Being and honour many saints.

TAY NINH TEMPLE
This elaborate building at Tay Ninh in Vietnam is the most important temple of the Cao Dai faith.

INDIGENOUS RELIGIONS

From Africa to the Americas, indigenous religions are found among remote peoples untouched by the major faiths. These religions, which include the widespread practice of shamanism, often involve contact with the spirits.

BELIEF IN PROTECTION
Followers of indigenous religions often carry objects – like this African nutshell doll – as protection against harm.

World celebrations

Throughout the year, in nearly every country or community, people celebrate special events with festivals. Many of these events are religious or have historic links to the farming seasons. Often, a festival is a joyful holiday with music, processions, delicious food and, sometimes, gifts.

▶ JANUARY

On 1 January, people around the world are eager to party as they welcome in a new year. In Rajasthan, India, it is time for the world-famous annual Camel Festival that takes place in the desert town of Bikaner.

NEW YEAR'S EVE
Firework displays light up cities all over the world as the old year turns into a new one.

BIKANER CAMEL FESTIVAL, INDIA
Wearing a colourfully decorated bridle, a camel waits to perform. Camels are a much-valued part of everyday life in Rajasthan.

▶ FEBRUARY

There is a lot of extravaga dressing up, with two big carnivals this month in Brazil and in Venice, Italy. It's also Chinese New Year, with two weeks of celebrations and family gatherings.

RIO CARNIVAL, BRAZIL
Costume parades, dancing competitions, loud music, and feasting last for five riotous day

◀ AUGUST

In August, it's holiday time for many. Pigs and a very messy tomato fight are among the fun events on offer. There are also arts festivals to enjoy. One of the most important is held in Edinburgh, Scotland.

FESTIVAL OF THE PIG, FRANCE
One of the funniest festivals is found in the French Pyrenees. People dress as pigs, race piglets, and challenge each other to make the most lifelike pig noises.

TOMATO BATTLE, SPAIN
La Tomatina, as it is called in Spain, takes place at the town of Buñol, near Valencia. Thousands gather for a mock fight with tonnes of squashy tomatoes.

EDINBURGH FESTIVAL
Drama, dance, music, and comedy are just some of the events at this Scottish cultural festival.

INDEPENDENCE DAY, USA
Decorated with the American Stars and Stripes flag, a festive cake takes centre table at a 4th July celebration.

BODY-PAINTING FESTIVAL, AUSTRIA
At this event, human bodies are transformed into amazing works of art. The festival includes competitions and displays from around the world.

◀ JULY

Heading the festivals is Independence Day on 4 July. This celebrates the day in 1776 when America declared its independence from Great Britain. In Siena, Italy, a historic horserace takes place. A body-painting festival in Austria is a popular modern event.

PALIO HORSERACE, SIENA
Bareback riders race through the streets of Siena. Each wears colours representing a district of the city.

RAMADAN AN EID AL-FIT
A Morocca shopkeeper sel trays of pastrie baked for Ei This holiday sweet treats en a month of fastir during Ramada

▶ SEPTEMBER

Mid-autumn Festival, Moon Festival, Harvest Festival: these are some of the names for feasts all over Southeast Asia at full moon. The celebrations were once held to give thanks for the rice harvest. Harvest celebrations are also an informal part of the Christian calendar.

HARVEST FESTIVAL
Fruit and flowers decorate a Christian church for Harvest Festival.

TET TRUNG THU, VIETNAM
Scary masks and dancing in the streets are for children to enjoy in Vietnam's version of the Mid-autumn Festival.

MOON FESTIVAL, CHINA
Rich pastries known as mooncakes are made for the autumn moon festival in China and other parts of Southeast Asia.

▶ OCTOBER

Homes light up in October. Diwali, the "festival of lights", is a big occasion in the Hindu calendar. The date varies, but often falls in October. On 31 October, things get spooky when grinning pumpkin lanterns appear for Halloween.

HALLOWEEN
Carving a lantern from a pumpkin is traditional at Halloween. The festival has ancient roots and developed from ceremonies held to honour the dead.

DIWALI
Hindu people light their houses with candles and oil lamps to symbolize the triumph of good over evil.

MARCH

CHINESE NEW YEAR
Hidden beneath the costume of a fantastic lion with huge swivelling eyes, performers dance to bring good luck for the new year.

VENICE CARNIVAL
On the last day of this annual two-week public event in Venice, people crowd the streets wearing elaborate masks and costumes.

The feast of St Patrick, patron saint of Ireland, falls on 17 March. The day of Holi, the Hindu spring festival, changes each year. The Jewish holiday of Purim varies, too, according to the Hebrew calendar.

ST PATRICK'S DAY
Many Irish people wear green on their saint's day, and celebrate with music and parades.

HOLI
Whatever the date of Holi, the fun is the same as people bombard each other with coloured powders and water.

PURIM
Shaking a wooden rattle is part of the religious service for Purim. The day remembers how Jewish people in ancient Persia escaped a deadly plot against them.

APRIL

Beware of practical jokers on 1 April, a day for making "April Fools" of everyone – or "April Fish" in France. More solemn are the major events of the Christian and Jewish calendars.

POISSON D'AVRIL (APRIL FISH)
On 1 April, children in France pin pictures of fish on their friends' backs for a joke.

PASSOVER
This festival remembers the freeing of the Jewish people from slavery 3,000 years ago. People eat a special meal including an egg, herbs, and a lamb bone.

EASTER
The Christian holiday celebrates Jesus Christ's resurrection after his crucifixion. Gifts of chocolate or sugar eggs symbolize rebirth.

JUNE

In northern regions, midsummer's day falls between 20 and 22 June. Many people mark the date with celebrations at sunrise. The start of the Muslim holy period of Ramadan can be in late June – the date depends on the rising of a new moon.

MIDSUMMER
The prehistoric monument of Stonehenge, on Salisbury Plain in Wiltshire, England, is a traditional place to watch the sun rise as midsummer's day dawns.

APPLE FLOWER FESTIVAL, DENMARK
Held on the small Danish island of Lilleø, this tiny festival celebrates the blossoming of the fruit trees.

WHITE NIGHTS FESTIVAL, ST PETERSBURG
An eagerly awaited highlight of the festival is the appearance on the Neva River of a sailing ship with bright scarlet sails.

MAY

People have long celebrated the warmer days and spring growth that come with May. During the three week White Nights festival in St Petersburg, Russia, revellers can stay up as late as they like – the nights are never completely dark at this time of year.

MAY DAY
In an age-old ritual, many British village communities erect a maypole on 1 May. The ribbons are wound round the pole as part of a dance.

MAY DAY WAS FIRST CELEBRATED BY THE ANCIENT ROMANS IN HONOUR OF FLORA, GODDESS OF FLOWERS

NOVEMBER

On Thanksgiving Day, Americans follow the tradition of the early European settlers, who gave thanks for the harvest every year. Today, Thanksgiving is mainly a family feast. In Mexico, people think of loved ones on the Day of the Dead – a time for happy memories.

THANKSGIVING
Figures from early American history parade in New York on Thanksgiving Day.

DAY OF THE DEAD, MEXICO
During this festival on 2 November, people buy paper skeletons and eat sugar skulls.

DECEMBER

In many countries and cultures, Christmas, Christ's birthday, is the time that children most look forward to, as they can expect presents and special food. There are also presents, games, and feasts at Hanukkah, the Jewish Festival of Lights, which often falls in December.

CHRISTMAS
A tree has been part of traditional Christmas celebrations for possibly hundreds of years.

HANUKKAH
One candle is lit on each day of this eight-day Jewish festival.

World languages

Spoken and written language allows us to communicate with one another. Around 6,000 languages are spoken across the world, and many people speak more than one language.

LANGUAGES
The three most widely used languages are spoken by nearly one quarter of the world.

1 MANDARIN
848 million speakers worldwide

2 SPANISH
339 million speakers worldwide

3 ENGLISH
335 million speakers worldwide

4 HINDI
260 million speakers worldwide

5 ARABIC
242 million speakers worldwide

GREETINGS
In all languages there is a way to greet someone. Here is how to greet someone in some of the world's most widely spoken languages. Not all languages are written using the same alphabet – a large number of scripts are used across the world.

سلام
salaam, **PASHTO**

你好
lee-ho, **MIN NAN**

xin chào
sin-chow, **VIETNAMESE**

မင်္ဂလာပါ
min-ga-la-ba, **BURMESE**

您好
nee-how, **MANDARIN**

Sampurasun
Sum-poo-rah-soon, **SUNDANESE**

侬好
nong hao, **WU**

নমস্কার
nômoshkar, **BENGALI**

سلام
salaam, **PERSIAN**

helo
hello, **MALAY**

你好
ngi-ho, **HAKKA**

നമസ്കാരം
nuh-mus-kāram, **MALAYALAM**

สวัสดี
sawasdee, **THAI**

ନମସ୍କାର
nuh-mus-kāra, **ORIYA**

مرحبا
marr-hah-bah, **ARABIC**

السلام عليكم
as-salām-alaykum, **URDU**

नमस्कार
nuh-mus-kār, **MARATHI**

你好
Ni Hao, **JIN**

નમસ્તે
nuh-muh-stay, **GUJARATI**

你好
néih-hóu, **CANTONESE**

வணக்கம்
vanakkam, **TAMIL**

こんにちは
konnichiwa, **JAPANESE**

ನಮಸ್ಕಾರ
namaskara, **KANNADA**

merhaba
mehr-hah-bah, **TURKISH**

你好
li hao, **XIANG**

प्रणाम
pra-naam, **BHOJPURI**

WHO SPEAKS WHAT?
Some languages are spoken in many countries around the globe. There are also many variations of major languages (dialects).

KEY
- Chinese (Mandarin, Cantonese, etc)
- Spanish
- Arabic
- Hindi
- English
- French
- Russian
- Portuguese
- English/Spanish
- Spanish/other
- Arabic/French
- French/other
- English/other
- Arabic/other
- Hindi/English/other
- Chinese/other
- Russian/other
- English/French
- Portuguese/other
- Other language
- Uninhabited land

SIGN LANGUAGE
People who cannot hear spoken language use hand signals to communicate. This is known as sign language. There are many different types of sign language.

HOW TO SAY "HELLO" IN BRITISH SIGN LANGUAGE

नमस्ते
nuh-muh-stay, **HINDI**

ꦱꦸꦒꦼꦁ2
halo, **JAVANESE**

السلام عليكم
as-salām-alaykum, **SINDHI**

assalamu alaykum
as-salam alay-keum, **UZBEK**

안녕하세요
ahn-nyeong-ha-se-yo, **KOREAN**

ਸਤਿ ਸ੍ਰੀ ਅਕਾਲ
sat-siri-akal, **PUNJABI**

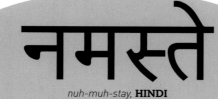
namaskārām, **TELUGU**

salam əleyküm
salām-alaykum, **AZERBAIJANI**

प्रनाम
pra-naam, **MAITHILI**

cześć!
cheshch, **POLISH**

akkam
ak-kam, **OROMO**

hello
ENGLISH

olá
oh-lah, **PORTUGUESE**

kumusta
coo-moos-tah, **TAGALOG**

Привіт
priveet, **UKRAINIAN**

здравствуйте
zdrast-wui-tyeh, **RUSSIAN**

kedu
kay-doo, **IGBO**

bonjour
boh-zhoo, **FRENCH**

hallo
ha-low, **GERMAN**

jambo
ja-m-boh, **SWAHILI**

no ngoola daa
no-ngoola-daa, **FULA**

ciao
chao, **ITALIAN**

ሰላም ደህና ነህ
tena-yste-lle'gn, **AMHARIC**

salut
sah-loot, **ROMANIAN**

hola
o-la, **SPANISH**

bawo ni
bah-wo nee, **YORUBA**

sannu
san-nu, **HAUSA**

The story of art

From the beginning of civilization, people in different cultures have produced art in many forms. They have used paint, stone, wood, metal, clay, and even their own bodies to show religious devotion, express ideas, or simply reflect the world around them.

► c.30,000–2500 BCE
PREHISTORIC ART
Early humans used charcoal and rock pigments to paint animals and figures on cave walls. Some made spray handprints by blowing paint through hollow bones. They also carved figures out of stone and animal tusks.

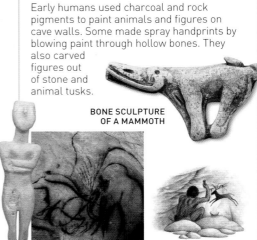

BONE SCULPTURE OF A MAMMOTH

PREHISTORIC FIGURE

CAVE PAINTING, FRANCE

DRAWING OF A CAVE ARTIST

► c.3000–539 BCE
OLDEST CIVILIZATIONS
Many beautiful examples of art have been found at the Royal Cemetery of Ur, which is in modern-day Iraq. They were created by skilled sculptors and jewellery makers in Mesopotamia, one of the oldest, and longest lasting, civilizations in our distant past.

GOLD ORNAMENT

GOLD AND BEAD WREATH

◄ c.500–1400
MEDIEVAL AND BYZANTINE
Metal and enamel work, carvings, and embroidery were prized in medieval Europe. Manuscripts were illuminated – lit up with decorations in bright pigments and gold leaf. Earlier Byzantine Christians produced icons of figures and frescoes of religious scenes.

BYZANTINE ALTAR MOSAIC

MOSAIC OF VIRGIN MARY, ISTANBUL

SILVER CUP

FRENCH TAPESTRY

ILLUMINATED MANUSCRIPT

◄ c.324–1450
ISLAMIC
Islamic artists decorated mosques with intricate patterns using tiles and mosaics. Modern Islam uses a similar approach – places of worship are beautifully patterned, but they never include images of people or animals.

THE GREAT MOSQUE, SPAIN

ISLAMIC BUILDING, ISRAEL

◄ c.1 CE–PRESENT
NATIVE AMERICAN
In Native American tribes, practical items like blankets and bags were so skilfully decorated with beads, feathers, and shells they became works of art. People also made tiny animal talismans and towering tree-trunk sculptures called totem poles carved with faces, animals, and birds. These arts continue today.

QUILLWORK BAG

TURQUOISE ANIMALS

CARVED FACE ON TOTEM POLE

► c.1350–1600
RENAISSANCE
Beginning in Italy, the Renaissance was a time when every form of art flourished. Artists were inspired by Ancient Greek and Roman works and produced fine paintings and sculptures that were full of grandeur, personality, and beauty. Venice became a centre for exquisite glasswork.

MONA LISA BY LEONARDO DA VINCI

PORTRAIT BY TITIAN

ITALIAN GOBLET

RENAISSANCE PENDANT

PIETA SCULPTURE BY MICHELANGELO

► c.1600–1800
BAROQUE AND ROCOCO
Baroque painting was all about drama. Artists painted realistic emotional scenes with intense colour and dramatic lighting. Originating in France, Rococo was a lighter style of architecture, furniture, and art that was elegant, graceful, and highly decorative.

EL GRECO PAINTING IN BAROQUE STYLE

ROCOCO FOUNTAIN

ORGAN WITH ROCOCO DECORATION

► c.1850–1900
REALISM AND IMPRESSIONISM
Realist painters wanted to create pictures of modern life and made ordinary working people the subject of their paintings. Impressionist artists tried to capture a moment, using delicate brushstrokes and dabs of colour to give fleeting impressions of flowers, landscapes, picnics, and parties.

RENOIR'S LUNCHEON OF THE BOATING PARTY

GOLD BULL'S HEAD
WITH SHELL INLAY

▶ c.3000–330 BCE
ANCIENT EGYPTIAN

The Ancient Egyptians filled elaborate tombs inside pyramids with statues, painted mummy cases, frescoes, and picture scrolls to help the dead in their afterlife. Painters had to show complete human forms so every figure combines a front and side view.

TOMB PAINTING

MODEL OF A GRANARY

RITUAL WATER JAR

HIGHLY DECORATED TOMB FIGURES

▶ c.2000–146 BCE
ANCIENT GREEK

The earliest frescoes and pottery, found in a Minoan palace on the island of Crete, are painted with colourful scenes of everyday life. Temples in Ancient Greece were decorated with marble friezes showing processions and beautifully carved columns.

DECORATIVE VASE

FRESCO OF A LEAPING BULL

DORIC, IONIC, AND CORINTHIAN COLUMNS

c.650 BCE–1900 CE
EASTERN

For more than 2,000 years, artists from India, China, and Japan have created beautiful objects using stone, ceramics, precious stones, and metals. Colourful Indian temples were lavishly decorated with figures of gods and goddesses. Serene Japanese prints on silk and parchment were known as "pictures of the floating world".

HINDU TEMPLE, INDIA

STONEWARE LION, MING DYNASTY, CHINA

HOKUSAI PRINT, JAPAN

HEAD OF THE BUDDHA, JAPAN

ORNATE FIGURE OF AN ELEPHANT, CHINA

◀ c.750 BCE–476 CE
ANCIENT ROMAN

Statues and busts (just the head) of emperors, famous people from the past, and gods and goddesses were popular in Ancient Rome. Wealthy people had gold jewellery, decorated pottery, and ornate glassware. The finest houses were decorated with mosaic floors and panels, and painted frescoes.

TERRACOTTA (CLAY) BUST

BEWARE OF THE DOG MOSAIC, POMPEII

FRESCO ON VILLA WALL, POMPEII

▶ 1880–1905

MONET'S GARDEN
Monet's paintings of his lily ponds captured changes in the light and seasons.

MURAL INSPIRED BY VAN GOGH'S THE STARRY NIGHT

NATURAL LIGHT
Using new portable easels and tubes of paint, artists left their studio to paint outdoors.

FIGURE BY RODIN
Rodin produced life-like figures that portrayed powerful emotions.

POST-IMPRESSIONISM

Painting got bolder, brighter, and freer in this period. Vincent Van Gogh poured his feelings into swirling landscapes created with thick brushstrokes and heavy paint. Others developed new techniques. Seurat's pointillist pictures were painted with millions of tiny dots of colour that blended together.

▶ c.1900–1950
EXPRESSIONISM AND SURREALISM

Expressionist painters used vivid colours and stark images, often squeezing the paint straight from the tube on to the canvas. Their pictures were not intended to show real life but express their personalities. Surrealist art turned the world upside down. Artists produced dream-like paintings and absurd objects like furry teacups and spiky irons.

"IF YOU UNDERSTAND A PAINTING BEFOREHAND YOU MIGHT AS WELL NOT PAINT IT"
SALVADOR DALI, SURREALIST ARTIST

▶ 1907–1960s
MODERN ART

Cubism was the beginning of modern art. Leading artist Picasso created startling figures with angular shapes that broke all the rules about colour, form, and perspective. Many years later in the United States, abstract expressionist artists invented action painting – splashing, smearing, or dribbling paint onto the canvas.

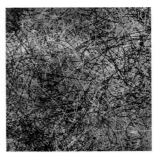

INSPIRED BY JACKSON POLLOCK

▶ 1970s–PRESENT
CONTEMPORARY

In contemporary art, anything goes. Painters use styles from the past and often rework and mix them together to show new ideas. Art can take many different forms. It can be a shed blown apart with all its pieces suspended in midair; a skull studded with diamonds; or lonely figures perched on buildings across a city skyline.

ANTONY GORMLEY'S EVENT HORIZON

MILLENIUM PARK FOUNTAIN, CHICAGO

Musical instruments

From very early times, people have enjoyed making music by beating, plucking, rattling, or blowing into instruments. Different groups of instruments are known as "families". In an orchestra, many of them come together to combine their sounds.

THE ORCHESTRA

Large orchestras have followed the same seating arrangement for their musicians since the 18th century. The various instruments are positioned according to type.

KEY

- Conductor
- First violins
- Second violins
- Violas
- Cellos
- Double basses
- Flutes
- Oboes
- Clarinets
- Bassoons
- Horns
- Trumpets
- Trombones and tubas
- Harp
- Drums
- Other percussion
- Piano

WOODWIND

These wind instruments are made of metal and plastic, as well as wood. Holes in the pipe are opened and closed with the fingers to change the notes. Some woodwind instruments use a vibrating strip, called a reed, as a mouthpiece.

PICCOLO

FLUTE

OBOE

Reed

CLARINET

COR ANGLAIS

BASSOON

CONTRABASSOON

BRASS

The brass section of an orchestra makes some of the loudest sounds. When brass players blow air into their instruments, they put their lips close to the mouthpiece to create vibrations. Many types of brass have button-like valves that are pressed down to alter notes.

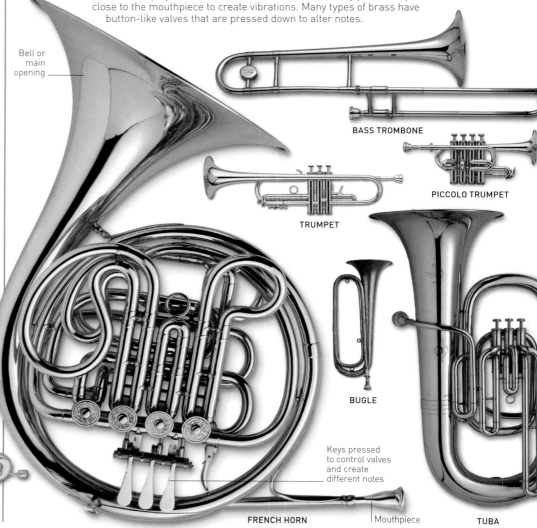

Bell or main opening

BASS TROMBONE

PICCOLO TRUMPET

TRUMPET

BUGLE

Keys pressed to control valves and create different notes

FRENCH HORN

Mouthpiece

TUBA

INTERNATIONAL INSTRUMENTS

Round the world, music-making involves a huge variety of traditional instruments. Many are unique to particular countries or cultures.

DHOLAK (INDIA)

CHIME (CHINA)

ANGKLUNG (INDONESIA)

CONGA DRUM (AFRICA)

CONGOLESE DRUM (AFRICA)

DARBUKA (MIDDLE EAST)

KAMANJAH (MIDDLE EAST)

KOTO (JAPAN)

RUAN (CHINA)

SARASWATI VEENA (INDIA)

RATTLE DRUM (CHINA)

LAMELLOPHONE (TANZANIA)

PERCUSSION

A percussion instrument is struck or shaken to keep a rhythm or create a tune. Percussionists usually play more than one instrument.

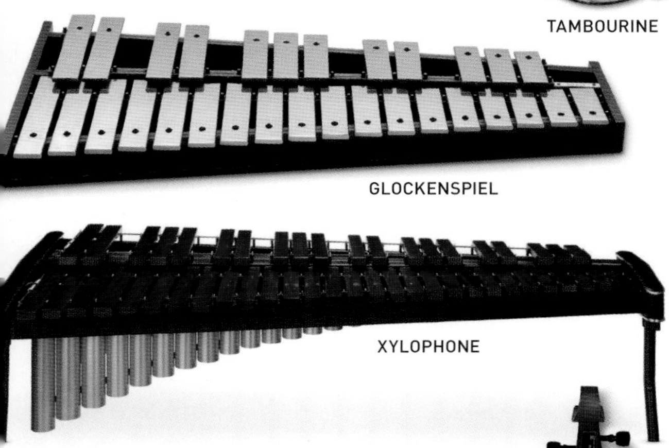

GLOCKENSPIEL

XYLOPHONE

TAMBOURINE

TRIANGLE

GONG

SNARE DRUM

TIMPANI

MARACAS

STRINGS

Several types and sizes of instruments are played with a bow drawn across a set of tightly stretched strings. They all have hollow wooden bodies that let the sounds vibrate.

Neck, where fingers press strings to create notes

Tuning pegs to adjust strings

MORE THAN 70 DIFFERENT PIECES OF WOOD ARE PUT TOGETHER TO FORM THE MODERN VIOLIN

PICCOLO VIOLIN

VIOLA D'AMORE

TENOR VIOL

BASS VIOL

VIOLIN

VIOLA

CELLO

DOUBLE BASS

KEYBOARDS

The piano is the most popular of a large group of instruments that are played by pressing keys or buttons. On a keyboard, a musician can play many notes at the same time.

Strings struck by hammer when keys pressed

Bellows

Keys

Pedals soften or lengthen notes

GRAND PIANO

ACCORDION

ELECTRONIC KEYBOARD

GUITAR FAMILY

A subset of the string family, guitars may have as many as 18 strings, but most have six. The strings are played with the fingers or a small tool called a pick.

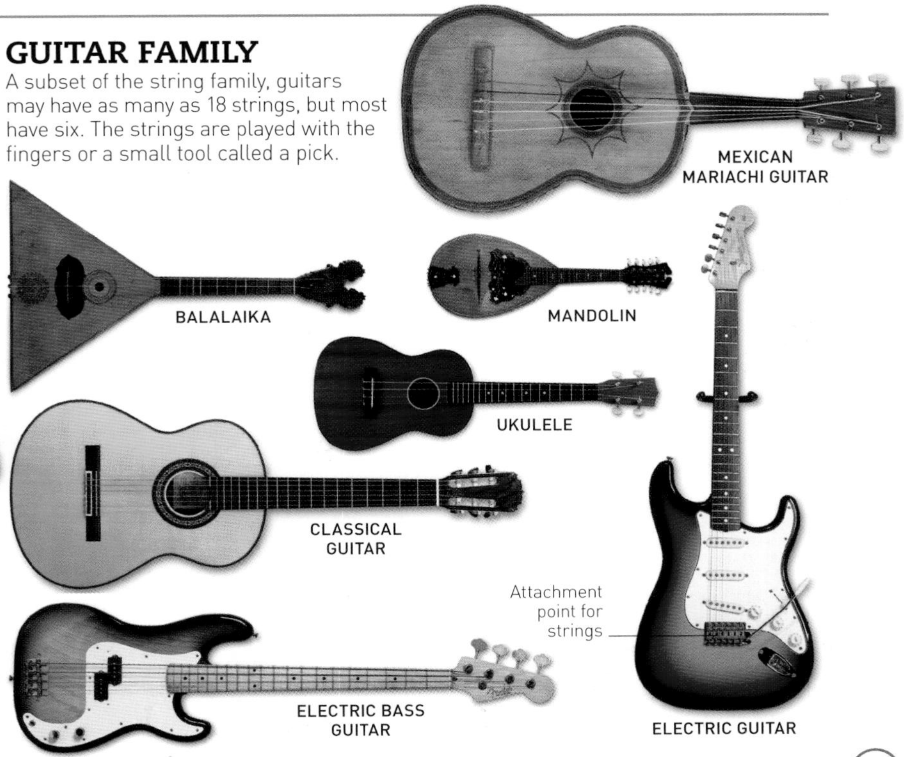

MEXICAN MARIACHI GUITAR

BALALAIKA

MANDOLIN

UKULELE

CLASSICAL GUITAR

Attachment point for strings

ELECTRIC BASS GUITAR

ELECTRIC GUITAR

How music works

Understanding how music works – music theory – is a vital part of learning how to read music and play an instrument. To play music, you need to understand its language – notes, pitch, rhythm, and harmony.

THE PIANO KEYBOARD

Each octave on the piano keyboard has seven white notes – A B C D E F G – and five black notes, grouped in twos and threes. A full-sized keyboard usually has around seven octaves. Its central C is called Middle C.

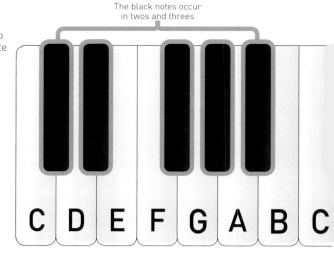

The black notes occur in twos and threes

THE PIANO
With its unique layout, the piano is a useful instrument for learning music theory. The pattern of black and white keys shows the relationships between notes.

The white note between a pair of black notes grouped in twos is always D

WRITING MUSIC

Music is usually written on five parallel lines known as a stave. Notes are placed on the lines, or in the spaces between them. The higher a note is placed, the higher its pitch.

THE FIRST KNOWN MUSIC WAS WRITTEN IN AN ANCIENT LANGUAGE CALLED CUNEIFORM, 3,400 YEARS AGO

ON THE LINES

IN THE SPACES

CLEFS

A clef is normally written at the start – the left-hand end – of every stave on the page. It fixes the pitches of the lines and spaces. The two most common clefs are the treble (or G) clef, and the bass (or F) clef.

TREBLE CLEF

BASS CLEF

THE G CLEF
The centre of the treble clef shows where G sits on the stave.

NOTES ON THE TREBLE CLEF
From G, the other notes on the stave can be worked out by going forwards or backwards through the musical alphabet.

THE F CLEF
The two dots of the bass clef show where F sits on the stave.

NOTES ON THE BASS CLEF
From F, the other notes on the stave can be worked out by going forwards or backwards through the musical alphabet.

NOTE VALUES

A note value is how long a note lasts for. It is measured in relation to other notes. Shown below – in descending order of length – are the five most common note values: semibreve, minim, crotchet, quaver, and semiquaver.

TIME VALUES
The chart below shows how the note values relate to each other. Each column represents one crotchet, so a semibreve lasts as long as four crotchets.

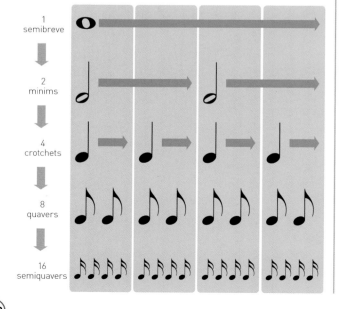

1 semibreve

2 minims

4 crotchets

8 quavers

16 semiquavers

BEAMS

Two or more consecutive quavers can be joined together with a thick line called a beam, which replaces the individual tails. Semiquavers or demisemiquavers can be joined in the same way. Beams make the rhythm easier to read.

Tail

QUAVERS =

SEMIQUAVERS =

Beam

DEMISEMIQUAVERS =

DOTTED NOTES

When a note is followed by a dot, it makes the note half as long again. The dotted crotchet below is 1½ times longer than a crotchet, and the dotted minim is 1½ times longer than a minim.

TIME SIGNATURES

Time signatures appear at the beginning of a piece of music. The top number indicates the number of beats in a bar, and the bottom number shows the note-value of each beat: 2 = minim, 4 = crotchet, 8 = quaver, and 16 = semiquaver.

2/4 Two crotchet beats to the bar

4/4 Four crotchet beats to the bar

3/2 Three minim beats to the bar

9/8 Nine quaver beats to the bar

3/4 Three crotchet beats to the bar

2/2 Two minim beats to the bar

6/8 Six quaver beats to the bar

12/8 Twelve quaver beats to the bar

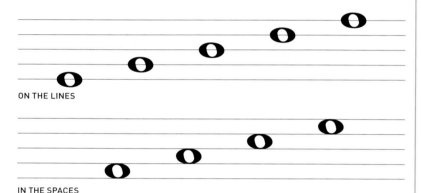

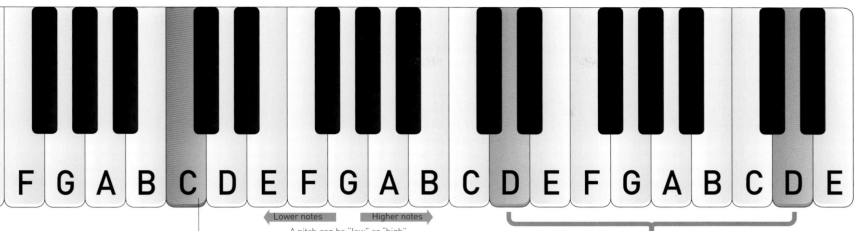

The C nearest the middle of a full-size keyboard is called Middle C

A pitch can be "low" or "high". On a piano keyboard, this works from left to right – the highest notes are at the right-hand end of the keyboard and the lowest notes are at the left-hand end

Lower notes   Higher notes

An octave is the distance from one note to the next one with the same letter name. These two Ds are one octave apart

SEMITONES

A semitone is the musical term for the interval, or gap, between notes that are immediately next to each other on the keyboard. A semitone means "half a tone" and represents a half step on the keyboard.

ON THE STAVE
This is how the three semitones shown on the keyboard are written on the stave.

TONES

A tone is the equivalent of two semitones. If two notes have just one note between them on the keyboard, they are a tone apart.

ON THE STAVE
This is how the three tones shown on the keyboard are written on the stave.

As the white notes B and C are only a semitone apart, a tone above B is the black note C♯

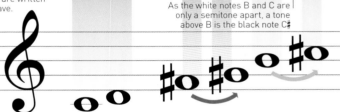

RESTS

Rests assign a time value to silences – gaps in the music during which a player or singer does not produce any sound. They work just like notes and have the same time values. When playing or writing music, the rests are as important as the notes.

TIME VALUES
The chart shows rests and how their time values relate to each other.

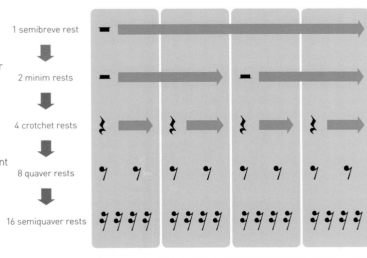

1 semibreve rest

2 minim rests

4 crotchet rests

8 quaver rests

16 semiquaver rests

TEMPO

The speed at which music is played is known as tempo. Tempo is usually indicated by descriptive terms. Shown here are some of the most common Italian terms for tempo and tempo changes.

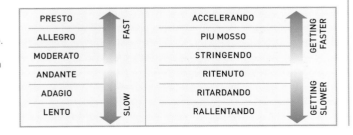

PRESTO	FAST	ACCELERANDO	GETTING FASTER
ALLEGRO		PIU MOSSO	
MODERATO		STRINGENDO	
ANDANTE		RITENUTO	
ADAGIO	SLOW	RITARDANDO	GETTING SLOWER
LENTO		RALLENTANDO	

SHARPS AND FLATS

Sharps and flats are symbols that raise or lower notes on the keyboard. Sharps raise a note by one semitone, and flats lower a note by one semitone. Notes that are not sharpened or flattened are called naturals.

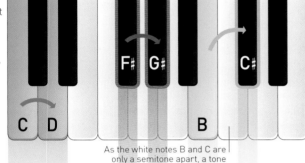

FLAT — Down a semitone

NATURAL

SHARP — Up a semitone

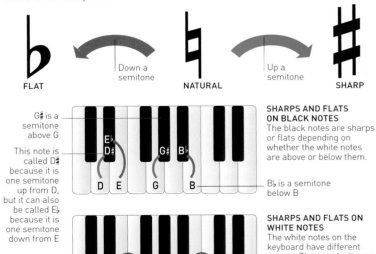

G♯ is a semitone above G

This note is called D♯ because it is one semitone up from D, but it can also be called E♭ because it is one semitone down from E

SHARPS AND FLATS ON BLACK NOTES
The black notes are sharps or flats depending on whether the white notes are above or below them.

B♭ is a semitone below B

SHARPS AND FLATS ON WHITE NOTES
The white notes on the keyboard have different names. They can be known as naturals, sharps, or flats.

This note is usually called C, but because it is one semitone up from B, it can also be called B♯

This note is usually called E, but because it is one semitone down from F, it can also be called F♭

Dance

All over the world and in every culture, people enjoy dancing – moving their bodies to music with a partner, in groups, or solo. People dance to tell stories, express their faith, show their patriotism, keep fit, get ready for battle or sport, celebrate an important event, compete, or purely for fun.

SACRED DANCE

Dance plays an important part in many religions. People include dance in their religious ceremonies or to communicate with their gods.

CORYBANTES
These Ancient Greek priests danced and drummed in armour.

BUDDHISM
Dancing figures are often used to decorate Buddhist shrines.

MUSLIM DERVISHES
Spin themselves into a state of ecstasy, so they can feel closer to god.

NATIVE AMERICANS
Danced to ask the gods for such things as rain or a good harvest.

SIVA NATARAJA
Hindu god Siva is often shown dancing at the creation of the world.

FOLK DANCING

People perform folk dances at festivals and celebrations. The dances are often accompanied by traditional music, and are passed down through generations.

FLAMENCO
A dramatic, rhythmic dance that originated in southern Spain.

ROMA DANCE
Often performed at family weddings and christenings.

LATVIAN DANCE
The Latvian Song and Dance Festival is a huge annual event.

EGYPTIAN DANCING
Ancient Arabic dance, usually performed by a solo woman.

IRISH DANCE
Often performed at competitions, either solo or in teams.

AFRICAN DANCE
African dance is often accompanied by drums and voices.

CLASSICAL DANCE

Classical dance is performed by trained or professional dancers. The focus is on formal steps and poses. These dances usually tell stories from literature or legend.

INDONESIAN
This style, called *bedhaya*, is performed only by women.

CAMBODIAN
A slow style, with smooth, wave-like movements.

KATHAKALI
South Indian dance-drama performed in elaborate make-up.

KABUKI
Japanese theatrical dance performed in colourful costumes.

BALLET
The classical dance form of most Western countries.

BALINESE
A story-telling dance form, always performed barefoot.

DANCE CRAZES

Some dance crazes caused outrage when they first appeared. In the 1780s people were shocked by the waltz because men and women embraced as they danced.

CANCAN
The cancan was a lively, high-kicking dance that became wildly popular in the ballrooms and music halls of Paris, France, in the 1830s.

JITTERBUG
An energetic, acrobatic couples' dance that originated in the USA in the 1930s. It spread to Europe via American servicemen during World War II.

TWIST
The twist was a 1960s craze. There were no steps to learn and no partner needed – dancers just wriggled and twisted along to the music on their own.

LINE DANCING
Dancers line up in a row and perform a pattern of steps together to country music. Line dancing started in the USA the 1970s but became a worldwide craze in the 1990s.

GANGNAM STYLE
An overnight dance sensation in 2012 when a video of Korean musician Psy performing his song of the same name went viral.

CANCAN

JITTERBUG   TWIST

LINE DANCING   GANGNAM

BOLLYWOOD STYLE

Bollywood films are famous for song-and-dance routines. In early films, dancers just acted out song lyrics, but the style is now a rich mix that borrows from the many different folk and classical styles of India.

Both arms are raised during the dance

Positions of hands and body tell a story, usually of love

BHARATANATYAM
A classical dance from south India, which features expressive hand movements and poses.

BHANGRA
A Punjabi folk dance, usually accompanied by a strong drum beat.

Kicks and jumps are often used

COSTUMES

The costume enhances a dancer's movements or helps set the scene of a story. Costumes are a traditional element of many dance forms and their design has changed little over time.

Jewelled headpiece

IRISH DANCER
Dresses have long sleeves and a short skirt, to emphasize leg movements.

BALLET
A short, sleeveless tutu shows off a dancer's form and technique.

INDIAN
Bharatanatyan costumes are based on Hindu temple sculptures.

BELLY DANCER
The *bedlah* consists of fitted bikini top, hip belt, and long skirt.

BALLROOM
Long dress with full, flowing skirt to enhance a dancer's movements.

DANCING SHOES

From the stomping drama of flamenco to the exquisite grace of ballet en pointe, wearing the correct footwear is essential.

BALLET

MALE TANGO

FEMALE TANGO

FLAMENCO

TAP

IRISH

BALLROOM

BALLROOM DANCING

Ballroom dancing is both a popular hobby and a competitive, professional sport. The two main categories in competition dance are ballroom dances such as the waltz and foxtrot, and Latin dances such as the tango.

Jangling bracelets draw attention to arm movements

SAMBA
A fast, rhythmic dance from Brazil.

RUMBA
The slowest of the Latin dances.

CHA-CHA
Originated in Cuba via the West Indies.

WALTZ
A popular, gliding dance from Austria.

TANGO
Dramatic dance from Buenos Aires, Argentina.

SALSA
Latin dance popular with amateurs.

PASO DOBLE
Inspired by Spanish bullfighters' moves.

STREET DANCE

New dance styles are always emerging from the streets of the world's cities. Breakdancing, or b-boying, came out of New York City in the 1970s and is still one of the most popular forms of street dance.

ONE-HAND ELBOW LEVER
Balance on one bent arm, holding the body straight.

FLARE
Breaker swings legs round him in a wide circle.

WINDMILL
Breaker rotates while swinging legs in a V shape.

HEADSPIN
Breaker balances on his head and spins rapidly.

HANDSTAND FREEZE
Breaker balances, then holds the position.

Facial expressions help tell the story

Intricate hand movements

ARABIC
Arabic dance uses quick, vibrating movements of the body and requires a lot of stamina.

TRADITIONAL BOLLYWOOD
Early Bollywood dance routines focused on acting out the lyrics of a song.

DANDIYA
A Gujarati folk dance where dancers hit dandiyas (sticks) together.

KATHAK
A classical dance from Uttar Pradesh in northern India.

SPORTING DANCE

Before a fight, Thai boxers perform a ritual dance called *Wai Khru Ram Muay*, to pay respect to their trainers and apologize in advance for their brutality.

Mongkhon (headband)

Ballet

Ballet started as an entertainment in the royal courts of Europe, and has grown into a breathtaking art form, enjoyed all over the world. Professional dancers work hard to reach the highest levels of fitness and artistry.

THE STORY OF BALLET

Ballet developed in France, which is why all the steps still have French names. It became a huge attraction in the great theatres of France, Italy, Russia, Scandinavia, and England.

1547
Italian Catherine de Medici becomes queen of France and brings an Italian style of dancing to the French court.

Catherine de Medici

1653
King Louis XIV dances the role of Apollo, the Sun god, in *Le Ballet de la Nuit* (The Dance of the Night).

Statue of Louis XIV of France

1661
First dance institution set up in Paris – l'Académie Royale de Danse.

1669
Dancer and director Pierre Beauchamps develops the five basic positions of the feet and arms.

Third position

1680
King Louis XIV starts staging regular opera-ballets at Versailles.

Palace of Versailles

1738
Imperial Russian Ballet School is founded in St Petersburg, Russia.

1832
La Sylphide, choreographed by Filippo Taglioni, opens in Paris, France.

1841
First performance of *Giselle*, danced by Italian ballerina Carlotta Grisi, takes place in Paris.

Mariinsky Theatre, home of the Russian Imperial Ballet from 1860

1877
Swan Lake, with music by Tchaikovsky, is performed by the Bolshoi Ballet in Moscow, Russia.

1890
The premiere of *Sleeping Beauty* is performed at the Mariinsky Theatre, St Petersburg.

1909
Ballet impresario, or organizer, Sergei Diaghilev forms the *Ballets Russes* company in Paris.

1913
The Rite of Spring, choreographed by Vaslav Nijinsky, causes outrage at its premiere in Paris.

1931
The Sadler's Wells Ballet (renamed the Royal Ballet in 1959) is formed in London.

Sculpture outside the Royal Opera House, home of the Royal Ballet

1964
Dancers Margot Fonteyn and Rudolf Nureyev receive a record 89 curtain calls after performing *Swan Lake* in Vienna, Austria.

ONLY MEN PERFORMED BALLET UNTIL 1681, WHEN MADEMOISELLE DE LAFONTAINE BECAME THE FIRST BALLERINA

YEARS OF TRAINING

Most professional dancers start young. After 8–10 years of dedicated training, only a few of the most talented students will join a ballet company (*corps de ballet*). The best dancers might progress to become a soloist or principal dancer.

BEGINNER
Dancers begin around age five, taking classes at a local studio.

BALLET SCHOOL
At the age of 11, the dancer is accepted at a ballet school.

APPRENTICE
At 16, the most promising students go on to three more years' study.

CORPS DE BALLET
The dancer joins a company, then progresses to minor roles.

PRINCIPAL
At this highest rank a dancer performs all the leading roles.

MAKING A POINTE SHOE

Female dancers wear special reinforced shoes so they can dance on the tips of their toes, a technique called *en pointe*. Dancers often embroider the toe area, to make shoes last longer and to help prevent slipping.

1 SHAPING THE UPPER
Layers of satin and stiff canvas are stitched together.

2 ADDING TOE BLOCKS
A leather sole is inserted, then layers of card, paper, and stiff fabric are pasted around the toe area to form a block.

3 SHAPING THE SHOE
The sole is stitched to the upper with thread. The shoe is then shaped with a special hammer.

4 ADDING RIBBONS
Traditionally, a dancer sews the ribbons on to her shoes herself.

CLASSIC BALLETS

The fashion for full-length ballets reached its height at the end of the 19th century. Many of the ballets from that time are still popular today.

SWAN LAKE, 1877
A handsome prince falls in love with a mysterious girl, only to discover that an evil magician has cast a spell on her.

GISELLE, 1841, ADAPTED 1884
A young girl is betrayed by the man she loves. She dies of grief, then comes back as a ghost and saves the life of the man who broke her heart.

THE FIREBIRD, 1910
Based on several Russian folk tales, it tells the story of how Prince Ivan and the magical Firebird overcome an evil magician called Kostchée.

COPPELIA, 1871
A light-hearted tale of a young man who falls for a life-sized doll, before realizing that his true love is the real, live girl next door.

THE NUTCRACKER, 1891
Toys magically come to life and take their owner on a journey to the Kingdom of Sweets, where the Sugar Plum Fairy lives, in this Christmas story.

COSTUME DESIGN

Costumes tell the audience about a character but must also allow a dancer to move freely. Below is the costume for a character from Greek myth called Eurydice, who is taken to the gloomy Underworld when she dies.

Fabric swatches

Colour samples

FROM SKETCHPAD TO STAGE
When Eurydice first appears, she is weighed down by a heavy cloak. The costume is designed so that she can remove it easily after she makes her dramatic entrance.

Wispy chiffon skirt suggests the spirit world

Cloak will be removed and hung up to become part of the set

THE BASIC POSITIONS

All the positions and steps in ballet are based on the five basic positions of the feet and arms. For all five foot positions, the feet are flat on the floor and turned out (pointing in opposite directions).

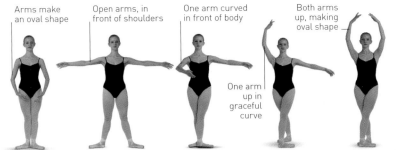

Arms make an oval shape

FIRST POSITION

Open arms, in front of shoulders

SECOND POSITION

One arm curved in front of body

THIRD POSITION

One arm up in graceful curve

Both arms up, making oval shape

FOURTH POSITION

FIFTH POSITION

AT THE BARRE

The barre is a handrail in the studio. Dancers hold on lightly to the barre so they can keep their balance while they concentrate on moves and positions.

DEMI-PLIE
Half bend the legs, heels flat on the floor.

ATTITUDE DEVANT
Stand on one leg, and raise the other leg in front, with knee bent.

RELEVE DEVANT
Balance on the ball of one foot, and bend the other leg at the knee.

CHANGEMENT

This jump goes straight up and down, with the front foot changing to the back in midair. The movement should be done with an easy bounce – this is called *ballon*. Practise several in a row to build up a stronger jump.

Start in the *demi-plié* position.

Jump, swap feet positions in the air.

Land softly in a deep *demi-plié*.

SISSONE OUVERT EN AVANT

A *sissone* is a jump starting from two feet. There are different kinds, but in this version, the legs open wide in the air, and then the dancer lands on one leg.

Start in a *demi-plié*, arms down.

Stretch legs wide apart while jumping forwards.

Land on one leg, keeping back straight.

A PRINCIPAL BALLERINA CAN GET THROUGH UP TO 12 PAIRS OF POINTE SHOES EVERY MONTH

ADAGE

Adage means "moving smoothly". Dancers put together a series of positions to make an exercise that improves balance and strengthens muscles.

TENDU DEVANT
Look to the front of the room.

ARABESQUE
Supporting leg is turned out.

ATTITUDE
Leg passes through first position.

CHASSÉ
Foot placed in wide fourth position.

RELEVÉ FIFTH
Feet in *demi-pointe* and arms lifted.

PAS DE CHAT

This means "cat step" in French. To perform it properly a dancer must spring quickly and land lightly and quietly, just like a cat.

Start in third position with *demi-plié*.

Push up from the floor, lifting one leg smoothly.

Spring into the air, bringing the feet together.

Land on the back foot, softly and quietly.

Bring the front foot down quickly into third position.

Male dancers always gaze at the ballerina

Strong knees and thighs are essential for supporting and lifting

EXPRESSING EMOTION
The *pas de deux* often portrays a romantic vision of love.

PAS DE DEUX

A *pas de deux* is a dance for two people, usually a man and a woman. It is a musical, physical, and artistic partnership between two dancers that can result in the most breathtaking moments in a performance.

SUPPORTING ACT
The male dancer supports the ballerina so she can balance *en pointe* for longer.

FISH DIVE
A lift in which the ballerina is supported with her back arched and arms outstretched.

Great buildings

The first great buildings were constructed for worship or for protection from invaders. In more recent times, many grand buildings are public spaces such as galleries and museums, or towering skyscrapers of offices and hotels.

▶ c.2560 BCE
GREAT PYRAMID AND SPHINX
The Great Pyramid was built as a tomb for Egyptian Pharaoh Khufu, and the Sphinx for his son, Khafre. Both were originally covered with smooth white limestone, and would have glittered in the sunlight.

THE GREAT PYRAMID AND SPHINX AT GIZA, EGYPT

▶ c.700 BCE
GREAT WALL
The Great Wall of China was built to keep out invaders. Various Chinese rulers extended it over hundreds of years, and it now stretches for an incredible 21,197 km (13,170 miles).

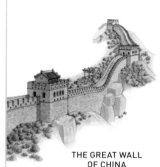

THE GREAT WALL OF CHINA

▶ c.1900 BCE
PALACE OF KNOSSOS
This was the largest centre of the Minoan civilization on the Greek island of Crete. Here, religious ceremonies may have been performed and political issues debated. By uncovering the remains, experts have worked out what the buildings would have looked like.

ARTIST'S IMPRESSION OF THE PALACE BUILDINGS

COPY OF A FRESCO FOUND AT KNOSSOS

◀ 1883
SAGRADA FAMILIA
This Roman Catholic church is Barcelona's most famous building. It was designed by the Spanish architect Antoni Gaudí, who died in 1926 when only a quarter of the church was built. It is expected to be completed by 2026.

SAGRADA FAMILIA, BARCELONA, SPAIN

◀ 1840
HOUSES OF PARLIAMENT
The United Kingdom's centre of government was built on the site of a palace, which burned down in 1834. The remains were incorporated into the new Gothic-style building. Construction took 30 years, and its architects died before completion.

THE HOUSES OF PARLIAMENT, LONDON, UK

◀ 1714
CHRIST CHURCH
This London church is one of six designed by Nicholas Hawksmoor in a style called English Baroque. It fell into disrepair in the 20th century but has been restored to its original glory, and its white stone facing gleams in the sunshine.

CHRIST CHURCH, LONDON, UK

◀ 1632
TAJ MAHAL
The Taj was built to be an elaborate jewelled tomb for the beloved wife of Mughal emperor Shah Jahan. It is known for its perfect symmetry: it is exactly as wide as it is high.

THE TAJ MAHAL, AGRA, INDIA

▶ 1930
EMPIRE STATE BUILDING
It took around 3,400 workers to complete the construction of this 103-floor Art Deco skyscraper in just 410 days. It was the world's tallest building until 1972, and remains New York City's most famous landmark. Every year, there is a race to the 86th floor.

EMPIRE STATE BUILDING, NEW YORK CITY, USA

▶ 1959
SYDNEY OPERA HOUSE
A multi-venue performing arts centre, Sydney Opera House was designed by Danish architect Jorn Utzon in a style called Modern Expressionism. The building's distinctive look comes from its one million self-cleaning, glazed white tiles.

SYDNEY OPERA HOUSE, AUSTRALIA

▶ 1971
POMPIDOU CENTRE
Housing a library, museum of modern art, and a centre for music research, the Pompidou is a high-tech arts centre. The different coloured parts are not just ornamental: green pipes indicate plumbing; blue ducts are for climate control; elevators, escalators, and staircases are red.

POMPIDOU CENTRE, PARIS, FRANCE

MODEL OF THE POMPIDOU

▶ 1993
GUGGENHEIM MUSEUM
The Guggenheim in Bilbao, Spain, is one of the world's most admired and popular buildings. Its architect, Canadian Frank Gehry, intended its shiny curves to appear random and sculpture-like.

THE GUGGENHEIM, BILBAO, SPAIN

40s BCE

PARTHENON

[I]s architects decided to make their temple [to] the goddess Athena the most impressive [in] Ancient Greece, and today it is one of the [gr]eat monuments of the ancient world. [Th]e Parthenon has many columns, and [is] decorated with carved panels and a [s]culpture frieze.

THE PARTHENON,
ATHENS, GREECE

▶ 80 CE

COLOSSEUM

This was the greatest amphitheatre in Ancient Rome. As many as 50,000 people gathered here to watch dramas, gruesome gladiator battles, and amazing spectacles. In the arena were passages, trapdoors, and hidden lifts to allow animals and men to appear from beneath the ground.

THE COLOSSEUM,
ROME, ITALY

▶ 537 CE

HAGIA SOPHIA

The cathedral church of Constantinople (now Istanbul), was the largest in the world for 1,000 years. It is famous for its massive dome, and for the ornate mosaics and marble pillars inside. Today, Hagia Sophia is a museum.

HAGIA SOPHIA,
ISTANBUL, TURKEY

▶ 1113

ANGKOR WAT

Meaning "City of Temples", Angkor Wat is the largest temple complex in the world. It was built to symbolize the home of the Hindu gods, Mount Meru. Its five towers represent the five peaks of the mountain, the walls its mountain ranges, and the moat the ocean.

ANGKOR WAT, SIEM REAP,
CAMBODIA

1609

BLUE MOSQUE

This mosque was built as an Islamic place of worship that would match the brilliance of the Hagia Sophia cathedral. Its design mixes traditional Islamic and Byzantine Christian architecture. It is named for its blue-tiled interior.

BLUE MOSQUE,
ISTANBUL, TURKEY

◀ 1552

ST BASIL'S CATHEDRAL

Built under the reign of Ivan the Terrible, this cathedral was designed to look like the flames of a bonfire rising up to the sky. It is famous for its unique, colourful, and ornate appearance.

ST BASIL'S CATHEDRAL,
MOSCOW, RUSSIA

◀ 1406

TEMPLE OF HEAVEN

This temple complex is intended to symbolize Heaven and Earth. Its most important building is the Hall of Prayer for Good Harvests, where sacred ceremonies were conducted by the Ancient Chinese emperors.

THE HALL OF PRAYER FOR GOOD
HARVESTS, BEIJING, CHINA

◀ 1333

HIMEJI CASTLE

Also known as White Heron Castle, Himeji is Japan's largest and best preserved castle. It was built as a fortress, and its multiple moats, fortified gates, and winding passages were designed to confuse and exhaust intruders.

HIMEJI CASTLE,
JAPAN

◀ 1238

ALHAMBRA PALACE

A palace and fortress built by Moorish (North African Muslim) kings of southern Spain, the Alhambra was designed to represent Paradise on Earth. There are enclosed landscaped gardens, and the palace is lavishly decorated.

THE ALHAMBRA,
GRANADA, SPAIN

▶ 1994

JIN MAO TOWER

Traditional Chinese and modern Western architectural styles are combined in this Shanghai skyscraper. Each tier flares outwards at its top like a pagoda-style roof. The tower is covered in glass and designed to be wind and earthquake resistant. There is a swimming pool on the 57th floor.

[T]HE GUGGENHEIM
[A]ND SURROUNDING
[B]UILDINGS

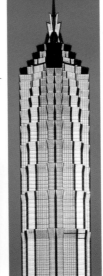

INSIDE THE JIN
MAO TOWER

JIN MAO TOWER,
SHANGHAI, CHINA

▶ 2004

BURJ KHALIFA

With 163 floors, Burj Khalifa is the world's tallest building. It is topped with a spiral minaret, like those on mosques. Its 24,348 windows are machine-cleaned, but the top of the spire is cleaned by hand, with the workers dangling from ropes.

BURJ KHALIFA, DUBAI,
UNITED ARAB EMIRATES

TOP 10 TALLEST SKYSCRAPERS

A skyscraper is a building used for offices, homes, or hotels that is higher than 150 m (450 ft).

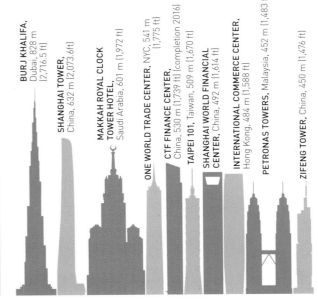

BURJ KHALIFA, Dubai, 828 m (2,716.5 ft)

SHANGHAI TOWER, China, 632 m (2,073.6ft)

MAKKAH ROYAL CLOCK TOWER HOTEL, Saudi Arabia, 601 m (1,972 ft)

ONE WORLD TRADE CENTER, NYC, 541 m (1,775 ft)

CTF FINANCE CENTER, China, 530 m (1,739 ft) (completion 2016)

TAIPEI 101, Taiwan, 509 m (1,670 ft)

SHANGHAI WORLD FINANCIAL CENTER, China, 492 m (1,614 ft)

INTERNATIONAL COMMERCE CENTER, Hong Kong, 484 m (1,588 ft)

PETRONAS TOWERS, Malaysia, 452 m (1,483 ft)

ZIFENG TOWER, China, 450 m (1,476 ft)

Great books

Thousands of years ago, stories were simply spoken aloud or told with pictures. As writing developed, tales were inscribed on stone, and then on parchment and paper. Great books transport us to different lives and are enjoyed by generations of readers all over the world.

▶ 2ND MILLENNIUM BCE

THE EPIC OF GILGAMESH

This poem was inscribed on clay tablets and is thought to be the first piece of written literature. It describes the journey of Gilgamesh, king of Uruk, who is on a quest with a wild man to fight evil.

"Humbaba's mouth is fire; his roar the floodwater; his breath is death."

▶ c.16TH–1ST CENTURY BCE

THE EGYPTIAN BOOK OF THE DEAD

This collection of drawings and magic spells was written over hundreds of years in Ancient Egypt. The spells were buried with the dead to help them in their next life in the Underworld.

A PAGE FROM THE BOOK OF THE DEAD

▶ c.4TH–2ND CENTURY BCE

INDIAN EPICS

Mahabharata by Vyasa and *Ramayana* by Valmiki are important Sanskrit poems that began as spoken songs. They tell stories about Indian culture, Hinduism, great wars, and exciting adventures.

A WARRIOR FROM THE MAHABHARATA

◀ 1908

ANNE OF GREEN GABLES

L M Montgomery tells a heart-warming tale about an orphan with a wonderful imagination. Anne is sent to a family who asked for a boy, but she thrives in her new home.

"Because when you are imagining you might as well imagine something worthwhile."

◀ 1894

SEVEN LITTLE AUSTRALIANS

This delightful story by Ethel Turner is about the mischievous Woolcot children, running wild at their home in Sydney.

BABY WOOLCOT WASHES THE KITTENS

◀ 1876

TOM SAWYER

THE ADVENTURES OF TOM SAWYER

Wily Tom Sawyer plays tricks on everyone but after he witnesses a murder, the games get serious. Mark Twain's adventures include graverobbers, children lost in caves, and a box of gold.

◀ 1861

GREAT EXPECTATIONS

Charles Dickens's story about Pip on his journey to becoming a gentleman includes bitter old Miss Havisham. She has been wearing her wedding gown ever since she was jilted at the altar.

"Ask no questions and you'll be told no lies."

◀ 1847

JANE EYRE

In Charlotte Brontë's novel, Jane Eyre has a harsh upbringing as an orphan. When she becomes a governess, she falls in love with her employer, Mr Rochester, who has a terrible secret in his house.

"I am no bird; and no net ensnares me."

▶ 1935

THE PENGUIN LOGO

PENGUIN PAPERBACKS

Most quality books were published with expensive hard covers until Allen Lane created Penguin paperbacks. He wanted people everywhere to be able to read good books in a format that they could afford.

▶ 1937

OF MICE AND MEN

John Steinbeck tells a sad, bleak story about two farmhands struggling to find work during the Depression in the USA. George tries to look out for his strong, slow-witted friend Lennie who dreams of farming rabbits.

LENNIE'S MOUSE

▶ 1937

THE HOBBIT

For this story, J R R Tolkien created a complete world called Middle Earth filled with hobbits, wizards, elves, dwarves, and trolls. On his quest to steal a dragon's treasure, Bilbo Baggins meets many dangers and finds a powerful magic ring.

THE RING

▶ 1943

THE LITTLE PRINCE'S HOME PLANET

THE LITTLE PRINCE

This magical little story from Antoine de Saint-Exupéry tells the tale of a pilot who is stranded in the desert. He comes across a little prince, who has fallen to Earth from another planet.

▶ 1945

ANIMAL FARM

George Orwell was making a political point with this story about animals taking over a farm to create an equal society. Things go badly wrong after Napoleon the pig seizes power.

NAPOLEON THE PIG

▶ 1947

THE DIARY OF A YOUNG GIRL

Anne Frank was 13 when she and her family went into hiding from the Nazis in World War II. The diary she wrote in their secret rooms has been translated into 70 languages.

ANNE FRANK'S DIARY

▶ c.2ND CENTURY BCE

INVENTION OF PAPER

Before the invention of paper by a resourceful Chinese civil servant called Cai Lun, writers used parchment, papyrus, or palm leaves.

PAPER AND BRUSH

▶ c.700–1500 CE

ARABIAN NIGHTS

Arabian Nights (also called *One Thousand and One Nights*) is a collection of captivating stories compiled over many centuries. Two of the best known are *Ali Baba and the Forty Thieves* and *Sinbad the Sailor*.

"Open Sesame!"

(Ali Baba and the Forty Thieves)

▶ c.750–1000

BEOWULF

Beowulf is an Old English poem about good and evil. The hero, Beowulf, destroys a terrible monster and then a dragon, but is killed during his last battle.

"When a chance came, he caught the hero in a rush of flame and clamped sharp fangs into his neck."

▶ 1440

THE PRINTING PRESS

The invention of the printing press by Johannes Gutenberg changed everything. Many more books were available, and ordinary people could own them for the first time.

THE PRINTING PRESS

▶ c.1595

ROMEO AND JULIET

William Shakespeare wrote 37 brilliant plays and many sonnets. One of his most famous plays, *Romeo and Juliet*, tells the tragic story of two young lovers whose families are fierce rivals.

"O Romeo, Romeo, wherefore art thou Romeo?"

ROMEO'S POISON AND DAGGER

1831

THE HUNCHBACK OF NOTRE DAME

Up in the towers of the Notre Dame Cathedral in Paris lives the hunchback Quasimodo. In Victor Hugo's story this tragic hero tries to save a kind gypsy dancer from death.

NOTRE DAME CATHEDRAL

◀ 1813

"Angry people are not always wise."

PRIDE AND PREJUDICE

Finding husbands for five daughters is a major challenge in the Bennet family. Jane Austen's complicated romance between Elizabeth Bennet and Mr Darcy is now a classic romance.

◀ 1812

GRIMMS' FAIRY TALES

The Brothers Grimm wrote many gruesome fairy tales with wicked characters that still frighten and thrill children today. *Little Snow White* and *Little Red Riding Hood* are two of the most famous.

"Mirror, mirror, on the wall, who in this land is the fairest of all?"

(Little Snow White)

◀ 18TH CENTURY

A TRADITIONAL CHINESE FAN

DREAM OF THE RED CHAMBER

This classic Chinese novel by Cao Xueqin is about the rise and fall of the aristocratic Jia family. It has a huge number of characters and paints a vivid picture of life in 18th-century China.

◀ 1605

DON QUIXOTE

Don Quixote sets out on his lanky horse Rocinante with his sidekick Sancho Panza on a donkey. Miguel de Cervantes' hero is in search of a knightly quest and a maiden to woo, but most of his adventures happen inside his head.

"Can we ever have too much of a good thing?"

1950

THE WARDROBE

THE LION, THE WITCH AND THE WARDROBE

C S Lewis set his adventures in Narnia – the mysterious world of ice and snow that four children discover through a door at the back of a wardrobe.

▶ 1952

CHARLOTTE'S WEB

Wilbur the pig is saved from slaughter by a supportive spider called Charlotte who weaves flattering messages about him in her web. E B White's heart-warming story has been a favourite for more than 60 years.

CHARLOTTE IN HER WEB

▶ 1960

THE MOCKINGBIRD IS A SYMBOL OF INNOCENCE

TO KILL A MOCKINGBIRD

Two children learn harsh lessons about equality in Harper Lee's explosive novel set in Alabama, USA. Their lawyer father defends a black man who is accused of a crime he did not commit.

▶ 1988

THE ALCHEMIST

Paulo Coelho's young shepherd, Santiago, tries to fulfil his Personal Legend by hunting for treasure. He learns valuable lessons on his journey.

SANTIAGO SEEKS TREASURE AT THE PYRAMIDS

▶ 1997

HARRY POTTER AND THE PHILOSOPHER'S STONE

The *Harry Potter* series by J K Rowling is about the adventures of a special young wizard called Harry and his schoolfriends. In this first story, an evil wizard hunts for the Philosopher's Stone so he can live forever.

THE SORTING HAT TELLS STUDENTS WHICH SCHOOL HOUSE THEY WILL BE IN

▶ 2005

THE BOOK THIEF

Markus Zusak's novel is narrated by death. He tells the touching story of a young girl who steals books in Germany during World War II.

BURNING BOOKS

Great thinkers

Throughout history, people have asked questions about the world and our place in it. Some great philosophers have come up with answers that have transformed our thinking – and others challenge us by posing new problems for us to think about.

▶ c.624–546 BCE
THALES "THE WISE"
Thales lived in Asia Minor (modern Turkey). He had the idea that water was the basic ingredient of everything, and that our world floated like a log in a universe of water.

▶ c.570–495 BCE
PYTHAGORAS
A Greek scientist, Pythagoras believed that everything in the universe could be explained by mathematics. He led a group of followers who obeyed his strict code about how to live, work, and honour the gods.

▶ c.563–483 BCE
SIDDHARTHA GAUTAMA
Known as the Buddha, or "enlightened one", he taught that nothing in the world is permanent. His goal was to end people's suffering, through teaching them the Eightfold Path to enlightenment.

"Even death is not to be feared by one who has lived wisely."

◀ 1712–78
JEAN-JACQUES ROUSSEAU
Rousseau said government is a contract between people and their rulers. If rulers ignore people's rights and freedoms, they break the contract and can be removed from power.

"Man was born free but everywhere he is in chains."

◀ 1711–76
DAVID HUME
Hume was a founder of "sceptical" philosophy, saying that there is nothing we can know for certain. He believed knowledge came only from direct experience, not from a person's ideas or religious beliefs.

◀ 1694–1778
VOLTAIRE
A French poet, playwright, and historian, Voltaire argued for free speech – that in a civilized society, everybody should have the right to say and think whatever they like.

◀ 1632–1704
JOHN LOCKE
Englishman Locke believed that people have the right to control their own body, and no one can tell them what to do with it. His ideas about power and freedom influenced lawmakers in the newly formed USA, who based the American Constitution of 1787 in part on Locke's ideas.

"Where there is no law, there is no freedom."

◀ 1596–1650
RENE DESCARTES
Descartes started a revolution in philosophy by doubting everything – including whether he really existed. He decided that as he had thoughts, someone must be thinking them – so he must really exist.

"I think, therefore I am."

▶ 1724–1804
IMMANUEL KANT
Unlike many philosophers of his time, Kant believed that knowledge of what is right and wrong is not born in us or given to us by God. We decide for ourselves what is morally right by using reason.

"Human reason is troubled by questions that it cannot dismiss, but also cannot answer."

▶ 1759–97
MARY WOLLSTONECRAFT
An English writer and teacher, she campaigned for women to have the same opportunities and rights as men. Her book, *A Vindication of the Rights of Women*, argued that girls should be educated as well as boys.

▶ 1806–73

JOHN STUART MILL
English economist and political thinker who believed that all people should be free to do whatever they choose, so long as it does not harm other people, or prevent them from doing what they want.

▶ 1818–83
KARL MARX
A revolutionary economist and thinker, Marx founded the theory of socialism, in which all the property, resources, and wealth of a country is owned by the public, and not by individual people.

▶ 1844–1900
FRIEDRICH NIETZSCHE
A German writer whose main philosophy was that people should aim achieve their full potent and be a "Superman" rather than an ordinary person.

551–479 BCE

CONFUCIUS

One of the most important early Chinese philosophers, Confucius taught that in order to live good and happy lives, people should respect their neighbours, honour their families, and obey their rulers.

"To study and not think is a waste. To think and not study is dangerous."

▶ 469–399 BCE

SOCRATES

One of the greatest Greek thinkers, Socrates devised a way of testing theories that involved asking lots of questions until he arrived at the truth. To him, the most important question of all was: "What makes a good life?"

"I am not an Athenian or a Greek, but a citizen of the world."

▶ 427–347 BCE

PLATO

Plato thought that our world is a faulty reflection of a perfect world that exists somewhere else. He founded the world's first university, the Academy, near Athens in Greece.

▶ 384–322 BCE

ARISTOTLE

Plato's pupil, Aristotle, is often called the first scientist. He believed that we should base our theories on what we have seen and experienced, rather than what we feel is true.

▶ 354–430 CE

AUGUSTINE OF HIPPO

Born in North Africa, Augustine was a Christian leader and thinker. He tried to explain why there is so much evil in our world, when God, who created it, is perfectly good.

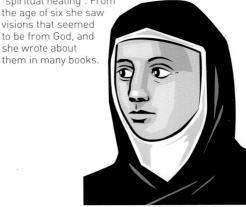

"Love the sinner and hate the sin."

1588–1679 ◀

THOMAS HOBBES

An English philosopher who believed that people are basically selfish. A civilized society needs to agree on a set of laws, then appoint a strong leader to make sure everyone obeys those laws.

1469–1527 ◀

NICCOLO MACHIAVELLI

An Italian writer and diplomat. He wrote *The Prince*, a book of advice for politicians. In it, he argues that sometimes it is right for a leader to do terrible things such as lying or even killing, if they are done for the good of his kingdom.

"The first method for estimating the intelligence of a ruler is to look at the men he has around him."

1225–74 ◀

THOMAS AQUINAS

A noble-born Italian monk, he wanted to prove God's existence through reason. He believed that it is obvious from observing the world that a supremely intelligent being must have created it, and this being must be God.

1126–98 ◀

IBN-RUSHD (AVERROES)

A Muslim philosopher from Cordoba in Spain. He studied Aristotle and Plato and tried to combine their scientific approach with Muslim religious views to create a unified idea of how the world works.

1098–1179 ◀

HILDEGARD OF BINGEN

A German writer, composer, and nun, Hildegard wrote about how to treat physical diseases by "spiritual healing". From the age of six she saw visions that seemed to be from God, and she wrote about them in many books.

▶ 1868–1963

W E B DUBOIS

An African-American historian, author, and campaigner, Dubois fiercely opposed the widely held view of the time that white people were a superior race. He believed that all people were equal and deserved equal rights, whatever their ethnicity or gender.

▶ 1889–1951

LUDWIG WITTGENSTEIN

One of the 20th century's most influential thinkers. He was especially interested in logic, and the connection between language and the world. He taught that we can only talk or write properly about things that exist.

▶ 1905–80

JEAN PAUL SARTRE

French writer and existentialist thinker. He believed that there is no God, and people have not been invented for any particular purpose: we must choose for ourselves what to do with our lives.

▶ 1908–86

SIMONE DE BEAUVOIR

French writer who argued that girls are not very different from boys when they are born. But because people treat women differently, they are forced to become submissive and obedient.

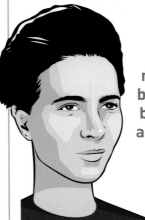

"One is not born, but rather becomes, a woman."

▶ 1930–2004

JACQUES DERRIDA

French philosopher who devised a way of thinking called "deconstruction". Language must be pulled apart, or deconstructed, to show how there are no fixed meanings to words. In fact, words get in the way of the search for truth.

"To pretend, I actually do the thing: I have therefore only pretended to pretend."

Food around the world

Every country has traditional food, based on local ingredients and handed-down recipes. Once upon a time you could get pizza only in Italy and sushi only in Japan. But today the world is like one huge café – with tastes from every continent available in big supermarkets and on city streets.

SOUTH AMERICA

Meat is a feast in South American countries, especially fine beef from cattle ranches on pampas grasslands. The continent's historic links with Spain and Portugal can be seen in stuffed empanadas, cheese-filled pastels, and colourful, spicy rice dishes.

TAMALES, BELIZE

TOSTONES, VENEZUELA

ARROZ CON POLLO, COLOMBIA

FEIJOADA, BRAZIL

PASTELS, BRAZIL

ACARAJE, BRAZIL

BLACK BEAN AND PUMPKIN SOUP, BRAZIL

EMPANADAS, BRAZIL

PUDIM DE ABOBORA, BRAZIL

ROAST GUINEA PIG, PERU

PORK BEAN STEW, BRAZIL

YERBA MATE, PARAGUAY

ICE CREAM WITH DULCE DE LECHE SAUCE, PARAGUAY

KIBBEH, ARGENTINA

DRY-RUB STEAK WITH CHIMICHURRI SAUCE, ARGENTINA

CEVICHE, PERU

NORTH AMERICA

People from many cultures have migrated to North America, introducing a wide range of food and recipes. The Thanksgiving roast turkey and pumpkin pie date back to the Puritan settlers, who cooked a feast of home-grown food to celebrate survival in their new land.

PUMPKIN PIE, CANADA

FRIED CHICKEN, USA

HAMBURGER, USA

HOT DOG, USA

SWEETCORN CHOWDER, USA

ROAST TURKEY, USA

FAJITAS, MEXICO

AFRICA

Food on this huge continent is full of flavours and scents – some from the Middle East and Asia. There are slow-cooked tagines and African curries, creamy dips with flatbread, and couscous with pomegranate seeds.

BRIK, TUNISIA

MECHOUIA, TUNISIA

SLADA BATATA HALVA, MOROCCO

TAGINE, MOROCCO

HARIRA, ALGERIA

COUSCOUS, TUNISIA

FERAKH MAAMER, MOROCCO

ZAHLOUK, MOROCCO

BSTILLA BIL DJAJ, MOROCCO

BABA GANOUSH, EGYPT

BOEREWORS, SOUTH AFRICA

GALINHA AFRICAN, MOZAMBIQUE

BOBOTIE, SOUTH AFRICA

BILTONG, SOUTH AFRICA

FUL MEDAMES, EGYPT

BLUEBERRY PIE,
USA

EUROPE

Traditional European dishes like Italian pizza and French coq au vin are served all over the world. A Mediterranean diet, rich in vegetables and olive oil, is the healthiest choice of all. But that doesn't stop people enjoying English fish and chips or spicy German sausage.

FISH AND CHIPS,
UNITED KINGDOM

ROAST BEEF,
UNITED KINGDOM

LIMBURGSE VLAAI,
THE NETHERLANDS

STOLLEN,
GERMANY

WALDORF SALAD, USA

ECLAIRS, FRANCE

QUICHE, FRANCE

COQ AU VIN, FRANCE

MOULES FRITES,
BELGIUM

SAUERKRAUT,
GERMANY

PICKLED HERRINGS,
GERMANY

GUMBO, USA

GAZPACHO, SPAIN

STRUDEL, AUSTRIA

GOULASH,
HUNGARY

BAKLAVA,
GREECE

BURRITOS, MEXICO

PAELLA,
SPAIN

FONDUE,
SWITZERLAND

WIENER SCHNITZEL,
AUSTRIA

SPAGHETTI
BOLOGNESE, ITALY

TIRAMISU,
ITALY

PIZZA,
ITALY

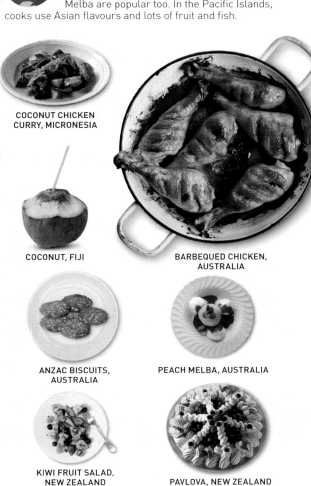

ASIA

Asian food has become popular everywhere. As well as spicy curries, there are delicately flavoured dim sum dumplings, spicy kebabs, and hand-rolled sushi.

PASKHA, RUSSIA

BORSCHT, RUSSIA

TONKATSU, JAPAN

AUSTRALIA AND OCEANIA

Barbecues are ideal for the outdoor life in sunny Australia. Ice cream puddings like Peach Melba are popular too. In the Pacific Islands, cooks use Asian flavours and lots of fruit and fish.

COCONUT CHICKEN
CURRY, MICRONESIA

KEBABS,
TURKEY

TABBOULEH,
LEBANON

SUSHI, JAPAN

TEMPURA, JAPAN

KULFI, INDIA

THAI GREEN CURRY,
THAILAND

DIM SUM, CHINA

COCONUT, FIJI

BARBEQUED CHICKEN,
AUSTRALIA

PANEER WITH DAHL, INDIA

SAMOSA, INDIA

KERALA FISH STEW,
INDIA

BANH MI, VIETNAM

PHO GA, VIETNAM

ANZAC BISCUITS,
AUSTRALIA

PEACH MELBA, AUSTRALIA

ALOO GOBI, INDIA

RINGRAH NA BHAJIA, INDIA

ICE KACHANG,
SINGAPORE

SATAY,
INDONESIA

NASI GORENG, INDONESIA

KIWI FRUIT SALAD,
NEW ZEALAND

PAVLOVA, NEW ZEALAND

Fruit

A fruit is the edible part of a plant that develops from its flowers. Each fruit contains a seed (or seeds) that is surrounded by flesh and enclosed in a skin or rind. Fruit is full of natural sugar and usually tastes sweet.

INSIDE A FRUIT

The flesh surrounding the seeds of a fruit is formed into layers: the central layer holds the seeds, while the outer layer is the skin or rind. The skin of some fruit, such as apples, can be eaten.

BERRY — Flesh or pulp, Seed, Thin skin

PIT FRUIT — Seed, Pit, Flesh or pulp

CORE FRUIT — Seeds inside the core, Flesh

CITRUS — Juicy segments, Pith, Leathery rind

MELON — Rows of seeds, Hard rind

BERRIES

A berry is a fruit with a seed, or seeds, that is produced from a single flower. The seeds are hidden in soft, often juicy, flesh. Many smaller berries have edible skins.

GUAVA

POMEGRANATE

PAPAYA

ELDERBERRY

BLACKCURRANT

BLUEBERRY

CRANBERRY

GRAPES

BANANA

PASSION FRUIT

KIWI FRUIT

CAPE GOOSEBERRY

TAMARILLO

PIT FRUIT

The hard stone of a pit fruit contains a single seed. Some pit fruit, such as raspberries, are actually made up of individual sections, each containing a seed.

CHERIMOYA

MANGO

CITRUS FRUIT

Most citrus fruits have a hard rind or skin. Citrus fruits are grown mainly for their delicious juice, which is held in the fleshy segments. These segments are enclosed in a soft, white layer of tissue known as the pith.

KUMQUAT

LEMON

CLEMENTINE

BLOOD ORANGE

KAFFIR LIME

KEY LIME

LIME

Central column

ORANGE

GRAPEFRUIT

CITRON

SHADDOCK

WATERMELON

PREADING EEDS

ruit seeds are spread in number of ways. They n be blown by the wind, rried by water, or pped when a fruit lls from a plant or ee. Often, seeds e spread by birds.

1 BIRD EATS FRUIT
Birds love to eat the bright fruits that hold the seeds.

2 BIRD PASSES SEED OUT
Once the bird has digested the fruit, it excretes the seed that was inside the fruit.

NEW TREE GROWS
The seed germinates in e ground and begins to form ew plant or tree.

SIZE COMPARISON

The jackfruit from Southeast Asia is the world's largest fruit. It can grow up to 90 cm (35 in) long and weigh up to 36 kg (79 lb).

JACKFRUIT

STINKIEST FRUIT

Many people consider the world's stinkiest fruit to be the durian. It can smell like rotten onions, but has a sweet, custard-like flesh.

DURIAN

ACCESSORY FRUIT

Some kinds of fruit grow differently from others. They are known as accessory fruit. The core fruit group is sometimes included within this category.

STRAWBERRY

STRAWBERRIES ARE PART OF THE ROSE FAMILY OF FLOWERING PLANTS

OCONUT

NECTARINE

LYCHEE

RAMBUTAN

PEACH

BLACKBERRY

RASPBERRY

DAMSON

PLUM

APRICOT

CORE FRUIT

These fleshy fruits have thin, often edible, skins. Their seeds are contained in the core at the centre of the fruit.

LOUQUAT

APPLE

PEAR

QUINCE

PINEAPPLE

BREADFRUIT

FIG

MELONS BELONG TO THE SAME PLANT FAMILY AS THE CUCUMBER AND HAVE BEEN GROWN SINCE ROMAN TIMES

MELONS

The melon originated in Africa. Each melon contains many seeds in the centre, which are surrounded by soft, sweet, juicy flesh. The hard skin is inedible.

CANARY MELON

CANTALOUPE

CRENSHAW MELON

HONEYDEW MELON

KIWANO

Vegetables

The word "vegetable" is not a scientific term. It is a word that people began to use hundreds of years ago to refer to plants that were grown to eat, rather than foraged from the wild. There are many different types, and they are rich in vitamins and minerals.

TYPES OF VEGETABLES

Vegetables are divided into groups according to the part of the plant that is eaten, for example roots, stems, leaves, pods, or flowers. Some are strictly "fruits", but because they are used in savoury cooking, are commonly called vegetables.

FRUIT

POD VEGETABLES

LEAFY VEGETABLES

FLOWERS AND BUDS

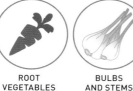
ROOT VEGETABLES

BULBS AND STEMS

COLOURS

You can often tell the health benefits of a vegetable from its colour. The colours of vegetables come from their natural pigments.

CHLOROPHYLL
Helps replenish red blood cells in the body.

CAROTENOIDS
Convert to vitamin A, which is good for eye health.

ANTHOCYANINS
Help protect the body's cells from damage.

LYCOPENE
Protects body cells and may reduce the risk of cancer.

POD VEGETABLES

Pod vegetables come from plants that produce fruits in the form of seeds or beans, nestled inside a pod. Many pod vegetables belong to a family of vegetables known as legumes. These vegetables are very high in protein.

OKRA

BROAD BEAN

LEAFY VEGETABLES

All vegetables have leaves, but "leafy vegetables" are the ones where we eat the leaves, rather than trim them off. The darker the leaves, the stronger the taste, and the richer they are in vitamins A and C and bone-strengthening calcium.

CABBAGE

AMARANTH

BRUSSELS SPROUTS

RED CABBAGE

SALAD ROCKET

BOK CHOY

CHICKWEED

FRUIT

These vegetables are all the fruit of a plant, and they contain the seeds it would use to reproduce. In this sense, they are very like apples and oranges, but these fruits contain less sugar and taste savoury, not sweet.

PEPPER

RED CHILLI

SQUASH

GOURD

BUTTERNUT SQUASH

MARROW

AUBERGINE

PUMPKIN

COURGETTE

FLOWERS AND BUDS

These vegetables are taken from plants that are grown for their edible flower heads or buds, such as broccoli and cauliflower. They are sturdy and high in fibre, which is good for the digestive system.

ARTICHOKE

CAULIFLOWER

BROCCOLI

WATER CHESTNUT

HAMBURG PARSLEY

SWEDE

DI SICILIA VIOLETTO CAULIFLOWER

ROMANESCO CAULIFLOWER

PARSNIP

"BROCCOLI" IS AN ITALIAN WORD THAT MEANS "LITTLE SPROUTS" OR "LITTLE SHOOTS"

RADISH

PURPLE FRENCH BEANS

LIMA BEANS

RUNNER BEANS

PEAS

LABLAB BEANS

DANDELION

LAMB'S LETTUCE

BEET GREENS

KALE

CURLY ENDIVE

KOMATSUNA

CAVOLO NERO

CHARD

LETTUCE

SPINACH

BROAD-LEAVED ENDIVE

LOOSELEAF CHICORY

ROOT VEGETABLES

These are the parts of the plant that grow underground, absorbing moisture and nutrients. This group includes roots, corms, and tubers, which are thickened, underground stems. The potato is a tuber.

POTATO

TARO

SWEET POTATO

TURNIP

BEETROOT

CARROT

BULBS AND STEMS

Stem vegetables are the edible shoots or stalks of plants, such as asparagus, celery, and fennel. Bulbs are the underground parts of plants that store their nutrients, such as onions, leeks, and garlic.

LEEK

CELERY

ASPARAGUS

KOHLRABI

SHALLOT

LOTUS STEM

WELSH ONION

SPRING ONION

PEARL ONION

FENNEL

LEMON GRASS

GARLIC

WHITE ONION

ONIONS

CHEESE-MAKING

The first stage in the making of any type of cheese is to curdle the milk. This means getting the milk to separate into solid lumps (curds) and a liquid called whey. The photographs below show the steps for producing a hard cheese such as Cheddar.

1 CURDLING THE MILK
A machine stirs an enzyme called rennet into the milk to speed curdling.

2 DRAINING AND HEATING
The milk curds are cut into cubes and the whey is allowed to drain off.

3 "CHEDDARING"
The curds are "cheddared" (piled up) to press out more moisture.

4 RIPENING
To shape the cheeses, the curds are put into moulds, then left to ripen.

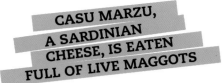
CASU MARZU, A SARDINIAN CHEESE, IS EATEN FULL OF LIVE MAGGOTS

ADDED FLAVOURS

Many people like to eat cheese just as it is. But cheeses are also made with added spices, fruit, and herbs to give them an interesting new taste.

ROSEMARY
CRANBERRIES
PAPRIKA
CHIVE
THYME
GARLIC
ASH

TOP CHEESE EATERS

The eight countries listed here are where to find the people who eat the most cheese per person per year (in kg/lb).

1 FRANCE
26.3 kg (58 lb) Favourites: Camembert and brie, both soft and creamy cheeses.

2 ICELAND
24.1 kg (53 lb) Favourite: Skyr, soft cheese with a yogurt-like texture.

3 GREECE
23.4kg (52 lb) Favourite: feta, tangy, white, and crumbly.

4 GERMANY
22.9 kg (50 lb) Favourites: Gouda, semi-hard and rich-tasting; and Bruder Basil, a semi-soft smoked cheese.

5 FINLAND
22.5 kg (49 lb) Favourites: Oltermanni, semi-soft and buttery; and Aura, blue and creamy.

6 ITALY
21.8 kg (48 lb) Favourites: Parmesan, nutty and grainy; mozzarella, made with buffalo milk; and Gorgonzola, blue-veined and crumbly.

7 SWITZERLAND
20.8 kg (46 lb) Favourites: Emmental, classic "holey" cheese; and Gruyère, firm and nutty.

8 AUSTRIA
19.9 kg (44 lb) Favourites: Bergkäse and Tilsiter, both with a strong taste and smell.

Cheese

Filling a sandwich, used in a sauce, or just nibbled, cheese is one of the world's favourite foods. It is delicious, nutritious, and made in so many varieties that there is a cheese to suit almost everyone. Most people have eaten only a few different cheeses, but there are thousands to try.

HARD CHEESE

This type of cheese is made from cooked curds pressed firmly into shape and left to age. The method removes as much moisture as possible from the curds and produces a solid cheese that keeps well. Semi-hard cheese has a higher moisture content.

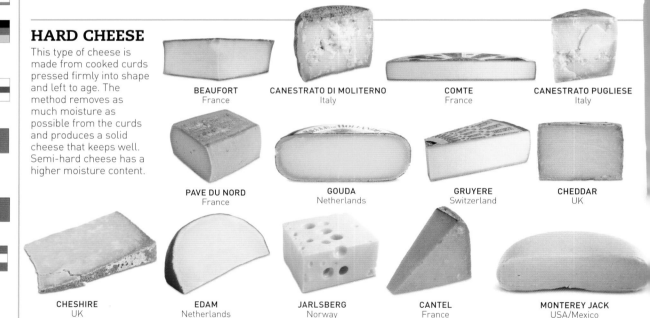

BEAUFORT
France

CANESTRATO DI MOLITERNO
Italy

COMTE
France

CANESTRATO PUGLIESE
Italy

PAVE DU NORD
France

GOUDA
Netherlands

GRUYERE
Switzerland

CHEDDAR
UK

CHESHIRE
UK

EDAM
Netherlands

JARLSBERG
Norway

CANTEL
France

MONTEREY JACK
USA/Mexico

SOFT CHEESE

The curds of soft cheeses are not cooked or pressed, but shaped and left to drain. Some types are eaten soon after making. Others are ripened until a wrinkly rind forms. Depending on the type of cheese, the centre may have a creamy or chalky texture.

RICOTTA AFFUMICATA
Italy

FETA
Greece

SUSSEX SLIPCOTE
UK

HOLY GOAT PANDORA
Australia

OLIVET CENDRE
France

MOZZARELLA
Italy

CHABICHOU DU POITOU
France

KETEM
Israel

BRIE DE MELUN
France

WABASH CANNONBALL
USA

WINNIMERE
USA

SAKURA
Japan

WHICH MILK MAKES CHEESE?

Most of the world's cheeses are made with milk from cows, goats, sheep, and buffalo. In dry regions with poor grazing, camels are an important source of milk. More rarely, cheese is made from the milk of horses, donkeys, yaks, and reindeer.

SHEEP

GOAT

COW

WATER BUFFALO

CAMEL

HORSE

BLUE CHEESE

The mouldy-looking streaks running through blue cheeses really are mould – but a type that is safe to eat. To produce blue cheese, the makers add mould spores to the curdled milk. After shaping the cheese, they pierce, or "needle", it to let in air and kickstart the mould's growth. Blue cheese, which can be hard or soft, usually has a strong flavour.

GORGONZOLA
Italy

STILTON
UK

ROQUEFORT
France

BAVARIA BLU
Germany

BLEU BENEDICTIN
Canada

BLEU DE CHEVRE
France

GAMONEDO
Spain

VALDEON
Spain

BARKHAM BLUE
UK

EMMENTAL
DE SAVOIE
Switzerland

Bacterial action forms holes as cheese ripens

Elastic texture

POSTEL
Belgium

CRESCENT DAIRY
FARMHOUSE
New Zealand

KASHKAVAL
Hungary

OSTIEPOK
Slovakia

SARDO
Argentina

ALLGAUER
BERGKASE
Germany

VASTERBOTTENSOST
Sweden

GRAVIERA
Greece

TIROLER
GRAUKASE
Austria

PECORINO
SARDO
Italy

BITTO
Italy

MANCHEGO
Spain

PECORINO
ROMANO
Italy

GAMALOST
Norway

CHEESE HISTORY

Cheese-making began long ago when people discovered, probably by chance, that curdled milk was good food. The cheese we eat today has a history of approximately 8,000 years.

8000 BCE

8000 BCE
People start keeping sheep and learn to milk them.

5500 BCE
Pots dating from this time in Europe may be the earliest cheese strainers.

4000 BCE
Evidence of dairy farming in the Sahara grasslands.

3500 BCE
Sumerian clay writing tablets mention curd making.

Ancient Sumerian script

2000 BCE
Egyptian tomb paintings show cheese being made.

300 CE
Cheese is sold and eaten throughout Europe.

50 CE
The Romans invent the cheese press.

1170
First reference to Cheddar, from Somerset in England.

1348
First reference to cheese from Parma, later known as Parmesan.

City Hall, Gouda

1697
First reference to Gouda, named after the Dutch town.

1791
French farmer Marie Harel invents Camembert cheese.

Statue of Marie Harel in Normandy, France

1815
First-ever cheese factory opens in Switzerland.

1860S
Mass-produced rennet makes cheese-making more consistent.

2000

2011
A 939 kg (2,070 lb) goats cheese takes the world title for the biggest cheese ever.

Bread

First eaten around 30,000 years ago, bread is a favourite food all around the world. Usually made with wheat or rye flour, it is easy to make and a great source of carbohydrates for energy. There are thousands of delicious varieties of bread, from flat and crisp to plaited and fluffy.

MAKING BREAD

Making bread is not difficult, although you need some strength to knead the dough and patience while it proves (rises). These steps show how to make a simple white loaf.

1 FLOUR Sift plain flour and salt into a bowl.

2 Add a mixture of water, milk, and yeast. Combine everything together until they form a dough.

3 Place the dough on a floured board. Let it rest for a few minutes. Then knead it for 5–10 minutes.

ROLLS

Rolls, and other forms of bread, come in all shapes and sizes. Many, such as bagels, have become popular all over the world.

WHOLEMEAL ROLL UK

PICOS ROLLS Spain

SKILLET BREAD USA

PIRAGI Latvia

WHO EATS THE MOST BREAD?

These ten countries eat more bread per person per year than anywhere else in the world.

1 TURKEY
104.6 kg (230.5 lb) per person per year. Favourites: bazlama, gözleme, and pide.

2 CHILE
96 kg (211.5 lb) per person per year. Favourites: marraqueta, hallula, and coliza.

3 ARGENTINA
76 kg (167.5 lb) per person per year. Favourites: pan de campo, pan de chapa, and chipas.

4 DENMARK
70 kg (154 lb) per person per year. Favourites: rye and pumpernickel.

4 GREECE
70 kg (154 lb) per person per year. Favourites: daktyla, lagana, and pitta.

4 POLAND
70 kg (154 lb) per person per year. Favourites: rye, wholegrain, flavoured breads, and bagels.

5 IRELAND
68 kg (150 lb) per person per year. Favourites: potato, soda, and barmbrack.

6 HUNGARY
60 kg (132 lb) per person per year. Favourites: lángos, pogácsa, and pretzels.

6 THE NETHERLANDS
60 kg (132 lb) per person per year. Favourites: wholegrain, rye, and suikerbrood.

7 GERMANY
57 kg (125.5 lb) per person per year. Favourites: rye, wholegrain, and wheat-rye.

> GERMANY HAS MORE THAN 1,300 VARIETIES OF BREAD, ROLLS, AND PASTRIES

LEAVENED BREAD

In leavened breads (where the dough rises), yeast or baking powder is added to the flour combined with a liquid like buttermilk to create carbon dioxide gas. This makes the bread light and airy. Thousands of different types of leavened bread are baked around the world.

PUMPERNICKEL Germany

SEVEN GRAIN BREAD USA

WHOLEMEAL COTTAGE LOAF UK

ZOPF Switzerland

CIABATTA Italy

BAGUETTE France

WHITE LOAF UK

SOURDOUGH LOAF Middle East

PANE DI PATATE Italy

PARTYBROT Germany

RAISING AGENT

Many types of bread are leavened, meaning that they have had something added to them to make them rise. The most common rising agent is yeast, which comes in various forms.

Compressed yeast

Powdered yeast

Dried yeast

MANTOU STEAMED BREAD China

HEFEZOPF Germany

PAIN A L'ANCIEN France

FOCACCIA BREAD Italy

PIZZA Italy

FLATBREADS

Most flatbreads do not contain yeast, although some, such as pitta bread and naan bread, are slightly leavened. Pitta bread opens up to form a pocket that can be filled with different ingredients. Other flat breads can be used like a plate and then eaten.

PITTA BREAD Middle East

PIDE Turkey

NAAN India

FLATBREAD Italy

CRISPBREAD Sweden

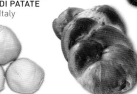

TORTILLA Spain

FLAVOURS FOR BREAD

Bread can be mixed with lots of different ingredients to make it taste savoury or sweet. Savoury breads can be flavoured with strong tastes, like onion and cheese. Sweet-flavoured breads often have fruit, nuts, and spices added to them.

[4] Put the dough into a clean bowl, cover with clingfilm and let it move (rise) for about three hours.

5 Punch the dough down while it is still in the bowl to take some of the air out.

6 Turn the dough out on to a floured board and knead it again for about two minutes.

7 Form the dough into the desired shape, or put it in a tin and cover with clingfilm and let it rise for 90 minutes.

8 Bake the bread for about 30 minutes in a pre-heated oven at 180°C/350°F/ Gas Mark 4 until it is golden brown and sounds hollow.

9 Turn the loaf out on to a wire rack and let it cool. Store the bread in a bread bin or tin so that it stays fresh.

PARKER HOUSE ROLLS
USA

BRIOCHE
France

BAGELS
Poland

GRISSINI
Italy

FAN TAN (BUTTERMILK ROLL)
France

PRETZELS
Germany

BRIOCHE NANTERRE LOAF
France

PUGLIESE BREAD
Italy

SEEDED RYE BREAD
Russia

BARMBRACK BREAD
Ireland

ANADAMA BREAD
USA

GLUTEN-FREE BROWN BREAD
USA

FOUGASSE
France

SPECIAL OCCASION BREADS

In many countries and within some religious groups, there is a tradition of baking special types of bread for certain occasions. Some recipes are everyday breads but with added ingredients such as fruit or nuts. Other varieties are only baked once a year.

HOT CROSS BUNS
UK – Easter

CIAMBELLA MANDORLATA
Italy – Easter

PANE DI PRATO
Italy

PANDORO BREAD
Italy – Christmas

PANETTONE
Italy – Christmas

SODA BREAD
Ireland

STOLLEN
Germany – Christmas

TSOUREKI
Greece – Christmas

GOZLEME
Turkey

HEFEKRANZ LOAF
Austria

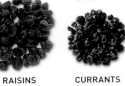

CHERRIES

CHOCOLATE

ONION

OLIVES

CHALLAH
Middle East –
Jewish Sabbath

MATZO
Middle East –
Jewish Passover

RAISINS

CURRANTS

SULTANAS

CARDAMOM

WALNUTS

PISTACHIOS

CHEESE

Pasta

Made from flour and eggs, plus a little water or olive oil, pasta has always been a very important food in Italy. Now it is popular throughout the world because it can be cooked in so many different ways. Pasta is also a great source of energy for our bodies.

MAKING PASTA

Pasta is not complicated to make, but it can take a little while. You can make it by hand, or you can use a food mixer. A pasta machine can be used to roll the pasta dough out and cut it into strips, depending on the shape that you want. You can use different types of flour, such as plain, semolina, buckwheat, or wholemeal flour.

1 ADD THE EGGS TO THE FLOUR
Make a well in the centre of the flour and then add the eggs.

2 MIX THE EGGS AN FLOUR TOGETHER
Combine the eggs and flour to form a dough, using a little olive oil or water to keep it moist.

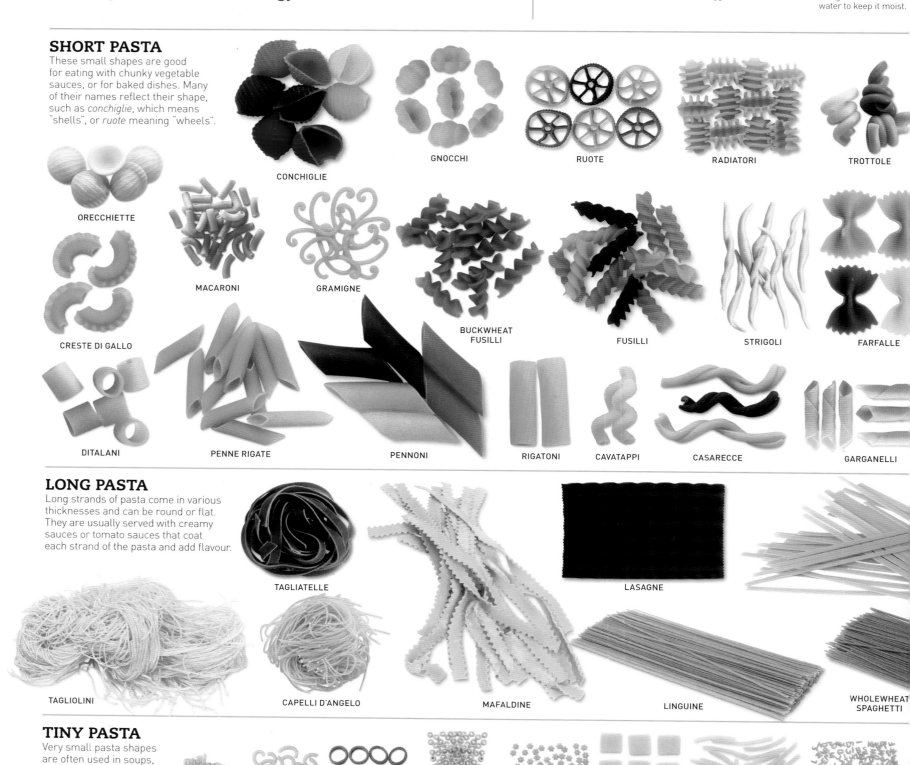

SHORT PASTA

These small shapes are good for eating with chunky vegetable sauces, or for baked dishes. Many of their names reflect their shape, such as *conchiglie*, which means "shells", or *ruote* meaning "wheels".

CONCHIGLIE

GNOCCHI

RUOTE

RADIATORI

TROTTOLE

ORECCHIETTE

MACARONI

GRAMIGNE

BUCKWHEAT FUSILLI

FUSILLI

STRIGOLI

FARFALLE

CRESTE DI GALLO

DITALANI

PENNE RIGATE

PENNONI

RIGATONI

CAVATAPPI

CASARECCE

GARGANELLI

LONG PASTA

Long strands of pasta come in various thicknesses and can be round or flat. They are usually served with creamy sauces or tomato sauces that coat each strand of the pasta and add flavour.

TAGLIATELLE

LASAGNE

TAGLIOLINI

CAPELLI D'ANGELO

MAFALDINE

LINGUINE

WHOLEWHEAT SPAGHETTI

TINY PASTA

Very small pasta shapes are often used in soups, or added to stews, because they are a quick and easy way to make the dishes more filling and serve more people.

RISONI

GRAMIGNA

ANELLI

ANELLINI

STELLINE

QUADRETTI

FILINI

ALFABETI

3 KNEAD
Use your hands
[t]o knead the pasta
[d]ough for about
[5]-7 minutes until
[it] is smooth.

4 REST THE DOUGH
Cover the dough in cling film and let it rest for 30 minutes. Then unwrap it and place it on a floured board.

5 FLATTEN THE DOUGH
Flatten the dough, using your hands and a rolling pin. Don't let the dough get too warm or floury.

6 ROLL THE DOUGH
Roll the dough out with a rolling pin or feed it through a pasta machine until it becomes thin.

7 PASTA STRANDS
Once the dough is thin enough, it can be cut into strips, or you can cut it by hand into different shapes.

WHO EATS THE MOST PASTA?

Nearly 13.5 million tonnes of pasta is produced worldwide each year. Here are the nine countries that eat the most pasta per person.

1 ITALY
26 kg (57 lb) per person per year. Italians eat 1,524,006 tonnes of pasta each year.

2 VENEZUELA
12.3 kg (27 lb) per person per year. Venezuela's total consumption is 350,213 tonnes each year.

3 TUNISIA
11.9 kg (26 lb) per person per year. Tunisia's total annual consumption is nearly 130,000 tonnes.

4 GREECE
10.5 kg (23 lb) per person per year. The Greeks consume around 120,000 tonnes of pasta annually.

5 SWITZERLAND
9.3 kg (21 lb) per person per year. Switzerland's total annual consumption is 73,130 tonnes.

6 SWEDEN
9 kg (20 lb) per person per year. Sweden's total consumption is just over 86,000 tonnes.

7 USA
8.8 kg (19 lb) per person per year. The USA is the world's largest consumer overall with a total of 2,700,000 tonnes of pasta each year.

8 CHILE
8.4 kg (19 lb) per person per year. Chile's total consumption is 144,000 tonnes each year.

9 PERU
8.2 kg (18 lb) per person per year. The Peruvians consume 250,000 tonnes annually.

STUFFED PASTA

Some pasta shapes are stuffed with a filling and sealed before they are cooked. Fillings can include creamy cheeses and vegetables such as spinach.

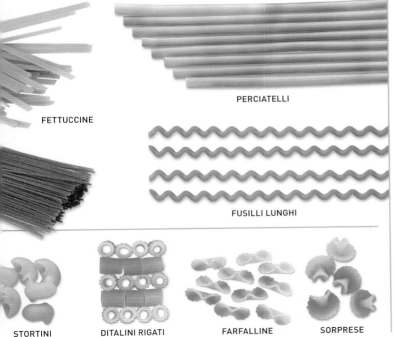

DISCHI VOLANTI

CAVATELLI

CAMPANELLE

STROZZAPRETI

PANSOTTI

CAPPELLETTI

CANNELLONI

LUNETTE

TORTELLINI

RAVIOLI

CARAMELLE

COLOURED PASTA

The basic ingredients of pasta don't change, but you can add different foods to pasta that will affect its colour and taste. Added flavours include garlic, herbs, and wine, as well as vegetables such as mushrooms.

FETTUCCINE

PERCIATELLI

FUSILLI LUNGHI

STORTINI

DITALINI RIGATI

FARFALLINE

SORPRESE

CURRY

HERBS

WILD MUSHROOM

TOMATO

RED WINE

SPINACH

ONION

EGG

THERE ARE MORE THAN 600 DIFFERENT SHAPES OF PASTA PRODUCED THROUGHOUT THE WORLD

Fish for food

All over the world, fish is an important part of people's diets. It contains protein, vitamins, and minerals. Fish can be cooked in many different ways or even eaten raw.

WHO EATS THE MOST FISH?

These ten countries eat more fish per person per year than anywhere else in the world.

1 MALDIVES
154 kg (339.5 lb) Favourites: skipjack tuna, yellowfin tuna, and mahi-mahi.

2 ICELAND
94 kg (207.2 lb) Favourites: haddock, halibut, herring, and plaice.

3 KIRIBATI
76.3 kg (168 lb) Favourites: lobster, yellowfin tuna, and skipjack tuna.

4 GUYANA
73 kg (161 lb) Favourites: crab, tilapia, and catfish.

5 JAPAN
71.9 kg (158.5 lb) Favourites: bluefin tuna, salmon, prawns, and eel.

6 FRENCH POLYNESIA
67.5 kg (149 lb) Favourites: tuna, mahi-mahi, octopus, sea urchin, and prawns.

7 SEYCHELLES
62.3 kg (137 lb) Favourites: octopus, tuna, squid, red snapper, and grouper.

8 NORWAY
61.9 kg (136.4 lb) Favourites: smoked salmon, prawns, trout, crab, cod, and herring.

9 PORTUGAL
58.7 kg (129.4 lb) Favourites: cod, sardines, octopus, squid, crab, lobster, clams, mussels, and oysters.

10 MALAYSIA
54.2 kg (119.4 lb) Favourites: prawns, crab, squid, cuttlefish, octopus, and sea cucumbers.

SUSHI AND SASHIMI

Raw fish is often used in Japanese dishes. Nigiri sushi uses rice formed into a rectangle with fish placed on top. Sashimi is very fresh, sliced raw fish. Maki sushi rolls are wrapped in seaweed called nori.

NIGIRI SUSHI

SASHIMI

MAKI SUSHI ROLLS

SALTED FISH, DRIED FISH

Fish does not stay fresh for long, particularly if it cannot be refrigerated. So fish is often preserved in salt or brine (very salty water), or dried to use later.

SALTED ANCHOVIES

BOMBAY DUCK (DRIED BUMMALO FISH)

DRIED SHRIMP

DRIED SCALLOP

SALTED COD

SALTED MACKEREL

SMOKED FISH

Fish can also be preserved by smoking in one of two ways. Hot-smoked fish are brined, dried, and then smoked quickly. Cold-smoked fish are brined and then smoked for 1–5 days.

ARBROATH SMOKIES (HADDOCK)

MUSSELS

KILN-ROASTED SALMON

OYSTERS

TROUT

MACKEREL

EEL

COLD-SMOKED SALMON

KIPPER

FINNAN HADDOCK

HALIBUT

WHITE HADDOCK

HERRING

YELLOW HADDOCK

ROUND FISH

Round fish have cylindrical bodies, making it possible to fillet (cut) pieces from both sides of their bodies. Depending on their texture, they are known as either white fish or oily fish.

Tail

CUTS OF SALMON

Tail fillet

Steak

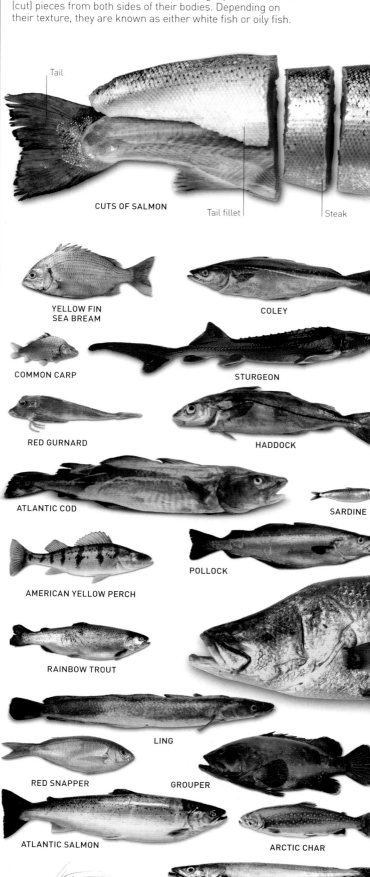

YELLOW FIN SEA BREAM

COLEY

COMMON CARP

STURGEON

RED GURNARD

HADDOCK

ATLANTIC COD

SARDINE

AMERICAN YELLOW PERCH

POLLOCK

RAINBOW TROUT

LING

RED SNAPPER

GROUPER

ATLANTIC SALMON

ARCTIC CHAR

HAKE

JOHN DORY

BLUE COD

Loin fillet

Head

FLAT FISH

Flat fish start life as small round fish, but turn on to their side as they grow. Flat fish are usually cut into long slices along their backbone. If they are large and thick enough, it is possible to cut steaks from them.

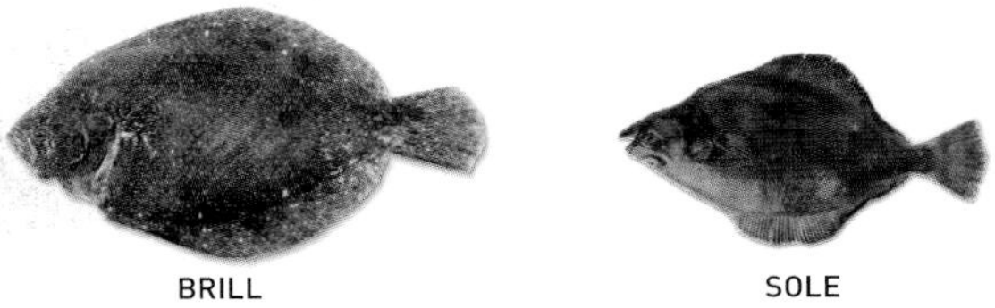

BRILL

SOLE

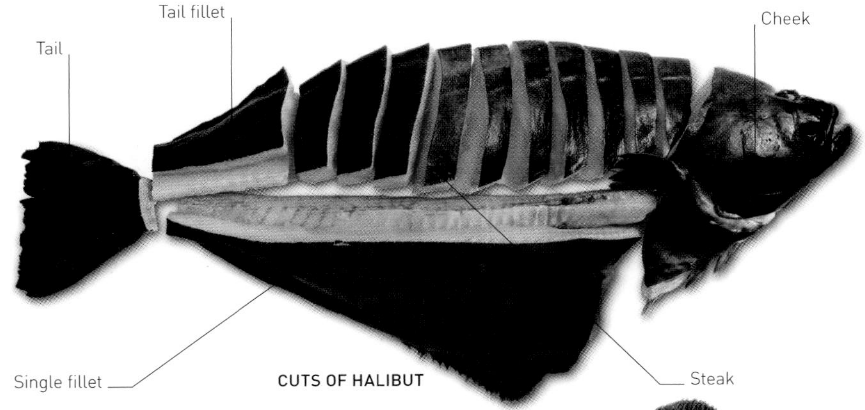

Tail

Tail fillet

Cheek

Single fillet

CUTS OF HALIBUT

Steak

TILAPIA

CATFISH

SAND WHITING

RED TILAPIA

DAB

ATLANTIC MACKEREL

ATLANTIC WHITING

ATLANTIC HERRING

TURBOT

PLAICE

HALIBUT

YELLOWFIN TUNA

FISH ROE

Roe is the name for the ripe eggs that are either found inside a fish's body or released outside it. Roe can be eaten raw or cooked. Sturgeon roe is highly prized and very expensive. It is made into caviar, by curing it in salt.

BELUGA CAVIAR

SEVRUGA CAVIAR

LUMP FISH ROE

FRESH COD ROE

SMOKED COD ROE

HERRING ROE (SOFT)

HERRING ROE (HARD)

SHELLFISH

Shellfish include marine animals such as oysters and mussels that live in shells, as well as creatures like lobsters, crabs, and prawns. They can be used in many recipes.

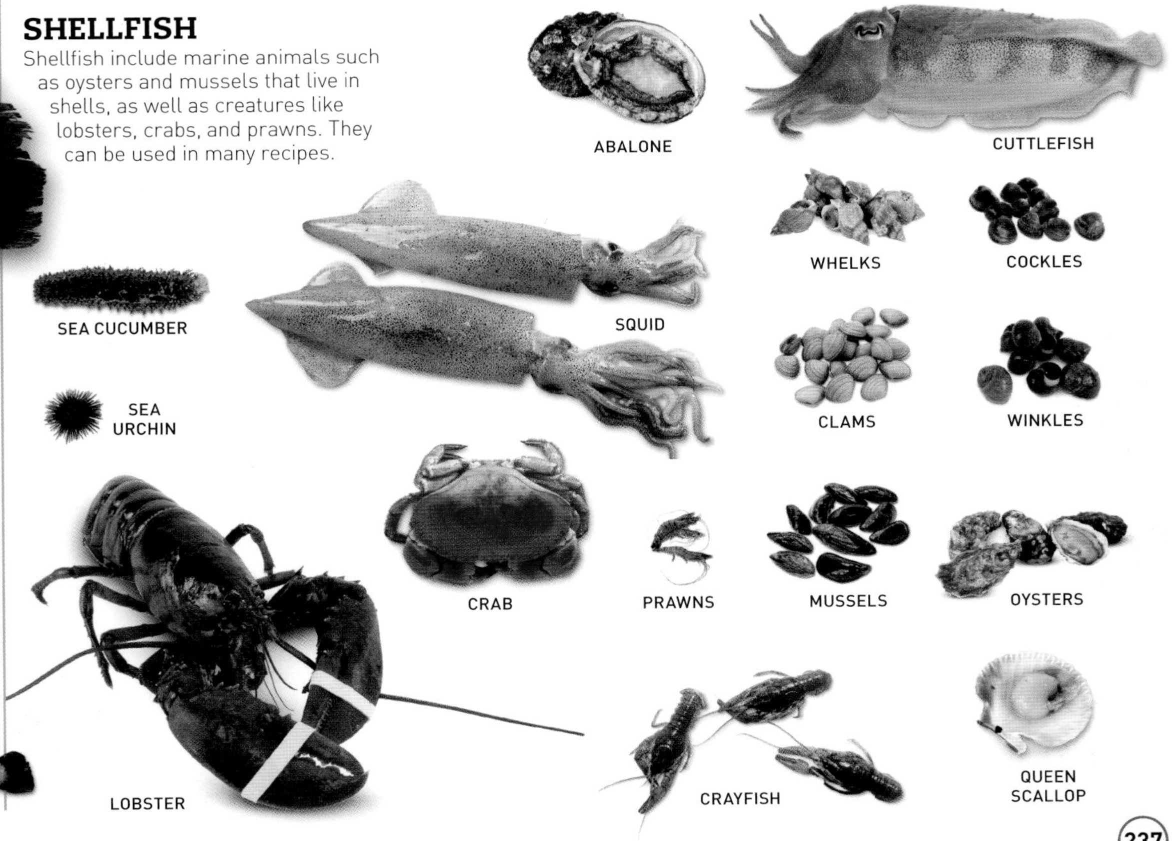

ABALONE

CUTTLEFISH

BARRAMUNDI

SEA CUCUMBER

SQUID

WHELKS

COCKLES

SEA
URCHIN

CLAMS

WINKLES

PIKE

RED MULLET

SEA BASS

MONKFISH

ANCHOVIES

CRAB

PRAWNS

MUSSELS

OYSTERS

MORAY EEL

BREAM

LAKE
TROUT

LOBSTER

CRAYFISH

QUEEN
SCALLOP

Meat

Humans have eaten meat for thousands of years. Animals such as cows, pigs, sheep, and chickens are reared on farms especially to provide us with meat. Other animals live in the wild and are hunted for their meat. A good source of protein, meat can be prepared and cooked in many ways.

MEAT CONTAINS MANY OF THE VITAMINS AND MINERALS THAT ARE IMPORTANT IN A HEALTHY DIET

WHO EATS THE MOST MEAT?

These ten countries eat more meat per person per year than anywhere else in the world.

1 URUGUAY
126.5 kg (279 lb) Favourites: beef, veal, and pork.

2 USA
124 kg (274 lb) Favourites: beef (especially steak), chicken, and pork (especially bacon).

3 CYPRUS
117.6 kg (259 lb) Favourites: chicken and pork (especially tenderloin and preserved forms).

4 SPAIN
113.1 kg (249 lb) Favourites: beef, pork (especially cured hams), and lamb.

5 DENMARK
112.4 kg (248 lb) Favourites: pork (minced and especially preserved forms) and beef.

6 NEW ZEALAND
109.9 kg (242 lb) Favourites: lamb and chicken.

7 AUSTRALIA
108.9 kg (240 lb) Favourites: lamb and beef.

8 CANADA
101.1 kg (223 lb) Favourites: beef, venison, pork (especially preserved forms), chicken, duck, and goose.

9 FRANCE
99.9 kg (220 lb) Favourites: beef, lamb, pork, chicken, and duck.

10 IRELAND
99.4 kg (219 lb) Favourites: beef, pork, and lamb.

BEEF

The meat from a cow is called beef. If the meat comes from a young cow under one month old, it is called veal. Some cuts of beef, such as steaks, are more popular than others and more expensive.

FILLET STEAK

RIB-EYE STEAK

FEATHERBLADE STEAK

BRISKET

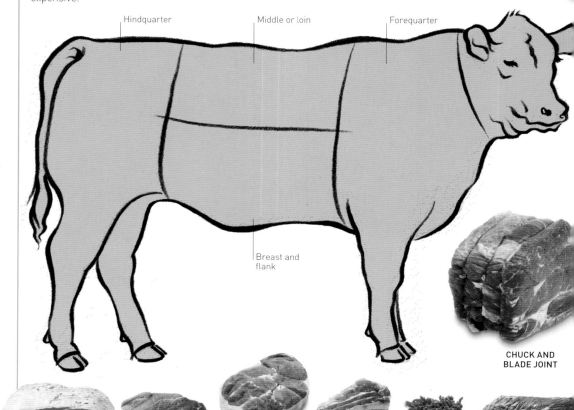

Hindquarter

Middle or loin

Forequarter

Breast and flank

CHUCK AND BLADE JOINT

RUMP

TOPSIDE STEAK

SLICED SHIN

SHORT RIBS

MINCE

HANGER STEAK

DICED VEAL

VEAL CHOP

VEAL ESCALOPE

VEAL TOPSIDE

SHOULDER ROAST

PORK

The meat from a pig is called pork. It can be cured to produce different types of bacon and ham as well as many other kinds of preserved meat products, such as salami.

RACK

TENDERLOIN

LOIN EYE STEAK

DOUBLE LOIN CHOP

HOCK

SAUSAGES

Forequarter

Middle

Hindquarter

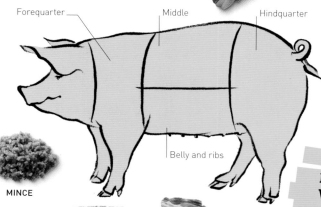

Belly and ribs

MINCE

IN 1920 A BUTCHER IN PARIS CREATED A PERFUME WITH THE POPULAR SCENT OF COOKED BACON

SPARE RIBS

PORK BELLY

LAMB AND MUTTON

The meat from a young sheep under a year old is called lamb. Meat from older sheep or goat is known as mutton. The cuts shown here can be from a sheep or a goat.

SHOULDER JOINT

SHOULDER CHOP

Middle or saddle

Forequarter

Leg

Breast and flank

LOIN

LOIN CHOPS

MINCE

RACK

LEG OF LAMB

SHANK

CHUMP CHOP

POULTRY

Birds that are raised domestically for food are all known as poultry. Types of poultry include chickens, ducks, turkeys, and geese.

TURKEY MINCE

TURKEY ROLL

WHOLE TURKEY

POUSSIN (SMALL CHICKEN)

CHICKEN BREAST

Wing

Breast

Leg

DUCK GOUJONS

WHOLE DUCK

DUCK BREAST

WHOLE CHICKEN

CHICKEN LEG QUARTER

CHICKEN THIGH

CHICKEN DRUMSTICK

DICED CHICKEN

WHOLE GOOSE

PRESERVED MEATS

Most meat can be preserved in different ways. It can be dried, smoked, or cured by soaking it in very salty water, or made into sausages such as salami that can be eaten raw. Pork is the meat that is preserved most often.

SALAME D'OCA

PANCETTA

JAMON

STREAKY BACON

KABANOS

BLACK FOREST HAM

KIELBASA LISIECKA

CHOURICO DE PORCO PRETO

SALAME TOSCANO

PASTRAMI

SALT BEEF

VEAL SALAME

HOFER RINDFLEISCHWURST

SMOKED VENISON

DROEWORS

GAME

"Game" refers to wild birds and animals that are hunted for food. This includes deer, the meat of which is called venison, and birds such as pheasants and pigeons.

SADDLE OF VENISON

Forequarter

Middle or saddle

Hindquarter

GROUSE

DICED VENISON

VENISON MINCE

VENISON FILLET

QUAIL

VENISON STEAK

PHEASANT

MALLARD

PIGEON

PARTRIDGE

TEAL

WOODCOCK

WHOLE HAUNCH OF VENISON

BONED HAUNCH OF VENISON, ROLLED UP

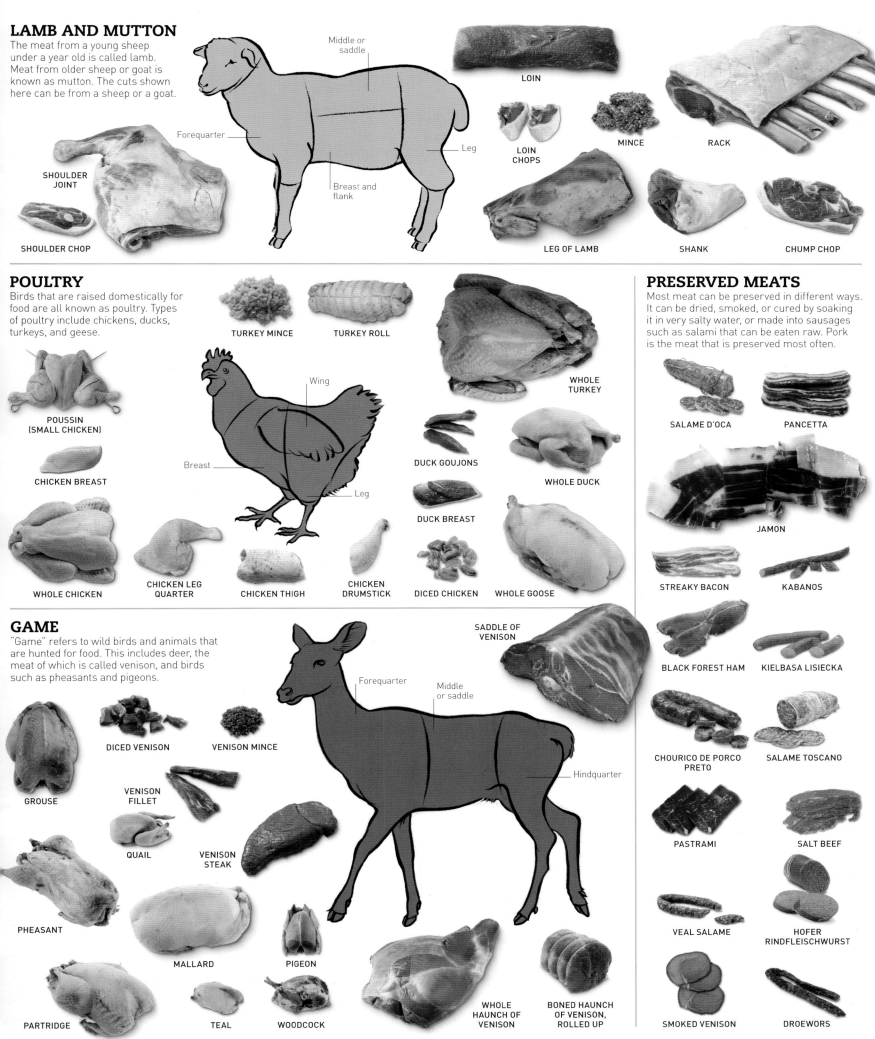

Men's fashion

The style of Western men's clothing, hair, and accessories changes as fast as women's fashion. Even centuries ago men were obsessed with fashion and loved to wear stylish clothes. They often spent more on clothes than women did.

▶ 2ND CENTURY BCE

THE ROMANS
Ancient Rome had strict clothing rules. Roman senators, part of the government, were at the highest level of society – they wore tunics called togas, and sandals.

BROOCH TO HOLD ROBE IN PLACE

ROMAN TOGA STUDDED SANDALS

▶ 5TH CENTURY CE

MEDIEVAL
Rich young men could become knights. They wore metal armour over their legs, while on top they wore a shirt made from metal mesh, called chain-mail. This made it easier for the knight to move and protected him from stab wounds.

LACE-UP CHAIN-MAIL

▶ 1550s

COURT STYLE
The kings of Europe set the trends, wearing new fabrics such as silk from China and Iraq, and cotton from India and Egypt. Clothes came in new colours, too, such as scarlet-red, as exotic dyes were imported from around the world.

◀ 1930s

ELEGANCE
Men dressed to show off their upper body, wearing jackets with padded shoulders and wide lapels to give the illusion of a strong chest. The athletic look was in fashion, so men took up sport to get in shape.

SWIMMING COSTUME

FEDORA HAT

PLUS FOURS AND POLO SHIRT

BAGGY SUIT

◀ 1920s

THE ROARING TWENTIES
Sport was the new trend, so many men dressed in a more casual style, ready for cycling, golf, tennis, athletics, and dancing. Short trousers called plus fours were a popular new fashion.

KNICKERBOCKERS WITH ARGYLE SOCKS

STRIPED ENAMEL CUFFLINKS

OPEN SUMMER SHOES

STRAW BOATER

BROGUES

TWEED CAP

ATHLETIC WEAR

PLUS FOURS AND KNITTED VEST

▶ 1940s

THE FORTIES
There were not many clothes for sale during World War II, as producing food and weaponry was more important. Men made do with fewer suits and dressed simply, although shoes and hats were still key accessories.

BAGGY TROUSER SUIT

TRILBY HAT

CASUAL ATTIRE

AVIATOR SUNGLASSES

SPECTATOR SHOES

▶ 1950s

SMART CASUAL
After years of wearing military uniforms, men wanted to relax and wear more casual clothes. Pinstripe, double-breasted suits were popular, and so were shorter Italian-style jackets. Young men developed their own style, and jeans were especially fashionable.

LEATHER JACKET

HOMBURG HAT

SUEDE SHOES WITH CREPE SOLES

COWBOY JEANS

FORMAL SUIT

▶ 1960s

THE NEW DANDIES
Young men wanted to show off and stand out. They wore slim, ankle-length trousers or jeans with tight-fitting shirts or sweaters. Pop music was a big influence on fashion and hairstyles.

BEATLES-STYLE SUNGLASSES

LEATHER COAT, SLIM TROUSERS

POINTED SHOES

LATE 1500s

ELIZABETHAN

Men's clothes became even fancier. Gentleman with money wore fitted velvet jackets with wide, frilly lace collars, and knee-length trousers called breeches with long silk or wool socks.

SUIT WITH RUFF

BREECHES WITH PADDED JACKET

1700s

ROCOCO

In Europe a new style came into fashion, Rococo, which was more glamorous than anything before. Men's clothes were richly decorated. They wore huge wigs and make-up to complete the look.

LINEN UNDERSHIRT

TIGHT WAISTCOAT

FRILLY BOW AND SLEEVES

SUIT WITH WHITE WIG

URS WITH FEATHERED HAT

SHORT TUNIC WITH COLOURED STOCKINGS

1900–10s

THE NEW CENTURY

Male fashion became plainer and more serious. More men worked in offices and dressed to fit in, not to stand out. They wore suits in dark colours with white shirts and ties.

SWIMMING CAP

BOWLER HAT

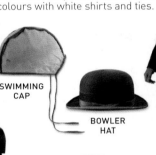

PANAMA HAT

WORK SUIT

FORMAL OUTFIT WITH TOP HAT

1850s

THE GENTLEMAN

Clothes became cheaper because they could be made by machine rather than by hand, so more men could afford to dress well. There were outfits for every occasion, and accessories such as hats, pointy shoes, and walking sticks were important.

EVENING OUTFIT

JACKET AND SLIM TROUSERS

SWIMMING COSTUME

WAISTCOAT AND POCKET WATCH

1800s

THE DANDY

Wealthy men of the 19th century wore top hats and curled their hair and moustaches. Their clothes were tight to show off their figure, and they changed outfits many times a day.

TIGHT JACKETS AND HIGH COLLARS

FITTED COAT WITH HIP POCKETS

1970s

FLARES AND PLATFORMS

Men experimented with fashion and enjoyed dressing up for fun in colourful patterned clothes. Extra-long flared trousers were worn with high platform shoes, and hairstyles were long and shaggy.

BIG SUNGLASSES

PLATFORM SHOES

CHECKED JACKET AND FLARES

FANCY PLATFORMS

1980s and 1990s

INDIVIDUAL STYLE

There were many looks to choose from in the 1980s and 90s. Suits had padded shoulders in the 1980s and became very slim in the 1990s. Many clothing styles were influenced by music such as punk and hip-hop.

PLAIN SUIT WITH PINK STRIPED SHIRT

COWBOY BOOTS

PUNK STYLE

2000s

ANYTHING GOES

Since the start of the new millennium, fashion for men has become very relaxed. Jeans and trainers are the most popular look. Other casual styles include chinos or khaki trousers, worn with polo shirts, graphic T-shirts, or sweatshirts.

SUNGLASSES

CLASSIC TRAINERS

JEANS AND POLO SHIRT

Women's fashion

Fashion is the style of what we wear, and how we wear it. The most important thing about Western fashion is that it changes. Hundreds of years ago, styles altered slowly, but now they move on very fast.

◀ 1300s
FASHION STARTS HERE
Women wore the same type of clothing for centuries, but by the 1300s fashion started changing more quickly and new dress styles were invented. There were strict laws on what to wear but women found ways to break the rules.

WOOL

MEDIEVAL DRESS

◀ 1400–1600s
RICH RENAISSANCE
Beautiful soft new materials, such as silk and velvet, became available to the rich. Skirts became wider, and mix-and-match clothes were popular. Sleeves could be untied and taken off for washing.

ORNATE HANDBAG

VELVET DAY DRESS

OUTDOOR SHOES

COURT DRESS

◀ 1940s
THRIFTY FORTIES
During World War II, material was scarce. Women dressed sensibly and learned how to make and recycle their own clothes. They still wanted to look stylish, using colourful accessories to add personality to plain outfits.

HAT WITH FLOWERS

LITTLE EVENING HAT

MAKE DO AND MEND

WAR ADVERT
To encourage women to make clothes last longer.

EMERALD-GREEN HEELS

HAIR TIED UP, KNEE-LENGTH DRESS

MATCHING HAT, GLOVES, AND SHOES

◀ 1930s
GLAMOROUS GOWNS
In this decade, fashion was inspired by Hollywood film stars. Long, slinky dresses were designed to create a slender look. Jackets had padded shoulders, which made the waist and hips look narrower.

WHITE SATIN EVENING DRESS

FLORAL DRESS

WIDE-BRIMMED STRAW HAT

ELEGANT LEATHER GLOVES

DRESS PATTERN

FITTED JACKET AND SKIRT

▶ 1950s
THE "NEW LOOK"
Designer Christian Dior created a new way of dressing in the 1950s. The look was very feminine, with a tight waist, swirling skirt, pearl necklaces, and earrings. Gloves and hats were almost always worn when leaving the house.

DAY HANDBAG

LONG SUIT DRESS

PEEP-TOE HEELS

▶ 1960s
THE SWINGING SIXTIES
London designer Mary Quant invented the mini skirt. Hems were the shortest they had ever been in the history of fashion. Shiny fabrics, space-age silver, knee high boots, and lots of eye make-up were popular.

PLASTIC ZIP-UP JACKET

SILVER BOOTS WITH POINTED TOES

POLKA-DOT MINI DRESS

STRIPED SEQUINNED MINI

1700s

THE FLAMBOYANT 1700s

French Queen Marie Antoinette became one of the first fashion celebrities. She loved clothing and often changed her outfits. Bright colours and ornate dresses were in fashion.

RED FOOTWEAR

HIGH-HEELED SHOES

DELICATE SILK BOOTS

DAINTY DANCING SLIPPERS

FORMAL DRESS, FRONT AND BACK

▶ 1850–1900s

THE VICTORIANS

Victorian women tried all sorts of tricks to change their body shape. They wore huge petticoats called crinolines under their skirts to make their hips look wide, or pads over their bottoms, called bustles. This made their waists look smaller.

1 CAGE CRINOLINE
Step into the crinoline and pull it up to the waist.

2 DOME SHAPE
Tie it at the waist. A skirt worn on top forms a dome shape.

BONNET WITH RIBBONS

FAN

CORSET WORN UNDER DRESS

TARTAN DRESS

BLACK GOWN WITH BUSTLE

1920s

THE JAZZ AGE

In the 1920s, more women worked, played sport, went to parties, and lived on their own. They wore loose, knee-length dresses, or trousers, so they could move freely, especially when dancing to jazz music.

UNEVEN HEMLINE

NO SLEEVES, PRETTY DECORATION

SIMPLE STYLE WITH STRIPES

SMALL, NEAT HAT

PATTERNED SILK SHOES

LACE-UPS FOR WALKING

PURSE WITH EGYPTIAN SYMBOLS

SPARKLY EVENING PURSE

SHORT HAIR, LONG BEADS, STRAIGHT DRESS

◀ 1900–20s

BELLE EPOQUE

During the Belle Epoque – French for "the beautiful era" – women wore pretty dresses with puffed sleeves, lace, frills, and feathered hats. Using special underwear, they created an S-shape body, with a big bust, tiny waist, and a big bottom.

LONG CORSET WORN UNDER DRESS

LACE-UP BOOTS

HIGH HEELS

SILK PURSE

LACE-COVERED DRESS

1970s

HIPPY STYLE

Bright colours, big patterns, big hair, and even bigger shoes were in fashion in the 1970s. Long skirts and dresses and wide flared trousers were worn with high platform boots or sandals. Indian-style accessories and decoration were also popular.

FLOPPY FLOWERY HAT

PATCHWORK MAXI DRESS

PLATFORM SANDALS

▶ 1980s and 1990s

THE STYLISH 80s AND 90s

Punk music and punk style ruled the streets in the 1980s. The look included ripped jeans, tight T-shirts, heavy black boots, and tartan skirts. By the 1990s, stretchy "body-con" dresses and all-black outfits were fashionable.

Shoulder pads

METALLIC STILETTOS

PUNK TARTAN MINI AND PINK LEGWARMERS

HEAVY BOOTS

TIGHT BODY-CON DRESS

HEAD-TO-TOE BLACK

▶ 2000s

ANYTHING GOES

In the new century, fashion is casual but creative. Jeans and trainers are the most popular outfit for young people – accessories add an individual touch. Styles from the past few decades are mixed to make new looks.

TAN LEATHER SATCHEL

BLUE BOWLING BAG

HIGH-TOP TRAINERS

CHUNKY-HEELED SANDALS

JEANS WITH CASUAL TOPS

Sports and hobbies

Ball sports

Ball games have been played for at least 3,500 years, and today there are hundreds of different kinds. Some can be played by a single person, while others involve as many as 30 players and need a huge pitch to play on.

MARBLE
Two players take turns to knock an X-shaped group of marbles from a large chalked circle, by throwing one marble.

SQUASH
A game played by two people on a walled, indoor court. Players use rackets to bounce the ball off the walls and floor.

TABLE TENNIS
This fast game is also known as ping pong. Two players hit a very light ball back and forth over a small net on a special table.

GOLF
Golf is played on huge grass cou with 18 holes. Gol use various club hit the small, dim ball into the hole

REAL TENNIS
The oldest racket sport, real tennis is played on an unusual indoor court. Players hit a felt-covered cork ball back and forth across a net, using wooden rackets.

TENNIS
Played on a variety of different surfaces. Players hit a felt-covered bouncy ball to each other across a net using tightly strung graphite or fibreglass rackets.

BOULES
Played outside, two teams throw large, very heavy, metal balls, "boules", towards a small target ball known as a "jack". The team that gets the ball closest to the jack wins.

HURLING
A traditional Irish game played on a grass pitch. Players use a flat-ended, curved stick to catch, bounce, and toss the ball to each other in order to score goals.

CRICKET
Two teams of 11 players each take turns to bat and field. Batsmen score "runs" by running between two areas, known as the wickets, while the other team tries to get them "out".

HOCKEY
Played on a large outdoor grass pitch by two teams of 11. Players pass the ball to each other using sticks with a hook-shaped end and try to score goals in their opponent's net.

SEPAK TAKRAW
Also known as kick volleyball, two teams of three players face each other on either side of a high net. The teams kick the ball over the net, winning a point if their opponents let the ball touch the ground inside the court.

HANDBALL
Two teams of seven players bounce and throw the ball to each other using only their hands, and try to score goals. Handball is played indoors and players can take a maximum of three steps while holding the ball.

VOLLEYBALL
Two teams of six players stand on either side of a high net. One player serves the ball over the net using his or her hand and the other team must hit it back. The teams try to hit the ball back and forth, but if the ball hits the ground the other team gets a point.

BEACH VOLLEYBALL
This form of volleyball is played by two teams of two or more players on a beach or sandy court. The ball must be hit, not caught; if it touches the ground, the other team wins a point.

DODGEBALL
Dodgeball is played indoors or outdoors on a small court divided into two equal sections. Two teams of six to ten players start with three balls each, and try to hit someone from the other team by throwing the ball at them. If they succeed, that player is out – the aim is to get all the opposing players out.

NETBALL
Netball is played by two teams of seven players on a hard indoor or outdoor court. Players must not run with the ball, they are only allowed to move one foot in order to turn and pass the ball to a team-mate. The aim is to throw the ball into a netted hoop and score a goal.

BASKETBALL
Two teams of five players move the ball up and down a court by bouncing the ball with one hand as they run, or by throwing it to another team member. The aim is to score goals by shooting the ball through one of the raised hoops that sit at either end of the court. A goal is known as a "basket".

HAND-PELOTA
One of many forms of pelota, hand-pelota is played on a court with two walls. The small, hard ball is hit with bare hands.

SNOOKER
This is played on a large, cloth-covered table with six pockets. Players take turns to knock the 22 balls into the pockets, using wooden cues (sticks).

POOL
Similar to snooker, but played on a smaller table with only eight balls. Two or four players use cues to knock the coloured balls into the pockets.

RACQUETBALL
A fast game, played on an enclosed indoor court. Two or four players use rackets to bounce the rubber ball off the four walls and the ceiling.

ROUNDERS
An outdoor bat-and-ball game for two teams of 11 players. The batting team try to score "rounders" by hitting the ball and running around four bases.

BANDY
Played on an ice rink, similar in size to a football pitch. Players use sticks to shoot an orange ball through nets at either end of the rink.

LACROSSE
A fierce outdoor sport in which two teams of ten players try to shoot a rubber ball into each other's goals using long sticks with nets at the top.

BASEBALL
Two teams of nine take turns to bat and field. Batters hit a ball thrown by the "pitcher" and then run around four bases. The fielding team tries to get the batting team "out".

POLO
Two teams of four players ride horses while trying to hit the plastic ball into a goal using long sticks called mallets. Games are divided into periods of time known as "chukkas".

CROQUET
An outdoor game, players use a small mallet to hit balls through metal hoops placed in the ground. Players take turns and must play the hoops in order; the first to finish wins.

SHOT PUT
Competitors take turns to throw a heavy metal ball (known as the "shot") from a standing position. The person who throws the shot the furthest wins.

SOFTBALL
Softball is a variant of baseball, played using a larger ball on a smaller pitch. It can be played inside or outside by teams of nine or ten. The ball must be pitched with an underarm motion.

BOWLS
Bowls can be played on an indoor or outdoor area known as a bowling green. Players try to roll weighted bowls as close as possible to a small ball, or "jack", at the end of the green.

FOOTBALL
Two teams of 11 players each try to score goals by kicking a football from one to another and then into netted goals at either end of a large grass pitch. Variants of the game can be played indoors or on the beach.

GAELIC FOOTBALL
In Gaelic football, two teams of 15 players can kick, "hand-pass" (hit), or run with the ball for up to four steps. A goal is scored by kicking or hand-passing the ball over the top of a high crossbar.

WATER POLO
This game is played in a swimming pool. Two teams of seven players throw the ball to one another while treading water. The aim is to throw the ball into a net guarded by a goalkeeper.

BOWLING
This is also called "ten-pin bowling" because players try to knock down ten long, bottle-shaped objects, known as pins. Players score points for the number of pins knocked down in each set, after having two attempts.

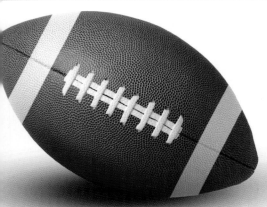

AMERICAN FOOTBALL
Played by two teams of 11 players on a large pitch, the aim is to get the ball into the other team's "end zone" and score a touchdown. The team with the ball has four chances to move the ball forwards by throwing or running with it in 10 yd (9 m) chunks. If it succeeds, it has four more chances to move another 10 yd (9 m). If it fails, the other team wins possession of the ball.

RUGBY
Two teams of 13 (rugby league) or 15 (rugby union) players try to move the ball down the pitch by running with it, passing it to team members, or kicking it. The opposing team tries to tackle the player with the ball to gain possession. Points are scored by getting the ball to the opposite end, or by kicking it through one of the tall, H-shaped goals.

AUSTRALIAN RULES FOOTBALL
This game is played by two teams of 18 players on an oval pitch. The aim is to get the ball to the opponent's end of the pitch and score points by kicking the ball through a set of goals. Players may use any part of their body to move the ball, but they cannot throw it. If they run with it, they must bounce it after every few steps.

Football

Football is one of the most popular sports in the world. Its appeal is its simplicity: all you need to play is a ball, and then you can play virtually anywhere – on grass, indoors, in the street, or even on the beach.

THE GAME
During a football match, two teams of 11 players try to kick a ball into each other's goal. The aim is to score more goals than the other team. If no one scores any goals, or the scores are equal at the end of the game, it is called a draw.

LASTS 90 MINUTES

45 45
TWO HALVES OF 45 MINUTES

HAS TWO TEAMS OF 11 PLAYERS

THE BALL
The first footballs were made of inflated pigs' bladders covered with leather. They were heavy and not very bouncy, especially if they got wet. Modern footballs are made of high-tech materials and are much lighter and bouncier.

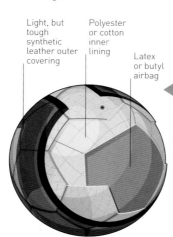

Light, but tough synthetic leather outer covering

Polyester or cotton inner lining

Latex or butyl airbag

THE PITCH
A football pitch must be flat and rectangular. The field of play is marked by white lines, and the goals must be a standard size. However, the length and width of the pitch may vary.

Technical area

Halfway line

Referee

Goal line

6 yard (5.5 m) box

Touchline

Fourth official

Assistant referee

9.15 m (10 yd)

16.5 m (18 yd)

45–90 m (50–100 yd)

90–120 m (100–130 yd)

Goal

5.5 m (6 yd)

Centre spot and centre circle

Penalty area

Penalty spot

Corner arc

PLAYERS AND POSITIONS
There are four main types of player on each team.

1 GOALKEEPER
Every team has a goalkeeper. If the goalkeeper is injured or sent off, he or she must be replaced.

2 DEFENDERS
Their job is to stop the other team scoring, so defenders are usually strong and good at heading and tackling.

3 MIDFIELDERS
The players in the middle of the pitch need good all-round ball skills as they have to defend and attack.

4 FORWARDS
Sometimes known as strikers, these players usually score most of the team's goals. They must be good at shooting.

FORMATIONS
Before a match, the manager organizes the players in a way that he or she thinks will help them to win. This is known as the formation. The formation is usually a set of three or four numbers, which show how many defenders, midfielders, and forwards there are. Often teams will start a match in one formation and then change during the game.

GOALKEEPER
Every team must have a goalkeeper, so he or she is not included in the formation.

4-4-2
In this basic formation there are four defenders, four midfielders, and two forwards. The two central midfielders have different roles – one defensive and one attacking.

3-5-2
This is an attacking formation. The two wide midfielders, often known as wing backs, have to help out in both defence and attack.

4-5-1
This is a defensive formation. There is only one striker, who receives support from the wide midfield players.

RULES OF FOOTBALL
During a match, a referee, assisted by officials on each touchline, makes sure the game is played fairly. Football has 17 official rules, or laws. Here are the three most fundamental rules, which apply whether you are playing in the park with friends, or in the World Cup.

○ **NO HANDS**
A goalkeeper is allowed to touch the ball with his or her hands during a match, but only in the penalty area. If another player touches the ball with his or her hand, the opposition wins a free kick. If a defender touches the ball with his or her hand in the penalty area, it is a penalty.

○ **FOUL PLAY**
If a player commits a foul, such as a bad tackle or a handball, a free kick (or penalty if it is inside the penalty area) is awarded to the opposition. For a bad foul or a deliberate handball, a player is shown a yellow card. If that player then commits a second yellow-card offence, he or she will be shown a red card and "sent off" from the pitch. For serious foul play, a player can be shown a straight red card.

○ **OFFSIDE**
The purpose of the offside rule is to make it harder for a side to score goals. Attackers cannot just stand by the goal waiting to score – there must be at least two defenders between them and the goal line when the ball is passed to them. One of these defenders is usually the goalkeeper. If a player is ruled offside, the defending team is awarded a free kick.

FIFA WORLD CUP
The Fédération Internationale de Football Association (FIFA) governs football around the world. Since 1932 FIFA has organized an international competition to find the best football team in the world. It is called the FIFA World Cup and the finals tournament is held every four years. So far, only eight different countries have ever won it.

BRAZIL
5 wins – 1958, 1962, 1970, 1994, 2002

URUGUAY
2 wins – 1930, 1950

GERMANY
4 wins – 1954, 1974, 1990, 2014

ENGLAND
1 win – 1966

ITALY
4 wins – 1934, 1938, 1982, 2006

FRANCE
1 win – 1998

ARGENTINA
2 wins – 1978, 1986

SPAIN
1 win – 2010

AROUND THE WORLD
FIFA has 208 members, but each continent, apart from Antarctica, also has its own football federation. These govern the game in the region and organize international competitions at club and country level.

UEFA (EUROPE) AND CAF (AFRICA) ARE THE LARGEST FEDERATIONS, EACH WITH 52 MEMBERS

ATTACKING SKILLS

The attacking team is the one in possession of the ball and which moves towards the opponent's goal. The players aim to pass the ball to each other and create a goal-scoring opportunity. They have to work together and try to avoid the opposing team. Here are some of the key ball skills attacking players need.

DRIBBLING
Running with the ball at the feet is known as dribbling. It is a vital skill required to beat an opponent.

SHOOTING
If a player is in a position to score a goal, he or she can use the inside or outside of the foot, but the top (instep) will produce the hardest shot.

CROSSING
A pass from the edge of the pitch to the centre is called a cross. A cross into the penalty area is hard to defend and can often lead to a goal.

HEADING
Heading the ball can be an attacking or defensive skill. Heading the ball with the middle of the forehead gives maximum power and control, and avoids injury.

OVERHEAD KICK

This is a really impressive way to score a goal. However, it is also a very difficult skill to master. A player has his or her back to the goal and must time the kick perfectly. It is best to practise this kick on soft ground to prevent injury.

1 LIFT OFF Raise your non-kicking leg in the air and push off with the other foot.

2 SCISSOR MOTION As you start to fall backwards, bring your kicking leg up. Your other leg should fall back to the ground.

3 STRIKE THE BALL When your back is parallel to the ground, strike the back of the ball with the top of your foot.

DEFENDING SKILLS

The team without the ball must do everything it can to stop its opponent from scoring a goal. Here are some of the skills a team may use to regain possession of the ball or prevent the other team from scoring a goal. Once the defending team has won the ball, it becomes the attacking team.

TACKLING
A defender can use his or her feet to take the ball away from the attacker. Known as a tackle, timing is very important. If the defender kicks the player instead of the ball, it is a foul.

MARKING
By staying close to his or her opponent, a defender might be able to prevent the attacking team making a pass or even intercept the ball. This is known as marking.

INTERCEPTION
By marking a player closely or guessing where an attacker is going to pass the ball, a defender may intercept it. He or she can then start an attack for their own team.

GOALKEEPING
The goalkeeper is the last line of defence. He or she can use any part of the body to prevent a goal. Goalkeepers need to be strong, agile, and able to react quickly when the ball is struck at them.

DEAD-BALL SKILLS

Corners, throw-ins, free kicks, and penalties are all dead-ball situations known as "set-pieces". Teams will spend a lot of time practising set-pieces as they are good goal-scoring opportunities.

CORNER
If a defender kicks the ball over the goal line, the attacking team is awarded a corner. It is taken from the nearest corner arc.

THROW-IN
When the ball crosses the touchline, whichever team kicked the ball last loses possession. The other team can then throw the ball and begin an attack.

FREE KICK
If a player commits a foul outside the penalty area, the other team will be awarded a free kick. The closer this kick is to the goal, the greater chance the attacking team has of scoring.

PENALTY
If a player from the defending team commits a foul inside the penalty area, the attacking team is awarded a penalty – a one-on-one shot against the goalkeeper.

PENALTIES

Here are the best places to aim for if you want to score a penalty, and the different ways you could strike the ball. Even if the goalkeeper guesses where you will shoot, he or she is unlikely to be able to save it – unless the shot is weak.

WHERE TO AIM YOUR PENALTY
■ Goalkeeper is likely to save, unless he or she dives too early.
■ Goalkeeper may be able to save if shot struck weakly.
■ Goalkeeper is highly unlikely to save.

HOW TO STRIKE THE BALL

PASS THE BALL
This type of penalty is best for accuracy. However, striking the ball in this manner could produce a weak shot that the goalkeeper could easily save.

CHIP THE BALL
Only a confident player should try this shot, which is aimed up and over the goalkeeper. This shot also requires great skill to get it on target.

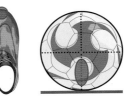

POWER SHOT
A powerfully struck penalty will always beat the goalkeeper – if it is on target. However, increased power also means less accuracy.

American football

Also known as gridiron in some countries, American football is one of the most popular sports in the United States. Professional football (the NFL) and college football are the most popular forms of the game.

THE GAME

Two teams of 11 players compete during four periods of play (known as "quarters"). The aim is to score points by advancing an oval ball into an opponent's end zone (to score a touchdown) or by kicking it through the goal posts (to score a field goal).

**LASTS
60 MINUTES**

**4 QUARTERS OF
15 MINUTES**

**HAS 2 TEAMS OF
11 PLAYERS**

EQUIPMENT

American football is a full-contact sport. Every part of the body needs to be protected against charging players. A helmet is the most vital piece of kit, as head clashes in a game are common. Players also wear body armour worn over soft shock-pads, which absorb any hard blows; this gives them a top-heavy appearance.

- Helmet
- Face mask
- Shoulder pad
- Chest pad
- Hip protector
- Thigh pad
- Knee protector
- Arm guard
- Neck guard

PADDING
A range of pads can be worn to protect specific parts of the body. The sort of protection a player wears often depends on the position in which he or she plays.

THE BALL
The ball is oval in shape. It is 28 cm (11 in) long, has a circumference of 71 cm (28 in) at its widest point, and weighs 425 g (15 oz).

SCORING POINTS

The objective in American football is to score more points than the opposition. Points can be scored in five ways.

O **TOUCHDOWN**
A touchdown is scored if a team advances the ball into the opponent's end zone. The ball can either be run over the line or passed to a team-mate in the end zone. A touchdown is the game's most valuable scoring play, worth six points.

O **POINT AFTER TOUCHDOWN**
After a touchdown, a team can score an extra point by kicking the ball through the goal posts.

O **TWO POINT CONVERSION**
Teams do not have to opt for a kick after scoring a touchdown. Instead, they could opt to score a try. In this instance, the team has a single play to score a touchdown. If successful, the team is awarded an extra two points.

O **FIELD GOAL**
A field goal is scored when the ball is kicked through the goal posts. It is worth three points.

O **SAFETY**
A safety, worth two points, is awarded if an opponent is tackled or spills the ball in his own end zone and it goes out of play.

THE FOOTBALL FIELD

The football field is bounded by long sidelines and shorter end lines, forming a large rectangle. End zones are located at either end of the field. The 100 yd (91 m) area in between is divided by lines that cross the field every 5 yd (4.9 m). Most fields are covered in grass, but some have an artificial surface.

THE CRISS-CROSS PATTERN OF LINES GIVES THE FIELD ITS "GRIDIRON" NICKNAME

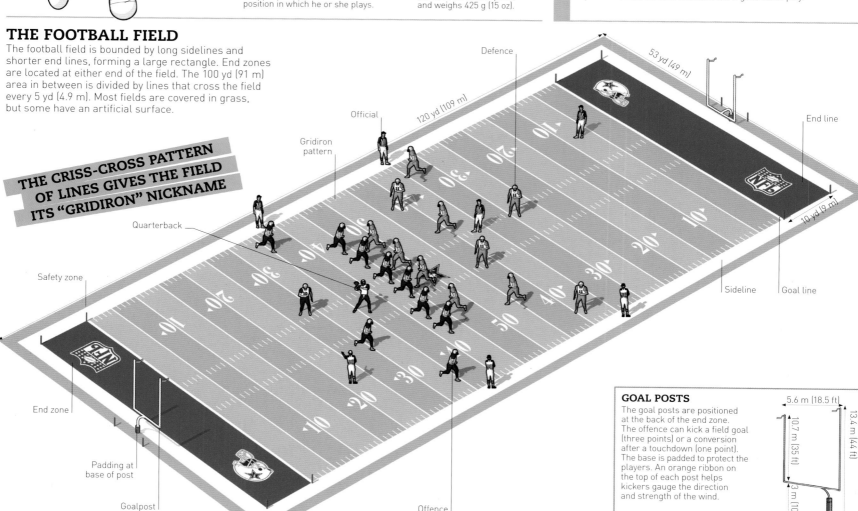

- Defence
- 53 yd (49 m)
- End line
- Official
- Gridiron pattern
- 120 yd (109 m)
- 10 yd (9 m)
- Quarterback
- Sideline
- Goal line
- Safety zone
- End zone
- Padding at base of post
- Goalpost
- Offence

GOAL POSTS

The goal posts are positioned at the back of the end zone. The offence can kick a field goal (three points) or a conversion after a touchdown (one point). The base is padded to protect the players. An orange ribbon on the top of each post helps kickers gauge the direction and strength of the wind.

- 5.6 m (18.5 ft)
- 10.7 m (35 ft)
- 13.4 m (44 ft)
- 3 m (10 ft)

0 YARDS AT A TIME

Territory and possession of the ball are the keys to success in American football. The team in possession of the ball is called the offence. It has four chances, called "downs", to advance the ball 10 yd (9 m) towards the opponent's end zone, either by running with the ball or by throwing it. If successful, the offensive team is awarded another four downs. If it fails to advance 10 yd (9 m), or if it loses possession of the ball during a play, possession of the ball passes to the defensive team.

BASIC DEFENCE

The aim of the defence is to stop the offence from gaining the 10 yd (9 m) they require to gain four new downs. Many teams use a formation called the 4-3 defence, in which four defensive linesmen line up in front of the three linebackers. Two safeties play behind to stop longer passes and runs, while two cornerbacks are positioned to cover any passes made to the wide receivers.

There are five positions in defence:
- **DE**   Defensive end
- **DT**   Defensive tackle
- **LB**   Linebacker
- **CB**   Cornerback
- **S**   Safety

BASIC OFFENCE

The "Standard I Formation" is a common attacking play using five offensive linesmen. The "I" refers to the line formed by the quarterback, fullback, and tailback, or running back. A tight end lines up on one side, with a wide receiver at each end.

There are eight positions in offence:
- **WR**   Wide receiver
- **TE**   Tight end
- **OT**   Offensive tackle
- **G**   Guard
- **C**   Centre
- **QB**   Quarterback
- **FB**   Fullback
- **TB**   Tailback, or running back

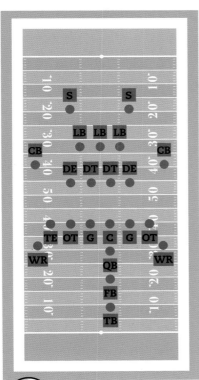

PLAYS

American football is punctuated by a series of plays, or downs. Offensive plays aim to advance the ball towards the opponents' end zone. Defensive plays aim to stop the offence moving forwards. Some of the most well-known plays are described below.

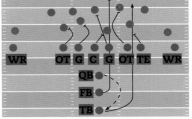

TAILBACK OFF-TACKLE
The tailback off-tackle is the most common running play in offence. The quarterback hands the ball to the tailback, who runs through a hole created by the offensive tackle and the tight end.

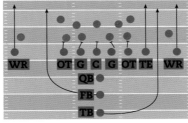

HAIL MARY
The Hail Mary is a passing play in which the quarterback throws a long ball towards one of a number of receivers. The play is often used as a last resort by a trailing team towards the end of the game.

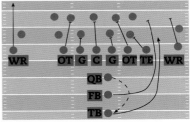

SWEEP
The sweep is an organized offensive running play in which a tailback receives the ball from the quarterback and then runs parallel to the line of scrimmage. This gives the fullback and offensive linesman time to create a gap for the tailback.

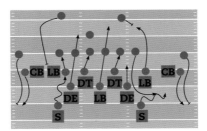

THE BLITZ
The blitz is a defensive tactic used to combat passing plays. The aim is to put the opposition quarterback under pressure by swamping the offence with defenders.

KEY SKILLS

Different positions require different skills. For example, quarterbacks need to be good at throwing; wide receivers must have lightning acceleration and be able to catch the ball; and defenders must be excellent tacklers and blockers.

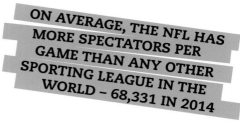

PASSING THE BALL
One of the most important duties of a quarterback is to pass the ball to a receiver. A strong, accurate pass is vital, as the quarterback may have to throw the ball over a long distance.

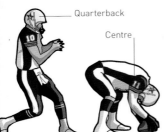
Quarterback
Centre

1 THE SNAP
The centre snaps the ball through his legs to the quarterback.

2 THE PASS
After collecting the ball, the quarterback grips the ball by the laces and passes it point first. The ball is spun as it is thrown, making it fly straight.

KICKING
All American football teams have a specialist kicker. His or her role is to kick for field goals or for the extra point following a touchdown. For a field goal attempt, the holder stands 7 yd (6 m) behind the centre, who snaps the ball to him. The holder catches the ball and sets it up for the kicker. The kicker steps forwards and swings his foot through the ball, aiming to send it between the goal posts.

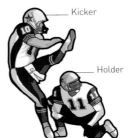
Kicker
Holder

ON AVERAGE, THE NFL HAS MORE SPECTATORS PER GAME THAN ANY OTHER SPORTING LEAGUE IN THE WORLD – 68,331 IN 2014

Defender
Wide receiver

CATCHING
All wide receivers must be able to catch the ball thrown by the quarterback. They sometimes do this running at full speed, and often while having to fight off a defender.

Offensive player
Defensive player

DEFENCE
The main task of a defender is to prevent the offensive side from advancing with the ball. He or she can do this by tackling the offensive player who is carrying the ball.

REFEREE'S SIGNALS

If a rule is broken during the course of a game, an official will bring play to a halt by waving a yellow flag. The referee then conveys the decision by using a hand signal and making an announcement.

INTERFERENCE
A penalty in which a player has interfered with another player during a play.

FIRST DOWN
The offence advances 10 yd (9 m) within four downs, so a new series of downs is called.

FALSE START
This is called when a member of the offence moves illegally before the ball is snapped.

OFFSIDE
A defensive player is on the wrong side of the line of scrimmage at the start of play.

HOLDING
A penalty in which a player of either side has illegally held an opponent.

ILLEGAL BALL TOUCH
A penalty in which the ball is illegally touched, kicked, or batted.

Baseball

Baseball is played in more than 100 countries around the world, including China, Japan, Venezuela, and Cuba. However, the game is often mostly closely associated with the USA, where it is one of the most popular sports.

THE GAME

Two teams take it in turns to bat and field. The batting team tries to score "runs" by hitting the ball and then running around four bases. The fielding team tries to get the batting team "out" (stop it scoring runs). Three "outs" ends the inning and the team with the most runs after nine innings wins.

NO TIME RESTRICTION

9 TURNS (INNINGS) EACH, PLUS EXTRA IF SCORE IS TIED

2 TEAMS OF 9 PLAYERS

EQUIPMENT

The most essential equipment for a game of baseball is, of course, the bat and the ball. As the ball can travel at speeds of up to 160 km/h (100 mph), some safety gear is also required.

BALL
A baseball has a tough rubber and cork core, surrounded by red cotton wool and covered with two strips of leather.

Red stitching

7.5 cm (3 in)

BAT
Professional bats are made from wood and usually weigh up to 1 kg (2.2 lb).

The barrel – where the batter strikes the ball

Tapered handle

Up to 101.5 cm (42 in)

CATCHER'S MASK
Face and head protection is essential for catchers. Batters also wear helmets to protect their heads.

GLOVES
Fielders wear a large, padded leather glove to make it easier and safer to catch the ball. The catcher also has a special mitt.

THE FIELD

The playing area is divided into the infield and the outfield. The infield is also known as the "diamond" and is where the batter, pitcher, and catcher all stand. It also contains the four bases and some fielders. The rest of the fielders stand in the outfield area.

IF A BATTER HITS THE BALL SO FAR THAT HE OR SHE CAN RUN AROUND ALL THE BASES IN ONE GO, IT IS CALLED A HOME RUN

HOME PLATE
To hit the ball, the batter stands in a batter's box next to the home plate, which also serves as the fourth base.

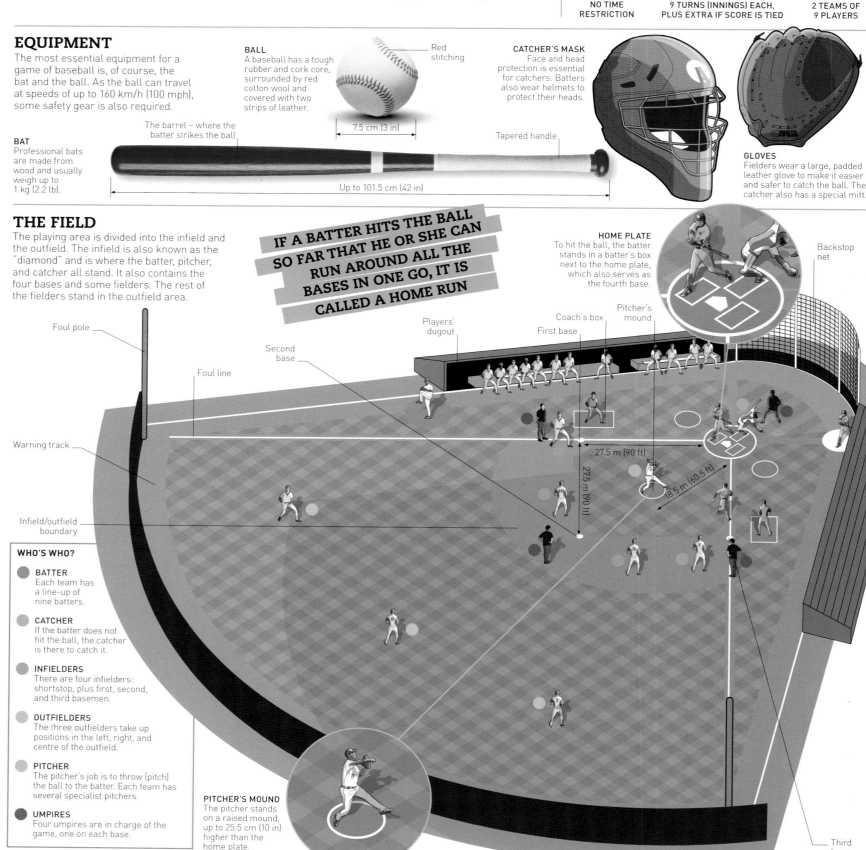

Foul pole

Second base

Foul line

Players' dugout

Coach's box

First base

Pitcher's mound

Backstop net

Warning track

27.5 m (90 ft)

27.5 m (90 ft)

18.5 m (60.5 ft)

Infield/outfield boundary

WHO'S WHO?

BATTER
Each team has a line-up of nine batters.

CATCHER
If the batter does not hit the ball, the catcher is there to catch it.

INFIELDERS
There are four infielders: shortstop, plus first, second, and third basemen.

OUTFIELDERS
The three outfielders take up positions in the left, right, and centre of the outfield.

PITCHER
The pitcher's job is to throw (pitch) the ball to the batter. Each team has several specialist pitchers.

UMPIRES
Four umpires are in charge of the game, one on each base.

PITCHER'S MOUND
The pitcher stands on a raised mound, up to 25.5 cm (10 in) higher than the home plate.

Third base

PITCHING

The pitcher's job is to get the batter out. He or she needs to make it difficult for the batter to hit the ball – known as a strike – or place the ball so that the batter will hit it where it will be caught easily.

1 WIND UP
The pitcher starts with his back foot on the pitching rubber and then raises his front leg to waist height.

2 STRIDE
He then plants his front foot firmly on the ground and swings his pitching arm back.

3 PITCH
Finally, the pitcher throws his arm forwards, releasing the ball when the arm is fully extended.

PITCH STYLES

The way that the pitcher grips or releases the ball can affect the speed, force, and angle of the pitch. Here are some common pitches.

FASTBALL
This is a popular pitch. Two fingers over the top of the ball allow it to be released at great speed.

STRAIGHT PITCH
A fastball usually goes straight towards the home plate.

CURVEBALL
A twist of the wrist gives this pitch topspin, which causes it to curve downwards at the last moment.

TAKING A TURN
The best curveballs cause the batter to swing at the wrong spot.

SLIDER
Gripped slightly off-centre, the slider is not quite as fast as a fastball, or as curved as a curved ball.

SPIN
A slider pitch swerves at the last moment, confusing the batter.

KNUCKLEBALL
The most difficult to learn, the knuckleball is gripped with two fingers on the top of the ball and pitched straight.

SLOW PITCH
A knuckleball moves so unpredictably that it is hard for the batter to time his or her swing.

> A CATCHER WILL SUGGEST OR "CALL" A PITCH STYLE TO THE PITCHER, BASED ON THE BATTER'S STANCE

STRIKE!

The pitcher must pitch the ball into the area known as the "strike zone". If the batter does not swing at all, misses the ball, or hits it into foul territory, the umpire at the home plate will call "strike". If a batter has three strikes, he or she is out, and it is the next batter's turn.

STRIKE ZONE
The strike zone is the area above the home plate between the batter's knees and the mid-point of his or her torso.

Home plate

BATTING

Batting requires strength, skill, timing, and the ability to out-think the pitcher. Most professional players are considered to be good hitters if they can safely hit three out of ten pitches.

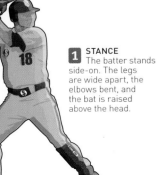

1 STANCE
The batter stands side-on. The legs are wide apart, the elbows bent, and the bat is raised above the head.

2 SWING
As the ball is pitched, the batter takes a big step forwards and swings the bat towards the ball.

3 FOLLOW-THROUGH
The batter completes the swing and then prepares to run to first base, if he has hit the ball.

Bat completes a full swing

Head up to check where the ball has gone

Hips rotate to generate power

WORLD SERIES

Every year the winners of the American League and the winners of the National League compete in a set of games, known as the World Series. These teams have won the most World Series, including some, such as the Giants, who have played in more than one city.

1 **NEW YORK YANKEES** 27

2 **ST LOUIS CARDINALS** 11

3 **PHILADELPHIA/OAKLAND/ KANSAS CITY ATHLETICS** 9

4 **BOSTON RED SOX AND NEW YORK/SAN FRANCISCO GIANTS** 8

5 **BROOKLYN/LOS ANGELES DODGERS** 6

6 **CINCINNATI REDS AND PITTSBURGH PIRATES** 5

7 **DETROIT TIGERS** 4

INTERNATIONAL BASEBALL

Baseball was dropped as an Olympic sport in 2008 and the last Baseball World Cup was held in 2011, so the most prestigious national competition is the World Baseball Classic. Launched in 2006, Japan won the first two competitions, but the Dominican Republic were victorious in 2013.

BASE RUNNING

As soon as the batter hits the ball, they need to start running to first base. However, they must reach the base before a fielder can throw the ball to a team-mate standing on the base.

TAG OUT
The fielder touches the batter with the ball before he or she reaches a base. Out!

SLIDE
The batter slides and touches the base before the base fielder can receive the ball. Safe!

> NICKNAMES FOR A HOME RUN INCLUDE: DINGER, TATER, LONGBALL, MOON SHOT, BOMB, OR GOPHER BALL

Basketball

Basketball is a fast-paced ball sport, invented in Massachusetts, USA, in 1891 as an indoor game to keep students fit during the winter. It was originally played by shooting the ball into fruit-pickers' baskets, which is how the sport got its name.

THE GAME

Two teams of five players each try to score points by shooting a ball through a hoop, which is 3.05 m (10 ft) above the ground. The winning team is the one that has scored most points by the end of the game.

LASTS
48 MINUTES

| 12 | 12 |
| 12 | 12 |
4 QUARTERS OF
12 MINUTES (NBA)

HAS 2 TEAMS OF
5 PLAYERS

EQUIPMENT

One of the attractions of basketball is that you need very little equipment to play – just a ball and two baskets. Players do not even need special clothing, just suitable shoes for running on court.

BALL
A modern ball is made of rubber or a synthetic composite covered in leather. It is 75–78 cm (30–32 in) in circumference and weighs 600–650 g (21–23 oz).

BASKET AND BACKBOARD
The basket is a 45 cm (18 in) hoop with netting hanging from it, mounted on a vertical backboard.

KEEPING SCORE

Spectators keep track of the score on a scoreboard. A basket made inside the three-point line scores two points. Baskets made from beyond the three-point arc score three points. When shooting a free throw, each basket made scores one point.

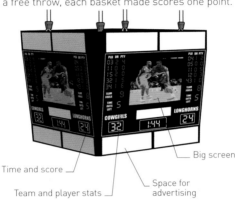

Time and score

Team and player stats

Space for advertising

Big screen

LAWS OF THE COURT

The NBA (National Basketball Association) governs the professional game in the USA. The NBA sets out only 12 basic rules, although each rule is divided into many clauses and subsections. Differing governing bodies worldwide have slightly different rules.

○ **PERSONAL AND TECHNICAL FOULS**
If a team commits a foul, the opposing team is given possession of the ball. If a team is fouled while shooting, they are awarded one or more shots at the basket. Fouls can be either personal – for example for pushing, blocking, or holding an opponent – or technical – for offences such as deliberate time-wasting or arguing with the referee. In the NBA, once a player has recorded six fouls, they may take no further part in the game.

○ **VIOLATIONS**
When a player breaks the rules, they commit a foul. For instance, players must dribble (bounce the ball in front of them) as they run. If they do not, they commit a foul known as "travelling".

○ **TIME LIMITS**
Basketball is designed to be a fast-moving, attacking sport. In the NBA, once in possession of the ball, a team must attempt a shot within 24 seconds; if it does not, possession passes to the other team.

THE COURT

A standard basketball court is a rectangle 15.2 m (50 ft) wide by 28.7 m (94 ft) long. Most, but not all, have a surface of polished wood. The various markings on the court help to regulate play.

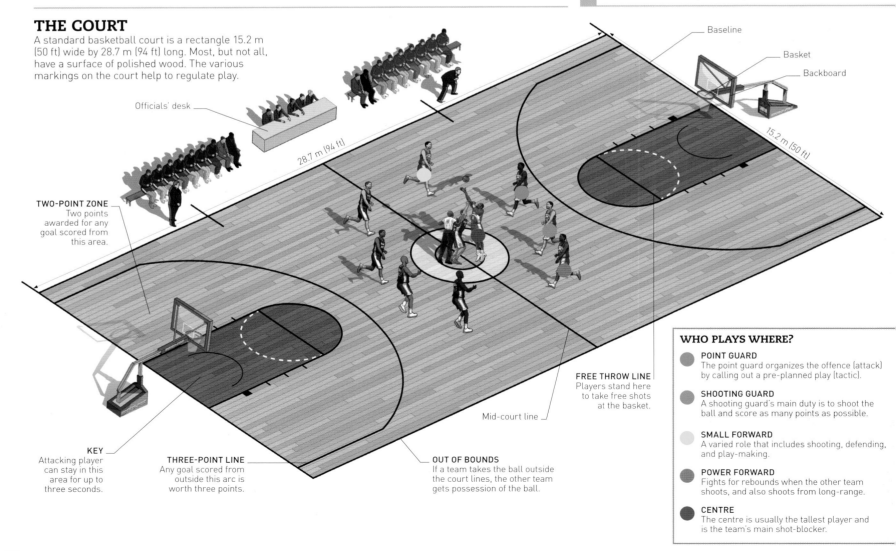

Officials' desk

Baseline

Basket

Backboard

28.7 m (94 ft)

15.2 m (50 ft)

TWO-POINT ZONE
Two points awarded for any goal scored from this area.

KEY
Attacking player can stay in this area for up to three seconds.

THREE-POINT LINE
Any goal scored from outside this arc is worth three points.

Mid-court line

OUT OF BOUNDS
If a team takes the ball outside the court lines, the other team gets possession of the ball.

FREE THROW LINE
Players stand here to take free shots at the basket.

WHO PLAYS WHERE?

● **POINT GUARD**
The point guard organizes the offence (attack) by calling out a pre-planned play (tactic).

● **SHOOTING GUARD**
A shooting guard's main duty is to shoot the ball and score as many points as possible.

● **SMALL FORWARD**
A varied role that includes shooting, defending, and play-making.

● **POWER FORWARD**
Fights for rebounds when the other team shoots, and also shoots from long-range.

● **CENTRE**
The centre is usually the tallest player and is the team's main shot-blocker.

SKILLS AND TECHNIQUES

All basketball players need good ball-handling skills. To be successful, a team needs to be able to pass to each other, dribble, shield the ball from opponents, and, most importantly, shoot baskets.

Ball is thrown hard and low

Ball passes under the defender's arm

BOUNCE PASS
Instead of throwing the ball straight from his chest, a player can bounce the ball to a team-mate. This makes it harder for an opponent to block or intercept the ball.

Wrist is angled to direct the ball downwards

Player holds ball in one or both hands

Player pushes upwards from standing foot

SLAM DUNK
The player runs up, jumps very high, and, with one or two hands, aims the ball downwards into the basket. The slam dunk is a popular shot because, as long as the player can jump high enough, its success rate is high.

The backboard is made of a shatterproof material called Plexiglas

The hoop must be strong enough to withstand players hanging from it

DRIBBLING
Dribbling is the name given to bouncing the ball continuously. A player must dribble while moving with the ball, or else they are penalized for travelling.

1 Using the hand furthest from your opponent, bounce the ball hard towards the ground.

2 Running forwards, control the ball with the fingertips as it rises back up towards you.

3 Keep your hand directly over the ball – if you touch the underside of the ball, you will be penalized.

MOVING
Once a player has stopped dribbling, he or she is not allowed to dribble for a second time. Instead, the player must keep one foot on the ground and pivot (swivel) on it before shooting or passing.

Pivot foot

1 The player stops dribbling or catches the ball. One of his feet must become the pivot foot.

2 The player swivels round on his pivot foot, looking for opportunities to shoot or pass the ball.

3 If a player drags his pivot foot or lifts it off the ground, he will be penalized for travelling.

PLAYING THE GAME
Basketball players require great athleticism, excellent hand-eye coordination, and, because it is such a fast-paced game, superb stamina. They also need to be tall. Players are rarely under 1.8 m (6 ft) and are often as tall as 2.1 m (7 ft).

Large hands enable a player to grip the ball one-handed

Number identifies player

Players wear loose vests and shorts, and air-cushioned trainers

BASKETS AND REBOUNDS
When a team scores a basket, the game restarts with the other team in possession of the ball behind the baseline under their own basket. If the shot is unsuccessful, the players compete for a "rebound". If the attacking team wins the ball, they can shoot again, but if the defending team wins it, they will try to move the ball to the other end of the court.

Strong leg muscles are essential for jumps

TIP-OFF
This is the name given to the jump ball that starts or resumes the game. The referee throws the ball up, and two players jump and try to tip it to a team-mate.

IN THE 1961–62 SEASON, WILT CHAMBERLAIN AVERAGED 50.4 POINTS PER GAME – THE HIGHEST SINGLE-SEASON TOTAL EVER

OFFICIALS' SIGNALS
A team of officials oversees a game. The timekeeper starts the clock when the ball is in play and pauses it whenever play is stopped. The shot-clock operator makes sure that the team in possession shoots within a certain time. There are two referees, who make gestures and signals to indicate aspects of play and breaches of the rules.

CHARGING
One arm out to the side indicates that an attacking player has run into a defender.

JUMP BALL
Both arms up mean that two players have a grip of the ball, so the referee is calling a jump ball.

TRAVELLING
Arms rotating indicate that a player has moved with the ball without dribbling it.

BLOCKING
Clenched fists against the waist signal that one player has blocked the way of another.

TWO-POINT SCORE
Left arm raised with two fingers showing indicates a two-point basket to the scorekeeper.

THREE-POINT SCORE
Both arms up, with three fingers up on each hand, signals a basket worth three points.

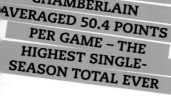
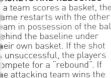

Racket sports

There are many different racket sports, but they all need similar skills: good hand-eye coordination, quick reactions, speed, fitness, and agility. Most racket sports can be played by two people (1 vs 1, known as singles) or four people (2 vs 2, known as doubles).

TENNIS
Players take it in turns to serve and can score points whenever their opponent fails to return a ball over the net or hits the ball out of play. Tennis (also known as lawn tennis) matches are made up of games and sets, with players needing to win six games to win a set. Matches can last for hours as a player must always win the final set by two games.

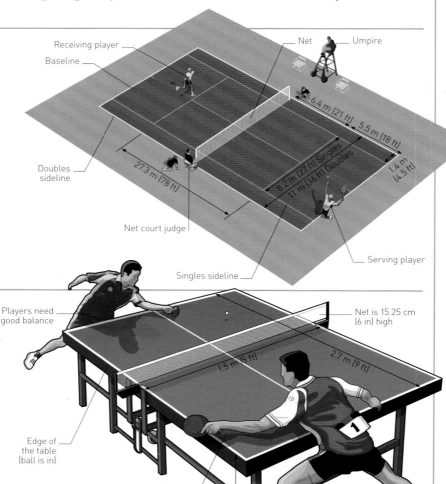

Receiving player

Baseline

Net

Umpire

6.4 m (21 ft)   5.5 m (18 ft)

Doubles sideline

27.3 m (78 ft)

8.2 m (27 ft) Singles
11 m (36 ft) Doubles

1.4 m (4.5 ft)

Net court judge

Serving player

Singles sideline

BEST OF THREE OR FIVE SETS

SINGLES OR DOUBLES

TABLE TENNIS
A player wins a point if his or her opponent cannot return the ball or if the return does not land on the table. The first player to score 11 points wins the game. However, if both players score 10 points, the first player to gain a two-point advantage wins the game. Table tennis is also known as ping pong.

Players need good balance

Net is 15.25 cm (6 in) high

2.7 m (9 ft)

1.5 m (5 ft)

Edge of the table (ball is in)

Players must not touch the table

76 cm (2.5 ft)

Players must react quickly

BEST OF FIVE OR SEVEN GAMES

SINGLES OR DOUBLES

SQUASH
Squash is played on a four-walled court and players take it in turns to serve. They can win points if their opponent fails to hit the ball after it has bounced once, or if they hit the ball out of bounds. A player needs 11 points to win the game, but if the score is tied at 10-10, a player needs to win by two points.

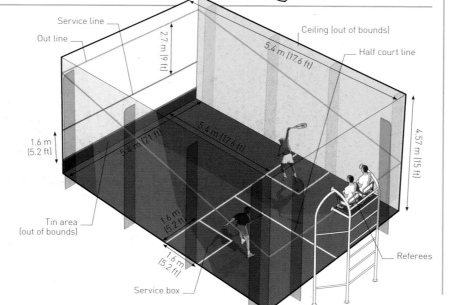

Service line

Out line

Ceiling (out of bounds)

2.7 m (9 ft)

5.4 m (17.6 ft)

Half court line

1.6 m (5.2 ft)

5.4 m (21 ft)

5.4 m (17.6 ft)

4.57 m (15 ft)

Tin area (out of bounds)

1.6 m (5.2 ft)

Referees

1.6 m (5.2 ft)

Service box

THE BEST OF 3 OR 5 GAMES

SINGLES (DOUBLES CAN BE PLAYED ON A BIGGER COURT)

TENNIS RACKET

TENNIS BALL
Tennis balls are made of rubber, covered in felt and weigh 56–59 g (1.9–2 oz). During a match, balls may be hit so hard that they lose their bounce and need to be replaced.

TABLE TENNIS BAT

TABLE TENNIS BALL
Made of celluloid and filled with gas, a table tennis ball weighs a mere 2.7 g (0.1 oz).

SQUASH RACKET

SQUASH BALL
Squash balls are made of hollow rubber. A coloured dot shows how fast or bouncy the ball is – orange is the slowest and blue the fastest.

BADMINTON

A player wins a point if his or her opponent fails to hit the shuttlecock or hits it out of play. The first player to win 21 points wins the game. However, if the score is tied at 20-20, a player must gain a two-point lead to win the game.

BEST OF THREE GAMES

SINGLES OR DOUBLES

BADMINTON RACKET

SHUTTLECOCK
The rounded base is made of cork covered in leather. The top has 16 feathers, which are often plastic.

Line judge (there are ten)

Doubles sideline

Net

Service judge

6.1 m (20 ft) Doubles

5.18 m (17 ft) Singles

Singles side line

Short service line

Umpire

13.4 m (44 ft)

1.98 m (6.5 ft)

0.76 m (2.5 ft)

Doubles service line

Singles service line

PRECISION AND POWER
Badminton shots can be softer than other racket sports due to the shape and weight of the shuttle. However, powerful smash shots are also effective.

REAL TENNIS RACKET

REAL TENNIS BALL
Heavier and less bouncy than a tennis ball, a real tennis ball is made of cork wrapped in felt. They are usually handmade.

If a player serves the ball into one of these windows, it's a point

A server who gets the ball in this grille wins a point

The receiving end

Net

Serving end

29.3 m (96 ft)

9.8 m (32 ft)

THERE ARE ONLY 50 REAL TENNIS COURTS IN THE WORLD AND NO TWO COURTS ARE IDENTICAL

REAL TENNIS

The scoring in real tennis (also known as Court Tennis) is similar to the modern game. However, the court is very different. It is enclosed on all four sides, and three of the sides have sloping roof areas. Courts also have several unusual features such as grilles and windows.

THE BEST OF THREE OR FIVE SETS

SINGLES OR DOUBLES

RACQUETBALL RACKET

6 m (20 ft)

12 m (40 ft)

Ceiling – the ball may hit here and still be in play

Front wall

Service box

4.5 m (15 ft)

45 cm (1.5 ft)

1.5 m (5 ft)

90 cm (3 ft)

1.5 m (5 ft)

4.5 m (15 ft)

6 m (20 ft)

Back wall

Referee

Judge

Judge

RACQUETBALL

Played on a similar court to squash, the objective of racquetball is to hit the ball so that an opponent cannot keep it in play. Points can only be scored by the server, but if the server fails to keep the ball in play, the serve passes to the other player. The first player to reach 15 points wins the game.

THE BEST OF FIVE GAMES

SINGLES, DOUBLES, OR "IRONMAN" (2 VS 1)

RACQUETBALL IS SO FAST THAT PLAYERS USUALLY WEAR GOGGLES TO PREVENT EYE INJURES

RACQUETBALL
Balls are made of rubber to make them bounce. They weigh about 40 g (1½ oz).

Tennis

Playing tennis is fun and helps you to gain some sporting skills. To play the game well, you have to be fast on your feet, quick-thinking, and sharp-eyed. World-class players make tennis exciting to watch, too.

THE MATCH

A tennis match is played in games and sets between two or four people. A game is a series of points won or lost, and a set is a series of games. The player who wins the best out of three or five sets is the match winner. Matches have no time limit.

NO TIME LIMIT

A MATCH CAN BE 3 OR 5 SETS

SINGLES: 2 PLAYERS
DOUBLES: 4 PLAYER

THE COURT

All tennis courts have the same measurements. They are marked by white lines that show the area in which the ball must land. Most courts are marked for both singles play (two players) and doubles (four players). A net divides the court into two equal ends. Around the playing area, various officials watch the match closely.

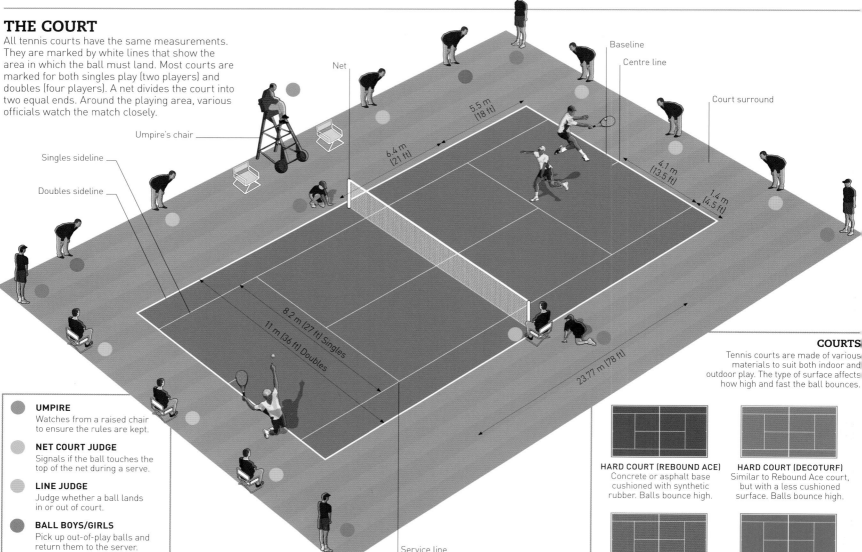

- Umpire's chair
- Singles sideline
- Doubles sideline
- Net
- Baseline
- Centre line
- Court surround
- 5.5 m (18 ft)
- 6.4 m (21 ft)
- 4.1 m (13.5 ft)
- 1.4 m (4.5 ft)
- 8.2 m (27 ft) Singles
- 11 m (36 ft) Doubles
- 23.77 m (78 ft)
- Service line

- **UMPIRE**
  Watches from a raised chair to ensure the rules are kept.

- **NET COURT JUDGE**
  Signals if the ball touches the top of the net during a serve.

- **LINE JUDGE**
  Judge whether a ball lands in or out of court.

- **BALL BOYS/GIRLS**
  Pick up out-of-play balls and return them to the server.

- **FOOT-FAULT JUDGE**
  Checks that a server does not step across the baseline before hitting the ball.

COURTS

Tennis courts are made of various materials to suit both indoor and outdoor play. The type of surface affects how high and fast the ball bounces.

HARD COURT (REBOUND ACE)
Concrete or asphalt base cushioned with synthetic rubber. Balls bounce high.

HARD COURT (DECOTURF)
Similar to Rebound Ace court, but with a less cushioned surface. Balls bounce high.

CLAY COURT
Balls bounce high on this surface but move at a relatively slow speed.

GRASS COURT
Balls move fast with a lower bounce. This surface can be slippery.

SCORING

Both players start with a score of zero, or "love". The first point you win scores 15. If you win a second point, the score is 30. A third point scores 40. One more point can win the game, provided you are already two points ahead of your opponent.

THE "LOVE" SCORE IN TENNIS MAY COME FROM "L'OEUF", FRENCH FOR "EGG" – WHICH IS ZERO-SHAPED

- Set markers
- Sets won
- Score for game in progress

	1	2	3	4		SETS	GAMES	POINTS
	6	7	6		R.FEDERER (1)	2	5	30
					VS.			
	0	6	7		R.NADAL (2)	1	8	40

- Completed sets
- Two sets were decided by tie-breaks
- Players' names
- Score for set in progress

TIE-BREAK

If the score is six games all, a tie-break is played. This game has special rules. A tie-break, and the set, is won when a player wins seven points and is at least two points ahead. There is no tie-break in the final set.

EQUIPMENT

Modern tennis equipment is made of lightweight materials that are strong and long-lasting. Rackets come in varying sizes. It is important to choose one that is the right weight for you and feels comfortable to hold.

BALLS
Frame

- Handle with cushioned grip

RACKET
Strings

THE SERVE

Also called the service, this stroke is the most important one to learn. Every point in a game starts with the serve. It is a tricky technique to master. Even professionals do not hit the ball over the net every time – but a server is allowed to have two attempts per point.

1 POSITION
Stand behind the baseline, just to the right of centre.

2 PREPARE
Turning sideways, hold the racket and ball in front of you.

3 TOSS
Toss the ball up and bend your racket arm back, ready to hit.

4 THROW
Throw the racket over your head and hit the ball. Follow through the stroke.

MAJOR WINNERS

The four biggest annual tennis tournaments, known as "Grand Slams", are: Wimbledon, the US Open, the Australian Open, and the French Open. Below are the top five singles Grand Slam winners.

1 STEFFI GRAF Germany – 22 wins

2 SERENA WILLIAMS USA – 19 wins

3 CHRIS EVERT USA – 18 wins

3 MARTINA NAVRATILOVA Czechoslovakia/USA – 18 wins

4 ROGER FEDERER Switzerland – 17 wins

FOREHAND DRIVE

Using the forehand is the skill that tennis players learn first. With practice, it can become a very powerful stroke. The ball must bounce once before you hit it.

1 RACKET BACK
Take the racket back and up, turn your shoulders to the side, and step forwards.

2 MEET THE BALL
Swing the racket forwards to meet the ball in front of your body. Hit the ball and follow through the stroke with the racket.

FOREHAND VOLLEY

Volley shots are played close to the net. Players must hit the ball before it bounces. The action is short, fast, and punchy, and does not use a big swing.

1 REACH
Stretch out your racket arm and step forwards. Watch the ball all the time.

2 SHORT FOLLOW-THROUGH
After making contact with the ball, finish the stroke with a short follow-through.

THE SMASH

The smash shot uses an action similar to that of the serve. It hits the ball as it comes down from high in the air, and requires fast thinking. You may have to spring up to reach the ball. Fully stretch your racket arm and reach up with the other arm. Drop the racket head behind your back and then accelerate it forwards to hit the ball.

Reach up with your opposite arm

Turn your body sideways and position yourself under the ball

BACKHAND DRIVE

You play this stroke when your opponent hits the ball towards the side opposite your racket arm.

1 SWING BACK
As the ball comes, turn your shoulders to the side and swing your racket back.

2 STEP
With a firm grip on the racket, step forwards to meet the ball. Stretch out your racket arm to hit the ball in front of your body.

3 FOLLOW THROUGH
Keeping the swing going, follow through the shot with your racket. Do not take your eyes off the ball until it is safely over the net.

Turn your shoulders to the side as you take the racket back

DOUBLE-HANDED BACKHAND
Two hands can give extra strength and power a backhand drive.

BACKHAND SLICE

Once you have mastered the basic backhand, you can try the more challenging backhand slice. A ball hit with this stroke spins and lands low, so it can take your opponent by surprise.

1 BACK
Take the racket back as you would for the backhand drive, with the head angled slightly up.

2 SLICE
Step into the shot and slip the head of the racket under the ball. Hit the ball when it is just in front of your body.

3 FOLLOW-THROUGH
Keep your arm straight and follow through with a short chopping movement. This part of the stroke is important, as it drives the ball forwards.

Athletics

The athletics arena is home to three main different sports styles: running, jumping, and throwing. Competitors need speed, stamina, agility, or strength, depending on their chosen event. All-round athletes have all these skills.

SET UP

Athletics events are also known as "track and field events". Running races take place on the track, and jumping and throwing events are held in an area known as the field. There are also two walking events on the track.

RUNNING

THROWING

JUMPING

ATHLETICS TRACK

The athletics area is marked out by a running track 400 m (328 yd) in circumference, with the field area for throwing and jumping events inside it. Shorter races use just one section of the track. In long-distance races, athletes circuit the track many times.

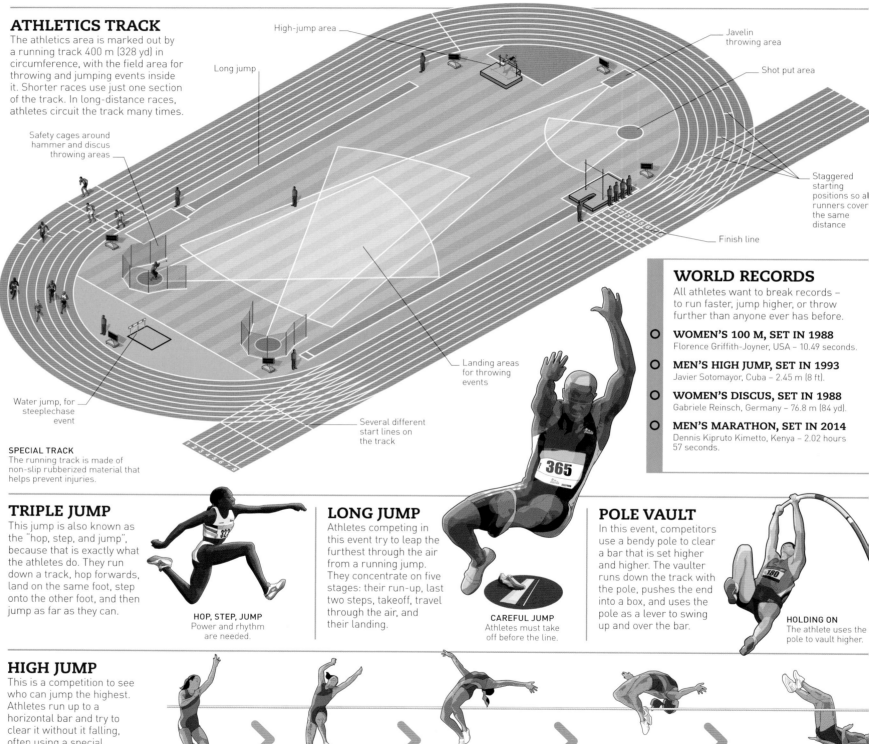

High-jump area

Long jump

Safety cages around hammer and discus throwing areas

Water jump, for steeplechase event

Javelin throwing area

Shot put area

Staggered starting positions so al runners cover the same distance

Finish line

Landing areas for throwing events

Several different start lines on the track

SPECIAL TRACK
The running track is made of non-slip rubberized material that helps prevent injuries.

WORLD RECORDS

All athletes want to break records – to run faster, jump higher, or throw further than anyone ever has before.

- **WOMEN'S 100 M, SET IN 1988**
  Florence Griffith-Joyner, USA – 10.49 seconds.

- **MEN'S HIGH JUMP, SET IN 1993**
  Javier Sotomayor, Cuba – 2.45 m (8 ft).

- **WOMEN'S DISCUS, SET IN 1988**
  Gabriele Reinsch, Germany – 76.8 m (84 yd).

- **MEN'S MARATHON, SET IN 2014**
  Dennis Kipruto Kimetto, Kenya – 2.02 hours 57 seconds.

TRIPLE JUMP

This jump is also known as the "hop, step, and jump", because that is exactly what the athletes do. They run down a track, hop forwards, land on the same foot, step onto the other foot, and then jump as far as they can.

HOP, STEP, JUMP
Power and rhythm are needed.

LONG JUMP

Athletes competing in this event try to leap the furthest through the air from a running jump. They concentrate on five stages: their run-up, last two steps, takeoff, travel through the air, and their landing.

CAREFUL JUMP
Athletes must take off before the line.

365

POLE VAULT

In this event, competitors use a bendy pole to clear a bar that is set higher and higher. The vaulter runs down the track with the pole, pushes the end into a box, and uses the pole as a lever to swing up and over the bar.

HOLDING ON
The athlete uses the pole to vault higher.

180

HIGH JUMP

This is a competition to see who can jump the highest. Athletes run up to a horizontal bar and try to clear it without it falling, often using a special technique called the Fosbury Flop (shown here). They land on a cushioned area to prevent injury.

1 TAKEOFF
The jumper pushes into the air from one leg.

2 MOVING UP
She starts to twist her body so that her back faces the bar.

3 ARCHING BACK
Her body arches backwards.

4 HIGH POINT
She kicks her legs up to clear the bar.

5 LANDING
She positions her arms in preparation for landing.

JAVELIN

Athletes compete to see who can throw the javelin (which is a bit like a "spear") the furthest down the field. Men throw a slightly longer javelin than women.

Javelin

SHOT PUT

The "shot" is a heavy metal ball that competitors try to throw ("put") as far as they can. At the beginning of each put, the shot is held close against the neck, and the shot putter spins around in a circle before hurling the shot forwards.

Women's shot
4 kg (8 lb 12 oz)

Men's shot
7.2 kg (16 lb)

HAMMER

The "hammer" in athletics is nothing like a normal hammer – it is a heavy metal ball attached by a wire to a handle. The thrower whirls the hammer around his or her head several times before releasing it. Men throw a heavier hammer than women.

Hammer

DISCUS

A discus is a fairly flat, heavy disc that spins through the air when it is thrown hard. The women's discus weighs 1 kg (2.2 lb) while the men's weighs 2 kg (4.4 lb). The winner is the person who throws it furthest.

1 PRELIMINARY SWING
Holding the discus in one hand, the athlete starts to swing it back and forwards.

2 TURNING CIRCLE
The athlete spins around one and a half times, gaining momentum.

3 RELEASE
At the front of the circle, the athlete sends the discus flying into the air.

4 FOLLOW-THROUGH
After releasing the discus, the athlete is careful to stay within the circle.

MULTI-PART EVENTS

In these track and field events, competitors need to be all-round athletes with a combination of skills.

○ **HEPTATHLON**
This two-day competition for women includes seven events: 200 m, 100 m hurdles, high jump, shot put, long jump, javelin, and 800 m.

○ **DECATHLON**
Men compete in ten events in this two-day competition: 100 m, long jump, shot put, high jump, 400 m, 100 m hurdles, pole vault, discus, javelin, and 1,500 m.

MIDDLE-DISTANCE RUNNING

These races are run over 800–3,000 m, and some, like the steeplechase, include hurdles and water jumps. The runners start off in lanes but do not usually have to stay in their lane throughout the race.

LONG-DISTANCE RUNNING

Races that are more than 3,000 m (3,280 yd) long are called "long-distance" races and demand great stamina. The events may take place in a stadium or along roads and paths. Many cities hold annual marathons, which are 42.2 km (26.2 miles) long.

DISTANCE EVENTS

There are eight Olympic middle- and long-distance events on the track. The 3,000 m steeplechase includes 35 jumps, seven of which are water jumps.

800 m	10,000 m
1,500 m	Marathon
3,000 m Steeplechase	20 km walk
5,000 m	50 km walk (men only)

SPRINT EVENTS

In the Olympics, there are eight sprint events. Some include hurdles.

100 m	110 m hurdles (men only)
200 m	400 m hurdles
400 m	4 x 100 m relay
100 m hurdles (women only)	4 x 400 m relay

SPRINTING

These fast races are run over distances from 100–400 m. Sprinters push off from the blocks and hit top speed almost immediately.

RUNNING ALONE
Most races involve individual runners.

RUNNING A RELAY
Teams of four run one leg of the race each, passing on a baton.

HURDLES
Competitors have to jump hurdles while running.

WHEN USAIN BOLT BROKE THE 100 M WORLD RECORD IN 2009, HE COVERED AN ASTONISHING 12.2 M (40 FT) PER SECOND

SPRINT START

In short sprints, getting off to a clean, fast start can make the difference between winning and losing the race.

1 READY
The sprinter gets ready by crouching and setting both feet firmly against the blocks.

2 GET SET
The athlete's body raises into a bridge, with the hips raised above the shoulders.

3 GO!
On the starter's gun, the sprinter explodes out of the starting blocks.

Winter sports

Sports have taken place on snow and ice for centuries. Today, most winter sports are variations of skiing, sledding, or ice skating. These sports have their own multi-sport tournament, the Winter Olympic Games, which takes place every four years.

EQUIPMENT
The standard equipment for alpine skiing includes skis (which have different shapes for different disciplines), poles, a helmet, goggles, boots, and bindings, which attach the boot to the ski.

GOGGLE
SKI BOOT
HELMET
BINDING
POLES
SKIS

ALPINE SKIING

Alpine skiing is an exhilarating sport of speed and skill. There are five types of alpine ski competition. Two of the disciplines – downhill and Super-G – focus on speed. Slalom and giant slalom are technical events, in which a competitor's skill will win the day. The fifth event, called combined (a mix of downhill and slalom), tests both speed and technique.

Helmet gives protection
Goggles reduce glare from the Sun
Skin-tight suit cuts down resistance
Gloves keep hands warm
Number on bib identifies skier
Alpine
35 SKI
DE-PLATE
Shin pads
High boots protect ankles
Ski binding
Edge of ski cuts into snow
Ski pole

TOP ALPINE SKIERS

○ **KJETIL ANDRE AAMODT (NORWAY)**
The only alpine skier to win eight Olympic medals, four of them gold – in Super-G (1992, 2002, 2006) and combined (2002).

○ **JANICA KOSTELIC (CROATIA)**
The only woman in history to win four Winter Olympic golds – three in 2002 and one in 2006.

○ **ALBERTO TOMBA (ITALY)**
The dominant technical skier of the late 1980s and early 1990s.

DIFFERENT COURSES
Every alpine-ski discipline tests different skills, so the courses for each are set out differently. A downhill course has the fewest gates (poles), whereas a slalom has many poles through which the skier must pass.

DOWNHILL
SUPER-G
GIANT SLALOM
SLALOM

THE WORD "SLALOM" COMES FROM THE NORWEGIAN WORD "SLALAM", MEANING "GENTLE SLOPE"

ALTERNATIVE SKIING METHODS

Freestyle skiing made its modern Winter Olympic debut in 1992. Disciplines include aerials, ski cross, half-pipe, and slopestyle. Cross-country skiers use alpine skiing and jumping techniques to complete courses up to 50 km (31.1 miles) in length.

CROSS-COUNTRY SKIING
Cross-country skiers use a variety of techniques to race over challenging terrain. These include the diagonal stride and double poling (below).

FREESTYLE SKIING
In 1992 moguls became the first freestyle skiing event to feature at the Winter Games.

1 POLES IN GROUND
2 PUSH
3 GLIDE

SNOWBOARDING

Developed in the USA in the 1960s, snowboarding has enjoyed an explosion in popularity in recent years. Inspired by skateboarding, skiing, and surfing, snowboarders descend a slope while standing on a ski-like board attached to their feet.

Helmet
Sweat shirt
Wrist guard
Glove

EQUIPMENT
Snowboarders need a board, boots, some bindings to attach the boots to the board, a pair of goggles, and a helmet.

BOOT
BINDING
SNOWBOARD

SNOWBOARDER
Professional snowboarders compete in various disciplines that test both speed (downhill) and acrobatic skills (half-pipe and quarter-pipe).

1 GRAB
2 BODY BEND
3 RELEASE

HALF-PIPE
Half-pipe events take place in a specially constructed U-shaped arena. Competitors perform tricks, such as the alley-oop (above), as they descend.

Entrance
Exit
HALF-PIPE
Snowboarder
Boot

SLOPESTYLE
Slopestyle sees participants navigate a downhill course littered with obstacles, such as jumps and rails (right). Scores are awarded for staying upright for the duration of the course and for the tricks performed.

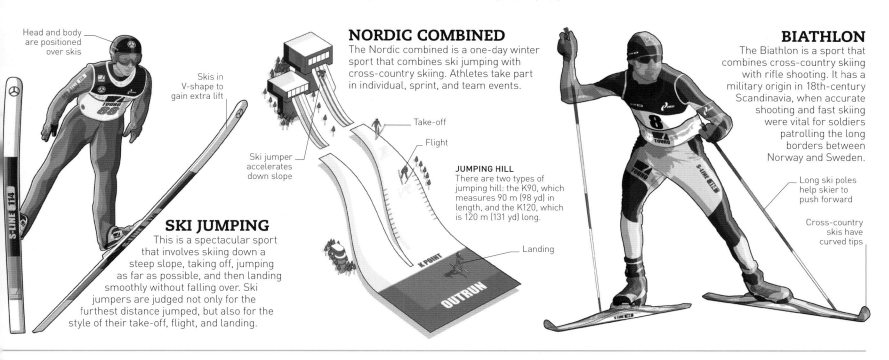

Head and body are positioned over skis

Skis in V-shape to gain extra lift

NORDIC COMBINED

The Nordic combined is a one-day winter sport that combines ski jumping with cross-country skiing. Athletes take part in individual, sprint, and team events.

Take-off

Flight

Ski jumper accelerates down slope

JUMPING HILL
There are two types of jumping hill: the K90, which measures 90 m (98 yd) in length, and the K120, which is 120 m (131 yd) long.

Landing

K POINT

OUTRUN

BIATHLON

The Biathlon is a sport that combines cross-country skiing with rifle shooting. It has a military origin in 18th-century Scandinavia, when accurate shooting and fast skiing were vital for soldiers patrolling the long borders between Norway and Sweden.

Long ski poles help skier to push forward

Cross-country skis have curved tips

SKI JUMPING

This is a spectacular sport that involves skiing down a steep slope, taking off, jumping as far as possible, and then landing smoothly without falling over. Ski jumpers are judged not only for the furthest distance jumped, but also for the style of their take-off, flight, and landing.

SLIDING SPORTS

Sliding sports are among the fastest winter sports. They include bobsleigh, luge, and skeleton. Competitors in each of these sports propel themselves down a specially constructed track and try to reach the bottom in the fastest time possible.

BOBSLEIGH
Bobsleigh was invented in Switzerland in the 19th century. The modern sport sees teams of two or four racing down ice-covered tracks in steerable sleds.

THE TRACK

All sliding sports take place on a specially constructed ice-covered track. The tracks feature left and right turns, S-curves, 180-degree bends (called "Omega"), and hairpins.

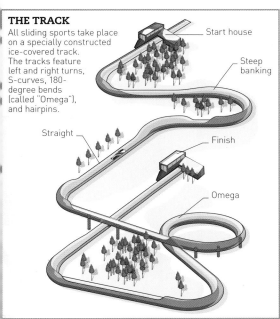

Start house

Steep banking

Straight

Finish

Omega

1 ROCK AND SLIDE
After taking up their positions, team members rock the sled and then push off down the launch pad.

2 FINAL PUSH
All members of the team must jump into the sled within 50 m (55 yd) of the start line.

3 FULL STEAM AHEAD
The driver sits at the front and steers the speeding sled.

LUGE
Luge athletes contest the fastest sport on ice. Lying feet first on their back on a fibreglass sled, they twist and turn down a track at breathtaking speeds of more than 135 km/h (85 mph).

Helmet and visor

Stainless steel runners

Helmet

SKELETON
Skeleton is the oldest sliding sport. It requires enormous courage. Athletes travel headfirst down the track on a 120 cm (48 in) long sled called a "skeleton".

Fibreglass base-plate

Sharp blades on bottom of runners

Athlete steers with feet

SKATING

Ice skating originated in Finland more than 3000 years ago. Originally, skates were made from animal bone strapped to the bottom of the foot. Today, competitive ice skating on steel blades has three disciplines: speed skating, ice dancing, and figure skating.

Bodysuit

Dance skates have shorter blades and higher heels

Costumes can be decorated

The female dancer must wear a skirt

SPEED SKATING
Speed skating sees athletes race on skates around an oval ice track. Events range from 500 m to 5,000 m.

Skate

ICE DANCING
Ice dancing competitions take place on an ice rink. It is a couples' event and judges give marks for each performance.

FIGURE SKATING
Single skaters or couples compete in two programmes: one to test their technical ability; the other to demonstrate artistic expression.

TOP FIGURE SKATERS

○ **GILLIS GRAFSTROM (SWEDEN)**
Won three consecutive men's singles gold medals at the 1920, 1924, and 1928 Winter Olympic Games.

○ **SONJA HENIE (NORWAY)**
Dominated the women's singles event, winning Winter Olympic gold in 1928, 1932, and 1936.

○ **JAYNE TORVILL AND CHRISTOPHER DEAN (UK)**
The British ice-dancing pair received the only perfect score in the event's history following their routine at the 1984 Winter Olympic Games.

Cycling

Cycling is a global sport, enjoyed by people of all ages. Most ride for fun, but many compete in disciplines such as track or road racing, or in BMX or mountain bike events.

Lightweight helmet

Breathable clothing

Gloves cushion the hands

MOUNTAIN BIKING

Mountain biking (MTB) is one of the newest cycling sports, started by cyclists riding off-road trails in California, USA, in the late 1970s. Cross-country mountain biking became an Olympic event in 1996.

RIDER PROFILE
As well as stamina and strong pedalling power, mountain bikers need balance and excellent technical skills to negotiate difficult off-road terrain.

ROUGH TERRAIN
Lifting the bike's wheels to get over an obstruction on the trail is known as bunny-hopping. The rider approaches the obstacle quickly, then lifts the handlebar and tucks his feet up under his body at the same time.

EVENTS

MTB is still quite a new sport and different types of competitions have been developed in recent years.

○ **CROSS-COUNTRY**
Riders race each other for a fixed number of laps of a circuit. The first to cross the finish line is the winner.

○ **DOWNHILL**
Competitors ride individually against the clock, down a hillside course. The fastest time wins.

○ **TRIALS**
Riders compete in various tests of poise, nerve, and artistry on their bikes, and are awarded points by judges.

○ **ENDURO**
Originating in France, a long-distance race in which only the downhill sections are timed and count towards the rider's finishing time.

MOUNTAIN BIKE
A mountain bike must be sturdy, to cope with bumpy trails, but still light enough to be manoeuvrable.

Low frame height makes it easier to climb at low speed

Up to 30 gears

Fat, knobbly tyres for good grip over rough ground

RIDER PROFILE
BMX riders need to be flexible and fit. Freestylers have style and creative flair.

Helmet with mouth guard

Gloves stop hands from slipping

Full-length trousers with padded knees

BMX

BMX (bicycle motocross) began as an offshoot of motocross (off-road motorcycle racing). Riders use specially designed bikes to perform freestyle tricks and stunts, or to race over a dirt track or obstacle course.

FLATLAND RIDING
A form of freestyle, flatland involves riders performing on flat surfaces with no ramps, jumps, or grindrails. It is probably the most technically demanding BMX discipline.

EVENTS

There are two types of competitive BMX riding – racing on dirt tracks and freestyle tricks.

○ **RACING**
Eight riders race in heats over a short circuit with different turns and jumps. The fastest riders then compete in the final race. BMX racing became an Olympic sport in 2008.

○ **FREESTYLE**
Divided into four main styles: base tricks (the basic moves); grind and lip tricks, performed on railings or the edge of a half-pipe structure; and aerial tricks, which are acrobatic turns and jumps in the air.

The rider uses his foot to keep the bike moving as he does a balancing trick

Stunt peg

DIRT TRACK
In a BMX race, riders complete a single lap of the course, which is laid out with various challenging features.

Banked turns or corners are called berms

Jumps are small, but closely packed together

Starting gate

Riders finish the course in 30–45 seconds

Finish line

BMX BIKE
Racing bikes are single-speed and designed for quick acceleration. Freestyle bikes are similar but often have stunt pegs attached, for riders to stand on when performing tricks.

Solid handlebar grips

Sturdy frame

Small wheels allow fast acceleration

Single gear

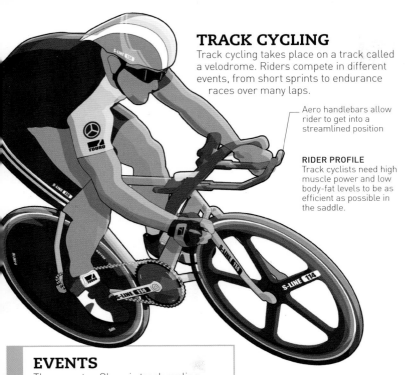

TRACK CYCLING

Track cycling takes place on a track called a velodrome. Riders compete in different events, from short sprints to endurance races over many laps.

Aero handlebars allow rider to get into a streamlined position

RIDER PROFILE
Track cyclists need high muscle power and low body-fat levels to be as efficient as possible in the saddle.

EVENTS

There are ten Olympic track cycling events, with men and women competing in each of the five events listed.

○ **INDIVIDUAL SPRINT**
Two riders race over three laps of the track.

○ **TEAM SPRINT**
Two teams of three riders race over three laps.

○ **TEAM PURSUIT**
Two teams of four riders race over 4 km (2.5 miles). Teams start on opposite sides of the track.

○ **KEIRIN**
Cyclists ride several laps behind a motorcycle pacemaker before sprinting to the finish.

○ **OMNIUM**
Twenty-four riders contest six different events: three sprints and three endurance races. The strongest overall rider wins.

MADISON
The Madison is a relay event for teams of two. When the riders change over, one uses his hand to propel the other into the race.

THE VELODROME
The velodrome track is oval and sloped, or "banked", so riders can achieve maximum speed.

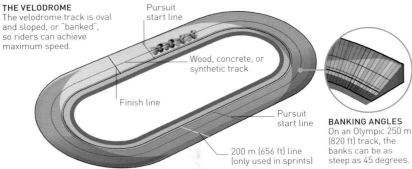

Pursuit start line

Wood, concrete, or synthetic track

Finish line

Pursuit start line

200 m (656 ft) line (only used in sprints)

BANKING ANGLES
On an Olympic 250 m (820 ft) track, the banks can be as steep as 45 degrees.

STANDARD TRACK BIKE
The standard bike is used for short races, while pursuit bikes with low-profile handlebars are used for endurance events.

Light, carbon-fibre frame

Drop handlebars

Single fixed gear

Aerodynamic disc wheel

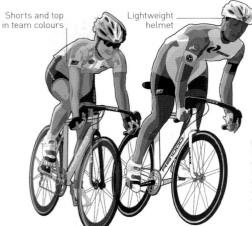

Shorts and top in team colours

Lightweight helmet

ROAD RACING

Road racing is one of the most physically demanding of all sports. Multi-stage races can cover thousands of kilometres in a few weeks and include all-day mountain climbs and 80 km/h (50 mph) sprints.

RIDER PROFILE
Road racers have an enormous capacity for physical and mental endurance. They must eat a balanced diet with a lot of carbohydrates – riders eat up to 6,000 calories on race days to maintain energy levels.

TOUR DE FRANCE

The Tour is the world's most famous road race. Riders cover about 3,500 km (2,175 miles) in 21 stages, finishing in Paris.

POLKA DOT JERSEY
Awarded to the King of the Mountains, the best climber.

WHITE JERSEY
Worn by the highest-placed young rider.

GREEN JERSEY
Awarded to the best sprinter.

YELLOW JERSEY
Worn by the overall leader.

RACE FORMATS

Road race formats range from one-day races to multi-stage endurance events. There are two Olympic events, the classic road race and the individual time trial.

○ **STAGE RACE**
A race over several stages in which the winner is the rider whose combined time is the quickest. May include sprint stages, mountain finishes, and individual or team time-trials.

○ **CLASSIC**
One-day races of up to 270 km (168 miles), often ridden over difficult terrain, such as cobbled roads.

○ **INDIVIDUAL TIME TRIAL**
Competitors race individually against the clock.

○ **CRITERIUM**
A high-speed race, on a city-centre circuit of less than 5 km (3 miles), over a set time (usually one hour) or a fixed number of laps.

ON THE ROAD
Riders race in teams. Team members work together during the race to help their leader to win, even if it means sacrificing their own chances of success.

Team car

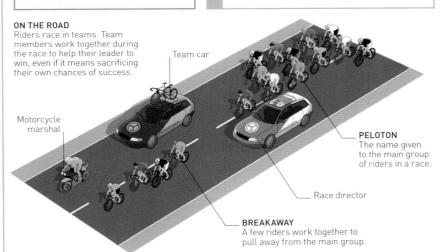

Motorcycle marshal

PELOTON
The name given to the main group of riders in a race.

Race director

BREAKAWAY
A few riders work together to pull away from the main group.

ROAD BIKE
Road bikes have to be strong, light, and comfortable enough to be ridden for long periods.

Integrated brake and gear levers

Carbon-fibre forks absorb minor bumps

Tubular tyres

Water sports

Water provides the perfect environment to show off sporting skills, from impressive tricks on a board to acrobatic dives into the water. Water sports are exciting and require great balance, strength, and endurance to keep control in the water.

SWIMMING

Many swimmers take part in races in swimming pools, but some will even cross seas or endure cold-water races in the peak of winter. Swimming requires agility and strength to move through the water as quickly as possible.

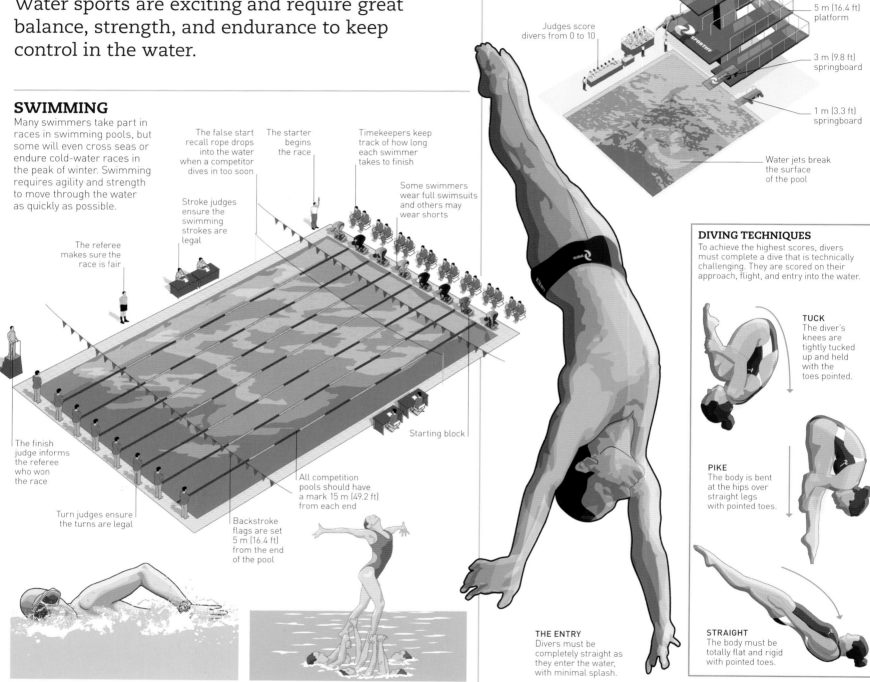

The false start recall rope drops into the water when a competitor dives in too soon

The starter begins the race

Timekeepers keep track of how long each swimmer takes to finish

Stroke judges ensure the swimming strokes are legal

Some swimmers wear full swimsuits and others may wear shorts

The referee makes sure the race is fair

Starting block

The finish judge informs the referee who won the race

Turn judges ensure the turns are legal

All competition pools should have a mark 15 m (49.2 ft) from each end

Backstroke flags are set 5 m (16.4 ft) from the end of the pool

SOLO SWIMMING
To glide through the water at great speed, swimmers must perfect their arm strokes and leg kicking so each movement propels them forwards.

SYNCHRONIZED SWIMMING
Synchronized swimmers must perform a graceful routine in perfect unison. Music is played both above and below the water to help them keep time.

SWIMMING STROKES
There are swimming competitions for all four types of swimming strokes. The fastest stroke is the front crawl. In the individual medley, swimmers must swim all four strokes.

FRONT CRAWL   BREASTSTROKE   BUTTERFLY   BACKSTROKE

DIVING

Competitive divers dive from a variety of heights. They must acrobatically twist and flip in the air before they hit the water. This requires great muscle strength, as divers must move their bodies like gymnasts.

Judges score divers from 0 to 10

10 m (32.8 ft) platform

7.5 m (24.6 ft) platform

5 m (16.4 ft) platform

3 m (9.8 ft) springboard

1 m (3.3 ft) springboard

Water jets break the surface of the pool

DIVING TECHNIQUES
To achieve the highest scores, divers must complete a dive that is technically challenging. They are scored on their approach, flight, and entry into the water.

TUCK
The diver's knees are tightly tucked up and held with the toes pointed.

PIKE
The body is bent at the hips over straight legs with pointed toes.

STRAIGHT
The body must be totally flat and rigid with pointed toes.

THE ENTRY
Divers must be completely straight as they enter the water, with minimal splash.

BALL SPORTS
A number of team ball sports take place in water, such as water polo and underwater hockey. In water polo, players must tread water for long periods of time. In underwater hockey, they need to be able to dive underwater.

WATER POLO
Teams score goals by throwing a ball into a net.

UNDERWATER HOCKEY
Teams use snorkels and a stick to get the puck into the goal.

BOARD SPORTS

Board sports are popular on lakes and along coasts, where people can use the power of the wind, waves, or boats to race along at high speeds or perform amazing tricks. They usually require excellent balance and strength to control the board and avoid falling off.

SURFING
Surfers need good balance to control a surfboard with their feet. The strength of the breaking waves pushes the board forwards.

KITESURFING
Kitesurfers use the power of the wind to speed across the water and jump high into the air.

WATER-SKIING
Water-skiers are pulled along behind a boat on one or two skis, or even barefoot. They compete in slalom, jumping, or trick events.

WAKEBOARDING
Wakeboarders are pulled along on a board by a boat and use the boat's wake to perform flips and jumps.

WINDSURFING
Windsurfers use a large sail to power them across the water in speed races or to perform impressive tricks.

FLOATER

The floater is a popular trick to help surfers gain speed when surfing a wave, or to clear a section of the wave. It is also a great way to set up for another trick.

1 When you have some speed, point the board towards the wave when it is starting to break.

2 Ride up to the lip of the wave at a 30-degree angle.

3 Switch your weight from your back foot to your front foot to turn on the lip of the wave.

4 Enter back into the wave by pushing your board flat on the face of the wave.

ROWING

Rowers face backwards and pull oars through the water to propel their boat as fast as possible. Typically, rowing is done in rivers or lakes, but some rowers even cross oceans.

SCULLING
In sculling, rowers have one oar in each hand.

There can be up to eight people in a rowing team

ROWING
In sweep-oar rowing, each rower is responsible for one oar.

WHITE WATER SPORTS

White water is made when rivers pass through rocky areas and create rapids. Adrenaline-seekers try to manoeuvre crafts such as kayaks, canoes, and rafts as they travel down the turbulent rivers in races, slaloms (winding races), or just for fun.

RAFTING
Groups can share the thrill of paddling an inflatable raft down the rapids.

CANOEING
Canoeists use a paddle with one blade and are either in a sitting or kneeling position in their boat.

A sprayskirt keeps the water out of the boat.

ESKIMO ROLL

Kayakers use an eskimo roll when they have capsized to turn the kayak the right way up.

1 LEAN FORWARD Lean against the kayak and hold the paddle out of the water.

2 SWEEP Sweep the paddle through the water and rotate your hips to pull the kayak up.

3 STABILIZE Use the paddle to make sure you are stable, then lift your head and body up.

KAYAKING
Kayakers use a paddle with a blade at each end to move quickly through the water.

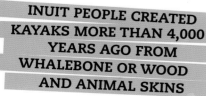
INUIT PEOPLE CREATED KAYAKS MORE THAN 4,000 YEARS AGO FROM WHALEBONE OR WOOD AND ANIMAL SKINS

Sailing

Sailing has been a mode of transport for thousands of years. Today, it is also an exciting sport and hobby, which requires quick thinking, confidence, and strength. Sailors take part in a number of competitive races around the world, although many sail the seas simply for fun.

ANATOMY OF A BOAT
Knowing the names for different parts of a boat is important when sailing, especially if you are part of a team. It helps you to communicate more clearly with each other so that you can travel faster and stay safe.

Main sail

Mast

Boom

Mainsheet

Stern

SAILING CLOTHING
Special clothing helps sailors keep warm and dry when on the water, especially in bad weather. A buoyancy aid or life jacket is worn to keep sailors safe if they fall into the water.

LIFE JACKET

BUOYANCY AID

DUNGAREES

JACKET

SAILING GLOVES

WETSUIT

DINGHY SHOES

FULL GLOVES

YACHTING BOOTS

NAVIGATING
Tides, currents, and shallow waters can make the ocean a dangerous place. Many sailors use GPS (Global Positioning System) to plan their course, but in case this fails, knowing how to navigate is a vital skill.

WIND DISPLAY
Shows the direction of the wind.

DEPTH DISPLAY
Helps sailors avoid water that is too shallow.

COMPASS
Helps sailors keep track of the boat's direction.

Dividers measure distance on chart

COURSE PLOTTER
The plotter shows which compass points to follow when it is placed over a map.

NAUTICAL CHARTS
Charts are detailed maps of a sailing area, with hazards and reference points shown.

YPES OF BOATS

oats are organized by class, which is determined by their
ngth. Small boats are ideal for short-distance racing, as they
ove quickly. Large boats are better for long-distance sailing as
ey can endure more treacherous seas than a small dinghy.
ere are some popular classes of boat.

LASER CLASS
A popular 4.2 m (14 ft)
dinghy for solo sailing.

470 CLASS
A 4.7 m (15.4 ft) dinghy
for a crew of two.

49ER CLASS
A 4.9 m (16 ft) dinghy with
CCA spinnaker for speed.

TORNADO CLASS
A 6.1 m (20 ft) catamaran
with two body sections that
increase the boat's speed.

**OCEAN RACER
(VOLVO 70) CLASS**
A 21.3 m (70 ft) yacht with
a 31.5 m (103 ft) mast.

AMERICA'S CUP CLASS
A 24 m (79 ft) yacht used
in the America's Cup race
between 1992 and 2007.

> SAILING FOR SPORT, RATHER
> THAN TRANSPORTATION
> OR WARFARE, BEGAN
> IN THE NETHERLANDS
> IN THE 1600s

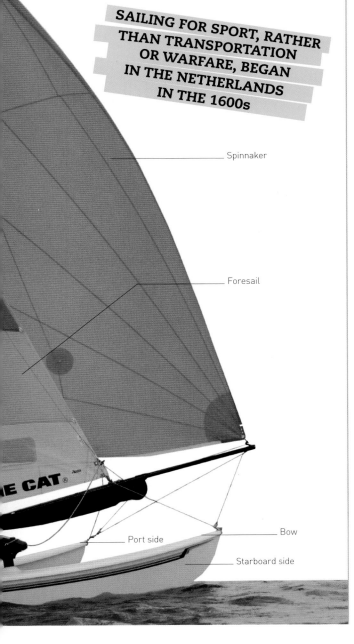

Spinnaker

Foresail

Port side

Bow

Starboard side

USING THE WIND

Sailors can adjust their sails to make the most of
the wind. The sails can be angled to capture the wind,
so the boat is pushed forwards in the direction it faces.
A sailing boat can travel in any direction except straight
into the wind (the no-sail zone).

KEY

→ **No-sail zone**
In this area the boat would be sailing
into the wind. The sails would not work
and the boat would not move.

--- **Close haul**
The closest a boat can sail to the wind
without entering the no-sail zone. Both
sails are pulled in tight to the centreline.

--- **Close reach**
Similar to a close-hauled course, but the
boat is turned away a little more from
the wind and the sails are loosened further.

--- **Beam reach**
Sails are eased halfway and the wind
is coming directly across the side of
the boat.

--- **Broad reach**
Sails are nearly full and the boat is on a
course away from the wind (downwind).

--- **Run**
Sails are full and the wind is directly
behind the boat.

WIND DIRECTION

Close haul

No-sail zone

Close reach

Beam reach

Broad reach

Run

TACKING AND GYBING

There are two ways of turning a boat: tacking and
gybing. Tacking is a safer, slower way of turning
as it allows more control of the sails. Gybing is
faster and is especially good for racing.

TACKING
Turn the boat to face upwind.

GYBING
Turn the boat to face downwind.

RECORD BREAKERS

Since sailing began as a sport several
hundred years ago, many sailors have
set impressive around-the-world
sailing records.

○ **JOSHUA SLOCUM (CANADA),
1895–98**
The first person to sail solo around the world,
with just three stops.

○ **ROBIN KNOX-JOHNSTON (UK), 1969**
The first person to sail solo around the world
without stopping.

○ **KAY COTTEE (AUSTRALIA), 1988**
The first woman to sail solo around the world
without stopping.

○ **ELLEN MACARTHUR (UK), 2005**
Became the fastest person to sail solo around
the world without stopping, in 71 days, 14 hours,
18 minutes, and 33 seconds.

○ **FRANCIS JOYON (FRANCE), 2008**
Broke Ellen MacArthur's record to become
the fastest person to sail solo around the
world without stopping, in 57 days, 13 hours,
34 minutes, and 6 seconds.

OCEAN RACING

Ocean races can be extremely challenging and dangerous. They require both
physical and mental strength, as sailors can be at sea for many weeks at a time.

ROUTE DU RHUM
Singlehanded racers must
work with fast winds in this
high-speed journey across
the Atlantic Ocean.

VOLVO OCEAN RACE
In this extreme race, nine-
person crews sail around
the world day and night.

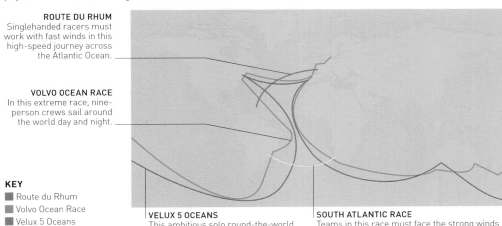

KEY
■ Route du Rhum
■ Volvo Ocean Race
■ Velux 5 Oceans
■ South Atlantic Race

VELUX 5 OCEANS
This ambitious solo round-the-world
race takes more than 100 days to finish.

SOUTH ATLANTIC RACE
Teams in this race must face the strong winds
and huge waves of the southern Atlantic Ocean.

Fishing

Rain or shine, anglers spend hours waiting for a fish to take their bait. Some eat their catch, but many throw the fish back. So what is the big attraction? Anglers enjoy the peace and quiet, pitting their wits against the fish, and having their skill rewarded.

WHERE TO FISH

There are three main types of fishing: freshwater fishing (sometimes called coarse fishing), saltwater fishing, and fly-fishing. In freshwater and saltwater fishing, anglers use baits and lures to attract fish. In fly-fishing, they use imitation flies instead. Freshwater environments include ponds, lakes, streams, and rivers. Fly-fishing can happen in fresh or salt water.

STILL WATER
Ponds and lakes are home to carp, pike, and other freshwater species. Anglers fish from the bank or a boat.

RUNNING WATER
Streams and rivers are the place to catch salmon, trout, bream, and perch. Anglers fish from the bank or wade in.

SALT WATER
Most saltwater fishing is from boats close to shore or out at sea. Anglers also sit on sea walls or wade in the shallows.

RODS, REELS, AND LINES

A simple stick or length of bamboo can work as a rod, with a line and hook tied on – but most anglers have high-tech rods made of fibreglass or carbon fibre. They come apart for easy carrying and are used with a reel to wind in and stow the line. Multiplier reels allow faster winding than fixed spools, as each turn of the handle spins the drum several times. Super-fast fly reels are used for fly-fishing.

MULTIPLIER REEL **FIXED-SPOOL REEL** **FLY REEL** **FISHING LINES**

FLOAT ROD (IN FOUR PIECES)

FISHING TACKLE

A tackle box with a handle is essential for transporting equipment and keeping it all organized. The best designs open out so that the compartments are tiered.

Artificial fly

See-through lid with handle

Lead shot

Float

Whistle to attract attention in an emergency

Lure

Float rig with hook

Catapult for launching bait into the water

Fishing line in different weights

Sharp scissors and other tools for tying flies

BAIT

Even everyday scraps of bread will attract fish, but there are better baits to use. Live types include worms and maggots. Sweetcorn, seeds, grains, and dog biscuits work well, too. "Boilies" are processed bait balls, high in protein, that come in many colours and flavours.

RED BOILIES **YELLOW BOILIES**

DOG BISCUITS **SWEETCORN** **WORMS** **WAX WORMS**

WEIGHTS

Weights help bring the end of the line close to the fish. Anglers use them to anchor the bait on the bottom or keep it at a particular depth. Most weights are made of a soft metal called lead. Different shapes do different jobs. The smallest – split shot – slots, or crimps, on to the line under a float to position it in the flow of water. The combination of the line, hook, bait, and weight is called a rig.

LEAD WEIGHTS

SPLIT SHOT

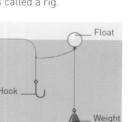
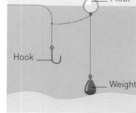

Float

Weight Bait

Hook

Hook

Weight

WIRE

HAIR RIG FOR CARP
Carp are wary fish. The bait is attached to the hook on a fine, weighted line. The fish sucks up the bait without feeling the hook.

CATFISH RIG
Catfish can be huge. Live bait is fixed to the hook. The baited rig is tied to a float that is secured by a weight on the riverbed.

CASTING

[F]ew people get the hang of casting straight [a]way, but practice makes perfect. Sending [t]he fly, lure, or bait to where the fish are takes [g]ood hand-eye co-ordination and strength.

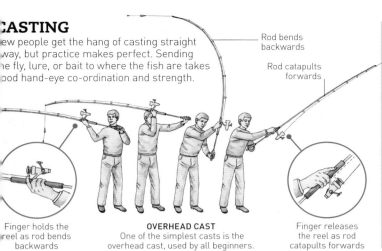

Rod bends backwards

Rod catapults forwards

Finger holds the reel as rod bends backwards

OVERHEAD CAST
One of the simplest casts is the overhead cast, used by all beginners.

Finger releases the reel as rod catapults forwards

BIGGEST CATCH

Big-game fishing happens out in the open ocean. Tuna, marlin, and swordfish are popular targets, and the aim is to catch the biggest fish possible. The record for the heaviest Atlantic bluefin tuna was set in 1932 by English fisherman Edward Peel, using a rod and line.

RECORD ATLANTIC BLUEFIN TUNA, 1932
362 kg (798 lb)

WEIGHING

All anglers want to know how much their catch weighs – so they can compete with each other, and with their own personal bests. For catch-and-release fishing, it is especially important to use scales that do not cause any extra distress.

TRADITIONAL SCALES   **PORTABLE SCALES**

LURES

[M]ade of plastic, metal, or wood, lures [a]re shaped and coloured to look like [ir]resistible little fish. Like a puppeteer, the [a]ngler works the line so the lures come to [li]fe. Any predatory fish that falls for one [fi]nds itself caught on the angler's hook.

WILD EYE SHAD

ZALT ZAM

ZANDER

PROFESSOR SPOON

SAMMY

ERNIE

FIRETAIL JELLYWORM

LURES ARE SOMETIMES DELIBERATELY DESIGNED TO LOOK DISTRESSED OR INJURED – LIKE EASY PREY

CHUG BUG POPPER

DEPTHS
Lures can be weighted to "swim" at different depths, so that they appeal to specific predators.

PIKE LURE
Pike will go for a lure at any depth. The lure has to be on a wire line as a pike has a fierce bite.

FLOATS

Like weights, floats help suspend bait or a lure at a particular depth in the water. Some come ready-weighted, but others are used with lead weights or shot. Lighter floats are ideal for still water. Fast-moving water needs heavier floats.

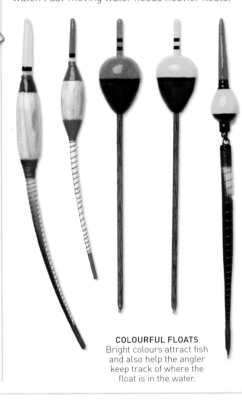

COLOURFUL FLOATS
Bright colours attract fish and also help the angler keep track of where the float is in the water.

UNUSUAL FISHING METHODS

People have caught fish throughout history, gathering food from rivers and the sea just as they hunted animals on land. Over the centuries, people came up with many weird and wonderful ways to catch fish.

○ **ON STILTS**
Stilt fishermen in Sri Lanka drive their poles into the sand just offshore, then perch at the top and cast their lines. This technique means they disturb the fish as little as possible.

STILTS

○ **USING SUCKER FISH**
Remoras are suckerfish that hitch a ride on larger fish. In Africa, some fishermen use them on their fishing lines. When they feel the remora has attached its sucker to a big fish, they haul it in.

○ **WITH DOGS**
Fishermen along the coast of Portugal traditionally used water dogs to herd fish into their nets.

PORTUGUESE WATER DOG

○ **USING CORMORANTS**
Chinese and Japanese fishermen use trained cormorants. A throat snare stops the birds swallowing bigger fish, but is loose enough to let them eat smaller ones.

○ **WITH DOLPHINS**
A pod of dolphins in Laguna, Brazil, helps the local fishermen by driving shoals of mullet towards the shore. The dolphins even leap out of the water to tell the people the right moment to cast their nets.

CORMORANTS

FLY-FISHING

[F]ly-fishing began as a way of catching river [s]almon and trout. Today, it is popular for a [h]uge range of fresh- and saltwater species. [T]he angler uses fake flies to tempt the fish. [S]ome are cast on to the surface of the water [(d]ry flies), and some into the water (wet flies). [F]lies can be lifelike (deceivers) or come in [c]razy colours (attractors).

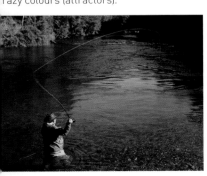

WRIST ACTION
In streams or rivers, the fly-angler aims to cast the fly upstream. Then it will gently drift downstream in a natural-looking way.

ADULT MAYFLY
(freshwater)

DAMSEL NYMPH
(freshwater)

CARP FLY
(freshwater)
Mimics dog-biscuit bait.

SUPER BUZZER SUPREME
(freshwater)
Looks like a midge pupa.

F-FLY
(freshwater)
Resembles a just-hatched insect stranded on the surface.

DEPTH CHARGE CZECH MATES
(freshwater)
Mimics a caddis fly larva.

SQUID WHITE
(saltwater)
Looks like a squid.

SURF CANDY FLY
(saltwater)
Imitates any baitfish.

WILLS SKITTAL TAN
(saltwater)
Imitates a shrimp.

CREASE FLY
(saltwater)

ATTRACTORS

Attractors are often brightly coloured. The fly-angler usually moves them around a lot to tempt fish to attack.

Legs make ripples on the surface

PIWI POPPER
(saltwater)

Rubber legs create movement

Big, buoyant eyes

CHERNOBYL ANT
(freshwater)

DEER HOPPER
(freshwater)

CACTUS BOOBY
(freshwater)

Combat sports

Many sports, both ancient and modern, have their roots in traditional fighting techniques. These combat sports teach strength and discipline, and help students learn how to defend themselves. Some are better known as martial arts.

TYPES OF COMBAT SPORTS

Some combat sports have developed from very old ways of fighting, while others have been around for just a few decades. Most focus on one of three types of attack: punches, kicks, and other strikes; throwing, holding, and pinning; or using weapons.

PUNCHES, KICKS, AND OTHER STRIKES

KUNG FU: TAOLU
Kung fu takes many forms. The most popular is taolu, a form of *wushu*.

KUNG FU: SANSHOU
Sanshou is a Chinese martial art similar to kickboxing. It is never practised with weapons.

KUNG FU: T'AI CHI
Based on slow, flowing movements, this is a gentle, meditative form of kung fu.

BOXING
The Ancient Greeks boxed, but modern boxing follows rules set 150 years ago in England.

THAI BOXING
Unlike Western boxers, Thai boxers attack with feet, elbows, and knees as well as fists.

CAPOEIRA
African slaves in Brazil developed capoeira. It looks like a dance, but it is really a form of self-defence.

TAEKWONDO
The name of this 20th-century Korean martial art means "the way of the foot and fist".

KARATE
Originating from Japan, karate is a form of self-defence. Practitioners do not use any weapons or props.

KARATE

THROWING, HOLDING, AND PINNING

JUJITSU
This Japanese martial art drew on ancient Indian and Chinese fighting techniques.

JUDO
Based on jujitsu, judo developed in the 1800s. It involves throwing, grappling, and striking.

SUMO WRESTLING
This sport is most associated with Japan, but it originated in China in the 3rd century BCE.

WRESTLING
As popular today as it was in Ancient Greece and Rome, wrestling involves one-to-one grappling.

SOMBO
Very like wrestling, this Russian combat sport also involves punches and kicks.

WRESTLING

USING WEAPONS

KALARIPAYIT
One of the world's oldest martial arts, kalaripayit developed in Ancient India.

FENCING
This sport developed from sword fighting in the 1500s. Many of its terms are French.

KYUDO
Samurai warriors practised an early form of kyudo, which is similar to archery.

ESKRIMA
Meaning "skirmish", eskrima was developed in the Philippines in the 16th century.

KENDO
Full of ritual, this Japanese sport is based on kenjutsu, an 11th-century form of sword-fighting.

KENDO

KUNG FU: TAOLU

Taolu is a form of kung fu in which competitors show off routines on a padded mat. Their moves include punches, balances, jumps, sweeps, and throws. Some moves are performed bare-handed, and some with weapons.

TAOLU WEAPONS
In taolu, competitors handle various traditional Chinese weapons. Working alone or in pairs, they aim to be as graceful as possible.

GUN (TYPE OF STAFF), 210 cm (7 ft)

JIAN (SWORD), 103 cm (3.4 ft)

DAO (CURVED SWORD), 98 cm (3.25 ft)

NANDAO (BROADSWORD), 97 cm (3.25 ft)

Swishing tassels emphasize the moves

Taijijian sword is 110 cm (3.6 ft) long

Chinese tunic worn over loose trousers

SEATED STANCE
In this stance, called *xie bu*, the competitor wraps one thigh over the other. The front foot stays flat on the floor.

CROUCH STANCE
This move, known as *pu bu*, is a very low squat. One arm arches over the head to counterbalance the crouching.

HORSE STANCE
This powerful position is known as *ma bu* in Chinese. The tops of the thighs must stay parallel to the floor.

BOXING

In boxing, two opponents try to punch each other, while avoiding punches themselves. They score points for different punches to their opponent's head and upper body. The winner is the boxer who scores most points or who knocks out his or her opponent.

Head bobs and weaves

Padded glove

Shorts

Boxing shoe

FIGHTING GEAR
Groin guards are optional, but gloves and mouth guards must be worn. Head guards are mandatory for women's contests.

GROIN GUARD

GLOVES

MOUTH GUARD

HEAD GUARD

JAB
A stiff jab is the basic punch used by all boxers. For a perfect jab, the boxer has to fully extend his arm.

HOOK
Hooks are delivered to the side of the head or body. The best hooks are those an opponent does not see coming.

UPPERCUT
This powerful punch is delivered on to the opponent's chin from below. It often results in a knockout.

JUDO

In the Japanese art of judo, two opponents (called judoka) try to throw each other to the ground, pin each other down, or force a submission. There are no weapons, and kicks and punches are not allowed.

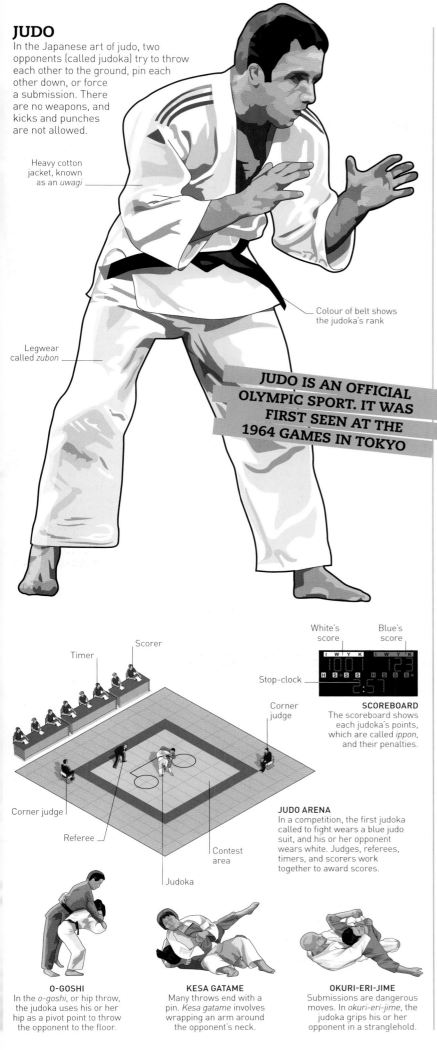

Heavy cotton jacket, known as an *uwagi*

Colour of belt shows the judoka's rank

Legwear called *zubon*

JUDO IS AN OFFICIAL OLYMPIC SPORT. IT WAS FIRST SEEN AT THE 1964 GAMES IN TOKYO

Timer

Scorer

White's score

Blue's score

Stop-clock

Corner judge

SCOREBOARD
The scoreboard shows each judoka's points, which are called *ippon*, and their penalties.

Corner judge

Referee

Contest area

Judoka

JUDO ARENA
In a competition, the first judoka called to fight wears a blue judo suit, and his or her opponent wears white. Judges, referees, timers, and scorers work together to award scores.

O-GOSHI
In the *o-goshi*, or hip throw, the judoka uses his or her hip as a pivot point to throw the opponent to the floor.

KESA GATAME
Many throws end with a pin. *Kesa gatame* involves wrapping an arm around the opponent's neck.

OKURI-ERI-JIME
Submissions are dangerous moves. In *okuri-eri-jime*, the judoka grips his or her opponent in a stranglehold.

SUMO

In sumo wrestling, the aim is to stay in the ring with only the feet touching the ground. The two opponents try to push each other off balance or out of the ring. The heaviest sumo star, Konishiki Yasokichi, weighed 287 kg (633 lb) and was known as the "Dump Truck".

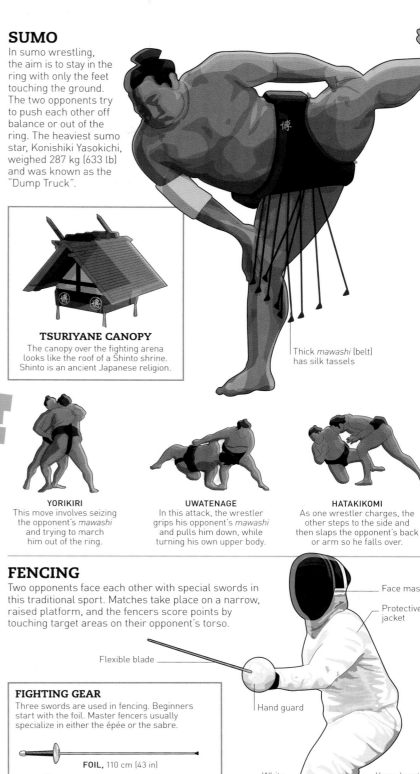

Thick *mawashi* (belt) has silk tassels

TSURIYANE CANOPY
The canopy over the fighting arena looks like the roof of a Shinto shrine. Shinto is an ancient Japanese religion.

YORIKIRI
This move involves seizing the opponent's *mawashi* and trying to march him out of the ring.

UWATENAGE
In this attack, the wrestler grips his opponent's *mawashi* and pulls him down, while turning his own upper body.

HATAKIKOMI
As one wrestler charges, the other steps to the side and then slaps the opponent's back or arm so he falls over.

FENCING

Two opponents face each other with special swords in this traditional sport. Matches take place on a narrow, raised platform, and the fencers score points by touching target areas on their opponent's torso.

Face mask

Protective jacket

Flexible blade

Hand guard

White breeches

Knee-length socks

Flat-soled trainers

FIGHTING GEAR
Three swords are used in fencing. Beginners start with the foil. Master fencers usually specialize in either the épée or the sabre.

FOIL, 110 cm (43 in)

EPEE, 110 cm (43 in)

SABRE, 105 cm (41 in)

ATTACK
The fencer extends his or her sword arm towards the opponent. A lunge forward adds force to the attack.

PARRY
The parry is a defensive move that blocks the opponent's attack and may expose him or her to a counterattack.

RIPOSTE
After a parry, the follow-up counterattack is known as a riposte. The name comes from the French word for "reply".

Knots

Knowing how to tie knots is a fun skill that is useful in many situations. For activities such as climbing or sailing, ropes tied with the right knots are vital for safety. More everyday uses for knots range from putting up a tent to making decorations or even tying shoelaces.

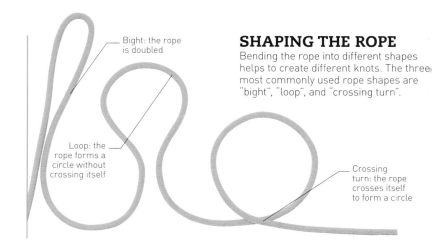

Bight: the rope is doubled

Loop: the rope forms a circle without crossing itself

Crossing turn: the rope crosses itself to form a circle

SHAPING THE ROPE
Bending the rope into different shapes helps to create different knots. The three most commonly used rope shapes are "bight", "loop", and "crossing turn".

FIGURE OF EIGHT

Easy to tie and untie, the figure of eight is a simple stopper knot that can be used to stop rope from slipping through a hole. It is an important knot for sailors and rock climbers.

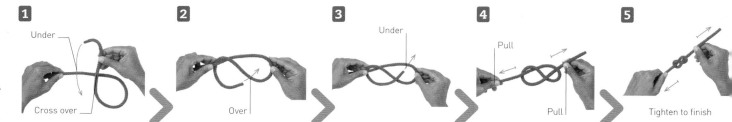

1 Under / Cross over
2 Over
3 Under
4 Pull / Pull
5 Tighten to finish

REEF KNOT

This binding knot is quick to do. It is used for securing rope or string around an object, so is perfect for tying up parcels. Reef knots are also known as square knots.

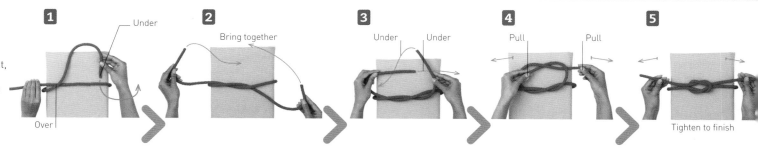

1 Under / Over
2 Bring together
3 Under / Under
4 Pull / Pull
5 Tighten to finish

CLOVE HITCH

The clove hitch is a binding knot that is used when only one end of a rope is available to work with. It is tied to secure the end of a rope to a post or similar, and is often used by climbers.

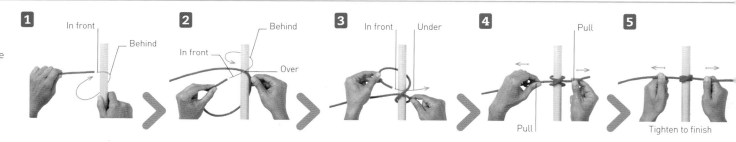

1 In front / Behind
2 In front / Behind / Over
3 In front / Under
4 Pull / Pull
5 Tighten to finish

ROUND TURN AND TWO HALF HITCHES

This is a weight-bearing knot that could be used for attaching a rope to a fixed object. For example, you could tie a swing to the branch of a tree using this knot.

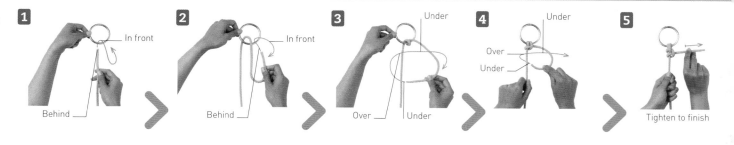

1 In front / Behind
2 In front / Behind
3 Under / Over / Under
4 Under / Over / Under
5 Tighten to finish

BOWLINE

The bowline is a handy loop knot with many uses, from mooring a boat to hanging up a hammock. It is quick to tie and untie.

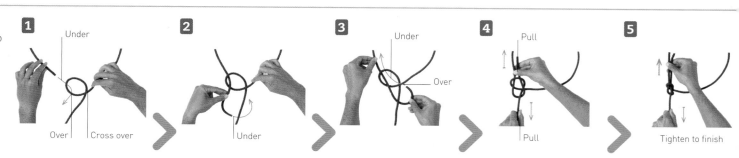

1 Under / Over / Cross over
2 Under
3 Under / Over
4 Pull / Pull
5 Tighten to finish

STOPPER KNOTS

These prevent a rope slipping through a hole or unravelling at the end. Stopper knots can also be used for decoration. Some are tricky to undo.

DIAMOND

STOPPER

SINK STOPPER

WALL KNOT

MANROPE

STEVEDORE

MONKEY'S FIST

MATTHEW WALKER

FIGURE OF EIGHT

BINDING KNOTS

Handy for many purposes, binding knots are particularly useful for tying things together in bundles. Some types are ideal for making bows on gift packages or tying shoelaces.

TIMBER HITCH

BOA

CLOVE HITCH

TURK'S HEAD

THIEF

PACKER'S

TRUE LOVER'S

REEF

SLIPPED REEF

SURGEON'S

GRANNY

TURQUOISE TURTLE

SLIPPED REEF DOUBLE

SAILOR'S CROSS

BEND KNOTS

These knots are designed to join two pieces of rope together. They are used by mountaineers on safety lines and other pieces of climbing equipment. Some bend knots secure fastenings between ropes of different thicknesses.

SHEET BEND

CARRICK BEND

BLOOD

TUCKED SHEET BEND

HUNTER'S BEND

LANYARD

WATER

DOUBLE SHEET BEND

FISHERMAN'S

HITCH KNOTS

A hitch ties a rope to something else, such as a pole or a ring. Fishermen often use hitches to fasten hooks on to fishing lines.

ROLLING HITCH

SHEEPSHANK

ICICLE HITCH

SHEER LASHING

SQUARE LASHING

KLEMHEIST

BUNTLINE HITCH

COW HITCH

ITALIAN HITCH

COW HITCH WITH TOGGLE

LOOP KNOTS

Loop knots are used to attach ropes to other objects. For this reason they are popular with climbers, sailors, and fishermen.

JURY MAST

PORTUGUESE BOWLINE

ANGLER'S LOOP

BOWLINE

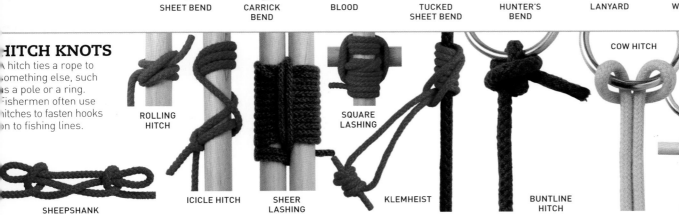
BASIC NET

THREADED FIGURE OF EIGHT

SPANISH BOWLINE

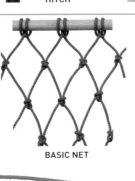
BLOOD DROPPER

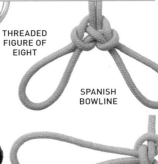
ALPINE BUTTERFLY

275

Games

Long before the Internet, computer games, and TV, people invented games. Board and card games have been around for hundreds or even thousands of years and are as challenging and fun to play today as they ever were.

CARDS FROM AROUND THE WORLD
European packs have 52 cards in four suits — hearts, clubs, diamonds, and spades. Other cards have pictures or shapes.

EUROPEAN CARD

TABLE-TOP GAMES
These competitive games have flat boards, small pieces, and can take hours of concentration before someone wins. Over the years, games like these became a focus for social get-togethers. They are still a great way to gather people round a table to have fun.

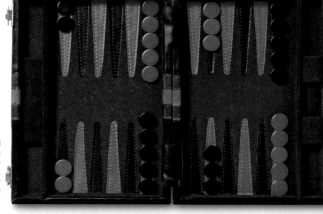

BACKGAMMON
This game for two players is one of the oldest in the world. It involves a mixture of strategy and luck as players roll dice and then decide how to move their counters. The winner is the first player to clear their pieces off the board.

CHINESE CHEQUERS
The aim of this game is to race your coloured pegs across the board to the opposite point of the star. You can move along one hole at a time or hop over pegs in your path.

SNAKES AND LADDERS
Players throw a die to move up the board and, hopefully, land on a ladder to skip rows. But watch out for the snakes!

GO GAME
Go starts with an empty board. Players place their stones where the lines cross to build territories. Or they surround and capture enemy stones.

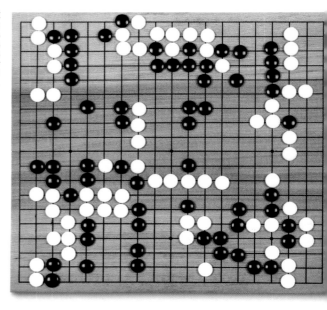

DRAUGHTS
The aim of this game is to grab all your opponent's pieces by jumping over them diagonally as you cross the board.

PLAYING PIECES
The earliest games were played with anything that came to hand — pebbles, shells, sticks, and bones. Nowadays, many games have written rules, boards, tiles, counters, marbles, or pegs.

MANCALA
There are hundreds of different versions of mancala. Players move seeds or stones along pits on the board and try to collect the largest store.

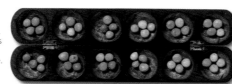

DOMINOES
A domino set has 28 tiles, each with two sets of spots representing numbers from zero to six. The players draw seven tiles and take turns to match the spots on tiles at the ends of a line. The winner is the first to get rid of their tiles.

MAHJONG
In this ancient Chinese game, four players take turns to pick up and discard tiles. The aim is to collect sets of different types.

PICK-UP STICKS
The sticks are dropped in a heap and each player in turn tries to pull a stick from the pile without disturbing the rest. The player with the most sticks wins.

SOLITAIRE
This aim of this game for one person is to clear the board by jumping marbles over each other to remove them. The game is complete when just one marble is left in the centre hole.

POPULAR CARD GAMES

In most games, winning is a mix of memory, skill, and luck in how the cards fall.

NAME	TYPE	PLAYERS	OBJECTIVE
Rummy	draw-and-discard	2 or more	combine cards into sets
Bridge	trick-taking	4 players	highest score
Poker	trick-taking	2 or more	hand rankings
Patience	building sets	1 player	complete all 4 sets
Canasta	draw-and-discard	4 players	highest score

JAPANESE HANFUDA OR FLOWER CARDS

A GAME OF CHESS

In a chess game, each player has a black or white army and takes turns to move pieces to attack the other player's king. The aim is to put the king into checkmate — a position where he cannot move to safety. Along the way, players capture enemy pieces and try to keep their own pieces safe.

CHESS CLOCKS
These clocks control the time spent on each move. The player stops his own timer after a move and starts his opponent's.

Black queen sits on black square

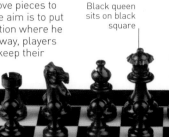

Light square in back corner is always on player's right-hand side

Front row has eight pawns

White queen sits on white square

King | Bishop | Knight | Rook

CHESS BOARD SET-UP
The 16 pieces sit on black and white squares in two rows with the eight pawns in the front row. In the back row, two bishops, two knights, and two rooks sit on either side of the queen and the king.

CHESS PIECES

There are 32 pieces in a set – 16 black and 16 white. Each player has one king, one queen, two rooks, two knights, two bishops, and eight pawns.

FULL SET OF BLACK PIECES

KING
The most valuable piece on the board, the king can move one square in any direction. It cannot move into a square occupied by a piece of the same colour or into "check" — a position where it is under threat by an opposing player.

QUEEN
The queen is the most powerful piece on the board. She can move in any direction and for any number of squares as long as her path is clear of her own pieces. If she captures an opponent's piece her move is over.

BISHOP
The bishop is topped by a mitre (bishop's head-dress). It can move any distance diagonally as long as its path is clear. The bishop starts on a light or dark square and must stay on the same colour throughout the game.

KNIGHT
The knight is useful because it can jump over pieces in its path. It moves two squares in any direction and then sideways one square to the left or right. In effect, it sits in the corner of a rectangle three squares by two and jumps to the opposite corner.

ROOK OR CASTLE
Sitting in the corner of the board at the beginning of the game, the rook (or castle) can move backwards, forwards, left, and right as far as it needs to. Its path has to be clear of pieces of the same colour. The rooks are often used to protect each other.

PAWN
Pawns are the smallest and least valuable pieces. Throughout the game, a pawn can move just one square at a time forwards from its starting position. But for its very first move, the pawn has the option of moving two squares forward.

GAMES THROUGH THE AGES

Archaeologists have found ancient game pieces that are more than 5,000 years old. Prehistoric people played games even earlier, with bones that were used like dice.

3100 BCE
The oldest known board game, Senet is a favourite pastime in Ancient Egypt.

Senet in tomb painting

Backgammon

3000 BCE
A board game similar to backgammon is played.

500 BCE
Pachisi, India's national game, is mentioned in the epic poem The Mahabharata.

200 CE
A pottery Go board from this era has been found in Shaanxi Province, China.

600s
An ancestor of the game of chess, Chaturanga is referred to in Indian writings.

700s
Fragments of early mancala games have been found in Eritrea, Africa.

Mancala

900s
Playing cards appear in China's Tang dynasty.

Hnefatafl

1230
The Scandinavian strategy game Hnefatafl is mentioned in the Norse Saga.

1200s
The first mention of the game of dominoes appears in a Chinese text.

Draughts

1492
A knight and lady are shown playing draughts in a medieval book.

Cribbage board

1600s
A card game called cribbage, played with a scorekeeping board, is invented.

c.1850
The Chinese game mahjong is created from earlier versions.

1886
The first World Chess Tournament is held.

1874
Parcheesi, a version of the ancient Indian game pachisi, is introduced to the USA.

Pachisi

1890s
Snakes and Ladders, based on an ancient Indian game, becomes popular in Victorian England.

1938
Criss Cross Words (later Scrabble) is invented by a US architect.

1970
A code-breaking game for two players called Mastermind is invented.

1978
Space Invaders becomes a blockbuster arcade video game.

1980
Arcade game Pac-Man is released in Japan.

1980
Rubik's Cube is launched and becomes the world's best-selling puzzle game.

Rubik's cube

1984
The Trivial Pursuit general knowledge game is a huge success.

2000
Computer gamers can set up home and choose how to live in The Sims, a follow-on from SimCity.

2004
World of Warcraft is created – a MMORPG (massively multiplayer online role-playing game).

2011
The multi-award-winning computer game Minecraft is released.

3100 BCE

2015

Magic

Magicians perform tricks and illusions to amaze an audience by making the impossible seem possible and the unbelievable believable. With practice and a little skill, anyone can learn a few magic tricks to impress friends and family. The golden rule of magic is never to reveal how your trick works.

PIECE OF ROPE

BOW TIE

BAG OF COINS

MAGIC TOOLS

All magicians have a few pieces of essential equipment in their tool box, as aids for tricks and for showmanship. A pack of playing cards and a set of cups and balls are probably the most important. Wands are also popular.

WAND

SCARVES

PACK OF CARDS

CUPS AND BALLS

TOP HAT AND RABBIT

DISAPPEARING COIN TRICK

In this vanishing trick, you will convince your audience that a coin has disappeared, when in reality it is hidden. You will need scissors, two sheets of paper or card, glue, a pencil, a handkerchief, a coin, and a clear plastic cup.

1 DRAW A CIRCLE
Place the plastic cup upside down on one of the pieces of paper or card and draw around it with your pencil. Cut out the circle.

2 GLUE THE CIRCLE
Glue the paper circle to the rim of the cup. You can discard the remains of the piece of paper or card.

3 PLACE THE OBJECTS
Place the cup upside down on the second piece of paper or card. Put the handkerchief and coin there too.

4 BEGIN THE PERFORMANCE
Now you are ready to begin the trick. Gather the audience, then put the handkerchief over the cup.

5 HIDE THE COIN
Completely cover the cup with the handkerchief and place it over the coin. You might want to wave your wand or say some magic words now.

6 SLOWLY REVEAL
Gently remove the handkerchief from the cup, taking care not to move the cup itself.

7 NO COIN!
If you are careful, your audience won't guess that the coin is actually underneath the paper circle.

WATER TO ICE

This is a simple transformation trick. You will need a paper cup, ice, sponge, scissors, and a small jug of water. Practise first so you know how much water your piece of sponge will absorb.

1 ADD THE SPONGE
Cut a piece of sponge to fit snugly inside your paper cup. This will absorb the water you pour in.

2 PLACE THE ICE
Put a few ice cubes on top of the sponge in the base of the cup. Gather your audience now, before the ice melts.

3 POUR THE WATER
Ask your audience to watch you pouring water from the jug into your cup, making sure they can't see into the cup.

4 VOILA!
Say some magic words or wave your wand, then tip the cup upside down and the ice cubes will tumble out.

MAGIC EFFECTS

There are thousands of different magic tricks and magicians are always thinking up new ones. All magicians perform their magic using effects. The simplest tricks rely on just one effect, but more complicated tricks use several effects at once.

PRODUCTION
Making something – or someone – appear out of nowhere.

VANISHING
The opposite of production – making a thing or person disappear.

LEVITATION OR SUSPENSION
Making something or someone appear to fly or float in midair.

PREDICTION
Seeming to know what is about to happen, such as which card will be picked.

TRANSFORMATION
Changing one thing into something else, such as a person into an animal.

RESTORATION
"Magically" repairing a torn or broken object.

ESCAPOLOGY
Escaping from restraints such as handcuffs, or traps such as cages.

TELEPORTATION
Moving something from one place to another without seeming to handle it.

MAGIC SKILLS

Entertaining the audience is a magician's first task. Once the audience is under his or her spell, the magician uses sleight of hand – distraction and deception – to make it appear that real magic is being performed.

SHOWMANSHIP
A good magician amuses and entertains the audience. Props such as scarves come in useful, and so does "patter" – telling jokes or asking questions.

SLEIGHT OF HAND
The magician takes advantage of "blind spots" in the audience's vision and uses fast, fluid hand movements to hide or disguise an action.

MAGICIANS

The first stars of stage magic invented their own amazing tricks. Today's top magicians continue this tradition, devising different illusions to delight and enthral audiences.

○ **THE GREAT LAFAYETTE (1871–1911)**
Lafayette was probably the most successful magician of his time. His speciality was dramatic illusions, often performed with his dog Beauty, a gift from Harry Houdini.

○ **HARRY HOUDINI (1874–1926)**
The greatest escapologist the world has ever known, Houdini could free himself from anything – handcuffs, leg irons, cages, straitjackets, prison cells, and even a sealed milk can.

HOUDINI

○ **DANTE THE GREAT (1883–1955)**
Dante's amazing shows of tricks and illusions included a huge cast of musicians, jugglers, acrobats, birds, and animals.

○ **CRISS ANGEL (1967–)**
"Magician of the Century" Criss Angel's stunts include walking on water, floating between two buildings, making an elephant disappear, and being run over by a steamroller while lying on a bed of glass.

○ **DAVID BLAINE (1973–)**
Blaine performs amazing feats of endurance such as being encased in ice, buried alive, or surrounded by deadly electric currents.

RAISING ACES

This teleportation trick makes it look as though you can conjure up the aces from a pack of cards. Carry out the first step in secret, then ask for a volunteer.

1 PREPARE THE DECK
Remove all four aces and place them on the top of the pack face down.

2 FOUR PILES
Ask your volunteer to divide the pack into four roughly equal piles. Keep track of which pile contains the aces.

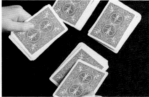

3 TOP THREE CARDS
Ask the volunteer to choose one of the three piles that don't contain the aces. Get him or her to take the top three cards and move them to the bottom of the pile.

4 DEAL ONE CARD
Have your volunteer deal one card from their pile on to each of the other three piles. Then repeat this for the other piles without aces, and finally for the pile with aces.

5 REVEAL THE ACES
Ask your volunteer to turn over the top card of each pile to reveal the four aces.

HEAT IS ON

This coin trick uses the effect of prediction to make your audience believe you have hidden mind-reading powers. You will need a bag of cool coins – put the coins in the fridge for a few minutes before you start.

1 GATHER THE AUDIENCE
Ask an audience member to pick a coin from the bag, hold it tightly and think hard about its appearance.

2 MIX THEM UP
Ask your volunteer to put the coin back in the bag, then tip out all the coins.

3 MISLEAD THE AUDIENCE
Pick up each coin and look at it, pretending to concentrate hard.

4 SHOW THE COIN
The coin that is warm to the touch is the one your volunteer picked up, of course!

THE MAGIC STRING

This trick uses the effect of restoration to appear to make a cut piece of string whole again. You will need a short length and a longer length of string and scissors.

1 SHORT STRING
Take the short length of string and hide it in the palm of your left hand.

2 LONG STRING
Place the longer length in your left hand below the shorter, so the shorter loop sticks out.

3 CUT THE STRING
Ask a volunteer to cut through the loop that's sticking out.

4 HIDE IT
Secretly tuck the cut pieces into the palm of your hand and pull out the long string.

5 RESTORE THE STRING
Show your audience the long string while keeping the shorter length hidden in your hand.

Horse riding

There are many ways to enjoy riding a horse, from playing team games and jumping over obstacles to going for a quiet canter in the countryside. Learning how to look after and handle a horse safely and correctly is part of becoming a good rider.

RIDING GEAR

A safety hat or helmet is the most important part of a rider's clothing. Boots should have a low heel to stop the feet from slipping through the stirrups. Chaps (leggings) worn over riding trousers or jodhpurs protect the lower legs.

SHOW JACKET

LONG BOOTS

PROTECTIVE HAT

GLOVES

HALF CHAPS

JODHPUR BOOTS

TACK

The equipment worn by a horse is known as tack. The bridle, which has a mouthpiece called a bit, allows the rider to control the horse's head. The saddle spreads the rider's weight evenly across the horse's back. There are many different styles of tack for different purposes.

Numnah absorbs sweat and helps to protect horse's back

Reins

Saddle

Bit passes through horse's mouth

Stirrup

Girth holds saddle in position

BRIDLE

WESTERN BRIDLE

RUBBER SNAFFLE BIT

JOINTED SNAFFLE BIT

JOINTED EGGBUTT SNAFFLE BIT

Curb chain

PELHAM BIT

Tongue groove

RUBBER PELHAM BIT

KIMBLEWICK BIT

RACING SADDLE

DRESSAGE SADDLE

ENGLISH SADDLE

WESTERN SADDLE

PUTTING ON A SADDLE

It is important to know how to put on a saddle correctly. A badly positioned saddle can hurt a horse's back and be unsafe for the rider. Both before and after mounting, the rider should check that the girth (the strap that goes under the horse's belly) is tight enough.

1 POSITION THE SADDLE
Place the saddle pad or numnah and saddle further forwards than the final position. Move both backwards together.

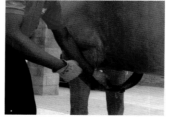

2 PICK UP GIRTH
Bring down the girth on the far side and pick up the end from the near side. Make sure it is not twisted.

3 FASTEN BUCKLES
Buckle the girth to the straps on the saddle. Pull it tight but without wrinkling the horse's skin.

GROOMING TOOLS

There are various specially designed tools for grooming horses. They include a stiff "dandy" brush and a rubber curry comb for cleaning off mud, softer brushes for removing dust and scurf, and a pick for dislodging dirt from hoofs.

HOOF OIL

HOOF PICK

HOOF OIL BRUSH

SWEAT SCRAPER

BODY BRUSH

DANDY BRUSH

SPONGE

RUBBER CURRY COMB

FEEDING A HORSE

The natural food of horses is grass, but a hard-working horse needs more. Extra foodstuffs include hay for fibre, grains such as oats, and nutritious pellets and mixes.

HAY

ALFALFA

PELLETS

COARSE MIX

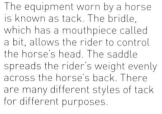

MOUNTING

or a new rider, the first challenge is getting into the saddle. earning how to mount a horse quickly and safely takes lots f practice. The rider should always begin from the left-hand r "near" side of the horse.

1 LIFT FOOT
Face the horse's rear. old the stirrup in the right and and put the left foot in it.

2 HOP
Hold the front of the saddle and hop round to face forwards. Use the right arm for support.

3 SPRING
Spring up and swing the right leg over the horse's back. Land gently in the saddle.

DISMOUNTING

Getting off a horse feels easier than getting on. However, for safety and the horse's comfort, the correct technique must be used. The rider dismounts on the near side and should never attempt to jump off while the horse is moving.

1 FEET OUT
Holding the front of the saddle, take both feet out of the stirrups and lean forwards.

2 SWING
Lift the right leg and swing it carefully over the horse's back.

3 SLIDE
Slide or drop down the horse's side and land lightly, facing forwards.

THE HIGH-JUMP RECORD FOR A HORSE IS 2.47 M (8 FT 1¼ IN)

JUMPING

Learning to jump on horseback is one of the biggest thrills for any rider. Most horses find it fun, too.

FOUR PACES

Horses have four main natural paces, or ways of moving at different speeds. These are walk, trot, canter, and gallop. At each pace, the horse's feet touch the ground in a repeated sequence of steps.

WALK: AVERAGE SPEED 5–6.5 KM/H (3–4 MPH)

TROT: AVERAGE SPEED 13–16 KM/H (8–10 MPH)

CANTER: AVERAGE SPEED 16–27 KM/H (10–17 MPH)

GALLOP: AVERAGE SPEED 40–48 KM/H (25–30 MPH)

HORSE SPORTS

Games and sports with horses are popular worldwide. They include racing, team games, and competitions between individual riders, such as jumping and cross-country events.

POLO
Team game in which riders strike a ball with mallets.

STEEPLECHASE
Race over obstacles such as fences and ditches.

DRESSAGE
Competition to show how well a horse moves.

   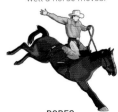

EVENTING
Sport combining dressage, cross-country riding, and showjumping.

HARNESS RACE
Racing with two-wheeled carts called sulkies.

HORSEBALL
Team game in which riders shoot a ball into a net.

RODEO
Contest based on traditional cowboy skills.

History

The first humans

Millions of years ago, a group of apes began to walk upright. They were our ancestors, the first human-like animals on the planet. Over time, their bodies adapted to walking upright and their brains grew larger, until finally they evolved into our species, *Homo sapiens*.

EARLY TOOLS
Early humans learned how to make tools by striking a stone with another one to make a cutting edge. Humans began to make different tools for different tasks, such as digging, sawing, or opening nuts.

SMALL HANDAXE

ANTLER HAMMER

FLINT BLADE

SAW

LATE ARRIVALS
Our planet was formed just over 4.5 billion years ago. If the whole of Earth's history were squeezed into an hour, most life forms would not develop until the last ten minutes. Humans would not appear until the very last fraction of the last second of the hour.

00:01 Earth's crust forms	**10:27** Oldest rocks on Earth's surface	**17:37** First bacteria	**41:45** First seaweed	**51:12** First jellyfish
53:25 First fish	**54:59** First insect	**57:07** First mammal	**59:58.8** First human ancestor	**59:59.9** First modern human appears

ON TWO FEET
Humans walk on two legs, unlike other primates (apes), who are either climbers or walk using all four feet. As a result of walking upright, humans' bodies have developed very differently from those of their ape relatives.

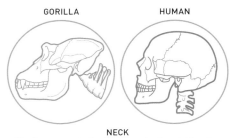

GORILLA   HUMAN

NECK
The human neck sits directly under the skull so the head balances at the top of the spine. A gorilla's neck meets the head from the side.

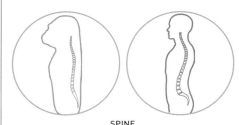

SPINE
The human spine has developed extra curves at the neck and lower back, so it can absorb the impact better when the person walks or runs.

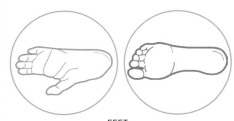

FEET
A gorilla's big toe is on the side of the foot, to help it climb trees. Human feet have aligning toes and longer heels, to support weight evenly while we walk.

OUT OF AFRICA
Homo sapiens, our species, first evolved in Africa around 150,000 years ago. About 100,000 years later, they began to move away to make new settlements, until humans were living on all the world's continents, except Antarctica.

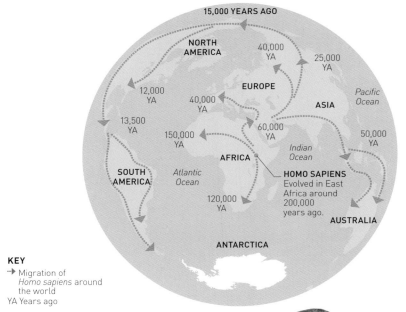

15,000 YEARS AGO

NORTH AMERICA — 40,000 YA
25,000 YA
EUROPE — 40,000 YA
12,000 YA
13,500 YA
150,000 YA
ASIA
Pacific Ocean
60,000 YA
50,000 YA
AFRICA
Indian Ocean
SOUTH AMERICA
Atlantic Ocean
HOMO SAPIENS Evolved in East Africa around 200,000 years ago.
120,000 YA
AUSTRALIA
ANTARCTICA

KEY
→ Migration of *Homo sapiens* around the world
YA Years ago

HOW TO MAKE A HANDAXE
It took skill and experience to select a suitable stone, then chip it to make a sharp, usable tool.

1 Selected stone is struck with a stone "hammer".

2 Large flakes are removed next to the first.

---

7 MYA (million years ago)
Sahelanthropus tchadensis
Thought to be last common ancestor of both chimps and humans.

6.1 MYA
Orrorin tugenensis
Possibly the first ape to walk on two legs.

4.1 MYA
Australopithecus afarensis
Thought to be the ancestor of the genus *Homo*, to which modern humans belong.

Australopithecus afarensis

2.2 MYA
Homo habilis
Called *habilis* (Latin for "handyman") because they may have been the first species to use tools.

600,000 YA
Homo heidelbergensis
Higher, broader skull to protect a larger brain than earlier species.

Homo sapiens

150,000 YA
Homo sapiens
Evolved in Africa, then spread worldwide, becoming the only surviving species of the *Homo* genus.

8 MYA   PRESENT

HUMAN ANCESTORS
About 7 million years ago, the ape family split into two branches – one would lead to chimpanzees, and the other was the line of human-like apes (hominins) that would eventually evolve into modern humans.

3.3 MYA
Australopithecus africanus
Ape-like, with a small brain but human-like teeth.

1 MYA
Homo erectus
As tall as modern humans, with a similar build.

Homo erectus

350,000 YA
Homo neanderthalensis
Excellent hunters and tool-makers who thrived in the colder climate of Europe.

Homo neanderthalensis

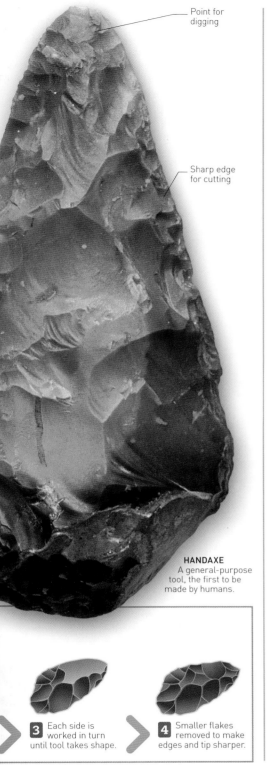

Point for digging

Sharp edge for cutting

HANDAXE
A general-purpose tool, the first to be made by humans.

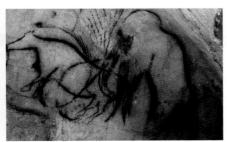

> **3** Each side is worked in turn until tool takes shape.

> **4** Smaller flakes removed to make edges and tip sharper.

HUNTER-GATHERERS
Early humans had to find food either by hunting animals, or by gathering wild plants. They developed tools to help them, from diggers for rooting out edible plants from the soil to harpoons for spearing fish.

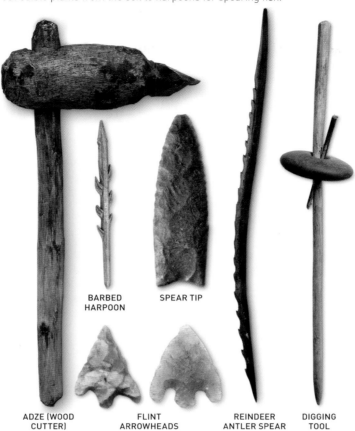

BARBED HARPOON

SPEAR TIP

ADZE (WOOD CUTTER)

FLINT ARROWHEADS

REINDEER ANTLER SPEAR

DIGGING TOOL

ANCIENT MONUMENTS
Many prehistoric sites still exist around the world. It is difficult to know exactly what some sites were used for, as they were built long before humans started keeping written records.

- **STONEHENGE, ENGLAND**
  A ring of gigantic stones, built about 5,000 years ago, as part of an ancient burial ground, or as a place of worship.

- **CARNAC, FRANCE**
  A small area of three fields, containing more than 3,000 granite megaliths (standing stones), arranged in rows.

- **GGANTIJA TEMPLES, MALTA**
  Two remarkably well preserved structures, built from limestone during the Neolithic Age (c.3600–3200 BCE).

- **GOBEKLI TEPE, TURKEY**
  The world's oldest known temple, built about 11,000 years ago near the ancient city of Şanlıurfa.

- **NEWGRANGE, IRELAND**
  A Neolithic burial site featuring a huge, circular mound containing a tomb and surrounded by 97 highly decorated stones.

STONE CIRCLE AT STONEHENGE

FIRST FARMERS
Gradually, humans learned that instead of moving around, constantly looking for food, they could stay in one place and become farmers, growing crops and raising animals to eat. Farming changed forever the way humans lived.

PART OF A BREAD OVEN

STONE SICKLE
For cutting crops.

TYPICAL BREAD

IRON SICKLE

BRONZE SICKLE

STONE AXE
Used to clear trees before planting crops.

REPLICA OF STONE QUERN
For grinding wheat to make bread.

ART
Early humans created the world's first art. They used paint made from coloured minerals in rocks to draw animals on the walls of their caves. They also carved animals or human figures out of rocks and bones.

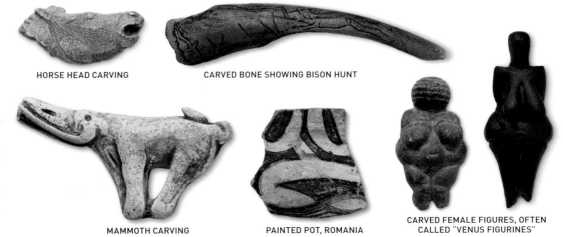

HORSE HEAD CARVING

CARVED BONE SHOWING BISON HUNT

CAVE PAINTING, FRANCE

MAMMOTH CARVING

PAINTED POT, ROMANIA

CARVED FEMALE FIGURES, OFTEN CALLED "VENUS FIGURINES"

MARBLE FIGURE, GREECE

BETWEEN TWO RIVERS

The region of Mesopotamia lay in the fertile flood plain between the rivers Tigris and Euphrates. The name Mesopotamia means "between two rivers" in Greek.

KEY
- Sumer region

SUMER
Sumer was not a single country but a collection of city-states that competed with each other for control of the region.

Early civilizations

The world's earliest civilization emerged more than 6,000 years ago in an area of Mesopotamia (modern-day Iraq) called Sumer. For the first time, people lived and worked together in cities, governed by a king who made laws that everyone had to follow.

FROM HUNTING TO FARMING

When roaming hunter-gatherers started planting crops, they began to settle in one place and made farming tools instead of hunting weapons. Villages, towns, and eventually cities were established.

PLOUGH

ADZE (TOOL FOR SHAPING WOOD)

ADZE HEADS

GREAT CITIES

As the Sumerian settlements grew, they formed cities, some of which became large and powerful city-states. Each city-state had its own leader, who ruled on behalf of the city's god.

○ **URUK**
Uruk was one of the first major cities in the world. Its most famous king was Gilgamesh, who was also the hero of one of the world's first known poems, *The Epic of Gilgamesh*.

○ **AKKAD**
This city was the centre of the world's first empire. In 2330 BCE, the Akkadians conquered many of their neighbouring city-states and took control of Mesopotamia.

○ **BABYLON**
The capital of the Babylonian Empire. At its peak around 550 BCE, the city's population was about 200,000.

○ **NIMRUD**
For a time, the capital of the Assyrian Empire. The magnificent palace of King Shalmaneser III covered over 50,000 sq m (538,196 sq ft) and had more than 200 rooms.

○ **UR**
Site of a huge ziggurat (pyramid-shaped temple) and the Royal Tombs, which contained some of the finest Mesopotamian art ever discovered.

THE SUMERIANS CREATED THE FIRST CALENDAR BY DIVIDING THE YEAR INTO 12, BASED ON THE MOON'S MOVEMENTS

BABYLON'S WONDERS

In 580 BCE King Nebuchadnezzar of Babylon built a number of huge buildings in his capital, turning Babylon into the most magnificent city in the ancient world.

ISHTAR GATE
Gigantic main entrance to the city, designed to inspire awe in visitors.

ETEMENANKI ZIGGURAT
Temple of Marduk, patron god of Babylon. Rebuilt after it was destroyed in about 689 BCE.

HANGING GARDENS
Majestic terraced garden, one of the Seven Wonders of the Ancient World.

CRADLE OF CIVILIZATION

The plain between the two great rivers of Mesopotamia was very fertile, with rich soil, a warm climate, reliable rainfall, and a wide range of plants and animals. It was the perfect place for early humans to put away their hunting spears and settle down in farming communities instead.

7000 BCE
People start to grow crops on a large scale in Mesopotamia.

5300 BCE
Large villages and small towns appear in Sumer.

Brick with inscription

3300 BCE
Sumerians invent a form of writing.

3000 BCE
Egypt: the pharaohs unite Egypt into a single state.

2334 BCE
King Sargon of Akkad conquers Sumer, creating the world's first empire.

Figure of Sumerian priest

c.2100 BCE
The great ziggurat (temple) built at Ur.

Ziggurat at Ur

539 BCE
Mesopotamia becomes part of Persia.

7000 BCE

500 BCE

4000 BCE
The Sumerians build several cities in southern Mesopotamia.

3200 BCE
Greece: earliest civilizations appear.

2800 BCE
Peru: earliest civilization in the Americas.

2600 BCE
Northwest India: Indus civilization reaches its peak.

2200 BCE
China: first kingdom established.

c. 2500–2000 BCE
Huge cemetery complex built at Ur.

1300–1200 BCE
Assyrians conquer much of Mesopotamia.

753 BCE
City of Rome founded.

Ornament from Royal Graves, Ur

Sedu (Assyrian god)

CODE OF LAW

King Hammurabi of Babylon laid down a set of strict rules that is one of the oldest recorded codes of law in the world.

NO RUNAWAYS
If you helped a slave to run away, you would be put to death.

HANDS OFF!
If a son hit his father, his hands would be chopped off.

TEMPLE OF DOOM
If you stole from a temple, you would be sentenced to death.

INVENTION OF THE WHEEL

Nobody knows exactly when the wheel was invented, but they were in use in Sumer by 3500 BCE. Sumerians used the wheel vertically on their chariots, and horizontally to make clay pots.

RECONSTRUCTION OF AN EARLY WHEEL

DAILY LIFE

Cups, bowls, and vases for everyday use were made of clay, but richer homes used vessels made of stone or metal. Silver was imported from nearby Anatolia to make luxury tableware.

BRONZE BULL'S HEAD

SILVER BOWL

STONE POT

ALABASTER VASE

SOAPSTONE TUMBLER

SCORPION DESIGN CUP

CYLINDER SEAL (LEFT) WITH IMPRESSION (RIGHT) OF GODS FIGHTING LIONS

GODS AND RELIGION

The Sumerians worshipped many gods, but the most important were the guardians of each city-state. Gods were worshipped in huge temples called ziggurats, which dominated the flat landscape for miles.

UTU
God of the Sun and of justice.

ENLIL
God of wind and storms.

EARLY WRITING

The first known form of writing comes from Sumer. The first symbols were recognizable pictures of objects (pictograms), but these developed into a system of simpler wedge shapes, called cuneiform.

PICTOGRAPH c.3100 BCE	CUNEIFORM c.700 BCE
≈	
WATER	
HAND	
BARLEY	
BREAD	
DAY	

WEALTH AND POWER

Much of the Mesopotamian art and crafts that survives today was found in a royal cemetery in the city of Ur. These treasures tell us about the skill and artistry of the craftsmen who made them, as well as the wealth of the people buried with their valuable possessions.

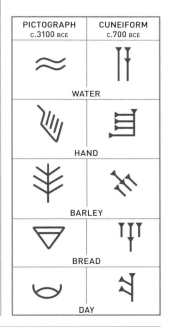

Hair comb

Gold willow leaves

Crescent-shaped earrings

Beaded cape

Belt

QUEEN PUABI'S FINERY

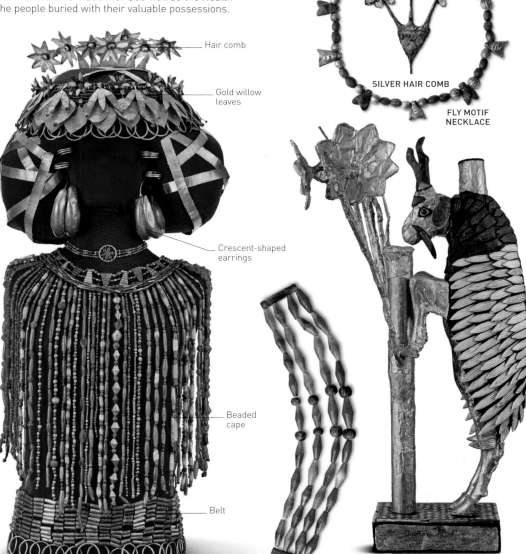

SILVER HAIR COMB

FLY MOTIF NECKLACE

BEAD BELT

"RAM IN A THICKET"
Gold, silver, shell, and lapis ram and shrub.

WAR AND WARRIORS

The different city-states of Mesopotamia competed with one another for land and vital resources, such as water, and this often led to fighting and war. Warring cities began to organize trained groups of men to fight – the world's first armies. Soldiers wore bronze or leather helmets, and carried large shields and bronze spears or bows and arrows.

ARCHERS ON A CHARIOT

FAMOUS PHARAOHS

The kings and queens of Ancient Egypt did not call themselves pharaohs, but that is the name we use today. They wielded an enormous amount of power. They made every law, held the title of highest priest in the land, and were worshipped as though they were gods.

KHUFU
Reigned c.2589–2566 BCE
Builder of the Great
Pyramid at Giza.

KHAFRA
Reigned c.2558–2532 BCE
Khufu's son. His face may
be the model for the Sphinx.

HATSHEPSUT
Reigned c.1473–1458 BCE
One of only a few
female pharaohs.

TUTANKHAMUN
Reigned c.1336–1327 BCE
The famous boy-king came to the throne when he was just nine years old. His fabulous gold mask was found in his tomb.

TUTHMOSIS III
Reigned c.1479–1425 BCE
Great military leader who
never lost a battle.

AMENHOTEP III
Reigned c.1390–1353 BCE
Helped to make
Egypt prosperous.

AKHENATEN
Reigned c.1353–1336 BCE
Rejected traditional
Egyptian gods.

RAMESES II
Reigned c.1279–1213 BCE
Ordered many huge
building projects.

CLEOPATRA VII
Reigned 51–30 BCE
Last pharaoh. Killed herself
after defeat by Rome.

Ancient Egypt

More than 5,000 years ago, two regions of the Nile river valley – Upper and Lower Egypt – were united under a common ruler. This was the birth of the empire of pharaohs and pyramids, one of the greatest powers of the ancient world.

PYRAMIDS

When an Egyptian ruler died the body was buried inside a massive pyramid. Taking up to 30 years to build, pyramids went through various changes of design over the centuries. People who were not royal were buried in simpler tombs.

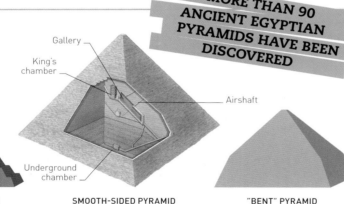

Gallery

King's chamber

Airshaft

Underground chamber

MORE THAN 90 ANCIENT EGYPTIAN PYRAMIDS HAVE BEEN DISCOVERED

MASTABA
Box-like brick or
stone grave.

STEPPED PYRAMID
An early model, built
in layers.

SMOOTH-SIDED PYRAMID
The classic structure, cased
with blocks of limestone.

"BENT" PYRAMID
Midway between
stepped and smooth.

THE RIVER NILE

Living along both banks of the Nile, the Egyptians occupied a rare fertile strip of land amid vast areas of desert. Their lives depended on the river. Regular flooding left deposits of rich soil that was excellent for farming grain crops.

ROWING BOAT
Wooden boats wer
used for transpor
and fishing.

Furled sai

Rudder fo
steering

MUMMY-MAKING

The Ancient Egyptians believed that a dead person's soul needed its body in the afterlife. Mummifying – which only the rich could afford – was an elaborate way of preserving a body to stop it crumbling away.

Priest wears
Jackal god mask

Linen
wrapping

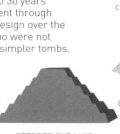

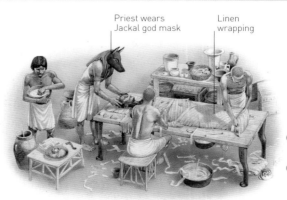

1 PRESERVING
After removal, the organs were preserved in canopic jars – pots topped with a god's head.

2 WASHING
Once dry, the body was washed in wine and rubbed with scents and oils.

3 PROTECTING
Protective amulets, like this symbolic pillar, were placed with the body.

4 WRAPPING
Strips of fine linen were wrapped around the entire body and coated with resin.

5 BURIAL
The mummy was put in an inner, body-shaped case and then an outer coffin, both decorated with pictures and symbols.

GODS AND GODDESSES

There were many gods and goddesses for an Ancient Egyptian to worship. This "family tree" shows how some of the major gods descended from Atum, who the Egyptians believed created everything.

EVERY TOWN IN ANCIENT EGYPT HAD ITS OWN LOCAL GOD

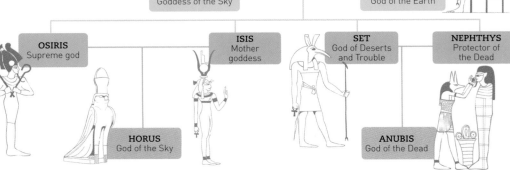

ATUM
Lord of Heaven

SHU
God of Air and Winds

TEFNUT
Goddess of Rain

NUT
Goddess of the Sky

GEB
God of the Earth

OSIRIS
Supreme god

ISIS
Mother goddess

SET
God of Deserts and Trouble

NEPHTHYS
Protector of the Dead

HORUS
God of the Sky

ANUBIS
God of the Dead

HIEROGLYPHS

Ancient Egyptian writing used pictures or signs called hieroglyphs. Each one could mean a sound, a word, or an action. The "alphabet" seen here shows some hieroglyphs and how they might be pronounced today. Instead of writing on paper, the Egyptians used flattened sheets of a type of reed called papyrus.

a	a	b	kh	h	tj	d	a/i
g	h	kh	j	k	m	n	w/u
p	k	r	sh	s	t	f	s

JEWELLERY

The Ancient Egyptians prized jewellery. Rings, necklaces, and amulets in the form of sacred symbols were popular. Jewellery worn by rich people was often made of gold and valuable stones.

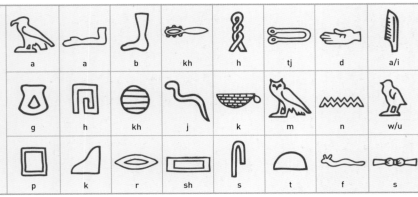

WINGED SCARAB AMULET

GOLD AMULET

EARRING

FINGER RINGS

BEAD NECKLACE

Mediterranean Sea
Nile Delta
LOWER EGYPT
· Giza
LOWER NILE
Red Sea
Abydos
UPPER EGYPT
Elephantine
SAHARA
NUBIAN DESERT

Egyptian Empire
1549–1069 BCE

HISTORY OF ANCIENT EGYPT

The Ancient Egyptian civilization lasted for more than 3,000 years, with hundreds of different rulers, both good and bad. Historians have divided up this very long timespan into major dynasties (ruling families), kingdoms, and periods.

3000 BCE

EARLY DYNASTIC PERIOD
c.3000–2686 BCE
Organized government under the rule of the pharaohs begins. People start to use hieroglyphs.

OLD KINGDOM
2686–2125 BCE
The great pyramids and the Sphinx are built at Giza.

The Sphinx at Giza

1ST INTERMEDIATE PERIOD
2160–2055 BCE
Many power struggles between dynasties.

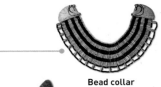
Slab for mixing ointment, made around 2000 BCE

MIDDLE KINGDOM
2055–1650 BCE
Life is more settled. Improved irrigation produces better crops.

Bead collar

2ND INTERMEDIATE PERIOD
1650–1550 BCE
More unrest, with wars and invasions.

Arrowheads

NEW KINGDOM
1550–1069 BCE
Egypt conquers many lands. Famous pharaohs include Tutankhamun.

Statuette of slave girl

3RD INTERMEDIATE PERIOD
1069–664 BCE
Assyrians conquer Egypt.

LATE PERIOD
664–332 BCE
Time of much temple building and animal mummifying.

Bronze statue, which may have held a cat mummy

PTOLEMAIC DYNASTY
332–30 BCE
Cleopatra VII, the last pharaoh, dies. Rome conquers Egypt.

30 BCE

Coin showing the head of Cleopatra

Painted mummy case, portraying the dead person

Scenes from the Underworld

Spread wings were a common decoration

Traditional sacred symbols of cross and pillar

The Ancient Greek civilization existed for 2,500 years. The Greeks built huge city-states, formed new colonies, and fought many battles before they were finally conquered by the Romans.

2200–1450 BCE
Height of Minoan palace culture in Crete.

Model of a Minoan house

1450 BCE
Mycenaeans invade Crete and occupy the Minoan palaces. They also build their own palace settlements in the Peloponnese region.

Fortified palace of Mycenae

1350 BCE
At the peak of the Mycenaean period, the city of Mycenae has a population of around 30,000.

Greek soldiers hid in a wooden horse to defeat the Trojans

1184 BCE
According to Homer, Greece defeats Troy in a war that has lasted more than ten years.

2500 BCE

MINOAN PERIOD
2500–1600 BCE
Minoan civilization flourishes in Crete. The Minoans are clever traders and build large palace complexes, but these are destroyed by invaders.

MYCENAEAN PERIOD
1600–1200 BCE
The Mycenaeans build fortified palaces. Armed with bronze weapons, they expand into Crete, but their cities fall to new invaders from the north.

DARK AGES
1200–800 BCE
The Mycenaean culture collapses around 1200 BCE, and Greece enters a dark age. Settlements become smaller and there are no written records.

Ancient Greece

The Greeks were one of the most advanced civilizations in the ancient world, inventing politics, philosophy, theatre, athletics, and the study of history. Their stories and plays still exist today, along with the remains of beautiful temples and buildings.

TROY

DELPHI

CORINTH — THEBES
OLYMPIA — ATHENS

MYCENAE

SPARTA

KNOSSOS

CITY-STATES
For most of its history, Ancient Greece was divided into city-states. Each city ruled the villages and farmlands around it with their own system of government and chose one god as a special protector.

WARRING STATES
The city-states of Athens and Sparta were bitter rivals and fought several wars against each other.

THE CITY-STATE OF ATHENS WAS 20 TIMES LARGER THAN THE SMALLEST GREEK COMMUNITIES

DAILY LIFE
Farmers and fishermen provided food, while in the city, traders sold leather goods, pots, weapons, and jewellery. Well-born women ran the household, helped by slaves.

SILVER ATHENIAN COIN

COIN FROM KNOSSOS

GOLD ALEXANDRIAN COIN

FISH PLATE

GOLD EARRING

REPLICA OF A GREEK PENDANT

MODELS DRESSED AS ANCIENT GREEKS

SMALL POT FOR OIL OR PERFUME

WINE JUG

SANDAL-SHAPED PERFUME BOTTLE

POWDER BOX

EARTHENWARE COOKING STOVE

CLASSICAL OIL POT

THE PARTHENON
This marble temple dedicated to the goddess Athena is one of the world's finest monuments. Built between 447 and 432 BCE, it has 85 Doric columns and a coloured frieze showing a procession.

Statue of Athena covered in gold and ivory

OLYMPIC GAMES
The Olympic Games were held in honour of the god Zeus. They took place every fourth year from 776 BCE at a site called Olympia.

DAY 1
On the first day of the games, competitors and judges swore an oath to compete fairly, and boys took part in running and boxing contests.

DAY 2
The second day was for chariot and horse races and the pentathlon – long jump, discus, javelin, running, and wrestling.

DAY 3
On the third day, 100 oxen were sacrificed to Zeus. Running races included the 200-metre "stade" race – the oldest contest in the games.

DAY 4
Wrestling and boxing filled the fourth day. Pankration was a kind of wrestling in which kicking and strangling were allowed.

DAY 5
On the final day, the winning athletes went to the Temple of Zeus to be crowned with olive wreaths.

800–775 BCE
The Greeks create new colonies in the eastern Mediterranean and southern Italy.

Greek trireme

750–700 BCE
The first great works of Greek literature are composed by Homer – *The Iliad* and *The Odyssey*.

Oil lamp decorated with images from *The Odyssey*

620–510 BCE
Many Greek city-states are ruled by tyrants who hold absolute power.

490 BCE
The Persian King Darius I invades Greece, but is defeated by the Athenians at the Battle of Marathon.

431–404 BCE
Sparta and Athens fight the Peloponnesian War, with great loss of life on both sides.

371 BCE
General Epaminondas defeats the Spartans at Leuctra. Thebes becomes Greece's most powerful city-state.

338 BCE
Philip, King of Macedon, defeats Athens and Thebes at Chaeronea, and conquers most of Greece.

334–323 BCE
Philip's son Alexander the Great invades and conquers the Persian Empire.

Alexander the Great on his horse Bucephalus

31 BCE
Rome captures all the Greek colonies, ending with Egypt in 31 BCE.

31 BCE

ARCHAIC PERIOD
800–500 BCE
By around 800 BCE, Greece begins to recover. City-states hold political power, backed by armies of citizen-soldiers. The Greeks begin to found colonies abroad.

CLASSICAL PERIOD
500–323 BCE
During the classical period, literature, art, politics, athletics, and theatre flourish, especially around the main centre, Athens.

HELLENISTIC PERIOD
323–31 BCE
Alexander the Great begins the Hellenistic Age in 323 BCE, and Greek culture spreads throughout the Middle East.

GODS

The Greeks had many gods, ruled over by Zeus and his wife Hera. Festivals and sacrifices were important in the daily religious life of the city-states. Women rarely had any role in public life, but a few were priestesses who played an important part in rituals and celebrations.

ZEUS

GREEK ALPHABET

The Ancient Greeks had an alphabet of 24 letters – the first to have vowels as well as consonants. The word "alphabet" comes from the first two letters, alpha and beta.

A	B	Γ	Δ	E	Z
ALPHA	BETA	GAMMA	DELTA	EPSILON	ZETA
H	Θ	I	K	Λ	M
ETA	THETA	IOTA	KAPPA	LAMBDA	MU
N	Ξ	O	Π	P	Σ
NU	XI	OMICRON	PI	RHO	SIGMA
T	Y	Φ	X	Ψ	Ω
TAU	UPSILON	PHI	CHI	PSI	OMEGA

GREAT THINKERS

Around 600 BCE, Greek thinkers began to use logic instead of religion to think about the world and how it works. Their ideas were the beginning of philosophy.

PYTHAGORAS (c.530 BCE)
A theorem for working out the length of the sides of a right-angled triangle still bears the name of Pythagoras. He also believed that numbers had mystical powers.

SOCRATES (469–399 BCE)
This Athenian philosopher taught his students to question the power of Athens' ruling classes. He was put to death for his views.

PLATO (427–347 BCE)
Socrates' pupil Plato believed people should live their lives trying to reach absolute moral goodness. His ideas are still studied today.

ARISTOTLE (384–322 BCE)
This pupil of Plato founded a school called the Lyceum. He wrote many important works about biology, zoology, physics, logic, and politics.

ARCHIMEDES (c.287–212 BCE)
This engineer and mathematician invented a screw pump that drew up water, and wrote a theorem to calculate the area of a circle.

PLATO

WAR AND ARMOUR

The main fighting force of the Greek city-states were hoplites, heavily armoured foot-soldiers who carried a large round shield, or *hoplon*. They fought in phalanxes (shield walls), several rows deep, to protect the soldiers.

WEAPON CALLED "KOPIS" IN SHEATH

HOPLITE ARMOUR

XIPHOS, ANCIENT GREEK SWORD

WARRIOR SHIELD (HOPLON)

SOLDIER'S AXE AND SANDAL

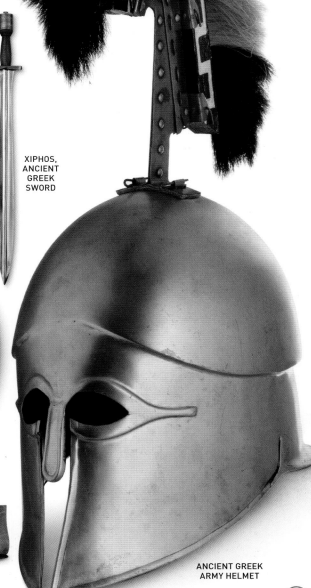

ANCIENT GREEK ARMY HELMET

Greek myths

Some of the oldest and best-known stories in the world are the myths of Ancient Greece. They are tales of gods and heroes, great loves, wars, daring adventures, and fabulous beasts. Some of them are told here. To the Greeks of long ago, the myths and the gods who appeared in them were very real.

THE GREEK GODS

In Greek mythology, the gods were powerful supernatural beings who could make anything and everything happen. There were 12 major gods and goddesses, of whom Zeus was king. The gods lived in their palaces on the top of snow-capped Mount Olympus, the highest mountain in Greece.

MOUNT OLYMPUS

HOW THE GODS BEGAN

The Ancient Greeks believed the creators of the world were Uranus, the Sky god, and Gaia, the Earth goddess. Uranus and Gaia had many children, including giants, monsters, and the Titans, first rulers of Earth. The Titans' children became gods and goddesses.

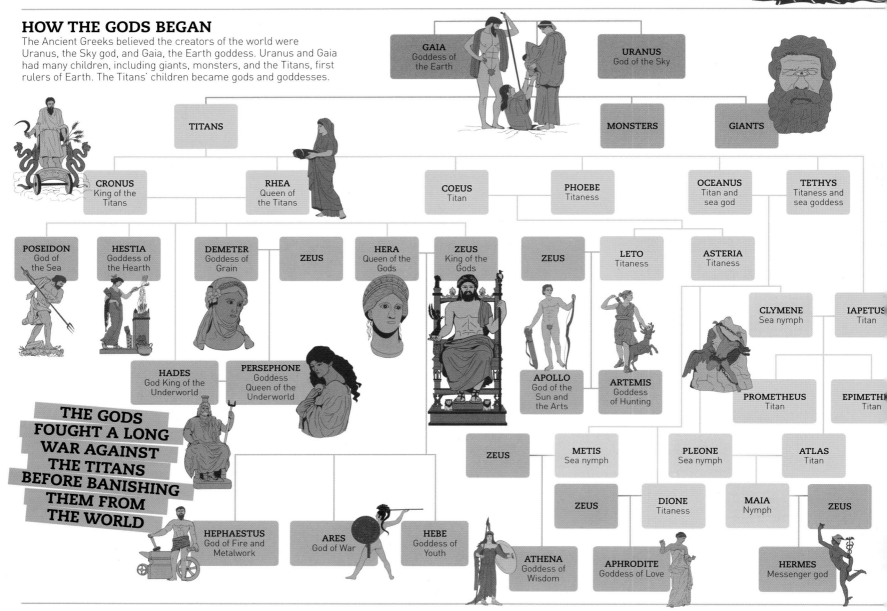

GAIA
Goddess of the Earth

URANUS
God of the Sky

MONSTERS

GIANTS

TITANS

CRONUS
King of the Titans

RHEA
Queen of the Titans

COEUS
Titan

PHOEBE
Titaness

OCEANUS
Titan and sea god

TETHYS
Titaness and sea goddess

POSEIDON
God of the Sea

HESTIA
Goddess of the Hearth

DEMETER
Goddess of Grain

ZEUS

HERA
Queen of the Gods

ZEUS
King of the Gods

ZEUS

LETO
Titaness

ASTERIA
Titaness

CLYMENE
Sea nymph

IAPETUS
Titan

HADES
God King of the Underworld

PERSEPHONE
Goddess Queen of the Underworld

APOLLO
God of the Sun and the Arts

ARTEMIS
Goddess of Hunting

PROMETHEUS
Titan

EPIMETHEUS
Titan

THE GODS FOUGHT A LONG WAR AGAINST THE TITANS BEFORE BANISHING THEM FROM THE WORLD

ZEUS

METIS
Sea nymph

PLEONE
Sea nymph

ATLAS
Titan

ZEUS

DIONE
Titaness

MAIA
Nymph

ZEUS

HEPHAESTUS
God of Fire and Metalwork

ARES
God of War

HEBE
Goddess of Youth

ATHENA
Goddess of Wisdom

APHRODITE
Goddess of Love

HERMES
Messenger god

THE UNDERWORLD

In the myths of Ancient Greece, the realm of the dead was known as the Underworld, a shadowy kingdom ruled by the god Hades. There were demons and monsters there. One of the most frightening was the three-headed dog Cerberus, who stood guard at the gates. The souls of those who had died were ferried to the Underworld in a boat across an ink-black river called the Styx.

CERBERUS

PUNISHMENTS FROM THE GODS

Many people were condemned to perpetual punishment in the Underworld because they had offended the gods. For example, Sisyphus, who had tried to become immortal, was made to push a huge rock uphill for ever. Tantalus, who insulted the gods, felt hungry and thirsty all the time, with food and drink just out of his reach.

TANTALUS

MYTHICAL BEINGS

Ancient Greek tales were full of weird creatures. There were beings called satyrs that had the upper body of a man but a lower half like a hairy goat, with hooves instead of feet. More noble were the wise centaurs, who were half man, half horse. A fire-breathing monster called the Chimaera was part lion and part goat, and had a serpent for a tail.

SATYRS

KING MIDAS

...n return for helping one of the ...ods, King Midas was granted ... wish. Greedily, he asked that ...verything he touched be ...rned to gold. When his food, ...rink, and even his daughter ...rned to gold, Midas begged ...r the gift to be taken away.

BELLEROPHON AND PEGASUS

The young hero Bellerophon rode a magical winged horse called Pegasus. Too bold and proud, he tried to fly up to the home of the gods. This so angered Zeus, he made Pegasus rear up and throw Bellerophon, who was injured. Lame and blind, he became a beggar.

THE TROJAN HORSE

Men inside horse

The Greeks defeated their Trojan enemies by trickery. Outside the city of Troy they left a huge wooden horse, which the Trojans seized. At night, men hidden inside the horse crept out to open the city gates for the Greek army.

THESEUS AND THE MINOTAUR

...he flesh-eating Minotaur, half ...an and half bull, was kept ...y King Minos of ...rete in a winding ...abyrinth, or maze. Every ...ear, Minos took 14 young ...eople from Athens to feed to ...is monster. Vowing to stop the ...aughter, the Athenian hero ...heseus found a way through the ...aze. As he went, he unrolled ... thread to mark his path. He ...ught and killed the Minotaur, ...nd then followed the thread to ...nd his way out of the maze.

DEMETER AND PERSEPHONE

Demeter, goddess of grain, had her daughter Persephone stolen by Hades, king of the Underworld. While she grieved, the crops all died. Hades agreed to send Persephone back every spring and summer, so that the corn and flowers could flourish. In winter, when she went back to Hades, nothing grew.

DEMETER

PERSEPHONE

MEDUSA

The Gorgon Medusa, a monster with snakes for hair, could turn people to stone with one look. Perseus, a son of Zeus, killed her. He avoided her gaze by aiming at her reflection in a shiny shield lent to him by the goddess Athena.

PROMETHEUS

The Titan Prometheus stole fire from the gods to give to humans. Furious, Zeus had him chained to a rock, where an eagle constantly pecked at his liver. Prometheus was supposed to stay chained for ever, but the hero Heracles rescued him.

JASON AND THE GOLDEN FLEECE

Jason was heir to a kingdom that had been taken from him in childhood. To earn his throne he had to steal the fleece of a magical golden ram. Jason found the fleece, but it was guarded by a terrible serpent. He asked the hero Orpheus to charm the serpent to sleep with music. Jason seized the fleece and was allowed to claim his throne.

PANDORA'S JAR

Zeus made a beautiful woman out of clay. He brought her to life and called her Pandora. When she married, he gave her the gift of a sealed jar, telling her not to open it. Pandora's curiosity got the better of her and she opened the lid. All the evil things in the world, such as hatred, disease, and war, flew out. Then one last tiny thing came out of the jar – hope for the future.

THE 12 LABOURS OF HERACLES

When the hero Heracles went mad and killed his wife, he was punished by being given 12 seemingly impossible tasks.

1 THE NEMEAN LION
The lion had such tough skin that no spear could pierce it. Heracles managed to strangle the beast.

2 SLAYING THE HYDRA
The Hydra was a many-headed monster. Every time Heracles cut off one of its heads, two new ones appeared. By sealing each wound he stopped more heads from growing.

3 THE KERYNEIAN HIND
After a long and gruelling chase, Heracles caught a golden-horned deer belonging to the goddess Artemis.

4 THE ERYMANTHIAN BOAR
Heracles defeated this ferocious boar by trapping it in a snowdrift.

5 THE AUGEAN STABLES
The filthy stables of King Augeas had never been cleaned. Heracles changed the courses of two rivers to wash all the dirt away.

6 THE STYMPHALIAN BIRDS
To get rid of some monstrous birds, Heracles frightened them into the air by playing castanets, and then shot them.

7 THE BULL OF KING MINOS
Heracles captured a huge and dangerous bull belonging to the king of Crete.

8 THE MAN-EATING MARES
Heracles tamed a herd of dangerous meat-eating horses by feeding their owner to them.

9 THE BELT OF HIPPOLYTA
Hippolyta was queen of the Amazon women and terrifying in battle. Heracles dared to steal her valuable belt.

10 THE CATTLE OF GERYON
Sent to the edge of the world, Heracles stole the cattle belonging to a giant herdsman.

11 GOLDEN APPLES OF HESPERIDES
In yet another theft, Heracles took the precious apples belonging to the daughters of Atlas, the giant who carried the world on his shoulders.

12 VISITING THE UNDERWORLD
In his final task, Heracles went to the Underworld and captured the three-headed dog, Cerberus, that guarded the gates. The hero was finally forgiven for his crime.

THE ODYSSEY

...mong the most often-told ...nyths are the adventures ...f the hero Odysseus. After ...ghting in the Greek war ...gainst the Trojans, ...dysseus spent many years ...n a dangerous sea voyage ...rying to get back home. The ...ourney of Odysseus and his ...ailors is described in the ...tory known as *The Odyssey*.

Odysseus's ships visit the lotus-eaters. These lazy people offer the sailors fruit that will make them forget the past.

Poseidon, the sea god, sends terrible storms to send the ships off course.

Circe, an enchantress, turns Odysseus's men into pigs and then back to men again.

Odysseus sails past the Sirens, who try to lure ships into dangerous waters with their song.

The sailors kill cattle on an island belonging to Helios the Sun god. Zeus strikes their ship with a thunderbolt, killing everyone but Odysseus.

Now the only survivor, Odysseus washes up on the island of the goddess Calypso, where he stays for seven years.

THE VOYAGE HOME

One-eyed giants called the Cyclopes keep the men captive and eat some of them. Odysseus blinds one of the giants and the crew escapes.

The giant Laestrygonians eat one of the sailors, and throw rocks at the ships, sinking all but one.

Odysseus visits the Underworld to find out his future. He has a vision of his homeland being invaded by enemies.

The ship sails the narrow channel between Scylla, a monster, and Charybdis, a whirlpool.

Odysseus finally returns home. He finds many men hoping to marry his wife, Penelope, and take his lands. Odysseus kills all the suitors and keeps his wife.

Ancient Rome

The Roman Empire was one of the greatest empires the world has ever known. At its peak, Rome's armies were almost unchallenged, and its emperors ruled a huge area – from Spain to the borders of Persia, and from North Africa to Scotland.

EXPANSION

Rome began as a humble hill-top settlement in central Italy, but before long, it had conquered Italy. It then took over the northern Mediterranean before expanding into much of northern Europe, North Africa, and the Middle East.

Roman Empire

1 **240** BCE
After conquering Italy, Rome seized the island of Sicily, by defeating the city of Carthage in the First Punic War.

2 **120** BCE
Forty years later, Rome took parts of Spain and North Africa in the Second Punic War. Victories against Macedonia gave it Greece.

3 **14** CE
By the end of the reign of Emperor Augustus, Roman armies had advanced into Egypt, Syria, and much of Europe.

ARMY

The Roman army was the ancient world's most effective fighting force. Professionally trained and armed, it had around 30 legions of 5,000 citizen-soldiers, each of whom served for 25 years.

BACKPACK
Roman soldiers carried cooking implements and tools to build a camp each night.

PUGIO
The Roman legionary dagger, or pugio, was around 20 cm (8 in) long. It was worn on the left hip.

GLADIUS
The Roman legionary sword, or gladius, was about 50 cm (20 in) long.

SHIELD
The legionary shield protected the whole body. Its edge could also be used to strike opponents.

HELMET
Roman helmets had a metal bowl to protect the head often with cheek pieces, and a horse-hair crest across the top.

ARMOUR
Body armour was usually formed of rectangular metal or leather strips.

KNEE GUARD
Greaves protected their knees from sword blows.

SANDALS
Soldiers wore leather sandals with nails hammered into the soles.

TACTICS AND FORMATIONS

The Romans were very effective foot (infantry) soldiers. Normally the legion would send a volley of arrows and javelins, before charging and fighting at close quarters. Very few enemies could defend themselves against them.

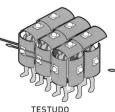
TESTUDO
Raised shields in the testudo, or "tortoise", defended against missiles dropped from above.

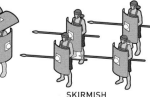
SKIRMISH
A skirmish formation was used for rapid advances or crossing difficult terrain.

ORB
The circular orb formation was used by small groups when surrounded.

CAVALRY DEFENCE
The front line held their javelins out at a 45-degree angle to defeat cavalry.

SOCIAL STRUCTURE

The emperor ruled the empire. He held enormous power but depended on the support of rich aristocratic families. Below them were ordinary Roman citizens. However, women and "foreigners" from places the Romans had conquered did not have citizenship and could not vote.

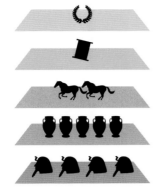

EMPEROR
The emperor (or emperors) was the ultimate authority.

SENATORS
Leading aristocrats served in the Senate.

EQUESTRIANS
Below senators were the less wealthy equestrians.

TRADERS AND WORKERS
Urban workers and merchants had little power.

FOREIGNERS
Outside Italy, most men did not have Roman citizenship.

SLAVES
Slaves had very few legal rights.

DAILY LIFE

The family played a central role in Roman life. Each household was ruled by the eldest adult male. Women carried out domestic chores and performed rituals to household gods.

GLASS BOTTLE

COLANDER

STONE GRINDER   OIL FLASK   RING

ENTERTAINMENT

Public entertainment was very important in Roman cities. Romans took part in religious festivals, or went to the theatre, public baths, and horse races. However, the most popular form of entertainment was gladiatorial contests in arenas such as the Colosseum in Rome.

COLOSSEUM
In this huge arena people came to see acrobats, wild beast fights, executions, and battles between gladiators.

GLADIATORS

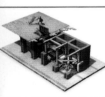
UNDERGROUND LIFT

EMPEROR'S BOX

Central sand-covered area where fights between gladiators took place

Underground passageways for holding gladiators and wild beasts

Entrance to tiers of seats for spectators

WHAT THE ROMANS DID FOR US

The Romans were brilliant engineers, builders, and scholars. Many essential things in our lives today were first introduced by the Romans.

PUBLIC BATHS
The Romans built large complexes for public bathing. These baths were the forerunners of the hammams used today in Islamic countries.

ROADS
The Romans created a network of paved roads that linked towns and cities. We still use many of these roads today.

THE GREAT BATH, ENGLAND

AQUEDUCTS
Roman engineers built channels, or aqueducts, to carry water from rivers to the cities. They erected great arched structures to keep the channels straight through dips and valleys.

ROMAN AQUEDUCT

○ **CALENDAR**
In their early calendars, the superstitious Romans avoided having months with even numbers of days because it was considered bad luck. Julius Caesar introduced a 12-month year with 365 days, which is close to the calendar we use today.

○ **LATIN**
Many European languages, such as French, Italian and Spanish, are descended from Latin, the language of the Romans.

○ **ROMAN NUMBERS**
The Romans had a numerical system that used letters to form numbers. We still use Roman numerals today on clocks and for important dates.

I 1	II 2	III 3	IV 4	V 5
VI 6	VII 7	VIII 8	IX 9	X 10
L 50	C 100	D 500	CM 900	M 1,000

TIMELINE

As their empire grew, the Romans' political system changed to meet the challenge of governing this vast area. They also fought many wars.

753 BCE
According to legend, the city of Rome is founded by Romulus and Remus, the twin sons of Mars, the god of war.

Statue of Romulus and Remus

509 BCE
Roman Republic is established after the overthrow of King Tarquinius.

261–241 BCE
Rome wins the first Punic War against the North African city of Carthage.

Soldiers in Carthage look at boats burning in distance

218–201 BCE
Carthaginian general Hannibal almost conquers Italy, but is defeated in the Second Punic War.

Head of Hannibal on a coin

44 BCE
Julius Caesar, Roman general and dictator, is assassinated after his victory in the civil war against his rival Pompey.

27 BCE
Julius Caesar's adopted son Octavian defeats his last rivals in a new civil war. He becomes the first Roman emperor and takes the name Augustus.

Bust of Julius Caesar

80 BCE
One of the great examples of Roman engineering, the Colosseum is finished. The largest amphitheatre in the empire, it seats 50,000 spectators.

Colosseum

395 CE
The Empire is permanently split into eastern and western halves, each ruled by a separate emperor.

Goths attacking Rome

410 CE
The Goths led by Alaric sack Rome. It is the first time in 800 years the city has fallen to a foreign invader.

476 CE
Romulus Augustulus, the last Roman emperor in the West, is overthrown. The eastern Roman Empire survives until 1453 CE.

ROMAN KINGDOM
750–510 BCE
Romulus kills his twin to become the first king of Rome. Later, the city is ruled by six kings. Under them, the city grows slowly. The last king, Tarquinius Superbus, is overthrown.

ROMAN REPUBLIC
507–27 BCE
Rome's kings are replaced by elected leaders. The republic lasts for nearly five centuries, until civil wars lead to its collapse.

ROMAN EMPIRE
27 BCE–395 CE
The final victor in Rome's civil wars takes power as Emperor Augustus. For the next four centuries Rome is ruled by a succession of emperors.

EASTERN AND WESTERN EMPIRE
395–476 CE
As the Roman Empire faces new threats, a single emperor cannot defend it. The rule is split between two emperors – one based in Rome and the other in Constantinople.

The Vikings

No one living between the 8th and 11th centuries welcomed a visit from the Vikings. These wild seafarers from Scandinavia caused widespread terror with lightning raids and looting. But as bold explorers, they travelled far and opened up a wider world.

CLOTHING

Tunics and trousers for men and long dresses for women were usual Viking wear. Most clothes were made of wool or linen and animal skins. Only the rich could afford silks and fancy accessories. The women wove and sewed everything.

CHILD MOTHER MERCHANT

RAIDING RECORD

The 300-year Viking history is marked out by raids, voyaging, and the colonizing of new lands.

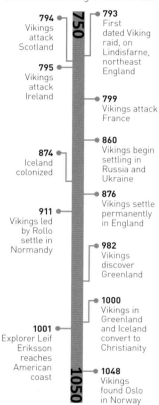

750

793 First dated Viking raid, on Lindisfarne, northeast England

794 Vikings attack Scotland

795 Vikings attack Ireland

799 Vikings attack France

860 Vikings begin settling in Russia and Ukraine

874 Iceland colonized

876 Vikings settle permanently in England

911 Vikings led by Rollo settle in Normandy

982 Vikings discover Greenland

1000 Vikings in Greenland and Iceland convert to Christianity

1001 Explorer Leif Eriksson reaches American coast

1048 Vikings found Oslo in Norway

1050

TREASURE

Every self-respecting Viking family had their special treasures. Rich folk prized finely crafted gold and silver jewellery. A typical adventurer, whether raider or trader, picked up ornaments and trophies in other lands.

HUNTING HORN
Made from the horn of an ox.

"EASTER" EGG
Christian symbol of rebirth from Russia.

BURIAL CHEST
Decorated oak chest made for a ship burial.

JEWELS
Rock crystal beads set in silver.

GOLDSMITH'S ART
Intricate brooch of twisted gold wires.

GAMING PIECE
Amber figure used in a board game.

ARMBAND
Solid silver arm ring with moulded beading.

BUCKLED UP
Patterned buckle plate.

MINI CUP
Tiny silver cup with engraved pattern.

LOKI
Shapeshifter and god of mischief.

ASK
First man, created from an ash tree.

ODIN
Norse god of wisdom and war.

THOR
Hammer-wielding god of thunder.

HEL
Goddess of the Underworld.

NORSE MYTHS

The ancient Norse myths explain how the world and the first people were created. The stories are full of dragons, magic, warring gods, and giants as wild as the Vikings themselves. According to Norse myth, there is a great battle still to come, which will end this world and start a new one.

RUNE ALPHABET

F U TH A R K H N I A S T B M L R

VIKING SOCIETY

At the top of the Viking social scale were the nobility, the uppermost being the jarls. Then came the freemen, such as warriors, craftsmen, and farmers. Lowest on the scale were slaves, or thralls, many of them prisoners of war.

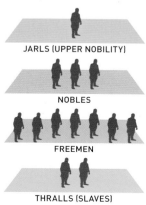

JARLS (UPPER NOBILITY)

NOBLES

FREEMEN

THRALLS (SLAVES)

RUNES

The Vikings used an alphabet of letters known as runes. These runes can be seen today carved into memorial stones, such as the famous Jelling Stones in Denmark, or as messages on pieces of wood and bone.

JELLING STONES
A copy showing pictures and runes.

FAR AND WIDE

The Vikings were skilled navigators. Sailing from what are now Denmark, Norway, and Sweden, they crossed open oceans in their small wooden boats. Their sea and land expeditions took them west to North America and east to Central Asia.

NORTH AMERICA

GREENLAND

ICELAND

KEY
▪ Viking homeland
▫ Viking settlements
→ Viking voyages

EUROPE

ATLANTIC OCEAN

Rigging

Square sail

Rowers work in pairs

FULL SAIL
A Viking ship used sails as well as manpower.

SPINNER

WARRIORS

HUNTER

ARCHER

HOME LIFE

No one had any privacy in a Viking home, known as a longhouse, which had one room or hall with a central fireplace. Here, everyone lived, ate, and slept. Wealthy households sometimes had extra rooms for cooking and weaving. Outside, there were animal barns, grain stores, and workshops.

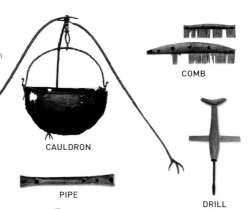

COMB

CAULDRON

PIPE

DRILL

HOLY CASKET
Container for Christian relics.

FANTASTIC BEAST
Gilded bronze fitting from a horse's bridle.

SILVER WARRIOR
Figure of a horseman bearing a sword.

ARMS AND ARMOUR

An axe, a sword, and sometimes bow and arrows were Viking battle gear. An iron helmet and a wooden shield warded off enemy blows.

HELMETS

SHIELDS

Welded iron plates

NORWEGIAN HELMET

Chain mail to protect neck

DAGGERS

ADVENTURERS

There are some famous heroes among the Vikings. Although their adventures took place more than 1,000 years ago, the legends of these chieftains live on.

○ **RAGNAR**
A hero of his day, he invaded Paris in 845. Stories say that he was later imprisoned in northern England, and left in a snakepit to die.

○ **BJORN JARNSMIDA**
One of the earliest known Viking explorers, he led raiding parties far and wide, attacking lands in Spain, France, Italy, and even North Africa.

○ **IVAR THE BONELESS**
Despite the unexplained name, Ivar was a vicious and powerful warrior. He invaded East Anglia in England in 869.

○ **ROLLO**
In the 9th century, this Norse chief founded a settlement in what is now Rouen in northern France.

○ **ERIK THE RED**
Originally Norwegian, he moved to Iceland from where he was banished for killings in 982. He founded the Norse colonies in Greenland.

○ **LEIF THE LUCKY**
Son of Erik the Red, Leif Eriksson made it all the way to North America in about 1001. He landed in present-day Newfoundland.

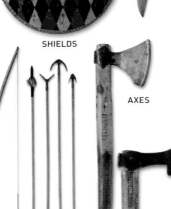
VIKING KNIFE

LEIF THE LUCKY

IT IS A MYTH THAT VIKINGS WORE HORNED HELMETS

ARROWS

LONGBOW

AXES

SWORDS

Unbleached linen

UNDERTUNIC AND LEGGINGS

THREE MAJOR CIVILIZATIONS

The Aztec civilization was based in what is now central Mexico. The Maya occupied southern Mexico, Guatemala, Belize, Honduras, and El Salvador. The Inca empire stretched 4,000 km (2,486 miles) along the west coast of South America.

KEY
- ■ MAYA
- ■ AZTEC
- ■ INCA

DIVERSE CULTURES

As well as the Maya, Aztec, and Inca civilizations, a rich mosaic of other peoples and cultures flourished in the region.

- **MAYA (c.2000 BCE–1697 CE)**
  Excelled at astronomy, and devised a way of writing using pictures. There are still millions of Maya in Central America today.

- **OLMEC (1200–400 BCE)**
  One of the earliest civilizations of Mesoamerica, their culture was based mainly on farming and trade.

- **ZAPOTEC (500 BCE–900 CE)**
  Based in southern Mexico. Ruled over 1,000 settlements in the region from its main city, Monte Albán.

- **TEOTIHUACAN (1–750 CE)**
  Built Teotihuacan, the largest and most impressive city in the ancient Americas.

- **NAZCA (100–800 CE)**
  Best known for the massive pictures and shapes (geoglyphs) they etched on the ground in southern Peru.

- **MOCHE (100–800 CE)**
  Built huge, mysterious pyramids, from mud bricks, that still dominate the countryside in northern Peru.

- **TOLTEC (750–1170)**
  Expert Mesoamerican architects and craftsmen. Built giant pyramids and palaces in their capital, Tula.

- **CHIMU (1000–1470)**
  Occupying a large area in the west of South America, they were skilled goldsmiths and architects. Eventually conquered by the Incas.

- **INCA (1150–1532)**
  Became the most powerful people in the Andes mountain region when they conquered the city of Cuzco in 1438. They went on to take over many other states for their empire.

- **AZTEC (1300s–1521)**
  Originally a wandering tribe, they founded the city of Tenochtitlan in 1325, which become the centre of their mighty empire.

Ancient Americas

Three great civilizations of the Americas flourished in different parts of the continent: the Maya and Aztecs in central America (Mesoamerica) and the Inca in the south, centred in modern-day Peru. These cultures, although different in many ways, all left behind beautiful art and the remains of spectacular cities.

MACHU PICCHU
A remote outpost of the Inca empire, up to half of its 143 buildings may have been used for religious ceremonies.

GREAT CITIES

Cities were built in a variety of places. The surrounding landscape and the building materials available had an effect on the look of the buildings. Cities were often dominated by huge temples and other religious buildings.

TIKAL
Major Maya city, inhabited from 600 BCE to around 900 CE.

CHICHEN ITZA
Maya city that was an important trading centre.

CUZCO
The religious and political capital of the Incas.

TEOTIHUACAN
City state that was destroyed mysteriously around 700 CE.

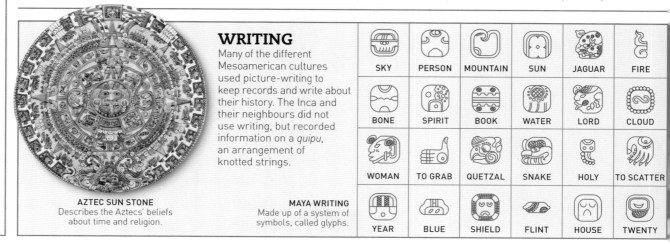

AZTEC SUN STONE
Describes the Aztecs' beliefs about time and religion.

WRITING

Many of the different Mesoamerican cultures used picture-writing to keep records and write about their history. The Inca and their neighbours did not use writing, but recorded information on a *quipu*, an arrangement of knotted strings.

MAYA WRITING
Made up of a system of symbols, called glyphs.

SKY	PERSON	MOUNTAIN	SUN	JAGUAR	FIRE
BONE	SPIRIT	BOOK	WATER	LORD	CLOUD
WOMAN	TO GRAB	QUETZAL	SNAKE	HOLY	TO SCATTER
YEAR	BLUE	SHIELD	FLINT	HOUSE	TWENTY

TIMELINE

The civilizations of the region lasted for 2,000 years, until European explorers and their armies wiped them out.

500 BCE
The Zapotec build Monte Alban as their capital and religious centre.

c.900–1000 CE
Toltecs build their capital at Tula, Mexico.

Toltec pottery

1325
Aztec city of Tenochtitlan founded on an island in Lake Texcoco.

Tenochtitlan marketplace

1519–21
Explorer and soldier Hernándo Cortés conquers the Aztecs for Spain.

Cortés meeting Aztec leader Moctezuma II

1542
The Spanish establish a capital at Merida and the Maya resistance comes to an end.

1400 BCE   1700 CE

1400 BCE
The Olmec build temples and carve colossal sculptures in northern Mexico.

350 BCE
First great Maya city of Tikal built in the rainforest of Guatemala.

Tikal temple

c.1300
Incas begin to expand their empire through the central Andes.

Cuzco, Inca capital

c.1438
Inca chief Pachacuti takes power. City of Machu Picchu is built.

Machu Picchu

1471
Tupac becomes king of the Incas and pushes far south to expand the empire.

1502
Moctezuma II begins his reign over ten million Aztecs. The empire is at its height.

1532
The Inca empire ends when Spanish warrior Francisco Pizarro captures and kills the Inca emperor, Atahualpa.

1697
The very last Maya outpost, Tayasal, falls to the Spanish.

GODS AND GODDESSES

The Mesoamericans and Incas worshipped many gods, most of them to do with nature or farming. People would ask the gods for good weather to make crops grow, or for better health for themselves and their families.

CHALCHIUHTLICUE
Aztec goddess of water and storms.

VIRACOCHA
Most important god of the Incas.

XOLOTL
Aztec god of death and lightning.

TZULTACAH
A group of Maya thunder-gods.

MAMA KILLA
Inca goddess of the moon.

MAIZE GOD
Unnamed, shaven-headed Maya god.

FUN AND GAMES

Ulama was a fast and furious ball game played by various cultures, including the Aztecs. We don't know the exact rules, but the aim was for two teams on a special court to try to put a ball through a ring set into a wall.

- Ring set 8 m (27 ft) high
- Solid rubber ball

RITUAL AND SACRIFICE

Sacrifice was a vital religious ritual. Animals and humans were offered up to feed the gods so that they would look after the earth.

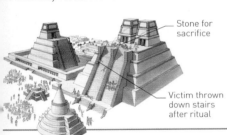
- Stone for sacrifice
- Victim thrown down stairs after ritual

AZTEC WARRIORS

War was a way of life for the Aztecs. Apart from gaining new land, the main reason for going to war was to capture enemy warriors for sacrifice to the gods.

AT 17, YOUNG AZTEC MEN WERE SENT OFF TO CAPTURE THEIR FIRST PRISONER

JAGUAR WARRIORS
For taking captives, Aztec warriors were awarded distinctive costumes.

AZTEC APPRENTICE WARRIOR
Carrying wooden spear tipped with sharp stone.

ART AND CRAFTS

The pottery, carvings, ceramics, and metalware left behind by the Mesoamerican and ancient Peruvian cultures are a valuable source of information about the way they lived, their ideas about life, and how and who they worshipped.

CARVED FROG
Aztec

MOTHER AND BABY
Teotihuacan, c.200 CE

CARVED JAGUAR BONES
Maya, 400 CE

JADEITE CARVING
Maya, 600–900 CE

JADEITE JAGUAR MASK
Olmec, 900–300 BCE

JADE MASK
Aztec, c.1420–1519

JADEITE FIGURE
Aztec, 1500–1530

PITCHER
Inca, 1476–1550

STIRRUP POT
Moche, 200–500 CE

MARBLE VASE
Maya, 600–1000 CE

GOLD CUP
Sicán (Andean culture)

FIGURE OF A WOMAN
Inca, c.1476–1550

GOLD LLAMA
Inca

KEY EVENTS

The Ottoman Empire expanded rapidly after it was formed, as the sultans set out to gain new territory for Islam, and also wealth to reward their followers.

1453
Mehmed II conquers Constantinople. The Byzantine Empire ceases to exist.

1514
Selim I invades northern Iraq and takes over most of the Middle East.

Selim I mosque, Istanbul

1571
Defeat at Battle of Lepanto stops Ottomans from expanding further west.

1914
Ottomans join World War I on the side of the Central Powers.

1923
The Ottoman Empire is dissolved and the Republic of Turkey is formed.

1300

2000

1354
Ottoman armies cross into Europe at Gallipoli.

1369
Ottomans capture Edirne, which becomes their capital.

1529
Army of Suleiman I besieges the Austrian capital, Vienna, but fails to conquer it.

1566
Suleiman I dies in Hungary. The Ottomans would advance no further into Europe.

1683
The Ottomans are defeated at the Battle of Vienna, starting the decline of the empire.

1300
The Ottoman Empire is founded by Osman I in Anatolia, northwest Turkey.

Edirne mosque

1538
Ottoman navy wins control of the eastern Mediterranean at the Battle of Preveza.

Suleiman I in battle

Modern Turkish flag

The Ottoman Empire

The Ottoman Empire was one of the biggest and longest-lasting empires in history. It was founded in the 14th century by Osman, a Turkish *ghazi* (Islamic warrior). Two hundred years later, the empire stretched over three continents: Africa, Asia, and Europe. It was ruled over by a series of powerful sultans, with the help of armies of slave-soldiers.

OTTOMAN CONQUERORS

By 1639 the Ottomans' conquest of most of the Middle East and North Africa made them the strongest Islamic power in the world.

CONQUESTS
- Up to 1512
- Up to 1520
- Up to 1566
- Up to 1639

The mosque has six minarets (towers for calling Muslims to prayer)

The vast courtyard is surrounded by 30 cupolas (mini-domes)

TOPKAPI PALACE
Built in 1460 for Mehmed II, Topkapi was the main palace of the sultans for 400 years.

POWERFUL SULTANS

The Ottoman Empire was ruled by descendants of the same family for 600 years. The sultans formed strong governments, and life under Ottoman rule was mostly peaceful and safe for ordinary citizens.

○ **OSMAN I (GAZI) (c.1258–1326)**
The founder and first sultan of the Ottoman Empire. A successful military general who extended Ottoman territory throughout his 27-year reign.

○ **MEHMED II (THE CONQUEROR) (1432–81)**
A great military leader, he captured Constantinople and conquered territories in Anatolia and the Balkans.

○ **SELIM I (THE GRIM) (1470–1520)**
Selim came to power after a civil war. He killed his brothers, and others who might have had a claim to the throne after his death, so that his chosen son, Suleiman, could become sultan.

○ **SULEIMAN I (THE MAGNIFICENT) (1494–1556)**
One of the greatest sultans. During his 46-year reign, the Ottoman Empire became a world power. Suleiman's reign was also a time of great achievements in in literature, poetry, art, and architecture.

○ **ABDULMECID I (1823–61)**
Responsible for an ambitious reform of the army, schools, and other institutions, Abdülmecid hoped this reform would make the declining empire competitive with other European countries.

SULEIMAN I THE MAGNIFICENT

THE SULTAN'S LOYAL MEN

The Ottomans operated a system called *devshirme* (gathering), in which Christian boys from conquered countries were made slaves, converted to Islam, and taught total loyalty to the sultan. They were then trained to do important jobs within the sultan's household and army.

> WHEN SULTAN MEHMED II TOOK POWER, HE PUT ALL HIS BROTHERS TO DEATH, TO PREVENT PLOTS AGAINST HIM

SCRIBES
Kept the sultan's records

VIZIERS AND GOVERNORS
Powerful political figures

BOY SLAVES

CLERICS
Islamic scholars

JANISSARIES
The sultan's elite troops

JANISSARY

MARK OF THE SULTAN

The tughra was the personal seal of the Ottoman emperors. All important documents, coins, and letters from the sultan carried a symbol, which was different for every ruler. The tughra was based on Arabic calligraphy. It was designed at the beginning of the sultan's reign and drawn by the *nişancı* (court calligrapher) on to court papers.

TUGHRA OF SULTAN MAHMUD II (reigned 1808–39)
It reads *Mahmud Han bin Abdulhamid muzaffer daiman*: "Mahmud Khan, son of Abdulhamid, is forever victorious".

daiman

muzaffer

Abdulhamid

Mahmud

bin

Han

MASTER BUILDERS

Ottoman rulers commissioned many magnificent palaces and mosques as symbols of their great power, as well as to show their devotion to Islam. Ottoman architects were inspired by both Islamic and European art, and their buildings are a lively mix of both traditions.

SULTAN AHMED MOSQUE, ISTANBUL
Also known as the Blue Mosque, for the blue tiles that decorate its interior. It was built between 1609 and 1616.

The central dome is 23.5 m (77 ft) in diameter

DOLMABAHÇE PALACE
Home to six sultans until the deposition of the last sultan in 1922.

AHMET FOUNTAIN
Public drinking fountain built by Ahmed III in 1728. The water is supplied from a pool inside the kiosk.

ART AND DECORATION

As the Ottoman Empire grew richer and more powerful, artists and craftspeople were in great demand to produce art and objects for the sultan's palaces. The town of Iznik was particularly famous for beautiful ceramic tiles and pottery, which were decorated with flowers and intricate plant motifs and Arabic script, mainly in vivid shades of blue and green.

IZNIK PLATE

IZNIK CERAMIC TILES

Sheath is decorated with more than 50 diamonds

Enamel flower motif

WEAPONS AND ARMOUR

During the reign of Suleiman I, the Ottoman army was the largest and most successful in Europe. The sultan's troops were highly trained, well disciplined, and equipped with the latest weapons and armour.

STEEL HELMET

HIDE AND COPPER CHICHAK (HELMET)

CUIRASS (BODY PROTECTOR)

CHAIN-MAIL ARMOUR

BREASTPLATE

MACE, DAGGER, AND SWORD

CAVALRY BOOTS

KALKAN (SHIELD)

JEWELS AND FINERY

The Ottomans' taste was influenced by the variety of cultures across their vast empire. Jewellery was ornate and generally mixed different metals and gems in one piece. Emeralds and jade were popular because green was associated with the prophet Muhammad.

Hilt is decorated with three Colombian emeralds

Five pieces of different shapes are engraved with verses from the Qur'an

TOPKAPI DAGGER
Made as a gift from Sultan Mahmud I to the ruler of Persia, Nadir Shah, in 1747.

SPOONMAKER'S DIAMOND
86-carat, pear-shaped diamond in gold and 49-diamond setting.

NECKLACE
1875–1925

The Mughal Empire

The Mughal Empire was founded by Babur, a Muslim prince and descendant of the Mongol conqueror Genghis Khan. The Mughals' enormous wealth and power can still be seen today in the many great monuments they left behind.

TIMELINE OF THE MUGHALS

1504
Babur captures the city of Kabul and becomes ruler of Afghanistan.

1526
Babur conquers Delhi in northern India. The Mughal age begins.

1540
Humayun, Babur's son, loses power to a rival Afghan dynasty but seizes it back in 1555.

1556
Babur's grandson, Akbar, becomes emperor.

1563
Akbar begins to pass laws granting Hindus religious and political freedom.

Akbar and his Hindu bride

1605
Jahangir becomes emperor on Akbar's death.

1613
British East India Company allowed to build a warehouse in Surat, Gujarat.

1627
Jahangir dies at the age of 58.

1632
Emperor Shah Jahan begins building the Taj Mahal as a memorial to his wife Mumtaz Mahal.

Tomb of Mumtaz Mahal

1657
Shah Jahan falls ill; a year later, his son Aurangzeb defeats his brothers and takes power.

1686
The East India Company starts a war with Emperor Aurangzeb over trading territory. After three years, the company admits defeat.

1707
Emperor Aurangzeb dies, triggering a period of rebellions.

1739
Nadir, Shah of Persia, captures Delhi. The Mughal Empire starts to decline.

1857
The last Mughal emperor, Bahadur Shah II, is deposed by the British for supporting the Indian Mutiny.

The Mughals originally came from Central Asia. At their height, they ruled all of what is now northern India, Pakistan, Afghanistan, and Bangladesh. Only a century later, they had lost nearly all their territory.

Indian Mutiny, 1857

MUGHAL EXPANSION

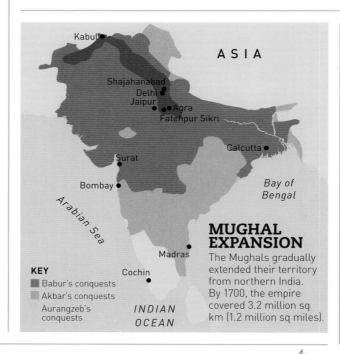

The Mughals gradually extended their territory from northern India. By 1700, the empire covered 3.2 million sq km (1.2 million sq miles).

KEY
- Babur's conquests
- Akbar's conquests
- Aurangzeb's conquests

MIGHTY MUGHALS

Babur and the strong rulers who came after him ensured that their empire grew steadily richer and more powerful.

- **BABUR (1483–1530)**
  A brilliant general, and also passionate about poetry and gardening. He wrote his own life story in the form of a diary, the *Baburnama*.

- **AKBAR (1542–1605)**
  Won the support of his people by setting fair taxes and promoting religious tolerance.

AKBAR'S TOMB

- **JAHANGIR (1569–1627)**
  A enthusiastic patron of the arts. His wife, Nur Jahan, was one of the most powerful women in Mughal history.

- **SHAH JAHAN (1592–1666)**
  Famed for the magnificence of his court, he built a new city, Shahjahanabad (now Old Delhi), as his capital.

- **AURANGZEB (1618–1707)**
  Expanded the empire by a quarter but the cost of military campaigns drained his treasury.

ARMOUR AND WEAPONS

Mughal warriors fought mostly on horseback, but they also used elephants that were specially trained to charge and trample the enemy during battle.

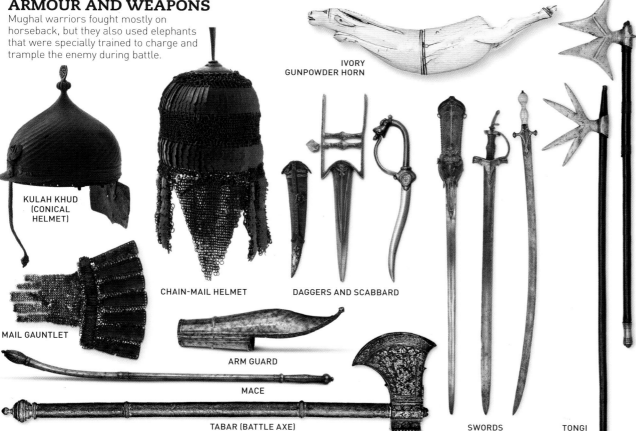

KULAH KHUD (CONICAL HELMET)

MAIL GAUNTLET

CHAIN-MAIL HELMET

IVORY GUNPOWDER HORN

DAGGERS AND SCABBARD

ARM GUARD

MACE

TABAR (BATTLE AXE)

SWORDS

TONGI

ASTRONOMY

Many Mughal emperors took a keen interest in science, mathematics, and especially astronomy. They built observatories and employed astronomers to produce detailed *zijes* (astronomical tables) and calendars.

JANTAR MANTAR OBSERVATORY, NEW DELHI (1724)
Built by order of the Emperor Muhammad Shah, to help create new astronomical tables.

Constellation Ursa Major, the Great Bear

Band representing the Zodiac

Longitude markings

BRASS CELESTIAL GLOBE (1790–9
Shows the positio of the stars an their constellation

ARCHITECTURAL WONDERS

The Mughals showed off their power by building many magnificent new buildings, mosques, and monuments. Architects took inspiration from Persian, Ottoman, Islamic, and Hindu traditions to create their own style.

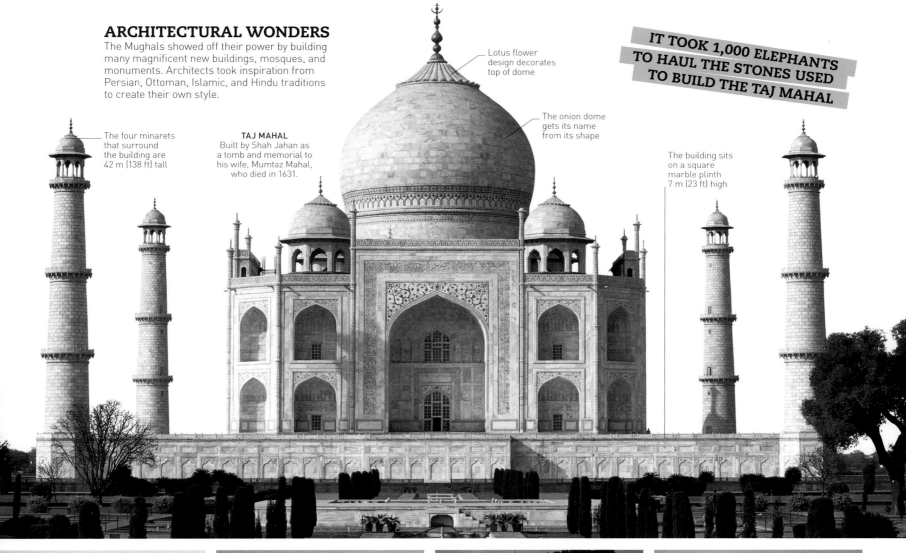

Lotus flower design decorates top of dome

The onion dome gets its name from its shape

The four minarets that surround the building are 42 m (138 ft) tall

TAJ MAHAL
Built by Shah Jahan as a tomb and memorial to his wife, Mumtaz Mahal, who died in 1631.

The building sits on a square marble plinth 7 m (23 ft) high

IT TOOK 1,000 ELEPHANTS TO HAUL THE STONES USED TO BUILD THE TAJ MAHAL

FATEHPUR SIKRI (CITY OF VICTORY)
Founded in 1571 by Akbar, to celebrate his military victories at Chittor and Ranthambore.

TOMB OF HUMAYUN
Built in Old Delhi in 1570, this magnificent garden tomb was the first major building of the Mughal period.

MOTI MASJID (PEARL MOSQUE)
Built in Old Delhi (1659–60) by Emperor Aurangzeb, the mosque is part of the Red Fort complex of buildings.

TOMB OF SAFDARJUNG
Completed in 1754 in New Delhi, this is one of the last great buildings of the Mughal Empire.

MUSLIM ART

Muslims were against showing people or animals in religious art, so sacred buildings were decorated with geometric patterns, plant and flower motifs, and decorative writing (calligraphy).

LEAF GEOMETRIC DESIGN

FLOWER DESIGN MARBLE INLAY

CALLIGRAPHY ON MOSQUE ENTRANCE

OCTAGON AND SQUARE PATTERN

DAZZLING CRAFTWORK

Art was greatly valued by the Mughals. The most skilled painters, craftworkers, jewellers, and textile designers from all over the empire were commissioned to produce exquisite works to adorn the emperor's palaces.

JADE BOWL

ENAMELLED KNIFE HILT

JEWEL-INLAID PENDANT

JADE JUG

Richly decorated borders were a tradition borrowed from Persian miniatures

MINIATURE PAINTING

Imperial Japan

The story of Japan's Imperial Age is filled with feuding clans and warlike samurai, constantly battling for wealth and power. But it was also a place where art and culture flourished, and where honour was respected above all.

RULE OF THE SHOGUNS

Although the ruler of Japan was the emperor, the country was really governed by the shogun. He was the most powerful of a group of wealthy, influential military generals called daimyo.

EMPEROR
The emperor was the deeply respected religious and cultural figurehead of Japan, but held little political power.

SHOGUN
The most powerful daimyo (military leader) and the real ruler of Japan. The first shogun seized power in 1192, and for most of the next 700 years Japan was ruled by a succession of shoguns.

DAIMYO
Wealthy clan leaders who each ruled a part of Japan. They kept their own armies, commanded by fearsome samurai warriors, and often fought each other for land or political power.

SAMURAI
Highly trained professional warriors, bound by a solemn oath of loyalty to their daimyo. In times when there were no wars to fight, the samurai perfected their skills in music, poetry, and art.

THE FULL TITLE SEII TAISHOGUN MEANS "GREAT GENERAL SUBDUING THE BARBARIANS"

FEARSOME WARRIORS

Japan's history was shaped by the military men who battled on behalf of warring clans.

○ **MINAMOTO YORITOMO (1147–99)**
After fierce struggles with rival clans and his own family, he finally became shogun in 1192. At his death seven years later, his son took over as ruler.

○ **SASAKI TAKATSUNA (1160–1214)**
Commander in the war between the Minamoto and Taira clans, he saved Yoritomo's life at the Battle of Ishibashiyama.

SASAKI TAKATSUNA

○ **NITTA YOSHISADA (1301–38)**
Resistance leader and general. At his final battle, he was surrounded by his enemies and, rather than be captured, he cut off his own head.

○ **TOKUGAWA IEYASU (1542–1616)**
After civil war, Tokugawa Ieyasu united Japan under his control. His descendants ruled for the next 260 years.

KATO KIYOMASA

○ **KATO KIYOMASA (1561–1611)**
A formidable military leader and devout Buddhist, he led a brutal campaign to rid Japan of Christianity.

NITTA YOSHISADA

MAGNIFICENT CASTLES

In the 16th century, noble families, who were often at war with their neighbours, built mighty fortresses to protect their land and armies. These magnificent castles also served as symbols of the clans' power and wealth.

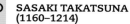
HIMEJI CASTLE
Also called the Castle of the White Heron, because its delicate, curved roofs resemble birds' wings.

FAITH AND WORSHIP

Most people followed a faith called Shinto – "the way of the gods" – a belief that all living things possess a divine spirit called *kami*. Worshippers held rituals and left offerings to the *kami* at specially built shrines all over Japan.

SHRINE ENTRANCE AT MIYAJIMA, SOUTHERN JAPAN
The gateway to a Shinto shrine is called a *torii*.

SAMURAI WARRIORS

Samurai were men of noble birth who were trained in all aspects of fighting and war. They were the only people allowed to carry a *katana* and a *wakizashi* (a pair of swords known collectively as *daisho*) in public.

The *Kabuto* (helmet) often featured a decorative crest

The *Mempo* was an iron mask used for protection and to scare enemies

Cheek and neck protector

Light armour, made from metal scales, allowed for easy movement

SAMURAI SUIT OF ARMOUR, 19TH CENTURY

SAMURAI CODE

Loyalty and honour were essential to the samurai. They lived by a strict, seven-point code called *Bushido*, which means "the way of the warrior".

GI	Integrity	**JIN**	Kindness
REI	Respect	**MAKOTO**	Sincerity
YU	Bravery	**CHUGI**	Loyalty
MEIYO	Honour		

WEAPONS AND ARMOUR

The samurais' favourite form of fighting was hand-to-hand combat with knives and swords. They were also expected to be skilled with bow and arrow, spears, and later, guns.

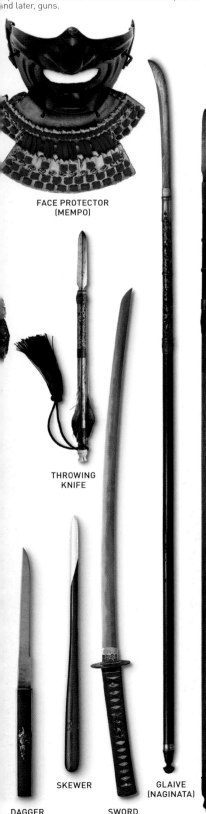

FACE PROTECTOR
(MEMPO)

THROWING
KNIFE

DAGGER
(WAKIZASHI)

SKEWER

SWORD
(KATANA)

GLAIVE
(NAGINATA)

SPEAR

ART AND CRAFTS

In 1603 the city of Edo (now Tokyo) became the capital of Japan. In the 260 years of peace that followed, art and culture flourished as never before. Edo artists and craftsmen produced beautiful work, from delicate ivory carvings to bold, colourful paintings and prints showing city life.

PRINTED
FAN
1858

BRASS LANTERN
18th century

WOODBLOCK PRINT OF EDO
BY UTAGAWA HIROSHIGE 1857

WRESTLER'S
NETSUKE 1800–50

TEA KETTLE
Edo period

CERAMIC
INCENSE
BURNER
1600–50

PORCELAIN
TEA BOWL
1700–50

MUSIC AND THEATRE

Going to the theatre and listening to music were popular pastimes for the wealthy. Noh theatre was a solemn form of storytelling, performed by actors in masks. Kabuki plays were much livelier and more dramatic.

KOTSUZIMI DRUM

NOTCH
FLUTE

BAMBOO
FLUTE

KOTO

KABUKI ACTOR, EDO PERIOD

SHAMISEN

ERAS AND EVENTS

Japan's Imperial Age began around 700 CE. Before then, the area was made of several smaller chiefdoms. The age effectively ended in 1868, when the modern era began. Japanese history is split into periods. A new period began at the start of the reign of a new emperor or with a similar major event.

700

NARA
710–94
Periods of Japanese history are often named after the capital cities used by rulers of that period. The city of Nara is Japan's first permanent capital.

1156 Civil war between several clans.

Woodblock print of Minamoto Tametomo fighting in the civil war

HEIAN
794–1185
Heian (now Kyoto) replaces Nara as Japan's capital in 794.

1192 After 30 years of civil war, Minamoto Yoritomo becomes shogun. The emperor's power is taken from him and he is reduced to a figurehead.

KAMAKURA
1185–1333
This period sees a huge rise in power of the daimyo and the samurai who serve them.

1281 Mongols attempting to invade Japan are forced back by a typhoon that the Japanese name *kamikaze*, or "divine wind".

Invading Mongols are forced back by a typhoon

KENMU
1333–36 Brief restoration of rule by an emperor.

MUROMACHI
1336–1568
Also known as the Warring State period, this is a time of rebellion and unrest.

1568 Oda Nobunaga seizes power in Kyoto. His army is equipped with muskets acquired from Portuguese traders.

**AZUCHI/
MOMOYAMA**
1568–1600
This period sees an end to the damaging internal conflicts the country has suffered.

c.1600 Art and culture flourish in the Edo period – beautiful objects are created by master craftsmen.

Folding war fan

EDO/TOKUGAWA
1600–1868
A long period of peace, during which Japan effectively cuts itself off from the rest of the world.

1603 Shogun Ieyasu sets up his capital in a fishing town called Edo, which will become Tokyo.

MEIJII
1868–1912

TAISHO
1912–26

SHOWA
1926–89

1639 Foreigners are forced to leave, beginning a 220-year period of complete isolation for Japan.

2000

HEISEI
1989–

RULING DYNASTIES

China was ruled by a series of dynasties, or families. Emperors were sometimes overthrown by rival clans or foreign invaders. When this happened, a new ruler took the throne and a new dynasty began.

1650 BCE

SHANG
c.1650–1046 BCE
China's first great ruling dynasty.

c.1500 BCE
Craftsmen learn large-scale production of bronze weapons and tools.

c.1250 BCE
Earliest evidence of writing in China.

c.1046 BCE
The last Shang ruler is defeated at the Battle of Muye.

Bronze wine beaker, Shang dynasty

ZHOU
c.1046–256 BCE
Feudal system begins: lords rule over the peasants who work on their estates.

Rice pot, Zhou dynasty

771 BCE
King You is killed and Haojing, the capital, is overrun by invaders. The Zhou court flees east.

551 BCE
Philosopher Confucius is born.

Confucius

WARRING STATES
481–221 BCE
As the Zhou decline, there is a period of struggle for control of China.

QIN
221–207 BCE
China is united under one emperor.

221 BCE
Warrior Zheng declares himself Emperor Shi Huang, ruler of all China.

214 BCE
Construction begins on the Great Wall.

Building the Great Wall

HAN
207 BCE–220 CE
Civil service is established, which will run China for the next 2,000 years.

105 CE
An imperial court official reports the invention of paper.

PERIOD OF DISUNITY
221–589
China is invaded and divides into separate states.

c.250
Buddhism is introduced to China.

SUI
581–618
China is reunified.

618
China's golden age begins, a period of great artistic and scientific developments.

TANG
618–906
China expands to become a great world power.

Horse figure, Tang dynasty

FIVE DYNASTIES AND TEN KINGDOMS
907–960
China is once again divided into north and south.

1100
China's population grows to about 100 million.

SONG
960–1279
Advances in technology bring wealth and prosperity.

Porcelain vase, Song dynasty

1279
Mongol invaders, led by Kublai Khan, conquer China.

Mongol warrior

YUAN
1279–1368
The conquering Mongols establish their own dynasty.

MING
1368–1644
Exquisite art and crafts are produced throughout the period.

1420
Beijing is named as the new capital of China.

1839–1860
In the Opium Wars, China and Western nations battle over trade.

Plate, Ming dynasty

QING
1644–1912
The empire declines steadily and is eventually overthrown.

1912
2,000 years of imperial rule come to an end when six-year-old emperor, Puyi, is deposed.

1912

Imperial China

China is one of the world's oldest civilizations, having lasted more than 4,000 years. It was an empire from 221 BCE until 1912, making it the longest-lasting empire in history.

ANCIENT WONDERS

The empire, with its vast wealth, technological skills, and unlimited manpower, created some of the biggest and most magnificent works of engineering and architecture ever made.

FORBIDDEN CITY
Enormous palace and fortress built in Beijing from 1406–21.

TERRACOTTA ARMY
8,000 life-size statues, buried along with Emperor Qin Shi Huang.

THE GREAT WALL
The final version of the Wall, built during the Ming dynasty to keep China's northern enemies out, was around 8,850 km (5,500 miles) long.

GREAT EMPERORS

Some strong emperors had long reigns, but many emperors were deposed or assassinated. At times, China was split among warring emperors.

QIN SHI HUANG (QIN DYNASTY, 259–210 BCE)
He conquered neighbouring states to become the first emperor of a unified China and founder of the Qin Dynasty.

HAN WUDI (HAN DYNASTY, 156–87 BCE)
Seventh emperor of the Han, he ruled for 54 years. During his reign, China's wealth and territory increased.

WU ZETIAN (TANG DYNASTY, 624–705 CE)
China's only female emperor. She was the wife of Emperor Gaozong, and took over from him when he became ill. Eventually, she declared herself China's sole ruler.

YONGLE (MING DYNASTY, 1360–1424)
The third Ming emperor, known for his ruthlessness and cruelty. He moved the Chinese capital from Nanjing to Beijing and built the Forbidden City.

KANGXI (QING DYNASTY, 1654–1722)
The longest-reigning emperor, he took the throne at the age of eight. His 61-year rule was a time of peace and prosperity for China.

EMPEROR YONGLE

GREAT INVENTIONS

Some of the world's greatest inventions and discoveries came from Imperial China, and many of those inventions are still in use today. Scientists and engineers were highly valued by the emperors.

SILK
c.4000 BCE

SHIP'S RUDDER
c.100 CE

WRITING

Writing by hand was considered an art form in China. It took calligraphers (professional hand-writers) years to learn how to make the 40,000 characters they needed to write the language.

CALLIGRAPHY SET

IN

THE DEVELOPMENT OF WRITING
Chinese characters have been simplified over their 4,000 years of use.

	HUMAN	WOMAN	HORSE	MOUNTAIN
ORACLE BONE 14th–11th century BCE	𔓕			
CLERICAL SCRIPT (LISHU) c.300 BCE	人	女	馬	山
MODERN SIMPLIFIED SCRIPT 1956	人	女	马	山

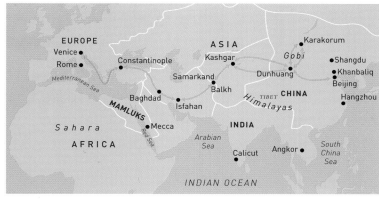

THE SILK ROAD

The Silk Road was a route that ran from China across Asia towards Europe. It was protected by the Chinese, so that traders from all over the world could use it safely. Chinese merchants became very rich by exporting goods such as silk, tea, porcelain, and spices.

KEY
— Silk Road

TAICHU CALENDAR

The traditional Chinese calendar dates back thousands of years. It was first officially recorded in 104 BCE, during the rule of Han Wudi.

ANIMAL YEARS
Each year is named after an animal. Every 12 years, the cycle starts over again.

> THE MORTAR USED TO BIND THE BRICKS OF THE GREAT WALL WAS PARTLY MADE FROM RICE FLOUR

PAPER
105 CE

EARTHQUAKE DETECTOR
132 CE

KITE
c.550 CE

GUNPOWDER
c.850 CE

THE THREE WAYS

Imperial China was generally tolerant of different religions. People were free to choose which of the three popular belief systems they wished to follow.

CONFUCIANISM
Followed the rules of Chinese thinker Confucius.

BUDDHISM
A philosophy begun by Buddha, a north Indian prince.

DAOISM
Daoists followed legendary Chinese philosopher Lao Zi.

MYTHS AND LEGENDS

Chinese mythology was a rich mix of traditional folk tales, legends based on real people, and stories adapted from Buddhist and Daoist teaching.

THREE SOVEREIGNS
According to legend, the first rulers of China.

SUN WUKONG
Monkey king with superpowers.

EIGHT IMMORTALS
Able to bestow life and destroy evil.

DRESSING UP

Rich people wore splendid robes, made of the finest silk. Peasants wore loose clothes made of hemp, a rough, scratchy fabric made from plant fibres.

JADE PENDANTS

IVORY FAN

CIVIL SERVANT'S HAT

SILK ROBE

ART AND CRAFTS

The exquisite creations of Chinese artisans were always in demand, both at home and abroad. Craftspeople enjoyed high status in society, above the merchants who sold their work.

GLAZED CAMEL
618–906 CE

IVORY PUZZLE BOX
1800–1900

BOTTLE
1736–95

PEWTER TEA CADDY
18th century

GLASS BOWL
1825–75

PORCELAIN TEAPOT
1662–1772

EMBROIDERED SHOES
Many women's feet were tightly bound, to make them as small as possible.

Medieval Europe

A thousand years of European history, from around the 5th to the 15th century, are known as the medieval era, or Middle Ages. This is often imagined as a colourful time of jousting knights and moated castles, but for most people life was hard.

WHAT THEY WORE

Most people dressed in wool and linen. The style and quality of their clothes told everyone whether they were rich or poor. Rich people wore bright colours, as well as expensive materials and furs.

NOBLEMEN

NOBLEWOMEN

KNIGHT IN DOUBLET AND HOSE

AN ORDINARY PERSON COULD BE FINED FOR WEARING PURPLE, WHICH WAS A COLOUR FOR ROYALTY ONLY

COURTIERS

PEASANTS

CHILD

BUILT TO LAST

Medieval architecture changed styles many times over the centuries. Some of the biggest and most impressive buildings from this period – such as castles, churches, and abbeys – are still standing.

BOLTON ABBEY
England

ST DEMETRIOS OF THESSALONIKI
Bulgaria

CHATEAU DE BEYNAC
France

TRAKAI ISLAND CASTLE
Lithuania

MONT-SAINT-MICHEL
France

HOLY TRINITY CHURCH
Slovenia

CHATEAU DE FOUGERES
France

BARDEJOV TOWN HALL
Slovakia

MAKING MUSIC

In medieval Europe, people of all classes enjoyed music, both as entertainment and in religious ceremonies. Many of their musical instruments developed into the ones we play and listen to today.

SHAWM

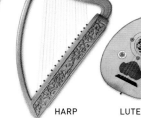
HARP

LUTE

HORN PIPES

REBEC

DOUBLE PIPE

WALKING LION

CASTLE

FOUR CROSSES

THISTLE

EAGLE

HARPY (DEMON)

COATS OF ARMS

A knight carried a set of symbols, or coat of arms, on his shield so that people could recognize him in full armour. The symbols were arranged under a system called heraldry. There were strict rules about colours and designs, and who was allowed to use them.

DRAGON

BEE

DOLPHIN

OWL

HUNTING DOG

REARING UNICORN

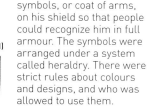
KNIGHT IN FULL ARMOUR

Visor can be raised and lowered

Guard for armpit

Moving plates at shoulder

Cuisse (thigh guard)

Poleyn (knee guard)

Greave (shin guard)

RELIGION

Medieval people had very firm religious beliefs. Europe was mostly Christian, but there were some Jews, and the Middle East was mainly Muslim.

RELIGIOUS IMAGE
This 13th-century stained-glass window was made for a French royal chapel.

THE CRUSADES

In a long-running series of wars called the Crusades, Christian European armies tried to drive Muslim rulers out of the Holy Land. They captured Jerusalem, only to lose the city again later.

ROUTES BY LAND AND SEA

- ■ 1st Crusade, 1096–99
- ■ 2nd Crusade, 1145–49
- ■ 3rd Crusade, 1189–92
- ■ 4th Crusade, 1202–04

TIMELINE

There is no clear beginning or end to the medieval period. Generally, it is dated from around the late 5th century to the middle of the 15th century.

Symbol of Islam

450

476 The Roman Empire in Western Europe ends. This is the approximate start of the medieval era also known as the Middle Ages.

570 Muhammad, Islam's most important prophet, is born.

732 At the Battle of Tours, European armies defeat Muslim invaders.

12th-century statue of Charlemagne

793 Vikings from Denmark, Norway, and Sweden begin their raids in northern Europe.

800 Charlemagne crowns himself emperor of Western Europe and builds a vast empire.

896 Alfred the Great defeats the Vikings, saving England from invasion.

French fortress built for William the Conqueror

1066 William the Conqueror of Normandy conquers the English at Hastings and becomes king of England.

Jewel with portrait of Alfred the Great

1096 Christian Crusaders start a long period of religious wars in the Holy Land.

Church inside Crusader fortress

1191 Richard I (the "Lionheart"), king of England, defeats Saladin, great ruler of Egypt and Syria.

1206 The Mongol Empire is founded by Genghis Khan.

Richard the Lionheart

1431 French heroine Joan of Arc is executed by the English and their French allies at the age of 19.

1453 The Turks take Constantinople, last outpost of the Eastern Roman Empire. This marks the approximate end of the Middle Ages.

1347 The disease called the Black Death begins and will kill about half the people in Europe.

1440s German craftsman Johannes Gutenberg invents the printing press.

1500

JOUSTING

A mock one-to-one fight on horseback, jousting was a dangerous sport. Two knights charged at one another, each trying to unseat the other with his lance.

Lance

Barrier, known as a "tilt"

JOUSTING HELMET

VAMPLATE (HAND GUARD)

LOCKING-GAUNTLET

ARMOUR AND WEAPONS

In the 12th century, knights wore chain-mail armour made from linked iron rings. By the 15th century, battledress was more often a suit of steel plates. Men fought with swords and long-handled weapons such as picks and axes.

CUIRASSIER

ARMET

BURGONET

BASINET

MAIL HELMET

MAIL JACKET

HORSE HEAD ARMOUR

GILDED PLATE ARMOUR

PLATE ARMOUR

POLE AXE

PICK

BATTLE AXE

DAGGERS

WAR HAMMER

HAND CANNON

CRIME AND PUNISHMENT

The law in medieval times was very brutal. Cruel instruments of torture were used both as punishments and to force people to admit guilt or divulge information. Many castles had a torture chamber hidden in their lower depths.

NECK SPIKER

THUMBSCREWS

IRON MASK

MOUTH SCREW

Castles

A castle was the imposing residence of a lord, built as a fortress, to withstand enemy attack. It was also a community where the lord and his family, his garrison of soldiers, and his many servants lived and worked.

TYPES OF CASTLE

The design of castles changed as weapons of attack developed. The earliest castles were built from earth and timber. Then, during the 12th century, lords began to build castles from stone. Although they took longer to build and more skill, they were much stronger and did not burn like wood.

MOTTE AND BAILEY
11th and 12th centuries. A wooden castle is built on a motte (mound), surrounded by a fortified enclosure.

CONCENTRIC
12th–15th century. A central fortress is surrounded by layers of stone walls.

STAR FORT
15th–20th century. Shape deflects cannon fire and allows defenders to fire from several angles.

INSIDE A CASTLE

A castle was like an enclosed village, with kitchens, gardens, stables, workshops, a chapel, and living space all contained within its walls. If the castle was surrounded by an enemy, the people inside had everything they needed to resist a seige for weeks, months, or even years.

Workshops

Vegetable gardens

Flags showed the lord's colours

GREAT HALL
The main room of the castle, where people ate, slept, and carried out castle business.

Circular towers

Thick stone walls

Moat

Battlements

DRAWBRIDGE
Could be raised to cut off outside access.

POSTERN GATE
Emergency side exit, in case the castle was invaded.

Inner wall

Outer wall

DUNGEONS
Underground chambers for holding prisoners and enemy captives.

CASTLES OFTEN HAD SECRET TUNNELS SO SUPPLIES COULD BE SMUGGLED IN DURING A SIEGE

BUILT FOR DEFENCE

Many castles had features to make it as difficult as possible for attackers to get inside. Towers were built on either side of the vulnerable gatehouse, so that defenders could rain missiles or boiling water down on uninvited visitors. Often the lord chose to site his castle on a hillside or clifftop so that he and his men had a good view of anyone approaching.

MOAT
A wide, steep-walled ditch around the castle, usually filled with water.

GATEHOUSE
The main entrance was often fortified by a movable iron grate called a portcullis.

ARROW AND GUN LOOPS
The thick walls had narrow slits through which a soldier could fire missiles at attackers.

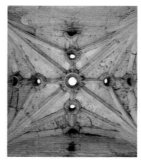

GATEHOUSE CEILING HOLES
Boiling water or other harmful liquids could be dropped on to intruders.

SPIRAL STAIRCASE
Narrow, spiral staircases meant that invaders could not easily use swords while climbing.

BUILDING A CASTLE

A master mason would be employed to plan and build a castle. The work could take years and provided jobs for many local people, from quarry workers and stone-porters to carpenters, and well-diggers.

Stonemason wears a coif (cloth cap) to show his profession

PULLEY WORK
Workers use a pulley to haul a basket of stone up to where it is needed.

SIEGE WEAPONS

There were two ways for attackers to overcome the defences of a castle. They could either take it by force by battering down the gate, climbing the walls, or tunnelling under the defences. Or they could surround the castle and starve those inside until they surrendered or died, which might take a long time.

TREBUCHET
Used to hurl heavy stones at castle walls.

LONGBOW
Used to shoot arrows at long range.

BOMBARD (CANNON)
Blasted walls with large stone balls.

BOMBARD
This British cannon, called the Mons Meg, was built in 1449 and is one of the largest ever made.

BALLISTA
Giant crossbow that fired huge arrows.

WHO'S WHO IN THE CASTLE

The household of a great castle in medieval Europe could easily contain 400 people. It was a busy place as servants, craftsmen, soldiers, and entertainers went about their various jobs.

THE LORD AND HIS FAMILY

GARRISON
The armed troops who were stationed in the castle to defend it.

CHAPLAIN
Led worship in the castle's chapel.

CONSTABLE
The lord's second-in-command, also called a castellan.

GONG FARMER
Dug and cleaned out the castle's toilets.

HUNTSMAN, FALCONER, DOG-KEEPER
Outside servants, each with a specific purpose on the lord's estate.

SEAMSTRESS
One of the many domestic servants who looked after the lord and his family.

PAGES, SQUIRES, AND KNIGHTS

Knights led the force that defended a lord's castle and lands. They were noblemen who pledged to fight for the lord whenever he needed them. In return, knights were paid well and granted lands of their own.

PAGE
A knight started his career at the age of seven, as a page. A page would serve meals and carry messages, as well as learning good manners and how to hold a weapon.

SQUIRE
At the age of 15, the page became a squire. He would clean his knight's armour and weapons, and accompany the knight to the battlefield. Squires were taught horsemanship and fighting skills.

KNIGHT
At the age of about 21, a squire would be made a knight at the ceremony of dubbing. Another knight, usually the squire's master, tapped the new knight on the shoulder with the flat of a sword, and announced him as a knight.

PAGE   SQUIRE   KNIGHT

CASTLE LIVESTOCK

The castle kept a variety of animals to provide food for the community. Chickens and geese lived in the courtyard, while larger animals grazed in the fields and were brought inside the castle walls at night to keep them safe.

COTSWOLD SHEEP

CHICKENS

LONGHORN COW

BAGOT GOAT

GOOSE

BOAR

CASTLES AROUND THE WORLD

The size, shape, and location of a castle were influenced by natural features such as mountains or lakes, the climate, what building materials were available, and how permanent the castle was intended to be.

HOHENZOLLERN CASTLE, GERMANY (19TH CENTURY)

BELMONTE CASTLE, SPAIN (15TH CENTURY)

SAUMUR CASTLE, FRANCE (10TH–16TH CENTURY)

KASTELHOLM CASTLE, FINLAND (14TH CENTURY)

QATRANA CASTLE, JORDAN (16TH CENTURY)

OKAYAMA CASTLE, JAPAN (16TH CENTURY)

THE REBIRTH OF EUROPE

The Renaissance began in northern Italy towards the end of the 14th century. Two hundred years later, its influence had spread all over the world.

c.1420
Architect Filippo Brunelleschi rediscovers perspective, meaning that objects can be drawn to look as if they are near or far away.

Arches drawn using perspective

1440
Johannes Gutenberg invents the printing press in Germany.

First printing press

1469
Lorenzo de Medici becomes head of the city-state of Florence.

Statue of Lorenzo de Medici

1472
Artist Leonardo da Vinci, aged only 20, is invited to join the Painters' Guild of Florence.

1486
Botticelli paints his masterpiece The Birth of Venus.

1498
Leonardo paints the mural The Last Supper for a convent in Milan.

1503
Pope Julius II commissions many artists, including Michelangelo and Raphael, to create work for him in Rome.

Statue on the tomb of Pope Julius II

1504
Michelangelo's statue of David is displayed in Florence.

1509
Dutch scholar Erasmus publishes his book Praise of Folly, which pokes fun at superstition.

1511
Raphael completes the fresco The School of Athens to decorate a wall in the Vatican, the Pope's palace.

1527
Rome is sacked by the army of Charles V, the Holy Roman Emperor.

1543
Doctor Andrea Vesalius publishes the first textbook about the human body and how it works.

Woodcut portrait of Andreas Vesalius

1546
Michelangelo appointed chief architect at St Peter's Basilica, Rome.

1550
Giorgio Vasari publishes a massive history of Renaissance art: The Lives of the Artists.

The Renaissance

The Renaissance is the name given to a time of huge cultural change in Europe, beginning in the late 14th century. Scholars rediscovered the writings of the Ancient Greeks and Romans, and this led to an explosion of new ideas about science, art, and politics.

WHERE IT BEGAN

The Renaissance began in the richest parts of Europe. The city-states of northern Italy were full of wealthy noblemen, bankers, and merchants who were eager to show off their wealth and power by supporting artists and inventors. In northern Europe, scholarship and new ideas flourished in the prosperous wool-trading regions of what is now Belgium, Germany, and the Netherlands.

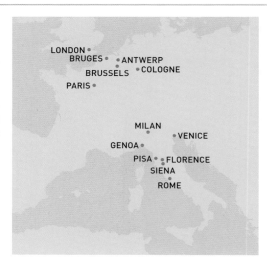

LONDON
BRUGES • ANTWERP
BRUSSELS • COLOGNE
PARIS •

MILAN
• VENICE
GENOA •
PISA • • FLORENCE
SIENA
ROME

KEY
• Major Renaissance cities

POWERFUL PATRONS

The Medici family were rich bankers. From 1434 they ruled the city of Florence, and commissioned artists such as Leonardo da Vinci and Michelangelo to produce many great buildings and works of art.

MEDICI COAT OF ARMS

RENAISSANCE MEN

During the Renaissance, many of the most influential people did not focus solely on one subject, but became expert in a range of disciplines.

○ **LEONARDO DA VINCI (1452–1519)**
A true all-rounder, Leonardo was a brilliant painter, inventor, sculptor, architect, and scientist. His Mona Lisa is probably the best-known painting in history.

○ **MARTIN LUTHER (1483–1546)**
German monk and university professor. He attacked corruption in the Roman Catholic Church, was excommunicated, and became a key figure in the Protestant Reformation.

○ **PARACELSUS (1493–1541)**
Swiss scientist who studied medicine and found that many doctors made patients worse rather than healing them. He used his knowledge of chemistry to develop new drugs and medicines.

○ **MICHELANGELO (1475–1564)**
Artist, architect, and sculptor who painted the ceiling of the Sistine Chapel, part of the Vatican in Rome. The ceiling contains more than 400 life-size figures and took four years to complete.

○ **NICCOLO MACHIAVELLI (1469–1527)**
A diplomat and writer from Florence. His book The Prince gave advice to ambitious politicians on how to succeed. The word "machiavellian" is still used today to describe ruthless or cunning behaviour.

FLYING MACHINE
Leonardo da Vinci's design for the ornithopter, a human-powered aircraft.

LEONARDO DESIGNED RECOGNIZABLE VERSIONS OF THE MODERN BICYCLE, HELICOPTER, AND PARACHUTE

SCIENCE AND DISCOVERY

A new method of approaching science began to take hold during the Renaissance, in which conducting experiments and gathering evidence were seen as the best ways to gain knowledge. This approach led to great progress in the sciences and to many new inventions.

PRINTED BOOK
Printing meant that scholars could publish their work more widely and exchange ideas with each other.

THEODOLITE
An instrument to help architects and builders to measure angles.

ASTROLABE
An ancient navigation aid, redesigned and widely used by Renaissance explorers.

MATCHLOCK MUSKET
The matchlock was a new way of firing a gun so that it could be operated by a single person.

WHEEL LOCK PISTOL
A method for firing the gun mechanically, rather than by a lit wick, it was safer and more portable than the matchlock weapon.

MUSICAL INSTRUMENTS

Music was the main form of entertainment in Renaissance Europe. Composers experimented with new instruments and different ways of singing in harmony.

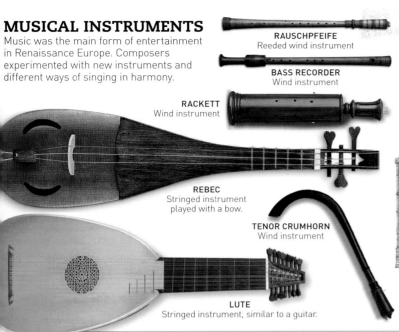

RAUSCHPFEIFE
Reeded wind instrument

BASS RECORDER
Wind instrument

RACKETT
Wind instrument

REBEC
Stringed instrument played with a bow.

TENOR CRUMHORN
Wind instrument

LUTE
Stringed instrument, similar to a guitar.

GOLDEN AGE OF ARCHITECTURE

Architects were inspired by the ruins of Ancient Roman and Greek buildings. They studied ancient writings on geometry and proportion in order to make buildings that were both beautiful to look at and suited to their purpose.

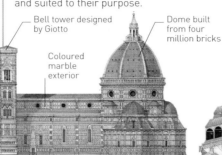

Bell tower designed by Giotto

Coloured marble exterior

Dome built from four million bricks

Single stone arch supports two arcades of shops

Dome designed by Michelangelo

DUOMO, FLORENCE
Completed in 1436, the *duomo* (cathedral) is topped by a huge, octagonal dome designed by sculptor and architect Filippo Brunelleschi.

RIALTO BRIDGE, VENICE
A late Renaissance masterpiece of architecture and engineering, completed in 1591.

ST PETER'S BASILICA, ROME
Over a 120-year period, many of Italy's finest architects worked on the building. It was completed in 1626.

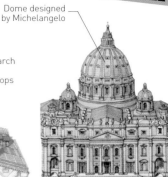

THE INTERIOR OF ST PETER'S BASILICA WAS DESIGNED TO HOLD UP TO 60,000 PEOPLE

A REVOLUTION IN ART

A way of thinking called humanism became popular during the Renaissance. Humanism's focus on the experiences and achievements of real human beings had a huge influence on artists. They started to portray people, including religious figures, as realistically as possible, and to place them in more everyday situations.

VIRGIN AND CHILD (c.1480)
Carlo Crivelli

MONA LISA (1503–06)
Leonardo da Vinci

FRESCO (WALL PAINTING) OF THE QUEEN OF SHEBA (1466)
Piero della Francesca

STATUE OF DAVID (1501–04)
Michelangelo

PIETA (MARY HOLDING JESUS) (1553)
Michelangelo

NEW ARTISTIC TECHNIQUES

Renaissance artists wanted their work to look realistic. They rediscovered ancient techniques and developed new ones to make their subjects and backgrounds look as much like those in the real world as possible.

LINEAR PERSPECTIVE
Perspective was used to give an artwork a sense of depth. For instance, if an artist drew a line of trees, he would make them smaller and closer together as they got further away from the foreground (front) of the drawing.

AERIAL PERSPECTIVE
Also called atmospheric perspective. It was a way of creating depth and distance, especially in a landscape, by making features paler and less detailed, the further away they got from the foreground.

HARMONY AND PROPORTION
Drawing objects so that they are precisely the right size when compared to each other. Artists rediscovered Ancient Greek and Roman writings, which set out how mathematics could be used to work out ideal proportions. A work of art created in this way would have perfect balance and harmony, they believed.

ADVENTURERS AND EXPLORERS

From the first sailing expeditions to rocket-propelled space travel, humans have always gone beyond the limits of their known world to see what else is out there.

c.2700 BCE
Egyptians build wooden ships capable of sea voyages. They begin trading with nearby countries.

334 BCE
Alexander the Great invades the Persian Empire, then continues east and north as far as modern-day Pakistan and India.

1001 CE
Viking Leif Ericsson reaches North America and makes a settlement in Newfoundland, Canada.

1488
Bartholomeu Dias of Portugal sails from the Iberian Peninsula to southern Africa.

1497
Vasco da Gama sails around the Cape of Good Hope to India.

1519–21
Portuguese Ferdinand Magellan is the first European to sail from the Atlantic Ocean to the Pacific Ocean.

Portuguese caravel (sailing ship)

1769
Captain James Cook discovers New Zealand.

Statue of Captain James Cook

1943
Jacques Cousteau invents the aqualung, an automatic air supply for divers.

1961
Yuri Gagarin becomes the first man in space.

2012
James Cameron reaches the bottom of the Mariana Trench, the deepest undersea location in the world.

1500–500 BCE
Phoenicians (from modern-day Israel and Lebanon) explore the Mediterranean, then as far as west Africa and Britain, looking for new trading partners.

Phoenician traders

1271
Marco Polo begins his exploration of China and Asia.

Marco Polo's China and Asia expedition

1492
Christopher Columbus lands in America and claims it for Spain.

Christopher Columbus's coat of arms

1577–80
Englishman Sir Francis Drake circumnavigates the globe (sails round the world).

Statue of Sir Francis Drake

1642
Abel Tasman explores Van Diemen's Land (now Tasmania).

1819
Augustus Siebe invents a helmet that enables divers to work at a depth of 60 m (196.8 ft).

Deep-sea diving helmet

1858
John Hanning Speke discovers Lake Victoria, Africa.

Arctic explorer's sealskin hood and gloves

1911
Norwegian Roald Amundsen and his team reach the South Pole.

Amundsen arriving at the South Pole

1969
Neil Armstrong, commander of USA's Apollo 11 mission, sets foot on the moon.

Apollo 11 commemoration badge

Exploration

The first explorers set sail in search of new places to buy and sell goods. Later, people led expeditions to get rich, to claim territory for their country or religion, to make scientific discoveries, or simply for the thrill of adventure.

EXPLORERS OF THE ANCIENT WORLD

The earliest explorers were the Phoenicians and the Egyptians, who wanted to find markets to trade their goods. Later cultures, such as the Romans and Vikings, also wanted to conquer new territories to expand their empires.

Rectangular sail on two curved beams

Oars were used when there was no wind

PHOENICIAN TRADING SHIP

VIKING LONGSHIP

Ships built from strong cedar wood from Lebanon

EGYPTIAN TRADING SHIP

THE AGE OF EXPLORATION

In the early 15th century, Portuguese sailors set out to find a sea route to Asia. This triggered a wave of exploration, as rival countries found new trading routes and established colonies all over the world.

KEY
- Magellan's route
- Other Spanish missions
- Portuguese expeditions
- English expeditions
- French expeditions
- Dutch expeditions

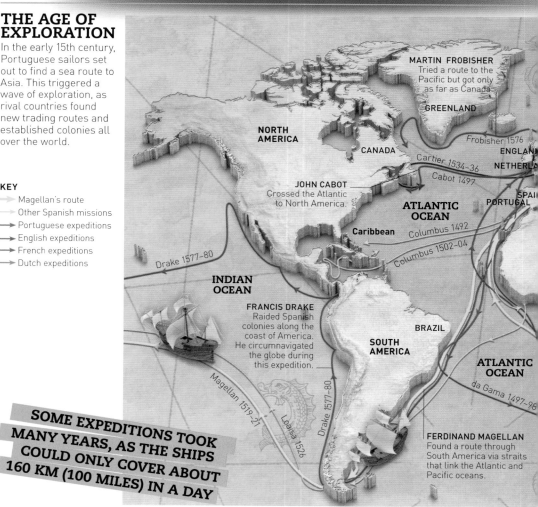

MARTIN FROBISHER
Tried a route to the Pacific but got only as far as Canada.

GREENLAND

NORTH AMERICA

CANADA

Frobisher 1576

ENGLAND

Cartier 1534–36

NETHERLANDS

Cabot 1497

JOHN CABOT
Crossed the Atlantic to North America.

ATLANTIC OCEAN

SPAIN

PORTUGAL

Caribbean

Columbus 1492

Columbus 1502–04

Drake 1577–80

INDIAN OCEAN

FRANCIS DRAKE
Raided Spanish colonies along the coast of America. He circumnavigated the globe during this expedition.

BRAZIL

SOUTH AMERICA

ATLANTIC OCEAN

da Gama 1497–98

Magellan 1519–21

Loaisa 1526

Drake 1577–80

FERDINAND MAGELLAN
Found a route through South America via straits that link the Atlantic and Pacific oceans.

SOME EXPEDITIONS TOOK MANY YEARS, AS THE SHIPS COULD ONLY COVER ABOUT 160 KM (100 MILES) IN A DAY

NAVIGATION TOOLS

Sailors exploring new territories had no maps to guide them, so they had to find their way by other methods. Navigators used a compass to find the right direction, and they calculated their position by observing stars and planets.

MAGNETIC COMPASS
18th century, Italy.

ASTROLABE
Allowed sailors to use the stars to navigate.

LODESTONE
The earliest type of magnetic compass.

GLOBE
For calculating routes and bearings.

TELESCOPE
Used to identify landmarks from a distance.

EARLY AIRCRAFT INSTRUMENT PANEL
Showed aircraft's height and speed.

SCIENTIFIC JOURNEYS

In the 19th century, the thirst for knowledge was so great that scientists and naturalists such as Charles Darwin embarked on long and dangerous trips to search out new species of animals or plants.

BEETLE SPECIMENS
Collected by Charles Darwin.

MICROSCOPE
Used by Charles Darwin in the 1830s.

INSECT DRAWINGS
Sketched by naturalist Henry Bates.

SNOUTFISH
Collected by explorer Mary Kingsley.

ADVENTURERS OF THE GOLDEN AGE

Exploration was a risky business, but the rewards were potentially huge. Successful explorers could expect fame, wealth, and personal favours from a grateful monarch.

- **CHRISTOPHER COLUMBUS (1451–1506)** Italian sailor Columbus was paid by King Ferdinand and Queen Isabella of Spain to find a sea route to China. Instead, in 1492, he found America and called it the New World.

- **VASCO DA GAMA (c.1460–1524)** A Portuguese explorer, he led the first expedition to sail round the Cape of Good Hope, at the tip of Africa, to India.

VASCO DA GAMA

- **FERDINAND MAGELLAN (1480–1521)** Magellan led the first expedition to sail all the way round the world. Unfortunately, Magellan himself did not make it home alive: he was killed in a battle between local tribes in the Philippines.

FERDINAND MAGELLAN

- **HERNAN CORTES (1485–1541)** A Spanish conquistador (soldier), Cortés first travelled to Mexico to set up a trading colony for Spain, but ended up destroying the entire Aztec Empire in Central America.

- **SIR WALTER RALEIGH (c.1552–1618)** An English adventurer who tried unsuccessfully to set up colonies in the New World, but who is best remembered for bringing tobacco back to Europe from the Americas.

SIR WALTER RALEIGH

ARCTIC OCEAN

Barents 1596–97

oughby 1553

SIBERIA

HUGH WILLOUGHBY AND WILLIAM BARENTS
Both sailed north of Siberia, but failed to find routes to the Pacific.

EUROPE

ASIA

CHINA

INDIA

PACIFIC OCEAN

AFRICA

Cabral 1500
da Gama 1497–98

Andrade 1517

Magellan 1519–21

Drake 1577–80

PHILIPPINES

Spice Islands

Loaisa 1526

VASCO DA GAMA
Reached India via Africa, returning to Portugal with cinnamon and pepper.

INDIAN OCEAN

Cape of Good Hope

Drake 1577–80

AUSTRALASIA

POLAR PIONEERS

In the 19th century, the cold, hostile regions of the Arctic and Antarctic were largely undiscovered. Explorers from many different countries joined the race to be the first to conquer the North and South poles.

INUIT (ESKIMO) KNIVES WITH BONE HANDLE
Made of steel from the abandoned ship of Sir John Franklin, who failed to find a sea route through the Arctic Ocean, north of Canada.

WINDPROOF HOOD
Worn by Sir Ernest Shackleton on his South Pole attempt of 1907–08.

CLASP KNIFE AND SEXTANT
Used by Captain Robert Scott on his South Pole expedition of 1912.

CROSS-COUNTRY SKIS
Used by Captain Scott in his first South Pole expedition, 1901–04.

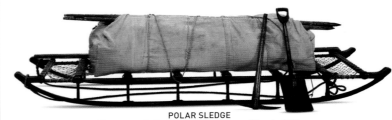

POLAR SLEDGE
Eight-man sledge from an Arctic expedition in 1875.

Revolutions

Political revolutions have occurred throughout history and can completely change society. Often violent, they typically occur when angry citizens rebel against their rulers to demand a fairer society, and frequently a different leadership. Revolutions can change existing power structures very quickly. However, their causes have usually been building over many years.

▶ 1566–1648
DUTCH REVOLT

In 1566–68, Dutch Protestants rose up against Catholic Spain, which had ruled the Netherlands since 1555, and declared independence. The revolt led to a long and bloody war with Spain that ended with Dutch independence in 1648.

ENGLISH CIVIL WAR TROOPER'S HELMET

ENGLISH CIVIL WAR

This period of intense political activity started when Parliament wished to restrict the authority of King Charles I. Civil war broke out and ended with the execution of the king in 1649. For ten years, England was a republic ruled by Lord Protector Oliver Cromwell.

MEDAL COMMEMORATING ENGLISH SUPPORT FOR THE DUTCH

▶ 1640–60

▶ 1648–53
THE FRONDE

A series of uprisings called the Fronde took place in France, initiated by the French Nobility and supported by the middle classes. They were rebelling against the King's absolute rule, and discontent later spread to the masses. After the Fronde failed, the King became even stronger.

STATUE OF KING LOUIS XIV

◀ 1945

HO CHI MINH: LEADER OF THE VIET MINH

AUGUST REVOLUTION

In 1945 Ho Chi Minh and his mainly communist force the Viet Minh set out to liberate Vietnam from French rule. They seized Hanoi and declared independence but French forces retaliated. This led to the First Indochina War and the start of bitter conflict in the region.

◀ 1936–39
SPANISH CIVIL WAR

This revolt against the Spanish government led to civil war. On one side were nationalists led by General Franco, backed by Nazi Germany and Fascist Italy. They fought Republicans: Communists, socialists, and anarchists, who were backed by the Soviet Union.

GENERAL FRANCO: DICTATOR OF SPAIN 1939–75

◀ 1930
BRAZILIAN REVOLUTION

Economic hardship, powerful landlords, and demands for workers' rights led to revolution in Brazil in 1930. A provincial governor called Getúlio Vargas seized power. A dictator at first, he introduced reforms that modernized Brazil and earned him the nickname "Father of the Poor".

GETULIO VARGAS: BRAZILIAN PRESIDENT 1930–45, 1951–54

◀ 1918–23
GERMAN REVOLUTION

A series of revolutions shook Germany immediately after World War I (1914–18). Communists Rosa Luxemburg and Karl Liebknecht led the Spartacists' uprising against the government, but it was brutally quashed. Later, extreme nationalists, led by Wolfgang Kapp, tried to seize power, blaming the Weimar Republic for betraying the German Empire.

◀ 1917

STATUE OF LENIN, BOLSHEVIK LEADER

OCTOBER REVOLUTION

Two revolutions happened in Russia in 1917. The first, in March, removed the tsar (ruler) and set up a provisional government. In the second, in October, the Bolshevik party, led by Vladimir Ilyich Ulyanov (Lenin), called for "peace, land and bread". They seized power and in 1922 set up the Soviet Union, the world's first Communist state.

▶ 1946–49
CHINESE REVOLUTION

From the 1920s onwards, there was a struggle for control of China between the Kuomintang, or nationalists, led by Chiang kai-Shek, and Communists under Mao Zedong. Civil war broke out in 1945, ending with a Communist victory in 1949.

MAO ZEDONG

▶ 1953–59

REVOLUTIONARY CHE GUEVARA BECAME A WORLDWIDE HERO

CUBAN REVOLUTION

An armed revolution led by Fidel Castro and Che Guevara overthrew the USA-backed dictatorship of President Batista. Cuba became a revolutionary socialist state and later a Communist country.

▶ 1956
HUNGARIAN REVOLUTION

After World War II (1939–45), Hungary became a Communist state, under the influence of the Soviet Union. In 1953 Imre Nagy, a moderate socialist, became leader, and in October 1956 he called for Hungary to become independent in an anti-Soviet uprising. The Soviet troops invaded Hungary and put down the uprising with great brutality.

▶ 1974
CARNATION REVOLUTION

On 25 April 1974, army rebel tanks rolled into Lisbon, Portugal, and seized control of the city's communications. They overthrew the government of Prime Minister Marcello Caetano, ending 50 years of dictatorship. The revolt was called the "carnation revolution" because the people gave carnations to the troops as they entered the city.

▶ 1974–77
ETHIOPIAN REVOLUTION

In September 1974, Mengistu Haile Mariam led an alliance of radical armed forces and police (the Derg) to depose the emperor, Haile Selassie. They executed the emperor and set up a Communist state. The coup was followed by years of bloodshed and civil war.

GRATEFUL LISBON CROWDS PRESENTED REBEL TROOPS WITH CARNATIONS

1775–83
AMERICAN REVOLUTION

In the mid-1770s American colonists revolted against British rule and "taxation without representation". They issued a Declaration of Independence. War broke out in 1775, ending in 1783 with the colonists winning independence and creating the United States of America.

THE US CONSTITUTION, DRAWN UP IN 1787

▶ 1789

THE STORMING OF THE BASTILLE, A PRISON IN PARIS, 14 JULY 1789

FRENCH REVOLUTION

This rebellion was against poverty, the nobility, and the royal family. In Paris revolutionaries demanding political change stormed the Bastille. A National Assembly was formed and the Declaration of the Rights of Man called for liberty, equality, and fraternity (brotherhood). King Louis XV and his wife, Marie Antoinette, were executed and France became a republic.

▶ 1791–1804
HAITIAN REVOLUTION

In the French colony of Saint-Domingue, former slave Toussaint L'Ouverture led slaves in a rebellion against slavery, burning plantations and killing their owners. Slavery was abolished on the island, which became independent Haiti.

L'OUVERTURE LEADING REVOLT AGAINST FRENCH PLANTATION OWNERS

▶ 1806–24
LATIN-AMERICAN REVOLUTIONS

Influenced by the American, French, and Haitian revolutions, Latin-American revolutionaries led by men such as Venezuelan Simón Bolívar and Argentinian José de San Martin rose up against Spanish colonial rule. By 1825 most of Latin America had gained independence.

SIMON BOLIVAR, KNOWN AS "THE LIBERATOR"

◀ 1911
XINHAI REVOLUTION

During the Xinhai Revolution, nationalists overthrew the Manchu dynasty in China, ending 2000 years of imperial rule. They set up a republic under Sun Yat-sen, although real power stayed in the hands of provincial warlords.

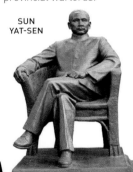

SUN YAT-SEN

◀ 1910–20
MEXICAN REVOLUTION

The Mexican Revolution started as a protest against the dictatorship of President Porfirio Díaz, but soon spiralled into an armed revolution that lasted around ten years. Led by Emiliano Zapata, Pascual Orozo, and Pancho Villa, the rebels fought to reform society.

> ### "IT IS BETTER TO DIE ON YOUR FEET THAN TO LIVE ON YOUR KNEES"
>
> EMILIANO ZAPATA, REVOLUTIONARY LEADER

◀ 1866–68

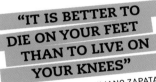

EMPEROR MEIJI RULED 1867–1912

MEIJI RESTORATION

Led mainly by young samurai, this revolution in Japan overthrew the Tokugawa shogunate (hereditary military rulers) and restored imperial rule under Emperor Meiji. The revolution led to reforms that modernized Japan.

◀ 1848
EUROPEAN REVOLUTIONS

Often called "the year of revolutions", in 1848 more than 50 uprisings broke out across Europe. Although these revolutions happened independently, people across the continent were banding together to demand political and social change and an end to monarchies. Thousands were killed as the uprisings were put down.

THE HUNGARIAN TRICOLOUR FLAG, A SYMBOL OF THE 1848 REVOLUTION

1979
NICARAGUA

In the 1970s there were extremes of rich and poor in Nicaragua. Supported by peasants, urban workers, and the middle-classes, the guerrilla troops of the Sandinista National Liberation Front (FSLN), threw out wealthy dictator Anastasio Somoza. They introduced new socialist reforms. Later, rebel groups called the Contras fought back against the Sandinistas, who lost power in 1990.

▶ 1980–81
SOLIDARITY IN POLAND

Revolution broke out in Poland when the independent trade union Solidarity organized workers' strikes, under the leadership of Lech Walesa. They wanted liberation from Soviet control, and their actions forced the Polish government to introduce reforms. Solidarity was banned but continued their resistance until they took power.

MONUMENT TO THE SHIPYARD WORKERS, GDANSK, POLAND

▶ 1986

YELLOW RIBBON

YELLOW REVOLUTION

The Yellow Revolution was a series of mass popular protests in the Philippines against the corrupt regime of President Marcos. In this non-violent revolution, more than two million Filipinos demonstrated for greater democracy, displaying yellow ribbons as a symbol of protest. Marcos departed and was replaced by Corazon Aquino.

▶ 1988–91
EASTERN EUROPE

By the late 1980s protests were spreading through the Soviet satellite states of Eastern Europe, as protesters demanded greater democracy. In Berlin demonstrators pulled down the hated Berlin Wall that divided East and West Germany, and by 1989 Communism had collapsed throughout Eastern and Central Europe.

FRAGMENT OF THE BERLIN WALL

▶ 2004–05
ORANGE REVOLUTION

Taking its name from orange banners and clothes of demonstrators, the Orange Revolution in Ukraine was made up of mass protests against the undemocratic election of a Russian-backed president. As a result the election was repeated and anticorruption candidate Yushchenko was elected.

▶ 2010–12
ARAB SPRING

Starting in 2010, a wave of pro-democracy uprisings took place in the Middle East and North Africa – Tunisia, Egypt, Libya, the Yemen, and Syria – that challenged some of the region's authoritarian governments. Protesters were met with violence, but regimes in Tunisia and Egypt were toppled.

> ### EACH DAY 5,000 TONNES OF PORRIDGE AND 10,000 LOAVES WERE SUPPLIED TO ORANGE REVOLUTION PROTESTERS IN UKRAINE

US presidents

Since the office was created in 1789, there have been 43 presidents of the United States, all men. To be eligible, a person has to be at least 35 years old and born either in the USA, or overseas to US-citizen parents. As well as being Head of State, the president is Commander-in-Chief of the country's armed forces.

GEORGE WASHINGTON
1789–97
Led army against the British in the American Revolution, then became the first president. Unanimously elected.

JOHN ADAMS
1797–1801
Helped draft the Declaration of Independence. Established the naval department, so he is remembered as the "Father of the Navy".

WILLIAM HENRY HARRISON
1841
The first president to die in office. He died of pneumonia only a month after he became president.

JOHN TYLER
1841–45
Vice-president who took the presidency on the death of William Henry Harrison, making him the first president to serve without being elected to office.

JAMES K POLK
1845–49
Greatly expanded the territory of the USA, adding Texas, Wisconsin, and Iowa as states, and taking over land in the west that would become New Mexico and California.

ZACHARY TAYLOR
1849–50
Successful military general who commanded US forces in the war against Mexico (1846–48). Died of cholera a year after taking office.

MILLARD FILLMORE
1850–53
Tried to make a compromise between the anti-slavery states and the slave-owning states in the south, but the peace was short-lived.

FRANKLIN PIERCE
1853–57
Allowed new states to decide for themselves whether to allow slavery, which angered many and edged the USA ever closer to civil war.

CHESTER A ARTHUR
1881–85
Brought in a law that meant that civil servants were hired purely for their ability rather than because of their political connections.

GROVER CLEVELAND
1885–89; 1893–97
The only president ever to serve two non-consecutive terms – he lost an election, then was voted back in again four years later.

BENJAMIN HARRISON
1889–93
Grandson of President William Harrison, during his term the country expanded and six new states were admitted to the Union.

WILLIAM MCKINLEY
1897–1901
Oversaw expansion of US territories, including Hawaii and Puerto Rico. Six months into his second term, he was assassinated.

THEODORE ROOSEVELT
1901–09
The youngest person to become president, at 42. Won the Nobel Peace Prize in 1906 for negotiating peace between Russia and Japan.

WILLIAM H TAFT
1909–13
A lawyer by profession, he set up the postal savings bank and passed a law allowing states to collect income tax.

DWIGHT D EISENHOWER
1953–61
Led the Allied armed forces in World War II. During his two terms of office, the US economy thrived.

JOHN F KENNEDY
1961–63
His work to reform civil rights and promote racial equality was cut short when he was shot dead in Texas.

LYNDON B JOHNSON
1963–69
Brought in the Civil Rights Act, but faced opposition for sending more troops into the war in Vietnam.

RICHARD NIXON
1969–74
Ended the Vietnam War and improved relations with the USSR. His term ended in disgrace after political corruption was uncovered.

GERALD FORD
1974–77
Unexpectedly became vice-president, then president, during an era of scandals. His honesty helped restore the image of the presidency.

JIMMY CARTER
1977–81
President during a difficult period for the USA, both at home and abroad. After his term in office, he became a respected statesman.

THOMAS JEFFERSON
1801–09
The main author of the Declaration of Independence, which stated that the colonies would no longer accept British rule.

JAMES MADISON
1809–17
Helped draw up the US Constitution, which set out America's laws and guaranteed certain rights for its citizens.

JAMES MONROE
1817–25
Remembered for the Monroe Doctrine, which declared that the USA would resist attempts by other countries to establish colonies in the Americas.

JOHN QUINCY ADAMS
1825–29
Son of a previous president, John Adams. After his presidency, he became a strong campaigner against slavery.

ANDREW JACKSON
1829–37
Before he took office, he became a national hero for leading the army that defeated the British at the Battle of New Orleans.

MARTIN VAN BUREN
1837–41
After financial panic and stock market crash led to economic depression, Van Buren became unpopular and was not re-elected.

JAMES BUCHANAN
1857–61
Like previous presidents, he tried to make peace between states on the slavery issue, but by the end of his term, civil war was looming.

ABRAHAM LINCOLN
1861–65
Opposed to slavery, he led the country during four years of civil war. Days after the war ended, he was shot dead by John Wilkes Booth.

ANDREW JOHNSON
1865–69
Put on trial by the Senate for violating the Tenure of Office Act, he escaped being removed from office by a single vote.

ULYSSES S GRANT
1869–77
A hero of the Civil War, he was an inexperienced politician whose presidency was overshadowed by scandal and corruption.

RUTHERFORD B HAYES
1877–81
After winning one of the closest presidential elections ever, he fought to end corruption in politics and public life.

JAMES A GARFIELD
1881
Shot dead after only 200 days in office, before he could carry out his promise to reform the civil service and other public bodies.

WOODROW WILSON
1913–21
Took the USA into World War I in 1917. After the war, he proposed the formation of the League of Nations to try to prevent future conflict.

WARREN G HARDING
1921–23
An unpopular president who was dogged by rumours of financial wrongdoing. He died suddenly, before an investigation could begin.

CALVIN COOLIDGE
1923–29
Honest, hard-working, and modest, he was fondly nicknamed "Silent Cal". Under his presidency, the US economy boomed.

HERBERT HOOVER
1929–33
Shortly after his election, the USA began an era of serious economic depression. Hoover was blamed and did not win a second term.

FRANKLIN D ROOSEVELT
1933–45
Led the USA through the Great Depression and World War II. He funded a plan to revive the US economy and help people out of poverty.

HARRY S TRUMAN
1945–53
Authorized the dropping of two nuclear bombs on Japan, which ended World War II. Took the USA to war with Korea.

RONALD REAGAN
1981–89
An ex-Hollywood star, he helped to end the Cold War. He was shot by a would-be assassin but recovered.

GEORGE H W BUSH
1989–93
An oil tycoon and ex-head of the CIA, he took the USA and its allies into the first Gulf War with Iraq (1990–91).

BILL CLINTON
1993–2001
Presided over a time of peace and prosperity, but his reputation was damaged by a scandal over a relationship with a White House worker.

GEORGE W BUSH
2001–09
After the terrorist attacks of 9/11, he ordered the invasion of Afghanistan and declared the War on Terror.

BARACK OBAMA
(2009–)
The first African American president. His healthcare reforms were disliked by opponents, and led to stalemate in government.

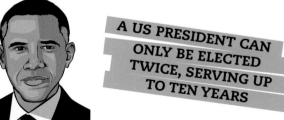

A US PRESIDENT CAN ONLY BE ELECTED TWICE, SERVING UP TO TEN YEARS

US Civil War

In the early 1860s, the USA, then known as the Union, was torn apart by war. The northern states had made slavery illegal and believed it should be abolished in the rest of the country. The southern states disagreed. Their landowners relied on African slaves to farm their tobacco and cotton. Some southern states felt so strongly, they left the Union.

EVENTS AND BATTLES

Less than a century after gaining its independence, the USA was in danger of breaking up. More than 50 major battles and 5,000 minor ones were fought before the Unionists finally won the war.

1860

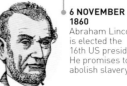

6 NOVEMBER 1860
Abraham Lincoln is elected the 16th US president. He promises to abolish slavery.

20 DECEMBER 1860
South Carolina withdraws from the Union. Six states follow by February 1861.

Abraham Lincoln

Confederate flag

ONE IN FOUR SOLDIERS WHO WENT TO WAR NEVER CAME HOME – MANY WENT MISSING

5 / 20 / 4 / 7	22 / 9	2.1 / 1.1
NUMBER OF STATES The new state of West Virginia formed during the war.	**POPULATION (IN MILLIONS)** The Union had 2.4 times more people than the Confederacy.	**SOLDIERS (IN MILLIONS)** Twelve per cent of all southerners fought in the war.

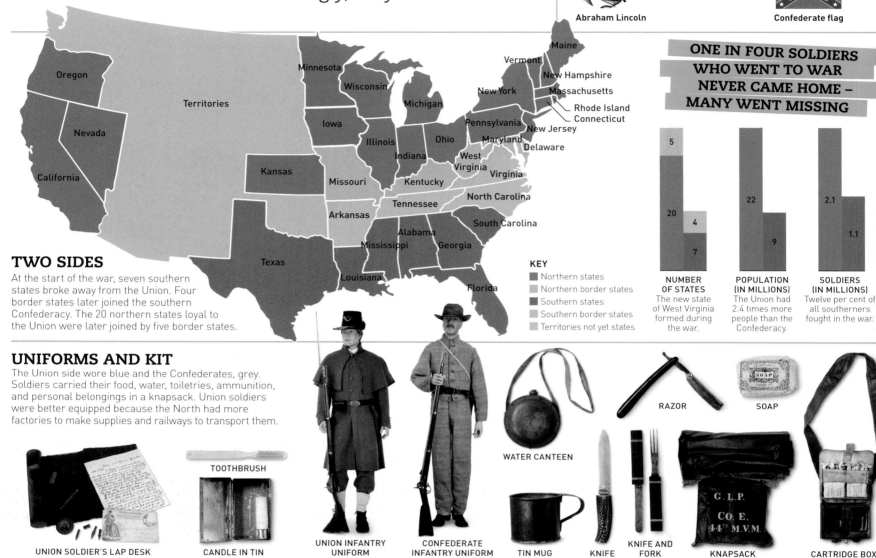

Map labels: Oregon, Territories, Nevada, California, Kansas, Texas, Minnesota, Wisconsin, Iowa, Illinois, Missouri, Arkansas, Louisiana, Michigan, Indiana, Ohio, Kentucky, Tennessee, Mississippi, Alabama, Georgia, Florida, Maine, Vermont, New Hampshire, New York, Massachusetts, Rhode Island, Connecticut, Pennsylvania, New Jersey, Maryland, Delaware, West Virginia, Virginia, North Carolina, South Carolina

TWO SIDES

At the start of the war, seven southern states broke away from the Union. Four border states later joined the southern Confederacy. The 20 northern states loyal to the Union were later joined by five border states.

KEY
- Northern states
- Northern border states
- Southern states
- Southern border states
- Territories not yet states

UNIFORMS AND KIT

The Union side wore blue and the Confederates, grey. Soldiers carried their food, water, toiletries, ammunition, and personal belongings in a knapsack. Union soldiers were better equipped because the North had more factories to make supplies and railways to transport them.

UNION SOLDIER'S LAP DESK

TOOTHBRUSH

CANDLE IN TIN

UNION INFANTRY UNIFORM

CONFEDERATE INFANTRY UNIFORM

WATER CANTEEN

TIN MUG

KNIFE

KNIFE AND FORK

RAZOR

SOAP

G.L.P. CO.E. 44TH M.V.M.

KNAPSACK

CARTRIDGE BOX

TRANSPORT INNOVATIONS

The 1830s had seen the birth of the railways. Both sides relied on steam trains to transport troops and supplies, but the North had more than twice as much track as the South. Other advances included the appearance of armoured steam warships, called ironclads, and early submarines.

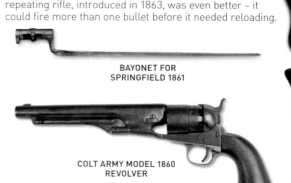

STEAM LOCOMOTIVE

CSS VIRGINIA (FIRST CONFEDERATE IRONCLAD)

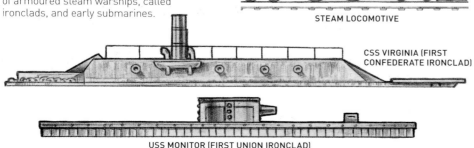

USS MONITOR (FIRST UNION IRONCLAD)

WEAPONS AND CONFLICT

The Civil War was the first in which large numbers of infantrymen were armed with rifles instead of muskets. Rifles shot further, and with greater accuracy. The repeating rifle, introduced in 1863, was even better – it could fire more than one bullet before it needed reloading.

BAYONET FOR SPRINGFIELD 1861

COLT ARMY MODEL 1860 REVOLVER

12–14 APRIL 1861
The first battle of the Civil War, fought at Fort Sumter, South Carolina, is a victory for the Confederates.

Union flag

11–16 FEBRUARY 1862
Ulysses S Grant leads a Union victory at the Battle of Fort Donelson, Tennessee.

Ulysses S Grant

4 JULY 1863
After a six-week siege, the Union army captures the city of Vicksburg, cutting off Arkansas, Louisiana, and Texas from the rest of the Confederacy.

15 NOVEMBER–21 DECEMBER 1864
Union General Sherman sweeps through Georgia, ending victoriously at the port of Savannah.

1 FEBRUARY 1865
Lincoln signs the 13th Amendment, which formally abolishes slavery in the USA.

9 APRIL 1865
Confederate General Lee surrenders to Union General Grant. The Civil War is over.

21 JULY 1861
The Union army is defeated at the first major battle of the war – the First Battle of Bull Run in Virginia. Almost 850 soldiers lose their lives (460 Union soldiers and 387 Confederates).

8–9 MARCH 1862
The Battle of Hampton Roads, off the coast of Virginia, sees the first combat between ironclad warships.

17 SEPTEMBER 1862
The Battle of Antietam takes place in Union territory near Sharpsburg, Maryland. With a total of 22,717 dead, wounded, or missing, it is the bloodiest single-day battle in US military history.

1–3 JULY 1863
The Union side halts the Confederates' advance at the Battle of Gettysburg, Pennsylvania.

8 NOVEMBER 1864
Lincoln is re-elected US president for a second term of office.

Lincoln Memorial

14 APRIL 1865
Lincoln is shot while at the theatre by John Wilkes Booth. He dies a day later.

AFRICAN AMERICAN SOLDIERS

Roughly a tenth of the Union army was made up of African American soldiers (179,000). There are no records of how many slaves were forced to fight for the South.

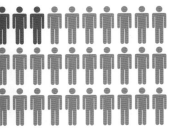
SOLDIERS IN THE UNION ARMY

KEY

African American soldiers   White soldiers

UNION FIGURES
The people on this side were loyal to the United States of America. They were nicknamed "Yanks" or "Yankees".

○ **ABRAHAM LINCOLN (1809–65)**
As US president, Lincoln led his country through the war, abolished slavery, and saved the Union.

○ **ULYSSES S GRANT (1822–85)**
General Grant led the Union army from 1862 onwards. After the war, he served two terms as president.

○ **JOSHUA CHAMBERLAIN (1828–1914)**
Chamberlain heroically led a crucial bayonet charge at Gettysburg.

○ **ROBERT SMALLS (1839–1915)**
A southern slave, Smalls freed himself, took over a Confederate ship, then fought on the side of the Union.

UNION GENERAL

CONFEDERATE FIGURES
People from the rebel states in the South broke away from the Union and formed a new country, the Confederacy.

○ **JEFFERSON DAVIS (1808–89)**
A soldier and senator, Davis was the president of the Confederate States of America.

○ **ROBERT E LEE (1807–70)**
Virginia-born Lee became the supreme commander of all the Confederate forces.

○ **JOHN BROWN GORDON (1832–1904)**
This fearless Confederate general was wounded so often that people said he must be invincible.

○ **BELLE BOYD (1844–1900)**
A notorious spy, Maria "Belle" Boyd gathered information from Union soldiers.

CONFEDERATE GENERAL

LIVES LOST
In total, an estimated 620,000 men lost their lives in the Civil War. Where possible, Union soldiers received a proper military funeral, but the military cemetery in Washington DC soon filled. Arlington, Virginia, the family estate of Confederate General Robert E Lee's wife, Mary, was taken over for the new state cemetery.

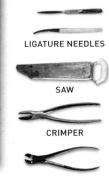
ARLINGTON CEMETERY

COMMUNICATION
Both Union and Confederate leaders made use of the newly invented electric telegraph. They could send messages to generals on the battlefield and receive updates on the fighting.

TIN OF COFFEE ESSENCE

BLOCK OF TEA

ROPE

SLEEPING CAP

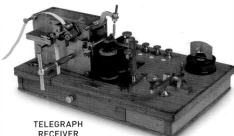
TELEGRAPH RECEIVER

MEDICAL ADVANCES
Although basic hygiene was still poor, great strides were made in treating the wounded. Horse-drawn ambulances transported casualties between field hospitals. Women worked as nurses on the battlefield for the first time.

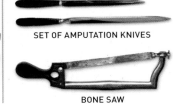
SET OF AMPUTATION KNIVES

BONE SAW

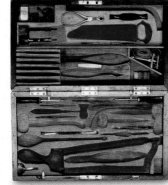
BOX OF INSTRUMENTS

LIGATURE NEEDLES

SAW

CRIMPER

FORCEPS

SPRINGFIELD 1861 RIFLE

CONFEDERATE COPY OF THE SPRINGFIELD 1861 RIFLE

SPENCER CARBINE (REPEATING RIFLE)

THE SPENCER CARBINE COULD FIRE SEVEN SHOTS IN 30 SECONDS

CONFEDERATE DRUM
Those too young to carry a rifle enlisted as drummer boys. During battle, their drum calls communicated commands to the men.

AGE OF IMPERIALISM

The growth of European empires spanned several hundred years, and led to wars, revolutions, and rebellions by those who were unwilling to be controlled by foreign nations.

1500s
The Portuguese and Spanish start to explore widely, especially around South America.

Model of a Portuguese caravel

1565
The Spanish establish the first European colony in what is now the USA. The first English colony is founded 20 years later in Roanoke.

1756–63
The Seven Years War sees Britain become the world's largest colonial empire, gaining America and India in the global conflict.

1775–81
The American states win independence from the British after the American War of Independence.

The American constitution

1810–26
Revolution in South America leads to most colonies freeing themselves from European rule.

1858–1947
British rule is imposed on India after the Indian rebellion of 1857 against the British East India Company.

1880–1914
European powers seek territory in Africa, invading and colonizing the continent in a "scramble for Africa".

1945
By the end of the World War II, the empires of Italy, Germany, and Japan collapse.

1947
The British make the first move to end colonialism by granting India independence after pressure from Mahatma Gandhi.

Statue of Mahatma Gandhi

1956
Disagreement over ownership of the Suez Canal in Egypt leads to the Suez Crisis. Britain and France lose their influence around the world.

1963
Independent African countries set up the Organization of African Unity to promote their economic, political, and cultural interests.

Flag of the Organization of African Unity

European empires

As European explorers sailed around the world in the 16th century, they claimed "new" colonies for their home countries. Nations built empires overseas and many became rich. However, the native people in these new empires were often treated very poorly.

WHY BUILD AN EMPIRE?

Many European powers considered themselves to be superior to the rest of the world and thought they were the best people to govern, develop, and civilize other nations.

EXPLORATION
People wanted to find new territories and trade routes.

NATIONALISM
Nations wanted to demonstrate their power and compete with others.

ECONOMY
There was a demand for new materials and new markets around the world.

RELIGION AND IDEOLOGY
Religious groups wanted to convert more people to Christianity.

BIGGEST EMPIRES

At their peak, some empires covered millions of square kilometres of land across the globe.

1 BRITISH EMPIRE
33.7 million sq km (13 million sq miles) in 1922.

2 SPANISH EMPIRE
19.4 million sq km (7.5 million sq miles) in 1740.

3 FRENCH EMPIRE
12.9 million sq km (5 million sq miles) in 1938.

4 PORTUGUESE EMPIRE
10.4 million sq km (4 million sq miles) in 1821.

5 ITALIAN EMPIRE
3.6 million sq km (1.4 million sq miles) in 1942.

THE IMPERIAL WORLD

During the Age of Imperialism, the world was constantly changing as countries struggled for land and power. Many nations had European rule imposed on them, while others rebelled and achieved independence. It was a turbulent time as global powers fought for territory and control.

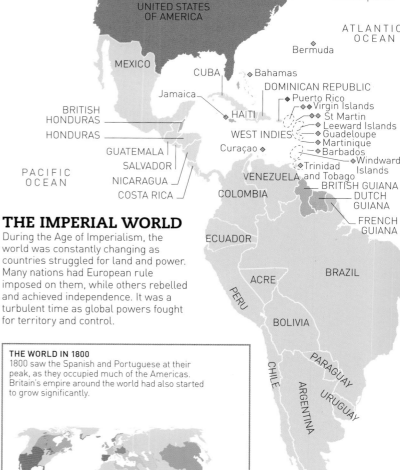

THE WORLD IN 1800
1800 saw the Spanish and Portuguese at their peak, as they occupied much of the Americas. Britain's empire around the world had also started to grow significantly.

TRADE

As Europeans claimed territories, they took advantage of the local resources, such as gold and spices, and traded them in markets around the world for profit.

IVORY
Africa and Asia

COFFEE
The Americas

GOLD
The Americas

COCOA
Central and
South America

**SPICES – PEPPER,
CLOVES, AND CINNAMON**
Asia

TEA
China and
India

COTTON
Asia and
the Americas

**SUGAR CANE
(SUGAR)**
The Americas

SLAVERY

Between 1500 and 1880, up to 12 million Africans were kidnapped from their homes and sold in the Americas as slaves. They were transported in slave ships and many died of disease and lack of food or water.

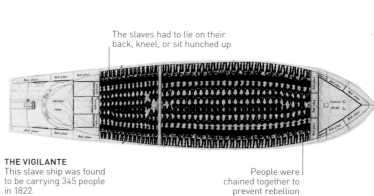

The slaves had to lie on their back, kneel, or sit hunched up

THE VIGILANTE
This slave ship was found to be carrying 345 people in 1822.

People were chained together to prevent rebellion

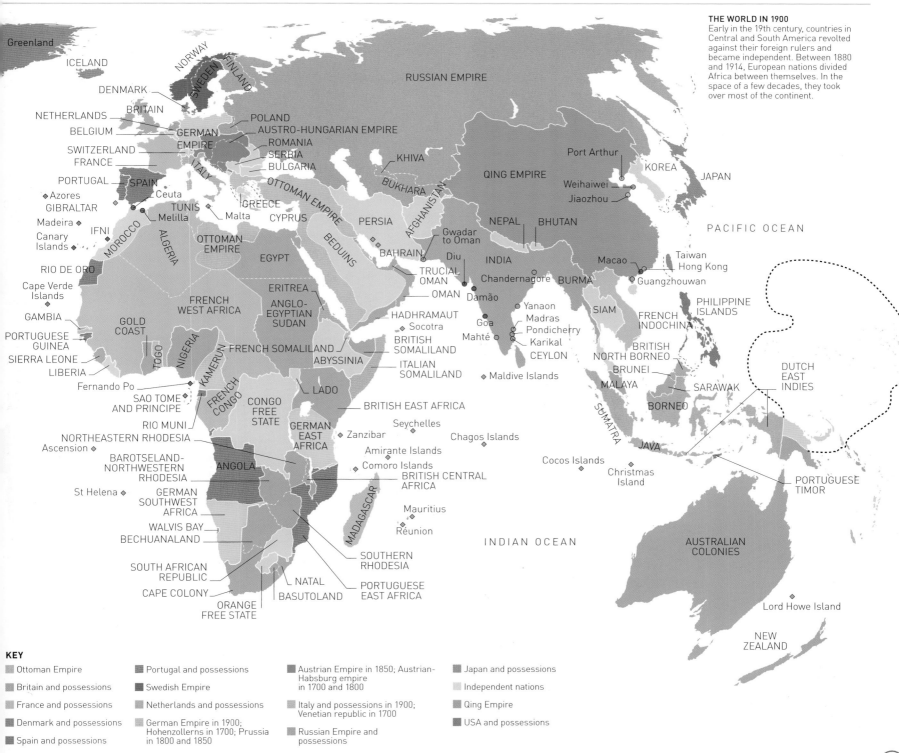

THE WORLD IN 1900
Early in the 19th century, countries in Central and South America revolted against their foreign rulers and became independent. Between 1880 and 1914, European nations divided Africa between themselves. In the space of a few decades, they took over most of the continent.

Greenland
ICELAND
NORWAY
SWEDEN
FINLAND
DENMARK
BRITAIN
NETHERLANDS
BELGIUM
GERMAN EMPIRE
POLAND
AUSTRO-HUNGARIAN EMPIRE
ROMANIA
SERBIA
BULGARIA
SWITZERLAND
FRANCE
ITALY
PORTUGAL
SPAIN
Ceuta
Azores
GIBRALTAR
TUNIS
Melilla
Malta
GREECE
CYPRUS
Madeira
IFNI
Canary Islands
MOROCCO
ALGERIA
OTTOMAN EMPIRE
EGYPT
BEDUINS
RIO DE ORO
Cape Verde Islands
GAMBIA
FRENCH WEST AFRICA
GOLD COAST
PORTUGUESE GUINEA
SIERRA LEONE
LIBERIA
TOGO
NIGERIA
Fernando Po
SAO TOME AND PRINCIPE
KAMERUN
RIO MUNI
FRENCH CONGO
CONGO FREE STATE
ERITREA
ANGLO-EGYPTIAN SUDAN
FRENCH SOMALILAND
ABYSSINIA
Socotra
BRITISH SOMALILAND
ITALIAN SOMALILAND
LADO
BRITISH EAST AFRICA
GERMAN EAST AFRICA
Seychelles
Zanzibar
Amirante Islands
Comoro Islands
BRITISH CENTRAL AFRICA
NORTHEASTERN RHODESIA
Ascension
BAROTSELAND-NORTHWESTERN RHODESIA
ANGOLA
St Helena
GERMAN SOUTHWEST AFRICA
WALVIS BAY
BECHUANALAND
MADAGASCAR
Mauritius
Réunion
SOUTHERN RHODESIA
PORTUGUESE EAST AFRICA
SOUTH AFRICAN REPUBLIC
CAPE COLONY
NATAL
BASUTOLAND
ORANGE FREE STATE
RUSSIAN EMPIRE
KHIVA
BUKHARA
QING EMPIRE
Port Arthur
Weihaiwei
Jiaozhou
KOREA
JAPAN
PERSIA
AFGHANISTAN
Gwadar to Oman
NEPAL
BHUTAN
BAHRAIN
Diu
INDIA
Macao
Taiwan
Hong Kong
TRUCIAL OMAN
Chandernagore
BURMA
Guangzhouwan
OMAN
Damão
HADHRAMAUT
Yanaon
Madras
Pondicherry
Karikal
SIAM
FRENCH INDOCHINA
PHILIPPINE ISLANDS
Goa
Mahté
CEYLON
BRITISH NORTH BORNEO
Maldive Islands
BRUNEI
MALAYA
SARAWAK
DUTCH EAST INDIES
SUMATRA
BORNEO
JAVA
Cocos Islands
Christmas Island
PORTUGUESE TIMOR
PACIFIC OCEAN
Chagos Islands
INDIAN OCEAN
AUSTRALIAN COLONIES
Lord Howe Island
NEW ZEALAND

KEY

Ottoman Empire	
Britain and possessions	
France and possessions	
Denmark and possessions	
Spain and possessions	
Portugal and possessions	
Swedish Empire	
Netherlands and possessions	
German Empire in 1900; Hohenzollerns in 1700; Prussia in 1800 and 1850	
Austrian Empire in 1850; Austrian-Habsburg empire in 1700 and 1800	
Italy and possessions in 1900; Venetian republic in 1700	
Russian Empire and possessions	
Japan and possessions	
Independent nations	
Qing Empire	
USA and possessions	

British monarchs

The history of England, and later Britain, is tied together by a string of kings and queens. Early on, royals could start wars, break from the Church, and punish the country's leaders. Today, the Queen has little power but upholds long and popular traditions.

▶ 757–1066
ANGLO-SAXONS

After the Romans left Britain in the 5th century CE, the land was attacked by invaders and split into warring kingdoms. The leader of one, Egbert, became the first king of England. Throughout the Saxon period, powerful kings fended off Viking raids, but England was ruled by Viking monarchs for over 25 years.

OFFA
757–96
The king of Mercia (central England) expanded his kingdom north and south and protected it by building a huge dyke along the Welsh border.

EGBERT
802–39
Originally King of Wesse[x], Egbert gradually increase[d] the power and influence [of] his kingdom. His authori[ty] was recognized througho[ut] most of England after he defeated Mercia and Northumbria.

757–96	OFFA	955–59	EADWIG
802–39	EGBERT	959–75	EDGAR
839–56	AETHELWULF	975–78	EDWARD II "THE MARTYR"
856–60	AETHELBALD	979–1013 AND 1014–16	AETHELRED II "THE UNREADY"
860–66	AETHELBERT	1013–14	SVEIN
866–71	AETHELRED I	1016	EDMUND II "IRONSIDE"
871–99	ALFRED "THE GREAT"	1016–35	CANUTE
899–924	EDWARD "THE ELDER"	1035–40	HAROLD I "HAREFOOT"
925–40	ATHELSTAN	1040–42	HARDICANUTE
940–46	EDMUND I	1042–66	EDWARD III "THE CONFESSOR"
946–55	EADRED	1066	HAROLD II

1485–1603 ◀
TUDORS

The Tudors ruled with an iron fist and were not always popular, but they fostered national pride and parliament grew in strength under them. The manufacturing and merchant classes rose in status, and architecture, literature, and theatre blossomed. Playwright William Shakespeare was a leading light.

ELIZABETH I
1558–1603
Strong-willed Elizabeth was a clever politician with loyal followers. Under her reign trade, exploration, and prosperity increased.

MARY I
1553–58
Nicknamed Bloody Mary, Henry VIII's eldest daughter burned protestants after she seized the throne, and restored the Roman Catholic Church.

HENRY VIII
1509–47
Famous for his six wives (he divorced two and beheaded two), Henry VIII made himself head of the Church of England and bankrupted his country.

1485–1509	HENRY VII TUDOR
1509–47	HENRY VIII
1547–53	EDWARD VI
1553	LADY JANE GREY
1553–58	MARY I
1558–1603	ELIZABETH I

1461–85 ◀
YORKISTS

This branch of the House of Plantagenets had a strong claim to the throne. After Richard of York was killed in the Battle of Wakefield (1460), his son Edward became the first Yorkist king. William Caxton invented the first printing press in this period.

1461–70	EDWARD IV
1471–83	EDWARD IV
1483	EDWARD V
1483–85	RICHARD III

RICHARD III
1483–85
The last English king to die on a battlefield, Richard III may have had a role in the death of his two nephews, the princes, in the Tower of London.

1399–1413	HENRY IV
1413–22	HENRY V
1422–61	HENRY VI
1470–71	HENRY VI

HENRY VI
1422–61 AND 1470–71
After losing his father's gains in France, a failing mind cost Henry VI the throne for a time.

▶ 1603–1749
STUARTS

This dynasty was dominated by political battles between King and Parliament, which ended with a civil war and a beheading. Although the Stuarts believed they had a god-given right to rule, they were tolerant of Catholics, and made peace with Spain. They were patrons of the arts and left a legacy of beautiful art and architecture.

JAMES I
1603–25
Scotland and England were united when this Scottish king took the throne. He ruled for long periods without Parliament, and was the target of Guy Fawkes's failed Gunpowder Plot.

CHARLES I
1625–49
This stubborn king believed in his divine right to rule and stamped on any opposition. Defeated by Oliver Cromwell in the Civil War, he was tried and executed by his parliament.

▶ 1649–59
COMMONWEALTH

For the first and only time in its history, England was a Commonwealth (or republic) without a king or queen. Ruled by puritan Oliver Cromwell and his Parliament, the country took Jamaica from the Spanish and defeated the Dutch at sea.

1649–53	REPUBLIC
1653–58	OLIVER CROMWELL (LORD PROTECTOR)
1658–59	RICHARD CROMWELL (LORD PROTECTOR)

OLIVER CROMWELL (LORD PROTECTOR)
1653–58
After Charles I was executed, this leading general established his own council of 15 and a parliament of 400. He was followed by his son Richard.

▶ 1660–1714
STUARTS

After Charles II was restored to the throne London suffered two disasters – a plague killed more than 100,000 people and a great fire destroyed most of the city. James II tried to restore the Catholic faith but fled when William of Orange was invited to restore rights in the Glorious Revolution.

1660–85	CHARLES II
1685–88	JAMES II
1689–94	WILLIAM III OF ORANGE AND MARY II (JOINTLY)
1694–1702	WILLIAM III
1702–14	ANNE

CHARLES II
1660–85
This "merry monarch" had many interests and many mistresses. He took a keen interest in architecture and science, and introduced the new sport of yachting to England.

▶ 1714–1901
HANOVERIANS

The Hanoverian dynasty saw many changes. Robert Walpole became the first Prime Minister to German-speaking George I, and Britain developed into an industrial society. By the end of Queen Victoria's reign, Britain's economic power was being challenged by other nations such as Germany and the United States.

1714–27	GEORGE I
1727–60	GEORGE II
1760–1820	GEORGE III
1820–30	GEORGE IV
1830–37	WILLIAM IV
1837–1901	VICTORIA

GEORGE I
1714–27
This German-born king faced rebellion in Scotland then scandal when a South Sea trading company went bust and ruined thousands of investors.

1066–1154

NORMANS

Originally Vikings who had settled in northwest France, the Normans were hungry for new land. William the Conqueror claimed the throne after he defeated Harold II at the Battle of Hastings. The Normans built castles and brought with them a feudal system of lords, who held land, and peasants, who worked it.

1066–87	WILLIAM "THE CONQUEROR"
1087–1100	WILLIAM II
1100–35	HENRY I
1135–54	STEPHEN

ALFRED "THE GREAT"
871–99
The only English king to be known as "The Great", Alfred was almost overthrown by Viking raiders but fought back, captured London, and expanded his original Wessex kingdom.

CANUTE
1016–35
This Viking king treated Danes and Saxons fairly and the country prospered. There is an old story that he proved he was an ordinary man by trying and failing to make the tide go back.

HAROLD II
1066
Harold II was appointed by his brother-in-law Edward the Confessor but his reign was short-lived. He died after being shot in the eye in the Battle of Hastings, and William I took the throne.

WILLIAM "THE CONQUEROR" 1066–87
Called "The Conqueror" because he conquered England, William was crowned king on Christmas Day 1066. He built the Tower of London and ordered a survey of land and people called the Domesday Book.

1399–1461

LANCASTRIANS

These three kings reigned through almost continual warfare. French territory was recaptured and then lost, and in the War of the Roses, the royal houses of Lancaster and York fought over the throne for 30 years.

HENRY V
1413–22
Henry V reclaimed lost territories in France when he defeated the French at the Battle of Agincourt, losing only 400 English lives.

HENRY IV
1399–1413
Returning from exile in France, Henry IV reclaimed the throne from Richard II. His reign was marked by many rebellions and revolts.

EDWARD I "LONGSHANKS"
1272–1307
This warrior king fought many battles to unite England and Scotland. A model parliament was formed during his reign.

HENRY III
1216–72
After provoking civil wars with his barons, Henry III was defeated by their leader de Montfort, who formed a parliament of lords, bishops, knights, and freemen.

1154–1399

PLANTAGENETS

Originating in Anjou, France, this dynasty took its name from a yellow flower (*Planta genista*) an ancestor wore in his hat. During much of their rule, England was at war with France and Scotland, and Wales and Ireland came under English rule. The Plantagenets laid the foundation for law and government by creating justices of the peace and the first parliament. They put the royal seal on a charter of rights called the Magna Carta.

JOHN I
1199–1216
John lost most of the territories in France and taxed his country heavily. The Magna Carta (great charter) was drawn up to settle the rights of people, Church, and monarchy.

1154–89	HENRY II
1189–99	RICHARD I "THE LIONHEART"
1199–1216	JOHN I
1216–72	HENRY III
1272–1307	EDWARD I "LONGSHANKS"
1307–27	EDWARD II
1327–77	EDWARD III
1377–99	RICHARD II

RICHARD I "THE LIONHEART"
1189–99
This crusading king spent most of his reign fighting for Christianity in the Holy Lands. Imprisoned by the Emperor of Germany, he was returned for a huge ransom and was eventually killed in France.

GEORGE III
1760–1820
The Americans won independence and England fought France in the Napoleonic Wars during George's reign.

WILLIAM IV
1830–37
Many more people got the vote under William IV, and slavery was abolished throughout the British Empire.

VICTORIA
1837–1901
This much-loved queen ruled for 64 years. After her husband Prince Albert died, she went into mourning but was coaxed back to public life.

1901–10

SAXE-COBURG-GOTHA

This dynasty of just one king is named after Queen Victoria's husband Prince Albert, who was the son of the Duke of Saxe-Coburg and Gotha. Edward became king at the age of 59 and reigned during the first years of the 20th century, when new inventions like the first automobile were taking Britain into the modern age.

EDWARD VII
1901–10
Edward was a social king who enjoyed sports, parties, and travel. He helped restore relations between France and England and built a new royal estate in Sandringham, Norfolk.

1910–

WINDSORS

George V changed his surname to Windsor during the World War I because of the strong anti-German feelings of his people. After Edward VIII gave up the throne to marry a divorced woman in 1936, his younger brother George VI was King through World War II. Queen Elizabeth II has reigned for more than 60 years.

1910–36	GEORGE V
1936	EDWARD VIII
1936–52	GEORGE VI
1952–	ELIZABETH II

GEORGE VI
1936–52
George VI was a good athlete and soldier, but this shy man with a stammer had not expected to be king. He managed to overcome his speech impediment and became popular during and after the war.

ELIZABETH II
1952–
The current queen remains head of the Commonwealth (former colonies) and is popular around the world. Prince William and Catherine, Duchess of Cambridge, and their children lead a new generation of royals.

The Industrial Revolution

In mid-18th-century Britain, a surge in new technology and inventions meant that fewer people were needed to farm the land. People moved from the countryside to towns, to work in the newly built mills and factories. This change in the economy, from farming to manufacturing, is known as the Industrial Revolution.

COAL AND IRON

For thousands of years, iron had been made by using charcoal from timber. But in 1709 Englishman Abraham Darby and his son developed a way of making iron using coal. Coal was easier to obtain than wood, so this discovery led to a huge growth in the production of iron to make tools and machinery, and to the opening of more mines to provide the coal.

IRONBRIDGE, SHROPSHIRE
Site of the world's first iron bridge, built by Darby's grandson in 1781.

STEAM POWER

The first steam engine was invented in 1712, to suck water from mines. Then, 60 years later, James Watt developed a way of using steam to drive factory machines. The age of steam had begun and would transform industry, travel, and home life, first in Britain and then all over the world.

DOUBLE-ACTING ENGINE IN A STEAMSHIP

Open valve — Piston rod pushes crankshaft

Boiling water turns to steam

Coal fire

1 FORWARD STROKE
Steam enters the cylinder through the open valve on the left and pushes the piston forwards.

Closed valve — Open valve

Water condensed from steam returns to boiler

Piston rod pulls crankshaft

2 BACKWARD STROKE
The steam now enters the cylinder through the valve on the right and pushes the piston back.

CANALS

The growth in manufacturing meant there were more goods to be transported around the country, and canals were the answer – man-made rivers, deep enough to cope with large, heavy barges. In 1761 an engineer called James Brindley built a 16 km (10 mile) long canal to carry coal direct from a mine in Lancashire to sell in Manchester in the UK. The venture made a fortune for the mine owner and sparked a boom in canal-building.

TRENT AND MERSEY CANAL
Originally called the Grand Trunk Canal, it cost £296,600 to build and opened in 1777.

CAEN HILL LOCKS
A series of 29 locks on the Kennet and Avon Canal in England were built in 1810 by John Rennie.

BIRTH OF THE RAILWAYS

Factories needed a constant supply of raw materials coming in and finished goods going out, and the railway was the perfect solution. Trains were much quicker than canal barges, and could carry much larger quantities of goods than road wagons. By the 1840s, fast and reliable steam engines were produced and became a symbol of the Industrial Revolution across Europe and America.

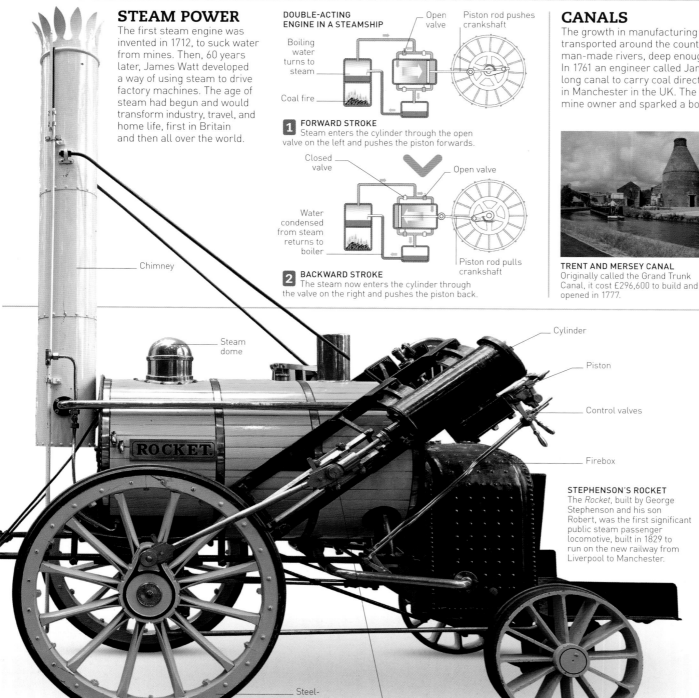

Chimney

Steam dome

Cylinder

Piston

Control valves

Firebox

Steel-rimmed wheels

Control rod

STEPHENSON'S ROCKET
The *Rocket*, built by George Stephenson and his son Robert, was the first significant public steam passenger locomotive, built in 1829 to run on the new railway from Liverpool to Manchester.

TREVITHICK'S LOCOMOTIVE
In 1808 Richard Trevithick built a "rail circus" in London and charged a shilling for a ride on *Catch Me Who Can*.

THE FACTORY AGE

Traditional industries such as cotton and textiles were transformed by the Industrial Revolution. Machines were developed that could make raw cotton into thread in a fraction of the time it had taken craft workers in the past. At first, the machines were powered by water, so mills and factories were built next to rivers. When steam replaced water power, the factories moved into towns.

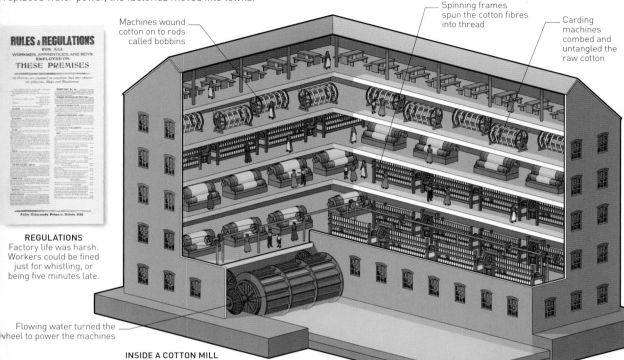

Machines wound cotton on to rods called bobbins

Spinning frames spun the cotton fibres into thread

Carding machines combed and untangled the raw cotton

REGULATIONS
Factory life was harsh. Workers could be fined just for whistling, or being five minutes late.

Flowing water turned the wheel to power the machines

INSIDE A COTTON MILL

THE NEW SPINNING MACHINES PRODUCED COTTON 1,000 TIMES FASTER THAN A HUMAN WORKER COULD

WORK CONDITIONS

Factory workers worked more than 12 hours a day, six days a week. At the start of the Industrial Revolution there were no laws to protect the health or safety of workers. Factories were hot and deafeningly noisy, and accidents and injuries were very common.

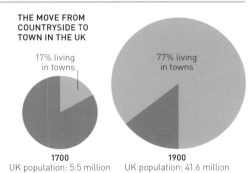

PIT CHILDREN
Children worked deep underground in coal mines, pulling heavy wagons along tracks.

WORKERS IN A COTTON MILL, 1859
A third of mill workers were children, aged as young as five. They wriggled between machines to clear blockages, which was strenuous and dangerous work.

- 50% women
- 24% girls
- 7% boys
- 19% men

RISE OF THE NEW TOWNS

As more and more factories were built, towns grew and housing, schools, and shops were built near to where people worked. Small towns quickly became large, factory-dominated cities, which attracted even more people in search of work.

THE MOVE FROM COUNTRYSIDE TO TOWN IN THE UK

- 17% living in towns
- 77% living in towns

1700
UK population: 5.5 million

1900
UK population: 41.6 million

FARM TECHNOLOGY

As the population grew, there was an increased demand for more food and more efficient, cheaper ways of growing it. Steam-powered ploughs and threshing machines appeared in the 1820s, then in 1831, American Cyrus McCormick invented a mechanical grain harvester.

SEED DRILL

STEAM THRESHING MACHINE

INDUSTRIAL PIONEERS

The Industrial Revolution was driven by engineers and inventors, many of whose ideas paved the way for the age of high technology in the 20th century.

- **RICHARD ARKWRIGHT (1732–92)**
  Invented the water frame for spinning thread or yarn, then set up the first water-powered cotton mill in England.

- **RICHARD TREVITHICK (1771–1833)**
  In 1804 Trevithick designed and built the world's first steam railway locomotive.

  RICHARD TREVITHICK

- **ELI WHITNEY (1765–1825)**
  American who invented a machine called the cotton gin, which revolutionized the cotton industry in America.

- **SIR HUMPHREY DAVY (1778–1829)**
  English chemist and inventor. He developed the Davy lamp, a light to help miners detect dangerous gases underground.

- **ISAMBARD KINGDOM BRUNEL (1806–59)**
  An engineer who built bridges, tunnels, railways, and the world's biggest ship at the time, the *Great Eastern*.

TIMELINE OF A REVOLUTION

The invention of steam power was a turning point in history. It also sparked major developments in other areas, including communications, transport, and construction.

1700

1709
Coke, a product of coal, is first used to produce iron.

Arkwright's mill in Derbyshire, UK

1712
Thomas Newcomen builds the first steam-powered engine.

1764
James Hargreaves invents the spinning jenny, a machine for spinning yarn.

1771
Richard Arkwright builds the first water-powered cotton mill.

Replica of Richard Arkwright's water frame

1774
James Watt develops the steam engine.

Replica of the Watt steam engine

1798
Gas lighting is introduced in factories, so they can operate throughout the night.

1800
Italian Alessandro Volta invents the first electric battery.

Volta's battery, called the "Voltaic Pile"

1805
Engineer Thomas Telford completes the Pontcysyllte Aqueduct, the longest and highest in Britain.

1807
The first commercial steamboat, *Savannah*, launches in America.

1815
Sir Humphry Davy invents a lamp that is safe to use in gas-filled mines.

Davy lamp

1825
The Stockton and Darlington Railway opens, the world's first public steam railway.

George Stephenson, engineer of the Stockton and Darlington railway

1837
The first electric communication device, the five-needle telegraph, is invented.

The electric telegraph, invented by William Cooke and Charles Wheatstone

1841
William Fox Talbot patents his invention of the "calotype" (photographic negative).

Fox Talbot's experimental camera

Early telephone by Alexander Graham Bell

1855
Englishman Henry Bessemer invents a machine to make steel cheaply.

1900

1876
Alexander Graham Bell invents the telephone.

RULES & REGULATIONS
FOR ALL
WORKMEN, APPRENTICES, AND BOYS
EMPLOYED ON
THESE PREMISES

World War I

In 1914 tensions that had been simmering in Europe came to a head. War broke out and quickly spread across the world. Fought between two powerful groups of countries (the Allies and the Central Powers), it was the biggest war the world had ever seen.

GERMAN FOKKER
Dr.I TRIPLANE

Timeline

1914

28 JUNE, 1914
Archduke Franz Ferdinand of Austria-Hungary is assassinated, with his wife, Sophie, in Serbia. A month later, Austria-Hungary declares war on Serbia.

12 AUGUST, 1914
One by one, countries take sides until war has broken out over most of Europe.

Lifebelt from the RMS *Lusitania*

7 MAY, 1915
Germany sinks the RMS *Lusitania*, a luxury British passenger ship, killing more than 1,000 passengers.

23 MAY, 1915
Italy enters the war on the side of the Allies and prepares to invade its neighbour, Austria-Hungary.

Italian army ID tag

1 JULY, 1916
The Battle of the Somme begins in France. By the time it ends in November, more than 300,000 men will die.

Battlefield site, Somme, France

17 DECEMBER, 1917
Following a revolution in Russia, the new government makes peace with Germany and leaves the war.

Russian helmet plate

3 NOVEMBER, 1918
German sailors mutiny. Austria-Hungary makes peace with the Allies.

28 JUNE, 1919
The Treaty of Versailles is signed and the war officially ends.

1919

Memorial to the missing (near Thiepval, France), built 1932

THE WAR TO END ALL WARS

When the war began, people believed it would be over quickly. In fact, it lasted for four years and more than 65 million men were called upon to fight.

SEPTEMBER–OCTOBER 1914
First trenches are dug along the Western Front in France and Belgium.

24 DECEMBER, 1914
British and German soldiers call an unofficial truce over Christmas.

APRIL 1915 – JANUARY 1916
The Allies fight Ottoman troops at Gallipoli, suffering disastrous casualties.

Ottoman army medal

12 FEBRUARY, 1916
Battle of Verdun begins.

Fortified turret, Verdun, France

31 MAY, 1916
The Battle of Jutland starts – the only major sea battle of the war. Britain claims victory, despite suffering heavy losses.

JANUARY 1917
Britain attacks the Ottoman Empire again, this time by landing in Palestine and pushing north through the desert to the city of Damascus.

6 APRIL, 1917
President Woodrow Wilson leads the USA into the war on the side of the Allies.

15 JULY, 1918
Second Battle of the Marne begins, near Paris.

3 AUGUST, 1918
The Allies win the Battle of the Marne. The German army collapses.

11 NOVEMBER, 1918
Germany agrees to an armistice and all fighting stops.

A CONTINENT AT WAR

The two main European arenas of the war were the Western Front, between Belgium and France, and the Eastern Front, which was mainly in Russia.

Atlantic Ocean

DENMARK
NETHERLANDS
NORWAY
SWEDEN
IRELAND
BRITAIN
BELGIUM
GERMANY
RUSSIA
SWITZERLAND
FRANCE
AUSTRIA-HUNGARY
PORTUGAL
SPAIN
ITALY
ROMANIA
SERBIA
BULGARIA
Black Sea
ALBANIA
GREECE
OTTOMAN EMPIRE
Mediterranean Sea
MOROCCO
ALGERIA

KEY
- Neutral
- Allied Nations
- Central Powers
- -- Western Front
- -- Eastern Front

EUROPE IN 1916

TAKING SIDES

By the end of 1914, almost all of Europe had taken sides in the war. Only a few countries remained neutral.

▪ ALLIED NATIONS   ▪ CENTRAL POWERS

	1914	1915	1916	1917	1918	1919
BRITAIN	▪	▪	▪	▪	▪	▪
FRANCE	▪	▪	▪	▪	▪	▪
ITALY		▪	▪	▪	▪	▪
RUSSIA	▪	▪	▪	▪		
UNITED STATES				▪	▪	▪
GERMANY	▪	▪	▪	▪	▪	▪
AUSTRIA-HUNGARY	▪	▪	▪	▪	▪	▪
OTTOMAN EMPIRE	▪	▪	▪	▪	▪	▪

CASUALTIES OF WAR

The cost of the war in human lives was enormous. More than 30 million men were killed or injured, and some battles were so devastating that thousands died in a single day.

AMBULANCE CART

1 JULY – 18 NOVEMBER 1916	21 FEBRUARY – 18 DECEMBER 1916	11 JULY – 10 NOVEMBER 1917
Battle of the Somme	Battle of Verdun	Third Battle of Ypres (Passchendaele)
1,219,201	976,000	848,614

TOTAL CASUALTIES FROM THE BLOODIEST BATTLES OF WWI

TRENCHES

Both sides built long trenches as a defence against long-range weapons. Soon, there was stalemate, with neither side able to advance into the other's territory. Life in the trenches was hard. Soldiers fought, ate, and slept there, sometimes for weeks on end.

MESS TIN

TRENCH AXE

SEWING KIT

GAS MASK

FOLDING SHOVEL

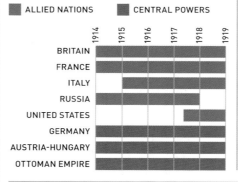

Artillery
Sandbags
BRITISH FRONT LINE
NO MAN'S LAND
23 m (25 yd) to 1.6 km (1 mile)
GERMAN FRONT LINE
Barbed wire
Officers' dugout
Bomb crater
Support trench
Communication trench

CROSS-SECTION OF A TYPICAL WORLD WAR I BATTLEFIELD

BRITISH SOPWITH PUP

GERMAN ALBATROSS D.Va

WAR IN THE AIR

Powered flight was barely ten years old when war broke out but the technology developed quickly. Soon, both sides were building fast fighter planes and giant bombers capable of carrying huge bombs.

ALTIMETER

FRENCH PILOT'S GOGGLES AND HELMET

WAR AT SEA

World War I was fought mainly on land, with very few major naval battles. The main role of the navies on each side was to protect merchant ships bringing in essential goods, as well as trying to stop the enemy from receiving supplies by sea.

HMS DREADNOUGHT

HMS SCOUT

GERMAN BATTLESHIP

> GERMANY'S GREATEST NAVAL WEAPONS WERE ITS SUBMARINES, KNOWN AS U-BOATS

TANK WARFARE

The tank was one of the most important inventions of the war. Although early tanks were unreliable and dangerous for crews working in them, their ability to power through enemy lines meant an end to the stalemate of trench warfare.

BRITISH MARK V TANK

ARMY RECRUITS

Millions of young men were either called up or volunteered to fight in the war. Countries such as Britain also relied heavily on recruits from their overseas colonies and dominions.

FRANCE

GERMANY

OTTOMAN EMPIRE

USA

ITALY

RUSSIA

TRENCH WEAPONS

Trench warfare called for weapons that could be used at very close quarters. Soldiers on raiding missions behind enemy lines carried daggers and knives so they could attack the enemy silently.

AMERICAN BAYONET

AMERICAN KNUCKLEDUSTER KNIFE

GERMAN BAYONET

PERCUSSION AND STICK GRENADES

HAND GRENADES

BRITISH NAIL CLUB

BRITISH SPIKED CLUB

GERMAN ROD

GERMAN CLUB

FIREARMS

The most widely used weapons were rifles and machine-guns. Machine-guns needed only a small crew, were reliable, and had a long range. This made them essential weapons in the trenches.

AUSTRIAN STEYR PISTOL

ITALIAN GLISENTI PISTOL

GERMAN LUGER PISTOL

GERMAN MOUNTED MACHINE-GUN

BRITISH LEE ENFIELD RIFLE

ITALIAN CARCANO CARBINE RIFLE

GERMAN SCHWARZLOSE MACHINE-GUN

BOMBARDMENT

Large field guns fired shells that exploded on impact. They had a long range and could be devastatingly effective but they were not very mobile and needed about ten men to operate them.

GERMAN GAS SHELLS

RUSSIAN MAXIM M1910 HEAVY MACHINE-GUN

BRITISH MORTAR SHELLS

FRENCH 75 MM FIELD GUN

GERMAN 77 MM FIELD GUN

THE COURSE OF THE WAR

At the beginning of the war, the Germans' progress seemed unstoppable, until a harsh winter and fierce resistance halted them in Russia. When the USA joined the war at the end of 1941, the tide turned. The Allies won victories in North Africa and the Pacific, then, in 1944, they landed in France and began to take back Europe.

Nazi flag

1 SEPTEMBER 1939 Germany, led by Nazi leader Adolf Hitler, invades Poland.

3 SEPTEMBER 1939 Britain and France declare war on Germany.

APRIL–JUNE 1940 Germany uses Blitzkrieg "Lightning War" tactics to take over France and most of Western Europe.

Statue of Winston Churchill

10 MAY 1940 Winston Churchill becomes Prime Minister of Great Britain.

JULY–OCTOBER 1940 Battle of Britain: German and British aircraft fight for control of the skies; Britain is the winner.

27 SEPTEMBER 1940 Germany, Italy, and Japan join forces as the Axis Alliance.

SEPTEMBER 1940–MAY 1941 The Blitz (German bombing raids on British cities) kills more than 60,000 civilians.

Statue of Theodore Roosevelt

8 DECEMBER 1941 President Roosevelt takes the USA into the war against the Axis Alliance.

7 DECEMBER 1941 Japan mounts a surprise attack on the US Navy at Pearl Harbor, Hawaii.

British child's gas mask

1939

World War II

In September 1939 Germany, led by dictator Adolf Hitler, invaded Poland and triggered World War II, the deadliest conflict in history. By the end of the war six years later, around 60 million people had been killed, more than half of them civilians. A large part of Europe was in ruins, and two Japanese cities had been obliterated by nuclear bombs.

AXIS vs ALLIES

The Axis alliance was formed in 1939 by Germany and Italy. In 1940 Japan joined and the countries formed the Tripartite Pact. The original members of the Allies were Britain and France, until 1940 when Germany invaded France and the French government was exiled to London. In 1941 the Soviet Union and the USA joined the Allies. In 1943 Italy surrendered, then changed sides to fight on the side of the Allies.

PRIMARY ALLIED FORCES
- GREAT BRITAIN
- FRANCE
- USA
- SOVIET UNION

PRIMARY AXIS FORCES
- GERMANY
- ITALY
- JAPAN

THEATRES OF WAR

For the first two years of the war, fighting raged across Western Europe, on the Eastern Front in Russia, and in North Africa. By the end of 1941, when the USA and Japan joined in, the conflict had spread to the Pacific and Southeast Asia. Few nations were able to stay neutral as war engulfed the whole world.

NOVEMBER 1942

ICELAND — North Atlantic Ocean — NORWAY — SWEDEN — FINLAND — USSR — North Sea — ESTONIA — LATVIA — LITHUANIA — EAST PRUSSIA — IRELAND — GREAT BRITAIN — GERMANY — POLAND — CZECHOSLOVAKIA — FRANCE — SWITZERLAND — AUSTRIA — HUNGARY — VICHY FRANCE — ITALY — YUGOSLAVIA — ROMANIA — BULGARIA — Black Sea — PORTUGAL — SPAIN — ALBANIA — GREECE — TURKEY — SICILY — Crete — CYPRUS — SYRIA — MOROCCO — ALGERIA — TUNISIA — Mediterranean Sea — PALESTINE — TRANSJORDAN — LIBYA

THE WAR IN EUROPE, NORTH AFRICA, AND THE MEDITERRANEAN

Germany began the war with the upper hand, rampaging through Europe and taking over a series of countries. Gradually, the Allies pushed back, and by 1943 Germany was in retreat.

KEY
- Allied areas
- Allied-occupied areas
- Axis countries
- Axis-occupied areas
- Axis allies
- Neutral countries

1941–45

USSR — MONGOLIA — MANCHURIA — KOREA — CHINA — JAPAN — ALASKA (US) — Bering Sea — Pacific Ocean — BURMA — THAILAND — INDOCHINA — PHILIPPINES — MALAYA — BORNEO — EAST INDIES — SUMATRA — JAVA — NEW GUINEA — PAPUA — HAWAII (US) — Indian Ocean — AUSTRALIA — Coral Sea — Southern Ocean

THE WAR IN THE PACIFIC AND ASIA

Japan joined the Axis countries in 1941 and quickly overran much of Southeast Asia, including Malaya and Singapore. The Allies fought back on land and sea, but it was superior airpower – and the dropping of two atomic bombs – that led to the Allies' victory.

KEY
- Allied areas
- Axis countries
- Axis-occupied areas
- Axis allies
- ⋯ Limit of Japanese advance

AIR POWER

World War II was the first war in which fighting took place as much in the air as on land or sea. There were three main types of planes: fighters, bombers, and transport planes.

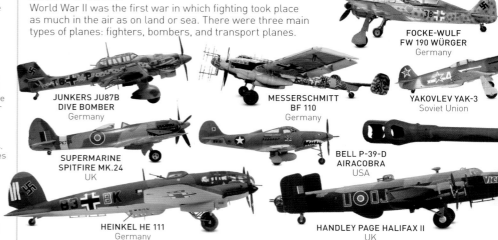

FOCKE-WULF FW 190 WÜRGER Germany

JUNKERS JU87B DIVE BOMBER Germany

MESSERSCHMITT BF 110 Germany

YAKOVLEV YAK-3 Soviet Union

SUPERMARINE SPITFIRE MK.24 UK

BELL P-39-D AIRACOBRA USA

HEINKEL HE 111 Germany

HANDLEY PAGE HALIFAX II UK

SMALL ARMS

Technology played a crucial role in the war, with both sides competing to produce weapons more efficient and deadlier than ever before. Rifles, machine-guns, mortars, and hand grenades were all improved during the course of the war.

LEE ENFIELD N0.5 MK 1 UK

HAND GRENADE USA

WALTHER P38 PISTOL Germany

VICKERS MARK IV MACHINE GUN UK

ORDNANCE QF 25-POUNDER UK

FIGHTING MEN

In most countries men were conscripted during the war, meaning they had to join the armed forces. Only those doing certain jobs, such as miners or farmers, or people in poor health were not required to join up.

BRITISH SOLDIER — **AMERICAN SOLDIER** — **SOVIET SOLDIER** — **GERMAN SOLDIER** — **JAPANESE SOLDIER** — **ITALIAN SOLDIER**

Timeline

4–7 JUNE 1942
The USA defeats Japan's navy at the Battle of Midway in the Pacific Ocean, halting the Japanese advance.

Soviet medal for the Battle of Stalingrad

2 FEBRUARY 1943
Soviet troops are victorious at Stalingrad and begin to march on Germany.

German V1 flying bomb, 1944

25 AUGUST 1944
Paris is liberated by the Allies from German occupation.

7 MARCH 1945
Allied troops cross the river Rhine and enter Germany.

Model of "fat man" atomic bomb, dropped on Nagasaki

6–9 AUGUST 1945
USA drops atomic bombs on the Japanese cities of Hiroshima and Nagasaki.

1945

Japanese Aichi D3A bomber plane

19 AUGUST 1942
Germany launches an attempt to take over the Soviet city of Stalingrad.

13 MAY 1943
The Axis armies in North Africa surrender.

25 JULY 1943
Italian dictator Mussolini is overthrown. A month later, the Allies invade mainland Italy, leading to Italy's surrender.

6 JUNE 1944
D-Day: Allied forces land in Normandy, France, and begin to advance inland.

Badge worn by Jews in Latvia

27 JANUARY 1945
Soviet army liberates the Auschwitz death camp in Poland.

7 MAY 1945
Following Hitler's suicide a week earlier, Germany surrenders.

15 AUGUST 1945
Japan announces its intention to surrender. On 2 September they sign the Instrument of Surrender, and World War II is officially over.

GERMAN ARMY BADGE
The Nazis used the swastika cross as their symbol.

HITLER AND THE NAZIS

Adolf Hitler was the leader of the Nazi (National Socialist) party. Nazis believed that Germans were naturally superior to what they called "inferior races". Hitler especially hated Jewish people, and blamed them for all Germany's economic and political problems.

CASUALTIES OF WAR

Both sides suffered terrible losses during the war. Poland lost 20 per cent of its population, and whole cities across Europe were left in ruins. The Nazis and their sympathizers executed six million Jewish people. This brutal, systematic murder is now known as the Holocaust. In Japan two nuclear bombs, dropped by the USA, caused mass destruction. In the city of Hiroshima, 65,000 people were killed, and in Nagasaki 40,000 lost their lives.

HOLOCAUST MEMORIAL IN BERLIN, GERMANY

PEACE MEMORIAL IN HIROSHIMA, JAPAN

APPROXIMATE TOTAL CASUALTIES PER COUNTRY	
SOVIET UNION	24 MILLION
CHINA	20 MILLION
GERMANY	6.6–8.8 MILLION
POLAND	5.6 MILLION
JAPAN	2.6–3.1 MILLION
YUGOSLAVIA	1 MILLION
ROMANIA	833,000
HUNGARY	580,000
FRANCE	567,600
PHILIPPINES	500,000–1 MILLION
ITALY	457,000
UNITED KINGDOM	450,700
UNITED STATES OF AMERICA	418,500
NETHERLANDS	301,000
GREECE	300,000–800,000
FINLAND	97,000
BELGIUM	86,100
CANADA	45,400
AUSTRALIA	40,500
BULGARIA	25,000
NORWAY	9,500

DURING THE BLITZ OF 1940–41, MORE THAN A MILLION HOMES IN LONDON WERE DESTROYED

LAND POWER

Advances in technology meant that armoured vehicles and tanks played a much bigger part in World War II than in previous conflicts. Panzer tanks, supported by air bombers, were the main power behind the Germans' swift and brutal takeover of most of Western Europe in the first months of the war.

UNIVERSAL CARRIER
UK

SHERMAN FIREFLY
UK/USA

M2 HALF-TRACK CAR
USA

BMW R12 MOTORCYCLE
Germany

WHITE SCOUT CAR
USA

STURMGESCHUTZ III
Germany

CHURCHILL TANK
UK

JAGDPANZER 38(T) HETZER
Germany

PANZERKAMPFWAGEN II
Germany

PANZERKAMPFWAGEN III
Germany

PANZERKAMPFWAGEN "TIGER" II
Germany

SEA POWER

Naval battles took place in both the Atlantic and Pacific oceans. In the North Atlantic, German U-boats (submarines) stalked and attacked the Allies' essential supply ships. In the Pacific, the USA took on the Japanese in a series of massive naval battles.

HMS AVON VALE
Escort destroyer, UK

HMS AGINCOURT
Battle class destroyer, UK

U-BOAT (SUBMARINE)
Germany

USS HORNET
Aircraft carrier, USA

I-400-CLASS SUBMARINE
Japan

HMS HOOD
Battlecruiser, UK

YAHAGI
Cruiser, Japan

PRINZ EUGEN
Heavy cruiser, Germany

The Cold War

After World War II, the USA and the Soviet Union (USSR) emerged as the world's most powerful countries. Although bitter enemies, the threat of nuclear destruction stopped them from declaring war. Instead, they each tried to weaken the other by spying, supporting other countries in conflicts, and developing new technologies.

NUCLEAR ARMS

After World War II, only the United States had nuclear bomb technology, but in 1949 the USSR successfully tested a nuclear device of its own. The nuclear arms race began, with both countries building more and more powerful weapons and stockpiling thousands of warheads.

NUCLEAR WEAPON STOCKPILES, 1950–2010
- ■ USA
- ■ USSR, then Russia after 1991

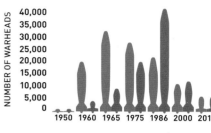

NUMBER OF WARHEADS: 40,000 / 35,000 / 30,000 / 25,000 / 20,000 / 15,000 / 10,000 / 5,000 / 0
1950 1960 1965 1975 1986 2000 2010

USS VIRGINIA (SSN-74) NUCLEAR SUBMARINE (USA)

AKULA-CLASS NUCLEAR SUBMARINE (USSR)

THE WORLD DIVIDED

As tensions grew between the two superpowers, they each tried to form alliances with other countries. By the mid-1950s, all of Europe and most of the world had chosen sides in the Cold War.

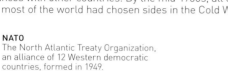

WARSAW PACT
Formed by the USSR in 1955, in opposition to NATO.

NATO
The North Atlantic Treaty Organization, an alliance of 12 Western democratic countries, formed in 1949.

USA | LUXEMBOURG | GREECE Joined 1952

BELGIUM | NETHERLANDS | TURKEY Joined 1952

CANADA | NORWAY | WEST GERMANY Joined 1955

DENMARK | PORTUGAL

FRANCE | UNITED KINGDOM

ICELAND | ITALY

EUROPE 1955
- ■ Warsaw Pact countries
- ■ NATO countries
- ■ Other USSR allies
- ■ Other USA allies

SOVIET UNION | ALBANIA Left 1962

BULGARIA

CZECHOSLOVAKIA

EAST GERMANY

HUNGARY

POLAND

ROMANIA

NATO LEADERS

In 1949 the USA brought together a group of countries to form a military union. NATO's aims were to stop the spread of Communism and help prevent future war in Europe. As the USA was the most powerful country in NATO, the US president was seen as its leader.

DWIGHT D EISENHOWER
Became US president in 1953. He promised help to countries who were under threat from the spread of Communism.

JOHN F KENNEDY
When Kennedy confronted the USSR in 1962 over weapons they held in Cuba, many feared that it would trigger a third world war.

RICHARD NIXON
Nixon started a slight thaw in the Cold War when he met the Soviet leader Leonid Brezhnev in 1972, to discuss reducing weapons.

RONALD REAGAN
The US president in charge at the end of the Cold War, Reagan signed a peace treaty in 1989 with Soviet leader Mikhail Gorbachev.

WARSAW PACT LEADERS

The Pact was an anti-NATO alliance between Communist nations. Communism was based on the belief that property should not be owned by individuals, but shared by everyone.

JOSEPH STALIN
Set the Cold War in motion by bringing much of Eastern Europe under Soviet control after World War II.

NIKITA KHRUSHCHEV
Tried to establish better relations with the USA, but was ousted as Soviet leader by rivals in 1964.

FIDEL CASTRO
Led a Communist revolution in Cuba in 1959. The USA supported many attempts to remove him from power.

MIKHAIL GORBACHEV
Became leader of the USSR in 1985, and introduced many reforms that helped bring an end to the Cold War.

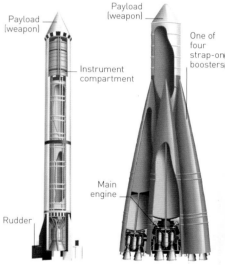

Payload (weapon)

Payload (weapon)

Instrument compartment

One of four strap-on boosters

Main engine

Rudder

PGM-11 REDSTONE (USA)
First missile to carry a live nuclear warhead.

R-7 SEMYORKA (USSR)
First intercontinental ballistic missile.

THE BERLIN WALL

After World War II, Germany's capital was divided up between the Allied countries – UK, USA, France, and USSR. In 1961 the Soviets built a 2 m (6.5 ft) high wall enclosing the three sectors of West Berlin to stop people escaping from the Communist Soviet sector to the Allied sector. The heavily guarded wall was finally demolished in 1989, at the end of the Cold War.

FRENCH SECTOR

BRITISH SECTOR | SOVIET SECTOR

AMERICAN SECTOR

KEY
— Berlin Wall

THE ENEMY AT HOME AND ABROAD

Espionage (spying) was an important Cold War tactic. Both sides developed military reconnaissance spy planes and anti-spy planes to counter the other's surveillance planes. They also deployed secret agents, whose job was either to uncover political and industrial information about the enemy, or to seek out spies and traitors in their own country.

LOGO OF THE CIA, USA'S COUNTER-INTELLIGENCE FORCE

LOCKHEED SR-71 BLACKBIRD RECONNAISSANCE PLANE

LOCKHEED U2 RECONNAISSANCE SPY PLANE

LOGO OF THE KGB, SOVIET SPY AGENCY

MIKOYAN-GUREVICH MIG-25 "FOXBAT" INTERCEPTOR PLANE

MIKOYAN-GUREVICH MIG-23 INTERCEPTOR PLANE

SPACE RACE

Both the USA and USSR desperately wanted to be world leaders in space exploration. They each poured huge amounts of money and resources into the race to be the first to land a man on the Moon.

FIRST SATELLITE TO ORBIT EARTH: USSR
On 4 October 1957, the Soviets launched *Sputnik I*. The USA launched their first satellite *Explorer I* four months later.

FIRST MAN IN SPACE: USSR
On 12 April 1961, Yuri Gagarin was the first man to orbit the Earth in his spacecraft, *Vostok I*.

COMMEMORATIVE STAMP SHOWING YURI GAGARIN

FIRST WOMAN IN SPACE: USSR
Valentina Tereshkova became the first female cosmonaut when she flew *Vostok 6* in 1963. It took the USA another 20 years to send Sally Ride up in the space shuttle *Challenger*.

FIRST "SPACE WALK": USSR
On 18 March 1965, Alexei Leonov spent about ten minutes floating outside his spacecraft, *Voskhod 2*. The Americans lost out again, by just three months.

FIRST PERSON TO LAND ON THE MOON: USA
On 20 July 1969, Neil Armstrong, Commander of the Apollo 11 moon mission, stepped out of the lunar landing module, *Eagle*, and on to the surface of the Moon.

MOON LANDING COMMEMORATIVE BADGE

VIETNAM WAR

In 1954 Vietnam was split when the Communists (Vietcong) in the North split from the South. The USA sent troops to help the South Vietnamese, leading to a 20-year war, which ended in victory for the Vietcong.

US MARINES HELMET

US MARINES ARMOURED VEST

US MARINES SUNGLASSES

M16 AUTOMATIC RIFLE (USA)

US MARINES CAMOUFLAGE JACKET AND TROUSERS

US MARINES TROPICAL BOOTS

VIETCONG HAT

VIETCONG FIGHTER'S TUNIC AND TROUSERS

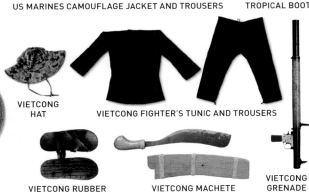

VIETCONG RUBBER SANDALS

VIETCONG MACHETE AND SCABBARD

VIETCONG GRENADE LAUNCHER

COLD WAR STORY

The Cold War divided Europe between democratic west and Communist east, and spread worldwide as both sides tried to undermine each other by influencing global events.

1945

FEBRUARY 1945
Yalta conference held to decide Germany's post-war future. Germany is split into four zones of Allied occupation.

MARCH 1946
British ex-prime minister Winston Churchill describes the division between Communist and non-Communist countries as an "iron curtain".

MARCH 1947
US President Truman declares the Truman Doctrine; that it was the USA's duty to fight Communism all over the world.

JUNE 1948
The Soviets try to squeeze the other Allies out of Berlin by blockading the city, forcing the Allies to airlift in supplies.

Memorial to Berlin Airlift

MAY–OCTOBER 1949
Communist East Germany and capitalist West Germany are founded.

OCTOBER 1949
Mao Zedong declares the foundation of the Communist People's Republic of China.

Book by Mao Zedong, Chinese communist leader

JUNE 1950
The Korean War begins; USSR and USA take opposing sides.

Sputnik satellite

OCTOBER 1956
The USSR invades Hungary to put down an anti-Communist uprising.

OCTOBER 1957
USSR launches Sputnik, the first satellite to orbit Earth.

AUGUST 1961
Soviets build the Berlin Wall.

OCTOBER 1962
USA and USSR face off in the Cuban Missile Crisis.

Statue of Che Guevara, one of Cuba's leaders at the time of the Missile Crisis

MARCH 1965
USA sends 200,000 troops to fight in Vietnam.

MAY 1972
USA and USSR sign a treaty agreeing to limit their nuclear weapons.

JULY–AUGUST 1980
USA boycotts the Moscow Olympic Games in protest at the Soviet invasion of Afghanistan.

DECEMBER 1987
USA and USSR agree to remove all medium- and short-range nuclear missiles.

NOVEMBER 1989
Berlin Wall is torn down.

Berlin Wall memorial

DECEMBER 1989
The Cold War is declared over.

1990

GLOBAL FLASHPOINTS

The effects of the Cold War were felt all over the world, as the USA and USSR backed different sides in various conflicts and uprisings.

KOREA 1950-53
The USA and United Nations backed South Korea, while USSR and China supported the Communists in the North.

CZECHOSLOVAKIA 1968
An attempted uprising against the Communist regime was violently put down by the USSR. The West disapproved, but did not intervene.

NICARAGUA 1979
When Sandinista revolutionaries overthrew the government, the USA funded a guerrilla war against the new regime.

AFGHANISTAN 1979
When the Soviets invaded Afghanistan, Afghan resistance fighters (Mujahideen) were secretly armed and funded by the USA.

Spies

Spying, or espionage, is all about finding out secret information, known as "intelligence". Spies have been operating for thousands of years. In ancient times, they sneaked into enemy camps to uncover their battle plans. If they were caught, they were killed. Spying is still a dangerous business. Secret agents carry weapons as well as the latest surveillance gadgets.

MATA HARI

THE FICTIONAL SPY JAMES BOND WAS CREATED BY IAN FLEMING IN 1953

Lighter flips open to reveal camera

LIGHTER CAMERA

CAMERAS
Used to photograph top-secret plans or provide evidence of a private meeting, the camera is an essential part of a spy's kit. These days, a secret agent can use a smartphone to take a snap without attracting attention. In the past, cameras had to be ingeniously concealed inside everyday objects.

WRISTWATCH CAMERA

INSECTOTHOPTER (FLYING SURVEILLANCE CAMERA)

MICRODOT CAMERA

DCD-1 (CIA SUBMINIATURE CAMERA)

WRAL (CIA SUBMINIATURE CAMERA)

MOLLY (CIA SUBMINIATURE CAMERA)

RADIOS
Radio allowed secret agents of the past to communicate quickly over long distances – they did so in code, because radio messages can be easily intercepted. Radio waves also transmitted sounds from listening devices, such as the one hidden in the hotel lamp below.

RADIO WRISTWATCH KGB

PORTABLE MILITARY RADIO

HOTEL LAMP TRANSCEIVER

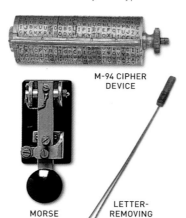
ATTACHE CASE RADIO

RECORDING DEVICES
With the help of bugs and other secret recording devices, spies can ensure that no conversation is ever private. Wiretaps allow an agent to listen in on phone conversations.

CIA WRISTWATCH MICROPHONE

MEZON RECORDING DEVICE

PEN-TOP MICROPHONE

CODES AND CIPHERS
Keeping communications secret and intercepting enemy messages were prime concerns during World War I and II. Codes allow words or instructions to be replaced by letters, numbers, or symbols. Ciphers are a clever kind of code, where a secret "key" encrypts the message.

HANDKERCHIEF WITH SECRET WRITING

M-94 CIPHER DEVICE

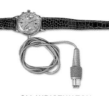
MORSE CODE KEY

LETTER-REMOVING DEVICE

GERMAN ENIGMA CIPHER MACHINE USED BY JAPANESE

GERMAN ENIGMA CIPHER MACHINE

WHO SPIES?

Most spies work for someone else – usually a government, a company, or another person. Spying is their job. It involves finding out information that others would rather keep hidden, and passing those secrets on.

GOVERNMENTS
Every government runs its own intelligence agency. The agency employs spies to gather information.

PRIVATE COMPANIES
Private intelligence agencies spy on behalf of individuals, companies, and governments.

POLITICAL GROUPS
Campaigners may work to find out "dirty" secrets kept by big companies or the government.

INDIVIDUALS
Some people spy without being hired. They may discover a secret and share it.

...AND WHY?

Spying is a risky business, so why do people do it? They are usually motivated by one of four reasons. Experts explain these using the term "MICE", which stands for Money, Ideology, Compromise, and Ego.

MONEY
Most spies do what they do for the money. Top spies are paid huge sums for the secrets they uncover.

IDEOLOGY
Some spy because of beliefs, or ideology. They work for a government or organization that shares their beliefs.

COMPROMISE
Sometimes people fall into spying because they have a secret of their own. They are blackmailed into the job.

EGO
A small number of spies are motivated by ego. They think being a spy will be glamorous.

CYBER SPIES

Computers and the Internet have changed the face of espionage. Cyber sleuths can now steal information remotely, by hacking into computers. Governments and companies take cyber espionage very seriously.

SECRET COMPARTMENTS

Spies need to be able to transport top-secret information, tickets, or messages without them being intercepted. Spies in World War I and II used special microdot cameras to shrink documents on to tiny pieces of film that could be concealed in the smallest hiding places.

Secret chamber

RING TO CONCEAL MICRODOTS

BOOT HEEL COMPARTMENT

COIN WITH SECRET COMPARTMENT

HOLLOW SOAP CASE TO HIDE DEVICES

WEAPONS

Used to threaten and wring out information, to silence an enemy for good, or for self-defence, guns and other weapons are an espionage essential. For some missions, they may be carried openly; on others, they must be carefully disguised.

.25 WEBLEY WITH SILENCER

PUSH DAGGER

GAS-FIRING CARTRIDGE ASSASSINATION WALLET

Strap attaches gun to arm

TIP OF POISON-PELLET CANE

SINGLE-SHOT ASSASSINATION DEVICE

Pen gun bullet

PNEUMATIC PEN GUN

TEAR-GAS PEN

SLEEVE GUN

CIA DEER GUN

GENERAL TOOLS

One challenge spies face is gaining entry to places where secrets are stored. Secret agents carry kit for breaking and entering, including fence cutters, key copiers, and lock picks.

LOCK PICK GUN

KEY PATTERN DEVICE

WIRE FENCE CUTTER

COVERT ENTRY KIT

INTELLIGENCE AGENCIES

Governments need spies to tell them about threats from other countries. Some also carry out surveillance on their own citizens.

○ **MSS, CHINA**
In 1983 China merged existing agencies to make its Ministry of State Security (MSS).

○ **RAW, INDIA**
Created in 1968, India's Research and Analysis Wing (RAW) reports directly to the Prime Minister, not Parliament.

○ **CIA, USA**
The Central Intelligence Agency (CIA) focuses on foreign threats to the USA.

○ **ISI, PAKISTAN**
Founded in 1948, Inter-Services Intelligence (ISI) collects information that affects Pakistani security.

○ **FSB, RUSSIA**
The Federal Security Service (FSB) was formed in 1995. It took over from the KGB after the fall of the Soviet Union.

○ **BND, GERMANY**
Germany's Federal Intelligence Service, or *Bundesnachrichtendienst*, was founded in 1956.

○ **DGSE, FRANCE**
Formed in 1982, the *Direction Générale de la Sécurité Extérieure* (DGSE) investigates threats to France.

○ **MI6, UK**
Formally called the Secret Intelligence Service, MI6 reports to the UK government and tracks terror threats.

○ **ASIS, AUSTRALIA**
The Australian Secret Intelligence Service (ASIS) was founded in 1952 to protect Australia's interests.

○ **MOSSAD, ISRAEL**
Formed in 1949, Israel's intelligence agency has around 1,200 employees.

Index

A

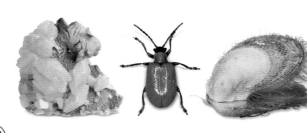

IJ

Acknowledgments

Smithsonian Enterprises:
President, Christopher A. Liedel
Senior Vice President, Carol LeBlanc
Vice President, Brigid Ferraro
Licensing Manager, Ellen Nanney
Key Accounts Manager, Cheryl Stepanek
Product Development Manager, Kealy Gordon

Consultants at the Smithsonian Institution:
National Museum of Natural History: Dr. Salima Ikram, Egyptology Unit Head, Department of Anthropology; Dr. William Fitzhugh, Curator of Archaeology and Director of Arctic Studies Center, Department of Anthropology; James Harle, Volunteer/Docent, Department of Botany; Dr. Jeffrey Post, Geologist, National Gem and Mineral Collection; Dr. Alexander Nagel, Research Associate, Department of Anthropology; Dr. Michael Brett-Surman, Museum Specialist, Department of Paleobiology; Dr. Benjamin J. Andrews, Research Geologist, Department of Mineral Sciences; and Dr. Don E. Wilson, Emeritus Curator, Department of Vertebrate Zoology.

National Air and Space Museum: Dr. Alex Spencer, Curator, Division of Aeronautics; Dr. F. Robert van der Linden, Chairman, Division of Aeronautics; and Dr. Andrew Johnston, Research Specialist, Center for Earth and Planetary Studies.

Smithsonian Project Coordinator: Cheryl Stepanek

Dorling Kindersley would like to thank the following people for their assistance with this book:
Bharti Bedi, Shaila Brown, Stella Caldwell, Steven Carton, Carey Scott, Virien Chopra, Chris Hawkes, Clare Hibbert, Kathryn Hill, Priyanka Kharbanda, Ann Kramer, Sam Priddy, Esther Ripley, and Sheryl Sadana, for additional editing; Claire Gell for jacket editorial; Tannishtha Chakraborthy, Mandy Earey, Fiona Macdonald, Isha Nagar, Pooja Pipil, Nidhi Rastogi, Damion Robinson, Tanvi Sahu, Mary Sandberg, Heena Sharma, Smiljka Surla, and Jacqui Swan for additional design; Mohammad Usman for hi-res assistance; Pawan Kumar for CTS assistance; Caroline Hunt for proofreading; Helen Peters for the index; Sakshi Saluja and Deepak Negi for picture research assistance; Peter Bull, KJA Artists, and Encompass Graphics for illustration; Stefan Podhorodecki and James Mann for photography. The publisher would also like to thank Mark Ryan and the Marylebone Cricket Club, Lord's Ground, for the use of their Real Tennis ball; and Jimmy Perrett and the Wandsworth Demons for the use of their AFL balls.

Picture credits
The publisher would like to thank the following for their kind permission to reproduce their photographs:

(Key: a-above; b-below/bottom; c-centre; f-far; l-left; r-right; t-top)

1 Dorling Kindersley: The Natural History Museum, London (cla); The Real Aeroplane Company (fcla); University of Pennsylvania Museum of Archaeology and Anthropology (c); Jari Peltomaki (ca/owl). Dreamstime.com: Eric Isselee (ca/Hermit crab); Karam Miri (ca). Fotolia: Jan Will (c/zebra). 2 Dorling Kindersley: Brooklands Museum (cr); Egyptian Museum, Cairo (fcla); Natural History Museum, London (ca); Paul Rackham (ca/Caterpillar); The National Music Museum (cl); The Natural History Museum, London (c); Christian Dior (c/bag); DB Schenker (c/DB Schenker Diesel); Durham University Oriental Museum (fcra, cl/war fan, c/Glass bowl); Forrest L. Mitchell / James Laswel (c/Libellula saturata). Fotolia: Shchipkova Elena (c/jaguar). 3 Dorling Kindersley: Dave King (cla); Motorcycle Heritage Museum, Westerville, Ohio (fcra); University of Pennsylvania Museum of Archaeology and Anthropology (c); Lister Wilder (c/Tractor); Jari Peltomaki (ca). Dreamstime.com: Am Wu / Amwu (c). 4 Dorling Kindersley: The Royal Academy of Music (br). Dreamstime.com: The Natural History Museum, London (bc). 5 Dorling Kindersley: Royal Green Jackets Museum, Winchester (bc); The Shuttleworth Collection (ftl); Linda Pitkin (fbr); Courtesy of Durham University Oriental Museum (tc/Fan). Dreamstime.com: Vtupinamba (tc). 6 Dorling Kindersley: 4hoplites; Natural History Museum, London (tl); Brooklands Museum (br); Greg and Yvonne Dean (br). 7 Dorling Kindersley: Durham University Oriental Museum (bc/Mummy mask Cartonnage). Fotolia: Eric Isselee (bc, fbr). Getty Images: felipedupouy.com / Photodisc (br). NASA: (ftr). 8 Dorling Kindersley: National Cycle Collection (fcla); The Science Museum, London (ca); National Railway Museum, York (clb). 9 Dorling Kindersley: RAF Boulmer, Northumberland (cla); The Science Museum, London; Dave King (cb). NASA: JPL-Caltech (ftl). 10 ESO: (c). NASA: CXC / SAO / J. Wang et al), Optical (DSS & NOAO / AURA / NSF / KPNO 0.9-m / T. Rector et al) (cb/rosette); Sally Hunsberger

(Lowell Obs.), Jane Charlton (Penn State) et al.; (r); ESA / Hubble and the Hubble Heritage Team (bc); ESA and the Hubble Heritage Team STScI / AURA)-ESA / Hubble Collaboration (bc/N90); ESA, ESO, & Danny LaCrue (cb). 11 ESO: E. Slawik (crb). NASA: (cl, clb); Johns Hopkins University Applied Physics Laboratory / Southwest Research Institute (cb); Johns Hopkins Applied Physics Laboratory (br). 12 ESO: NASA, ESA, and A. Simon (Goddard Space Flight Center) (clb). NASA: (ca, cra). 13 NASA: ESA, and L. Lamy (Observatory of Paris, CNRS, CNES) (cb); JPL (cra, crb). 14 NASA: Goddard / MIT / Brown (bl). 15 NASA: (crb). 16 Dorling Kindersley: Dave Shayler / Astro Info Service Ltd (fcl/Apollo 7, fcl/Apollo 10, fcl/Apollo 11, fcl/Apollo 14, fcl/Apollo 15, cl/Apollo 8, cl/Apollo 12, cl/Apollo 16, cl/Apollo 9, cl/Apollo 13, cl/Apollo 17). ESA: C. Carreau / ATG medialab (cr/Rosetta). NASA: JPL-Caltech (fbr); (fcl/Apollo 1, clb, bl, bc, ca, cra, cr/Mariner 10, cr/Messenger, crb, br); ESA / Alex Lutkus (fcr). 17 ESA: ISRO / ISAC (br). NASA: JPL-Caltech (ftr); NSSDC Photo Gallery (ftl/Luna 10); (tl/Apollo 15, tl/Prospector); NASA's Goddard Space Flight Center (tl/Orbiter); NASA AMES / Corby Waste (tr/Surveyor); NSSDC (tr/Mariner 9, fcra); NASA AMES (fcr/Pioneer 11); JPL (fcl, c/Magellan, fbr); ESA (fcr/Cassini, cl/Venus Express); (fclb, cb, fbl). courtesy Virgin Galactic: (br/SpaceShipTwo). 18 ESO: (bc); Digitized Sky Survey 2 (cla); Igor Chekalin (ca). Mike Lewinski: (fcla). NASA: CXC / SAO / F. Seward et al. (fcr/chandra); JPL-Caltech / R. Gehrz (University of Minnesota) (fcra); ESA / ASU / J. Hester (fcr); Swift / E. Hoversten, PSU (fcr/Nebula). NRAO : AUI (tr). The Library of Congress, Washington DC: (fcrb, bl). 19 Dr.Seth Shostak: (cl). ESA: Scott Ferguson (tc). ESA / Hubble: ESA, N. Evans (Harvard-Smithsonian CfA), and H. Bond (STScI) (tc/polaris). ESO: Y. Beletsky (tr/venus); B. Tafreshi (twanight.org) (ftr). Mike Lewinski: NASA: (br); James Spann (cla); JPL-Caltech / Space Dynamics Lab (cla); JPL-Caltech / UCLA / MPS / DLR / IDA (bl); ESA SOHO team (bc). NOAA: (cla/aurora7, cla/moondog, cla). 20 Dorling Kindersley: NASA (ca). Dreamstime.com: Igor Chekalin (crb, bc); Mihai-bogdan Lazar (cla); Valerio Pardi (cl); Neutronman (c); Vladimir Il'yin (cr, bl); Sdrart (cb); Procyab (fbr). ESA / Hubble: NASA, ESA, Digitized Sky Survey 2 (br); NASA (cb/M71). NASA: ESA, and STScI (cra). 22 Dreamstime.com: Mihai-bogdan Lazar (cl); Neutronman (cra); Pere Sanz (c). ESA / Hubble: NASA, ESA, and the Digitized Sky Survey 2. Acknowledgment: Davide De Martin (cla); ESO, ESA / Hubble and Digitized Sky Survey 2: Davide De Martin (ca); NOAO / AURA / NSF (bl); David Malin (Anglo-Australian Observatory). (bc); NASA, ESA, Z. Levay (STScI) and A. Fujii (br). 24–25 NASA: (c). 25 Dorling Kindersley: Stephen Oliver (crb). Dreamstime.com: Carla F. Castagno / Korat_cn (cra). ESO: Iztok Bončina / ESO (cl). Fotolia: Dario Sabljak (cr). NASA: DOE / Fermi LAT Collaboration, CXC / SAO / JPL-Caltech / Steward / O. Krause et al and NRAO / AUI (fcra). The Library of Congress, Washington DC: (fbr). 26–27 Dorling Kindersley: The Science Museum, London (c). 27 Dorling Kindersley: The Science Museum, London (tc). Dreamstime.com: Derektenhue (cra); Vitalyedush (fcr); Zirconicusso (fcrb). The Library of Congress, Washington DC: 29 Dorling Kindersley: Board of Trustees of the Royal Armouries (clb); Durham University Oriental Museum (cb). The Library of Congress, Washington DC: (bl). 30 Dorling Kindersley: The Natural History Museum, London (tl/Lithium, cla/Peridot, cb/Cerium); The Science Museum, London (cl/Strontium). Dreamstime.com: Robyn Mackenzie (cla/cheese). Fotolia: Bram J. Meijer (fcl). 31 Dorling Kindersley: Brett Critchley / BCritchley (c/lens); The Natural History Museum, London (ca/Diamond, cra/Fluorite); Stephen Oliver (ftr, cra/Scuba); The Science Museum, London (ca/Microprocessor, fcr/Light bulb, cr/bromine, cb/Battery). Dreamstime.com: Nikkytok (clb/greenlight). Fotolia: Pablo H. Caridad (clb/Poison). 33 Alamy Images: Paul Fleet (cl). Dorling Kindersley: David Patterson and Bob Andersen (crb). Dreamstime.com: 3quarks (cl). Fotolia: Jose Gil (c); Eric Isselee (br). NOAA: Shawn Dahle, NOAA's Alaska Fisheries Science Center (ca). 41 PunchStock: (tr). 42 Dorling Kindersley: Blists Hill and Jackfield Tile Museum, Ironbridge, Shropshire (tr); The Science Museum, London (fcra, ca). The Library of Congress, Washington DC: (ftr). 43 Alamy Images: stu49 (cra). Dorling Kindersley: Ruth Jenkinson (bc); The Science Museum, London (tl, cla). Dreamstime.com: Scanrail (tc); Stephen Vanhorn / Svanhorn4245 (clb). Fotolia: Alexandr Mitiuc (tl). The Library of Congress, Washington DC: Charles Milton (ca/Herman). 44 Dorling Kindersley: The Shuttleworth Collection, Bedfordshire (br); Natural History Museum, London (tc); Durham University Oriental Museum (tr); The Museum of London (tc/spear); Vietnam Rolling Thunder (cb); The Science Museum, London (clb). 44–45 Dorling Kindersley: The Science Museum, London (c). 45 Dorling Kindersley: Maidstone Museum and Bentliff Art Gallery (tl); The Science Museum, London (c, cr, tr, cra); The Museum of English Rural Life, The University of Reading (tc). 50 Dorling Kindersley: John Mould (cla); Mark Surman (clb). 51 Dorling Kindersley: R. Florio (cr). 52 Dorling Kindersley: James Coward (br); Doubleday Swineshead Depot (fcla, fcl, cl, ca, c/PTO Shaft); Keystone

Tractor Works (c/Thieman, ftr/Moline); Rabtrak (c/YTO 180, crb/Felderman, fcrb/Soils 20); Derek Mellor (tc); Paul Rackham (bc, cra, fcrb/International T-20); Happy Old Iron, Marc Geerkens (crb/Georges Vidal); Robin Simons (fcra); Paul Holmes (fcr); Piet Verschelde (fbr). 53 Dorling Kindersley: James Coward (ca); Daniel Ward (ftl, tl, cla, fcra/McDonald Imperial); Roger and Fran Desborough (tc, fcrb, fclb); The Shuttleworth Collection (tr); Andrew Farnham (fcla/Massey-Harris); Mary and Brian Snelgar (cra); Lister Wilder (c); Robert Crawford (ftr); Happy Old Iron, Marc Geerkens (fcra/Pavesi America); Paul Rackham (fcla/Titan, fcr, fbl, clb, bc); Henry Flashman (bl); Richard Mason (fbr/Doe Triple-D); David Wakefield (fbr/JCB). 54–55 Fotolia: Yahia Loukkal (b). 54 Dorling Kindersley: DaimlerChrysler AG (fcl, clb). Fotolia: Masek (bl). 55 Dorling Kindersley: James River Equipment (clb, crb); Yorkshire Air Museum (cl); James Rivers (br). 56–57 Dorling Kindersley: Railroad Museum of Pennsylvania (S12 Switcher); Ribble Steam Railway / Science Museum Group (Deltic). 56 Dorling Kindersley: Didcot Railway Centre (c/King Edward II, br/GWR Hall Class); Virginia Museum of Transportation (tr/Whitcomb, bc/VGN Class SA No. 4); The National Railway Museum, York / Science Museum Group (clb/Rocket, bl/Wren, bl/Ner Clas XL No 66); Ffestiniog & Welsh Highland Railways (clb/Taliesin, cb/Merddin Emrys); National Railway Museum, York (crb/LB & SCR B1 Class, bl/Mallard); Ribble Steam Railway / Science Museum Group (bc/Hunslet Austerity); Harzer Schmalspurbahnen (br/DR Class 99.7376). 57 Dorling Kindersley: DB Schenker (cb/BR Class 92); Musee de Chemin de Fer, Mulhouse (tl/Bugatti Railcar); Harzer Schmalspurbahnen (tl/DR Class Kö, tc/GHE T1); Railroad Museum of Pennsylvania (tr/Type NWZ, cla/Conrail No.2233, c/No. 800, c/PRR Class GG1); Didcot Railway Centre (tl/BR Class 08); Ribble Steam Railway / Science Museum Group (tc/BR Class 05, ca/D9500 Class 14, cra/Sentinel, cl/0-4-0); Virginia Museum of Transportation (tr/Norfolk and Western 41, ca/N&W EMD GP9 Class); Eisenbahnfreunde Traditionsbahnbetriebswerk Stassfurt (cra/DR V15, cla/DR V60, cl/DR E04, clb/DR Class 243, br/Shunter); Hitachi Rail Europe (cb/Javelin); The Science Museum, London (bl/Puffing Billy). Dreamstime.com: Mamahoohooba (crb/Maglev). 58 Dorling Kindersley: Charlie Garratt (clb); Nigel Cocks (cra); The National Motorcycle Museum (cl, cl/Triumph Trophy TR6, c/Royal Enfield, clb/Ivy Three, fbl); Phil Crosby and Peter Mather (c); Micheal Penn (bl); Peter Hodson (bc). 58–59 Dorling Kindersley: The National Motorcycle Museum (ca); Wayne MacGowan (c). 59 Dorling Kindersley: Charlie Garratt (c); The National Motorcycle Museum (tc, cr, cb, bc); Brian Chapman and Chris Illman (tc/Weslake, fcrb/Mighty Mouse); Motorcycle Heritage Museum, Westerville, Ohio (tr, clb); George Manning (cla, ca, crb); Neil Mort, Mott Motorcycles (ca/Ducati); Justin Watson (cr/Honda); David Jones (cr/Moto guzzi); Ian Bull (br); National Motor Museum, Beaulieu (fcrb, ca). 60 Dorling Kindersley: Tony Agar (ca/Mosquito); Sarl Salis Aviation (tc/DVII); Royal Airforce Museum, London (Hendon) (tc/FW 190, tr/ME262, tl/Pup, tc/Bulldog, ca/Spitfire, cla/S.E.5A, cla/Dolphin, cl/Vimy); Brooklands Museum (tl/Camel); Gatwick Aviation Museum (tc/P-38, c/B-25, c/Vulcan, clb/Wellington); Midlands Air Museum (tr/F-86); Commemorative Air Force, Mesa, Arizona (cla/Nieuport 17, clb/B-17); Paul Ford (cla/Dr 1); RAF Museum, Cosford (cla/Mustang); Planes of Fame Air Museum, Chino, California (ca/A6M Zero, ca/Yak-9); Yorkshire Air Museum (cra/Hawker Hunter); Matthew Boddington (cl/B.E.2c); RAF Battle of Britain Memorial Flight (c/Lancaster); Keith Warrington, Sutton Coldfield Model Makers Society (cl/JU87B); Pima Air and Space Museum, Tuscon, Arizona (cb/B-58A). 60–61 Dorling Kindersley: Royal International Air Tattoo 2011 (B-52). 61 Dorling Kindersley: Royal Airforce Museum, London (Hendon) (cla/F-35 Lightning); Pima Air and Space Museum, Tuscon, Arizona (tl/Tomcat); John Wilkes, Model Exhibition, Telford (tl/Harrier); Dave Gait (tc/Douglas DC3); Nationaal Luchtvaart Themapark Aviodome (tc/F27 Friendship); Brooklands Museum (tc/Concorde); Flugausstellung (tc/L-1049, ca/Comet 4C); Golden Apple Operations Ltd (ca/Stearman); The Real Aeroplane Company (cra/J/1N Autocrat, c/Pitts 51S); Philip Powell (cra/F177RG Cardinal); Richard Seeley (c/Gipsy Moth); Hamblin Jet, Luton Airport (cr/Learjet 45); The Shuttleworth Collection (c/JetRanger); RAF Boulmer, Northumberland (cr/Sea King); Fleet Air Arm Museum (cb/Westland Wessex, crb/Westland Lynx). Dreamstime.com: Patrick Allen / Ratmandude (cb/Bell UH-1); Wayne Mckown / Mckown (cl/B2); Darkmonk (cra/Airbus A380); Ivan Cholakov / Icholakov (crb/Black Hawk). U.S. Air Force: Senior Master Sgt. Joy Josephson (cl/A-10 Thunderbolt II). 62 Dorling Kindersley: Brooklands Museum (bl); City of Norwich Aviation Museum (cl); Flugausstellung (fclb). NASA: U.S Air Force (clb); (br). The Library of Congress, Washington DC: (cr). 63 Dorling Kindersley: Nationaal Luchtvaart Themapark Aviodome (tr); Roy Palmer (clb). Dreamstime.com: Darkmonk (br). The Library of Congress, Washington DC: (cb). U.S. Air Force: (cr, crb, bl). 64 Dorling Kindersley: Trek UK Ltd (ca). 65 Dorling Kindersley: National Cycle Collection (tl, tc, tr, cra, cla); (tr/Swift safety bicycle). 66 Dorling Kindersley: The Natural History Museum, London (cla). 67 Dorling Kindersley: Natural History Museum, London (cra); Mike Read (cla). Dreamstime.com: Jeff Grabert / Jgrabert (cra/margay). Fotolia: Eric Isselee (ca). 68 Dorling Kindersley: Natural History Museum, London (fcl); Neil Fletcher (ftr); Booth